For Reference

Not to be taken

from this library

DICTIONARY OF THE NEW TESTAMENT

DICTIONARY OF THE NEW TESTAMENT

✦

XAVIER LÉON-DUFOUR

Translated from the second (revised) French edition by

TERRENCE PRENDERGAST

HARPER & ROW, PUBLISHERS

SAN FRANCISCO

Cambridge London
Hagerstown Mexico City
Philadelphia São Paulo
New York 1817 Sydney

DICTIONARY OF THE NEW TESTAMENT. English translation copyright © 1980 by Harper & Row, Publishers, Inc. All rights reserved. Printed in the United States of America. No part of this book may be used or reproduced in any manner whatsoever without written permission except in the case of brief quotations embodied in critical articles and reviews. For information address Harper & Row, Publishers, Inc., 10 East 53rd Street, New York, NY 10022. Published simultaneously in Canada by Fitzhenry & Whiteside Limited, Toronto.

FIRST EDITION

Designed by Jim Mennick

Library of Congress Cataloging in Publication Data

Léon-Dufour, Xavier.
DICTIONARY OF THE NEW TESTAMENT

Translation of *Dictionnaire du Nouveau Testament.*
Includes index.
1. Bible. N.T.—Dictionaries. I. Title.
BS2312.L413 1980 255.3 79-3004
ISBN 0-06-062100-1

---

80 81 82 83 84 10 9 8 7 6 5 4 3 2 1

TRANSLATOR'S DEDICATION

For my mother
and to the memory of my father

Contents

Charts and Illustrations

Translator's Preface

Father Léon-Dufour's *Dictionnaire* has already been translated into several other languages. Although English-speaking readers have had to wait a little longer for this translation, the delay has allowed for use, throughout, of the second French edition of 1978. This revised version incorporated over a thousand modifications, expansions, corrections, and additions—mostly of a minor sort—all of which have been reflected in this translation.

In the rearrangement of the *Dictionary* to suit the English word order, very few modifications had to be made. The fact, however, that metric measurements are new or strange to some English-speaking countries led to the inclusion, along with the metric originals, of standard measurement equivalents, wherever this seemed called for.

I wish to express my thanks to Mr. John Loudon, of Harper and Row, for his considerable patience with delays in the translation schedule, the result of academic and other pressures on me; to Rev. Lloyd J. Robertson, President of Atlantic School of Theology, for his understanding of the pressures which the translation project placed on my performance of academic duties; to Rev. John Driscoll, to Sr. Virginia Turner and to the Sisters of St. Paul's Convent, Herring Cove, for their help with technical aspects of the manuscript; and to the Mrs. Anne Bonang, Moira Hughes, Marilyn Moore, and Lynn Theriault, for their care in typing the handwritten manuscript.

The translation is dedicated to my mother and to my father's memory: by their lives of faith they "translated" the New Testament for me in so many ways.

TERRENCE PRENDERGAST, S.J.

Halifax, Canada
15 August 1979

Author's Preface

Some seven years ago, Paul-André Lesort challenged me with a project: to put at the public's disposal a manageable resource that would answer questions raised by a reading of the New Testament. I was intrigued, but terrified. Hadn't my experience with the preceding *Dictionary of Biblical Theology* been enough? But when the reader's advocate persisted, I decided to set myself to the task and take on the wager. Could a reader of the New Testament, whether a believer or unbeliever, easily find answers to questions raised by the text?

The New Testament, which is this dictionary's field of inquiry, is a literary collection whose writing was spread out over barely fifty years. This short span of time allows us to regard this body of writing as a unified conceptual whole. The difficulty involved, and its interesting feature, is that this work is based on two civilizations, one belonging to Semites and one belonging to Greeks. In the dictionary we try to indicate the connections between these two kinds of thought. Since in this dictionary we are interpreting a contemporary idiom which is itself a translation of the Greek, we have to try to bridge the gap separating a twentieth-century outlook from one belonging to the first century. This is not achieved by imagining that we can bridge so great a gulf (after all, we cannot situate ourselves within the context that belonged to the first Christians), but only by attempting to relate ourselves to one another, something which is the basic precondition of a healthy understanding of any text.

An introduction precedes the word list proper, a feature unique in this kind of a work, and one which was conceived by Paul-André Lesort. Its purpose is twofold. First, it attempts to give the reader an opportunity to discover what is left unsaid in the New Testament. The New Testament presupposed the existence of the mental furniture of the time: the land and its people, some earlier history, the Mediterranean world and its cultural heritage, the varied aspects of life (political, juridical, economic, domestic, cultural), and, finally, the religious patterns of Israel's own faith. All of these established facts, which are generally not made explicit in the New Testament, are quite indispensable to the reader. When tied to this kind of a backdrop, the New Testament stops floating without an anchor in the world of human beings.

The introduction's other goal is to gather together the content of the separate entries which are scattered throughout the word list. One of the faults of any dictionary stems from the dictionary genre itself. It is a collection of words arranged in alphabetical order, offering entries that are geared to give meaning to words, but which, by that very fact, are isolated from one another in such a way that their connections are not immediately apparent. In this dictionary, the arrows placed at the bottoms of the entries invite the reader to tie related terms together. Reaching a synthesis, however, is not always an easy task. So, in addition, the introduction endeavors to organize those aspects of a single topic which are scattered throughout the word list, such as what matters were relevant to marriage, or to the various social levels, or to cultural life in Jesus' time. Quite frequently, the entries themselves are cross-referenced to the introduction so that the reader might supplement the entry or see the entry in question in its total context.

The word list itself requires a bit of explanation—first of all, of the choice of words. We estimate that out of a possible 5,500 Greek words found in the New Testament we have retained *all* the terms (a thousand, and then some) which require an explanation, historical-geographic, archeological, literary or theological. This truly is a dictionary, an exhaustive one. However, we have had to drop the bulk of personal and place names which are cited only once or which scarcely have a bearing on an understanding of the text. In numerous cases we chose one or another English word because of its prominent place in current speech, setting aside terms which had to be let go (unless they could be handled through arrows directing the reader to words treated elsewhere). We have first of all set about indicating the Greek word used by the New Testament text and, on occasion, an antecedent Hebrew word from the Old Testament. Sometimes an etymology of the various words has been given.

Ordinarily, words are discussed according to their specific shades of meaning, for it is important to dispel any confusion which certain verbal relationships involve. Here are some examples of terms which have been related to one another through word chains. Faith—fidelity—hope—patience—persecution—perseverance—trust. Boldness—glory—pride—trust. Envy—jealousy. Agony—anguish—care—fear.

Sometimes, in order not to lengthen the number of entries excessively and in order to preserve a synthetic view on several topics, we have had to proceed to thematic groupings. This was the case with animals, fabrics, precious stones, vices, virtues, etc.

On still other occasions, the English word included several Greek or Hebrew words, thereby revealing the ambiguity found in such terms. This was the case with ark, abyss, nether world, folly, slander, newness, age, etc.

Numerous entries inform the reader about various fields. In the historical category these are quite varied—for example, adoption, emancipation, anathema, chronology, centurion, collection, Council of Jerusalem, prefect, procurator, province, tetrarch—ideas about which one has problems remembering the precise facts. At this point, I turn to entries dealing with places and persons, in order to point out the many informative discoveries of an archaeological kind, such as those relating to marketplace, copper and bronze, mirror, Nag Hammadi or Qumran. Basic exegetical concepts have been set forth, such as those relating to literary genre, criticism, a literary unit, the agrapha, the apocryphal writings, a canon of the Scriptures, the deuterocanonical writings, parable and allegory, structure. We have even tried to provide in modern terms the equivalents of certain ticklish ideas such as eternity, time, the end of the world, myth, predestination. Where appropriate, a need was felt to sketch, from the theological thickets in which they are imbedded, traces of such core concepts as God, Christ, the angels or redemption, along with all their associated ideas.

The entries have been set up on two levels, first a continuous text, then a series of biblical references. For readers looking for quick information, the text will undoubtedly be adequate to the task, but those who want to deepen their understanding of the meaning given can turn to the references provided in abundance. Sometimes they will uncover, through the references to the Old Testament, the term's depth, its roots in the biblical tradition. At other times, they will verify or fill in the text's hastily provided information. Unless they wish only to uncover the meaning of a difficult word encountered in the New Testament, readers may leaf through the book without tiring themselves. But they should not be afraid to be carried along by the interplay of arrows which may take them well beyond the original word's definition. Charts and maps (for which we thank Bernard Lagaillarde) will facilitate the task. In a single glance readers can grasp the books of the Bible, the apocryphal writings, the connections that may be established between hours and watches of the day and night, etc.

To carry this project off well, it was necessary to avoid several pitfalls. I have tried to transform entries into one long sentence, stringing scriptural texts end-to-end, a concordance set to prose. (I have to mention the great help rendered by the incomparable *Concordance du Nouveau Testament,* published by Cerf in 1970).[1] The entries do not intend to retrace the history of Caesarea or of Peter in the New Testament. Rather they are to inform the reader who wants to understand whatever is taken for granted in what he or she is reading. In the case of the introduction it was possible to sketch the broad outlines of a theology of the Old Testament and of the state of Jewish thought at the time of Jesus. Thus, it was possible to provide a complete (even if not an exhaustive) backdrop to the basic understanding needed by every reader of the New Testament.

To accomplish this work, an enormous task for one man, there had to be help and support from a large number of people. I wish to thank all of them. To begin with, Jacqueline Thevenet, who edited a first version of the entries on places and persons, as well as a good number dealing with common names. Then, those who assembled various parts of the introduction: Jean-Pierre Berger for Roman and Hellenic questions, Michel Sales and Bernard Corbin for Jewish questions. Even after these things were done, there remained a great deal of work, which took more than three years to finish. It was then that Renza Arrighi improved the rough drafts of the entries and brought together other documents needed for the introduction. If I mention these details, it is to explain how, in fact, over and above the theological entries which had been reserved to me from the outset, I had to bring together and unify the whole work. For this reason I assume full

1. *Modern Concordance to the New Testament,* ed. Michael Darton (New York: Doubleday, 1976), is an English adaptation of the French *Concordance.*—Trans.

responsibility for the entire content of this Dictionary. Moreover, without speaking any further about the many suggestions made by Paul-André Lesort and Jean-Pie Lapierre, I also want to mention two first-rate specialists by name: Charles Morel, who watched over the accuracy of the etymologies, and Joseph Trinquet, whose solidly grounded competence was linked to a patient and minute reading of the entire manuscript. Finally, ahead of time, I want to express my thanks to the readers, who, through their use of it, will help me improve this work, a labor that was conscientiously and courageously shaped in the hope that it might be of help to them.

X.L.-D.

Lyons-Paris
September 1968–August 1975

Abbreviations of Books of the Bible

Acts	Acts of the Apostles
Am	Amos
Bar	Baruch
1 Chr	1 Chronicles
2 Chr	2 Chronicles
Col	Colossians
1 Cor	1 Corinthians
2 Cor	2 Corinthians
Dn	Daniel
Dt	Deuteronomy
Eccl	Ecclesiastes
Eph	Ephesians
Est	Esther
Ex	Exodus
Ez	Ezekiel
Ezr	Ezra
Gal	Galatians
Gn	Genesis
Hb	Habakkuk
Hg	Haggai
Heb	Hebrews
Hos	Hosea
Is	Isaiah
Jas	James
Jer	Jeremiah
Jb	Job
Jl	Joel
Jn	John (Gospel)
1 Jn	1 John
2 Jn	2 John
3 Jn	3 John
Jon	Jonah
Jos	Joshua
Jude	Jude
Jgs	Judges
Jdt	Judith
1 Kgs	1 Kings
2 Kgs	2 Kings
Lam	Lamentations
Lv	Leviticus
Lk	Luke
1 Mc	1 Maccabees
2 Mc	2 Maccabees
Mal	Malachi
Mk	Mark
Mt	Matthew
Mi	Micah
Na	Nahum
Neh	Nehemiah
Nm	Numbers
Ob	Obadiah
1 Pt	1 Peter
2 Pt	2 Peter
Phlm	Philemon
Phil	Philippians
Prv	Proverbs
Ps	Psalms
Rv	Revelation
Rom	Romans
Ru	Ruth
1 Sm	1 Samuel
2 Sm	2 Samuel
Sir	Sirach
Sg	Song of Songs

1 Thes	1 Thessalonians	Tb	Tobit
2 Thes	2 Thessalonians	Wis	Wisdom
1 Tim	1 Timothy	Zec	Zechariah
2 Tim	2 Timothy	Zep	Zephaniah
Ti	Titus		

Abbreviations and Symbols

A.D.	*anno Domini* (in the Christian era)
Aram.	Aramaic
B.C.	before Christ (prior to the Christian era)
f.	and the following verse
Gk.	Greek
Heb.	Hebrew
Intr.	Introduction
Lat.	Latin
N.T.	New Testament
O.T.	Old Testament

*	The word is treated in a Dictionary entry.
→	A cross reference either to entries or to paragraphs of the Introduction which situate or complement the entry.
□	Indicates the exhaustive nature of the N.T. references for the word treated in the entry.
△	Indicates the exhaustive nature of the N.T. references for the term treated in the footnote.
[ ]	Encloses a word not found in the text of the N.T.
=	Designates the parallel texts in other gospels.
( )	The N.T. passages so indicated in the footnotes are not found in all manuscripts.

Transliterations of Greek and Hebrew

GREEK

α	alpha	a
β	beta	b
γ	gamma	g
δ	delta	d
ϵ	epsilon	e
ζ	zēta	z
η	ēta	ē
θ	thēta	th
ι	iota	i
κ	kappa	k
λ	lambda	i
μ	mu	m
ν	nu	n
ξ	xi	x
ο	omicron	o
π	pi	p
ρ	rho	r(rh)
σ ,ς	sigma	s
τ	tau	t
υ	upsilon	y(u)
φ	phi	ph
χ	khi	kh
ψ	psi	ps
ω	omēga	ō
‛	(rough breathing)	h

HEBREW

א	aleph	’
ב	beth	b
ג	ghimel	g
ד	daleth	d
ה	he	h
ו	waw	w
ז	zayin	z
ח	heth	h
ט	teth	th
י	yod	y
כ	kaph	k
ל	lamed	l
מ	mem	m
נ	nun	n
ס	samek	s
ע	ayin	‘
פ	pe	p
צ	sade	ṣ
ק	qoph	q
ר	resh	r
שׂ	sin	s
שׁ	shin	sh
ת	taw	t

VOCALIZATIONS

◌ַ	(pathah)	a
◌ָ	(qames)	â
◌ֵ	(sere)	é
◌ֶ	(seghol)	è
◌ְ	(shewa)	e
◌ִ	(hireq)	î (i)
◌ֹ	(holem)	ô (o)
◌ֻ	(shureq)	û (u)

INTRODUCTION

OUTLINE OF THE INTRODUCTION

A. The *pax romana*
B. Sea routes
C. Land routes
4. The social context
A. Noblemen and knights
B. People and citizens
C. Freedmen
D. Slaves
5. The cultural context
6. The religious context
A. The worship of Rome
B. Eastern religions
C. Philosophical mystery cults
D. Astrology and magic
E. The Jews
7. The spread of the Christian faith

V. THE CULTURAL HERITAGE
1. Cosmology
2. Anthropology
3. Languages
A. Aramaic
B. Hebrew
C. Greek

VI. POLITICS AND THE LAW
1. Civil status
A. Jews
B. Resident aliens
C. Slaves
2. Government
3. Finance
A. Civil taxes
B. Religious taxes
4. Law and justice
A. The powers
a. The Great Sanhedrin
b. Other tribunals
B. Civil law
a. Personal law
b. Matrimonial law
c. The law of succession
d. Damages and interest, debts
C. Penal law
a. Procedures
b. Crime and punishment
c. The death penalty

VII. Economic Life

1. Natural resources
   - A. Agriculture
   - B. Sheepherding and fishery
   - C. Mineral resources
2. Trades
3. Business
4. Rich and poor

VIII. Family Life and the Home

1. The basics
   - A. The Jewish house
   - B. Clothing
   - C. Personal hygiene
     - a. Cleanliness
     - b. Cosmetics
     - c. Hair grooming
   - D. Nutrition
     - a. Diet
     - b. Cooking
2. Family life
   - A. The family and others
   - B. The foundation and life of the home
     - a. Marriage
     - b. Men
     - c. Women
     - d. Couples
     - e. The widowed
   - C. The stages of life
     - a. Birth
     - b. Girls
     - c. Boys
     - d. Adults
     - e. Old age
   - D. Sickness and death

IX. Culture

1. Traditions
2. Education
3. Writing manner and the communication of news
4. Acquaintances
5. The arts
6. Music
7. Dancing
8. The theater and amusements
9. Greek culture

X. The Faith of Israel
1. The Covenant
2. God
3. The people

XI. Religious Movements
1. The Sadducees
2. The Pharisees
3. The Essenes
4. The Zealots
5. The people of the land and their confraternities

XII. The Holy Scriptures and God's Word
1. The Law and contemporary Israel
A. The Torah
B. The traditions of the Elders
C. The guardians of the Law
2. Israel and messianic expectations
A. Prophecy and apocalyptic
B. The coming of the reign of God
C. Messiah
3. The wisdom tradition and contemporary revelation

XIII. Worship
1. Places of worship
A. The Temple and its personnel
B. The synagogues
2. Acts of worship
A. Sacrifices
B. Prayer
a. Daily prayer
b. The weekly sabbath
3. The annual liturgical cycle

XIV. Morality
1. God's Law
A. Ritual purity laws
B. Neighbors
C. The exterior law and the interior law
2. Observance of the Law
A. Man's freedom and God's judgment
B. Sin, expiation and conversion

XV. The New Testament
1. The text
2. Books and the Book
3. Interpretation

I. THE HISTORICAL CONTEXT

Biblical texts critically examined allow the historian to specify the major historical eras which underlie them. In addition, some of their findings are confirmed by extra-biblical documentation. Whether the interpretation given to these established events be one of belief or unbelief, the following points can be affirmed.

1. Before Jesus

A. From the year 63 B.C. Palestine* was occupied by the Romans and was integrated within the Empire. Herod* the Great (40–4 B.C.) and his descendants (Archelaus,* Antipas and Philip,* then Herod* Agrippa) were nothing less than vassals of a power that was unstable and imaginary. As far back as the eighth century B.C. the people of Israel had already lost their national independence. The ancient Israelite Kingdom with its two halves, the North and the South, had been destroyed by Assyrian (721) and Babylonian (587) invasions. Once deported, the people lived in exile* until the victory of the Persian King Cyrus, who authorized their return (538). But those repatriated lived no less under domination, first under the Persians, then under Alexander the Great (332) and his successors, the Seleucids. On the other hand, some Jews remained in foreign lands, thereby forming the initial core of the Jewish Diaspora* in the whole Mediterranean basin.

B. Judaism* was the name given to the Jewish milieu in both its religious and cultural manifestations, which date from the post-exilic period of Israel's history (after 538). It was characterized by Israel's resistance to any influence from other civilizations which might tend to absorb or change it. The people's religious heritage and original traditions were jealously preserved through scrupulous observances. At the very most, foreign contributions were an enrichment of it, having been integrated without disadvantages to the purity of the faith and traditional thought patterns.

C. This astonishing spiritual success knew a particularly glorious episode: the Maccabean* Wars (167–164 B.C.). The Syrian* king Antiochus Epiphanes (175–164) had tried to destroy the Jewish religion and force the people to adopt Greek customs. The victory of the Maccabees was the victory of the Jewish Law; for it always served to accentuate even more the distinction between Jews and their pagan neighbors. From 142 to 63 B.C. Israel rediscovered political independence under the Hasmonean descendants of the Maccabees. Pompey* put an end to this by seizing Jerusalem* (63) after his conquest of Syria and its annexation to the Roman Empire. He established the Hasmonean prince Hyrcanus II as High Priest* and "ethnarch*" (63–40). In fact, it was his Idumean minister, Antipater, who governed in his name, thereby opening a way for his son Herod.

D. Herod* the Great became "King of the Jews" in 40 B.C. with Rome's help, this was particularly so because his non-Jewish background made him unacceptable to the Jews. On his death (4 B.C.), it was once again through Augustus'* intervention that Herod's three sons succeeded him following the terms of his will: Archelaus* (4 B.C.–A.D. 6) got Judea,* Idumea and Samaria,* Herod* Antipas (4 B.C.–A.D. 39) Galilee and Perea, Philip* (4 B.C.–A.D. 34) Gaulitania, Iturea* and Trachonitis.* Although in Palestine people continued to call them kings, Archelaus had the title ethnarch and the two others tetrarch.* Herod the Great's grandson, Herod* Agrippa I, managed to reunite the ancient dominion from 37 to A.D. 41. After his death in 44, Judea experienced no other authority except that of the emperor's officials.

E. Attempted revolts against the Roman occupation occurred on several occasions, one by Theudas* (probably a short time after the death of Herod the Great in 4 B.C.), that of Judas the Galilean (at the time of Quirinius' census,* in A.D. 6–7), those which took place under the governments of Fadus (about 44), Cumanus (48–52), Felix* (52–60). The most violent uprising, directed by the Zealot* movement, burst out in 66. An insurrectionist government was then established in Jerusalem. The "Jewish War" lasted four years; after desperate resistance, it ended with the destruction of Jerusalem and the Temple* by the legions of Titus* in 70 and the dispersion of Jews throughout the world.

2. JESUS OF NAZARETH. Jesus* of Nazareth was not a mythical figure. His existence is topographically located in Palestine, more particularly in Galilee,* as well as chronologically dated (through his baptism by John) in the fifteenth year of the reign of Tiberias Caesar (Lk 3:1), that is in the year* following the first of October 27 (or the nineteenth of August 28). The Baptist's ministry, which appeared to be that of a prophet,* enjoyed immense popularity and stirred up a unique movement, one which looked for conversion* to God in expectation of his imminent coming and judgment; it took place in the desert of Judea, not far from Jerusalem. John had been baptizing in the Jordan, either at Bethany* (Jn 1:28), or at Aenon (3:23), a place located near Salim (to the east-north-east of Shechem). It was in the period of this great prophet's influence that Jesus must have begun his own ministry.

The other major reference point in Jesus' history is his death on Golgotha.* It clearly happened on a Friday, very probably on the eve of the feast of Passover, the fourteenth or fifteenth of the month of Nisan.* The most likely dates are April 7, 30, or April 3, 33.

Between his baptism by John and his violent death, Jesus traveled the length and breadth of Galilee and Judea, calling on his contemporaries to prepare for the imminent coming of the Kingdom* of God. By his miracles* and proclamation he aroused a messianic* enthusiasm that threatened to erupt into a political uprising. But Jesus wanted only to cast a seed into the hearts of his disciples which, in germinating, would break down the barriers that hemmed in the religious leaders of his era. His message was the Good News of that love which had to reign on earth as in heaven.

This history did not pass completely unnoticed by the historians of the time.

Thus, in a text which we can reestablish despite the transformations made by Christian editors, Josephus* mentions not only Jesus' success and his condemnation to the cross by Pilate, but also the fact that his disciples did not stop loving him because "he appeared to them alive after his death" (*Jewish Antiquities,* XVIII, 3:3). In fact, after the Passover occurrences, the disciples carried on in a manner which contrasted radically with their discouragement at Jesus' death: they believed that Jesus was risen.*

3. The Primitive Community. The first Christian community came to birth in Easter faith. The historian finds in the origin of this faith neither a phenomenon of mass delusion nor one of mythical story-telling, but rather the sober declaration of privileged witnesses.* These witnesses proclaimed the crucified Jesus, whose death had left the disciples crippled and fearful, as the Lord* forever alive: he had been raised from the dead.

A. The first community was Judeo-Christian, that is, all of its members were Jews. Right away the preaching* of the apostles in Jerusalem touched the Aramaic*-speaking residents, who were strict observers of the Mosaic Law, as well as Greek-speaking Jews of the Diaspora* called Hellenists.*

The community gathered around its center, the College of the Twelve,* the witnesses of the Risen One. Peter* enjoyed exceptional prestige. Among the earliest of the disciples were the brothers* of the Lord (1 Cor 9:5; Gal 1:19) who, although members of his family in the broad sense, had been opposed to his ministry initially. They were venerated as those who had been close to Jesus.

In their adherence to the same faith the believers differed in their attitudes, according to their respective milieus. The Hebrews, having no inclination to withdraw from Judaism,* continued their practiced observance of laws and prayers. They gathered around James,* the most influential of the "brothers of the Lord." On the other side, the Hellenists, whose leader was Stephen,* criticized the overvaluation of Jewish worship and preached its spiritualization. A certain tension must have existed between the two groups; though banal in itself, the conflict over table* service may be an echo of it (Acts 6:1–6).

B. Stephen's diatribe against the Temple (Acts 7) unleashed the Jewish religious authorities' already latent persecution against this new sect (cf. Acts 24:5; 28:22). First the Hellenists, then Peter, perhaps the Twelve also, had to leave Jerusalem.

This dispersion inaugurated the Christian mission, first to the Jews, about A.D. 34–36 in Samaria,* then in various cities of Judea and Galilee. From Jerusalem the Apostles sent Peter and John* to put their seal of approval on the beginning of this work by calling down the Holy Spirit upon the new converts. But a decisive step still had to be taken, the admission of pagans to the Christian community.

C. It was on the occasion of one of his pastoral journeys that Peter understood (and later admitted to the Jerusalem group) that the same gift of God had been given to the pagans* (Acts 10:1–48; 11:4–18). The expansion reached a new stage: in Phoenicia, Cyprus* and, finally, at Antioch* (Acts 11:19). It was in this city that the young sect, set free from Jewish pressure, came of age: there, for the first time, the disciples of Jesus were called "Christians*" (11:26) and were said to celebrate the worship of the Lord (13:2).

The primitive community, then, had two poles: Jerusalem and Antioch. Tension broke out: some "conservatives," the Judaizers* from Jerusalem, wanted to impose circumcision* on pagan converts as a requirement for salvation. In order to resolve the conflict, a gathering took place in Jerusalem in the year 48, one which we may designate as the first "Council.*" It was really the Mother Church which settled the issue once and for all, but in a catholic sense: the pagan converts would not be held to observance of the Law of Moses (Gal 2:1–10), even if they were later prevailed upon to keep some minimal Jewish observances (Acts 15:23–29). This exposition is not prejudicial to the tradition,* the precision of which was attested to by a large number of living links; the collection* was the tangible sign of the unity of the churches (Acts 11:28–30; 1 Cor 16:1–4). In any case, the latter were from that time on many and vigorous.

4. PAUL. Paul* of Tarsus was the principal actor in this drama of evangelization and radical universalism. An exemplary Jew and a persecutor of Christians before his encounter with Christ, he travelled in the course of his three missionary journeys between 48 and 60 through Asia,* Macedonia* and Greece;* as a prisoner he came to the isles of Crete* and Malta, ending up in Rome. With his fellow workers he founded a large number of churches. In communion with one another, these were structured in the following way: as their progress was constantly being followed up by their founder, generally they were headed by presbyters* set apart by the laying on of hands.* Gradually, Ephesus* and Rome* were the churches which became the poles of the universal Church. More than anyone else, Paul had to confront the problem of Jewish observances; he vigorously reacted to the vacillations of Peter, who, at Antioch, did not dare disregard the keeping of dietary laws (Gal 2:11–14). First and foremost a theologian, Paul stressed the equality of Jew and pagan under the dominion of sin* and in the attraction of grace*: for everyone salvation is the free gift of God's mercy in Christ. The Jews clearly were chosen* first, the Law* having been merely a provisional regime and a powerless one; in fact, faith,* which preexisted the Law among the patriarchs, was the only way to salvation. To submit oneself to former observances was to fail to recognize Jesus Christ as the sole mediator in whom there is henceforth "neither Greek nor Jew, neither circumcised nor uncircumcised, neither barbarian nor Scythian, neither slave nor free" (Col 3:11).

5. EXPANSION. The expansion of Christianity appears surprising: it was characterized by a rapid spread unequalled in missionary history and by its encounter with the pagan world, toward which the Jewish religion remained uncompromising. Simultaneously this was favorable and hostile territory for the new faith (cf. Intr. IV.7). Until about the year 60, evangelization was concentrated first of all in the synagogues*: there Christ was proclaimed at the time of the sabbath* celebrations which the Jewish community of the place and

THE EMPERORS OF ROME, THE HIGH PRIESTS OF ISRAEL, THE KINGS AND GOVERNORS OF PALESTINE, THE LEGATES OF SYRIA

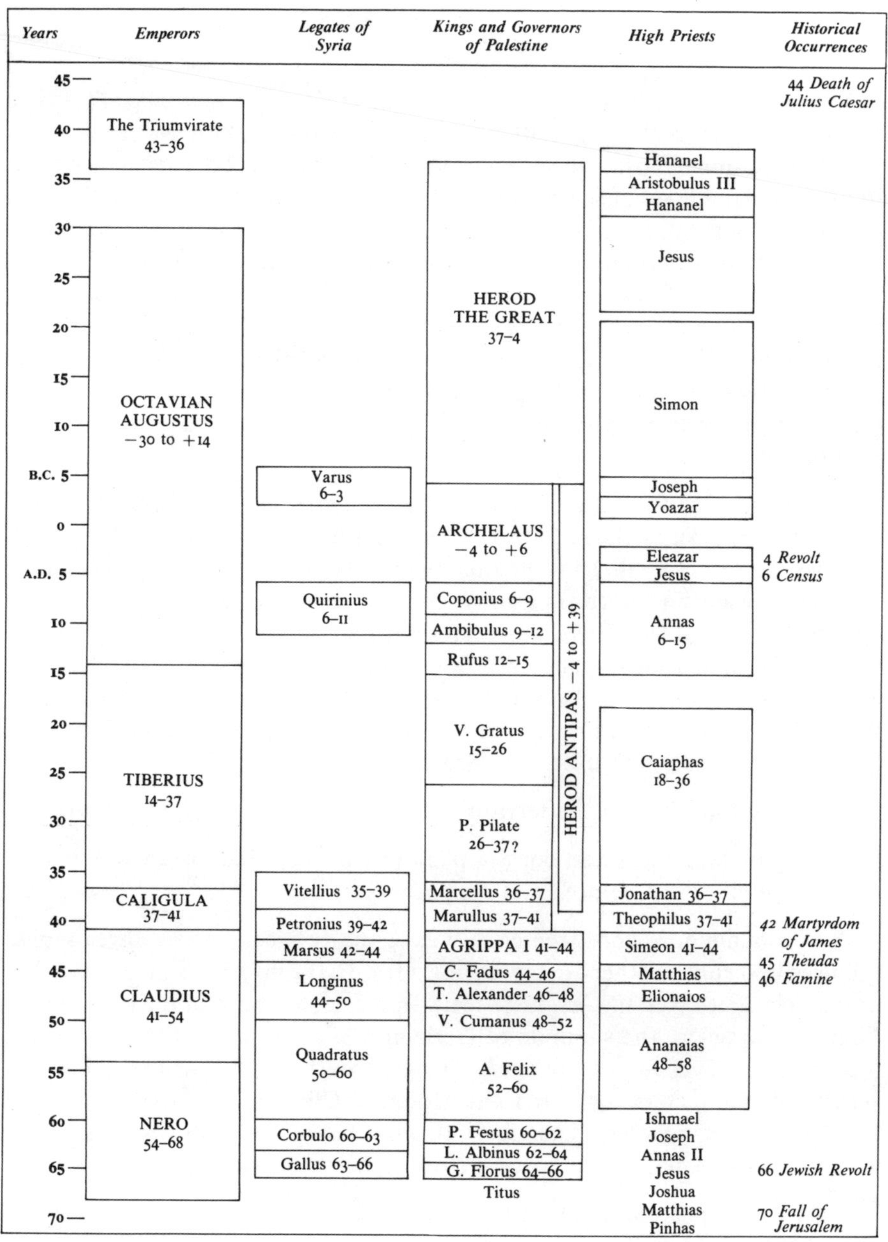

Years
Emperors
Legates of Syria
Kings and Governors of Palestine
High Priests
Historical Occurrences
45
40
35
30
25
20
15
10
B.C. 5
0
A.D. 5
10
15
20
25
30
35
40
45
50
55
60
65
70
The Triumvirate 43–36
OCTAVIAN AUGUSTUS −30 to +14
TIBERIUS 14–37
CALIGULA 37–41
CLAUDIUS 41–54
NERO 54–68
Varus 6–3
Quirinius 6–11
Vitellius 35–39
Petronius 39–42
Marsus 42–44
Longinus 44–50
Quadratus 50–60
Corbulo 60–63
Gallus 63–66
HEROD THE GREAT 37–4
ARCHELAUS −4 to +6
HEROD ANTIPAS −4 to +39
Coponius 6–9
Ambibulus 9–12
Rufus 12–15
V. Gratus 15–26
P. Pilate 26–37?
Marcellus 36–37
Marullus 37–41
AGRIPPA I 41–44
C. Fadus 44–46
T. Alexander 46–48
V. Cumanus 48–52
A. Felix 52–60
P. Festus 60–62
L. Albinus 62–64
G. Florus 64–66
Titus
Hananel
Aristobulus III
Hananel
Jesus
Simon
Joseph
Yoazar
Eleazar
Jesus
Annas 6–15
Caiaphas 18–36
Jonathan 36–37
Theophilus 37–41
Simeon 41–44
Matthias
Elionaios
Ananaias 48–58
Ishmael
Joseph
Annas II
Jesus
Joshua
Matthias
Pinhas
44 Death of Julius Caesar
4 Revolt
6 Census
42 Martyrdom of James
45 Theudas
46 Famine
66 Jewish Revolt
70 Fall of Jerusalem

numerous God-fearers* took part in. Ordinarily, only a small number embraced the new preaching; thereafter, hounded and persecuted missionaries carried the message to the pagans* with the help of the earliest converts, who already belonged to the local scene. The Christian Church distinguished itself amid the pagans by its faith in the one God of the Covenant* and his envoy Jesus Christ, but as well by its moral life, characterized by charity* and purity.*

II. THE LAND

1. In the first century the "land of Israel" (Mt 2:20) was officially called Judea* (Lk 4:44; Acts 10:37); after the Jewish revolt of 135 it was improperly called "Palestinian Syria," then "Palestine." Although its "borders" are difficult to fix, it was made up of several regions: Judea in the narrow sense of the term (including Idumea), Samaria,* Galilee* and Perea (or "the territory across the Jordan"). It was bordered on the southeast by the desert of Arabia,* on the south by the Sinai* desert, on the west by the Mediterranean, on the north by Lebanon, and on the northeast by the Decapolis,* Iturea* and Trachonitis.* It formed a quadrilateral of about 250 kilometers (150 miles) in length by 40 to 140 kilometers (25–85 miles) in breadth, covering some 25,000 square kilometers (9,700 square miles), approximately the size of Sicily or the state of New Hampshire.

2. Various rock formations characterized the ground from the sandstone of the Jordan Plateau to the red sand of the coast and the basalt in the region of Tiberias.* Overall, chalky soil predominated. Its porous nature accounted for the lack of water in the rivers during summer as well as the number of wells, particularly in Galilee. There was rock on the surface of the land, from which fact there stemmed a vast quantity of stones and a meager amount of arable land. The country's underground resources were quite poor. In the absence of iron, some layers of copper and basalt were mined. Salt* was provided in abundance by the waters of the Dead Sea or "Sea of Salt" (Gn 14:3; Dt 3:17).

3. The terrain divided the territory into four parallel longitudinal strips:

A. On the Mediterranean coast a plain (Shephelah, Sharon) in which were located the cities of Caesarea and Joppa.

B. A mountainous zone, the extension of the Lebanon, where three ranges followed upon one another at varying altitudes. To the north, the hills of Galilee, around Nazareth (500 meters, 1,640 feet). In the center, beyond the break in the Plain of Esdraelon, the summits of Gerizim (881 meters, 2,890 feet) and Ebal (940 meters, 3,084 feet) in Samaria. To the south, in Judea, the heights of Jerusalem (790 meters, 2,592 ft.), the Mount of Olives (812 meters, 2,664 feet) and Hebron (1,027 meters, 3,370 feet); this last massif led to the expression "to go up to Jerusalem"; on the eastern slope it fell off toward the Dead Sea.

C. A long depression below sea level, the deepest in the world, carved by the course of the Jordan. The river, gushing forth at the foot of the Anti-Lebanon range, at an altitude of 45 meters (148 feet) descends in a steep slope toward the Lake of Gennesaret (Tiberias) at 210 meters (689 feet) below sea level and, crossing the Plain of Ghor (where there are oases), snakes in countless meanderings to the Dead Sea (−392 meters, −1,286 feet).

D. East of the Jordan Valley, the table-land of present-day Jordan.

4. A. With the great diversity of landscape there were corresponding contrasts in climate, from the subtropical (where the effects of the sea were mixed in) to the mountainous and the desert. Each region differed more or less from the others according to its own humidity index. Overall, however, and except for the Jordan trench area, the country's climate was temperate, marked by two seasons: from April to October a totally dry summer, from November to March a winter in which rain might fall for sixty days.

B. Although dreaded for its violence (the rarer it was, the more torrential it could be), rain was crucial for the earth's bountifulness, especially an early rain in October or a late rain in April (Jas 5:7). The rainfall depended on winds blowing from the west (cf. Lk 12:54). The coast was the most favored region, followed by the central mountain crest with a total precipitation rate, for example in Jerusalem, that approximated that of Paris (575 millimeters, 23 inches); the shielded eastern slope, by contrast, quickly became the arid Judean desert regions and the dry Jordan Plain. In summer, the same winds from the west brought abundant nocturnal dews which nourished the vegetation. Conversely, the wind from the southeast (the *hamsin,* the sirocco) blasted the air with heat (cf. Lk 12:55). In addition to the prevailing winds there were also local breezes, which occasionally brought with them violent whirlwinds and stirred up hazardous storms in the basin of Lake Tiberias (cf. Mt 8:24).

C. Temperatures were less determinators of the seasons than were the rains. They remained mild in winter (from 8° to 12° C., 48° to 56° F.), tolerable in summer (from 21° to 29° C., 74° to 90° F.), except in the Jordan depression (as high as 50° C., 122° F.). However, the daily divergence in temperature was quite pronounced, possibly reaching a variation of 20° C. (36°F.) between noon and midnight. The nights were cool, even on the threshold of summer (cf. Mk 14:67).

5. The vegetation in Jesus' time was not the same as in our day. The numerous forests have today practically disappeared through man's use or from the foraging of goats; plants have been imported over the centuries: the prickly pear (from Mexico), the eucalyptus (from Australia), sunflowers and tomatoes (from America). For the remainder, the vegetation was generally subtropical like today: oak, terebinth, plane, red carob, cyprus and juniper trees. In the Jordan Valley it became tropical (palm* trees) but in the southern deserts it was reduced to hardy thickets. In the month of March the greenery burst forth almost everywhere: tulips and gladioli, wind-flowers that quickly fade away (Mt 6:28). Among fruit-bearing trees, three especially were cultivated and were so characteristic of the country that they occasionally symbolized Israel: the olive,* the fig,* the vine.* Among cereals, wheat* and barley* were predominant, serving as the basis of nourishment. There remain only the vegetable crops to mention: beans, lentils, onions, leeks, eggplant, sweet peppers, different kinds of lettuce.

6. Wild fauna abounded in the country. In the desert, various kinds of cats (among which was undoubtedly the lion*: cf. I Sm 17:34; Jer 49:19) were a reminder of its proximity to the African continent. Besides the invasions of grasshoppers* and the bites of serpents,* the natives feared the fox and shepherds the wolf. Flies, worms* and insects swarmed in the countryside. There was a great variety of birds. Fish,* from species akin to those known in Egypt, constituted the riches of the Jordan and of Lake Tiberias (the Sea of Galilee). Oxen, bulls and fowl were abundant; sheep* and goats* made up large flocks, occasionally guarded by a dog* (at that time, it was a half-wolf, snarling and half-famished). The camel* became rare, while the ass,* much more vigorous than in our countries, served as the customary mount (Mt 21:7), particularly in the mountains, or as the beast of burden (Mt 21:5); horses* were not used except by the Romans.

III. THE PEOPLE

1. From the remotest periods of antiquity Palestine was inhabited. Nomadic Semites,* originating from diverse family stocks, were known to have been there as early as the start of the third millennium. Around the fifteenth century B.C. the Hebrews drove out the Canaanites* (or Phoenicians) to settle in the land that had been promised to their fathers; they did this in accordance with the covenant* established by God with Abraham, Isaac and Jacob. They were conscious of being a unique people,* chosen, charged to make manifest among men worship* of the one God; however, they did not thereby have at their disposal a land isolated from the world. Following upon as well as prior to their occupation, the Mediterranean coastland remained the almost required pathway for going from Egypt to Mesopotamia and back. This country, then, was a crossroads of the nations; in succession it experienced invasions by the Assyrians (721), Babylonians (587), then the occupation by the Greeks (322) and Romans (63). Despite all this, and small though she was, Israel, through a remnant* that was faithful, preserved her faith in the one God.

2. The Various Population Groupings

A. The term *Hebrews** may perhaps derive from the name of a nomadic tribe, the Apiru (2000 B.C.); according to Jewish tradition, this word is related to the root *'avar,* "to pass," pointing to the destiny of this people which was to be continually on the move and also had as its vocation the "causing (of others) to pass" from ignorance to knowledge of the one God.

B. This people was also Israel,* from the name given by the nocturnal visitor to Jacob after his wrestling with God (Gn 32:29), that is, according to its popular etymology, the one who had been face to face with God and who was destined to prevail over men.

C. To this latter name, which is more specifically religious, there came to be associated that of Jew,* a generalization consequent upon the return from the Exile (538) and further specifying the settling of the people in its homeland. In this period in fact, the Judeans, the descendants of the tribe of Judah,* preserved intact their faith and traditions, while other tribes* allowed themselves to be tainted by the pagan environment. As it happened, this word came to designate a people who included the inheritors of the promise,* without thereby having to be resident in Judea.

D. For their part, the Galileans,* the inhabitants of the north (formerly occupied by the tribes of Asher, Naphtali, Issachar, and Zebulun, and the first to be invaded [in 721] by the pagans), scarcely represented the authenticity of the Jewish faith, mixed in as they had become with strangers. From this fact came the name Galilee, *Gelil-hag-goyyîm:* "circle of the nations" (Is 8:23; Mt 4:15). Within this land of rugged Jewish peasants, with a peculiar dialect (Mt 26:73), there rose up revolutionaries, less fiery than the rigorists of Judea but more fiery in the purity of their nationalism.

E. The Samaritans* were considered to be heretics. Strictly speaking, the antagonism between Jews and Samaritans does not go back to the secession from Israel* (935), which led to the setting up of the Northern Kingdom (1 Kgs 12); above all it derived from the return from the Exile* in Babylon (538).

The Judeans henceforth had as neighbors people of pagan origins who, though they had certainly adopted the beliefs of the Israelites who had stayed on in the country during the deportation period, limited divine revelation to the five books of Moses.* Moreover, after having built a sanctuary around the year 330 on Mount Gerizim, they centered their worship there rather than in Jerusalem. Even though their temple had been destroyed in 128 B.C., they held that they had always remained true worshippers of Yahweh (cf. Jn 4:20). In Jesus' time the Jews had been outraged by Herod's conduct in rebuilding the capital of Samaria and giving it the name of the emperor Augustus* (Sebaste).

F. We cannot say of the Idumeans (whose name, according to popular etymology derived from Edom—Esau, son of Abraham) that they belonged to the Jewish people, despite all efforts at their Judaization. Having dwelt for only a short time in the region to the south of Judah* and Hebron, they remained "cousins" of the chosen people. Notwithstanding this, it was an Idumean, Herod the Great, who presided over the destiny of Judea for thirty-six years.

G. Pagans, such as the indigenous Canaanites and, especially, the Greeks, were numerous in Palestine. From the fourth century, under Alexander, many cities had no Jews or anything Jewish: such were the Greek cities of the Decapolis,* situated east of the Jordan River, between the Sea of Galilee and the Dead Sea, which had successfully resisted Jewish pressure; others were on the coast, from Acco (Acre) as far as Gaza by way of Caesarea; others as well were in Galilee, Tiberias (founded in Jesus' time in 17–22) and the capital, Sepphoris. We cannot really speak of the Romans as a part of the population: they were the "occupiers," resident in garrisons, most notably in Caesarea, Jerusalem and

Acco. The pagans, whatever their origins, Canaanite or Greco-Roman, were the majority in cities, except for Jerusalem. It is therefore mistaken to imagine the "holy land" as a country where with one accord people rendered worship to the one only God. The presence of these non-Jews had to favor the universalism proclaimed by Jesus.

H. Among Christians a distinction must be drawn between those of pagan background and those of Jewish background, Judeo-Christians and Judaizers. It is difficult to give an exact count of the population of Palestine in Jesus' time. The Jews properly so-called could not have been more than a half million in number; in adding on to their numbers the Samaritans, the Idumeans and those of the Decapolis, we arrive at the figure of barely a million.

3. THE DIASPORA. The Jewish Diaspora,* or the totality of Jews scattered throughout the entire empire, suggests that we not remain satisfied with the preceding facts. The "Jewish people" cannot in fact be limited only to the inhabitants of Palestine. Very early on, the Israelites emigrated. Suffice it to take note of the Assyrian and Babylonian deportations,* the foundation of the colony of Elephantine near Aswan in Egypt in the fifth–fourth century B.C., the volunteers enlisted in the army of Alexander in Mesopotamia (fourth century), the Jewish mercenaries of Antiochus interned in Italy, the temple of Leontopolis in Lower Egypt (third century), and, finally, commercial enterpreneurs. Jews were found in particularly large numbers in Rome and Alexandria.

The number of Jews living in the Roman Empire has been estimated at seven or eight million, about eight to ten percent of the empire's population. These Jewish communities were able to engage in the economic and political life of various states, with the result that some even became intimates of the emperor. On the whole, they remained faithful to their ancestral faith, as did Philo,* the great philosopher of Alexandria (13 B.C.–A.D. 45/50). They even tried to radiate their faith, for example by translating the Bible into Greek (the Septuagint*) between 250–150 B.C., or by attracting proselytes,* the God-fearers,* such as Cornelius* (Acts 10:1). They opened up a fertile field for future believers.

IV. THE MEDITERRANEAN WORLD

1. THE HISTORICAL CONTEXT. In the first century B.C. the *pax romana* inaugurated a new period in the history of the Mediterranean world. Conflicts which tore apart peoples and kingdoms gave the Romans successive occasions to intervene and impose their authority; in the case of Judea, it was rival leaders who appealed to the Roman power to settle the conflicts or to obtain protection. In Rome and throughout Italy* the triumphs of Caesar* (48 B.C.) and Octavian (31 B.C.) put an end to a protracted civil war. The republican government which ruled Rome during earlier centuries was transformed by Caesar into a personal dictatorship and progressively by Octavian into an absolute monarchy. The term *imperium,* which previously signified the executive power of the consul, the chief of the army, henceforth stood for the sovereign's *(imperator)* authority over subject peoples, Egyptians or Gauls, Greeks or "barbarians.*" This authority was not limited in time, place or extent. The era of violent conflicts was ended; from the Rhone to the Euphrates Rome claimed to be the guarantor of public order and unity.

2. THE POLITICAL CONTEXT. By means of a complex administration, a vast overhaul progressively took place. What typified the Roman government in occupied countries was, on one side, the centralization of authority in the governor's hands, and on the other, a differentiation among statutes accorded to the conquered peoples. This ability to differentiate respected local circumstances; it depended also on Rome's selection of her representatives, through whom Rome ensured the pursuit of her inclinations and interests.

A. At the top was the emperor.* In the New Testament era he had not yet acquired the legal importance he would achieve beginning with the next century. Nonetheless, elected for life as he was, he was in theory the first citizen *(princeps)* and magistrate; his magistracy applied to the whole empire. The eastern populaces considered him king in the Hellenistic sense, namely that he was a distinguished individual who had received his power from God; in Rome he was the religious leader, the supreme pontiff. Thus, Octavian (63 B.C.–A.D. 14), the first emperor, was called Augustus*: "worthy of reverence," and after his death became, by apotheosis, a divine being. From this time on emperor worship (or worship of "Rome") became common throughout the empire; recognition was given thereby to the Roman power's achievement in suppressing local tyranny, political corruption or disorder, and the establishing of conditions favorable to the economic and social life of the conquered peoples. The emperor was inviolable; in addition to his power over the whole empire, he exercised his protection over private individuals by the possibility, which all (Roman) citizens* had, of their making appeal to him on any judicial decision. He thereby gained considerable influence.

B. The provinces.* Each occupied country became a Roman province: a senatorial province when, after having been pacified, it was administered by the Senate; an imperial province when, still requiring the presence of troops, it was answerable more explicitly to the person of the emperor who was commander-in-chief of the army.

a. The senatorial provinces (Asia,* the principal one, Achaia,* Cyprus,* and Macedonia*) each had a governor* with the title of proconsul (for example, Sergius Paulus,* Gallio:* Acts 13:6-12; 18:12-17) at its head. His office, a two-year term, concerned itself with the smooth functioning of justice and the collection of taxes. Moreover, judicial measures already in force were respected to the extent that they did not contravene Roman law. Only the most serious sanctions, and notably the death penalty, were kept from local officials and had to be referred to the governor. The levying of taxes required the taking of a census* and a land registry to assess fortunes: personnel, "the tax collectors,*" were recruited and controlled by "general contractors."

b. The imperial provinces (for example, Syria*) were administered by a legate* (for example, Quirinius*) named by the emperor for an indeterminate time (Acts 24:10). Certain regions, especially, were confided to a prefect* who, from A.D. 42, was called a "procurator*": thus, Pontius Pilate,* Felix* or Festus* (Mt 27; Acts 24:27). These officials had troops and military powers at their disposal. They were accompanied by a cohort* which did guard duty for them. The praetorium* where they administered justice served as a type of military command-post.

c. In addition, the emperor reserved to himself the right of granting to provinces of his choice some semblance of autonomy through his recognition of local assemblies (municipal or provincial). These served as counterweights to the personal power of Roman magistrates. Sustained by the central power, they paradoxically reinforced loyalty toward Rome. Another means used to encourage this kind of loyalty was the granting of Roman citizenship* to a particular individual or category of persons, more rarely to entire cities. One could buy this privilege or possess it by hereditary right (Acts 22:28). This title had great worth; it made one exempt from corporal punishment (Acts 16:37) and forced labor, withdrawing its holder from local jurisdiction and legitimizing direct appeal to the emperor (Acts 25:10,12,21,25).

C. Cities and communities. The internal status of each province* varied according to the relationship Rome established as a consequence of its judgment or inclinations. This differentiation was in effect particularly at the level of cities which, in the situation obtaining earlier, frequently had functioned as autonomous entities.

Afterwards, cities could be ranked according to a very precise hierarchy. Several cities, some repopulated after the civil war by Roman veterans (such as Corinth*) were privileged; designated a "colony*" or "Roman municipality," they were likened to the cities of Italy, and some of their residents, who were descended from Roman colonists, enjoyed a majority of the rights of Roman citizens* (the free residents of Rome and Italy).

Other cities enjoyed only certain rights. These privileged cities, however, were lost in the number of towns, large and small, where only the aristocracy were liable to acquire one or another of a citizen's rights. These towns had their own organization and possessed their own citizenship and occasionally magistracies, as in Tarsus,* Ephesus,* Smyrna.* They administered a territory more or less extensive, all the while depending, in the last analysis, on the Roman magistrate to whom the province* had been entrusted. Finally, in territories which were not responsible to any city, some communities which formed an ethnic or religious enclave, the vestige of an organization predating the Greek conquests, maintained a separate status. So regarded were the Galatians* and numerous small protectorates which Rome tended to administer more and more directly (the kingdom of Herod, the tetrarchy* of Lysanias, the Decapolis*). By exception, certain important temples (that of Jerusalem among others) enjoyed special status and, occasionally, their own territory. In all cases, the residents were held to the payment of taxes,* for the country as such belonged to the Roman occupier.

3. The Economic Context

A. In the age of the *pax romana* the Mediterranean world in its entirety enjoyed an economic prosperity that was notable in comparison with the past, even if it remained the possession of privileged groups. The public works, theaters, new shrines, large numbers of restored cities, and several famous industries, attest it. The cessation of wars and a unified administration and monetary system explain this progress, but one factor played a decisive role: the network of communication roads spread everywhere in the empire. Rid of brigands, this network encouraged commercial relations already traditional in the Mediterranean as well as "international" trade of every sort.

B. The principal links were the sea routes. In fair weather, the average speed was four to six knots. The sea lanes served chiefly to deliver wheat (which fed Rome), but also spices, metals, and slaves. The cost of transportation was less expensive than on the land routes. Only luxury goods made use of the inland roads. Maritime trade between Rome and Alexandria was preferential and quite regular. Numerous Alexandrian ships called at Rhodes* or put into the southwest of Asia,* present-day Turkey. Another major sea lane ran from Rome to the Black Sea or present-day Asia. Corinth* played an important redistribution function within it. The emperor Nero undertook, without achieving his goal, to dig a canal through the Isthmus of Corinth to ease traffic. Other major axes (Rome-Carthage, Rome-Southern Gaul, Rome-Spain) are not mentioned in the New Testament.

C. The land routes, which the apostles followed, linked one country with another. Leading to the principal ports, they linked the cities of the interior with the maritime routes. A road from Petra to Caesarea passed through Jerusalem, and a road from the Tigris and Euphrates valleys ended at Antioch after passing through Damascus. There had already been a road network in Asia Minor; the Romans used it, improving it with solid pavement and developing its outline. The journey from Antioch to Rome, for example, became relatively easy. Passing through Tarsus and Ephesus, a traveller reached Macedonia by sea, then crossed the Balkans as far as Illyria, to Dyrrachium opposite Brindisi; from there one could embark for Italy. Care for the construction and maintenance of the roads was the responsibility of the governor of the province. Paid for by the taxes of the residents, they were worked on by the legionnaires and convicts. Highway distances were computed in miles* (1,500 meters) written on milestones beginning in the capital city. Besides Rome, these included Lyons in Gaul, Ephesus in Asia, and Carthage in Africa. One could travel on horseback (thirty to fifty miles a day) or on foot (twenty-five miles a day).

4. The Social Context. The two extremes of the social ladder, the ancient nobility and the slaves, maintained their traditional statuses, but the intervening positions, persons free by birth or franchise, were transformed; a profound change took place that affected the whole social structure. The aristocratic regime, which typified republican Rome, moved toward a transformation into a democratic regime through access to the magistracies opened up to citizens of various social classes.

A. The newer nobility which came into being comprised high magistrates named by the emperor, in spirit much more open than the ancient nobility (for example, Gallio,* the proconsul of Achaia and brother of Seneca, Acts 18:12-17), while the higher fringe of freemen formed the class of knights. This latter, distinguished by the possession of a certain level of wealth, was immersed in business and administration. It was from the ranks of the knights that the emperor recruited officials for the imperial provinces. Their successes retained an individual character, for the class to which they belonged did not yet enjoy any prestige. Thus the knights, of which Pilate* was one, were more grasping and more sensitive to charges that might be brought against their administrations.

B. The other freemen, the *plebs,* held positions in keeping with their resources: peasants, craftsmen, merchants, lawyers, orators, educators, doctors. If they hailed from the provinces, they could become Roman citizens* through the payment of a large sum of money. Thereafter they could serve in the army or in the lower echelons of government.

C. Moreover, a new social class mingled with theirs, that of the freedmen,* released from slavery. Acts of emancipation were multiplied at the beginning of this era. Motivated by a humanitarian concern, emancipatory actions allowed entry to economic or administrative levels heretofore restricted. Freedmen rose to important posts in the political field; eager to rid themselves of any trace of servitude, they formed a dynamic social class, very useful to a world under construction. In Rome their number was a third that of the free men.

D. The slave,* at the lowest rung of the ladder, was for the ancient world an object *(res),* a "tool" (Aristotle). Subject to his master's capriciousness, he enjoyed not a single civil right, not even that of marriage. He did not even have religious rights, but was excluded from civic worship. In Rome there was one slave for every two free men; in 5 B.C., this amounted, according to certain estimates, to the presence of 280,000 slaves for a citizenry of 560,000. At Alexandria, out of a population of nearly one million, only 300,000 men were free. In Athens three out of every four residents were slaves.

5. THE CULTURAL CONTEXT. In extending its power to countries surrounding the Mediterranean, Rome found a world already culturally unified, at least on the surface, whatever other partitions and tensions held sway among the ethnic and social groupings. This cultural unification was due to the Hellenization brought about by Alexander the Great (336-323 B.C.) throughout his conquered territories, and by the dynasties that succeeded him.

The business colonies, established just about everywhere on the Greek coasts, were joined by more than seventy new cities. The ancient cities were progressively Hellenized. Except in the most remote countrysides, Greek* became the common language (*koinē**) and, at Rome, the language of the cultured gentry. Education was increasingly inspired by the Athenian model. The customs of Greece and her philosophical currents (Epicureanism,* Cynicism, Stoicism*: cf. Acts 17:18) spread through the mingling of people (in business, the army, through itinerant philosophers and artists). Hence the Greek culture was grafted onto many Oriental civilizations. Hellenism* is the name given to the civilization and culture which issued from this encounter and the interchange thus effected. It was a composite culture, certainly inferior (if such an evaluation is possible) to that of ancient Greece, but characterized by an astonishing openness, a cultural eclecticism, of which the religious context of the era offers one of the best illustrations.

6. The Religious Context

A. We have already made mention (Intr.IV.2.A) of the worship* of Rome or of the emperor in the occupied countries, deriving from the oriental understanding of the sovereign. This cult did not supplant existing religions and did not pose as a rival to them. As a kind of state religion, it was the expression of political unity and of loyalty to Rome. Resembling them in nature, it even associated itself with the civic cults which formerly thrived in these Hellenic cities. Each center gathered around a deity out of which it forged a symbol of itself and which, occasionally, was the only vestige of its past glories. Such were Athena in Athens, Artemis* in Ephesus, and Apollo at Cyrene.* The civic assemblies did not come together without a preliminary sacrifice to the god, and civic festivals involved cultic celebrations. The priests,* with a role exclusively ritualistic, were officers with the same title as other civic officials. The gods of the most influential cities attracted foreigners in pilgrimages* and their sanctuaries supported many an industry. Other cults had a more extensive sphere of influence by virtue of their long traditions. Such were those of Apollo at Delphi, to which one came for consultation before a perilous journey, a marriage, or a business or political venture, or that of Zeus at Olympus, renowned for the games celebrated every five years and where all of Greece became aware of its unity.

B. Then again, the Oriental religions at the beginning of the Christian era were adopted by or infiltrated into Greek and Hellenized cities, and even into Rome, despite the rather severe measures taken by the Senate. Their gods were not protectors of the city: their worship, with its ritual practices, personally assured the individual of the divinity's succor, particularly in time of sickness. The principal religions of this kind were conceived in Egypt (Isis, Osiris, Horus), in Syria* (Atargatis, Adonis), and in Phrygia* (Cybele). These cults were distinguished by their attention to the rhythms of nature, the resurgence of life in vegetation and fertility. They demanded no moral or doctrinal reform. Their rites, whose shape was occasionally orgiastic and always appealing to the senses (music, noise, pomp-filled ceremonies, ecstatic happenings), brought about what the believer looked for. A distinction was made between the simple faithful and the initiates. The latter took part in secret rites, called mysteries,* which represented the vicissitudes associated with the gods and, in letting the initiate commune with the divine experience, assured him of prosperity now and sometimes happiness hereafter.

C. There were also philosophical mysteries, whose rites "re-presented" a doctrine and which constituted a search for that wisdom* by which one might live without suffering too much and also attain to immortality.* This concurred with a particular view of the world and of human destiny. In this view, the soul* is the offspring of an exalted heaven, but has become contaminated through union with matter. Once purified, it will ascend again to its original element. According to some interpreters, such mystery cults came to influence Paul's theology during his travels through Asia Minor, but historians today reject this view because of the major differences, intrinsic to these oriental mystery religions, which distinguish them from the Christian faith. Like amulets, pagan initiation rites protected believers automatically. They were effective once and for all without reference to a believer's subsequent moral life. Above all, the cult participant sought his own happiness or his own immortality, in such a way that love (his for God and God's for him) was missing.

D. The action of the gods (as well as salvation when it was ultimately achieved) pertained to the cosmic or astral sphere. Astrology held great sway at all levels of society. Stars* determined an individual's life. Mankind was delivered to blind fate, against which the choice of favorable days was his only protection. There was also a belief in demons,* whether the several types of intermediaries between the gods and men or independent ones, most often of a malicious sort (cf. Eph 6:12). Out of these beliefs magical* practices, mostly of Babylonian or Egyptian origin (cf. Acts 19:19), developed.

E. The Jews, a few of whom dwelt just about everywhere in the Hellenistic world, stood radically apart from the rest of people because of the integrity of their faith and their observance of the Law.* On the one hand, they enjoyed special privileges: their own courts, their councils of elders, their synagogues, permission for circumcision, and exemption from emperor worship. This last duty was occasionally replaced by offerings. Augustus himself once made an offering of sacrifices to Yahweh. The God of the Covenant* remained the only Savior; every other god was reckoned false, nonexistent.

The Greco-Roman world's opinion of these singular and intransigent Jews took two forms: on the one hand a fear or dislike, on the other an attraction. On the negative side one may not speak of anti-Semitism as such, for this racial problem was unknown at the time. Nor was it, in the syncretistic religious environment, an intolerance toward the Jewish faith as such. Rather, the very number of Jews (in Alexandria they occupied two of the five city quarters) and the incomprehensible exclusiveness with which they held back from mingling with non-Jews, when combined with their refusal to share even in civic cults, stirred up mistrust and occasionally hatred. The historian Tacitus (A.D. 55–120) presented a caricature of their history and their customs. At Rome in the year 50, the Jewish community was struck with a decree of expulsion (cf. Acts 18:2) which extended toward them the same Senate mistrust that earlier had been shown to Greek rhetoricians and philosophers banned on several occasions (in 173, 161, and 155 B.C.). More positively, on the other hand, many pagans were drawn to the synagogue* and participated in its services without the Jews having had to enlist them through any kind of missionary activity. The Jews called these people God-fearers.* Some reached the point of becoming proselytes,* that is, members of the Jewish people through complete adherence to Jewish observances. They severed themselves from any contact with their own native people. The piety of the synagogue offered what the civil or oriental religions and the various philosophies could not: the discovery of a unique God,* more powerful than fate, the Creator of the world and the Lord of history; a light for moral conduct and a wisdom which coincided with their religious impulses; a God who, above all, heard the poor and rendered justice and mercy; and, finally, the hope of a sure salvation.

7. The Spread of the Christian Faith

A. One remains surprised at the speed and extent of the spread of the Christian faith reflected in the New Testament, especially in the Acts of the Apostles. Without doubt the *pax romana,* the mingling of peoples and ideas, and the relative security of travel provide a partial account for the ease with which the Christian preachers were able to reach the very diverse communities in the Mediterranean basin.

The Jewish Diaspora* played a still greater role. In the first instance, it was in the synagogues* that the Apostles, and chiefly Paul, proclaimed Christ. They definitely thought that it was to the Jews in the first place that the message was to be proclaimed (Acts 13:46; Rom 1:16), but in doing this they were at the same time evangelizing pagans, the many God-fearers* who frequented the services and who were thus already "turned towards God, leaving idols behind" (cf. 1 Thess 1:9). The preaching in the synagogues, even when it aroused strong opposition, always brought some believers, Jews or pagans, to conversion.* Immediately formed into a fraternal community, the Christian faith spread out into their respective environs.

The Christian proclamation was welcomed chiefly by the poor, notably slaves.* Excluded from the cults of the city (cf. Intr. IV.4.D), these people often had turned to the Oriental cults and now, suddenly, they found the best in Christianity: "he who had been but an object became a person and became aware of his own dignity" (Festugière). In the cultured classes spiritual disquiet had been articulated through the questioning of society by philosophical currents, particularly by the recently arrived Stoicism,* which espoused interiority, and by Cynicism, which led to a scorn of values such as wealth.

B. Nonetheless, obstacles to popular acceptance of Christianity were numerous. The Israelite (including the proselyte*) had to renounce his assurance of salvation through descent from Abraham, and his identification mark, circumcision, as well as his worldly certitude of being through the Law "a guide to the blind, the educator of the senseless" (Rom 2:19).

In addition, a strict partitioning of Greco-Roman society resisted cultural unification. Despite the new concept which inserted each city, formerly an absolute unit, into a totality which embraced the universe, and for which man, as such, found himself a citizen of the world (an idea which catholicity, the universality of the Church, inherited), it remained a task for the apostles to confront ethnic and social groups which were often closed and tension-creating communities. We observe that the welcome or rejection of the Gospel, considered apart from the secret thoughts of the persons involved, was often a function of the mentality of the evangelized groups and of the personality of the preacher. The reactions in Athens, Corinth, Ephesus or among the Galatians differed according to dominant historical and social factors.

It was on this base of antagonism, Jewish and pagan both, that the Church developed its message of charity, of the abolition in God through Christ of any kind of exclusiveness. It was also in this context that the Church had to stir up the communitarian unity of the converts from various backgrounds: rich and poor, unlettered and cultured, Jews, Greeks and barbarians.*

V. THE CULTURAL HERITAGE

1. COSMOLOGY. Jews and Christians inherited a cosmology that was common to the Middle East, but which had been reinterpreted to agree with monotheism. The universe,* first of all, was not a cosmos in the Greek sense, that is, a well-ordered organism, but rather a totality which only its relationship to the Creator unified. We find the phrases "heaven and earth" (Mt 5:18), "all things" (1 Cor 15:28), or, in its triple dimension, "the heavens, the earth, the underworld" (Phil 2:10; Rv 5:3,13) used to designate it.

At the time of creation* God split the primordial ocean, the abyss,* in two. Between these halves, the earth* formed a great plain. On its horizon, upon columns, reposed the firmament, a kind of solid cupola to which the sun,* the moon,* and the stars* were attached in order that they might mark off the seasons, days and years. Above the firmament the waters* of the (celestial) ocean were driven back but would water the earth through sluice-gates. Beyond the waters was the invisible heaven* (Am 9:6) where God dwelt on his throne (Mt 5:34; Rv 4:2) with the angelic courts. From there he watched over the inhabitants of earth. From there he could descend. There the glorified Jesus went to reascend. There believers have their true dwelling-place. Beneath the earth were found the primordial waters, an ocean of gentle water out of which the springs issued, giving life to plants. Below the earth, perhaps in the primordial ocean, the dwelling-place of the dead was located, the netherworld* (Jb. 38:16–17; Rom. 10:7). In the abyss the rebellious angels (Lk 8:31; 2 Pt 2:4; Rv 9:1–3,11) and the Beast* (Rv 11:7; 17:8) were imprisoned. At the end of the world the firmament will lose its consistency; it will vanish (2 Pt 3:7,10). The luminaries will become unhinged (Is 34:4; Mk 13:24–25; Rv 6:14–15). Afterward, a new heaven and a new earth will appear (2 Pt 3:12–13).

2. Anthropology. Semitic* thought patterns belong in association with those spiritual groups who put the emphasis on man's unity rather than on a multiplicity of constitutive principles. In practice, their view of a creator God kept the biblical writers from getting caught up in a timeless gnosis.* For them man is not a god who has fallen into matter, who is striving to remember the heavenly realms.

A. Man* so continually receives his existence from God that one cannot describe him without reference to the God who holds him in existence. Thus, biblical anthropology is essentially religious. No individual exists by himself. Naturally related to the entire universe, man finds himself essentially related to other human beings. His first object of thought is humanity as a whole and then, more specifically, the people to whom he belongs. The Christian sees in Jesus Christ the new Adam,* the Man par excellence in whom every person finds meaning.

B. Man is not an amalgam of body and soul, but rather expresses his being wholly through his body,* his heart,* his soul,* his spirit,* his flesh.* Dualistic Greek philosophy touched Semitic thought structures only lightly; many biblical words are weighted with a depth of meaning that eludes the hurried Western reader today.

3. Languages

A. In Jesus' time the language commonly spoken in Palestine was not Hebrew but, as had been the case for several centuries, Aramaic,* a Semitic language related to Hebrew. This idiom, originally proper to some royal cities of the Middle East absorbed by the Assyrian conquest in the eighth century B.C., had become the language of diplomacy and trade from Mesopotamia to the Mediterranean and had ended by supplanting the native languages while it was diversifying according to the regions, both western (Palestinian-Christian, Targum,* Samaritan, Palestinian Talmud*) and eastern (Syriac, Babylonian Talmud). A village of Syria near Damascus (Ma'lūlā) still speaks it today.

B. An ancient language, Hebrew* had been the written religious language and, so it appears, continued to be understood by Jews: prayers were ordinarily said in Hebrew and the texts of Qumran* are, for the most part, written in it. Thus Mt 27:46 reports in Hebrew the call to God *(Eli)* uttered by Jesus on the cross (Mk 15:34). To facilitate comprehension of the liturgical texts of the Old Testament, regular use was made of Aramaic paraphrases (Targums*), of which two had become official versions; these date from the return from the Exile (sixth century B.C.).

C. Due to the Roman occupation it seems quite likely that, at least in Jerusalem, Jews knew a little Greek* and, eventually, Latin (cf. the inscription on Jesus' cross: Jn 19:20). Big business had to make use of Greek, and the pilgrimages* to the Temple brought into Palestine a large number of Jews from the Diaspora* who themselves spoke Greek. It is thought that Jesus' message, delivered in Aramaic, could have been expressed, from the start of the apostolic proclamation, in the Greek of the gospel tradition, particularly when we recall that from the earliest period of the Church there were Hellenists* in the Christian communities. The believers who had come from the Diaspora transposed into Greek the sayings of Jesus and the narratives about Jesus. Aramaic and Hebrew are Semitic languages, following a logic different from that of Indo-European languages such as Greek, logic expressed in symbols, word-pictures. In Semitic languages, ideas are not expressed in abstract conceptual form, but through concrete terms rich in multiple meanings. In the Greek translation of the Septuagint* (a version of the Old Testament, dating from 250 to 150 B.C.) or of the gospels, the richness of Semitic words is not always evident. This holds for the many words featured in this dictionary, for example, glory, truth, peace, blessing, and so forth.

VI. POLITICS AND THE LAW

Palestine was occupied territory, subject to the exigencies of the Roman power. It representated a special case in the Empire for two reasons.

The Jews comprised not only the roughly 500,000 inhabitants of Palestine, but also the seven to eight million in the Diaspora,* who constituted about ten percent of the Roman Empire. Gathered together in tightly knit communities, the Jews of the Diaspora enjoyed an official status, recognized by the Roman authorities. A good many bore the title of Roman citizen* and some occupied important positions within the emperor's immediate entourage. Worldwide Judaism was a power which reinforced the standing of the little nation of Palestine and allowed it to be assured of support in high places.

Israel viewed its politics in a singular way: it was a "theocracy." In its eyes Yahweh alone gave commands, with the established authority (the Sanhedrin* and the High Priest*) being merely his representatives. Religion, politics, and law were inextricably interwoven.

For this double reason, Rome judged it good to take cognizance of Israelite law and to accord to Israel a status of its own, one through which the nation enjoyed certain privileges which differentiated it from the other provinces of the Empire.

1. Civil status

A. The Jews

a. It was through circumcision* that one became a member of the Jewish people. Nonetheless, belonging to Israel had to be verified by two other criteria, the Israelite origin of one's ancestors and the observance of the Law. Hence, the frequent genealogical references in the Bible (Ru 4:18–22; 1 Chr 5:30–41; 6:18–29; Mt 1:1–17; Lk 3:23–38). It was thought that only members of "pure" families were the heirs of Abraham* (cf. Mt 3:9), that is, assured of the pardon and protection of God and the promise of messianic salvation. In addition, it was necessary not to be implicated in an action that could involve a violation of the Law* (for example, unjust gains) or the non-observance of certain ordinances, or, simply, a legal blemish. Even in the choice of table companions the Jews of

Jesus' time excluded everyone who did not belong to Israel. Held at a distance and not enjoying (or at least not entirely) civil rights were the circumcised who were of pagan background (the proselytes*), those who were engaged in contemptible trades, and illegitimate children (cf. Jn 8:41). Through a special dispensation from Rome, Jews were exempt from military service.

b. An Israelite woman* did not have civil status equal to a man's. Perpetually a minor, she could not give testimony in court, nor acquire or bring about justice, not even as her husband's heir. Despite this, she found protection in the Law (cf. Intr. VIII.2).

B. Resident aliens.* The ancient inhabitants of Palestine, who stayed in the country after the Israelite conquest, and the small number of immigrants were held in disrepute and most often were indigent. The Old Testament associated them with the most destitute, "the widows and orphans," and provided protective measures for them (Dt 24:17-21). Though free men and not slaves, those who were pagans in background could not share all civil rights. Mixed in with the active life of Israel, they were held to sabbath* observance and were admitted under certain conditions to participation in religious feasts.* Some, by conversion to the Jewish faith and by circumcision, became proselytes,* but even then their civil rights, although broader, were never equal to those of Jews. Their burial place was separate.

C. The slaves.* A Jew could become a slave as the consequence of an act of theft or, more often, through an insolvent debt, but, this only for a maximum period of six years (Ex 21:2–11; Dt 15:12). His condition, which was in no way a dishonorable one, resembled that of a wage-earner taken on for a long term by a wealthy property owner. Pagan slaves, on the other hand, whether they had been purchased or were born to the servants of a family, were such for life. The number of either kind is hard to establish; doubtless it was far smaller than in Greece or Rome.

2. Government

A. Rome observed the sensitivities of the Jews. The governor* did not reside in Jerusalem but at Caesarea; he went up to the Holy City on the occasion of major festivals to oversee the crowds. The troops, few in number and made up of Romans, Gauls, or Spaniards, resided in Syria. Nonetheless, a Roman guard from 700 to 1000 strong (Acts 21:27–40) was maintained in Jerusalem. In Judea there were only auxiliaries of Greek, Syrian or Samaritan extraction. In effect, the Jews were exempt from military service (cf. Intr. VI.1.A.). Because of Israel's repugnance for any divinizing of the human form, troops entering Jerusalem were instructed to conceal the insignia which bore the emperor's effigy; only the silver Roman denarius* was stamped with the head of Tiberius (cf. Mt 22:19). Coins struck in Judea bore, along with the name of the sovereign, only symbols borrowed from Judaism. Probably civil servants and military officials initiated levies that were badly received (Mt 5:41).

B. Roman authority was likewise tolerant of Jewish sensibilities. On the one hand, the Law's* prohibition of any dealing with pagans* (Lk 7:3) preserved a strict separation. Thus, Pilate had to come out of the praetorium* to hold discussions with the Jews who kept their distance (Jn 18:28) and, to enter the house of the centurion Cornelius,* Peter had to be instructed by a vision (Acts 10:28). On the other hand, various direct taxes* weighed on the people who were already burdened by the Temple tribute*; in addition the censuses* (three of them between 28 B.C. and A.D. 14) made them feel the yoke. Also, agitators relatively frequently stirred up trouble against the occupying forces. Paul saw matters differently: for him the *pax romana* was a factor favorable to the spread of the Christian message which led him to ask for submission to its authority* (Rom 13:1,5).

3. Finance

A. Civil taxes*

a. From the time of Solomon (1 Kgs 4:7) Jews paid taxes: the country was divided into twelve administrative districts, each of which in turn had to make provision for the royal coffers. After the Babylonian Exile, a tax had been levied by each succeeding pagan occupying power (2 Kgs 15:20; 23:35; Ezr 4:13; Neh 5:4). The local rulers, Herod the Great (for his political prestige) and his successors, the tetrarchs,* themselves had levied sometimes exorbitant demands of tribute.

b. In New Testament times the Roman taxes were direct and indirect. Direct taxes, levied by agents of the imperial treasury, related to real estate and were paid in kind. In addition, through "capitation" (a head tax), each person was taxed according to the assessed value of his fortune (Mt 22:17). Indirect taxes were custom* duties and town dues. Five-year contracts awarded their levying concessions to general contractors who, assisted by local agents (the publicans*), acted as guarantors for the overall payment.

B. Religious taxes

a. The Temple tax, the equivalent of a half-shekel* or a didrachma* (Mt 17:23), had to be paid during the month preceding Passover by all Jews, including those in the Diaspora.* This cared for the upkeep of the sanctuary and of the priests in its service.

b. The *tithe,** which the Levites* levied, corresponded to one-tenth of the produce of the earth (Dt 14:22-23). Without its payment, the produce was held to be impure and its consumption a sin. The payment of the tithe was done with joyous hearts; the offering of the first fruits* was even a feast, both rural and religious (Dt 26:1-11).

4. Law and Justice

A. The powers

a. The Great Sanhedrin,* a type of permanent commission which sat twice weekly at Jerusalem in the Temple, might go back, not to Moses (Nm 11:16) nor likely to Ezra, but to Antiochus III (223–187 B.C.); it was instituted under John Hyrcanus (134–104 B.C.).

The High Priest* was its president. The 71 members were elders* (representing the leading families), the former high priests, as well as Sadducees* (all of the priestly class) and, less numerous, scribes* and doctors* of the Law, Pharisees.*

Its function was religious and political. In the first instance, it was the highest court for crimes against the Law* and simultaneously a theological academy which established doctrine, set the liturgical calendar* and controlled all aspects of religious living. On the political side, the Sanhedrin voted on the laws, had a police force at its disposal, and regulated relations with the occupying power. For a hearing, twenty-three members constituted a quorum. In the case of a night session for a serious offense, no imposition of the death penalty could be pronounced until the next morning's session.

The Romans officially recognized the Sanhedrin's power to draw up cases and pronounce sentence according to Jewish law. However, in a case involving the death penalty, the Sanhedrin was obliged to obtain ratification from the Roman authority.

The political function of the Sanhedrin passed out of existence in 70; the religious Sanhedrin was then transferred to Jamnia (today's Jabné, 20 kilometers [13 miles] south of Jaffa); then to Tiberias.*

b. The other tribunals. Through decentralization, which Josephus* attributed to the legate Gabinius (63–55 B.C.), four cities (Gadara, Amath, Jericho, Sepphoris) each had twenty-three-member courts of justice. In addition, throughout the country, wherever a community regularly gathered, little sanhedrins composed of three members, including a judge (Mt 5:25), customarily handled less significant cases and inflicted the scourging* penalty (Mt 10:17).

B. Civil law

a. The law concerning persons. Here several distinctions are important. Only the free adult male enjoyed the full privileges of civil law. Sons before the age of majority (in principle at the age of twenty, but often later) and slaves were placed under the authority of the family head. Women were held to be inferior to men; commitments which they undertook could be nullified by their husbands (cf. Intr. VIII.2.B.c). Resident aliens* had a status that was still more inferior and they remained marginal to society; even so, legislation afforded them protective measures (Lv 24:22; Dt 24:17).

b. The law of marriage. Two kinds of unions were forbidden: marriage with a non-Jewish woman (the law of endogamy) and consanguineous unions (bound by restrictions set forth in very precise legislation). The levirate* law prescribed for a man the duty of marrying the widow of his brother, if he died without issue, in order to assure him a posterity (Mt 22:25).

c. The law of succession. Inheritances passed to male descendants, a double portion going to the firstborn* (cf. Dt 21:17 and Lk 15:12). Under the influence of Hellenistic law, the making of wills* began (cf. Gal 3:15). The rabbis* carefully articulated the conditions for their validity.

d. Though the above factors manifest little precision, because of the great importance which Jews accorded to reciprocal relationships touching on matters of justice,* very precisely detailed legislation was in effect for questions of damages and interest (cf. Ex 21–22), buying and selling, loans, wages and debts.

C. Penal law. Israelite legislation was distinguished by the religious element involved in it and, when we compare it with the Mediterranean codes of law of that time, by its humanitarian dimension. Rooted in the Law, that is in God's instruction to his people, its every prescription found justification in this motivation.

a. Procedures. In the first instance a complaint had to be brought forth by an accuser. Proof was not recognized by the deed, no matter how flagrant. There had to be two eye-witnesses* to confirm the crime (Dt 19:15; Mt 18:16). Their responsibility in the matter implicated them so seriously that, in instances involving the death penalty by stoning, they had to be the first to cast stones. Neither women, minors, nor slaves could act as witnesses. A lawyer or witnesses in his favor presented a defense for the accused. For judgments, a simple majority was enough to acquit, while for capital punishment an absolute majority plus two was mandatory.

b. Crime and punishment. The most severe and most harshly punished crimes were those against God or the holiness of his people. These implied by their nature what we would call a threat to national security. The following were such crimes: idolatry,* magic* (or even divination), blasphemy,* violation of the sabbath,* murder (because of the spilled blood), adultery* or, in addition, any formal disobedience to ecclesiastical law such as not circumcising a son or not celebrating Passover. In all these cases, the stipulated penalty was death. In Jesus' time, however, capital punishment had to be ratified by the Romans.

For crimes and offenses posing a threat to the human person, property or the family's or an individual's good name (cf. Mt 5:22), account was taken of the degree of seriousness involved and the law of talion* applied: eye for eye, tooth for tooth (Ex 21:24; Mt 5:38). As unmerciful as this might appear, the talion measure represented progress over the customs of antiquity (Gn 4:23f.), because it set a strict equivalence between the offense and the penalty.

c. Among the Jews, the death penalty* was carried out by stoning.* Other methods were decapitation, strangulation and death by fire. Crucifixion* was introduced under the Roman occupation. Other sentences were, on one side, prison* (notably that of insolvent debtors), and on the other, scourging* or beating, which had to be stopped before the victim succumbed.

VII. ECONOMIC LIFE

1. Natural Resources

A. Agriculture. As in the majority of ancient countries, agriculture was the principal resource and activity of New Testament Palestine. The land, frequently won over for farming from the rocky terrain (Mt 13:5), was cultivated to its maximum in the fertile plains, where the yield could be strikingly abundant (cf. Mt 13:8), and on the tended hillsides and terraces. Field work began as soon as the October rains softened the earth. The peasant guided a wooden plow (Lk 9:52) with its iron plowshare as he prodded the yoked cattle or asses with the goad. Seeding was done by hand. Harvest,* threatened by drought, blistering winds, birds and parasites, took place before Passover in the case of barley* and between Passover and Pentecost for wheat.* Since scythes had not yet been invented, the ears of grain were cut in handfuls with iron reaping hooks. The milling, assisted by single or yoked beasts of burden, generally took place on the village threshing floor, which was an open air place. With the night breezes to help, the grain could be separated from the chaff through use of a winnowing fan* (Mt 3:12). The wheat was gathered into pits or into actual barns (Mt 6:26).

The vines,* the peasant's most precious possession, prospered on the hillsides; their cultivation required several years' care before bearing fruit and constant attention afterwards. Vineyards required a press* for the production of wine. From a tower (Mt 21:33) built in the middle of his vineyard, in which he lived during the summer, the owner warded off thieves and foxes. The olive* tree and the fig* tree were constantly replanted, the former for oil,* indispensable for cooking, for perfumes* and medicines; the latter for shade and for figs, eaten either fresh or dried.

B. Herds of goats* and sheep* were an important source of revenue (meat, milk, leather, wool). Fish* abounded in the rivers and lakes (except for the Dead Sea). There was (chiefly in Galilee) a thriving fishing* industry, organized into corporations with owners and workers (Mk 1:20). There was no deep-sea fishing.

C. Mineral resources were limited to several copper mines in the region of modern-day Aqaba, in operation from the royal era, and the extraction of basalt (Dt 3:11). This latter, called "ironstone" and used in the absence of iron for various tools, was used to make millstones* and other, chiefly agricultural, implements. It gave rise to a somewhat extensive industry.

2. Trades. Trades, especially those of craftsmen, were geared to the needs of the times and were handed down from father to son. They were related to the production of foodstuffs and the manufacture of clothing* (weavers, fullers,* dyers, tailors), of household and agricultural equipment (welders, potters), of jewels and precious objects needed for worship (goldsmiths, jewellers), and of perfumes* for the Temple liturgy or daily use. To all of these must be added the cadres of Temple tradesmen, notably those associated with its construction, maintenance and ornamentation, a considerable group who were well paid and helped by funds from the Temple treasury when unemployed. In New Testament times, Judaism had a high regard for apprenticeship and the practice of a trade. Jesus' first disciples had been fishermen (Mt 4:18) who, after Jesus' death, at first returned to their original trades (Jn 21:3). Paul, like many scribes* who had recourse to a profession to make a living (e.g. baker or tailor), was a tent maker (Acts 18:3). Some trades, however, were not well regarded, out of moral considerations, if they appeared to present opportunity for theft (such as a conveyor of merchandise) or from a sense of physical repugnance (tanners, it seems, were such because of the odor of the leathers) or because they made it difficult to observe the Law (here, again, the tanners, or shepherds*).

3. Business. Palestinian ports were of minor importance, for the Jews did not take to the seas. Businessmen made use of Greek, Phoenician and Roman ships. In compensation, the country located at the crossroads of eastern Asia, of Egypt and Arabia was crisscrossed by highways, both longitudinal and transversal, so it benefited from multiple encounters. Despite the danger from brigands, numerous caravans of camels and asses exported agricultural products and perfumes* or imported from Greece, Arabia, Mesopotamia, and even India, precious fabrics,* glass, metals, aromatics,* as well as slaves, particularly from Syria. The big businessman appeared to be fairly prosperous, his revenues allowing him to assemble vast rural estates. The small businessman looked after provisions in the cities (especially Jerusalem), access to which, except via the main highways, remained difficult. Custom* houses were set up not only on the borders, but also in the markets. Purchases were made with Roman or local coins.* Bartering was also carried on. The very large number of pilgrims who came to the Temple were a source of income for Jerusalem and they brought to the Temple the tax prescribed annually for every Jew. Because of the materials it used, its requirements of wood, cloth and precious stones* and animals for community or private sacrifices,* the Temple had a key role in the business life of the city.

4. Rich and Poor. The separation between social classes was considerable. The sovereign and his court, the big merchants, the landowners, the chief tax collectors and the priestly aristocracy led a life of ease, and occasionally of luxury. Banquets brought together a large number of feasters (Mt 23:6). In Jerusalem, there was a custom of inviting the poor of the street to a meal on the occasion of a city-wide celebration or for the feast of the Passover (cf. Lk 14:13).

Craftsmen and the ordinary priests constituted a type of middle class. Small farmers, impoverished by the concentration of landholdings in the hands of the rich, were often in debt. Among the dispossessed, the day-laborers lived, more or less well, on their daily wages (equal to a denarius* plus meals) while those who could not work—the infirm—were provided for by charitable organizations. In fact, alms* played an important role in Jewish life.

The various taxes* weighed heavily and, placing the bulk of the people in a precarious situation, prevented attainment of the modest way of life to which the country, in principle, was capable.

In such a setting, Jesus did not systematically write off the rich*; he even called them to follow* him, proposing to them as an ideal the life of the dispossessed (Mt 19:16–29), or the life of the birds of the air (Lk 12:22–31). He put them on guard against that possession of riches which led them to forget their mortal condition and to forget the poor* (Lk 12:16–21; 16:19–31). Accordingly, without our being able to know precisely its cause, the primitive community seems to have had economic difficulties (Acts 6:1) and Paul had to come to its aid with a collection* for the needs of the Mother Church of Jerusalem (Rom 15:25–26; 1 Cor 16:1–4; 2 Cor 8–9; Gal 2:10).

VIII. FAMILY AND HOME LIFE

1. The Basics

A. The Jewish house. From the rare traces that have been preserved we are able to conjecture that ordinarily houses were made of coarse, baked bricks, less often of stone. Among the poor, they consisted of a single room with annexed storerooms in which were kept wheat and jars of water. Among the more comfortable there was a courtyard surrounded by rooms. In the courtyard was a cistern or, in its absence, water jars for ritual ablutions* (cf. Jn 2:6). There were few windows and the inside was rather dark, which led to the use of lampstands* and the presence, even among the poorest, of an oil lamp* that always remained lit. Houses in cities of the Diaspora* seem to have had larger windows (cf. Acts 9:25; 20:9; 2 Cor 11:33). Their foundations were set on rock, with bricks resting upon stones (Mt 7:24). The roof was flat, formed of branches mixed with earthen clay and small pebbles; it could easily be broken into (Mk 2:4) and required frequent repairs. Surrounded by a parapet, it served as a terrace, useful in several ways—for sleep on summer nights, for household chores, conversation and prayer. If it was solid, a guest room was built on it, called an upper room (Acts 1:13; 9:37; 20:8) which was cooler than the rooms below. The ground floor of the house was ordinarily leveled earth; the door, made of wood, was strengthened with a bolt and a latch, and could be opened with the help of a key made of wood with iron points. On the door post hung a *mezuzah,* a tube containing parchment on which the text of Dt 6:4–9; 11:13–21, the *Shema Israel,* was written (cf. Intr. XIII.2.B.a.). Its furnishings consisted of a table for meals, couches or benches on which one could stretch out to eat, beds (couches or rugs, with cushions) and closets. The kitchen had an oven for bread, a stove with two grates, and many utensils made of baked earth or copper.

B. Clothing. Beginning with the royal period, Israel made use of wool,* linen,* and cotton. Corps of specialized tradesmen wove the fabrics, naturally colored, bleached white or colored purple,* scarlet,* blue or brown. Clothes* were loose-cut, draped over the body rather than fitted. Their beauty depended on the quality of the fabrics* (Lk 7:25; Rv 19:8) and embellishments such as embroidery and jewels (cf. Jas 2:2). Fringes* and phylacteries* added a note of piety. The principal garments were the tunic,* held together by a belt,* and the cloak.* The primitive sack cloth* was transformed into a fabric which was tied up around the loins as an undergarment.

The headdress consisted of a piece of material covering the head, falling loosely over the shoulders or rolled up, like a turban or a veil*; it was kept on all day. Shoes,* made of leather of varying degrees of suppleness, occasionally studded with nails, were removed at the sanctuary and in homes.

C. Personal hygiene

a. Jewish tradition demanded of all a strict cleanliness. Washing* feet, dusty from the roads, and hands took place at the house entrance or before meals (Mk 7:3–4; Lk 7:44). Also the whole body was washed* frequently, using water from streams or cisterns and, in the cities, pools* or bath houses, these latter having been introduced by the Romans. Above all hygiene was a religious precept. Before prayer in the Temple one had to wash and change one's clothes. Ritual ablutions were stipulated for the removal of any legal defilement.*

b. From ancient times, perfumes* held a major place in Jewish life, either out of social convention (Lk 7:46) or to alleviate the discomforts of the heat.

c. Hair* care was important: to leave one's hair unkempt or to shave one's head signified mourning* or sadness.* To leave one's hair uncut was one of the features of a vow (cf. Acts 21:23–24). Women braided or elegantly adorned their long hair (cf. 1 Tim 2:9).

D. Nourishment

a. The produce of the ground, milk products, and fish constituted, with bread,* the staple foodstuffs. Roast meat, particularly lamb or kid, was served at a feast or banquet. Among drinks wine* held a privileged place at special meals. Red, occasionally spiced or sweetened with honey and from various productions, it was kept in goatskins or jars. It had to be filtered and mixed with water before being drunk (cf. Mt 23:24).

Moreover, in New Testament times numerous dietary restrictions continued to hold sway, the origins of which may be sought in the religious character associated with meals.* Thus, pork,* camel,* shellfish, all insects with the exception of certain kinds of locusts* (cf. Mt 3:4), and all meats* of an animal which had not been slaughtered and bled or any which had been sacrificed to idols, rendered the one who partook of them "unclean.*" The sorting of the fish mentioned in Mt 13:48 might refer to such prescriptions, ones against which Paul had to wrestle (cf. Rom 14:14).

b. Cooking was reserved for the women or for slaves: each day the grains were ground at the millstone,* flour kneaded, mixed with leaven* or not, then baked in the oven to obtain bread.* Pastries were appreciated; honey served as sugar. In addition to salt,* many spices added flavor to dishes which were cooked in oil. Kitchen utensils were made out of baked earth or copper. During the meal which was taken together, bread shaped like a disc served as a plate. It was also dipped into sauces which were set in the middle of the table.

2. Family life

A. The family and others

The family or the house* (cf. Neh 7:4) depended on the patriarchal model to such an extent that it was known as "the father's house" *(bêt ab).* Under the father's authority or, upon his death, that of the eldest son, it included the grandparents, the spouses, the children (legitimate or not) as well as the servants and the foreigners living in. Less extensive than that of the patriarchs, this resident family remained the fundamental nucleus of society, and individuals kept alive their sense of lineage so well that the conversion of the head of the family involved that of its members (Jn 4:53; Acts 10:2; 11:14; 18:8; 1 Cor 1:16). The family was also the worshipping unit for the Passover (Ex 12:3–4). Family solidarity was expressed in the *gô'èl** tradition, the redeemer,* defender and protector of family and individual interests.

The members of the family were all brothers.* Opposite them were grouped the others who were termed neighbors*: other Jews, resident aliens,* slaves, the pagans. Relations with others were severely limited according to blood relationships. Clearly also, the family circle tended to expand under the sacred law of hospitality. Despite this, it was Jesus who would definitely break the tight circle: in Jesus Christ all are brothers.*

B. The foundation and life of the home

a. It is within the framework of the family that one has to situate the institution of marriage.* A wife was sought above all among near relations without infringing on the obligations of the incest prohibition (Lv 18:6) but also, despite prohibitions, among foreign clans. There were marriages of attraction, but ordinarily, owing to the very young age of the future spouses (the rabbis set 12 years as the girl's minimum age and 13 as the boy's), it was the parents who arranged the marriage. It fell to the parents to discuss the price of the *mohar* (cf. Gn 29:15–16; 34:12), a sum of money which the future groom had to pay to the father of the girl, not for the purchase of his wife, but as compensation given to her family. He usually used this amount to provide a trousseau for the young girl. Once these dealings were complete, the two young people were engaged, that is they were legally bound to one another, without yet living together (cf. Mt 1:18–20).

Finally, after a period that is hard to define exactly (one year?), the wedding ceremony took place, a purely civil, not religious rite. A contract was drawn up in which there was featured a formula like that found in the Wadi Murabba'at: "You will be my wife." The feast ordinarily took place in the fall after harvest. The references scattered throughout rabbinic literature do not allow us to pinpoint precisely the features of a wedding party. According to the most probable data, the groom was accompanied by his companions (Mt 9:15), among whom one, his closest, served as the "master of the ceremony" (Jn 3:29). He went to his bride's home. The young woman, veiled and surrounded by her bridesmaids, after receiving her parents' blessing (cf. Gn 24:60), joined the wedding train which went to the groom's paternal home where the merrymaking extended late into the night. According to another custom which Palestinian customs at the turn of the twentieth century seem to confirm, the groom, occasionally delayed by last-minute details of the wedding contract with his parents-in-law, only at a late hour appeared at his paternal home where his bride, veiled and with her bridesmaids (Mt 25:10), waited for him. Then the marriage was consummated.

The celebrations (the banquet, dancing, amusements) were extended for a week, sometimes two, bringing together all the neighbors, usually in the husband's house.

b. From then on, the man exercised absolute power *(oikodespotēs)* over the newly constituted home.

c. The woman* recognized her husband as her lord (*ba'al:* Gn 18:12) and master *(âdôn),* while the man, basing his view on certain biblical texts (Ex 20:17; Dt 5:21) considered his wife as his property, like his house, his servant or his donkey. Although the woman was protected by the law from possible abuse (Dt 21–22), she remained in every way legally the dependent of her husband (cf. Intr. VI.1.A.b.). She was responsible for hard domestic work (bread, water, oil, fabrics) or she kept the herds and worked the fields. Her esteem grew in relation to the number of her children and her capacity for work.

d. Despite this inequality, the couple could live according to the desire of the Creator (Gn 2:18,24), especially if they were blessed with the gift of sons; children were to respect their mother* as well as their father* (Ex 20:12). Should the woman prove to be sterile, a concubine could come to be introduced into the home—for monogamy was still the ideal of Jewish marriage (cf. Prv 5:15–19; 31:10–31; Eccl 9:9; Sir 26:1–4). If the woman were caught in adultery,* she could be put to death or else the husband could send her away by writing out a dismissal note (Mt 5:31; cf. Dt 24:1,3; Is 50:1; Jn 8:3) so that she could legally remarry. The motive for such a dismissal could occasionally be benign. For her part, the woman could not ask for a divorce* (Mk 10:12 implies Greco-Roman practices).

e. A widow* stayed with her sons in her husband's family. If she were without children, she could equally stay there according to the levirate* practice (Dt 25:5–10) by which her brother-in-law (Lat. *levir*) would marry her and raise offspring to perpetuate the deceased's name (Ru 4:5,10). In the absence of a *levir,* she could remarry outside the family and, in anticipation, might return to her parents' home.

C. Stages of life

Generally, the ancients divided human life into seven-year periods. Here briefly are the distributions into seven phases made by Hippocrates: the little child (0–7), the child (7–14), the adolescent (14–21), the young man (21–28), the mature man (28–49), the aged man (Gk. *presbytēs*) (49–56), the old man (over 56). If one may judge by the facts of the Bible or those of Qumran,* among the Jews the reckoning was similar. At 13 the young Jew had to observe the Law*;

at 20 years he could give testimony and, ordinarily, got married; at 25 or 30 he had to take up his role in the community. The Levite* exercised his ministry from 25 to 50 years of age, the priest and judge from 30 to 60. In any case the age of 50 or 60 marked a transition point in life; the *Damascus* Document* gives a reason: "At 60 years men are deprived of their intelligence prior to the completion of their days" (X:9a). The maximum lifetime was from 70 to 80 years (Ps 90:9f.).

a. On the birth of the Jewish baby there is nothing noteworthy. Without doubt labor pains were ordinarily severe (Is 26:17; Jer 22:23; cf Gn 3:16), but the delivery, necessary as it was (Is 13:8; 1 Thes 5:3), was a source of joy (Jn 16:21). The baby was washed, rubbed with salt,* and wrapped in swaddling clothes. Ordinarily it was breast-fed by its mother, then, two or three years later, weaned (Gn 21:8; 2 Mc 7:27). On the eighth day the child received its name* and if male was circumcised* (Lv 12:3; Lk 2:21); thus was it introduced into the chosen people.

b. Up until their marriages, girls remained with their mothers and helped with the housekeeping tasks or in tending the flock (Gn 29:6).

c. The boys' education was carried on under the guidance of the father* of the family. Through working with his father and in keeping the family traditions, the child was little by little initiated into the religious traditions of his people. His father taught him the commandments of Yahweh: "You will repeat them to your sons; you will also tell them to them seated in the house or walking on the road, as well upon lying down as when you are standing up" (Dt 6:7). At the occurrence of sabbath, daily prayer, a circumcision, Passover, etc., he explained the rites to his son and told him of their meaning: "When your son asks you in days to come, 'What is the meaning of this custom?' you will tell him, 'It was Yahweh's power that caused us to come out of the land of Egypt' " (Ex 13:14). Finally, he recounted to him the great deeds Yahweh did for his people. At thirteen years and a day the child became a *bar-miṣvah* ("a son of the commandment"): he was held to observance of the law, prayers, fast days. Finally, after a period of time at school (cf. Intr. IX.2), the child remained at his father's side as he introduced him to his trade (cf. Jn 5:19–20).

d. Adults, whether they belonged to a priestly family, to the lay nobility or to the common folk, were all governed in all of their activities by family traditions. These latter, in the majority of cases, determined their occupations and their rank in the city: priesthood, elder's* function, trade, agriculture, craft. Nonetheless, through study every Jew could become a doctor* of the Law. Whatever their state, the adult life was entirely characterized by veneration of the Law. In social relations—extending even into the realm of thoughts and feelings—a concern to please Yahweh guided one's existence; hence, the asceticism of and fidelity to religious prescriptions were ordinarily the inspiration for judgment and conduct.

e. Right into extreme old age* the head of the household maintained his proper authority over his own (cf. 1 Pt 5:5); the young had to have a regard for the elderly (1 Tim 5:1), particularly since wisdom was sure to reside in them.

D. Sickness and death

a. The New Testament mentions a large number of sicknesses* and infirmities: fever,* malaria, diseases of the skin (sores, gangrene, leprosy*), defective organs (those of the blind,* one-eyed, short-sighted, deaf,* mute,* stutterers, paralyzed, lame,* weak, sterile), various maladies (rheumatism, hemorrhage, strokes, dropsy, dysentery), nervous conditions (the epilepsy of the lunatic,* madness*). Through insufficient hygiene and preventative medical measures, diseases spread easily, despite the Law's prescriptions in the area of cleanliness (cf. Intr. VIII.1.C) and in spite of the severe restrictions that fell upon specific illnesses, e.g. lepers. Among the remedies devised we may note the use of oil and ointments, wine acting as a disinfectant (Lk 10:34) and a strengthener (1 Tim 5:23) or an eye-lotion (Rv 3:18). The doctor's* profession does not seem to have been too highly regarded (Mk 5:26; Lk 8:43). Jesus readily healed the sick (Mt 10:8; 11:5; Jn 9:3) and Christians designated healing* as one of the charisms* (1 Cor 12:28).

b. Death.* According to biblical anthropology, the deceased continued to exist in his totality in Hades,* in a state diminished but not annihilated by death. In order to assure his peace, funeral rites and, above all, burial* were required even through the corpse and the tomb* rendered those who touched them ritually impure.* In contrast with her neighbors, Israel rejected every form of worship of the dead. Her rites, as acts of piety, were to be free of every kind of magic.*

The dead person's eyes were closed as if in sleep; the corpse was washed (Acts 9:37), anointed with perfumes (Jn 19:40; cf. Mt 26:12; Mk 16:1), then wrapped in a shroud* (Mk 15:46); linen* wrappings bound together the hands and feet, while a facecloth* covered its face (Jn 11:44). The body was afterwards exposed on a bier inside the house and the mourning* customs, chiefly lamentation, began.

For the burial* the bier was borne in a long funeral procession to the cries of weeping women toward the tomb where the corpse was laid to rest in the earth itself. Neither embalming (in the strict sense) nor cremation were practiced in Israel.

IX. CULTURAL LIFE

1. Tradition.* In Israel, as in other ancient civilizations, the culture was expressed and handed down primarily in oral form. Gatherings of the elders, conversations at the city gates, at banquets or under the Temple porticoes—these kept alive the knowledge of national and religious traditions. Characteristically, the usual manner of proceeding was by way of the question; the replies, well-honed, were learned by heart. Later on, collections preserved the sayings of the elders. In commenting upon them, the wise man* and the scribes* instructed the people and guided their moral life. The Bible, constantly repeated and reinterpreted, remained the source of all knowledge.

2. Education. Besides the education received in the family (cf. Intr. VIII.2.C.c), from the age of five children attended schools which met in the synagogues. One of the members of the little sanhedrin (cf. Intr. VI.4.A) held the position of teacher. He made use of the mnemonic techniques of his age: parallelism, antitheses, repetition, assonance. Jesus did not speak to the crowds in any other way than this. The gospels time and again offer examples of this manner of proceeding: "Whoever exalts himself will be humbled, he who humbles himself will be exalted."

All teaching* focused on the Bible, whether reading, writing, geography or history. The child learned biblical Hebrew, very close to his Aramaic language. Through chanting the verses of Scripture, he learned songs and music. At ten years of age he left school to learn, most often, his father's trade.

3. The Manner of Writing and of Communicating News

A. A large number of Jews in Jesus' time knew how to read and write (cf. Mt 27:37; Mk 12:16ff.), even though they frequently turned to professional scribes. Writing* was done on clay tablets (Lk 1:63) with a stylus, and on parchment (what we would call books) with a quill soaked in an ink that was barely fluid, composed of soot and gum. The parchments were kept rolled around a wooden rod. They were unrolled for reading (Lk 4:17; cf. Heb 10:7).

B. For correspondence, people used papyrus, which was scarce and expensive; a rough material, it was difficult to write on. Sometimes recourse was had to a calligrapher to whom one would give dictation. Paul must have dictated his letters, since he occasionally states that some passage or other is from his own hand (Gal 6:11; cf. Rom 16:22). An ancient letter* used stereotyped formulas, according to a set pattern: (1) mention of the sender's name as well as (2) the recipient's, (3) a thanksgiving, (4) development of the letter, (5) farewell and final good wishes (for health, happiness, etc.). A seal* was attached as the signature. Closed and sealed, the letter was ordinarily carried by a courier or a merchant traveller. The Sanhedrin* had special messengers at its disposal (cf. Acts 28:21). Only Roman officials had access to the postal network organized by Rome.

C. To communicate orders or news the authorities made use of wall posters. The notice attached to Jesus' cross may be an instance of this custom. Most of all, however, news was communicated by word of mouth.

4. Learning. The divine Law and wisdom* were the privileged domains Jewish thought scrutinized. The quest for knowledge for its own sake, a characteristic of the Greeks, was something almost impossible for Israel. Even the elementary sciences, essential for life, were not autonomous but rather integrated within a religious perspective. Accordingly, a rudimentary astronomy allowed for the establishment of a liturgical calendar*; geography, which was more of a cosmology, located Israel in the center of the world (cf. Intr. V.1); mathematics served the calculations which were applied to the Bible, and numbers* had a symbolic value. On the other hand, over against the views of the neighboring nations, natural forces for the Jews were not sacred sources of power nor objects of taboos or fears: they were merely creatures subject to their Creator. In this regard, the biblical vision disengaged, on behalf of human learning, a field free of any prohibition.

5. The Arts

A. The prohibition against every representation of Yahweh (cf. Ex 20:4; Dt 5:8: "You shall not make an image* . . .") accounts for the singular absence in Israel of the modeling arts, painting and sculpture. Only decorative motifs and precious objects adorned the Temple (Ex 35:31). On the other hand, in Jesus' time architecture was an imported art, first of Greek, then of Roman origin; hence Herod's imposing constructions.

B. In compensation for the above, the genius of Israel was concentrated and deployed in the word, oral and written. The Old Testament is not only a religious document, in many of its texts it is also a literary creation of great beauty. The varied feelings of man, the bewildering encounters with God or the inexhaustible wonders of creation are described therein with an intensity, a joy, an immediacy whose tone is unique in the treasury of world literature. Whether it be in prose or poetry, the language of the Bible, although relatively restrained, is animated by an incantatory rhythm from which there issues a power that is often poignant. Rejecting any kind of abstraction, it was by means of images that were simple, close at hand and drawn from the concrete circumstances of daily life that this language led to the depths of reality. There everything was animated by the living and life-giving God, whose presence gives movement, meaning and salvation to all that lives; such, notably, was the case with the concise moderation shown in the gospels. Accordingly, one may speak of the mystery of biblical language.

6. Music. Unlike the situation with regard to the plastic arts, music played a big role in family and social life in Israel. It characterized every feast (Lk 15:25) and played a part in the ceremonial of funerals (Mt 9:23). In worship it expressed praise in most excellent fashion.

Song* was its principal form; it was rich in half tones, in the unison, which was accompanied by various bodily movements (such as hand-clapping, or dancing, in which rhythm counted above all). The Psalms* were sung, notably at the Passover meal (Mt 26:30). In the Temple, cantors were responsible for the principal services. Christian prayer was often sung (Acts 16:25; Col. 3:16; Eph 5:19).

For the various musical instruments, see cymbal,* flute,* harp,* trumpet,* zither.*

7. Dancing. Dancing,* loved by Jews as by all the peoples of the Orient, always accompanied by musical instruments and almost always by song, was performed in groups (except in certain instances [Mt 14:6]), at times of rejoicing (Lk 15:25), at vintage time, at weddings. Religious dance (cf. 2 Sm 6:14) is not mentioned in the New Testament, but we know that, by custom, cadenced movements accompanied chanted prayer.

8. THE THEATER AND AMUSEMENTS

A. The theater was an import from abroad. Several Hellenistic cities possessed one and it seems that Herod built one in Jerusalem. Theaters were also used for public assemblies, such as at Ephesus on the occasion of a riot (Acts 19:29–32).

B. Despite much leisure time (through religious ordinances a third of the year was lost to work), the Jews do not seem to have elaborated their own particular amusements. Music and dancing, riddle contests and public lectures may, nonetheless, be presupposed. Liturgical activities, in a liveliness that was constantly renewed, oriented the people toward contemplation. Cruel and violent games, loved by the Romans, were never practiced in Israel.

9. GREEK CULTURE. Without doubt, Greek culture exercised an influence in Palestine in the time of Jesus. Herod's successors endowed several cities (Caesarea, Tiberias) with new buildings: stadiums, pools, etc., and changed their names to Greek or Roman ones (thus Samaria became Sebaste). Business transactions and crowd displacements at the time of Temple festivals fostered numerous interchanges. One could hear Greek spoken in the streets. Still, the people of Palestine remained closed to this penetration, small market-towns and villages were hardly touched at all. Despite his varied journeyings, Jesus' ministry was carried out in these areas in a traditional Jewish milieu. It was an entirely different situation with the birth of the Church.

X. ISRAEL'S FAITH

1. THE COVENANT. At the origin of Israel's existence lay the certitude of an event known as the Covenant.* God chose Israel to reveal himself to her and to make this privileged people his witness to the nations of the entire world. The initiative redounded to God alone who predestines* (Rom 11:2), but the commitment was reciprocal; if Israel were obedient to God's will,* God would give her his blessing.* God made known what he loved, first in the Law written in Moses' tablets and handed on to the priest-levites, then through the voice of the prophets and sages, then through the interpretations of the priests and scribes, lastly and definitively through his son Jesus, through the Holy Spirit poured into our hearts. Despite the degradations it suffered through the course of centuries, the Covenant told of the projected communion between Yahweh and his people. Two formulas were equivalent to one another: "Israel, the people of Yahweh" and "Yahweh, the God of Israel."

2. GOD. In this relationship, God was recognized as the Creator* of heaven and earth, the unique God* in the face of a polytheism all around. Here is what the believer proclaimed each day: "Hear, O Israel! The Lord our God is Lord alone" (Dt 6:4 = Mk 12:29). Idols* were nothing; God alone was the Living One and he spoke to his people.

Judaism did not systematically describe its faith in a "theology" (discourse about God); instead it spoke of God in an anthropomorphic way, giving him its feelings and ways of looking at things. In this way it stammered out the ineffable nearness of God. But it was not duped by its language and it safeguarded the divine transcendence, even if it was done only by its refusal to fashion any image of God or to pronounce the Name* of Yahweh.* The very many names given him struggled to tell one or another of the divine relationships with men and the universe: the Lord, the Heavenly One, the Everlasting One, the Most High, the Glory, the Eternal One. Jesus preferred that of Father, for it spoke best of the mercy,* which constituted the being of God, and broke out of the national exclusivism within which later Judaism wished to lock him.

3. THE PEOPLE. Through the Covenant relationship which God established with her, Israel became a people.* It had no other principle of cohesion than God himself. Such was her grandeur, such also was her paradox: without ceasing to be a nation* among others, it was the nation chosen from among all others by the God whose Covenant was to be extended to all men. Jesus discovered himself at odds with the nationalistic tendency which refused to accept the provisional and figurative* character of the national epoch of God's people. It was in the relationship of Israel to other nations that the destiny of the people of God was to be played out. The remaining noteworthy feature is that what characterized this people was its awareness of its election* and its mission. In her turn, the Church of Jesus thought itself to be the true Israel,* continuing to exist only through the God who chose her and sends* her forth, but also discovering herself bound to Jesus and open to all men. Jesus did not abolish the Law and the Prophets, but he brought them to their fulfillment,* through his sacrifice* sealing a covenant of all men with God the Father.

XI. RELIGIOUS MOVEMENTS

Palestinian Judaism in the time of Jesus did not constitute a monolithic and uniform religion. Within the bosom of the same faith in Yahweh, the Jewish people diversified into a multiplicity of spiritual movements, indeed into religious parties. All believers did not necessarily belong to one or another of these groupings; but these exercised a determining influence within the religious and socio-political life of Israel.

Of these diverse "currents," only one was properly speaking heretical and cast out as such from the Jewish community, the group of Samaritans.* These, in fact, regarded no other book as holy except the Pentateuch.* They did not recognize in the Temple of Jerusalem the true dwelling-place* of God, but offered their sacrifices on Mount Gerizim in Samaria. With regard to the Herodians,* they did not constitute a religious party but a political group favorable to King Herod. Similarly, the scribes* were merely officials in the service of the Law. Official Judaism knew two principal parties: the Sadducees and the Pharisees. Marginal Judaism offered two important sects*: the Essenes and the Zealots.

1. In Palestine the Sadducees* represented the party of opportunists, that of the established order (formed under Hyrcanus I: 135–104 B.C.), willingly collaborating with the Roman occupier, since the latter allowed the exercise of a religion which was, in other respects, quite conservative. An aristocratic party, the offspring generally speaking of the sacerdotal caste, the Sadducees revealed themselves quite scornful of the people. Their influence was felt chiefly in worship and liturgy. It scarcely was exercised outside the Jerusalem Temple. Unlike the Pharisees, only the written Law (Pentateuch and Prophets) was normative for religion in their eyes; they read it in a manner that was literal and quasi-juridical, stressing the penal and present-day aspects of the doctrine of retribution. Josephus* and the New Testament (Mt 22:23; Acts 23:8) relate that they did not await the coming of the Messiah and that they rejected more recent beliefs: resurrection, the existence of angels. From the political viewpoint they had no fears of rapprochements with Hellenism,* doubtless because of a thought pattern which was authentically faithful to the Covenant, namely, the universal diffusion of Jewish thought. But this degenerated into a political concern to preserve the nation to the detriment of rigorous faithfulness to the Law. Their attitude differed profoundly from that of the Pharisees, but they joined together with them in opposition to Jesus. It appears that it was they who took on the responsibility of arresting Jesus (Mk 14:53).

2. The Pharisees* (about 6,000 strong) constituted the prevailing party. They were the heirs of the pious* of the period following the Maccabean War (after 125 B.C.) and staunch upholders of the Law, as it was restored by Ezra* at the time attempts were made to Hellenize Palestine, especially by Antiochus Epiphanes (175–164 B.C.). After supporting an active political nationalism for some 150 years, these laymen showed themselves intent above all in obeying the Law of the Lord. Guided by a very high religious ideal, they wanted to practice strictly all the prescriptions of the Law, if necessary by explaining and multiplying them with the help of oral traditions to which they also assigned a normative value. They found their recruits among the doctors* of the Law and among the scribes* who helped believers apply the Law to daily life. Scattered through the length and breadth of Palestine, they exerted a strong influence, particularly by means of the synagogues, over the people who, for their part, loved and esteemed them. Alone of all the parties, they survived the destruction of Jerusalem and its Temple in A.D. 70.

The delicate flower of Judaism in the time of Jesus, they were the true inheritors of the Mosaic tradition,* as may be inferred from their fidelity even at the price of a martyr's death. Unlike the Sadducees and the Zealots, their conduct was exclusively religious. Concerned for justice, they tried to practice the Law at its best and, to achieve this, they had recourse to the traditions of the elders* which they believed went back to Moses himself, having been faithfully handed down from one generation to another. According to Josephus,* they believed in the resurrection of the body and in a final judgment, as well as in angels and spirits. Neither fatalists nor laxists, they reckoned that man could practice the will of God. Finally, they shared a messianic hope common to the Jewish people and awaited, with the coming of the Messiah, the liberation of their nation, the punishment of the wicked and the return to the Holy Land of all dispersed Jews. In waiting for this day of victory, they were solicitous to win to the Jewish faith converts from the whole world.

Jesus severely criticized the excesses of the Pharisees, as a prophet* would have done, and as John the Baptist did. Their rigor in interpreting the Law, their concern more for its letter than for its spirit, frequently led them to misunderstand God's immense goodness and to reject in spiteful fashion the people who could not practice their religion in the Pharisaic manner. Jesus surely shared the profound concerns of Pharisaism but he felt obliged to reproach their casuistic intransigence which, for the sake of more or less valuable traditions, ended up by making the Law impossible to observe. This is the "Pharisaism" which the gospel tradition systematized in order to indicate the enduring tendency of every religious movement. Despite the above, there was no lack of Pharisees to sympathize with Jesus during his earthly life (Lk 13:31), to defend the first Christians (Acts 5:34), or to accept the Christian faith, notably Paul (Acts 15:5; Phil 3:5).

Confronted by Jesus, the Pharisees were jealous of the influence he acquired with the people, and they balked at the virulent attacks of this prophet. But this was not the deepest motivation for their opposition. It is striking to note that the Pharisees do not seem to have intervened directly in the arrest and passion of Jesus. But they could not admit, either, the intolerable claim that Jesus made in healing on the sabbath and in forgiving sins as Yahweh did. John clearly states this in depicting their opposition under the designation "the Jews*": "the Jews sought to kill him because he not only violated the sabbath, but also called God his own Father, making himself the equal of God" (Jn 5:18). It was because of their conception of God that they had to reject Jesus.

3. The Essenes* did not constitute an official party like the two preceding ones. According to Josephus, they truly were monks who lived in seclusion in the deserted parts of the country. Indeed, it seems that we may identify them with the monks who lived in the environs of the Dead Sea, near Ain Feshka, modern-day Qumran.* Even though they are never mentioned in the New Testament, the manner of their existence and thought can be reconstructed. Thus, the Synoptics* interpret the ministry of John the Baptist in the light of Second Isaiah,* a reading familiar to Qumran. The differences, however, cannot be ignored. Considering themselves as "the small remnant*" of the "pure," they carried on a common life in the desert, working during the day, praying and meditating on the Scriptures at night. Sharing of goods, meals in common, celibacy—such were their practices. Even though there was a lay majority among them, the priests held the leading role in the monastery. They practiced the same celebrations as official Judaism, without observing the same calendar*; they showed themselves to be as hostile to the Temple worship as to its priesthood, both of which they reckoned to be impure. Unlike the Pharisees, they were attuned to the apocalyptic* aspect of revelation, incorporating within it as well elements deriving from Iranian dualism* (good/evil).

4. The Zealots* shared the views of the Pharisees, but their faith doubled into a militant nationalism. Mixing politics and religion, their fanaticism expressed itself in terrorist acts that had it out not only for the Roman occupying force but also for their co-religionists, whom they judged too lukewarm. It was a Zealot insurrection in A.D. 66 that provoked the Roman repression and the fall of Jerusalem. This party is not attested with certitude until after 44; some associate it with the Galileans, who, during the census of Quirinius (about A.D. 6), revolted under the leadership of Judas the Galilean (Acts 5:37); but these bands of "hired assassins" do not seem to have been organized into a party before 44. Jesus, despite several violent statements (Mt 10:34), had nothing in common with the conduct of the Zealots (cf. Mt 26:52–53).

5. The people of the land *('am hâ-ârèṣ)* designated, in the time of Ezra*/Nehemiah, the Judeans who stayed on in the land during the exile and had become indifferent toward the Law. In the first century, this term of reproach was applied to the ignorant, whose piety was inferior and morality negligent, particularly in the matter of prescriptions of ritual purity (Jn 7:49). On the opposite side of the coin, it seems that there were confraternities *(habbērîm)* that bound themselves vigorously to the laws of purity* and from time to time organized fraternal gatherings.

XII. THE HOLY SCRIPTURES AND GOD'S WORD

In the course of the centuries, the Word* of God had been consigned to writing so that in the time of Jesus a collection of writings was considered as "the Law and the Prophets" (Mt 5:17; Lk 24:27) or "the Law, the prophets and the holy writings," that is, "*the* Book," the Bible* (cf. the prologue of Sirach; 1 Mc 12:9; 2 Mc 8:23), the Scripture (Ezr 6:18), distinct from what was known as the oral commentary of the Law (Neh 8:8). This collection constituted the canon* of the Scriptures.

The Hebrew Bible includes twenty-four books, arranged in three sections: (1) the *Torah* or "Law," with the five books which make up the Pentateuch*; (2) the *Nebiim,* eight in number, four "earlier prophets" (Joshua, Judges, Samuel and Kings), and four "latter prophets" (Isaiah, Jeremiah, Ezekiel, and the twelve minor prophets, counted as one); (3) the *Kethubim,* eleven in number, comprised of three poetic books (Psalms, Job and Proverbs), five "rolls" which were read on different feasts*: Ruth (Pentecost), the Song of Songs (Passover), Ecclesiastes (Booths), Lamentations (the destruction of the Temple), Esther (Purim); finally, three other writings (Daniel, Ezra/Nehemiah, Chronicles). The fixing of the canon was gradual: from before the third century B.C. for the first two sections, between the fourth and second centuries B.C. for the third section. At the Council of Jamnia (A.D. 90–100) seven books of the Greek Bible were excluded, along with certain additions proper to the Greek Bible.

The Greek Bible included certain works today referred to as apocryphal, some of which were adopted by Christians (Judith, Tobit, 1 and 2 Maccabees, Wisdom of Solomon, Wisdom of Sirach and Baruch, additions to Esther and Daniel) while others were rejected by them in the seventh century (1 Ezra, 3 and 4 Maccabees, Odes of Solomon, Psalms of Solomon). As the table of books which follows indicates, the Greek translation modified the Hebrew sequence. The "Writings" were redivided according to their genre, either within the books called "historical" (such as Joshua, Judges, Kings, Ruth, Chronicles, Ezra, Nehemiah, Esther, Judith, Tobit and Maccabees) or amid the Prophets (thus Baruch, Lamentations, Daniel). It subdivided certain books* (such as Samuel, Kings). Finally, the text offered some notable differences in the text of some passages.

In Jesus' eyes as in those of every Jew, these books were inspired* and always had to be held in relation to the Word* of the Living God, who is their source and gives them meaning. The relationship between Writing and Word gets transposed into the relationship which unites Scripture and Tradition,* the latter modulating the interpretation of the letter according to the era. There remains the always thorny problem of actualization (how does this divine text concern me today?) which in Jesus' time manifested itself through the many references to the traditions of the elders, the abuse of which ended up in the voiding of Scripture and the Word of God themselves.

In the time of Jesus and the primitive Church, Scripture consisted in what we today call the Old Testament. Jesus was filled with reverence for it, even though he seems not to have quoted it except in cases of controversy*; otherwise, he never concerns himself with the letter but is content to give its meaning. The first Christians, for their part, fastened on justifying their experience of the Risen One and of removing the scandal* of the cross by appealing to prophecies and discovering in them the unity of God's plan* (Lk 24:44; Acts 3:18; 8:32).

1. The Law and Contemporary Israel

A. The Law* or Torah referred to a teaching which communicated divine revelation, destined just as much to illuminate intellects as to direct existence. The predominant meaning ended by being that of the practical rule, that of law in the modern sense of the word. The abuses and subtleties, in which later rabbis* delighted, imposed a false image of the Law, reducing it to a storehouse of jurisprudence. The Law was before all else the expression of what the Living God desired, of what Israel had to do to be faithful to the Covenant.* In fact, it did not contain only prescriptions, but also the history of the Covenant. On the other hand, out of this tangle of commandments, for the most part religious, it is futile to try to derive a civil law code.

Also, it is difficult, if not impossible, to reduce the Law to a few essential commandments. Rather, let us admit that it possessed two attributes: it revealed the fundamental beliefs (Covenant, one God, Israel's call) and it promulgated

BIBLES: THE THREE OLD TESTAMENT VERSIONS

The Hebrew Bible		*The Greek Bible*	*The Latin Bible*	*Abbreviations*
A. TORAH (5)		*A. LEGISLATIVE AND HISTORICAL WRITINGS*		
Beréshith	In the beginning	Genesis	Genesis	Gn
W^{e}éllè sh^{e}môth	These are the names	Exodos	Exodus	Ex
Wayiq^{e}râ	And he called	Leyiticon	Leviticus	Lv
Way^{e}dabbér	And he spoke	Arithmoi	Numbers	Nm
Ellè hadd^{e}bârîm	These are the words	Deuteronomion	Deuteronomy	Dt
B. FORMER PROPHETS (4)				
Y^{e}hôshûa‘		Iēsous	Joshua	Jos
Shoph^{e}tîm		Kritai	Judges	Jgs
		Routh	Ruth	Ru
		Basileiōn I–II	Kings I–II	1–2 Sm
Sh^{e}mu'él I–II		Basileiōn III–IV	Kings III–IV	1–2 Kgs
M^{e}lâkîm I–II		Paraleipomenōn I–II	Chronicles I–II	1–2 Chr
		(Ezra I)		
B.' LATTER PROPHETS (4)		Ezra II	Ezra	Ezr
		Ezra III	Nehemiah	Neh
Y^{e}sha‘yâhû	Isaiah	Esther [+*suppl.*]	Tobit	Tb
Yirmeyâhû	Jeremiah	*Ioudith*	Judith	Jdt
Y^{e}hèzq'él	Ezekiel	*Tōbit*	Esther	Est
Nebi'îm XII	Twelve Prophets[1]	*Makkabaiōn* I–II		
		(Makkabaiōn III–IV)		
		B. BOOKS OF WISDOM		
C. KETHOUBIM = Writings (11)			Job	Jb
T^{e}hillîm		Psalmoi	Psalms	Ps
Yôb		(Odai)		
M^{e}shâlîm		Paroimiai	Proverbs	Prv
		Ekklēsiastēs	Ecclesiastes	Eccl
		Aisma	Song of Songs	Sg
		Jōb		
Rûth		*Sophia Salōmōnos*	Wisdom	Wis
Shir hashîrîm		*Sophia Sirach*	Sirach	Sir
Qohèlèth		(Psalmoi Solomōntos)		
Eicâ				
Esther		*C. BOOKS OF PROPHECY*		
		Dōdeka prophetai[1]		
Dâniy'él		Ēsaias	Isaiah	Is
Ezra/N^{e}hèmia		Ieremias	Jeremiah	Jer
Dib^{e}rey hayamîm		*Barouch*	Lamentations	Lam
		Thrēnoi	Baruch	Bar
		Epistolē Ieremiou	Letter of Jeremiah	
		Iezekiēl	Ezekiel	Ez
		Sousanna [= *Dn 13*]	Daniel 1–14	Dn
		Daniēl [+ 3:24–90]		
		Bel kai Drakōn [= *Dn 14*]	Twelve Prophets[1]	
			Maccabees I–II	Mc I–II

In italics: the deuterocanonical* writings. Within parentheses: the apocryphal* writings.

[1]The Hebrew order of the TWELVE PROPHETS: Hosea (Hos), Joel (Jl), Amos (Am), Obadiah (Ob), Jonah (Jon), Micah (Mi), Nahum (Na), Habakkuk (Hb), Zephaniah (Zep), Haggai (Hg), Zechariah (Zec), Malachi (Mal). The Greek Bible puts Amos and Micah in the second and third places respectively, with corresponding realignments of the other books.

rules for existence. It listed a large number of ordinances which had no value except for a given era and civilization, the nomadic for example. Along with the great interpreters of his day, such as Hillel, Jesus distilled the essence of the Torah when he told the scribe that the greatest commandment was to love God, and that the second was like it, to love one's neighbor as oneself (Mt 22:37–39). Moreover, Jesus protested against interpretations designated as "the traditions of the elders" (Mt 15:2f.,6).

B. The traditions of the elders* formed an integral part of the Torah,* insofar as they were handed down. The written Law was always accompanied by "the Law which is in the mouth," destined, as it was, to explain it and to give its meaning. The necessity of this tradition* derived from the very nature of the original Torah. As instruction concerning doctrine and practice, it had to be transmitted to the faithful. Ezra* entrusted it to the doctors* of the Law, laymen who were knowledgeable in the Torah (Neh 8:9). They endeavored in their turn to fit Law and life together, bringing to birth a traditional interpretation, which they took pains to prove went back to Moses* and, through him, to God himself.

A series of word pairs characterized this enterprise: to transmit/to receive *(mâsar/qibbêl),* to speak/to hear *(âmar/šhema'),* to give/to receive *(nâtan/lâqah).* Above all, lists of decisions were established, ever longer and longer, which one had to to be concerned with "repeating" (*shânah,* whence *Mishnah**). Thus, there were added to the Scriptures "the traditions which Moses bequeathed" (Acts 6:14; cf. Mk 7:5; Gal 1:14). This "oral law" was oriented toward a worthwhile goal. One must also note that it carried in its wake the excesses which Jesus condemned, denouncing as he did the quibbles of the lawyers who allowed the overturning of the Law itself. They ended up substituting a human interpretation for the divine decision.

C. The guardians of the Law were, however, vigilant. The greatest example was a permanent commission sitting in Jerusalem, the Great Sanhedrin, while minor sanhedrins ensured the observance of the Law in the villages (cf. Intr. VI.4.A).

In the first century, the authorized interpreters of the Torah were no longer the priests, but the scribes,* the lawyers* or doctors* of the Law. Ezra* and the author of Sirach* had been scribes. These laymen were learned men who, originally simple copyists, became enforcers by virtue of their profound knowledge of the Law. They had acquired this learning in one of the schools *(bet-ha-midrash)* conducted by the most famous doctors of the Law, such as Gamaliel,* who was Paul's teacher. The teaching consisted of a vast commentary on Scripture, called Midrash,* which had as its goal the actualization of the inspired text, while explaining it and giving it practical applications. There were two principal kinds of midrashim: *halakah,* a commentary on the Torah which aimed at furnishing juridical rules, and *haggadah,* which commented on or even embellished narrative and edifying texts. A third kind of commentary was *pèshèr,* one which strove to show forth the present significance of a biblical text. This last procedure was freely employed by the evangelists, who sought out what had been foretold about the Christ in the Scripture and been proclaimed by Jesus himself in the synagogue of Nazareth (Lk 4:16–22). At the conclusion of his studies, the new scribe could himself comment on the Scripture and also preach. If he had proven his fidelity in the observance of the Law, he was in his turn recognized as a doctor of the Law and could gather disciples around himself.

These doctors were venerated with the name rabbi,* that is "teacher." Rigorous observers of the Law, they vowed their lives to commenting upon the Scriptures in the synagogues,* giving instruction under the Temple porticoes, gathering disciples* whom they taught to love the Law. They sat on the sanhedrin and established Israel's jurisprudence. From the year 70, they formed a caste of rabbis and began the Talmudic* literature.

D. At least in its origins Christianity did not evolve in this direction. Jesus had reproached the scribes, as he had the Pharisees, for their often blameworthy casuistry. Above all, he had shown how the Law had to be "kept," namely by fidelity to Jesus' very own commandments.* In addition, the handing on of these commandments was no longer assured simply by some literal "repetition," but by the Holy Spirit who undertook to revive its memory and to bring the former time into the present.

2. Israel and the Messianic Expectation

A. Prophecy and apocalyptic

a. In the first century worship of the Torah and admiration for Moses had eclipsed the great prophets. These latter were piously mentioned and relegated to a past which had been shut off for almost 400 years. Apparently they had been run aground, whereas the rabbis maintained the authenticity of the Law. Only Elijah* preserved a place apart, for he had to come back at the end of time as the forerunner of the Messiah. To him was assigned the role, among others, of resolving juridical questions which had remained insoluble. This fact highlights the Christian innovation which gave such importance to the prophets.

In effect, if the Torah does indicate God's will,* which guarantees the Covenant, it does not specify *when* the final blessing will be bestowed. The chosen people had always lived in the expectation of a definitive amelioration of their lot. This hope was founded on the divine promises* and took on its complexion according to the various eras and contingencies: the Day* of the Lord, the days of the Messiah,* peace,* joy,* salvation,* the redemption* of Israel.

b. Before the doctors of the Law became the official interpreters of the will of God, two major traditions held sway in succession (despite the fact that they interfered with each other): prophecy and apocalyptic. The prophets,* who had been commanded to proclaim in Yahweh's name the way of life fitting each age, timelessly corrected popular hopes* of a nationalistic or earthly type of Messiah in order to preserve unsullied the true messianic expectation. The apocalypticists,* who revealed what lay hidden, took up the slack. These visionaries strove to divine precisely the time of the Day's* arrival and painted its coming in vivid colors. Apocalyptic literature, already extant in the prophetic writings of Ezekiel, includes, in addition to Daniel,* apocryphal* works which, though not preserved in the Jewish canon, exerted a great influence between the third century B.C. and the first century A.D. Chief among these were the collection attributed to Enoch* (except for the "Parables" which derive from the first century A.D.), the Jubilees* (dating from about 125 B.C.), the Testaments* of the Twelve Patriarchs (100 B.C.), the Ascension of Isaiah* (first century B.C.), the Apocalypse of Baruch* (A.D. 70–100) and the Apocalypse of Ezra* (A.D. 70).

Discussion continues on the origins of eschatological* conceptions, that is, those ideas which deal with the end of time. What seems clear is that, however different the modes of speech and however varied the provenance of the writings, one fundamental conviction prevailed; while Israel in one sense *already* had possession, she still did *not yet* enjoy that possession irretrievably. This structure, which undergirds hope,* holds true for Christian as well as Jew. What differs is the reality designated to be *already* and *not yet.* This feature, properly speaking a temporal aspect, is characteristic of all eschatology.

c. Like the prophet, the seer wanted to give meaning to the present moment and to history; unlike the prophet, however, he accepted time* in its totality. While in faith situating himself at the end of time, he returned by means of a literary device to a unique past time, letting Adam, Enoch, Moses, and Elijah speak. Striking up against that wall which is the end of history as humans know it, he is forced to find another language to maintain the distinction between the two worlds, that of man and that of God. Time stands still, and any before/after structure is no longer adequate to distinguish the present from the time to come. Therefore, he has to have recourse to a different relational structure, that of below/above. Moreover, the Hebrew term *'ôlam* (in Greek *aiōn;* in English aeon,* age*) conceals a great deal of the ambiguity of the Jewish thought-world. It possesses both a temporal meaning (the world already here/the world to come) as well as a spatial one (the earthly world/the heavenly world). In every case, whether under the form of prophetic hope or under that of an anticipated future, Israel's waiting foscused on two realities, the Kingdom of God and the person of the Messiah.

B. The coming of the rule of God. When John the Baptist and Jesus proclaimed that "the rule of God is very near," they were responding to the common expectation of Israel. This expectation was oriented in various directions according to the Jewish milieu. For some, among whom were some of Jesus' disciples (Lk 19:11; 2:38; Acts 1:6), the arrival of the rule* of God consisted in the restoration of the chosen nation; for others, it was expressed by a rule of a thousand years of prosperity (cf. Rv 20:4–6), while for still others, finally, it was a hidden, spiritual dominion, in the heart.

Apocalyptic environments brought forth two particular features. Before all else, the rule of God is universal, cosmic, to such an extent that its conception is properly spiritual but its realization cannot be effected except temporally. On the other hand, seers proposed to unlock the divine secrets by measuring out the time still to go until the end—cosmic catastrophes, tribulations of every kind, as well as precursory signs* which would ensure that one would not be surprised by the end of the world.

Jesus held to the imminent coming of the reign (kingdom) of God, but he rejected all calculations and every description. The "eschatological discourse" (Mk 13) is a protest against this kind of speculation, which deflects one away from what is essential—conversion.* Jesus did not suppress expectation. He did not identify the Church, which he wished to establish, with the kingdom of God. The Church* is but a provisional moment within the coming of the reign of God.

C. The person of the Messiah. Generally, expectation of God's rule was bound to the expectation of a mysterious person entrusted with the task of establishing the kingdom. Messianic depictions were quite varied. Most of the time, people hoped for the coming of a personal messiah, the son of David. Sometimes, as at Qumran,* he doubled as two persons, the Messiah* Son of David,* and hence a temporal king, and the Messiah son of Aaron, thereby a High Priest. One discovers again the fundamental duality of Judaism: royalty and priesthood. Often also, the Messiah would have a precursor, such as the prophet Elijah.

According to another apocalyptic current of thought, people waited for the coming of the Son* of Man, a suprahuman figure who derived from the vision of Daniel* 7:13–18 and had been taken up and still further spiritualized by the literature ascribed to Enoch.*

Jesus, it would appear, did not explicitly present himself under one title or another; he was content to raise questions about himself. He avoided allowing himself to be taken for a "messiah" who might appear to be a political liberator, but he did make use of designations such as "the Son of Man" and "the Son." According to some observers, he must have evoked the appearance of the Servant* of God proclaimed in Second Isaiah. Prophecy and apocalyptic both are represented in his thought.

The early Christians hardly ever preserved the title Son* of Man, but further specified the designation "the Son" as "the Son of God," and conferred on Jesus the title of Christ* or Messiah,* which was no longer ambiguous from the moment believers could no longer attribute temporal royalty to a crucified man. Among other titles given to Jesus by the Christian faith is that of Lord.*

3. The Wisdom Tradition and Contemporary Revelation. At the time of Jesus, the doctors of the Law had not only eclipsed the prophets, but seem also to have presumed to become the sages of their day. In reality, they confiscated Wisdom to the advantage of the Law, attributing to the latter what tradition had said of Wisdom. Nomism (from the Gk. *nomos,* law) or legalism did not, however, put a halt to sapiential currents. These were manifest in pious circles and even in rabbinic literature. It is clear that the New Testament has close ties with the wisdom tradition.

A. As in the cultures of the ancient Orient and of the entire world, the Bible retained traditions of wise men who were experts in the art of living well. Of such a type are the maxims collected in Proverbs, Ecclesiasticus or Wisdom, the reflections of Job or of Ecclesiastes, just as in the Egyptian Proverbs of Amenem-Ope (about 1000 B.C.) or the Wisdom of Ahikar (about 680 B.C.). Two differences should be noted: biblical wisdom* is essentially oriented toward a religious perspective. It also contests human wisdom's pretension of bringing happiness. In this line of thought, Jesus offers himself as a greater than Solomon (Mt 12:42), and Paul puts human wisdom at odds with the folly of the cross (1 Cor 2), underlining the problem of the relationship between philosophy* and revelation.*

B. The teacher of wisdom taught with the help of maxims, parables,* and riddles which caught the disciple's attention and invited him to question his teacher. Thus was born a wisdom genre which made itself felt also under the apocalyptic manner of revelation* (for example, Dn 2:28–30, which speaks of the "revelation of divine mysteries*"). The teaching of the sages was an appeal to listen and to draw near to the teacher (Prv 9:1,6; Sir 24:18,21). So spoke the Jesus who retained equally the doctrine of the "two ways*" and offered an answer to personal problems.

C. In the biblical writings, Wisdom became personified, a divine reality present at the time of creation (Prv 8:22–31), assisting God in the mastery of history (Wis 10:1–11:4), to such an extent that it is difficult to distinguish it from God in the midst of his activity in the world. This conception of Wisdom's pre-existence* is the basis of the Christology which sees in Jesus the firstborn* of every creature (Col 1:15–18), the reflection of God's being (Heb 1:3).

XIII. WORSHIP

The faith of Israel did not tolerate two ways of life, one religious, the other secular, because the whole people was set apart, dedicated to God. Jewish life was wholly penetrated by the prescriptions of the Law. One example should suffice to illustrate this point: circumcision,* which symbolized the Covenant, at the same time indicated a belonging to Yahweh and to Israel. It was a rite and at the same time a family tradition, carried out by the father of the family and not in the sanctuary.

The circumcised people nonetheless accorded a special place to a life of worship.* To enter into communion with God and to show its fidelity to the Covenant, the people designated as sacred* certain places (Temple, synagogue), certain persons (priests, levites), certain objects (altar, ark), certain times (sabbath, feasts), certain actions (sacrifices, pilgrimages, circumcision, prayers), certain ordinances (fasting, bans). The very multiplication of these "consecrations" risked concealing their goal and making them degenerate into magic.*

1. Places of Worship

A. The temple and its personnel

a. Like other religions, Israel built a holy edifice where God made himself present to men to receive their worship and to allow them to share in his life. From its origins, Israel was conscious of the inherent ambiguity in every one of God's dwellings* among men. Two traditions ran together, one celebrating the grandeur of the Temple, God's habitation in the midst of men, the other recalling that God cannot inhabit a human building. The Temple* mentioned in the New Testament was not the one Solomon had had built. That one had been destroyed in 587 B.C. (2 Kgs 25). Rebuilt after the return from exile (520–516), the "second Temple" was desecrated by Antiochus Epiphanes in 167. In 20 B.C., Herod the Great undertook the rebuilding of the Temple which Jesus knew. Magnificent as it was, "Herod's Temple" evoked wonder (Mk 13:1). The works were not completed until A.D. 64. Six years later, it was destroyed (August 6, 70). While the Jews lamented its ruin and, deprived of a sacrificial cult, carried on their prayer in synagogues, the Christians, who at first had also frequented the Temple, began to worship in their own buildings.

b. The Temple personnel included as many as 20,000 men. The priestly* hierarchy had been fixed for three centuries and was comprised of three ranks, the High Priest,* the priests,* and the Levites.* To all of them were entrusted the cultic and ritual observances, but also various other tasks including that of the police and Temple finances.

B. The synagogues. Seemingly, the synagogues* made their appearance during the exile in Babylon (587–538); in any case, at the time of Ezra* (400 B.C.). Deprived of the Temple, the irreplaceable place of sacrifices, the exiles came together to pray and to hear God speak through the Law. While the Temple was unique, synagogues multiplied, even at Jerusalem (Acts 6:9). In Jesus' time one was found in each Palestinian village of importance and in the Diaspora.* Rome had thirteen. Two factors seem to have come into play, the need to secure places for prayer (without contradicting the law of unity which wished only one place of sacrificial worship) and the need to teach the people. A significant feature of Judaism, synagogues were not exclusively reserved for religious functions. Just as the Great Sanhedrin* sat in the Temple, so also did the local sanhedrin gather at the synagogue. Trials were held there and punishments were meted out (Mt 10:17; 23:34). Christian churches were not successors to the Temple (this was effected in the body of Christ and in the Holy Spirit), but to the synagogues.

2. Acts of Worship

A. Sacrifices. These constituted the essence of the external Temple worship: the perpetual sacrifice* (incense* at morning and evening, the daily holocaust*), supplementary sacrifices on the sabbath and feast days, finally all those which the Law required of Jews on various occasions (offering of the firstborn,* the purification of women after childbirth, the healing of a leper*) and those which were voluntarily offered. Despite resemblances which these sacrificial rites shared with pagan sacrifices, a radical difference distinguished them from one another, namely the notion of God which they presupposed. Yahweh, the creator of all, had no need of anything; sovereign Lord, he could not be bound; he himself reunited within his Covenant the one who by expiation* came to recognize his debt or his sin and wished to enter once again into communion with him.

B. Prayer. Prayer* made explicit the relationship of an individual or a people who sought to abide with God. It formed an integral part of Israel's worship. Communitarian and personal, it punctuated Jewish existence by its key times, each year, each month, each week, each day. The Psalms,* inspired by God for his people, are a constant element of it. Imbued with trust, they reveal all the dimensions of prayer. They express, in exultation as well as in trial, dependence on the God of the Covenant.

a. Daily prayer. In the morning before every other activity, then at night, every adult (except women and slaves) was obliged to pray. For this he wrapped himself in a shawl and tied his phylacteries* to his forehead and his left hand. He turned toward Jerusalem, toward the Temple. Aloud he recited two prayers, a prayer of blessing and the *Shema Israel:* "Hear, O Israel: The Lord our God is Lord alone. You will love the Lord your God with all your heart, with all your soul and with all your strength. And these commandments which I give to you today will be in your heart. You will drill them into your children, and you will speak of them when you are in your house, when you go on a journey, when you lie down and when you get up. You will bind them to your hand to serve as a sign to yourself, and they will be on your forehead between your eyes. You will write them on the door-posts of your house and on your gates" (Dt 6:4–9; cf. 11:18–21; Nm 15:37–41). Then came the long prayer, today called *Shemoneh Esreh,* the "Eighteen [Benedictions]" of which the first three and the last three must have been recited by Jesus and by the Apostles.

b. The weekly sabbath.* The seventh day of the week, beginning on Friday at sundown, was entirely consecrated to the Lord. People rigorously stopped all work to pray and rest in memory of God's rest* after the creation of the world, at least according to the tradition handed down by Ex 20:8–11. Friday, the preparation* day (Parasceve), people cleaned house and set about making necessary purchases so that the sabbath meals, which were eaten cold, could be prepared with care. The sabbath was a day of joy for families and one had to dress up in fine clothes. At the appointed hour, believers gathered together in the synagogues to pray and to hear the reading and exposition of the Scriptures, while at the Temple a special liturgy took place.

3. The Annual Liturgical Cycle

A. At the beginning of each month* there was the rite of the new moon* (neomeny). September's new moon inaugurated the religious year. The year was marked off by major feasts; an essential element of Judaism, they fostered the faith and the unity of the people.

B. Four feasts* predominated: Passover,* Pentecost,* Booths,* the Day of Atonement.* The first three, agrarian in origin (the first sheaf, the first of the cereal harvest, the first vintage), had as their goal in Jesus' time a remembrance of the historical happenings which were foundational for Israel's life—the going out from Egypt, the gift of the Law on Sinai (according to a post-70 tradition), the wandering in the wilderness. They included a pilgrimage,* since every Jew was obliged in principle to celebrate them in Jerusalem. They brought together in overwhelming joy enormous crowds, notably for the Passover, "the Feast." The fourth solemnity, one of an exclusively religious character, sought purification of sins and reconciliation with God.

C. Secondary feasts reinforced national pride and piety; such were the feasts of Dedication* and Purim ("the lots"), in memory of the Jews' deliverance by Esther (Est 9), whose celebrations produced a carnival of sorts.

D. The significance of and ritual for these feasts are the background which helps to make the meaning of numerous New Testament texts intelligible.

XIV. MORALITY

1. God's Law. The Torah* specified what had to be the conduct of those who wished to enter into the Covenant of God: nothing could escape the divine judgment. Therein lay the difference between the Torah and the philosophical schools; the latter set forth a choice; in the Law God imposed his commandments.* So, the pious Jew had to express his faithfulness to the Covenant by his conduct, had to sanctify and glorify God's Name* in pagan eyes, had to concretely reveal his love. Accordingly, he tended toward "imitating God," showing himself like him "merciful and compassionate."

A. Ritual purity* laws determined what was clean or unclean (pure or impure) in different realms: wars, sexuality, death, certain sicknesses, certain foods, certain animals. They were in effect prior to their codification in the Torah and had become transformed there into specifically religious ordinances. These prohibitions acquired the value of divine commandments and, little by little, were transformed into moral precepts so that they came to be associated with God's holiness (Lv 11:44). They had as their basic purpose the preservation in holiness* of the people whom the holy God had elected by setting them apart from other people: thus, they affirmed even more clearly that God alone was holy.

However, the laws of purity led to numerous excesses. First of all, they reinforced the nationalist and exclusive character of Jewish religion by rendering pagan adherence to Jewish monotheism almost impossible. Peter had to wrestle against this very narrowness (Acts 10:9–11:18). Afterwards they fostered, among those who were observant, a sharpness and an affectation which were intolerable (in the third century A.D. they went so far as to count out 613 commandments, of which 365 were negative and 248 positive) and such formalism that the practitioners learned how to twist the Law. Following the prophets' lead, Jesus was unable to tolerate this (Mt 15:1–20), and refused to consider such precepts as binding. He focused his attention on interior attitudes, something which led the early Christians to see the ritual purity laws as merely an outward sign of an inward holiness.

B. Neighbors* occupied a large place in the Torah, but these did not thereby refer to just any people. One's neighbor was one's brother,* his compatriot, but not so the foreigner* or the Samaritan. If one gave evidence of humanity and good will toward a non-Jew, this was to keep the peace, to "make the Lord's name holy" and to reply to deeply felt appeals for charity. In carrying out to its goal the evolution already begun, Jesus broke down the barriers dividing people; henceforth my neighbor was anyone who drew near to me in difficulty.

Among Jews, life was regulated by obligations of strict justice and morality (sincerity, respect for another's welfare, respect for one's oath). Before all else, one had to be solicitous for one's neighbor's honor, especially to preserve conjugal community, or in instances of public insult* or scandal.* Jesus revealed in simple terms the depth of these ordinances by seeing in them the very root of moral activity.

The obligations of charity* set upon everyone the serious obligation of performing certain "good works*": to feed the hungry, to practice hospitality, to care for widows and orphans, to clothe those in need, to visit the sick or imprisoned, to bury the dead. Jesus continued these obligations, but gave his meaning to them when he declared: "For you did these things to me" (Mt 25:40). He conferred on them an absolute value when he declared that the second commandment was as important as the first (Mt 22:39–40). One cannot say that he loves God if he does not love his neighbor (cf. 1 Jn 3:10–14).

C. The exterior law and the interior law. These levels show up within the revelation of God's Law.* The prophets, particularly Jeremiah and Ezekiel, had proclaimed that, because the law written on stone had not been observed, one could only hope that one day God would inscribe it on hearts. Paul showed that this expectation had come true through the Holy Spirit who had been given (2 Cor 3:3). Between this hope and its realization stood the commandment* of Jesus, which recapitulated the ancient Law (Dt 30:14). Jesus crystalized the Law in the hearing of his word; this meant believing in him and loving the brethren without reserve. Once again it was the Holy Spirit who alone bestowed the knowledge and accomplishment of this commandment.

2. Observance of the Law

A. Man's freedom and God's judgment were the presuppositions of moral action, imbedded as these were within a covenant context. Man was free* and could choose between that good and evil which the Torah or the Gospel revealed to him. Nonetheless, there dwelt within man a penchant towards evil, which tempted him to move towards sin. This is what Paul clearly stated in Rom 7:7–24, through the illumination and power of the Holy Spirit, who had been given. In the case of the Jew who had no knowledge of this gift, he knew only that man is never tempted beyond his powers and that he can overcome the evil inclination through his own will. On the contrary, for Paul, who had been persuaded that no one can do justice* through his own works,* man under the Law and without the Holy Spirit is irremediably headed toward certain death.

On God's side, he rewards or punishes in accordance with man's conduct. To each commandment, whether it be a prohibition or an obligation, there is bound the retribution* which will follow, that is, a blessing* or a curse* (Dt 28). It seems certain that Jesus shared this belief (Mt 16:27), but he saw the recompense to consist in God's unique gift of himself personally (cf. Mt 6:4,6,18) within the perspective of a heaven to come. For the Jew, on the contrary, the earnings came to man already here below according to a kind of strict retributive justice; hence the principle, "There is no death without sin, nor suffering without transgression," a principle which bore in its wake terrible consequences with regard to man's ultimate responsibility for sickness (cf. Jn 9:2). Still, there were very many wise men who, following Job's lead, preferred to give up on clarifying the unfathomable mystery of the suffering and death of the just and to wait patiently for retribution to be worked out beyond death. In every regard, the Israelite believed firmly that God, faithful to his Covenant, would one day execute his just judgment.*

B. Sin, expiation and conversion. Israel was acutely conscious of the sin which she ceaselessly committed in transgressing the Law, something which was equivalent to rejecting God personally. To sin was to reject God's will* by violating one of his commandments,* whether this be by deliberate intent or not. Rendered unclean, the sinner could not be reconciled with God or enter once again into the Covenant relationship except by an expiatory* sacrifice.

For involuntary transgressions which involved legal impurity, these actions momentarily excluded from worship* the persons who were implicated. With the coming of the Gospel, these laws of purity* tended to give way to the invitation to be aware of one's responsibility in the realm of sin.*

If a man willingly transgressed the Law, he had to obtain pardon for his sin by returning to God through various ritual means (prayers* and sacrifices*), through bodily afflictions (sickness and death were reckoned as "love's reproofs"—Hos 11:4), through acts of penitence* and conversion, that is, by turning back to God, implying sincere confession* of one's sins, the firm resolve not to commit them anew, the redressing of one's conduct and the reparation, where needed, of the wrong done to one's neighbor. John the Baptist, Jesus, and the first Christians did not proclaim any other way, but they did focus the attention on love of God and love of one's neighbor.

XV. THE NEW TESTAMENT

1. THE TEXT. The New Testament contains twenty-seven books* of varying lengths, all written in Greek by a variety of authors and at different times in the course of the first century. It was transmitted in innumerable manuscripts. The most ancient manuscript containing the entire New Testament, *Sinaiticus,* dates from the fourth century. The most ancient complete manuscript of John goes back to the beginning of the third century. The most ancient papyrus of a fragment is dated to the year 135. Important variants affecting its meaning are few in number; we mention only Mk 16:9–20; Lk 22:19b–20, Jn 5:3b–4; 8:1–11. Establishing the text is carried out by means of textual criticism.*

2. BOOKS AND THE BOOK. The books are arranged both according to their literary genre* (gospels, acts, letters, apocalypse) and their greater or lesser lengths. Four gospels* are recognized, as well as one book of Acts* of the Apostles, thirteen epistles* which make up the "Pauline Corpus,*" one Epistle to the Hebrews,* seven general epistles and one Revelation* (Apocalypse). All the works were written by believers with the objective of edification.

These books, moreover, constitute only one book and exclude anything that is apocryphal.* The New Testament canon,* fixed during the second century (with a few particular exceptions, such as Hebrews and Revelation), seems to have had as its motive not the inspired* nature of the books, nor even the fact that they were judged orthodox, nor their attribution to apostolic* authors, but rather the recognition that they all were, and they alone, "universally received" in the churches of the time.

These books were divided into chapters according to a system proposed by Stephen Langton and alluded to in 1226; the chapters themselves were further divided into verses by a printer, Robert Estienne, in the course of a hasty journey that brought him from Lyons to Paris in 1551.

3. INTREPRETATION. The New Testament has been handed down as a text to be interpreted by exegetes. This exegesis* is done on texts of varying lengths, first of all, on pericopes* or small passages, narratives or speeches isolated within the framework of their literary context. Exegesis then examines writings as they constitute a whole, whether as a complete work (such as each of the gospels) or according to the writer to whom they are ascribed (such as the Pauline literature). Finally, to the degree that one can conceive of the New Testament as a whole, exegesis treats the totality of the New Testament. On this last level it becomes evident that such an enterprise requires a search for terminology broad enough to unify the viewpoints of such diverse works.

The work of interpretation has known and passed through different ages and phases: that of dogma, work done in the name of belief or unbelief; that of criticism,* which has its starting point in literary analysis; that of history, which appeals to the milieus in which the writings were formed *(Formgeschichte,* Redaktionsgeschichte*);* finally, that of hermeneutics,* which is open to any of the many possible meanings of the text. Most recently, structural analysis has presented a new way of looking at the text. While still finding its way, it nonetheless remains promising, even if it possesses rather limited objectives.

The historico-critical method considers the text under the aspects of its growth and its transmission (in technical parlance, under its "diachronic" aspect—the evolution of linguistic features in time). This view presupposes that the interpreter respects the meanings which words possess at each stage of evolution. In fact, words belong to a system of relations, to a language which constitutes a whole at any given time. We may designate the totality of such linguistic features which are reckoned as forming a system at a particular time in the evolution of language as the "synchronic" aspect. And so, a synchronic study (which some prefer to call "structural") leads us to read a text as it is in itself, prior to any consideration of its history. To take bearings on the possible meanings of a text, criticism successively undertakes a synchronic study, which enables it to uncover the "structure" of the passage; then, a diachronic study, which aims at reconstructing the evolution of its structures, and finally a functional study which inserts the text into the sociological milieu which gave it birth. These short pointers on the current directions of critical study are an invitation to the reader to deepen, if he or she judges it appropriate, these difficult questions of method when reading the biblical text.

WORD LIST

Aaron Gk. *Aarōn,* Heb. *aharôn.* The brother of Moses,[1] who presided at the erection of the golden calf,[2] but in whom tradition saw especially the ancestor of the priestly order,[3] the High Priest above all others,[4] the intercessor who turned aside the divine wrath.[5] The Essenes* awaited the Aaronic Messiah, a sovereign messiah-priest. Like Aaron, Christ was called by God to function as High Priest;[6] his priesthood was not of the same order but was analagous to Aaron's, one superior to his, like Melchizedek's.[7]

[1]Ex 4:14. [2]Ex 32:1-6; Acts 7:40. [3]Ex 28:1; Nm 17:16-26; Lk 1:5; Heb 9:4. [4]Sir 45:6-22. [5]Wis 18:21-25. [6]Heb 5:4. [7]Heb 7:3,11-21 □.

→ High Priest—Melchizedek—priesthood.

Abaddon Heb. *Abaddôn:* "ruin, destruction." In the O.T. the place of perdition where the dead dwelt,[1] personified alongside Death.[2] An angel* of the Abyss,[3] whose Greek name *Apollyōn* meant "destroyer."

[1]Jb 26:6. [2]Jb 28:22. [3]Rv 9:11 □.

→ abyss—death—netherworld.

abandon Gk. *eg-kata-leipō:* "to leave, to quit," with a tone of the rupturing of personal relationships. The word was frequently used by the Septuagint* to tell of the vicissitudes of the Covenant.* Men abandoned Yahweh,[1] while Yahweh promised not to abandon his chosen, his faithful one, but always to be with him.[2] Also, the Jew ceaselessly offered praise that God had not abandoned him.[3] From the cross on which he desired to stay, Jesus died crying out: "My God, My God, why have you abandoned me?"[4] Insofar as these words agree with Psalm 22:1, it does not seem appropriate to soften them by supposing that Jesus secretly uttered the conclusion to the Psalm which told of the triumph of life.[5] Jesus died with a "why" on his lips, but he uttered this why while speaking to God and while supposing him to be present. In this way, he manifested his faith to the end, that is, right into death's shadows.[6] His answer did not come until after his death, in the centurion's confession[7] or in Peter's declaration on Pentecost.[8] Jesus did not cheat in dealing with death. Paul perhaps hinted at a similar abandonment from the side of men.[9]

[1]Jgs 2:12; 1 Sm 8:8; 12:10; 1 Kgs 9:9; 11:33; Jer 1:16; 2:13; cf. Heb 10:25. [2]Dt 4:31; 31:6,8; Jos 1:5; 1 Kgs 6:13; Ps 37:28,31; cf. Heb 13:5. [3]1 Kgs 8:57; Ps 27:9; 38:22; 119:8. [4]Mt 27:46 (= Mk 15:34). [5]Ps 22:30f. [6]Phil 2:8. [7]Mk 15:39. [8]Acts 2:27,31. [9]2 Cor 4:9; 2 Tim 4:10,16.

abba An Aramaic term corresponding to the Hebrew. *âb:* "father," the equivalent of "papa," used in the nominative and vocative cases. A form of address to God not used in the O.T. or in later Judaism, but one characteristic of Jesus. The invocation of the Christian who, through the Spirit, knows himself to be a son.[1]

[1]Mk 14:36; Rom 8:15; Gal 4:6; cf. 2 Cor 6:18 □.

→ father.

Abel Heb. *hèbèl:* "breath, vanity." The younger son of Adam and Eve, murdered by Cain, his older brother,[1] because of his works, which God held to be acceptable; a type of the persecuted just* man.[2] His poured out blood* was eloquent before God, but that of Jesus was still more so.[3]

[1]Gn 4:1-8; 1 Jn 3:12. [2]Mt 23:35 (= Lk 11:51). [3]Heb 11:4; 12:24 □.

Abilene Gk. *abilēnē.* The territory of the city of Abila, which has vanished today, to the northwest of Damascus, in the Antilebanon. The tetrarchy* of Lysanias until A.D. 37, it was given to Herod* Agrippa I from 37 to 44, administered by a Roman procurator until 53, then annexed to the kingdom of Agrippa* II, incorporated in the year 100 within the Roman province of Syria.*[1]

[1]Lk 3:1 □.

ablution Gk. *baptismos.* A water purification rite, effected among other ways by a bath.[1] Not to be confused with a sprinkling.*

[1]Mk 7:4; Lk 11:38; Heb 9:10 □.

→ Intr. VIII.1.C; XIV.1.A. bath—baptism—pure—wash.

abide **1.** Gk. *menō.* In numerous passages, particularly Johannine ones, to abide signifies not only "to stay, to sojourn, to reside, to inhabit," but also alludes to that abode which the divine Wisdom* sought out for itself among men.[1] A great dream once existed of seeing God dwelling among his people. According to the rabbis, the *Shᵉkînâh* signified the house, the dwelling-place of God. This dream became a reality in Jesus Christ (note the probable word play in the Gk. *skēnoō,* which possessed the same consonants as the Heb. *Shᵉkînâh:* "to pitch a tent*"[2]). John liked to set forth the new relationship uniting man with God, no longer like that of someone who faced another, but expressed now through the image of a mutual indwelling.[3]

[1]Sir 24:7f.; cf. Jn 1:9-11. [2]Jn 1:14. [3]Jn 14:23; 15:4-7; 1 Jn 2:14,27; 3:6,9,24; 4:12f.,15f.

2. In the sense of "to subsist" or "to not pass away at all," a variety of Greek terms was used. What did not disappear was Christ; the foundation stone,*[4] his word;[5] faith, hope and love.[6]

[4]Mt 7:24f. (= Lk 6:47-49); 1 Cor 3:14; Eph 2:20-22. [5]Mt 24:35 (= Mk 13:31 = Lk 21:33). [6]1 Cor 13:8-13.

Abomination of Desolation Gk. *to bdelygma tēs erēmōseōs,* a term uniting the image of "the disgusting thing" (Gk. *bdelyros:* "disgusting"), impure,[1] idolatrous,[2] with that of "devastation" (from the Gk. *erēmoō:* "to render desolate"[3]). The expression originally described the altar of Zeus (or his statue), erected in 168–167 B.C. by Antiochus IV Epiphanes in the Temple of Jersalem.[4] In Matthew and Mark[5] it was taken up again as a sign of the end of the ages*;

Luke, who passed over it, made it correspond with the historical fact of the "devastation" of Jerusalem.[6] Paul equated it with the person of the Unholy One, the Adversary, the Lost One.[7]

[1]Gn 43:32; Lv 11:43; 18:22; Rv 17:4f. [2]1 Kgs 11:5; 2 Kgs 23:13; Prv 15:8; Rom 2:22. [3]Mt 12:25 (= Lk 11:17); Rv 18:17,19. [4]Dn 9:27; 11:31; 12:11; 1 Mc 1:54,59; 2 Mc 6:2. [5]Mt 24:15 (= Mk 13:14) □. [6]Lk 21:20. [7]2 Thes 2:3f.

→ Intr. I.1.C.—Antichrist—Dedication.

Abraham Gk. *Abraam,* Heb. *Abrâhâm,* from the Babylonian: "he loves the father" or from the Aram.: "the Father [God] is lifted up." A native of Haran, in northern Mesopotamia, or of Ur of the Chaldees; the ancestor of the chosen people,[1] he lived in approximately the nineteenth century B.C. (?). His personality dominates the entire Bible, even to the extent that one of the divine names is "the God of Abraham, Isaac and Jacob."[2] From his life's course the N.T. particularly emphasized his faith, which was manifest on several occasions: his home-leaving,[3] the promise to him of a posterity and his sacrifice of Isaac.[4] Abraham was the "friend of God,"[5] the father of believers, and so, of all the nations.[6]

[1]Gn 12–25. [2]Mt 22:32 (= Mk 12:26 = Lk 20:37); Acts 3:13,32 △. [3]Heb 11:8. [4]Gn 15:6; 22:1-19; Heb 11:17,19; Jas 2:21. [5]Is 41:8; Jas 2:23. [6]Mt 3:9 (= Lk 3:8); Jn 8:33-39; Rom 3:27–4:25; Gal 3:6-29.

→ covenant—faith.

abyss **1.** Gk. *a-byssos:* "without bottom" (Gk. *bythos, byssos:* "bottom of the sea"[1]).

[1]2 Cor 11:25.

2. An underground place where the dead dwelt;[2] a chasm (Gk. *chasma*[3]) there separated the wicked from the just.

[2]Rom 10:7. [3]Lk 16:26 △.

3. A place where the demons were imprisoned,[4] under tyranny by a king,[5] of which the Beast* was a type;[6] Satan* was imprisoned there for a thousand years.[7]

[4]Lk 8:31; Rv 9:1f. [5]Rv 9:11. [6]Rv 11:7; 17:8. [7]Rv 20:1,3 △.

4. Other Greek words—*siros:* literally "a cavity in the earth, an underground receptacle for grain"; *tartaroō:* "to plunge into Tartarus," a verb deriving from the name which designated the netherworld in Latin mythology.[8]

[8]2 Pt 2:4 △.

→ Intr. V.1.—netherworld.

accomplish

→ fulfill.

Achaia Gk. *Achaia.* The territory situated in the southern part of modern-day Greece, subjected to the Romans in 146 B.C. Following the division of the provinces* carried out by Augustus* in 27 B.C., Achaia was a senatorial province (like Macedonia,* with which it formed an association of Greek states), without economic or political importance. It was at Corinth* that a proconsul governed, while Athens* remained the prestigious homeland of Hellenism. It was evangelized by Paul.[1]

[1]Acts 18:12,27; 19:21; Rom 15:26; 1 Cor 16:15; 2 Cor 1:1; 9:2; 11:10; 1 Thes 1:7f. □.

→ Cenchreae—Gallio—Map 3.

[Acts of the Apostles] The second half of Luke's work which attempted to show how the Good News proclaimed and lived out and related in the first part, the gospel of Luke, came to be fulfilled in its transmission by Jesus to the pagan nations. It was not a history of the Church, nor even one about its first mission fields, but rather was a theological work, edited about the year 80, probably with pagan readers in mind.

→ Intr. I.3–5; IV.7; XV.2.—Luke.

Adam Gk. *Adam,* Heb. *âdâm* (related to *adâmâ:* "earth"): "the earthy one." In the O.T., the term sometimes referred to the man created by God,[1] but ordinarily referred to the human collectivity.[2] Adam was the man* in whom every man had to recognize himself as called to intimacy with God in spite of his sin.*[3] In the N.T., except for one or two references to the common ancestor of men[4] and several reflections on the conduct of women[5] or on the meaning of marriage,[6] interest focused on setting Adam face-to-face with Jesus Christ.* Similar in that both had a universal role, they differed in their origins, whether that of death or life.[7] With terminology inherited from his era, Paul spoke of Adam as a figure* of the Christ, without thereby affirming a historical reality in our modern sense of that word.

[1]Gn 4:25; 5:1,3-5; 1 Chr 1:1; Tb 8:6; Sir 49:16 △ and, perhaps, Gn 2:20; 3:17,21; Wis 10:1f. [2]Jb 14:1; Ps 8:5; 104:14ff. [3]Gn 2–3. [4]Lk 3:38; Jude 14; cf. Acts 17:26. [5]1 Tim 2:13f. [6]Gn 2:24; cf. Mt 19:4-6; Eph 5:31. [7]Rom 5:12-21; 1 Cor 15:20-22, 45-49 □.

→ creation—man—myth.

adjure Gk. *omnymi, omnyō.*

→ oath.

adoption Gk. *hyiothesia* (from *hyios:* "son" and *tithēmi:* "to put, place, consider as"): "the action of establishing as a son," a technical term of legal language in Greece and at Rome. Although not mentioned in the Mosaic legislation, adoption was not unknown in Israel.[1] According to Roman law this was carried out by a purchase before witnesses. Jews considered that they themselves had obtained a filial adoption from God.[2] Christians reckoned that a similar occurrence had taken place in Jesus[3] through the Spirit who made believers sons in truth,[4] even if the fullness of that adoption was at the same time envisaged as future.[5]

[1]Gn 16:2; 48:5f.; 50:23. [2]Rom 9:4,25f.; 2 Cor 6:18. [3]Rom 8:15; Gal 3:26; Eph 1:5; Heb 12:5-8; Rv 21:7. [4]Gal 4:5-7; 1 Jn 3:1f. [5]Rom 8:23 □.

→ child—Son of God.

adore **1.** Lat. *adorare,* from *orare,* a term belonging to religious and juridical language: "to pronounce a ritual formula, prayer or petition," from which we get *ad-orare:* "to address a prayer to." Popular etymology linked the word to *os:* "mouth." The Greek word *pros-kyneō* (from *pros:* "before, turned towards" and *kyneō:* "to kiss"), implied the gesture of bending forward to kiss the hands or feet, signifying: "to prostrate oneself." Occasionally, the term was preceded by the expression "to fall at the feet of or on one's face,"[1] in the ancient world a disposition common when in the presence of a sovereign or master.[2] When used in ancient pagan worship, the term probably meant "to kiss, to incline oneself so as to cast a kiss from one's hands to" the image of the god. Hence, its derived meaning was: "to adore," a meaning which the term assumed in the Greek and Roman world. The Septuagint* made use of it; although there was not among the Jews any representation of Yahweh, prostration expressed the fact that one recognized God's presence and sovereignty and was willingly entirely submissive to his will.[3]

[1]Mt 18:26; Acts 10:25; 1 Cor 14:25; Rv 4:10; 7:11; 11:16. [2]cf. Is 51:23; 2 Kgs 1:13. [3]Ps 96:9; 99:5.

2. As was the case in the O.T., the N.T. stressed that adoration was a duty[4] and that it was due by all men[5] to God alone.[6] It was typical of life in heaven.*[7] When used without an object, the term refered to worship* in the Temple.[8] Jesus foretold an adoration of the Father in spirit and truth, thereby suppressing localization of any kind of worship.[9]

[4]Mt 4:10 (= Lk 4:8 = Dt 6:13). [5]1 Cor 14:25; Rv 14:7; 15:4; cf. Rom 14:11; Eph 3:14. [6]Acts 10:25f.; Rv 19:10, 22:8f. [7]Rv 4:10; 5:14; 7:11ff. [8]Jn 12:20; Acts 8:27; 24:11; cf. Jn 4:20. [9]Jn 4:20-24.

3. Directed towards the earthly Jesus, gestures of prostration indicated recognition of a higher power[10] in him or else they were a mockery of him during his passion.[11] Accordingly, the term expressed the Church's faith.* So, it was also used of the child honored by the Magi[12] and in reference to the Risen One.[13]

[10]Mt 8:2; 9:18; 14:33; 15:25; 20:20; Mk 5:6; Jn 9:38. [11]Mk 15:19; cf. Mt 27:29. [12]Mt 2:2, (8), 11. [13]Mt 28:9,17; Lk 24:52.

4. The devil* and his representations demanded or received prostration[14]; following Jesus' lead,[15] believers refused to give it to them, even at the cost of their lives.[16]

[14]Mt 4:9 (= Lk 4:7); Rv 9:20; 13:4,8; 19:20. [15]Mt 4:10 (= Lk 4:8). [16]Rv 13:15; cf. Rom 11:4.

5. Another such term was: to kneel (Gk. *gonypeteō:* "to fall on one's knees"). Similar to prostration, the gesture of bending the knee symbolized homage and supplication.[17] It was often associated with prayer.[18] By this gesture, all men will recognize that Jesus is Lord.[19]

[17]Mt 17:14; Mk 1:40; 10:17. [18]Lk 22:41; Acts 7:60; 9:40; 20:36; 21:5. [19]Phil 2:10.

→ fear—God-fearer—kiss—piety—prayer.

Adramyttium Gk. *Adramytteion.* A port city of Mysia,* opposite Lesbos.[1]

[1]Acts 27:2 □.

→ Map 2.

adultery Gk. *moicheia* (of uncertain etymology). **1.** The law forebade adultery, that is, sexual relations between a man (married or not) and a married woman,* for such a relationship violated the proprietary right which a husband had over his wife.[1] The two offenders had to be put to death, generally by stoning* on the part of the community, all of whom were affected by the crime.[2] Jesus extended to the man what formerly held only for the woman[3] and went so far as to condemn desire* which was already adulterous.[4] Adultery was one of the vices* which closed off entry into the Kingdom[5]; even so, God can forgive it.[6]

[1]Ex 20:14,17; Mt 19:18 (= Mk 10:19 = Lk 18:20); Lk 18:11; Rom 2:22; 7:3; 13:9; Jas 2:11. [2]Lv 20:10; Dt 22:22-24; Jn 8:3-5. [3]Mt 5:32; 19:9; Mk 10:11f.; Lk 16:18. [4]Mt 5:27f.; cf. Prv 6:20-35. [5]Mt 15:19 (= Mk 7:22); 1 Cor 6:9f.; Heb 13:4; 2 Pt 2:14. [6]Jn 8:3-11; cf. Mt 21:31f. △.

2. In the figurative sense, and following the lead of the O.T. prophets,[7] the N.T. uses this term to describe a people who were disbelieving and unfaithful to God.[8]

[7]Ez 16:15-34; Hos 2–3. [8]Mt 12:39; 16:4 (= Mk 8:38); Jas 4:4; Rv 2:22 △.

→ Intr. VIII.2.B.d.—debauchery—divorce—marriage—prostitution—spouse—vices.

advent

→ Day of the Lord—parousia.

adversary Gk. *anti-keimenos:* "one who is set opposite, the enemy," the opponent;[1] Satan was the Adversary above all others.[2] Similarly, with the Gk. *en-antios,* "vis-a-vis, contrary," which can as readily be predicated of elements such as the wind,[3] men,[4] forces[5] or Satan.[6] The Greek *anti-dikos* designated the "opposing party,"[7] which might also mean Satan.[8]

[1]Lk 13:17; 21:15; 1 Cor 16:9; Gal 5:17; Phil 1:28; 1 Tim 1:10. [2]2 Thes 2:4; 1 Tim 5:14 △. [3]Mt 14:24 (= Mk 6:48); Acts 27:4. [4]Acts 17:7; 28:17; 1 Thes 2:15; Heb 10:27. [5]Acts 26:9; Col 2:14. [6]Ti 2:8 △. [7]Mt 5:25 (= Lk 12:58); Lk 18:3. [8]1 Pt 5:8 △.

→ Satan.

advocate

→ Paraclete.

aeon The Greek *aiōn* (Heb. *'ôlâm*) has two meanings: a) "duration, length of time, age.* Through this word the O.T. attempted to overcome the extent of a lifetime's length or, when God was under discussion, to tell of one who was eternal (Gk. *aiōnios*); b) world.* The apocalyptic* of late Judaism distinguished two aeons: "this one" which had to pass away and which was subject to tribulation, and "that one" which has yet to come and which will be a kingdom of justice and peace.[1]

[1]Mt 12:32; Mk 10:30 (= Lk 18:30); Eph 1:21; Heb 6:5.

→ age—eternal—time—world.

afraid

→ fear.

Agabus Gk. *Agabos.* A Christian prophet of Jerusalem. He foretold two events: a famine and Paul's arrest.[1]

[1]Acts 11:27f.; 21:10f. □.

agape Gk. *agapē:* "love." A fraternal meal liturgical in character, in the course of which the Eucharist was celebrated. Attested from the end of the second century (Tertullian), perhaps from the beginning of it (Ignatius*), this custom would have been extant in the first century[1] and have had its origin in the Christian meals at Corinth,* whose disorders Paul denounced.[2] The meal, which was incorrectly named the "joyous agape," was not the original form of the Eucharist, in contrast to the sacrificial meal. The agape seems often to have degenerated into carousings and was forbidden in the fourth century, to disappear entirely in the seventh century.

[1]Jude 12 □. [2]1 Cor 11:20,22. [3]cf. Acts 2:46; 20:7. [4]cf. 2 Pt 2:13.

→ breaking of bread—Eucharist—meal.

age A translation of the Heb. *'ôlâm* and of the Gk. *aiōn,* from the same root as *aei:* "always" (cf. Lat. *aevum, aeternus*).

1. Properly speaking, the term did not designate a period of a hundred years nor even a long determinate period of time; it was the equivalent of eternity.*[1]

[1]2 Cor 9:9; Heb 5:6; 1 Pt 1:25.

2. The expression "age upon age" is a Hebraism, similar to "song of songs"; it has the same meaning as "forever" and points to an unlimited time, whether it be past or future.[2]

[2]Rom 16:27; Heb 1:8; Rv 4:9.

3. The word can also designate the world,* whether present or to come.[3]

[3]Mt 12:32; Eph 1:21.

→ aeon—eternal—time.

age (old)

→ old age.

agony Gk. *agōnia:* "wrestling, combat, turmoil of soul, disquiet, anxiety." Faced with his impending death, Jesus was in the throes of anguish,* a word which more precisely expresses the meaning of the term which was chosen by Luke.[1]

[1]Lk 22:44 □; cf. 2 Mc 3:14-21; 15:19.

agora Gk. *agora:* "assembly," from which derive "the place of assembly, the public square."[1] At Athens the market was a place decorated with trees; it was divided into quarters which were assigned to diverse corporations of merchants and contained varied institutions (the senate, tribunal, temples, etc.).[2]

[1]Mt 11:16 (= Lk 7:32); 20:3; 23:7 (= Mk 12:38 = Lk 11:43 = 20:46); Mk 6:56; 7:4; Acts 16:19; 17:5. [2]Acts 17:17 □.

→ public square.

[agrapha] Gk. *agrapha (logia):* "unwritten sayings" (*a* privative and *graphō:* "to write"). Sayings of Jesus missing from the canonical* gospels but known through tradition. Agrapha are reckoned to be authentic according to several criteria: the quality of their transmission, the absence of tendentious invention in them, their nonalteration of canonical sayings. Here are several, in addition to 1 Thes 4:16f., whose authenticity* is under discussion. "There is more joy in giving than in receiving"[1] is often considered to be a proverb which circulated through the Greco-Roman world and was attributed to Jesus; "Love your brother as your very own soul, guard him as the pupil of your eye";[2] "The rich man began to scratch his head and the matter did not suit him. And the Lord said to him: 'How can you say, "I have fulfilled the law and the prophets"? For it is written in the law: You shall love your neighbor as yourself! Behold now how large a number of your brothers, children of Abraham, are covered with filthy rags and are dying of hunger, while your house is brimming over with goods and absolutely nothing spills over for them!' ";[3] "That same day Jesus saw a man doing some work on the sabbath. He said to him, 'If you know what you are doing, you are blessed. But if you do not know it, you are cursed and a transgressor of the law' ";[4] "He who is close to me is close to the fire. He who is far from me is far from the Kingdom";[5] "If your brother has sinned against you with a word and has made you honorable amends, receive him back seven times a day. Simon said to him, 'Seven times a day?' The Lord answered him and told him, 'Yes, I tell you even seventy-seven times seven times! For even among the prophets, after they had received the anointing of the Holy Spirit, there was found to be sin in speech' ";[6] "Pray for your enemies, for, whoever is not against you is for you. Whoever keeps himself distant from you today will be close to you tomorrow";[7] "Ask for great things and God will give you little things as well";[8] "Be expert money-changers."[9]

[1]Acts 20:35 [2]*Gospel of Thomas** 25; cf. Lv 19:18; Mt 19:19 [3]*Gospel of the Nazarenes* in Origen: *On Matthew* 15:14; 19:16–22. [4]Lk 6:5, according to *Codex D.* [5]*Gospel of Thomas* 82; cf. Mk 9:49; Lk 12:49; 1 Pt 1:7; Rv 3:18. [6]*Gospel of the Nazarenes,* in Jerome, *Against*

Pelagius 3:2; *On Matthew* 18:21f. [7]*Papyrus Oxyrhynchus* 1224. [8]Clement of Alexandria, *Stromateis* I, xxiv, 158:2. [9]Quoted in Origen: not trustworthy bankers, but people who can discern good and evil.

Agrippa Gk. *Agrippas,* Lat. *Agrippa.*

1. Herod Agrippa I.

→ Herod.

2. Herod Agrippa II (27–94), son of Herod Agrippa I. In 53, king of Chalcis, a small principality of Lebanon, which he exchanged for the ancient tetrarchy* of Philip and Abilene.* He was reproached for his incestuous relationship with his sister Berenice,* for his complicity with the Romans and his ambiguous, if not favorable, attitude toward Christians.[1]

[1]Acts 25:13–26:32 □.

Akeldama

→ Hakeldama.

[Akkadian] The Semitic* language of the inhabitants of the country of Akkad in north Babylon, which held a preponderant role in the period around 2250 B.C.[1]

[1]Gn 10:10.

Alexander Gk. *Alexandros:* "he who protects men."

1. The son of Simon of Cyrene and the brother of Rufus.[1]

[1]Mk 15:21 □.

2. A Jew of the high priestly family.[1]

[1]Acts 4:6 □.

3. A Jew of Ephesus.[1]

[1]Acts 19:33 □.

4. A Christian apostate.[1]

[1]1 Tim 1:20 □.

5. A smelter, the adversary of Paul, whom some identify with 3 or 4 above.[1]

[1]2 Tim 4:14 □.

alien

→ stranger.

[allegorization] A process by which one confers one or more meanings onto features of a narrative or of a parable* which they ordinarily would not have had. Thus, "the Lord of the house" *(ho kyrios tēs oikias)* becomes "your Lord" *(ho kyrios hymōn).*[1]

[1]Mt 24:42 and Mk 13:35.

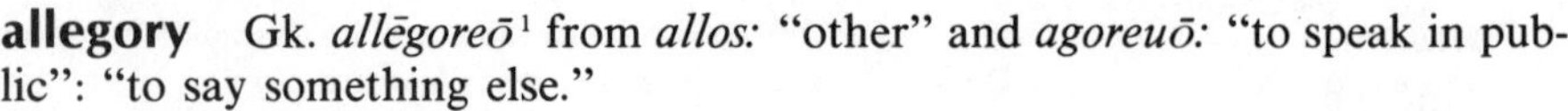

allegory Gk. *allēgoreō*[1] from *allos:* "other" and *agoreuō:* "to speak in public": "to say something else."

[1]Gal 4:24 □.

1. Within a narrative, an extended metaphor* wherein each detail receives its own proper meaning: so, in the parable* of the Good Shepherd in Jn 10:1–5: the shepherd, the sheep, the door, the sheepfold, the doorkeeper.

2. Distinct from a symbol,* which translates a reality, it gives expression to an idea in the form of an image.

Alleluia Gk. *Allēlouia,* from the Heb. *hallelûyâ,* meaning "Praise Yah (Yahweh)." A liturgical acclamation at the beginning or ending of certain psalms.*[1] A shout of praise* proclaimed by the elect to celebrate God's final triumph.[2]

[1]Ps 111–117. [2]Rv 19:1,3,4,6 □.

alms, almsgiving Gk. *eleēmosynē,* a word signifying "pity, mercy" and associated, consequently, with God's compassion;[1] a word translating the Heb. *ṣ^edâqâ:* "justice," probably because almsgiving was a means of re-establishing the justice that God desired on the earth (giving to all beings what they need), despite the many beggars* known to the Orient.[2] Along with prayer and fasting, almsgiving was one of three fundamental Jewish practices which rendered pleasing to God someone, even a non-Jew, who performed this action without ostentation;[3] it was an act of worship*[4] which purified.[5] Jesus praised it,[6] practiced it[7] and demanded it of his disciples.[8] The primitive Church even tried to organize a sharing of goods with the poorest,[9] and Paul undertook a collection.[10] But, without love it was in vain.[11]

[1]Lk 6:36,38. [2]Mk 10:46 (= Lk 18:35); Jn 9:8; Acts 3:2f.; cf. Lk 16:3. [3]Mt 6:2-4. [4]Acts 9:36; 10:2,4. [5]Lk 11:41. [6]Mk 12:41-44. [7]Jn 13:29. [8]Lk 12:33; 16:9. [9]Acts 4:32–5:11; 6:1-6. [10]Acts 11:29f.; 24:17; Rom 15:28; 1 Cor 16:1-4; 2 Cor 8–9; Gal 2:10. [11]1 Cor 13:3.

→ beggar—collection—mercy—poor.

aloes Gk. *aloē.* A perfume extracted from a precious oriental wood (without any connection with the medicinal plant bearing the same name). Rarely was it used in its pure form; in the Bible it was always mixed with another perfume, such as myrrh.*[1]

[1]Ps 45:9; Prv 7:17; Sg 4:14; Jn 19:39 □.

→ perfume.

Alpha and Omega The first and last letters of the Greek alphabet. The expression meant the first and the last in history,[1] the beginning and the end of all that existed.[2] A divine title,[3] attributed to Jesus Christ.[4]

[1]Is 41:4; 44:6; 48:12; Rv 1:17; 2:8; 22:13. [2]Rv 21:6; 22:13. [3]Rv 1:8; 21:6. [4]Rv 22:13 □.

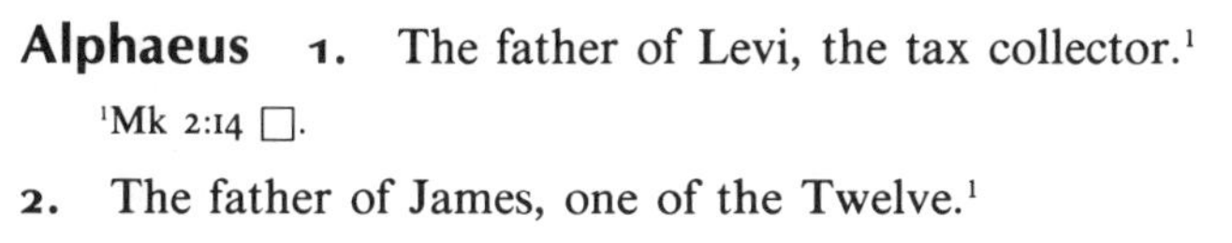

Alphaeus **1.** The father of Levi, the tax collector.[1]

[1]Mk 2:14 □.

2. The father of James, one of the Twelve.[1]

[1]Mt 10:3; Mk 3:18; Lk 6:15; Acts 1:13 □.

altar Lat. *altare, altaria* (to be linked with *adoleo:* "to cause to burn"), translating the Gk. *thysiastērion* (from *thysia:* "sacrifice").

1. As the durable witness to a favor, specifically to a divine appearance,[1] the Jewish altar signified God's presence; sanctifying the offerings, it was the place where communion between the faithful and God was realized;[2] hence the respect owed to it.[3] Its four corners, shaped like horns,[4] constituted its most sacred aspect. In the gospels, the term simultaneously meant the altar of holocausts* and the altar of incense.* The altar of holocausts, which was built out of stone in the Temple enclosure, was square; since it was elevated, one went up to it by means of a ramp. The altar of incense, situated within the Holy* Place, was made of cedar covered with gold.[5]

[1]Gn 12:7f. [2]1 Cor 10:18. [3]Mt 5:23f.; 23:18-20. [4]Rv 9:13. [5]1 Kgs 6:20; 7:48; Lk 1:11.

2. Christians had an altar of their own, which had supplanted the preceding ones.[6] Also, the primitive Church did not use a particular altar, but rather communicated at the table of the Lord's sacrifice.[7]

[6]Heb 13:10. [7]1 Cor 10:16-21.

→ sacrifice.

amen A Hebrew word, from the root *'mn:* "to show oneself firm, stable." It signified not only a wish, "So be it!" but an affirmation, "It's a fact!" as Luke's translation of it suggests: "In truth" *(alēthōs, ep'alētheias).* [1] The word came into use on solemn occasions, generally liturgical ones, to affirm what had just been said,[2] particularly after an act of praise that had been pronounced by the congregation.[3] It is noteworthy that Jesus used it, since he was used to speaking Aramaic*; he made use of it particularly in words which gave expression to the tension between his hope[4] and his opposition to Pharisaism.*[5] In his speeches, the amen, duplicated by John,[6] became a solemn invocation attesting to the truth* of what he said and (replacing the prophetic "thus says Yahweh") to the authority of the revealer.* Jesus Christ was the Yes of God himself, who realized in his person all of God's promises.*[7]

[1]Lk 4:25; 9:27; 12:44; 21:3. [2]Nm 5:22; Dt 27:15-26; Neh 8:6; Ps 41:14; Jer 11:5. [3]1 Chr 16:36; Ps 106:48; Rom 1:25; 9:5; 11:36; 16:27; Gal 1:5; Heb 13:21; Rv 5:14. [4]Mt 10:23; 19:28; 24:34; 25:40. [5]Mt 6:2,5,16; 8:10. [6]Jn 1:51; 3:3,11. [7]Is 65:16; 2 Cor 1:19-21; Rv 3:14.

→ faith—truth—yes.

Ananias Gk. *Ananias,* from the Heb. *hananyâ:* "Yahweh is favorable."

1. A Christian Jew of Jerusalem, the husband of Sapphira, who tried to deceive the Apostles.[1]

[1]Acts 5:1,3,5 □.

2. A Christian Jew of Damascus, who baptized Saul.[1]

[1]Acts 9:10-17; 22:12 □.

3. The High Priest (A.D. 47–59) and president of the Sanhedrin* which tried Paul.[1]

[1]Acts 23:2; 24:1 □.

anathema Gk. *ana-thema:* "what one places above [the altar, the Temple]," consequent upon a votive offering.[1] In the Septuagint* the word translated the Heb. *hérèm,* which designated what was consecrated* exclusively to God, and forbidden to secular usage.[2] It meant to deliver oneself to God's judgment* and to exclusion from the community, if one did not tell the truth*[3] or if one failed to fulfill one's promise*;[4] it also meant to deliver someone over to God's judgment.[5]

[1]Lk 21:5. [2]Lv 27:28f.; Jos 6:17,21. [3]Mt 26:74 (= Mk 14:71); Rom 9:3. [4]Acts 23:12,14,21. [5]1 Cor 12:3; 16:22; Gal 1:8f.; Rv 22:3 □.

→ corban—excommunicate—pure—sacred.

Andrew Gk. *Andreas,* a Greek name. The brother of Simon Peter,[1] a native of Bethsaida[2] and a resident of Capernaum,[3] he had been a disciple of John the Baptist and one of the first two disciples to follow Jesus.[4] One of the Twelve.*[5]

[1]Mt 4:18 (= Mk 1:16). [2]Jn 1:44. [3]Mk 1:29. [4]Jn 1:40. [5]Mt 10:2 (= Mk 3:18 = Lk 6:14); Mk 13:3; Jn 6:8; 12:22; Acts 1:13 □.

→ apostle.

angel Gk. *aggelos,* a functional name which meant a "messenger."[1] Nothing was implied thereby about the specific nature of an angel. The Bible presupposed the existence of God's angels, who contributed to the structuring of the created universe. Through angels, our gaze is extended beyond visible things; through them God's glory* reveals itself, as his presence and his transcendence also do. Further, it is important not to represent in a material way these celestial beings, who themselves are called "the Glories."[2]

[1]Mt 11:10; Mk 1:2; Lk 7:24,27; 9:52; Jas 2:25 △. [2]2 Pt 2:10; Jude 8 △.

1. "The Angel of the Lord" is mentioned in the prologue and in the epilogue of Matthew,[3] once in Luke and four times in Acts.[4] He was the same as the Angel of Yahweh, who scarcely was different from Yahweh* revealing himself here below in a visible form.[5]

[3]Mt 1:20,24; 2:13,19; 28:2. [4]Lk 2:9; Acts 5:19; 8:26; 12:7,23. [5]Gn 16:7; 21:17-19; comp. Jgs 6:11 with 6:14.

2. Angelology, or talk about angels, rooted itself in Oriental mythological representations according to which God was surrounded by a court of the "sons* of God" or the Seraphim, a celestial army intended to heighten his glory and to locate it in a height inaccessible to humans.[6] The messengers sent by God proclaimed God's presence at work among men. In the course of centuries their number tended to be multiplied, so that their functions in the celestial court (such as archangels or the Cherubim*[7]) could be specified and they could be designated by proper names: Michael,* Gabriel,* Raphael.[8] The meaning of this tradition was the simultaneous revelation of God's transcendence and his immanence in the whole world.

[6]Jb 1:6; Is 6:2f.; Rv 5:11; 7:11. [7]1 Thes 4:16; Heb 9:5; Jude 9. [8]Tb 3:17; 12:15; Lk 1:19,26; Rv 12:7.

3. The N.T. does not question angelic representations, but curbs their proliferation. In the gospels, angels appeared at Jesus' service here below[9] or were envisioned at the time of his last coming;[10] they stressed the personal worth of children or of converted sinners;[11] their state in the heavenly court[12] helps us to comprehend the nonterrestrial condition of the chosen ones.[13]

[9]Mt 4:11; Mk 1:13; Lk 22:43; Jn 1:51; cf. Mt 26:53. [10]Mt 13:39,41,49; 16:27; 24:31 (= Mk 13:27); 25:31; 2 Thes 1:7; 1 Tim 3:16. [11]Mt 18:10; Lk 15:10. [12]Lk 12:8f.; 16:22. [13]Mt 22:30 (= Mk 12:25; Lk 20:36).

4. Christ was superior to the angels.[14] Paul, who was aware of classes of angels,[15] wrestled against the excessive place which the syncretistic Colossian* milieu tended to accord to them: there they had proposed intermediary powers* in order to screen God's too brilliant light and to furnish many mediators*; Paul also developed a Christology which set Christ above these Dominations.*[16]

[14]Heb 1:4-13; 2:2-16. [15]Rom 8:38f.; 1 Cor 15:24; Eph 1:21; Col 1:16. [16]Col 1:15; 2:18; cf. Rv 19:10; 22: 8f.

5. Opposed to the angels, who were God's messengers, the N.T. recognizes the angels of Satan,* who acted to men's detriment, but who will be conquered definitively.[17]

[17]Mt 25:41; 2 Cor 11:14; 12:7; 1 Pt 3:19,22; 2 Pt 2:4; Jude 6; Rv 9:11; 12:7,9.

6. The "angels of the churches"[18] in the book of Revelation are variously interpreted. Some see in them angels responsible for protecting the community,[19] or others, taking them in a metaphorical sense, see them as the churches' "genies" or the leaders of the communities.

[18]Rv 1:20; 2:1,8,12,18; 3:1,7,14 △. [19]cf. Dn 10:13.

→ demon—devil—Dominations—glory—spirit.

anguish Unlike fears and cares, anguish meant a profound disquiet and uncertainty in the face of the future and of death. Several Greek terms spoke of this condition of soul. One could be oppressed, plunged into distress (Gk. *stenochōria*),[1] hemmed in, choked, blocked, dominated by fear (Gk. *synechomai*),[2] anxious over the battle's outcome (for example in the face of death [Gk. *agōnia*][3]), or finally, in its ultimate form, have a heart which lacked courage before an inescapable position (Gk. *aporia*).[4]

[1]Dt 28:53; 2 Cor 4:8; 6:4,12. [2]Mt 4:24; Lk 8:37; 12:50; 2 Cor 5:14; Phil 1:23. [3]2 Mc 3:14-21; 15:19; Lk 22:44 △. [4]Hos 13:8; 2 Mc 8:20; Wis 11:5; Lk 21:25; 2 Cor 4:8.

→ agony—care.

animals Gk. *zōa,* the plural of *zōon* (From *zēn:* "to live"): "living beings," and *thēria,* the plural of *thērion:* "wild beast." The N.T. mentions:

—among the quadrapeds (Gk. *tetra-pous*): the ass,* the bear, the bull, the calf, the camel,* the dog,* the foal of an ass, the fox, the he-goat,* the heifer, the horse,* the lamb,* the lion,* the ox, the panther, the pig,* the sheep,* the sow, the wolf;

—among the birds: the crow, the dove,* the eagle,* the hen and its chicks, the pigeon, the turtledove,* the vulture*;

—among sea animals: the fish,* the "monster";

—among reptiles: the asp, the dragon,* the serpent,* the viper;

—finally, mention is made of gnats, grasshoppers,* moths,* scorpions,* worms.*

→ Intr. II.6.—beasts; Beast—Living Ones.

Anna Gk. *Anna,* translating the Heb. *hannâ:* "full of grace." The name of Samuel's mother[1] and of a widowed Jewish prophetess.[2] The apocryphal* name of the mother of Mary, Jesus' mother.

[1]1 Sm 1:2–2:21. [2]Lk 2:36 □.

Annas Gk. *Annas,* translating the Heb. *hananyâ:* "Yahweh has had pity." The High Priest* from A.D. 6,[1] a member of an eminent priestly family, the father-in-law of Caiaphas* and perhaps the leader of the Sadducees.* Although deposed by the governor Valerius Gratus in A.D. 15, it was to him that Jesus was brought immediately following his arrest;[2] he was part of the sanhedrin* which tried Peter and John.[3]

[1]Lk 3:2. [2]Jn 18:13,24. [3]Acts 4:6 □.

anoint 1. Gk. *aleiphō:* "to smear" (with oil, with perfume). A gesture with various interpretations: the beauty and health of the body,[1] joy,[2] a mark of honor,[3] the healing of a sick person.[4]

[1]Ru 3:3; 2 Chr 28:15; Mt 6:17. [2]Jdt 10:3; Dn 10:3. [3]Ps 23:5; Is 61:3; Mk 16:1; Lk 7:38,46; Jn 11:2; 12:3. [4]Mk 6:13; Jas 5:14 △.

2. Gk. *chriō,* Heb. *mâshah,* a verb restricted to cultic consecration.* Its usage depended perhaps on the gesture's recognizable symbolism: oil* penetrates everything, even stone.* Thus, through consecration, a king,* a priest,* a prophet,* an altar* were specially set apart.[5] The anointing would confer on the king the Spirit's power,[6] making him the "Anointed One" (Heb. *mashîah* = the Messiah*) of the Lord; the N.T. applies to Jesus the O.T. texts concerning the anointing of the king-priest.[7] A priestly anointing was not narrated of Jesus, because he was the High Priest, not like Aaron* but according to the order of Melchizedek.*[8] While a prophetic anointing had been attributed to Jesus, it was related to his baptism.[9] Finally, because the Christian has been "anointed" in baptism, the oil of anointing (Gk. *chrisma*) remains in him; it is God's Word received from Christ under the Holy Spirit's movement or else it is the Holy Spirit himself, through whom he is instructed about all things.[10]

[5]Ex 30:29f.; 1 Sm 10:1,6; 1 Kgs 19:16. [6]1 Sm 16:13. [7]Ps 2:2; 110:1; Acts 4:25-27; Heb 1:8f. [8]Lv 4:5; 8:12; Heb 5:5-10. [9]Is 61:1; Lk 4:18-21; Acts 10:38; cf. Lk 3:21f. [10]1 Jn 2:20,27; cf. Jn 14:26; 2 Cor 1:21.

→ Christ—heal—Messiah—oil—perfume.

Antichrist Gk. *antichristos* (from *anti:* "contrary to" and *Christos:* "Christ"), a Christian neologism fashioned after the pattern of *antitheos:* "the anti-god." The word is proper to the Johannine writings in which it sometimes designates Christian apostates,[1] sometimes a mysterious personality who concealed himself behind them.[2] The totality depended on a much broader and earlier O.T. concept: powers hostile to God, which have been at work from the origins of the world, will reveal themselves in a special way at the time of the end*;[4] one may detect here an influence from Persian and Babylonian myths about the battle between the gods and monsters. This personality is variously titled in the N.T.: false Christs and false prophets,[5] the most ungodly one, the most damned one, the Adversary,[6] the two Beasts.[7] Not having to reveal itself except at the end of time, this personification was supratemporal[8] all the while carrying on its activity through intermediaries; it could not be incarnate in some one historical person or other, but the concept allowed for the designation of men who were opposed to the establishment of Christ's kingdom[9] and for the knowledge that it would be overcome on the last day.[10]

[1]1 Jn 2:18. [2]1 Jn 2:18,22; 4:3; 2 Jn 7 □. [3]Jb 9:13; Ps 74:13; 89:10f.; Is 51:9. [4]Ez 38–39. [5]Mt 24:24 (= Mk 13:22). [6]2 Thes 2:3-8. [7]Rv 13. [8]2 Thes 2:3-12; Rv 13. [9]1 Jn 2:18-22; 4:3; 2 Jn 7 [10]2 Thes 2:8.

→ Abomination of Desolation—beasts, Beast—Gog—numbers.

Antioch Gk. *Antiocheia,* from *Antiochos,* a frequent name of Seleucid kings (312–125 B.C.).

1. *Antioch of Pisidia.* Despite its name, the territory of Antioch (a Roman colony* from the time of Augustus) was situated in Phrygia.* Its essential role was that of watching over Galatia.* Jews were numerous there. Paul stayed there on three occasions.[1]

[1]Acts 13:14,44,50; 14:19,21; 2 Tim 3:11 □.

→ Map 2.

2. *Antioch of Syria.* Established by Seleucus in 300 B.C., the city had been the Seleucids' capital when Alexandria was that of the Ptolemies. The home of Hellenistic civilization, Antioch was the capital of the Roman province of Syria (64 B.C.). The third city of the Empire (after Rome and Alexandria) it numbered some 300,000 inhabitants, about ten percent of whom were Jews. The homeland of Nicolas.[1] Evangelized by Hellenist* Christians, then by Barnabas* and Paul,*[3] it was, along with Jerusalem, one of the two leading centers for the spread of the faith. There for the first time the disciples were given the name of Christians.*[4] It was the Antioch community that sent out Paul to proclaim Christ to the Mediterranean world,[5] and that Paul rejoined on his return from his first two missions.[6] There was played out a controversy between Christians of Jewish and pagan backgrounds: about meat* sacrificed to idols[7] and on Peter's dealings with the pagans.[8]

[1]Acts 6:5. [2]Acts 11:19f. [3]Acts 11:22,26. [4]Acts 11:26. [5]Acts 13:1-3. [6]Acts 14:26; 15:35f.,40; 18:22. [7]Acts 15:22f.,30. [8]Gal 2:11 □.

→ Intr. I.3.C; IV.3.C.—Ignatius of Antioch—Syria—Map 2.

Antipatris Gk. *Antipatris.* A city sixty kilometers (37.5 miles) northwest of Jerusalem where Paul, threatened with death by Jews from the capital, stopped before being taken to Caesarea.[1]

[1]Acts 23:31 □.

→ Map 4.

apocalypse **1.** Gk. *apokalypsis* (from *apo* "far from, aside from" and *kalyptō* "to cover, veil"): "what relates to a revelation," "revelation" concerning the divine judgment, a mystery, the person of Jesus.[1] A special charism with which the Spirit endows certain believers.[2]

[1]Mt 11:25,27 (= Lk 10:21f.); 16:17; Lk 17:30; Jn 12:38; Rom 1:17f.; 2:5; 8:18f.; 16:25; Gal 1:12; Eph 1:17; 3:3; 2 Thes 1:7; 2:3. [2]1 Cor 14:26,30; 2 Cor 12:1,7; Gal 2:2.

2. The term describes a literary* genre that is characterized by the revelation of secrets concerning the end of time and the course of history, through the medium of unusual settings and, often, through pseudonymity. Such, in addition to Isaiah 24–27 and the Revelation of John, were the Book of Enoch,* the Fourth Book of Ezra,* the Apocalypse of Baruch* or the collection of eschatological sayings of Jesus which are known as the "Synoptic* Apocalypse."[3]

[3]Mt 24 (= Mk 13 = Lk 21).

→ Intr. XII.2.A. b-c; XII.2.B.

3. The Book entitled the "Apocalypse" or Book of Revelation[4] came from the environs of Ephesus, behind which stood the authority of the apostle John. There are two theories about its dating: the period following the persecution of Nero (65–70) or the end of Domitian's reign (91–96). It is not very helpful to link the various visions described in the book with specific events or people. In accord with its literary genre, the work does not reveal future kingdoms, but rather the hidden meanings and enduring significance of history in which the drama of salvation is being played out ever anew through the clashing actions of its many actors. The book is a deuterocanonical* writing.

[4]Rv 1:1.

→ Intr. XV.

[apocryphal writings] **1.** Gk. *apokryphos* (from *kryptō:* "to hide" and *apo:* "far from, aside"): "withdrawn from sight, secret." Writings resembling canonical books, but not belonging to the canon* of the Scriptures. Protestant Christians call them "pseudepigraphal writings" (from the Gk. *graphē:* "writing" and *pseudēs:* "liar"): "writings whose titles are untrue." They reflected the

THE APOCRYPHAL WRITINGS OF THE OLD TESTAMENT

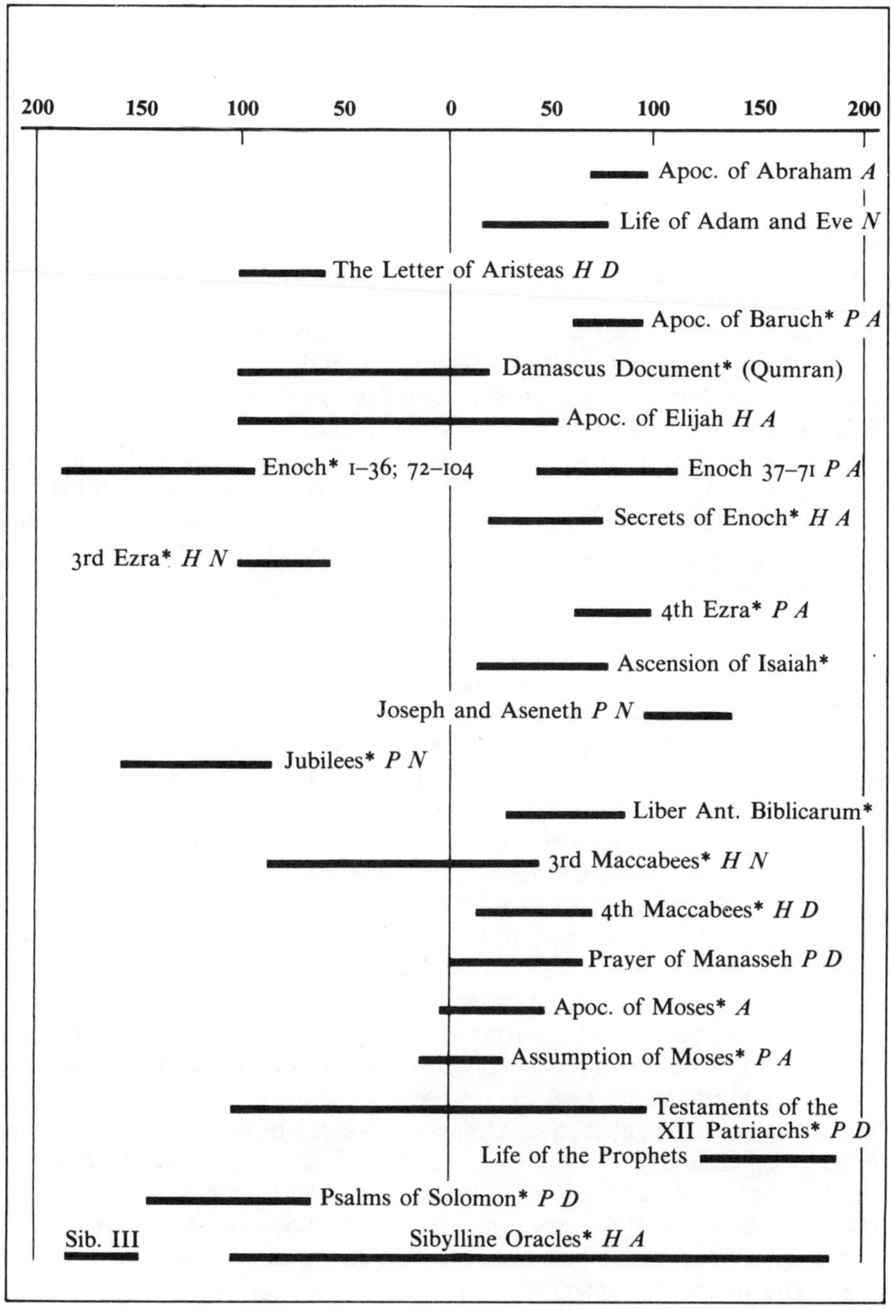

The works are listed from top to bottom according to the alphabetical order of the proper names. The horizontal bars indicate their approximate dates. *A* = apocalyptic; *D* = didactic; *H* = Hellenistic; *N* = narrative; P = Palestinian.

thought-patterns and hopes of the Jewish people during the two centuries which preceded and the century that followed the beginning of the Christian era, as well as deviations from the Christian faith in the first centuries. The following list does not include the approximately twenty texts to which the Fathers of the Church made allusion but which have been lost to us today.

2. The O.T. apocryphal writings were of Palestinian (P) or Hellenistic (H) origin. They exercised a real influence on the primitive Christian literature (thus, Jude cited the Assumption of Moses in verse 9 and the Book of Enoch in verses 14–15). Some even contain Christian interpolations. These texts, often fragmentary, ordinarily have come down to us in translated versions. The dates of their composition are approximate.

3. The N.T. apocryphal writings are later than the first century.
3.1. The apocryphal gospels attempted to fill in the lacunae presented by the canonical* gospels, particularly with regard to Jesus' infancy and his passion. Ordinarily, they reflected popular theology of the time and often betrayed gnostic* tendencies. They have had a tremendous influence on popular piety and on religious art. Among the gospels of a synoptic type we may mention: the *Gospel of the Nazarenes* (before 180), the *Gospel of the Hebrews,* that is deriving from Greek-speaking Christians of Jewish background (end of the second century, Aramaic translated into Greek), the *Gospel of the Egyptians,* that is, deriving from Christians of a pagan background (before 150), the *Gospel of the Ebionites* (before 150, in Greek), the *Gospel of Peter* (a Greek fragment from before 150). We add also the collection of diverse sayings which make up the *Gospel of Thomas** (second century).

Among fictional gospels we mention: the *Proto-Gospel of James* (on the Savior's infancy, Greek, around 150), the *Gospel of Pseudo-Matthew* (Latin, fifth to sixth centuries) the *Dormition of the Virgin,* the *History of Joseph the Carpenter* (earlier than the fourth century, in Coptic, Arabic and Latin), the *Arabic Gospel of the Childhood* (late), the *Gospel of Nicodemus* (fourth century, including the *Acts of Pilate* on the passion of Jesus and the *Descent into Hell*). Finally, two forgeries: the *Gospel of Basilides,* the *Gospel of Marcion,* and two poorly named works: the *Gospel of Truth* and the *Gospel of Philip.*
3.2. The "acts" continued the narrative of the Acts of the Apostles by recounting chiefly the travels and miracles of the Apostles: John (before 200), Paul (before 200), Peter (180–190), Thomas (about 150), Philip, Bartholomew, Barnabas and Thaddeus were all the heroes of a narrative.
3.3. The epistles tended to develop the privileges of certain churches or to develop some point or other of doctrine. The *Third Epistle to the Corinthians,* the *Letter of the Apostles* (150–180), the *Epistle to the Laodiceans,* the *Epistle to the Alexandrians,* the *Correspondence of Paul with Seneca,* the *Epistle of Barnabas* (after 130), the *Kerygma of Peter,* the *Kerygma of Paul.*
3.4. The apocalypses intended to encourage their readers to face the future. Peter, Paul, Thomas, Stephen and John all had one each attributed to them.

→ agrapha—Bible—deuterocanonical writings—Nag Hammadi—Thomas (Gospel of).

Apollos Gk. *Apollōs,* a shortened form of the name *Apollōnios.* A Jew of Alexandria, perhaps from the school of Philo,* a disciple of John the Baptist, well versed in the Scriptures, then a very successful Christian preacher.[1] Some exegetes attribute to him, without solid basis, the Epistle to the Hebrews.*

[1]Acts 18:24; 19:1; 1 Cor 1:12; 3:4–6:22; 4:6; 16:12; Ti 3:13 □.

apostasy Gk. *apostasia,* from the verb *aph-istamai:* "to separate oneself from." With a spatial meaning[1] as well as a figurative one: men separate themselves from God,[2] that in which apostasy properly speaking consists,[3] and God puts himself at a distance from the ungodly.[4]

[1]Lk 2:37; Acts 22:29. [2]Dt 32:15; Jer 2:19; Lk 8:13; 1 Tim 4:1; Heb 3:12. [3]2 Thes 2:3. [4]Lk 13:27.

→ scandal.

apostle Gk. *apostolos* (from *apostellō:* "to send, to appoint"): "someone sent," an emissary, a delegated official entrusted with a mission[1]—not simply a person who propagates a doctrine or devotes himself to a cause.

[1]Jn 13:16; Acts 9:2; 2 Cor 8:23.

1. In the wide sense, ambassadors of the Risen Christ on whom the Church was founded,[2] possessing authority (but not superiority) over the communities, that is, one of pastoral service.[3]

[2]1 Cor 15:7; 2 Cor 5:20; Gal 1:19; Eph 2:20; 4:11; 1 Thes 2:7. [3]Acts 20:28; 1 Cor 9:19; 1 Pt 5:2-5.

2. In the narrow sense, one characteristic of Luke's account, they were the Twelve,* the apostolic college charged with witnessing to the fact that the Risen One was the same Jesus of Nazareth whom they had known.[4] The N.T. furnishes four lists of them,[5] identical in names but different in their order. First of all, the four who were the first to be called: Peter, Andrew, James and John. Then, a second group of four: Philip, Bartholomew, Matthew and Thomas. Lastly, James, Thaddeus (or Jude), Simon and Judas Iscariot. Peter always comes at the head of the list, Judas always at the end of it. This college was completed after Judas'* defection, but not on the occasion of the death of James.[6]

[4]Except Lk 11:49; Acts 14:14. [5]Mt 10:2-4; Mk 3:16-19; Lk 6:14-16; Acts 1:13. [6]Lk 6:13; Acts 1:15-26; 12:2; Rv 21:14.

3. Paul was in an extraordinary way the "Apostle to the Gentiles."[7]

[7]Rom 11:13, cf. Acts 9:15; 22:21; Rom 1:5; Gal 1:15f.; 2:8; Eph 3:8; 1 Tim 2:7.

→ Church—ministry—send.

[apostolic age] The era covered by the authority of the Apostles,* extending a little beyond the end of the first century.

appearance Gk. *eidos* (from a root meaning "to see"). What is, properly speaking, seen,[1] for example, according to Luke, the bodily aspect of the dove*[2] or the face of Jesus.[3] In the same sense, one judged according to the appearance (Gk. *opsis:* "view"),[4] according to the face (Gk. *pros-ōpon:* "in front of one's view"),[5] one appreciated something according to the aspects that were seen (Gk. *horasis,* the act of seeing).[6] Generally, one should not confuse the appearance, which designated the reality insofar as it was perceived, with the form* which expressed the reality itself.

[1]2 Cor 5:7. [2]Lk 3:22. [3]Lk 9:29. [4]Jn 7:24. [5]2 Cor 5:12; 10:7. [6]Rv 4:3; cf. Acts 2:17; Rv 9:17.

→ face—form—see.

appearances of Christ 1. In the year 55[1] Paul handed on a very primitive list of appearances, one that may have been made up of two groups: Cephas* and the Twelve*; James and the Apostles. To these, an appearance to five hundred brethren has been added. In addition, the evangelists mention appearances to individuals: to Mary and the women,[2] to the disciples at Emmaus,[3] and to seven disciples at the lakeside.[4] By distinguishing the recipients of the appearances we are able to delineate two types: official appearances,[5] beneficial to the apostolic college (and several others), whose accounts focus on the mission which established the Church; and private appearances,[6] given to some person or other and whose special purpose was to narrate their recognition of the one who appeared. The appearance to Saul of Tarsus[7] belongs in a separate category.

[1]1 Cor 15:3-7. [2]Mt 28:9f.; Mk 13:9-11; Jn 20:11-18. [3]Mk 16:12f.; Lk 24:13-35. [4]Jn 21:1-23. [5]Mt 28:16-20; Mk 16:14-20; Lk 24:34,36-53; Jn 20:19-29. [6]= notes 2,3,4. [7]Acts 9:3-19; 22:6-21; 26:12-18; 1 Cor 9:1; Gal 1:13-17.

2. The gospel accounts belong neither to the apocalyptic* genre (there is neither revelation of secrets nor any extraordinary setting) nor to the category of biographical memoirs (it is impossible to coordinate them in time or place; nor were there any souvenir snapshots). Rather, as an analysis of the accounts shows, they attempted to convey a unique experience by communicating its theological meaning. Various terms describe the encounter of the Risen One with his disciples: the most important, because it stressed the Risen One's initiative is "he let himself be seen; he made himself seen" (Gk. *ōphthē*);[8] then the verbs to see,[9] appear,[10] reveal,[11] to grasp hold of,[12] and to know.[13] The accounts themselves are varied, sometimes featuring a sudden approach,[14] at other times a slow discovery.[15] In all cases, there were three characteristic phases, the Risen One's initiative,[16] a spontaneous recognition by the disciples,[17] and a mission charge.[18] From Christ's initiative came the objectivity of the encounter in the eyes of the disciples: faith was the consequence, not the origin, of the experience. The description of a gradual recognition allowed for the paradoxical assertion of the Risen One's new condition; he was simultaneously removed from the normal limitations of earthly life and yet sensibly present to people. The mission given offered meaning to the future and described Jesus' new mode of presence.

[8]Lk 24:34; Acts 13:31; 1 Cor 15:5-8. [9]Mt 28:7,10; Mk 16:7,11,14; Jn 20:18,20,25,29; 1 Cor 9:1. [10]Mk 16:9,12,14. [11]Gal 1:16. [12]Phil 3:12. [13]Phil 3:8,10. [14]Mt 28:9; Lk 24:36; Jn 20:-19,26. [15]Lk 24:11,13-32; Jn 20:11-18,25-29; 21:1-7. [16]Mt 28:9,17f.; Mk 16:9,12,14; Lk 24:-15-17,36; Jn 20:14f.,19,26; 21:4f.; Acts 1:3; 9:3f.; 22:6f.; 26:12-14; Gal 1:15f.; Phil 3:12. [17]Mt

28:9,17; Lk 24:31,37-45; Jn 20:16-18,19,25,28; 21:7,12. [18]Mt 28:10,18-20; Lk 24:46-49; Jn 20:17f., 21-23; 21:15-17; Acts 1:8; 9:15f.; 22:14f.; 26:16-18; 1 Cor 9:1f.; 15:8-11; Gal 1:16,23.

60481

3. According to Luke, the appearances to the Apostles lasted forty* days;[19] with this number he emphasized their function as a prototype: the time of the appearances was the period of the foundation of the Church.[20] Luke did not say that Christ would cease revealing himself; for he himself located the appearance to Saul of Tarsus after the Ascension. He gave a different color to the accounts of appearances to the apostles: an apocalyptic* style, glory, an emphasis not on the Jesus who lived but on the existing Church.[21] By contrast, Paul linked the appearance to himself with that given to the Eleven[22] and described it in a manner which differed from Luke's accounts.[23]

[19]Acts 1:3. [20]Lk 24:44-49,50-53; Acts 1:2; 10:41f.; 13:31. [21]Acts 9:3-5; 22:6-11; 26:13-18. [22]1 Cor 9:1; 15:8. [23]Gal 1:16; Phil 3:12.

4. Among the recipients of the appearances John situated the future believers:[24] these have not seen what the disciples saw, but they know that these witnesses saw him. Their faith rests on the witness of the first disciples, in knowing that they were met by the Risen One; in their turn they are met by the Jesus who lives after his death and who dwells in them.[25]

[24]Jn 20:29. [25]Jn 14:19-23.

→ Ascension—exaltation—resurrection.

Appius (Forum of) Gk. *Appiou phoron.* A place some sixty-four kilometers (forty miles) south of Rome.[1]

[1]Acts 28:15 □.

→ Map 3.

apron Gk. *lention* (from the Latin, *linteum.*) A piece of fabric that could serve as a tablecloth or as a hand towel for washing.[1]

[1]Jn 13:4f. □.

Aquila and Priscilla Gk. *Akylas, Priskilla (Priska).* Christian spouses of a Jewish background. Expelled from Rome* in 49–50 by edict of the Emperor Claudius,* they were tentmakers at Corinth* when they became Paul's* hosts, then his fellow workers.[1]

[1]Acts 18:2f.,18f.,26; Rom 16:3f.; 1 Cor 16:19; 2 Tim 4:19 □.

Arabia, Arabs The collective Hebrew noun *arab* designated the nomads of the Syro-Arabian desert.[1] Arabia (Gk. *Arabia*) indicated, from the second century B.C., the territory of the Nabatean* kingdom which ran alongside Palestine, from the Red Sea to Damascus, including within it Mount Sinai.[2] There were Arabs (Gk. *Arabes*) in Jerusalem on Pentecost.[3] Paul withdrew into Arabia after his conversion.[4]

[1]Is 13:20; Jer 3:2. [2]2 Mc 5:8; Gal 4:25. [3]Acts 2:11. [4]Gal 1:17 □.

Lincoln Christian College

[Aramaic] A Semitic* language related to Hebrew; the one most widely spoken in Palestine in the time of Jesus; thus, *talitha qoum* (Mk 5:41), *ephphatha* (Mk 7:34), *Marana tha* (1 Cor 16:22).

→ Intr. V.3.A.

Archelaus Gk. *Archelaos.* The son of Herod the Great* and Malthake (from about 23 B.C. to A.D. 15), brother of Herod Antipas,* ethnarch* of Judea, Samaria and Idumea in 4 B.C. Accused of tyranny and scandal, he was exiled to Vienne (Gaul) in A.D. 6. His territory then became a Roman province.*[1]

[1]Mt 2:22 □.

→ Intr. I.1.A.—Herod.

[archetype] An original (from the Gk. *archē:* "beginning") which serves as a model or "prototype" (from the Gk. *typos:* "imprint"). The term may be applied to persons or to concepts.

Archippus Gk. *Archippos:* "head of the cavalry"(?). One of the recipients of the Epistle to Philemon* and Paul's collaborator at Colossae.*[1]

[1]Col 4:17; Phlm 2 □.

Areopagus Gk. *ho Areios pagos:* "the hill of Ares [the god Mars]," to the west of the Acropolis of Athens.* The hill had lent its name to the city council, a high religious tribunal that sat there at its origin but which, in Paul's time, held its sessions at the Royal Portico, near the agora.* It seems that Paul's speech on the unknown god was given not on the hill but in front of the council.[1]

[1]Acts 17:19,22 □.

Aretas IV The Nabatean* king from 8 B.C. to A.D. 40. His daughter had been given in marriage to Herod Antipas,* but she had been repudiated around 27. It was during his reign that Paul fled from Damascus.[1]

[1]2 Cor 11:32 □; cf. Mt 14:3f. (= Mk 6:17f.); Acts 9:25.

→ Arabia.

Arimathea Gk. *Arimathaia.* A city to the northwest of Jerusalem, probably identical with the Rama(thaim) of the O.T. The home town of Joseph* who buried Jesus.[1]

[1]1 Sm 1:1; Mt 27:57; Mk 15:43; Lk 23:51; Jn 19:38 □.

→ Map 4.

Aristarchus A Christian from Thessalonica* and Paul's faithful companion.[1]

[1]Acts 19:29; 20:4; 27:2; Col 4:10; Phlm 24 □.

ark Lat. *arca,* translating the Gk. *kibōtos.*

1. *Noah's Ark* (Heb. *tébâ*). The vessel (length: 150m. [492 ft.], width: 25m. [82 ft.], height: 15m. [49.2 ft.]) in which Noah* survived the flood.*[1] A figure* of Christian baptism.*[2]

[1]Gn 6:13–8:19; Mt 24:38; Lk 17:27; Heb 11:7. [2]1 Pt 3:20 △.

2. The *Ark of the Covenant* (Heb. *arôn*). A wooden chest which was said to have contained the "tablets of the Covenant" or the Law, on which the Decalogue* had been carved.[3] The portable sanctuary of the Hebrews in the desert and the visible sign of God's presence.[4] Set down within the Holy of Holies* of Solomon's Temple and covered over with a golden lid, it was the propitiatory.*[5] Later on it disappeared, probably at the time of the Temple's destruction in 587 B.C.

[3]Dt 10:1f.; 1 Kgs 8:9; Heb 9:4. [4]Nm 10:35f.; 1 Sm 4:3-7; Rv 11:19 △. [5]Ex 25:17-21.

arm (of the Lord) Gk. *brachion (tou Kyriou).* A metaphor of God's power intervening in the history of his people "with outstretched arm."[1]

[1]Dt 4:34; Is 52:10; 53:1; Lk 1:51; Jn 12:38; Acts 13:17 □.

Armageddon The place where, according to Rv 16:16, the kings of the whole world will come together for the final war. This Hebrew name probably linked the Hebrew word *har,* "mountain," and the equivalent of Megiddo, a city in the Plain of Esdraelon where many kings of Israel, such as Josiah, perished;[1] it symbolized the ultimate catastrophe.[2] The context of Rv 16:16 contains overtones of the "mountain of Assembly"[3] where Gog, the eschatological* enemy,* is to perish.[4]

[1]Jgs 5:19; 2 Kgs 9:27; 23:29f. [2]Zec 12:11. [3]Is 14:13. [4]Ez 38:2,4; Rv 20:8.

armor

→ combat.

army (heavenly)

→ Sabaoth.

aromatics Gk. *arōma.* A scented vegetable substance used in the manufacture of perfumes.* It is difficult to be specific about its nature.[1]

[1]Mk 16:1; Lk 23:56; 24:1; Jn 19:40 □.

→ Intr. VII.3.

Artemis The Anatolian goddess who bore this Hellenistic name was a deity distinct from the Greek goddess of the same name, who was identified with Diana, the huntress. The colleague of Ashera and Astarte, at Ephesus* she was the "Great Mother" of nature, the symbol of fertility.[1]

[1]Acts 19:24-35 □.

→ Intr. IV.6.A.

as Gk. *assarion.* A Roman coin made of copper. For a day's labor, one could receive 16 as.[1]

[1]Mt 10:29 (= Lk 12:6) □.

→ coins.

Ascension A scene reported by Luke[1] and mentioned in the conclusion to Mark.*[2] Two aspects were featured in it. In its function of separation (Gk. *di-istēmi*),[3] it told of the cessation of a certain way of relating to one another between Christ and his disciples, until the parousia.* In its mention of an elevation on high *(ep-airō)*[4] or an ascent *(ana-)* to heaven (Gk. *ana-bainō,*[5] *ana-lambanō,*[6] *ana-pherō*[7]), it symbolized the exaltation,* the glorification or the Lordship* of the Christ who was present to the whole universe.

[1]Lk 24:51; Acts 1:3-11. [2]Mk 16:19. [3]Lk 24:51. [4]Acts 1:9; cf. Mt 9:15 (= Mk 2:20 = Lk 5:35); Jn 14:2f. [5]Jn 6:62; 20:17; Rom 10:6; Eph 4:8-10; cf. Acts 2:34. [6]Mk 16:19; Lk 9:51; Acts 1:2,9,11,22; 1 Tim 3:16. [7]Lk 24:51.

→ Exaltation of Christ.

ashes Gk. *spodos.* Like dust which was simultaneously an image of sin and of man's fragility,[1] ashes on which one sat or with which one covered one's head, expressed penance* and mourning.*[2] The ashes of a heifer were sprinkled* in major instances of legal purification.*[3]

[1]Gn 18:27; Jb 30:19. [2]Is 58:5; 61:3; Jer 6:26; Mt 11:21 (= Lk 10:13). [3]Heb 9:13 □.

Asia Gk. *Asia.* In the N.T. it designates that part of Asia Minor (modern-day Turkey) that had been a Roman senatorial province* since 129 B.C. It included Mysia,* Lydia, Caria and Phrygia*; but sometimes in Acts,* Phrygia is named separately and Asia often means no more than the edge of the sea.[2] More dynamic and more open in the East than the province of Achaia,* it was, with Ephesus* as its center,[3] the true home of Hellenism* both economically and intellectually. The seven churches of Asia mentioned at the beginning of Revelation*[4] show that the principal cities of this province had been evangelized when this book was written.[5]

[1]Acts 2:9. [2]Acts 16:6; 27:2. [3]Acts 19:26f. [4]Rv 1:4. [5]Acts 6:9; 19:10,22; 20:4,16,18; 21:27; 24:19; Rom 16:5; 1 Cor 16:19; 2 Cor 1:8; 2 Tim 1:15; 1 Pt 1:1 □.

→ Map 3.

Asiarch Gk. *asi-archēs:* "a leader of Asia.*" Not the governor of the Roman province,* but a priest* named annually to preside at provincial worship of the emperor and Rome. The title was kept after leaving office.[1]

[1]Acts 19:31 □.

aspersion

→ sprinkling.

ass Gk. *onos, hypozygion* ("under the yoke"). One of the domestic animals most highly prized among the Israelites. It was not the horse,* a warrior mount, but the peaceful family ass (or even the offspring of the she-ass [Gk. *pōlos*]) on which the Messiah would come.[1]

[1]Zec 9:9; Mt 21:2,5,7 (= Mk 11:2,4,5,7 = Lk 19:30,33,35); Jn 12:14f.

assembly Various words refer to a group of people who "join together" (Gk. *syn-erchomai*)[1] in a single place and for a common purpose; they may be applied indiscriminately to a secular grouping or to a religious assembly whether Jewish or Christian. The Greek word *plēthos* stressed the idea of a multitude or collectivity.[2] The Greek word *dēmos* retained the nuance of a public assembly of the people,[3] as did the rarer term *agoraios.*[4] With regard to the more frequent terms, *synagōgē* and *ekklēsia,* they have in view the same reality, that of a religious (rarely a secular[5]) assembly: *synagōgē* being that of the sanhedrin,*[6] Christians,[7] or even of the heavenly gathering;[8] *ekklēsia* was predicated of the Hebrews in the desert[9] and, ordinarily, of Christian gatherings.[10]

[1]Mk 14:53; Jn 18:20; Acts 1:6; 10:27; 16:13; 19:32; 22:30; 28:17; 1 Cor 11:17f.,20,33f.; 14:23,26 △. [2]Acts 6:2,5; 15:12,30; 19:9; 23:7; cf. Lk 23:1 △. [3]Acts 17:5; 19:30,37; cf. 12:22 △. [4]Acts 19:38 △. [5]Acts 19:32,39f. △. [6]Mt 26:57; Lk 22:66; Jn 11:47; Acts 4:5. [7]Acts 15:6,30; Jas 2:2. [8]2 Thes 2:1. [9]Acts 7:38 △. [10]1 Cor 11:18; 14:4f.,12,19,28,34f.; Heb 2:12; 12:23.

→ agora—Church—people—synagogue.

Assos A port on the northwest coast of modern-day Turkey, in ancient Mysia* (province* of Asia).[1]

[1]Acts 20:13f □.

→ Map 2.

assurance

→ confidence.

[Assyrian] A Semitic* language of the upper Tigris region. Its name derived from the city Asshur,[1] the capital before Nineveh, of the Assyrian Empire.

[1]Gn 10:11.

Athens Gk. *Athēnai.* The ancient capital of Attica (Greece) whose role had been a preponderant one in the development of the ancient civilization; it had lost all political grandeur from the fourth century B.C. on. Although it preserved the prestige of its past and its culture, it was, when Paul came to the Areopagus,* no more than the capital city of the Roman province* of Achaia.*[1]

[1]Acts 17:15f.,21f.; 18:1; 1 Thes 3:1 □.

→ Map 2.

athlete A word derived from the Greek verb *athleō:* "to wrestle," used in the strict sense as well as figuratively[2] to describe Christian combat. This latter reality was also described by another Greek term, *agōnizomai:* "to engage in combat."[3]

[1]2 Tim 2:5. [2]Phil 1:27; 4:3; Heb 10:32 □. [3]1 Cor 9:25.

→ combat.

[Atonement (Feast of the)] **1.** Although the N.T. does not refer to this Jewish feast, the idea of expiating* which underlies it was constantly at hand, not under its essential feature of fasting (this feast was still called "the Fast"), but under the redemptive function of Christ the High Priest.

2. The Day of Atonement *(Yom Kippur),* celebrated at the September equinox, was a day of solemn penance* established by God[1] for the expiation of all the transgressions and defilements of the year that had not been pardoned. The High Priest* himself had to handle the liturgical functions and he entered the Holy of Holies*[2] to do so. The first rite was that of the *sacrifice* of expiation:* the High Priest sacrificed a bull for his own sins and those of his family, then a goat for the sins of all Israel. Then with the blood* of the sacrificed animals, he sprinkled the people, the altar* of holocausts, the Holy Place* and the Holy of Holies. The second ceremony was that of the scapegoat*: the High Priest extended his hands* over the head of another goat, laying upon it all the sins of the community, whereupon the animal was led to the desert so that it could "bear on itself in an uninhabited land all the iniquities of the nation."[3]

[1]Lv 16:29f. [2]Heb 9:3,25; 13:11. [3]Lv 16:22.

3. Jesus Christ, the definitive High Priest, through his intercession*[4] has obtained God's great pardon*: henceforth man is pleasing to God, that which had been the goal and meaning of *Yom Kippur.*

[4]Heb 5:7; 7:25; 9:24.

→ Intr. XIII.3.B; XIV.B.—expiate—fast—feast—pardon—propitiatory—sin.

Attalia Gk. *Attaleia.* The port of Pamphilia where Paul and Barnabas* embarked for Antioch in Syria.*[1]

[1]Acts 14:25 □.

→ Map 2.

Augustus Gk. *Augoustos,* from the Latin, translating the Gk. *sebastos:* "worthy of reverence," as a god would be. The imperial title, equivalent to "His Majesty" with a nuance of divine personality. It was conferred on January 16, 27 B.C. on the first Roman Emperor (31 B.C.–A.D. 14), Caius Julius Caesar Octavianus (63 B.C.–A.D. 14), the grandnephew of Julius Caesar.* His successors —of whom Nero was one—kept the title. Samaria* had been named Sebaste.*[1]

[1]Lk 2:1; Acts 25:21,25; 27:1 □.

[authentic] **1.** What derives from some author (a word of Jesus, a narrative of Luke's) or belongs to some book (verses of Matthew).

2. Something whose truth or authority cannot be contested.

Authorities

→ Dominations.

authority Gk. *ex-ousia* (to be linked with the participle of *ex-estin*): "it is permitted, to be free from. . . ."[1] The word indicated that the power* possessed or received could not be exercised except within the framework of a specific juridical, political, social or moral order.[2] God set the course of history,[3] disposed of the creatures he had made,[4] delegated his power to men[5] or to messengers, who were angels or others.[6] The devil attempted to overthrow him.[7] Jesus' authority was bound up with the mission he had received from God: in him it was found to be perfect trust and startling freedom.[8] It was by means of it that he cured the sick, drove out demons and proclaimed the Good News.[9] He delegated this same authority to his disciples;[10] in serving men, he showed them how it was to be exercised.[11] Constituted as Lord, he received it from God in a definitive manner.[12] Christ did not withdraw authority from magistrates;[13] nevertheless, although "everything is permitted" the believer, this was not so that he might fall into someone else's power.[14]

[1]Mt 12:2,10; 22:17. [2]Acts 8:19; 9:14; 26:10,12. [3]Acts 1:7. [4]Lk 12:5; Rom 9:21. [5]Jn 19:11; Rom 13:1f. [6]Rv 6:8; 9:3,10,19. [7]Lk 4:6; 22:53; Eph 2:2; Col 1:13; Rv 13:2,4,12. [8]Mt 21:23-27 (= Mk 11:27-33 = Lk 20:1-8); Jn 5:27; 10:18; 17:2. [9]Mt 7:29; 9:6 (= Mk 2:10 = Lk 5:24); 9:8; Mk 1:27 (= Lk 4:36). [10]Mt 10:1. [11]Mt 20:25-28 (= Mk 10:42-45 = Lk 22:24-27). [12]Mt 28:18. [13]Rom 13:1-3; Ti 3:1. [14]1 Cor 6:12; 8:9; 9:4-18; 10:23.

→ Intr. VI. 2.B.—liberty—power.

Azotus The Greek name *(Azōtos)* of the O.T. city of Ashdod, located between Gaza and Joppa. This city and its territory were evangelized by Philip,* one of the Seven.*[1]

[1]1 Sm 5; Acts 8:40 □.

→ Map 4.

B

Baal Heb. *ba'al:* "master, owner." The name of Mediterranean deities. The prophets wrestled against the Baalization of the cult of Yahweh.[1] The word is in the feminine because Baal had been assimilated to "shame" (Gk. *aischynē,* Heb. *bôshèt*).[2]

[1]1 Kgs 18; 19:18. [2]2 Kgs 21:3; Jer 2:8; 12:16; Rom 11:4 □.

Babylon Gk. *Babylōn,* Heb. *Bâbèl.* A very ancient city of South Mesopotamia to which Judah was deported in 586 B.C.[1] Having symbolized from O.T. times the city of a power inimical to God,[2] in the N.T. it cryptically refers to Rome.*[3]

[1]Mt 1:11f.,17; Acts 7:43. [2]Gn 11:9; Is 13:1. [3]1 Pt 5:13; Rv 14:8; 16:19; 17:5; 18:2,10,21 □.

bank Gk. *trapeza:* the "table" of the money-changers,* which Jesus overturned in the Temple.[1] Banks and bankers were alluded to by Jesus, who did not criticize the making of interest, however, even though it had been disapproved of by the Law.[2]

[1]Mt 21:12 (= Mk 11:15 = Jn 2:15). [2]Ex 22:24; Dt 23:20; Mt 25:27 (= Lk 19:23) □.

baptism Gk. *baptisma/baptismos,* from *baptō,* a verb gradually limited to meaning "dyeing" and relaced by *baptizō:* "to moisten, to plunge into."

1. A rite common to many religions (water* was purifying and a source of life) which had been adopted by the Essenes* under the form of a daily bath symbolizing efforts towards a pure life and aspirations for purifying grace; it was also practiced by Jews on the occasion of the admission of proselytes* into the people of Israel. The baptism of John the Baptist* differed from others on two scores: it was proffered to all and was not to be repeated; it indicated a summons to conversion* and was an anticipation of messianic baptism in Spirit and fire.[1] It continued as a practice of baptist sects long after John's death.[2] The gospel tradition tended to tone down the Baptist's activity in favor of stressing his role as the Precursor.[3]

[1]Mt 3:6-12 (= Mk 1:4-8 = Lk 3:3-18); 21:25 (= Mk 11:30 = Lk 20:4); Lk 7:29f.; Jn 1:25-33; 3:23; Acts 1:22; 10:37; 11:16; 13:24. [2]Acts 18:25; 19:3f. [3]Comp. with Mt/Mk: Lk 3:21; Jn 1:32.

2. Jesus was baptized by John,[4] an action interpreted as his desire to be in solidarity with the sinners[5] whose sin he took away. Jesus himself conducted a baptismal rite[6] through his disciples, a baptism which cannot be assimilated to John's nor to that of the Spirit, but one which was "in the name of Jesus."[7]

[4]Mt 3:13-17 (= Mk 1:9-11 = Lk 3:21f.). [5]Mt 3:14f.; Jn 1:29. [6]Jn 3:22. [7]Jn 3:23-30; 4:1f.; cf. Acts 2:38.

3. From its earliest days the Church baptized[8] in the name* of Jesus,[9] that is, as a way of one's belonging to Jesus through the Lord's power;[10] she understood the importance of this ministry of hers by tracing it back to a command of the Risen One.[11]

[8]Acts 2:41; 8:12,16,36,38; 9:18; 10:47f.; 16:15,33; 18:8; 19:5; 22:16; 1 Cor 1:13-17; 15:29; Heb 6:2. [9]Acts 2:38; 8:16; 10:48; 19:5. [10]Acts 22:16; 1 Cor 10:2; 12:13; Eph 4:5. [11]Mt 28:19.

4. Various interpretations have been given to this rite. Baptism was a sign of the unity of believers[12] all of whom were called to live the very life of Christ.[13] It plunged the catecheumen into Christ's death and became the demand for a new life, following in the pattern of the Risen One.[14] It was a new birth,[15] a seal,[16] an illumination,[17] a new circumcision,[18] a bath of regeneration:[19] to be in Christ was to be a new creation.*[20]

[12]Eph 4:5. [13]Gal 3:27. [14]Rom 6:3-5; Col 2:12; 1 Pt 3:18-21. [15]Jn 3:5. [16]2 Cor 1:22; Eph 1:13; 4:30. [17]Eph 5:8-14; Heb 6:4. [18]Col 2:11. [19]Ti 3:5. [20]2 Cor 5:17.

5. A metaphor referring to Jesus' passion.[21]

[21]Mk 10:38f.; Lk 12:50.

→ Intr. XI.3.—ablution—bath—Spirit of God—water.

Barabbas Gk. *Barabbas,* from the Aram. *bar abbâ:* "son of the father." The leader of a revolutionary band and a murderer, whose first name was Jesus. The Jews preferred the setting free of Jesus Barabbas to the release of Jesus Christ.[1]

[1]Mt 27:16f. (= Mk 15:7); 27:20f.,26 (= Mk 15:12,15 = Lk 23:18); Jn 18:40; cf. Acts 3:14 □.

Barachiah Gk. *Barachias:* according to Matthew, the father of Zechariah.[1]

[1]Mt 23:35 □.

barbarian Gk. *barbaros:* "stranger." In its origins it was an onomatopoeic word designating one who jabbered away. In antiquity the term referred to those who spoke Greek or Latin poorly. So, it did not possess a contemptuous shade of meaning; in the first instance it meant a "stranger": the Barbarian was to Greeks and Romans what the Gentile was to Jews.[1]

[1]Acts 28:2,4; 1 Cor 14:11 □.

barley Gk. *krithē.* A grassy plant that abounded in Palestine and was harvested in the spring; the offering of a sheaf of barley as the first fruits* inaugurated the sabbaths* of the paschal feast days. Less expensive than wheat,* it was used to make the poor man's bread.[1]

[1]Lv 23:11; Ru 3:15; 2 Kgs 4:42; Jn 6:9,13; Rv 6:6 □.

Barnabas Gk. *Barnabas,* a name of uncertain etymology; according to Acts 4:36, "the son of encouragement." The surname of Joseph, a levite* native of Cyprus,* one of the first Christians and a model of detachment. An "Apostle,*" a "prophet and a doctor," he played an important role in regard to Saul,* who had recently come to Christ, and in Antioch's* relations with Jerusalem.[1]

[1]Acts 4:36; 9:27; 11:22,30; 12:25; 13:1f.,7,43-50; 14:12-20; 15:2-39; 1 Cor 9:6; Gal 2:1-13; Col 4:10 □.

barren

→ sterility.

Barsabbas Gk. *Barsabbas,* from the Aram. *bar sâbâ:* "son of the exalted one" or *bar shabbâ,* "son of the sabbath." A surname of Joseph* (5) and of Jude* (7).[1]

[1]Acts 1:23; 15:22 □.

Bartholomew Gk. *Bartholomaios,* from the Aram. "son of Tolmai." One of the Twelve,* always mentioned in association with Philip and the one whom some, from the ninth century on, have identified with Nathanael.[1]

[1]Mt 10:3 (= Mk 3:18 = Lk 6:14); Acts 1:13; cf. 2 Sm 13:37 □.

[Baruch (Apocalypse of)] An O.T. apocryphal* writing, dating from the first century A.D. Composed in Hebrew, it has not been preserved except in the Syriac and in a Greek fragment. Its thought was close to that of rabbinical theology. It tried to give an answer to questions on the reasons for Jerusalem's destruction and to the problem of sin insofar as these issues were related to the eschatological judgment.

bath Gk. *loutron* (from *louō:* "to wash, to bathe," *louomai:* "to bathe, to take a bath"). A complete bath was taken in certain circumstances.[1] Unlike the washing of a part of the body,[1] it symbolized perfect purity.* The believer has been purified of his sins through the blood of Jesus*[3] and through the bath of baptism.*[4]

[1]Acts 9:37; 16:33; cf. 2 Pt 2:22. [2]Jn 13:10. [3]Rv 1:5. [4]Acts 22:16; 1 Cor 6:11; Eph 5:26; Ti 3:5; Heb 10:22 □.

→ Intr. VIII.1.C.—baptism—pure—wash—water.

bath (measure) Gk. *batos,* Heb. *bat,* occasionally translated as an "earthenware jar" or a "barrel." A Hebraic measurement of liquid capacity, corresponding to the Greek measure* (Gk. *metrētēs*) equal to 36.44 liters (38.6 quarts).[1]

[1]Lk 16:6 □.

→ measures.

battle

→ combat.

beasts, Beast Gk. *thērion* (the same root as Lat. *ferus:* "wild"), translating the Heb. *hayyâ:* a "living" and, more particularly, a "dangerous animal."

1. A wild beast.

→ Intr. II.6.

2. For ancient man beasts (also called the "Living Ones,*" Gk. *zōa*)[1] were sometimes the bearers or mediators of a power greater than man's, one that was either evil or favorable to him.[2]

[1]Heb 13:11; 2 Pt 2:12; Jude 10. [2]Mk 1:13; 16:18; Rv 4:6-9; cf. Gn 3:1-3; Ez 1:5-25.

3. According to some biblical texts, which echo Oriental mythologies, God's Adversary at the beginning or end of the world was a Beast, a serpent,* dragon,* fabulous animal.[3] This Beast obeyed Satan* and duplicated itself according to need, producing, along with the Dragon, the satanic triad;[4] but its defeat was assured.[5] The book of Revelation details its work and its fall.[6]

[3]Jb 9:13; 26:12; Ps 74:13f.; 89:10f.; Is 27:1; 51:9; Rv 12:9f.; 20:2. [4]Rv 16:13. [5]Rv 15:2; 19:19f. [6]Rv 11:7; 13; 14:9,11; 16:2,10,13; 17; 20:4,10 □.

→ animals—Antichrist—Living Ones.

beatitude

→ happy.

Beelzebul Gk. *Beelzeboul.* An old Phoenician deity.[1] A term probably deriving from the Heb. *Baal-z^e^bûl,* exalted lord, Baal* the Prince. According to rabbinical texts, he was the lord of the dunghill, the lord of sacrifices offered to idols. Or else it was a word deformed into *Baalzeboub,* the lord of the flies. The prince of demons.*[2]

[1]2 Kgs 1:2-16. [2]Mt 10:25; 12:24 (= Mk 3:22 = Lk 11:15); 12:27 (= Lk 11:18) □.

beg, beggar Gk. *pros-aitēs* (from *aiteō:* "to ask"). "Better to die than to beg!"[1] was said because begging was a "shame"[2] and a curse.[3] Rare in ancient Israel where family bonds were quite tight, beggars had become numerous;[4] often blind,* they kept to the sides of roadways[5] or near to the Temple gates.[6]

[1]Sir 40:28. [2]Lk 16:3. [3]Ps 109:10. [4]Dt 15:7. [5]Mk 10:46 (= Lk 18:35). [6]Acts 3:2 □.

beget **1.** Gk. *tiktō,* used in the biological sense of the term, and, in speaking of a woman: "to give birth to a child";[1] it was never used in a spiritual sense.

[1]Mt 1:21ff.; Lk 1:31ff.; Gal 4:27; Rv 12:2-5.

2. Gk. *gennaō* (the causative of *gignomai*): "to cause to be, to engender." A term used equally for physical begetting as well as for adoption.* But, unlike neighboring religions which freely retained sexual representations to speak of relationships between the deity and men, the O.T. speaks only of adoption to refer to the God who begets: of such a kind are the references in the Psalms which look to the anointing* and enthronement of a king-messiah.*[2] In the N.T., similarly, the begetting of Jesus, which was always mentioned in reference to Ps 2:7, does not refer to his birth, but to his baptism,* or his resurrection.*[3] Similarly, in relation to believers, it is a case of their "birth" or "rebirth" in faith.[4]

[2]Ps 2:7; 110:3. [3](Lk 3:22;) Acts 13:33; Heb 1:5; 5:5. [4]Jn 1:13; 3:3-8; 1 Pt 1:23; 1 Jn 2:29; 3:9; 4:7; 5:1,4,18.

3. Paul, heir to the Jewish tradition, considered that he had begotten some in the faith[5] or that he possessed spiritual sons.[6]

[5]1 Cor 4:15; Phlm 10; cf. Gal 4:19. [6]1 Cor 4:17; 1 Tim 1:2; 2 Tim 2:1; 1 Pt 5:13.

→ born, reborn—child—genealogy—race.

Belial, Beliar Gk. *Belial* or *Beliar,* of uncertain etymology, probably "the good-for-nothing." In the *Testaments of the XII Patriarchs** it referred to Satan*; at Qumran,* to the spirit of darkness.[1]

[1]2 Cor 6:15; cf. Ps 18:5 □.

believe

→ faith.

beloved Gk. *agapētos.* When it was applied to Jesus, it served as a messianic* epithet; it was similar to the adjectives "only" and "chosen.*" It described Jesus' special filial descent.[2] When used to refer to believers, as it frequently was, it referred to the love of God[3] and of the brethren,[4] a love of which they were the objects. On the "beloved disciple," cf. disciple* (3).

[1]Compare Mt 12:18 and Is 42:1; Mt 17:5 (= Mk 9:7) and Lk 9:35. [2]Mt 3:17 (= Mk 1:11 = Lk 3:22); Mk 12:6 (= Lk 20:13); 2 Pt 1:17 □. [3]Rom 1:7. [4]Acts 15:25; Rom 16:5; Jas 1:16; 1 Jn 2:7.

→ election—love—Son of God.

belt Gk. *zonē.* A long piece of material or leather, sometimes richly decorated,[1] generally helpful in tucking up the flaps of a tunic* in order to facilitate walking or work.[2] Metaphorically, to have one's loins girt meant to reveal oneself as perfectly available.[3] The belt could carry various things, one of which was the wallet.*[4] The same Greek word also indicated a girdle.*[5]

[1]Ex 28:4; Rv 1:13; 15:6. [2]Ex 12:11; 2 Kgs 4:29; Lk 12:37; 17:8; Jn 13:4f.; 21:7; Acts 12:8. [3]Jer 1:17; Lk 12:35; Jn 21:18; Acts 21:11; Eph 6:14; 1 Pt 1:13. [4]2 Sm 20:8; Ez 9:2; Mt 10:9 (= Mk 6:8). [5]Mt 3:4 (= Mk 1:6) □.

→ clothing.

Benjamin Gk. *Beniamein,* Heb. *Bin-yâmîn:* "son of the right [hand]" or "son of the South." The second son of Jacob* and Rachel, whose favorite child he was after Joseph.* The eponymous* ancestor of one of the twelve tribes* of Israel, the one from whom king Saul and Saul (Paul) of Tarsus were descended.[1]

[1]Gn 35:18; 42:4; Acts 13:21; Rom 11:1; Phil 3:5; Rv 7:8 □.

Berenice Gk. *Bernikē* (born in A.D. 28). The older daughter of Herod Agrippa.* At 20, the widow of her uncle Herod,* king of Chalcis, she lived with her brother Agrippa II,* married Polemon, king of Cilicia, then returned to Agrippa. She shared a liaison with Titus,* when he came to conduct the Jewish war.[1]

[1]Acts 25:13,23; 26:30 □.

Beroea Gk. *Beroia.* A city of Macedonia, today's Werria; the native city of Sopater.[1] When he was chased out of Thessalonica, Paul went there with Silas.*[2]

[1]Acts 20:4. [2]Acts 17:10-13.

→ Map 2.

Bethany Gk. *Bēthania,* according to a popular etymology: "the house of the poor man" or "of Ananias."

1. A large town about three km. (two mi.) east of Jerusalem,*[1] on the road to Jericho,* on the eastern slope of the Mount of Olives.*[2] Today's El-Azarieh, an Arab deformation of Lazarus' name. The village of Simon* the leper, of Martha* and Mary,*[3] well-known to Jesus,[4] the place where he raised up Lazarus[5] and whence Jesus went up to heaven.[6]

[1]Jn 11:18. [2]Mk 11:1 (= Lk 19:29). [3]Mt 26:6 (= Mk 14:3); Jn 11:1; cf. Lk 10:38. [4]Mt 21:17; Mk 11:11f. [5]Jn 12:1. [6]Lk 24:50 □.

→ Map 4.

2. According to John, a small market-town on the west bank of the Jordan where John* had been baptizing.[1]

[1]Jn 1:28; cf. 3:23,26; 10:40 □.

Bethlehem Gk. *Bēthleem,* of uncertain etymology: "the house of Lahmu" (an Akkadian* deity) or "the house of bread." An important village of Judea,*[1] about eight km. (five mi.) south of Jerusalem,* called "the city of David*"[2] because he had received his royal anointing there.[3] According to prophecy and according to the gospels, the place of the Messiah's birth.*[4]

[1]Mt 2:1. [2]Lk 2:4,11,15. [3]Ru 1:2,19; 4:11; 1 Sm 16:4,18. [4]Mi 5:1; Mt 2:5f.,8,16; Lk 2:15; Jn 7:42 □.

→ Map 4.

Bethphage Gk. *Bēthphaguē.* A hamlet on the eastern slope of the Mount of Olives,* probably to the north of Bethany.*[1] Jesus sent there to search for the foal of an ass* on which he was to make his entry into Jerusalem.

[1]Mt 21:1; Mk 11:1; Lk 19:29 □.

→ Map 4.

Bethsaida Gk. *Bethsaida,* cf. Aram. *béth-ṣaydâ:* "the house of provisioning" *or* "of the fishery." A village of Galilee,* north of the lake, erected into a city with the name Julias by the tetrarch* Philip.* Modern-day Et-Tell.[1]

[1]Mt 11:21 (= Lk 10:13); Mk 6:45; 8:22; Lk 9:10; Jn 1:44; 12:21 □.

→ Map 4.

betrothed Held to their promise, betrothed persons were considered as spouses.*

→ Intr. VIII.2.B.a.

Bethzatha, Bethesda Gk. *Bēthesda,* Lat. *Bethzatha.* A pool located to the north of the Jerusalem Temple esplanade. Excavations at the Church of Saint Anne have permitted the reconstruction of two water reservoirs separated by a 6.5 m. (21.3 ft.) colonnade, with the complex having been encircled by four colonnades which measured respectively; to the east, 49.5 + 40 m. (162.4 + 131.2 ft.); to the south 65.5 m. (215 ft.); to the west, 40 + 48 m. (131.2 + 157.5 ft.); to the north, 50 m. (164 ft.). From these, we can fill out the allusions to five porticoes mentioned in John.[1] It had formerly been a pagan place of healing.

[1]Jn 5:2 □.

→ pool—Map 1.

[Bible] Lat. *Biblia:* "book," coming from the Gk. *ta biblia:* "the books." A collection of works considered as inspired by God and constituting the canon of the Scriptures. For Jews, the Bible includes twenty-four works; for Protestants, who retain works written in Hebrew but subdivide them according to the Greek Bible, it includes thirty-nine O.T. books and twenty-seven N.T. ones; for Roman Catholics, who also retain works written in Greek, it includes forty-six O.T. books and twenty-seven from the N.T.

→ Intr. XII; XV.—apocryphal writings—book—canon—deuterocanonical writings.

bier

→ coffin.

blaspheme **1.** Gk. *blas-phēmeō* (from *blas,* related to *blabē:* "wrong" and *phēmi:* "to speak"): "to injure, speak ill of, calumniate." Directed at the holy God, whose Name* the Jews avoided even pronouncing, blasphemy and profanation of holy things, faults typical of the pagans,[1] were punished with death by stoning.*[2] In addition, one had to avoid provoking blasphemy.[3] The term, according to secular Greek usage, could have the meaning of great insults, in actions or speech, against God, his way,* or those he sent.*[4]

[1]2 Kgs 19:4,6,20-22; Rom 2:24; Rv 13:6. [2]Lv 24:16; Acts 6:11. [3]1 Tim 6:1; Ti 2:5. [4]Acts 13:45; 18:6; 1 Tim 1:13; 1 Pt 4:4; 2 Pt 2:2; Rv 2:9; 16:9.

2. The principal cause of the accusation against Jesus, who attributed to himself a divine authority,* namely, the power to forgive sins.[5] A rejection of Christ's power and word.[6]

[5]Mt 9:3 (= Mk 2:7 = Lk 5:21); 26:65 (= Mk 14:64); Jn 5:18; 10:33. [6]Acts 18:6.

3. Blasphemy against the Holy Spirit consisted in attributing to the devil* the exorcisms* effected by Jesus; according to others, it signified opposition to the God who intervened at the end* of time to forgive sins and save men. To take this position is to wander away from the God who forgives.[7]

[7]Mt 12:31f. (= Mk 3:28f. = Lk 12:10).

→ curse—injure—insult—slander.

blessed, blest

→ happy.

bind and loose Gk. *deō kai lyō.* This expression has to be understood in the light of Jewish customs. The synagogue held to a practice of excommunication,* pronouncing its judgment by "binding and loosing," as, for example, by loosing a vow to which someone had been bound. The expression is applicable to the disciplinary sphere (excommunication) and to doctrinal or juridical decisions. In Matthew 16:19, Peter possesses the power to ordain conditions for entry into the kingdom of heaven. In Matthew 18:18, the ecclesial community receives the same power. In John 20:23, the Risen One uses other words: "to retain and to forgive" to speak of the same reality.

→ loose.

bishop

→ episcope.

Bithynia Gk. *Bithynia.* The ancient kingdom of Asia* reunited to Pontus* by Pompey in 64 B.C. to form the senatorial province* of Bithynia and Pontus. Paul was unable to get there, but, according to Pliny the Younger's* testimony, Christians were numerous there around the year 110.[1]

[1]Acts 16:7; 1 Pt 1:1 □.

→ Map 3.

blessing Gk. *eulogia* (from *eu:* "well" and *legō:* "to speak"): "praise."[1]

1. Generally, the term preserves a Semitic substrate of the Hebrew word it translates, *b^erâkâ:* more than a word, it was an act through which a gift was handed over, particularly, at the outset of the biblical tradition, the gift of life.*[2] To bless was to speak and communicate the divine gift.[3] Also, one could inherit* a blessing.[4]

[1]Rv 5:12; 7:12. [2]Gn 27:25-30. [3]Nm 6:24-26; Dt 28:3-6. [4]Gal 3:8; 1 Pt 3:9.

2. God was, in the most excellent fashion, one who blessed.[5] The blessing found its apex in the Christ who bestowed the Holy Spirit, the ultimate inheritance.[6]

[5]Mt 25:34; Heb 6:7. [6]Acts 3:25; Gal 3:14; Eph 1:3; Heb 12:17.

3. Man responded to God's blessing with thanksgiving,* with Eucharist.*[7] The man who blesses God carries that blessing back to its source.[8] So, Jesus blessed his disciples,[9] but it was not maintained that he "blessed the bread":[10] he "pronounced a blessing over bread and the cup."[11] When one blesses someone this is done in God's name, the one who alone can bless and integrate it within the course of one's very life.[12] Finally, man can recognize that someone or other has been blessed by God.[13]

[7]1 Cor 10:16. [8]Lk 1:64; 2:28; 24:53; Eph 1:3; Jas 3:9; 1 Pt 1:3. [9]Mk 10:16; Lk 24:50f. [10]Exception: Lk 9:16. [11]Mt 14:19 (= Mk 6:41); 26:26 (= Mk 14:22); Lk 24:30. [12]Lk 1:42; Rom 12:14; 1 Cor 4:12; 1 Pt 3:9. [13]Mt 21:9 (= Mk 11:9f. = Lk 19:38 = Jn 12:13); 23:39 (= Lk 13:35); Lk 1:42.

→ curse—happy.

blind Gk. *typhlos.*

1. Quite widespread in the East, blindness, which was chiefly caused by a purulent eye disease, was held to be a punishment from God.[1] Even though the Law recommended care of the blind,[2] the blind were often reduced to the state of being beggars.*[3] Their cure, which was quite rare, was reckoned to be a great miracle.*[4]

[1]Ex 4:11; Jn 9:2; Acts 13:11. [2]Dt 27:18. [3]Mk 10:46; Jn 9:1. [4]Jn 9:16.

2. When related to the prophetic portrayal of salvation as light,*[5] blindness symbolized spiritual darkness* and hardening.*[6] Also, in restoring sight to the blind, Jesus furnished a sign* of the messianic times.[7] One who recognized him[8] understood that Jesus was the light of the world;[9] like Paul, such a one was disposed to receive back his sight.[10]

[5]Is 35:5. [6]Is 6:9f.; Mt 15:14; 23:16-26; Jn 9:41; 12:40; Rom 2:19; 2 Cor 4:4; 2 Pt 1:9; 1 Jn 2:11; Rv 3:17. [7]Mt 11:5 (= Lk 7:22). [8]Jn 9:39; cf. Mt 13:16f. [9]Jn 9:5. [10]Acts 9:8,17f.; 22:11,13; Rv 3:18.

→ eye—harden—light—see—sickness.

blood Gk. *haima.*

1. The blood was life*[1] and life was God's.

[1]Lv 17:11-14.

2. Therefore, one could not drink blood along with butchered meat.[2] When sprinkled on the altar,* in some instances blood rendered a sacrifice expiatory.*[3] But only the blood of Jesus was efficacious,[4] for Christ himself was the propitiatory*;[5] his blood was that of the Covenant* for the forgiveness* of sins,[6] the one drunk in the eucharistic meal.[7]

[2]Dt 12:23f.; Acts 15:20,29. [3]Heb 9:7; 13:11. [4]Heb 10:4,19. [5]Rom 3:25. [6]Ex 24:6-8; Mt 26:28 (= Mk 14:24). [7]Jn 6:53f.; 1 Cor 10:16.

3. One could not shed innocent blood with impunity,[8] for God would avenge it.[9] But Jesus voluntarily shed his own blood, thereby, renewing the Covenant.[10] This was the significance of the precious blood which gushed forth from Jesus' side.[11]

[8]Mt 23:29-36; 27:4,24f. [9]Rv 6:10; 19:2. [10]Is 53:12; Lk 22:20. [11]Jn 19:31-37; 1 Pt 1:19; 1 Jn 5:6-8.

4. The expression "flesh and blood" designated man in his earthly state.[12]

[12]Sir 14:18; Mt 16:17; 1 Cor 15:50; Gal 1:16; Eph 6:12; Heb 2:14.

→ sacrifice.

bloody sweat In Gethsemane* during his agony,* "the sweat (of Jesus) became like clots of blood (Gk. *thromboi haimatos*) which fell (Gk. *katabainontes*) to the ground."[1] Toward the end of the third century the passage was found to be missing from several manuscripts; without doubt it had been removed out of some theological scruple. It is difficult to be precise about the nature of the phenomenon, even though some would want to liken it to hemathidrosis, a sweat whose rosy hue derives from the passage of hemoglobin into the sweaty secretions.

[1]Lk 22:44 □.

boast, boasting

→ confidence.

body Gk. *sōma* translated the Heb. *bâsâr* which was also rendered *sarx:* "flesh." According to contemporary use, this word described the unity of flesh and bone which an individual daily had at his or her disposal[1] and which was to become a corpse[2] at death (generally, Gk. *ptōma*[3]). Yet, at times among the Greeks, it meant that which brought unity to the plurality of bodily members.[4] Ordinarily, according to the Bible, the body was that through which man entered into relationships with his brethren and with the universe; it constituted his ability for self-expression.

[1]Mt 5:29f.; 6:22f. (= Lk 11:34,(36), 25 (= Lk 12:22f.); 1 Cor 5:3; 7:34; 9:27; 13:3; Gal 6:17; Jas 2:16. [2]Mt 27:52,58 (= Mk 15:43 = Lk 23:52 = Jn 19:38); Lk 17:37 (cf. Mt 24:28); 23:55; 24:3,23; Jn 19:40; 20:12; Acts 9:40. [3]Mt 14:12 (= Mk 6:29); 24:28 (cf. Lk 17:37); Mk 15:45 (cf. 15:43); Rv 11:8f. △. [4]Rom 12:4; 1 Cor 12:12-26.

1. The body designated the person in his or her external and visible aspect,[5] so that this word could be regarded as interchangeable with the personal pronoun.[6] Its dignity inhered, above all else, in its procreative power.[7] The "sin against the body"[8] probably referred to a sin against the human body in its self-expression. There was no list of sins against the body, but only one listing those of the flesh.[9] Nonetheless, the body was that intermingling of forces which flesh and spirit are.

[5]Rom 6:12; 12:1. [6]Comp. 1 Cor 6:19 and 3:17; or 1 Cor 6:15 and Eph 5:30. [7]Rom 1:24; 4:19; 1 Cor 6:13-20; 7:4. [8]1 Cor 6:18. [9]Gal 5:19.

2. Without calling into question the dignity of the body, Paul offered a particular theology of the body. The flesh, indwelt by sin,*[10] had enslaved the body. Thereafter it remained a "body of sin," since sin was able to dominate the body[11] and deliver this same body over to death.[12] In that case, the body became identified with wicked flesh*; it described the human person become a slave of sin.

[10]Rom 7:20. [11]Rom 6:6,16. [12]Rom 7:24; 8:10. [13]Rom 6:12; 8:13.

3. But Christ took on the "body of flesh"[14] and his body became the place in which reconciliation* was effected. The believer saw "his body of sin destroyed";[15] he was stripped of that carnal body destined for death.[16] From that point on he could glorify God in his own body and "offer his body" as a living act of worship.*[17] In incorporating us within himself, Christ thereby made our bodies to be his very own body. Also, unlike the flesh, the body was to rise.*[18] Wretched being though it might now be, it would be transfigured,* not by a simple transition but by a true bursting forth[19] into a body of glory,* that is, into a spiritual body.[20]

[14]Col 1:22. [15]Rom 6:6. [16]Col 2:11. [17]Rom 12:1; 1 Cor 6:20. [18]Rom 8:11; 1 Cor 6:14. [19]2 Cor 5:8. [20]1 Cor 15:44; Phil 3:21.

→ Intr. V.2.B.—Body of Christ—bone—flesh—man—soul—spirit.

Body of Christ Gk. *sōma tou Christou.*

1. The body* of Jesus. During his earthly life Jesus expressed himself through his own body like any other man;[1] this body, after being handed over to death,[2] was no longer to be found on the morning after the sabbath.[3] This was because it had become the temple* of the new worship,*[4] a spiritual body.[5] Through his own glorious* body, our wretched bodies will one day be transfigured.*[6]

[1]Mt 26:12 (= Mk 14:8); Heb 10:5; cf. 1 Jn 4:2. [2]Mt 27:58 (= Mk 15:43 = Lk 23:52 = Jn 19:38); Lk 23:55; Jn 19:40; Rom 7:4; Col 1:22; Heb 10:10; 1 Pt 2:24. [3]Lk 24:3,23; Jn 20:12. [4]Jn 2:18-22. [5]1 Cor 15:44. [6]Phil 3:20f.

2. *The eucharistic body.* * Jesus used this expression to indicate his new, eucharistic* presence,[7] one in which we share so that we may constitute one only body.[8]

[7]Mt 26:26 (= Mk 14:22 = Lk 22:19 = 1 Cor 11:24). [8]1 Cor 10:16f.

3. *The body of Christ.* This expression knew earlier, preparatory stages. First of all Paul, in a Hellenistic* manner of speaking, described believers as multiple members whom Christ had brought into the unity of a single body.[9] At the same time, he considered every Christian as one of Christ's members;[10] here his thinking was Semitic. It was also such when, in the Captivity Epistles,* he ended up with a conception of the Church* as the Body of Christ, joining together Jews and pagans;[11] the Church progressively gives expression to Christ along with its stages of growth.[12]

[9]Rom 12:4f.; 1 Cor 12:12-27; cf. Gal 3:27. [10]1 Cor 6:15. [11]Eph 1:22f.; 2:14-16; 3:6; 4:4; 5:23,30; Col 1:18,24; 2:17,19; 3:15. [12]Eph 4:12,16.

bone Gk. *osteon:* "bone, remains."[1] The expression "flesh* and bone" pointed to the earthly body in its totality, what allowed a man to enter into a relationship with others; whence, a meaning of close kinship. The Risen One was not a ghost, since he entered upon visible relationships with his disciples.[3] On the cross Jesus had been the true paschal lamb* whose bones were not to be broken.[4]

[1]Mt 23:27; Heb 11:22. [2]Gn 2:23; 29:14; Jgs 9:2; 2 Sm 19:13. [3]Lk 24:39. [4]Ex 12:10,46; Nm 9:12; Ps 34:21; Jn 19:33 □.

→ body—flesh.

book Gk. *biblion, biblos:* "(Egyptian) papyrus," hence: "roll, book."

1. A roll of parchment or codex of papyrus on which were consigned and linked together the words and thoughts of God or men. In antiquity a book included from 1,800 to 3,000 stichoi (lines of thirty-five or thirty-six letters, such as those in the Greek hexameter). In this way the Torah* had gotten subdivided into five books: Genesis and Deuteronomy constituted their own natural units (seventy-eight and sixty pages of Hebrew in Kittel's edition), the rest was divided into three other parts (sixty-six, forty-four and seventy-two pages). Similarly, Samuel, Kings and Chronicles were each subdivided into two "books." The N.T. "books" were determined according to their authors, recipients and contents.

2. The word took on a different meaning according to its subject. Thus, in the N.T. reference is made to the Book of the Covenant,[1] the Book of the Law,[2] that of Moses,[3] Isaiah[4] or the Psalms,[5] as well as that of the Gospel or Revelation of John.[6] The function of these books was similar to that of Scripture: to witness, to recall and to confirm prophetic words.[7]

[1]Ex 24:7; Heb 9:19. [2]Dt 28:58,61; Gal 3:10. [3]2 Chr 25:4; Mk 12:26. [4]Lk 3:4; 4:17. [5]Lk 20:42; Acts 1:20. [6]Jn 20:30; Rv 1:11. [7]Dt 31:26f.; Is 30:8; Jer 36; Rv 22:7,9,18f.

3. In the metaphorical sense, there is a "book of life,"[8] a book in which are inscribed men's actions in anticipation of judgment* day;[9] in the end, there is the sealed book which only the Lamb can open: probably the book in which have been consigned God's actions in the course of his people's history and his plan* which is fulfilled in Jesus Christ.[10]

[8]Ex 32:32f.; Ps 69:29; Dn 12:1; Lk 10:20; Phil 4:3; Rv 3:5; 13:8; 17:8; 20:12,15; 21:27. [9]Dn 7:10; Rv 20:12. [10]Ez 2:9f.; Rv 5:1-10; cf. 2 Cor 3:14-16.

→ Intr. IX.3.—Bible—Scripture.

Booths (Feast of) Heb. *Sukkôt,* Gk. *skēnopēgia* (from *skēnē:* "tent" and *pēgnymi:* "to drive in (stakes), to set up").

1. An autumn feast,* at harvest time[1] or at vintage time,[2] with the intention of thanking God by offering him a basket full of fruit.[3] Afterwards called the Feast of Tabernacles or Tents to recall the huts made of branches under which people camped during the harvest, as well as those erected in Jerusalem throughout the seven days of the feast, which was concluded with an eighth day.[4] From this practice there derived a further, supplementary sense: the commemoration of the wandering in the desert, during which the Hebrews took shelter under tents.[5]

[1]Ex 23:16. [2]Jgs 9:27. [3]Dt 26:2. [4]Lv 23:34-36; Nm 29:35; Jn 7:2 □. [5]Lv 23:42f.

2. A week of rejoicing among the people, with supplementary libations and sacrifices. In addition to rendering thanks to God, the liturgy culminated on the seventh day with a petitionary prayer for rain*: a libation ritual with water drawn from the pool of Siloam,* with readings from the Exodus miracle accounts and prophecies proclaiming, under the symbol of the fountainhead, the spiritual renewal of Zion.*[6] On that day, Jesus presented himself as the one able to slake thirst.[7] In proclaiming that Jesus is the light of the world, John 8:12 could have been making an allusion to the evening light ritual, during which sacred dances were performed.

[6]Zec 14:16-19; Ez 47:1-12; Is 12:3. [7]Jn 7:37f.

→ Intr. XIII.3.B.

born, reborn As was the case in the majority of religions, the Bible expressed its faith in another life through the symbol* of new birth, bestowed already here below by the deity. It differed radically in its conception of it: this was not a case of a magic initiation rite which would transform one's human nature, but was an act of God which made Israel his firstborn* from the very time of the going-out from Egypt*[1] and one which promised definitive renewal through a Law* written on the heart.[2] According to late Judaism, baptism* made of the proselyte* one newly born.

The N.T. specifies that the believer "was begotten" (Gk. *gennēthēnai ek,* the passive of *gennaō:* "to beget") of the Spirit and water[3] or from above.[4] This last affirmation also underlies the Greek when mention was made of the believer "having been reborn" (Gk. *ana-gennaomai*) by the power of the Resurrection*[5] or by the divine Word.*[6] Finally, through the Greek *palin-genesia:* "re-generation" at the end of time,[7] the individual was situated within the wider history of the "new creation."[8] This regeneration took place equally well at baptism;[9] thanks to a seed of incorruptibility, which the believer henceforward bore within himself, he had been invited to a new life.[10]

[1]Ex 4:22; Dt 32:6,18f. [2]Ez 36:26f. [3]Jn 3:5f.,8. [4]Jn 3:3,7. [5]1 Pet 1:3. [6]1 Pt 1:23; cf. Jas 1:18. [7]Mt 19:28; cf. Rv 21:5. [8]2 Cor 5:17. [9]Ti 3:5. [10]1 Jn 3:9; cf. 1 Jn 2:29; 4:7.

→ baptism—beget—child—new—son of God.

bosom

→ breast.

brambles Under this term were indicated various shrubby trees (acacia, acanthus, hawthorn, holly, jujube, thistle, thorn, but not the cactus, nor the Barbary fig, which were imported later), all of them prickly; stress was laid on their bushiness (Gk. *batos*[1]) or on their thorns (in Gk. *akantha:* "sharp-pointed" or *tri-bolos:* "with three points"[2]). The N.T. does not distinguish among these terms.[3] Very common in the Mediterranean and semi-desert or subtropical regions,[4] thickets and the scrub of thorn bushes had to be weeded out before sowing and burnt, either to fertilize the earth or as fuel.[5] Metaphorically, the thorny bushes stood for what was opposed to receiving revelation.[6]

[1]Mk 12:26; Lk 6:44; 20:37; Acts 7:30,35 △. [2]Mk 7:16; Heb 6:8 [3]Comp. Mt 7:16 and Lk 6:44. [4]Intr. II.5. [5]Jer 4:3; Mt 13:7 (= Mk 4:7 = Lk 8:7). [6]Mt 7:16 (= Lk 6:44); 13:22 (= Mk 4:18f. = Lk 8:14); Heb 6:8.

→ crown (of thorns).

brass Lat. *aes:* "copper." Today, an alloy of copper and zinc, the composition of which dates from the thirteenth century A.D. Mistakenly identified with bronze* (Gk. *chalkos*).[1]

[1]1 Kgs 7:13f.; Jer 1:18; 1 Cor 13:1; Rv 18:12.

bread Gk. *artos.*

1. A foodstuff made from barley* flour (more common than corn, wheat*) and leaven.* Cooked on a plate or in the oven, it took on a shape of a disc (also capable of serving as a saucer) or a loaf; it resembled a stone.[1] It was what one could not forego, the basic nourishment,[2] so much so that it often was a synonym for a meal.*[3] It was never cut with a knife, but was broken by hand with the intention of being shared: to share bread was to give it,[4] it was to join together and to indicate the union of those sharing in a meal.[5]

[1]Mt 7:9 (= Lk 11:11); cf. 4:3 (= Lk 4:3). [2]Am 4:6; Mk 3:20; Lk 11:5; 15:17. [3]Lk 14:15; Acts 2:42. [4]Is 58:7; Jer 16:7. [5]Ps 41:10; Mt 14:19 (= Mk 6:41 = Lk 9:16 = Jn 6:11); 26:26 (= Mk 14:22 = Lk 22:19 = 1 Cor 11:23); Jn 13:18; 1 Cor 10:16.

2. The bread, which man needs every day, God gives to everyone who asks him for it.[6] The heavenly manna* which satisfies[7] is a figure* of the eschatological* food, the definitive gift.[8]

[6]Mt 6:11 (= Lk 11:3); 2 Cor 9:10. [7]Mt 14:20 (= Mk 6:42 = Lk 9:17 = Jn 6:13; cf. 6:26). [8]Ps 78:23-25; Is 30:23; Jer 31:12; Lk 22:16; Rv 2:17.

3. As a privileged metaphor,* it suggests the Word of God,* man's true life,[9] which had already been prefigured by the manna.* Jesus was the "bread of life" in person, the one who alone gives life,[10] the bread he gave his disciples on the night before his sacrifice.*[11] In distributing it to crowds in the desert Jesus taught his disciples how to share the Word and the Eucharist* superabundantly.[12]

[9]Dt 8:3; Am 8:11; Mt 4:4 (= Lk 4:4). [10]Jn 6:35-47. [11]Mt 26:26 (= Mk 14:22 = Lk 22:19 = 1 Cor 11:23). [12]Mt 14:13-21 (= Mk 6:32-44 = Lk 9:10-17); 15:32-38 (= Mk 8:1-9); Jn 6:1-15.

→ communion—Eucharist—manna—meal—unleavened bread.

breaking of bread Gk. *klasis tou artou.* In breaking (not cutting) and in distributing bread over which a blessing* had been said, the father of the family began the table fellowship which the fact of eating together had become.[1] Taken up by Jesus on the occasion of his last meal,[2] the gesture of breaking bread has occasionally been used by Christians to refer as well to the eucharistic meal*: such may have been the case in the Emmaus narrative.[3]

[1]Mt 14:19 (= Mk 6:41 = Lk 9:16); 15:36 (= Mk 8:6). [2]Mt 26:26 (= Mk 14:22 = Lk 22:19 = 1 Cor 11:24). [3]Lk 24:30,35; Acts 2:42,46; 20:7,11; 27:35; 1 Cor 10,16 □.

→ bread—Lord's Supper—meal.

breast Gk. *stēthos:* "breast,"[1] *mastos:* "bosom."[2]

[1]Rv 15:6. [2]Lk 11:27; 23:29; Rv 1:13 △.

1. "To beat one's breast" (in Gk. *typtō to stēthos*) was a gesture of repentance or of sadness.[3] With *koptomai* (without a complement) it was the equivalent of "to lament."[4]

[3]Is 32:12; Ez 23:34; Na 2:8; Lk 18:13; 23:48. [4]Mt 11:17; 24:30; Lk 8:52; 23:27; Acts 8:2; Rv 1:7; 18:9.

2. To lean on the breast of a friend at a meal during which one reclined and was not seated, was a gesture of intimacy.[5] Another word to convey the same disposition, Gk. *kolpos:* "bosom."[6]

[5]Jn 13:25; 21:20. [6]Jn 1:18; 13:23; cf. Lk 6:38; 16:22f. △.

breath

→ spirit.

bronze Gk. *chalkos.* An alloy of copper and tin. The bronze age succeeded the stone age, from 3,000 to 1,200 B.C. Smelted,[1] hammered or chiseled, it was fashioned into plates,[2] objets d'art,[3] idols,[4] coins.[5] It was worth less than gold or silver,[6] unless one of these metals was used as part of its composition (*chalkolibanon:* "polished brass").[7]

[1]2 Tim 4:14. [2]Mk 7:4. [3]Rv 18:12. [4]Nm 21:9; Dn 2:32; Rv 9:20. [5]Mt 10:9 (= Mk 6:8); Mk 12:41. [6]Jer 6:28; Ez 22:18; 1 Cor 13:1 □. [7]Rv 1:15; 2:18 △.

brother Gk. *adelphos.*

1. In its proper meaning, men who were the offspring of the same mother's womb. By extension, members of the one same family,[1] the one same tribe,*[2] the one same people,[3] over against those who were strangers.*[4] In the metaphorical sense, persons linked spiritually by similar feelings,[5] a covenant,*[6] faith in Israel's God[7] or in Jesus Christ.[8]

[1]Gn 13:8; 14:14; 29:15; 1 Chr 23:22. [2]2 Sm 19:13. [3]Ex 2:11; Dt 25:3. [4]Dt 1:16; 15:2f. [5]2 Sm 1:26. [6]Am 1:9. [7]Acts 2:29. [8]Jn 21:23; Acts 1:15; Gal 1:2; Phil 4:21.

2. Jesus recognized his brothers in all those who do the will* of the Father.[9] In God's family[10] Jesus is the firstborn of a multitude of brothers,[11] who have become sons by adoption.* This brotherhood (Gk. *adelphotēs*)[12] is constituted by brotherly love* (Gk. *phil-adelphia*),[13] in spite of some who are unworthy[14] or false brethren who may worm their way in.[15] It is open to all men[16] who can be reborn by the word of God and the Holy Spirit.[17] Finally, in the New Adam,* the New Man* symbolizes a universal brotherhood that will be brought about at the end of time.[18]

[9]Mt 12:46-50. [10]Eph 2:19. [11]Rom 3:29. [12]1 Pt 2:17; 5:9 □. [13]Rom 12:10; 1 Thes 4:9; Heb 13:1; 1 Pt 1:22; 3:8; 2 Pt 1:7 △. [14]1 Cor 5:11. [15]2 Cor 11:26; Gal 2:4 △. [16]Mt 5:47. [17]Jn 3:3; 1 Pt 1:23. [18]Rom 5:12-21; cf. Eph 2:15f.; Col 3:10f.

→ child—neighbor.

brothers of Jesus **1.** The N.T. indicates the existence of Jesus's brothers and sisters, among whom were James and Joseph (Joses), Jude and Simon.[1] They were not disciples* of Jesus during his earthly life.[2] After Easter they were members of the Jerusalem community and were then called "brothers of the Lord": James, who was favored with an appearance* of the Risen One, was their leader.[3]

[1]Mt 13:55f. (= Mk 6:3). [2]Mk 3:31-35; Jn 7:3-10; cf. Jn 2:12. [3]Acts 1:14; 1 Cor 9:5; 15:7; Gal 1:19.

2. The expression does not necessarily designate brothers* according to the flesh, at least if one takes account of Oriental practices which extend this term to more distant relatives.[4] Greek usage is not sufficient to contradict this tradition of Palestinian origin. Finally, James and Joseph (Joses) seem to be sons of a Mary* distinct from the mother of Jesus.[5]

[4]Gn 29:12ff. [5]Mt 27:56 (= Mk 5:40); Jn 19:25.

bucket

→ pitcher.

build up Gk. *oikodomeō* (from *oikos:* "house" and *demō:* "to build"), often linked with its opposite *katalyō:* "to destroy, demolish."[1] Underlying the metaphorical usage was the fact that the same Heb. verb *bânâ* signified "to construct" a house or a family.[2] God was the builder above all others;[3] Christ was the architect of his Church,[4] of his body,[5] of the Holy City.[6] An apostle, and even every Christian, collaborated with the unique builder of God's building,[7] into which he himself was integrated.[8] One did not build oneself up,[9] but only built up the community,[10] and this not through knowledge but by love.[11]

[1]Jer 1:10; 24:6; 31:28; Mt 26:61 (= Mk 14:58); 27:40 (= Mk 15:29); Jn 2:20. [2]2 Sm 7:5,11. [3]Acts 20:32; Heb 11:10. [4]Mt 16:18. [5]Eph 2:20-22; 4:11-16. [6]Rv 21. [7]1 Cor 3:5-17; 2 Cor 10:8; 12:19; 13:10. [8]Col 2:7. [9]1 Cor 14:4f. [10]Rom 14:19; 15:2; 1 Cor 14:12,17,26; Eph 4:29; 1 Thes 5:11. [11]1 Cor 8:1; 10:23.

bury **1.** In the strict sense, to carry from one place to another, to gather up (Gk. *ek-komizō, syn-komizō*),[1] or to place in the tomb (Gk. *thaptō, entaphiazō*). An essential filial duty which, nevertheless, gave way to a call from Jesus.[2] The expression "to die and be buried" spoke of the seal burial placed on a death by preserving the memory of a deceased person[3] with a monument (Gk. *mnēma*).

[1]Lk 7:12; Acts 8:2 △. [2]Mt 8:21 (= Lk 9:59f.). [3]Gn 25:8f.; 35:8; 1 Kgs 2:10; Lk 16:22; Acts 2:29; 1 Cor 15:4.

2. According to some interpreters, Paul saw in baptism* by immersion an analogy with a burial to sin;[4] it remains difficult to substantiate this point.

[4]Rom 6:4; Col 2:12.

→ Intr. VIII.2.D.b.—coffin—mourning—tomb.

bushel Gk. *modios,* Lat. *modius.* A Roman measure of solid capacity, equalling about 8.75 liters (7.9 dry quarts). This receptacle could be used by the poor as a dish or as a holder in which to put food.[1]

[1]Mt 5:15; Mk 4:21 (= Lk 11:33) □.

→ measures.

buy back, ransom Gk. *agorazō (ex-agorazō)*[1] and *lytroō*.[2] The first term derived from the image of a purchase, the second from that of "deliverance." The verb *ex-agorazō* may also mean "to share partnership in,"[3] while the words from the root *lytron* are reserved for designating whatever pertains to "deliverance," the redemption of God's people by God and by Jesus Christ.

[1] 1 Cor 6:20; 7:23; Gal 3:13; 4:5; 2 Pt 2:1; Rv 5:9; 14:3f. △. [2] Mt 20:28 (= Mk 10:45); Lk 24:21; 1 Tim 2:6; Ti 2:14; 1 Pt 1:18. [3] Eph 5:16; Col 4:5 △.

→ liberate—ransom—redemption.

C

Caesar Gk. *Kaisar,* from the Lat. *Caesar.* The surname of the Julia family, made famous by Julius Caesar (100–44 B.C.). Along with "Augustus,"* the official title of the Roman Emperor.[1] The "friends of Caesar" were courtiers closely linked with his person.[2] In Phil 4:22 the "house of Caesar" designated personnel in the "emperor's service."

[1]Mt 22:17 (= Mk 12:14 = Lk 20:22); Lk 2:1; 3:1; Jn 19:15; Acts 25:21. [2]Jn 19:12.

→ emperor.

Caesarea Gk. *Kaisareia,* the name of cities so called to honor Caesar* Augustus.*

1. *Caesarea in Palestine.* A port of Palestine built in 12–9 B.C. by Herod* the Great thirty km. (nineteen mi.) south of Haifa. From the year 6, the residence of the Roman prefect/procurator* and his garrison.[1] Philip* (who had his home there[2]) and Peter went there on missions.[3] Paul went there on several occasions,[4] and lived there as a prisoner for two years.[5]

[1]Acts 10:1; 23:23,33; 25:1,6,13. [2]Acts 21:8. [3]Acts 8:40; 10:24; 11:11; 12:19. [4]Acts 9:30; 18:22; 21:8,16. [5]Acts 25:4 □.

→ Map 4.

2. *Caesarea Philippi.* A city situated at the foot of Mount Hermon, at the wellspring of the Jordan River. Rebuilt around 2–1 B.C. by Herod Philip II* on the remains of the Paneion (a grotto dedicated to the god Pan). Modern-day Banias.[1]

[1]Mt 16:13 (= Mk 8:27) □.

→ Map 4.

Caiaphas Gk. *Kaiaphas.* Bearing Joseph as his first name and being Annas'* son-in-law, he was High Priest* from 18 to 36. A Sadducee,* he willingly collaborated with Pilate.* He presided over the trials* of Jesus and the Apostles.[1]

[1]Mt 26:3,57; Lk 3:2; Jn 11:49; 18:13f.,24,28; Acts 4:6 □; cf. Mt 26:51 (= Mk 14:47 = Lk 22:50),58 (= Mk 14:53 = Lk 22:54), 62f. (= Mk 14:60f.), 65 (= Mk 14:63); Mk 14:66; Jn 11:51; 18:10,15,16,19,22,26; Acts 5:17.

Cain Gk. *Kain,* from the Heb. *qaîn:* "blacksmith [?]," the ancestor of the Kenites (?).[1] The firstborn son of Adam and Eve. Out of jealousy he killed Abel,* uncovering the hatred* that from the beginning lurked in the hearts of men;[2] he is a type of the wicked man, the one who hates his brother, the just one.[3]

[1]Nm 24:21f. [2]Gn 4:1-16; Heb 11:4. [3]1 Jn 3:12,15; Jude 11 □.

[calendar] 1. The manner of subdividing time varied with civilizations. Israel seems to have adopted first of all the lunar calendar of the nomad: a year with 354 days totaling twelve months* (alternatively having twenty-nine and thirty days), each month beginning at the time of the new moon.* In Jesus' time, the official calendar took cognizance of the solar calendar of the farmer: it ended up having 364 days in its year, a supplementary month being added every three years to the twelve lunar months, or, as a variation that began with Seleucus (fourth century B.C.), seven supplementary months were added every nineteen years. According to the solar calendar, feasts regularly fell on the same day of the week: Passover on a Wednesday, Pentecost on a Sunday.

2. According to a Babylonian practice, the civil year began with the first month of spring, called Nisan.* Nevertheless, from the beginning Israel had set the start of its year in September, at the end of agricultural work; a vestige of this custom may be seen in the ancient liturgical calendar which began with the feast of the September new moon "at the end of the year" (Ex 23:16), rather than with the feast of Passover (Lv 23:5).

3. Various eras were known in antiquity. The era of Olympiads began on July 1, 776 B.C. The Roman era began with the foundation of Rome *(a[b] U[rbe] c[ondita]: a. U.c.)* on January 1, 753 B.C. The Seleucid era began on October 1, 312 B.C. The Christian era had been set by an Armenian monk, Dennis the Little (in A.D. 526) on March 25, 754 *a. U.c.* In Jesus' time it was reckoned that the world had been created for some 5,000 or 4,000 years. The Julian calendar

YEARS: HOW TO COMPUTE THEM

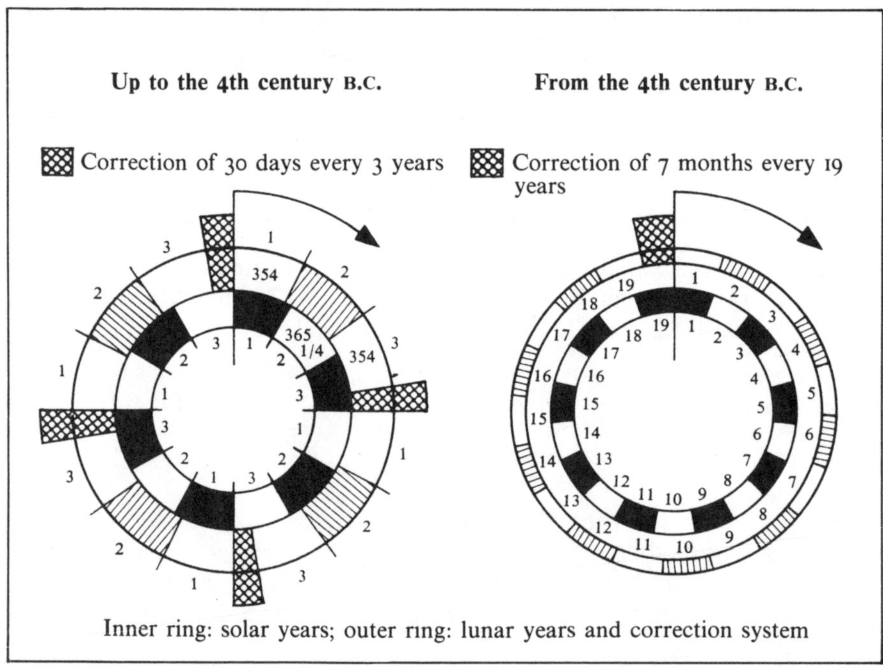

Inner ring: solar years; outer ring: lunar years and correction system

(named after Julius Caesar, who established it in 45 B.C.) determined the existence of leap years (the sixth day before March 1 was repeated every four years). The Gregorian calendar (named for Pope Gregory XIII, who established it in 1582), in order to bring the Julian calendar into harmony with the sun, suppressed ten days between October 4 and 15, 1582; at that time it was determined that the century years would not be leap years unless their dates were divisible by 400, so that up until 2099 the Julian calendar will remain thirteen days behind the Gregorian calendar. The modern Jewish calendar in effect today has the year 5,741 begin on September 11, 1980.

4. At Qumran* the calendar was a solar one (twelve months of thirty days, with an intercalary day every three months). The year always began on the same day of the week, normally a Wednesday, and Passover* did as well. According to this practice, the Last Supper could have been celebrated on a Tuesday and not on Thursday.

→ chronology—day—feast—month—week—year.

call

→ vocation.

camel

camel Gk. *kamēlos,* Heb. *gâmâl.* One of the most ancient saddle and draft animals known in the Near East; one of the signs of wealth among Bedouins.[1] One could use its hair to make clothing.*[2] Its great size was proverbial, either in itself[3] or in comparison with the tiny gnat.[4]

[1]Gn 12:16; 30:43; Jgs 6:5; Is 60:6. [2]Mt 3:4 (= Mk 1:6). [3]Mt 19:24 (= Mk 10:25 = Lk 18:25). [4]Mt 23:24 □.

Cana Gk. *Kana,* from the Heb. *qânè:* "reed." A village of Galilee,* located not at Kafar Kenna but at Hirbet Qana, some fourteen km. (nine mi.) northeast of Nazareth. According to John, it was there that Jesus changed water into wine.[1]

[1]Jn 2:1,11; 4:46; 21:2 □.

→ Map 4.

Canaan In the O.T. the expression "land of Canaan" designates a sufficiently indeterminate geographical entity: Palestine* properly speaking and also the Syrian* coast. It also referred to the land* promised to the Hebrews.[1]

[1]Gn 11:3; Ex 3:8; Is 19:18; 23:11.

Cananaean, Canaanite

1. Gk. *Kananaios,* Simon's surname. Although the Greek does no more than transcribe the Aramaic *qan'ânayâ,* this surname designated him as someone who was animated by "ardor." The parallel, Lk 6:15, writes "Simon called the Zealot."[1]

[1]Mt 10:4 (= Mk 3:18) □.

2. Gk. *Chananaios,* a resident of Canaan, a generic term for a Phoenician.[1]

[1]Mt 15:22; cf. Mk 7:26 □.

Candace Gk. *Kandakē.* A dynastic name, like Pharaoh, of the sovereigns of Meroe, the kingdom of southern Nubia or Ethiopia.[1]*

[1]Acts 8:27 □.

candelabra

→ lampstand.

[Canon of the Scriptures] Gk. *kanōn:* "rule," whence, "rule of faith." A list of biblical books officially recognized by the Jews and the Church as inspired* by God.

→ Intr. XII; XV.—Bible—deuterocanonical writings.

canticle

→ psalm—song.

Capernaum Gk. *Kapharnaoum,* Heb. *Kephar nâhûm:* "Nahum's village," four km. (2.5 mi.) to the west of the Jordan's* opening into the Lake of Gennesaret.* A frontier post on the state borders of the tetrarchs* Herod* and Philip,* the seat of a Roman garrison, but one not Hellenized as Magdala* or Tiberias* had been. Capernaum was "Jesus' city," the hometown of Peter and Andrew. Modern-day Tell Hum.[1]

[1]Mt 4:13; 8:5 (= Lk 7:1); 11:23 (= Lk 10:15); 17:24; Mk 1:21 (= Lk 4:31); 2:1; 9:33; Lk 4:23; Jn 2:12; 4:46; 6:17,24,59 □. Cf. Mt 9:1; Mk 1:33.

→ Map 4.

[capital punishment] Stoning* was the capital punishment in Israel. Decapitation[1] and crucifixion,* as well as being put to death by the sword,[2] call attention to Roman customs.

[1]Mt 14:10; Mk 6:16,27; Lk 9:9 △. [2]Acts 12:2.

→ Intr. VI.4.A.a and C.c.

Cappadocia Gk. *Kappadokia.* A region at the center of modern-day Turkey. A Roman province* since 17 B.C.[1]

[1]Acts 2:9; 1 Pt 1:1 □.

→ Map 3.

captive Gk. *aichmalōtos* (from *aichmē:* "point, spear, battle," and *haliskomai:* "to be taken"): "a prisoner of war, a captive." Used in a general sense of prisoners.*[1] As a recollection of the deportation* of the Jews to Babylon and their return,[2] man was said to be a captive of sin;[3] but Jesus came to deliver him and make him his own captive.[4] In addition, captivity was a terrible punishment which foretold the end* of time,[5] but one from which God delivered through Jesus Christ.[6]

[1]Rom 16:7; Col 4:10; Phlm 23. [2]Is 45:13; Jer 1:3; Ez 1:1f. [3]Rom 7:23; cf. 2 Tim 3:6. [4]Eph 4:8; cf. 2 Cor 10:5. [5]Jer 15:2; Lk 21:24. [6]Is 61:1; Lk 4:18.

→ deportation—exile—liberate—prison—slave.

care **1.** An ambiguous word that can mean either solicitude or disquiet; the two Greek words can have this same double meaning, *melo (ML)* points rather to a sense of occupation, concern, interest borne, whereas *merimnaō (MR)* looks more in the direction of the meanings of preoccupation and disquiet. The distinction was well illustrated in two cases, first that of Martha and Mary,[1] and then in God's care in the face of man's anxiety.[2]

[1]Comp. Lk 10:40 (*ML*) and 10:41 (*MR*). [2]1 Pt 5:7 (*MR* + *ML*).

2. The expression often came with a positive coloring when it concerned solicitude shown to men or for the Church:[3] more frequently, this time in negative fashion, in order to tell of those things which no one cared about.[4] Occasionally, the dividing line between the former meaning and the latter one floated somewhat.[5]

[3]Lk 10:34f.; 15:8; Acts 27:3; 1 Tim 3:5; 4:15 (*ML*); 1 Cor 12:25; 2 Cor 11:28; Phil 2:20 (*ML*). [4]Mt 22:5,16 (= Mk 12:14); Mk 4:38; Jn 10:13; 12:6; Acts 18:17; 1 Cor 9:9; 1 Tim 4:14; Heb 2:3; 8:9 (*ML*). [5]1 Cor 7:32-34 (*MR*).

3. Jesus condemned cares that made people anxious,[6] most especially cares of the world;[7] this was so that one might be able in faith to come to a state of authentic freedom.

[6]Mt 6:25-34 (= Lk 12:22-26); 10:19 (= Mk 13:11 = Lk 12:11) (*MR*); Lk 21:14 (*ML*). [7]Mt 13:22 (= Mk 4:19 = Lk 8:14) (*MR*). [8]1 Cor 7:21 (*ML*); Phil 4:6 (*MR*).

→ anguish—trust.

carpenter A word which improperly translates the Gk. *tektōn* (from which "architect" comes), because woodworkers were almost unknown in Palestine. In its broad sense, the Gk. referred to a worker or craftsman who worked on a pre-existing material, whether of wood, stone or even metal: a "tailor" of stone, a mason, a sculptor, etc.[1]

[1]Wis 13:11; Sir 38:27; Is 40:19f.; Jer 10:3; Mt 13:55; Mk 6:3 □.

catechesis, catechize Gk. *kat-ēcheō:* "to cause to be retained in the ears," to inform,[1] hence, "to instruct." The noun "catechesis" does not exist in the N.T. To catechize was to teach the essential facts of Jesus' life;[2] an instruction that probably was given as a follow-up to proclamation (Gk. *kēryssein*) of the Gospel,* either preparatory to baptism or immediately following it. In similar fashion to what happened among the Jews when they gave instructions on the Law,[3] the teaching of doctrine (Gk. *didachē*) on a more or less searching level[4] developed out of the catechetical context.

[1]Acts 21:21,24. [2]Lk 1:4; Acts 18:25. [3]1 Cor 14:19; Gal 6:6. [4]Mt 28:20; Acts 2:42.

→ preach—teach.

Catholic Epistles

→ Epistles (Catholic).

cenacle

→ upper room.

Cenchreae One of Corinth's* three ports, to the east of the isthmus, on the Saronic gulf. It allowed navigators coming from the Orient to clear Corinth without going around the southern part of Greece* with its dangerous coastlines. At Cenchreae, where Paul was in transit on his return from his second voyage, there was a church in which Phoebe was the deaconess.[1]

[1]Acts 18:18; Rom 16:1 □.

→ Map 2.

census Lat. *census,* Gk. *apographē.* The numbering of residents which permitted the levying of taxes.* The census of Quirinius* in A.D. 6–7 provoked the rebellion of Judas the Galilean against this expression of the provinces'* dependence on Rome.[1] Luke mentions the census which brought Joseph and Mary to Bethlehem in 7–6 B.C.;[2] he ascribed it to Quirinius perhaps because the operation in A.D. 6–7 was the only notorious one, perhaps also because Quirinius, who had been consul from 12 B.C., frequently received postings in the East and so could have been responsible for a census.

[1]Acts 5:37. [2]Lk 2:1-5 □.

→ Intr. VI.2.B.—Quirinius.

centurion Gk. *kentyriōn, hekatontarchēs:* "one who commanded a hundred." A subordinate Roman officer, taken from the ranks. He commanded a century of from sixty to one hundred men, but he could be detached for administrative or judiciary tasks, especially in the distant provinces* such as Judea.* More independent than the magistrates in regard to local conditions, he appears in the N.T. as an upright man: such a one was Cornelius.[1]*

[1]Mt 8:5,8,13 (= Lk 7:2,6); 27:54; Mk 15:39,44f.; Lk 23:47; Acts 10:1,22; 21:32; 22:25f.; 23:17,23; 24:23; 27:1,3,6,11,31,43 □.

Cephas Gk. *Kēphas,* from the Aram. *képhâ:* "rock," translated into Greek not as *petra* but as *Petros,* the surname given by Jesus to Simon* and generally used by Paul.[1]

[1]Jn 1:42; 1 Cor 1:12; 3:22; 9:5; 15:5; Gal 1:18; 2:9,11,14 □.

→ Peter.

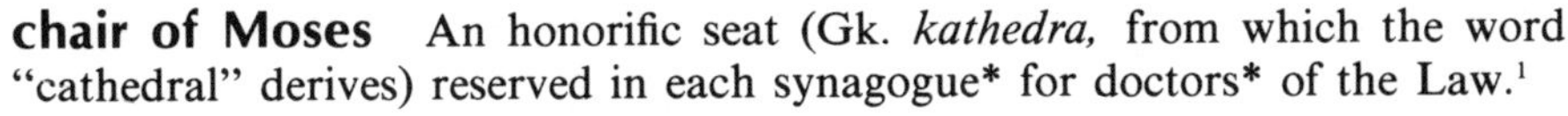

chair of Moses An honorific seat (Gk. *kathedra,* from which the word "cathedral" derives) reserved in each synagogue* for doctors* of the Law.[1]

[1]Mt 23:2 □.

[Chaldean] The language of the inhabitants of Babylon.* Because of Dn 2:4, the term referred, among the rabbis and in Christian writings, to biblical Aramaic.*

charism Gk. *charisma* (from *charizomai:* "to please" and *charis:* "grace, what one rejoices in").

1. The broad sense: the free gifts* given by God—generally a spiritual gift, the Holy Spirit, salvation in Jesus Christ, eternal life, the privileges of Israel, liberation from a danger.[1]

[1]Rom 1:11; 5:15f.; 6:23; 11:29; 2 Cor 1:11.

2. The technical sense: a free gift appropriated by one person or another, which allowed him to accomplish through the Spirit* activities suited to the community's good.[2] These charisms were ordered to the building up* of the Body of Christ*; although they had to be the object of a discernment of spirits,* they were desirable in the ministries of charity.*[3] It is difficult to establish a common list of the charisms.[4]

[2]Rom 12:6; 1 Cor 1:7; 7:7; 1 Tim 4:14; 2 Tim 1:6; 1 Pt 4:10. [3]1 Cor 12:4,9,28,30f. □. [4]Cf. Rom 12:6-8; 1 Cor 12:28-30; Eph 4:11.

→ gift.

charity Lat. *caritas* (derived from *carus:* "dear, of great price"), translating the Gk. *agapē:* "love," which can have God or one's neighbor as its object.[1]

[1]1 Cor 13.

→ almsgiving—love.

chastise, chastisement

→ punish, punishment.

Cherubim Gk. *cheroubin* (the plural of *cheroub*), from the Heb. *keruḇîm,* the plural of a word whose Akkadian* root *karâbu* meant "to bless" and which produced the participle *karibu:* a Mesopotamian deity of second rank. Mysterious heavenly beings represented under the form of winged lions with human faces; servants of Yahweh[1] and supporters of the divine majesty.[2]

[1]Gn 3:24; Ps 18:11; Ez 28:14; 41:18f. [2]Ex 25:18-22; 1 Sm 4:4; Ps 80:2; Heb 9:5 □.

→ angels—Living Ones.

[chiasm] Gk. *chiasma:* crossing. The distribution of words in a sentence or the arrangements of elements of a pericope* in such a way that they correspond two by two around a center that is not always explicit: A B C D ⊠ D[1] C[1] B[1]

A[1]. Example: "He who wishes to save his life [A], will *lose* it [B], He who *loses* his life for my sake [B[1]], will find it [A[1]]" (Mt 16:25).

chief priests Equivalent to high priests.*

child 1. The littlest one (Gk. *nēpios*), the youngest child, considered a weak and defenseless human being, not yet making use of reason, simple and without experience. A term associated with that of the nourishment of one who still drank milk,[1] it was opposed to the concepts of an adult,[2] a stable judgment,[3] and to educated people[4], to teachers[5] and the perfect.*[6] The Greek word *brephos* more precisely designated the child at its mother's breast,[7] the one just born[8] who fed on milk:[9] of such kind was the tender childhood[10] which Luke saw in the children brought to Jesus.[11]

[1]Mt 21:16f.; 1 Cor 3:1f.; Heb 5:12. [2]1 Cor 13:11; Gal 4:1,3. [3]Eph 4:14. [4]Mt 11:25f. (= Lk 10:21). [5]Rom 2:20. [6]1 Cor 3:1f.; Heb 5:12f. [7]Lk 1:41,44. [8]Lk 2:12,16; Acts 7:19. [9]1 Pt 2:2. [10]2 Tim 3:15. [11]Lk 18:15.

2. The little one (Gk. *pais* and its diminutive *paidion*) would be a young boy from seven to fourteen years of age,[12] one whom Jesus saw as a type of the true disciple,[13] probably in what he was, that is, a poor* person, fully dependent, and one who received everything as a gift and not as something due.[14] The disciple of Jesus, thus, had to return to the state of childhood.[15] A term which also signified a servant.*

[12]Lk 1:59; 2:43; 8:51,54; 11:7. [13]Mt 19:14; cf. 10:42; Mk 9:41. [14]Mk 10:15. [15]Mt 18:3; cf. Jn 3:5.

3. The child, in the sense of a boy or girl (Gk. *teknon,* derived from *tiktō:* "to beget"). He remained in an affective relationship with his parents,[16] who were to show him tenderness[17] and might expect obedience from him.[18] The word also denoted "descent"[19] and often carried along a metaphorical meaning, with notes of the affection linking two persons.[20] It was even a term used to speak of God's children, his "begotten ones."[21] Finally, it could bear the meaning of belonging to a group[22] or could indicate the presence of a quality.[23]

[16]Mt 7:11 (= Lk 11:13); 10:21 (= Mk 13:12); 18:25; 19:29; 21:28; 27:25; Lk 15:31; 23:28. [17]Eph 6:4; Col 3:21. [18]Eph 6:1; Col 3:20. [19]Mt 3:9 (= Lk 3:8); 23:37 (= Lk 13:34); Jn 8:39; Rom 9:7f.; Gal 4:31. [20]Mk 2:5; 10:24; Jn 13:33; Gal 4:19; 1 Jn 2:1,12,28; 3:7,18; 4:4; 5:21. [21]Jn 1:12; Rom 8:16f.,21; 1 Jn 3:1f. [22]2 Jn 1:4,13. [23]Eph 2:3; 5:8; 1 Pt 1:14; 2 Pt 2:14.

4. The son (Gk. *hyios*): this appellation linked up with the previous one on several scores. It also revealed the relationship which bound one to his parents,[24] to ancestors,[25] to a teacher.[26] By a Semitic turn of phrase, "son of" followed by a name, could also express a sense of belonging to a group (a companion, a follower of . . .)[27] or could designate a state or quality (violent, peaceful, belonging to a particular world . . .).[28] Occasionally this term (as was not the case with *teknon*) showed the distance towards parents which a disciple could and had to take when called by Jesus.[29] Finally, it characterized the freedom of those who had become sons of God[30] through adoption.*[31]

[24]Mt 20:20; Mk 10:45; Lk 1:13. [25]Mt 1:20; Lk 19:9. [26]1 Tim 1:2; 1 Pt 5:13. [27]Mt 8:12; 9:15; 12:27; 13:38; 17:25; 23:15; Acts 3:25; 23:6. [28]Mk 3:17 (cf. Lk 9:54); Lk 10:6; 16:8; 20:34,36; Jn 12:36; 17:12; Acts 4:36; 13:10; Eph 2:2; 5:6,8; 1 Thes 5:5; 2 Thes 2:3. [29]Mt 10:37; Lk 12:53. [30]Rom 8:14,19; Gal 3:25f.; 4:7. [31]Rom 8:15.

→ Intr. VIII.2.C.a-c.—adoption—father—son of God.

choose

→ election.

Chorazin Gk. *Chorazin.* A city situated in the mountains of Galilee,* about three km. (two mi.) to the northwest of Capernaum.[1]

[1]Mt 11:21 (= Lk 10:13) □.

→ Map 4.

Christ Gk. *Christos* (from *chriō:* "to anoint"), translating the Heb. *Mâshiah:* "anointed one." A surname given to Jesus: "the Christ." When the word was used by Paul without the article, it was the equivalent of a proper name.

→ anoint—Jesus Christ—Messiah.

Christian Gk. *christianos,* deriving from *christos:* a disciple or votary of the Christ,* as the Herodians* had been supporters of Herod. The name, quite rare in the N.T., was bestowed for the first time at Antioch*: it seemingly came about with Roman authorization,[1] for the Jews designated the sect members by the name of Nazarenes*[2] and the Christians called themselves brothers, disciples, believers.

[1]Acts 11:26; 26:28; 1 Pt 4:16 □. [2]Acts 24:5 △.

[chronology] From the Gk. *chronos:* "time, length of time" and *logos:* "science, speech": that science which seeks to fix the dates of historical happenings.

1. The N.T. frequently indicates relative chronologies: "the fifteenth year* of the reign of Tiberias";[1] "after forty years";[2] "for two years."[3] The establishment of an unknown date is dependent on a second date to which the event in question refers. In certain instances, for example "the third day,"* the writer did not wish to specify a date, but merely wished to indicate by this number* that the event was a crucial part of God's plan.[4]

[1]Lk 3:1. [2]Gal 2:1. [3]Acts 28:30. [4]Gn 22:4; 42:18; Ex 19:11,16; Mt 16:21; 17:23; 20:19; Lk 13:31-33.

2. An absolute chronology is very difficult to arrive at, but occasionally it can be tied to a year close by. The birth of Jesus is ordinarily tied to two facts: the death of Herod which took place in 4 B.C. and the census* of Quirinius which we can fix in 7 or 8 B.C., a date which would correspond with that of Jesus' birth. The beginning of the preaching of John the Baptist,* fixed in the fifteenth year* of Tiberias' rule, is dated either from August 19, A.D. 28 (by Roman reckoning) or from October 1, A.D. 27 (by Syrian reckoning); historians lean toward the latter. The date of Jesus' death is determined by the coincidence of 14–15 Nisan* with a Friday, something which occurred in the years 29, 30, 31, 33, 34. April 7, A.D. 30 and April 3, A.D. 33 have the largest number of proponents.

3. A Pauline chronology is determined by beginning with a definite date: Paul's stay in Corinth. Actually, Paul stopped there during the proconsulship of Gallio, the brother of Seneca, after which he sojourned there eighteen months (Acts 18:11): this is the relative chronology. We can also arrive at an absolute chronology, thanks to an inscription discovered at Delphi in 1905 which reproduced a letter of the Emperor Claudius when he had been "acclaimed" for the twenty-seventh time. Through another inscription found at Rome's Major Gate (the Aqua Claudia) which fixed the twenty-seventh acclamation prior to August 1, 52 and by means of a third inscription (found at Kys in Caria), which fixed the twenty-sixth acclamation during the twelfth year of Claudius' reign (between January 25, 52 and January 24, 53), we can date the twenty-sixth acclamation between January 25 and August 1, 52. Since, in virtue of a decision taken by Claudius in 42, the procurators took office at the new moon in the month of April, we reckon that Gallio was already in office at Corinth in April 52. If, moreover, Paul had been brought before the proconsul after having stayed eighteen months at Corinth, and since he had to embark in the summer before the bad weather came, Paul seemingly must have arrived at Corinth towards the end of 50 and left it in August-September 52.

Analogous reasoning allows us to assert that Paul left Caesarea for Rome during the winter of 59–60, at the beginning of the procuratorship of Festus. It is more difficult to date Paul's "conversion." According to Gal 1:18; 2:1, it went back 14 + 3 years before the Council of Jerusalem* (48/49); according to Jewish calculations (a year* begun equalled a whole year), the interval is brought back 12½ + 1½ = 14 years, which would lead us to the year 34/35. For other dates, consult the chart, p. 126. Remember, when consulting it, that all dates are approximate, by one year at least.

Church 1. Gk. *ekklēsia.* In profane Greek: "a political assembly of the people";[1] in biblical Greek, the word translated various Hebrew terms: *qâhâl* (from *qôl:* "voice"): "the (liturgical) gathering of Israel,"[2] or *'édâ* (from *yâ'ad:* "to determine," from which came *mô'éd:* "set time, feast"): "assembly." *Qâhâl* and *'édâ* are also translated by *synagōgē* (from *syn:* "together" and *agō:* "to push"): "the gathering,"[3] used in a special way at Qumran* to designate the eschatological community of the chosen ones. In Aramaic, one could say either *'dtâ* or *k^e^nichtâ,* or even *qehâlâ.*

[1]Acts 19:32,39f. [2]Dt 4:10; Jos 8:35; Neh 8:2. [3]Nm 16:3; Dt 5:22.

2. Why does the N.T. prefer *ekklēsia* to *synagōgē?* Our answer has several facets. *Ekklēsia* was chosen by the Septuagint* in numerous cases to render the Hebrew term *qâhâl,* probably because of the similarity of the sounds in the two words, perhaps also because of its etymology (from *ek-kaleō:* "to convoke"), to designate the "holy convocation" of the people of God.[4] On the other hand, Jews preferred *synagōgē* (letting *ekklēsia* fall into disuse), chiefly to describe the local

assemblies of the Diaspora.* From that time on, Christians distinguished themselves even more from Jews and were better able to point to the universalism implied by their "assembly."

[4]Ex 12:16; Lv 23:3; cf. 1 Cor 11:18.

3. It is not possible within the confines of a short note to detail the history of the word *ekklēsia.* However, the following are some salient features of it. From their beginnings, Christians were aware of belonging to an assembly called together by God in Christ Jesus. They spoke of it from the start by referring to "the Church which is at Jerusalem, at Antioch, at Ephesus, etc.;"[5] thereby they indicated the unique assembly "of God" located in one place or another. The plural "the churches" put the accent on the multiplicity of such locales, without thereby diminishing the conviction that it was the sole Church of God.[6] This was the way Paul expressed himself in his earliest letters.[7] With the epistles to the Colossians and the Ephesians, the Church took a particular shape as a reality in this world, but also one whose existence depended uniquely on God, who ceaselessly gave her life,[8] and whose function was that of proclaiming the reign and kingdom of God with which she was not strictly identified.[9]

[5]Acts 8:1; 13:1; 18:22; 20:17,28. [6]Acts 15:41; 16:5. [7]Rom 16:1; 1 Cor 16:1,19. [8]Eph 1:22; 3:10; 5:23-25,27,29,32; Col 1:18,24. [9]Mt 16:19; 18:18; 1 Cor 11:26; Eph 5:27; Rv 21:3,5.

4. The word *ekklēsia* is missing from the gospels, except for two passages in Matthew.[10] Thus we might ask whether the term itself was articulated by Jesus of Nazareth. The little flock gathered together by Jesus[11] was the origin of the Apostolic Church and, even if these two Matthean texts might belong to a later redaction, there is nothing therein which is against the notion that Jesus proclaimed the existence of a "Church," which we ought not to associate with the "holy remnant" of Qumran* but rather ought to take to mean the true Israel of God. Although attempts of specialists to find an Aramaic equivalent (Aram. *k*ᵉ*nichtâ*) on the lips of Jesus have not found assent among all scholars, Jesus did announce and found "his Church." This term may be rendered in English by "assembly" or "community," but this can be done only on the condition that we thereby understand a relationship with God[12] or Jesus Christ[13] to underlie this word, a fact which precludes its use to designate an ordinary social organization.

[10]Mt 16:18; 18:17. [11]Lk 12:32. [12]1 Cor 1:2; 11:16,22; 2 Cor 1:1; Gal 1:13; 1 Thes 2:14. [13]Rom 16:16; Gal 1:22.

→ Intr. I.3–5; IV.7; X.3; XII.2.A.—apostle—assembly—Body of Christ—Israel—ministry—people—reign—synagogue.

[Church Fathers] Christian authors from the first centuries, who, by the union of their holiness and their teaching, exercised a spiritual paternity in the Church. The Apostolic Fathers form a scarcely homogenous group of writers in the post-apostolic age, some of whose principal texts were some of the following: the *First Epistle of Clement of Rome* (96), the *Second Epistle of*

Clement (about 150), the seven *Letters of Ignatius of Antioch* (towards 115), the *Epistle of Barnabas* (either 95, or 115, or even 135), the *Shepherd of Hermas* (about 140), the *Letter of Polycarp* (end of the first century), the account of the *Martyrdom of Polycarp* (156?), the *Didache* (end of the first century), the writings of Papias (90–135), the *Apology of Quadratus* (120), the *Letter to Diognetus* (second century?).

Cilicia Gk. *Kilikia.* A coastal region of the southeastern part of modern-day Turkey, a Roman province* since 57 B.C., with Tarsus* as its principal city.[1]

[1]Acts 6:9; 15:23,41; 21:39; 22:3; 23:34; 27:5; Gal 1:21 □.

→ Map 3.

circumcision Gk. *peritomē* (from *temnō:* "to cut," *peri:* "all around").

1. Removal of the foreskin.* An ancient custom among the Egyptians, Edomites, Ammonites, Moabites and Israelites, but not among the Assyrians, Chaldeans, or Philistines. It symbolized membership in a community.

2. Among the Hebrews, a religious rite linked to Abraham,* the father of the people,[1] prescribed for the eighth day after birth[2] and holding priority over sabbath* observance.[3] A physical sign of the Covenant* with Yahweh, it symbolized integration into the Jewish religious life. Hence, the metaphor "circumcision of the heart" used to speak about fidelity to Yahweh.[4] The uncircumcized (Gk. *akrobystia*) was a synonym for a pagan, and the circumcized was a similar term for an Israelite.[5]

[1]Gn 17:8-14; Rom 4:10-12. [2]Lv 12:3; Lk 2:21; Acts 7:8; Phil 3:5. [3]Jn 7:22f. [4]Dt 10:16; Jer 9:25; Rom 2:29. [5]Rom 15:8; Gal 2:7f.; Eph 2:11; Col 4:11.

3. The primitive Church refused to impose Jewish circumcision on converted pagans.[6] Paul showed that faith* had rendered it useless, for only Christ saved.[7] True circumcision was interior, not one done by man's hand; it was identified with conversion* to Christ.[8]

[6]Acts 15:1-20. [7]Rom 3:30; 4:9; 1 Cor 7:19; Gal 5:2,6; 6:15. [8]Phil 3:3; Col 2:11.

→ Intr. IV.7.B; VI.4.C.b—baptism—faith—foreskin.

[citation] A passage of Scripture reported in a text with the aim of clarifying it: thus, Mt 1:22f. quotes the verse found at Is 7:14.

citizen Each Greek or Hellenized* city* (Gk. *polis*) had its own right to citizenship (Gk. *politeia*). The title of citizen (Gk. *politēs*) gave to its residents (for example, the Galatians) a superior status in relation to that of populations still unable to adapt themselves to an urban "civilization."[1] Roman citizenship (Gk. [*anthrōpos*] *Rōmaios*), above all in the east, was a supplementary promotion. Rare as it was, in principle it ratified a recognized attachment to the Roman cause.[2] Outside of Italy* it scarcely conferred any fiscal advantages, but it gave one the possibility of lodging an appeal from any tribunal* to the imperial tribunal.[3] The emperors jealously watched over this right, which made of every citizen a virtual obligee of theirs.[4]

[1]Acts 21:39. [2]Acts 22:28. [3]Acts 25:11,20f.,25; 26:32. [4]Acts 16:37f.; 22:25-29; 23:27.

→ Intr. IV.2.B.c; IV.4.—city.

city Lat. *civitas:* a coming together of men who enjoy the same rights and who participate to varying degrees in the administration of their common interests; the city is distinct from a "town," a term which designates an ensemble of inhabited houses. The Gk. *polis* corresponded to both meanings. That of "city" appeared to be the quite probable interpretation when one spoke of the "city of the nations,"[1] of the "heavenly city"[2] or, with the derivatives of the word, of "the rights of the city"[3] and of "citizenship."[4]

[1]Rv 16:19. [2]Heb 13:14. [3]Eph 2:12. [4]Phil 3:20.

→ Intr. IV.1.c.—citizen.

Claudius Gk. *Klaudios,* Lat. *Claudius.* Tiberius Claudius Nero (10 B.C. to A.D. 54), grandson of Augustus* and nephew of Tiberius*; the fourth Roman emperor from the year 41 on. During his reign there occurred a famine in 48 and, in 49–50, a decree by which Jews were expelled from Rome, facts which have been confirmed by the historians Dio Cassius, Tacitus and Suetonius.[1]

[1]Acts 11:28; 18:2 □.

clean

→ pure, impure.

Cleopas, Clopas **1.** Gk. *Kleopas* (a Gk. abbreviation of *Kleopatros*). One of the two disciples of Emmaus. Some identify him with Clopas.[1]

[1]Lk 24:18 □.

2. *Klōpas* (Semitic name: *qlôpha*). The husband (or father?) of Mary,* the mother of James the Little* and of Joseph* (or Joses). Improbably identified with Alphaeus.*[1]

[1]Jn 19:25 □.

cloak **1.** In its current sense, a translation of the Gk. *phailonēs,* Lat. *paenula,* a kind of hooded cape, a cape with a cowl, a jacket covering the bust.[1]

[1]2 Tim 4:13 □.

2. Often it translated the Gk. *himation,* Lat. *toga:* a rectangular piece of woolen or linen material, not sown, with an opening for the arms, that was thrown over the shoulders or wrapped abound the body;[1] it was taken off to keep oneself more alert[2] and could serve at night as a covering.[3] It did not designate a "coat" in the modern sense, but more generally the outer clothing,* in contrast with the tunic,* the undergarment.[4] It was a kind of vest strung over the shirt, indispensable for formality and manners. When used in the plural, the word should be translated by the generic term "clothing."[5]

[1]Acts 12:8. [2]Mt 24:18; Mk 10:50; Acts 7:58; 22:20. [3]Ex 22:25f.; Dt 24:12f.; Mt 5:40 (= Lk 6:29). [4]Mt 24:18 (= Mk 13:16); Lk 22:36; Acts 9:39. [5]Mt 17:2 (= Mk 9:3 = Lk 9:29); 21:7f. (= Mk 11:7f. = Lk 19:35f.); 26:65; 27:31 (= Mk 15:20 = Jn 19:2), 35 (= Mk 15:24 =

Lk 23:34); Mk 5:28,30; Lk 7:25; 24:4; Jn 13:4,12; 19:23f.; Acts 1:10; 7:58; 10:30; 14:14; 16:22; 18:6; 20:33; 22:20,23; Jas 5:2; 1 Pt 3:3; Rv 3:4f.,18; 4:4; 16:15.

→ clothing—dress—tunic.

cloth Gk. *sindōn.* Material woven of flax or wool and serviceable as clothing or as a veil.[1]

[1]Mk 14:51f. □.

→ shroud.

clothe, clothing Various Greek words correspond to these terms. The generic term is *en-dyō:* "to cause to enter into," hence *en-dyma:* "clothing"; *peri-ballō:* "to cast about, to envelop"; *amphi-azō:* "to put around (*amphi*)." Various garments are mentioned. Those which were undergarments were the tunic* and girdle.* Those which were outer garments, with their translations that are quite approximate, were: cloak* (coat), dress,* suit, military cloak,* belt* and shoes.*[1]

[1]Mt 6:30; 11:8 (= Lk 7:25) □.

1. Clothing was the primordial condition of existence.[2] God provided for it and freed one from disquiet about it.[3] There was an obligation to clothe the poor.[4]

[2]Sir 29:21; Rom 8:35; 1 Tim 6:8; 2 Tim 4:13; cf. Acts 20:33. [3]Mt 6:25,28f.; Lk 12:22,27. [4]Ez 18:7; Mt 25:36,38,43; Lk 3:11; Acts 9:36,39; Jas 2:15; cf. Mt 5:40.

2. As a constitutive element of social life, clothing signified the dignity of the person[5] and the distinctions between the sexes;[6] it was descriptive of some individuals: the prophet,[7] the king,[8] the High Priest,[9] the rich and the poor,[10] a wife,[11] the upright woman,[12] the man who was mocked.[13] Its manner varied according to circumstances: work,[14]* feast* day,[15] pomp,[16] mourning* and penance,*[17] finally, glory.*[18]

[5]Mt 27:28; Lk 8:27,35; Jn 21:7; Acts 10:30; 12:8; Rv 1:13. [6]Dt 22:5; 1 Cor 11:5-15. [7]Zec 13:4; Mt 3:4 (= Mk 1:6); 7:15; Rv 11:3; cf. Mt 11:8. [8]Acts 12:21; Rv 17:4; 18:16; cf. Mt 6:29 (= Lk 12:27). [9]Lv 21:10. [10]Lk 7:25; Jas 2:2f. [11]Rv 19:8. [12]1 Tim 2:9; 1 Pt 3:3. [13]Mt 27:28; Lk 23:11; Jn 19:2.[14]Mt 24:18; Lk 17:8. [15]Mt 22:11f.; Lk 15:22. [16]Mk 12:38. [17]Mt 11:21 (= Lk 10:13). [18]Mt 28:3.

3. Since clothing formed a unity with the person,[14] it expressed one's being by means of certain gestures and in certain metaphors.* Some symbolic actions were current in Israel: "to touch" the outfit of a messenger from God was to come into contact with his power;[20] "to tear" one's garments was to express one's sorrow or one's anger;[21] "to shake off" (the dust from) one's clothing was to break with persons one was leaving behind.[22] To take off one's clothes could be a miming of death.[23] Some expressions were metaphorical: "to wash" or "to soil" one's clothing was equivalent to purifying oneself or sinning;[24] "to gird up" (the loins) was to keep oneself ready;[25] "to keep" one's clothing was to keep vigilant.[26]

[19]Jude 23. [20]Mk 5:27-30 (= Lk 8:44; cf. Mt 9:20f.); 6:56; Acts 19:12; cf. 1 Kgs 19:19. [21]Mt 26:65; Acts 14:14. [22]Acts 18:6. [23]Jn 13:4. [24]Rv 3:4; 22:14. [25]Lk 12:35. [26]Rv 16:15.

4. Within the biblical perspective, clothing signified man's definitive integrity or the renewal of his being when reunited to God. The garments of skins with which God clothed the nakedness of the first parents, who had become ashamed of themselves, indicated the integrity that was hoped for.[27] Paul multiplied metaphors he had borrowed from the clothing imagery to describe a Christian's actual transformation,[28] one who by baptism had been clothed again with Christ himself,[24] as well as to speak of a reclothing of his body that was still to come.[30] Heavenly creatures had appeared in resplendent outfits;[31] and so had the transfigured Jesus.[32] White garments symbolized the newness of the being (or the state) of the elect.[33]

[27]Gn 3:21. [28]Rom 13:12; Eph 4:24; 6:11,14; Col 2:11; 3:9f.,12; 1 Thes 5:8; cf. Lk 24:49. [29]Rom 13:14; Gal 3:27. [30]1 Cor 15:53f.; 2 Cor 5:2-4. [31]Lk 24:4; Rv 15:6; 19:14. [32]Mt 17:2 (= Mk 9:3 = Lk 9:29). [33]Rv 3:5,18; 4:4; 6:11; 7:9,13.

→ Intr. VII.2; VIII.1.B.—combat—fabrics—linen—purple.

cloud

1. Gk. *nephelē,* in its proper sense: a cloud foretelling rain*[1] or bringing about a shadow.*[2]

[1]1 Kgs 18:44f.; Lk 12:54. [2]Is 25:5; Jude 12.

2. Similtaneously opaque and luminous, it revealed the God who was present without also unveiling his mystery.[3]

[3]Ex 13:21f.; 19:16-20; 1 Kgs 8:10-13; Mt 17:5 (= Mk 9:7 = Lk 9:34f.); 1 Cor 10:1f.

3. An element of the panoply of eschatological* theophanies*[4] which went along ("with" or "in")[5] it or which bore ("upon")[6] it.

[4]Acts 1:9; Rv 1:7; 10:1; 14:14. [5]Dn 7:13; Mk 13:26 (= Lk 21:27); 14:62; Rv 11:12. [6]Mt 24:30; 26:64; 1 Thes 4:17; Rv 14:14-16 □.

→ shadow.

Cnidus

Gk. *Knidos,* modern-day Cap Krio, between the isles of Cos and Rhodes, on the southwest coast of Asia Minor.[1] The vessel that transported Paul as a prisoner attempted, in vain, to shelter there.

[1]Acts 27:7 □.

→ Map 2.

coat

→ cloak.

cockcrow

Gk. *alektorophōnia,* from *alektōr:* "cock," and *phonē:* "voice.*" The end of the third watch* (three o'clock in the morning*).[1]

[1]Mk 13:35 □; cf. Mt 26:34 (= Mk 14:30 = Lk 22:34 = Jn 13:38); 26:74f. (= Mk 14:68,72 = Lk 22:60f. = Jn 18:27).

→ day—hour.

cockle

→ darnel.

coffin Gk. *soros.* Coffins discovered in Palestine were foreign in origin. The dead, wrapped in a shroud,* lay in state; they then were carried on a kind of bier or litter to tombs, in which they were laid to rest just as they were.[1]

[1] 2 Sm 3:31; Lk 7:14 □.

→ Intr. VIII.2.D.b.—bury.

cohort Gk. *speira,* Lat. *cohors.* Including from 600 to 1,000 men each and commanded by a tribune,* the cohort was the basic unit of the Roman legion* (ten cohorts per legion, six centuries per cohort). There were also auxiliary cohorts distributed in provinces* that were disturbed or of strategic importance; they were recruited outside of Italy* and only their cadres were Roman. One cohort permanently ensured the surveillance of Jerusalem. Another one accompanied the procurator* in his movements and protected his residence.[1]

[1] Mt 27:27 (= Mk 15:16); Jn 18:3,12; Acts 10:1; 21:31; 27:1 □.

[coins] **1.** Prior to the minting of coins, payments were made with set weights* of precious metals. This explains the fact that certain coins (the mina, the shekel, the talent) kept the names of the weight measurements. In principle, then, the talent* was the weight of metal which a man could carry; it was divisible into sixty minas* and the mina into sixty shekels. According to the Babylonian scale of weights, the talent weighed 30.3 kilograms (66.4 lb.).

2. Various kinds of coins (copper, silver and gold) were in circulation in Palestine in Jesus' time. The Greek monetary system, introduced into Israel during the Seleucid period and made general after Alexander the Great's conquest, coexisted there alongside the Roman monetary system, that of the occupying power. In addition, pilgrims, soldiers and merchants brought with them coins peculiar to one country or another. Whether there was a peculiarly Jewish coinage system remains a controverted question. To strike coins presupposed some state of independence, something which was scarcely the case in Israel's history after the monarchy, a time for which no coinage is attested. On the other hand, a Jewish shekel was known, one which may go back to the Persian domination or, as is more commonly supposed, to the Maccabean* era. For their part, the Hasmoneans and principally Herod the Great and his successors were able to mint copper coins, and the Roman procurators did as much. In both cases these coins were exclusively meant for local circulation. The N.T. does not designate by name an explicitly Jewish coin. The unspecific expression "piece of silver" has sometimes been translated by "shekel" (a term associated with Jewish coins) or, erroneously, by "denarius" (a Roman coin); uncertainty on the matter persists.

Greek and Roman coins are explicitly named in the N.T. For Greek coinage, the base unit was the silver drachma,* divided into six silver obols* and into forty-eight copper pieces. Two drachmas were equal to one didrachma*; four drachmas made one tetradrachma, sometimes called a stater.* There also existed a copper piece of infinitesimal worth, the lepton,* "mite," equal to one-seventh of a copper piece. Very large sums were reckoned in talents* and minas,* 6,000 and 100 drachmas respectively. Roman money had as its unit the silver denarius,* which was divided into four brass sesterces and sixteen copper as.* The as* was divisible further into four quadrants.*

3. Since the grades and weights of the different pieces when newly minted remain unknown, their respective values cannot be determined except in a relative way. A guess concerning their purchasing power would be even more conjectural. The figures given in the following table only furnish an order of the coins' sizes and a set of equivalences within a total system.

collection

1. Gk. *logeia* (from *legō:* "to gather together"): "a gathering" of wealth to come to the aid of the poor. The term, however, is scarcely at all used in the N.T.[1] Three other terms describe charitable activity, beginning with that union which bound brothers together in the faith: *diakonia:* "service,"[2] *koinōnia:* "[putting into] communion"[3] and *leitourgia* (from *leitourgeō:* "to officiate in worship"): "ministry."[4] Two other terms show charity's origin and its result: *karpos:* "fruit,"[5] *charis:* "free gift."[6] The theme of "eagerness" *(spoudē)*[7] was associated with them, just as Christ's example also was.[8]

[1]1 Cor 16:1f. △. [2]Acts 11:29; Rom 15:25,31; 2 Cor 8:4,19f.; 9:1,12f. [3]Rom 15:26; cf. Acts 2:44; 2 Cor 8:4. [4]2 Cor 9:12; cf. Rom 15:27. [5]Rom 15:28. [6]1 Cor 16:2f. [7]2 Cor 8:8,(17,)22; cf. Gal 2:10. [8]2 Cor 8:9.

2. The two collections mentioned (several times) in the N.T. were in favor of the Judeo-Christian* brethren: for those in Judea, at Antioch;[9] for those in Jerusalem, in Galatia, at Corinth, in Macedonia and Achaia.[10] Paul, who promoted the second one, attached a particular importance to it, seeing in this gift and its acceptance[11] a sign of the unity achieved between communities of pagan and Jewish origins. These collections may be set in relation to the Jewish custom of a religious tax* paid to the Temple of Jerusalem.

MONEY EQUIVALENCIES

SILVER	talent	1										
	mina	60	1									
	stater (shekel)	1,500	25	1								
	didrachma	3,000	50	2	1							
	drachma (denarius)	6,000	100	4	2	1						
COPPER	(sesterce)	24,000	400	16	8	4	1					
	(dipondius)	48,000	800	32	16	8	2	1				
	as	96,000	1,600	64	32	16	4	2	1			
	(semis)	192,000	3,200	128	64	32	8	4	2	1		
	quadrant	384,000	6,400	256	128	64	16	8	4	2	1	
	lepton	768,000	12,800	512	256	128	32	16	8	4	2	1

[9]Acts 11:28-30. [10]1 Cor 16:1-4; 2 Cor 8–9; cf. Rom 15:25-28. [11]Rom 15:31.

→ Intr. I.3.C; VII.4—alms—charity—communion.

collector of taxes

→ publican.

colony Gk. *kolōnia,* from the Lat. *colonia* (from *colere:* "to cultivate"). The term described certain towns where Roman soldiers had been settled and who consequently enjoyed the rights of Roman citizens.* One such was Philippi.[1]

[1]Acts 16:12 □.

→ Intr. IV.2.C.

Colossae Gk. *Kolossai.* A city of Phrygia,* in the Lycus Valley, which has vanished today. Epaphras* founded a church there.[1]

[1]Col 1:2 □.

→ Map 2.

[Colossians (Epistle to the)] Written by Paul, most probably during his captivity at Rome (61–63) or in an earlier one at Caesarea (58–60), to the Church of Colossae,* on the occasion of a doctrinal kind of crisis. According to some scholars, its authenticity* is doubtful.

→ Intr. XV.—Epistles.

combat 1. War (Gk. *polemos*), in the strict sense, is not mentioned in the N.T. except in apocalyptic* contexts, save in Lk 14:31 (and in Jas 4:1f.: fierce disputes among brothers). Military expeditions and campaigns (Gk. *strateia*) sometimes take on a metaphorical meaning: Paul considered himself as having companions in arms[1] and asked Timothy* to be a good soldier;[2] Christian life was a rugged battle,[3] one needed to be clothed with armor (Gk. *pan-oplia*) in order to resist the devil,*[4] who had been despoiled of his own weapons by Jesus, the Lamb of God.*[5] For this combat, weapons (Gk. *hopla*) were indispensable:[6] a breast-plate,[7] helmet,[8] shield[9] and sword.[10]

[1]Phil 2:25; Phlm 2. [2]2 Tim 2:3f.; cf. 1 Cor 9:7. [3]2 Cor 10:3f.; 1 Tim 1:18; Jas 4:1; 1 Pt 2:11; cf. Rom 7:23. [4]Eph 6:11,13. [5]Lk 11:22; Jn 1:29. [6]Rom 6:13; 13:12; 2 Cor 6:7; 10:4; 1 Pt 4:1. [7]Eph 6:14; 1 Thes 5:8. [8]Eph 6:17; 1 Thes 5:8 △. [9]Eph 6:16 △. [10]Eph 6:17.

2. The sporting games of the stadium[11] were an honor for ancient man, especially for the Greeks; the Olympic Games were every four years and the Isthmian Games at Corinth every two years. They included boxing (Gk. *pykteuō*),[12] wrestling (Gk. *palē*),[13] jumping, the discus, the javelin and, above all, the race, which varied from twelve to twenty-four stadia in its length.[14] Sporting combat (Gk. *agōn*) could describe the Christian's struggle to resist sin and to stand firm in the faith.[15] Exercises (Gk. *gymnazō*) such as these were recommended.[16]

[11]1 Cor 9:24. [12]1 Cor 9:26 △. [13]Eph 6:12 △. [14]1 Cor 9:24,26; cf. 2 Tim 4:7; Heb 12:1. [15]Lk 13:24; Rom 15:30; 1 Cor 9:25; Phil 1:30; Col 1:29; 2:1; 4:12; 1 Thes 2:2; 1 Tim 4:10; 6:12; 2 Tim 4:7; Heb 12:1,4; Jude 3 △. [16]1 Tim 4:7f.; Heb 5:14; 12:11 △.

→ athlete.

Comma (Johannine)

→ Johannine Comma.

commandment Gk. *entolē* (from *entellomai:* "to command, to prescribe"), Heb. *miṣwâh.*

1. This term referred to a specific precept of the Law (Gk. *nomos*) or Christian life.[1] Ordinarily it was used to stress the personal nature of the ordinance; this was not an article within a collection but rather was a challenge.[2] The word also allowed for the description of what was essential in the Law.[3]

[1]Mt 5:19; Mk 10:5; Lk 1:6; 23:56. [2]Mt 15:3 (= Mk 7:8f.); 19:17 (= Mk 10:19); 1 Cor 7:19; 14:37; Eph 2:15. [3]Mt 22:36,38,40 (= Mk 12:28,31 = Lk 18:20).

2. John, who restricted *nomos* to its meaning of Jewish law, kept the positive aspect of the Law. Through his use of *entolē* the love of the Father was expressed and revealed in the commandment; through it the believer entered into communion with the Father.[4] As the common tradition had already expressed it,[5] Jesus' unique commandment was love;[6] this love found its source in the mutual love of Father and Son, and its model was shown in the behavior of Jesus of Nazareth.[7]

[4]2 Jn 4–6. [5]Rom 13:9; Eph 6:2. [6]Jn 13:34; 14:15,21; 15:10,12,14,17; 1 Jn 2:3f.; 7f.; 3:23f.; 4:21; 5:2f.; cf. Rv 14:12. [7]Jn 10:17f.; 12:49f.; 14:31; 17:26.

→ Intr. XII.1.D.—law.

communion Gk. *koinōnia* (from *koinos:* "common," *koinoō:* "to put in common"): "the action of having in common, to share, to participate in" (Gk. *met-echō:* "to have with"), community, sympathy. Communion with the altar,* as well as with the body* and blood* of Christ, was something expressed by means of two sets of terms.[1] One set was participation in Christ,[2] in the Spirit,[3] in the divine nature, in the one same life of faith.[5] Another set was translated by fraternal union,[6] the placing of goods in common use,[7] the collection* on Jerusalem's behalf.[8]

[1]1 Cor 10:16f.,18,20f. [2]Phil 3:10; 1 Pt 4:13; Heb 3:14. [3]2 Cor 13:13; Phil 2:1; Heb 6:4. [4]2 Pt 1:4. [5]Ti 1:4; 1 Jn 1:3. [6]Acts 2:42; 2 Cor 1:7; Phil 4:14; 1 Jn 1:6f. [7]Acts 2:44; 4:32; Gal 6:6; 1 Tim 6:18; Heb 13:16. [8]cf. Rom 12:13; 2 Cor 8–9.

→ collection—cup—Lord's Supper.

[concordance] **1.** An alphabetical table furnishing all the words of a particular textual corpus so that they can be compared and grouped. Since the sixteenth century there have been concordances to the Bible in Hebrew, Greek, and Latin.

2. For translations of the Bible into modern languages such word concordances have to be fashioned according to a thematic arrangements because there are no official translations in these languages. The *Concordance to the New Testament,* published in 1970 by G. Bardy, O. Odelain, P. Sandevoir, and R. Séguineau, combined an index of 5,594 N.T. Greek words within 358 major themes from the families of French words; one single French word could in fact correspond to several Greek words.

3. A *Concordance to the Synoptic Gospels* was published in 1956 by X. Léon-Dufour. By using seven colors, it presented a concordance not of words but of synoptic* pericopes,* a feature which allowed each gospel passage to be taken in at a single glance within its very own status (its relationship to the rest of the gospel in which it was included) as well in its synoptic status (its relationship with the two other gospels).

4. Concordances should not be confused with "gospel harmonies," an ancient term used to indicate gospel synopses* so constructed as to make apparent that the gospels agreed among themselves. Nor ought a concordance be confused with "concordism," a theory of interpretation which strove to make biblical texts be in harmony, cost what it might, either among themselves or with secular disciplines; they were led to this by failing to recognize those viewpoints that were peculiar to the Bible or even to understand the literary genres* that were typical of the Bible's texts.

condemn This word properly translates several Greek terms which have no Hebraic equivalents: *katakrinō,*[1] *kataginōskō,*[2] *dikazō*[3] and the adjective *epithanatios:* "condemned to death."[4] In other cases, the verb "to condemn" is in its context an interpretation of the verb *krinō:* "to judge,"[5] a fact which often makes one hesitant in translating it.[6]

[1]Mt 12:41f.; 20:18; 27:3; Mk 10:33; 14:64; 16:16; Lk 11:31f.; Jn 8:10f; Acts 16:37; 22,25; Rom 2:1; 5:16,18; 8:1,3,34; 14:22f.; 1 Cor 11:32; 2 Cor 3:9; 7:3; Ti 3:11; Heb 11:7; 2 Pt 2:6 △. [2]Gal 2:11; Ti 2:8; 1 Jn 3:20f. △. [3]Mt 12:7,37; Lk 6:37; Acts 25:15; Jas 5:6 △. [4]1 Cor 4:9 △. [5]Mt 23:33; Mk 12:40; Lk 20:47; 23:40; 24:30; Jn 5:29; Acts 13:27; Rom 3:8; 13:2; 1 Cor 11:29,34; Gal 5:10; 1 Tim 3:6; 5:12; 2 Pt 2:3. [6]Jn 3:17-19; 12:47f.; Rom 2:1,3; 14:3f.,10,13a; Col 2:16; Jas 4:11f.

→ judgment.

condition A possible translation of the Gk. *morphē:* form.*

confess, confession of faith Gk. *homologeō:* "to speak *(legō)* similarly, or in agreement with[1] *(homos),"* to be suitable to, to commit oneself to,[2] to recognize,[3] to proclaim openly.[4] A term from secular juridical language. With the meaning of attestation through affirmation and negation, the word reinforced a public declaration.[5] Following the Septuagint* (which added on the prefix *ek*), the term was the equivalent of praising God (Heb. *yâda'*).[6] Applying its secular use to the religious sphere, it signified "to publicly proclaim" one's faith,[7] whence those "confessions of faith" which scholars have recognized as underlying the actual N.T. texts.[8] Finally, to confess one's sins was not only to admit the wrongs one had done against God, but also to declare his divine holiness:[9] thus, Peter's action when face to face with Jesus.[10]

[1]Lk 22:6. [2]Mt 14:7. [3]Heb 11:13. [4]Acts 7:17; 24:14. [5]Mt 7:23; 10:32 (= Lk 12:8); Jn 1:20; Rv 3:5. [6]Mt 11:25 (= Lk 10:21); Lk 2:38; Rom 14:11; 15:9; Heb 13:15. [7]Mt 10:32; Jn 9:22; 12:42; Acts 23:8; Rom 10:9f.; 2 Cor 9:13; Phil 2:11; 1 Tim 3:16; 6:12f.; Ti 1:16; Heb 3:1; 4:14; 10:23; 1 Jn 2:23; 4:2f.,15; 2 Jn 7. [8]Rom 1:3f.; 10:9; 1 Cor 12:3; 15:3-5; 1 Thes 1:10; 1 Tim 6:12. [9]Mt 3:6 (= Mk 1:5); Acts 19:18; Jas 5:16; 1 Jn 1:9. [10]Lk 5:8.

→ lips—witness.

confidence This word translates two Greek terms with different meanings, which were occasionally brought together.[1] *Parrēsia* (from *pan:* "all" and *rhēma:* "word"): "the ability to speak everything," whence "openness, candor, courage, assurance," describing a noble attitude which originates in an awareness of election*[2] and which was characteristic of a Christian's conduct as, formerly, it had characterized Jesus' conduct;[3] it manifested itself in an upright bearing, the head held high, and, especially, in clear speech and confident behavior.[4] *Kauchēsis,* which may also refer to boasting,[5] should not be translated uniformly as "pride": essentially it means self-confidence, trust, or glorying in someone or something in order to exist faced with one's self, others, God himself.[6]

[1]Heb 3:6. [2]Lv 26:13. [3]Mk 8:32; Jn 7:26; 10:24; 11:14; 16:25,29; 18:20; Acts 2:29; 4:13,29,31; 9:27f.; 13:46; 18:26; 19:8; 28:31; Eph 6:19f.; 1 Thes 2:2; cf. 2 Cor 4:13. [4]Acts 14:3; 2 Cor 3:12; 7:14; Eph 3:12; Phil 1:20; 1 Tim 3:13; Phlm 8; Heb 4:16; 10:19-35; 1 Jn 2:28; 3:21; 4:17; 5:14. [5]Rom 3:27; 4:2; 11:18; 1 Cor 1:29; 3:21; 5:6; 2 Cor 12:1; Gal 6:13; Jas 4:16. [6]Rom 2:17,23; 5:2,3,11; 15:17; 1 Cor 9:15,16; 15:31; 2 Cor 1:12-14; 5:12; 7:4,14; 8:24; 9:2,3; 12:1-9; Gal 6:4-14; Phil 1:26; 2:16; 3:3; 1 Thes 2:19; 2 Thes 1:4; Jas 1:9.

→ glory—liberty—pride—trust.

consecrate In the O.T., the term *hagiazō* does not signify "to consecrate" in the sense of "to make sacred," except when it describes cultic* acts performed by men;[1] when God is the subject of the verb it means "to elect,"* "to assign a mission to."[2] In the N.T. this Greek word should never be translated by "consecrate" since this term is no longer adequate to describe Christian cultic activity. In particular, we note that Jesus asked the Father to "sanctify" his disciples, just as he had "sanctified" himself.[3] In a word, Christians are not "consecrated," but "saints."

[1]Ex 29:37. [2]Sir 45:4; Jer 1:5. [3]Jn 10:36; 17:17,19.

→ holy—pure—Nazirite—sacred—sacrifice—worship.

conscience Gk. *syneidēsis* (without a corresponding Heb. term). A power of practical judgment by which one declares that this is (or was) for oneself either good or bad. For example, Job could say that his heart reproached him about nothing.[1] The Greek word borrowed by Paul from the religious language of his era expressed that reflexive judgment demanded by a biblical notion of the heart.* In speaking of the "law written on the hearts of pagans," Paul described that consciousness which they had when performing by nature what the Law* ordained;[2] God's plan was written in the heart of everyone, even before revelation definitively gave it a precise form: man was born into a dialogue with God[3] and in his activity he reacted more or less in accord with God's plan.

Conscience was not autonomous (based on human knowledge of what was good and evil) but "theonomous": man's judgment was always subject to God's.[4] Only faith enlightened a conscience,[5] which could then reckon itself good and irreproachable.[6]

A good conscience made one free,[7] but freedom itself was conditioned by the exigencies of the consciences of others[8] and by God himself.[9] The word is used in a sacrificial context by the Epistle to the Hebrews.[10]

[1]Jb 27:6. [2]Rom 2:14f. [3]cf. Rom 1:19-21. [4]1 Cor 4:4; 2 Cor 4:2; 5:11. [5]Rom 13:4f.; 1 Tim 1:5,19; 3:9; 4:1f.; 2 Tim 1:3; Ti 1:15. [6]Acts 23:1; 24:16; Rom 9:1; 2 Cor 1:12; Heb 10:22; 13:18; 1 Pt 3:16,21. [7]1 Cor 10:29. [8]Rom 14:15-20; 1 Cor 8:7-13; 10:23-29. [9]1 Cor 6:12; 1 Pt 2:19. [10]Heb 9:9,14; 10:2 □.

→ heart.

[controversy] A literary genre* in which a searching discussion on an open question was recounted: thus, Mt 22:15–22.

conversion Lat. *conversio:* a "turning back." The Gk. *epi-strephō:* "to re-turn,[1] to come back," and the Gk. *meta-noia:* "change *(meta)* of mentality *(nous),*"[2] both correspond, in the N.T., to the Heb. *shûb,* which characterized prophetic proclamation.[3] The English terms "turning back" and "conversion" are preferred to the term "penance" which chiefly suggests a penalty suffered for a fault to be "repented of" (Gk. *meta-meleisthai*), an idea which is inadequate for expressing the radical transformation of one's being and the fruits of conversion.

[1]Mt 12:44; 24:18; Lk 2:39. [2]Heb 12:17. [3]Jer 18:8; 24:7; Ez 33:9,11; Am 4:6-12. [4]Mt 3:8 (= Lk 3:8) Acts 26:20; Eph 4:23.

1. Following the prophets, John the Baptist* required of everyone who had himself baptized, that he re-turn in the direction of the imminent reign* of God,[5] while Jesus, in his turn, proclaimed the same demand in the face of the God who was presently at work in him:[6] he possessed the power to forgive sins[7] and reminded people that God rejoiced at every conversion.[8] After he had risen, he entrusted to his disciples the mission of proclaiming conversion.[9]

[5]Mt 3:2 (= Mk 1:4 = Lk 3:3),11; Acts 13:24. [6]Mt 4:17; 11:20f. (= Lk 10:13); 12:41 (= Lk 11:32); Lk 5:32. [7]Mt 9:6 (= Mk 2:10 = Lk 5:24). [8]Lk 15:4-32; Rom 2:4; 11:22; 2 Tim 2:25; Rv 2:5,16,21; 3:3,19. [9]Lk 24:47.

2. The primitive community likewise called for a turning aside from idols*[10] in order to cling to God and to Christ[11] through baptism and the remission of sins.[13] This definitive act could not be renewed[14] and, yet, everyone was constantly being called to conversion, Peter first of all.[15] The term conversion can be transposed, for example, into a return to the state of children[16] or, in John's gospel by such an expression as "to go to, to follow, Jesus."[17]

[10]Acts 14:15; 1 Thes 1:9. [11]Acts 9:35; 11:21. [12]Acts 2:38; cf. Rom 6:4; Eph 5:26; Ti 3:5. [13]Acts 3:19; 5:31. [14]Heb 6:6. [15]Lk 22:32; 2 Pt 3:9. [16]Mt 18:3. [17]Jn 1:43; 8:12; 10:27; 13:36.

→ Intr. XIV.2.B.—baptism—hardening—pardon—penance—repentance.

copper

→ bronze.

corban

→ korban.

Corinth Gk. *Korinthos.* The ancient Greek city on the isthmus of the same name, razed in 146 B.C., but rebuilt in 44 B.C. by Julius Caesar; the capital of the province* of Achaia* and a Roman municipality. By reason of its two other ports (one of which was Cenchreae*) which gave out onto two seas, Corinth was a hub of communications between East and West and a great economic center. Its social contrasts were marked (two-thirds of its population were slaves*) and its morals were so dissolute that the verb *korinthiazesthai* (to act like a Corinthian) meant "to live a life of debauchery." Cosmopolitan city that it was, the attachment to Hellenism* was less dominant a factor there than elsewhere; it was located at a crossroads of Greek and Oriental religions; worship of Aphrodite flourished there. Paul sojourned there for some eighteen months around 50–52.[1]

[1]Acts 18:1,8,10,27; 19:1; 1 Cor 1:2; 2 Cor 1:1,23; 6:11; 2 Tim 4:20 □.

→ Intr. IV.2.C; IV.6.—Achaia—Apollos—Cenchreae—Map 2.

[Corinthians (Epistles to the)] In the first letter (which, in fact, was the second: cf. 1 Cor 5:9), Paul wrote from Ephesus,* around 56, to the community of Corinth where the insertion of the Christian faith into a pagan culture had stirred up numerous problems. The second letter (which, in fact was the fourth: cf. 2 Cor 2:3; 7:8), was written from Macedonia,* around 57, to the same recipients whom Paul, after suffering violent blows, counted on returning to visit.

→ Intr. XV.

Cornelius A centurion* of the cohort* garrisoned at Caesarea.* He was the first pagan God-fearer* to convert.[1]

[1]Acts 10:1-31 □.

[Council of Jerusalem] A frequently used name for the gathering which took place in 48/49 at Jerusalem and which was described by Luke in Acts 15. In fact, the narrative of Acts 15 seems to have combined two events originally independent. James seems to be informing Paul in Acts 21:25 about the terms of a decree decided upon sometime earlier and about which mention had never been made in letters he would have received. Also, many scholars think that there were two gatherings in Jerusalem. One was concerned with the requirement of the Jewish law for those converts who were of pagan origin (Gal 2:1–10; cf. Acts 15:1–4); the other, later than the incident that took place at Antioch,* specified in a decree what were to be the relationships between Christians of Jewish background and those who were of pagan background (Gal 2:11–14; Acts 15:29).

court (outer)

→ outer court.

covenant Gk. *diathēkē* (from *dia-tithemai:* "to dispose of") a juridical act by which someone disposed of his goods. This Greek term renders in a better fashion than *syn-thēkē:* "bilateral treaty," the special sense of the Hebrew *berît,* which in the O.T. generally described a covenant between two unequal parties, which was typical of the vassal treaties. In a vassal treaty the more powerful partner promised to protect the weaker one, on condition that this latter undertook to serve the former[1] under Yahweh's watchful gaze.[2] Thus, an oath created solidarity between the partners: God would be faithful to his promises; the people undertook to observe the stipulations. On such observance depended either a blessing* or curse,* the concluding aspects of the covenant.[3] However, in all of this the notion of contract never predominated over the aspects of gift* or promise.*[4]

[1]2 Sm 3:12. [2]1 Sm 20:8; 23:18. [3]Ex 19:5,8. [4]Gal 3:15; Heb 9:16f.

1. The Covenant God made with Abraham,[5] his people Israel,[6] and David[7] was irrevocable and eternal,[8] for God's fidelity* could not depend on the unfaithful deeds of men.[9] In Paul's eyes, this then raised the scandalous question of Israel's unbelief* when faced with Jesus Christ.[10] These "convenants" had been expressed in various terms, but all were linked by the initiative which Yahweh had taken one day: circumcision* and the Law* were but stipulations added later.[12] One had to ceaselessly remind oneself of God's activity.[13]

[5]Gn 15:18; 17:2-11; Lk 1:72f.; Acts 7:8; Gal 3:15-18; cf. Heb 6:13. [6]Ps 105:10; Acts 3:25; Rom 11:27; Heb 8:10; 10:16. [7]2 Sm 7:5-16; Ps 89:4f.; Is 55:3; Acts 13:34. [8]2 Sm 23:5; Is 55:3; Ez 37:26; Heb 13:20. [9]Dt 7:9; Jer 31:35-37; 2 Tim 2:13; Heb 10:23. [10]Rom 3:3; 11:27. [11]Rom 9:4; Eph 2:12. [12]Dt 5:15; 8:2. [13]Lk 1:72; 22:19; 1 Cor 11:24f.

2. The Covenant with the people had been sealed in the blood* of the cultic sacrifice* offered by Moses.[14] It was this Covenant that Jesus alluded to when he spoke of his "blood of the Covenant."[15] It was that one which the Epistle to the Hebrews* described in order to emphasize that it had been betrayed by Israel[16] and that Jesus thus had contracted a "better,"[17] a "new"[18] Covenant; it was not Moses but the Christ who alone was mediator* of this Covenant.[19] Unlike the O.T. in which the cultic meal followed upon the Covenant, in the N.T. the eucharistic institution precedes the sacrifice of the cross, one in which the Covenant which established the Church is consumed.[20]

[14]Ex 24:8; Zec 9:11. [15]Mt 26:28 (= Mk 14:24). [16]Heb 8:9; 9,15. [17]Heb 7:22; 8:6. [18]Jer 31:31; Heb 8:8; 9:15; 12:24. [19]Heb 7:22; 8:6; 9:15; 12:24; 13:20. [20]Ex 24:11; Lk 22:20; 1 Cor 11:25.

3. According to another line of the tradition, the Covenant, which had been expressed by circumcision and the Law and had been misunderstood by Israel, would one day have to be written on the heart.*[21] Paul recognized this new covenant in the gift of the Holy Spirit.[22] He vigorously set the two covenants in opposition to each other; one had led to the slavery* of the Law and the other one was that of the liberty* of the children of God.[23]

[21]Jer 31:33; 2 Cor 3:3,6. [22]Ez 36:27; 2 Cor 3:6; Eph 1:13; 2:18; 1 Thes 4:8. [23]Gal 4:22-31.

4. Again, according to another, more personalist line of tradition, "the covenant in my blood" was the one in which Jesus—according to Luke and Paul—foretold his sacrifice and fulfilled the covenant sealed by the Servant of Yahweh*[24].

[24]Is 49:8; 53:12; Lk 22:20; 1 Cor 11:25.

5. Equivalences to and transpositions of the covenant were numerous. Promise,*[25] reconciliation* of the people with its God,[26] God's dwelling among men,[27] communion* with the Father,[28] God's kingdom,*[29] all of these corresponded to the traditional covenant formula: "You will be my people and I will be your God."[30]

[25]Acts 13:23; Gal 3:16,18; Eph 2:12. [26]Rv 21:3. [27]2 Cor 6:16. [28]Jn 20:17. [29]Lk 22:29. [30]Ex 29:45; Lv 26:11; Ez 37:27; 2 Cor 6:16; Rv 21:3.

→ Intr. X.1–2—law—promise—testament.

covetousness Gk. *epithymia.* All the while preserving the at times neutral meaning of "to desire strongly,*" the N.T., nonetheless, regularly confers on this term a pejorative moral sense: that of "excessive desire." Jewish tradition was familiar with the "evil inclination," "the spirit of perversion" which was at the heart of man. Of such a kind was that original covetousness[1] which entailed as well the passions in general[2] (another word for passion was *pathos*[3]), particularly in the sexual order.[4] Covetousness was mostly bound up with the flesh,*[5] with sin[6] and the world,[7] once with Satan[8] and once also with wealth[9] (in this last instance the N.T. prefers to use the word *pleonexia:* "greed"*).

[1]Rom 7:7; 13:9; cf. Ex 20:17; Jas 4:2; 1 Jn 2:16f. [2]Mk 4:19; Rom 1:24; 1 Cor 10:6; Col 3:5; 1 Thes 4:5; 1 Tim 6:9; 2 Tim 2:22; 3:6; 4:3; Ti 3:3; 1 Pt 1:14; 2 Pt 3:3; Jude 16,18. [3]Rom 1:26; 7:5; Gal 5:24; Col 3:5; 1 Thes 4:5. [4]Mt 5:28. [5]Rom 13:14; Gal 5:16,24; Eph 2:3; 1 Pt 2:11; 4:2f.; 2 Pt 2:10,18. [6]Rom 6:12; 7,8; Jas 1:14f. [7]Ti 2:12; 2 Pt 1:4; 1 Jn 2:16f. [8]Jn 8:44. [9]Acts 20:33.

→ Intr. XIV.2.A.—desire—greed—vices.

creation Gk. *ktisis* (from *ktizō:* "to found, to establish, to build, to create") Heb. *bârâ.*

1. In the beginning God founded (Gk. *katabolē:* "foundation"; from *ballō:* "to cast" and *kata:* "towards below") the world, a world which he pre-existed,[1] with a view to his interventions in the history of men.[2] Like a potter,* he "modeled, fashioned" (Gk. *plassō*)[3] Adam and Eve; he "made, fashioned" (Gk.

poieō)[4] them as he had the universe.[5] The creator (Gk. *ktistēs*)[6] was the one "having created" (Gk. *ktisas*),[7] who had organized everything by his word,*[8] calling into existence what was not.[9] The creator God did not limit himself to this original act,[10] but ceaselessly kept his creatures alive[11] and guided them towards himself,[12] giving them meaning and goodness[13] and thereby securing their trust.[14]

[1]Jn 17:24; Eph 1:4; 1 Pt 1:20. [2]Mt 13:35; 25:34; Lk 11:50; Heb 4:3; 9:26; Rv 13:8; 17:8 △. [3]Gn 2; Rom 9:20; 1 Tim 2:13 △. [4]Mt 19:4 (= Mk 10:6). [5]Acts 4:24; 7:50; 14:15; 17:24; Rom 1:20; 9:20f.; Heb 12:27; Rv 14:7. [6]1 Pt 4:19 △. [7]Mt 19:4; Rom 1:25; Eph 3:9; Col 3:10. [8]Heb 11:3. [9]2 Mc 7:28; Rom 4:17. [10]Mk 10:6; 13:19; 1 Cor 11:9; Heb 9:11; 2 Pt 3:4; Rv 4:11; 10:6. [11]Acts 17:28; 1 Tim 6:13; Heb 1:3. [12]Rom 11:36; 1 Cor 8:6; Heb 2:10; 4:13. [13]Rom 1:20,25f.; Eph 4:24; 1 Tim 4:3f. [14]Acts 4:24; Rom 8:39.

2. What was new in the N.T. is, first of all, that Jesus himself, having been intimately associated with God the Father, is himself the creator, model and goal of all things.[15] Moreover, in Christ a new creation had been inaugurated.[16] Hence, a parallelism in the following instances: Jesus is the new Adam,*[17] the head of a redeemed humanity.[18] All men were "created in Christ Jesus with a view to good works."[19] In addition, the whole universe,* whose sinful structure* was ceaselessly dissolving[20] but to whom Good News was being proclaimed,[21] would have access in him to the glorious liberty* of the children of God[22] and all would be made new.[23]

[15]Jn 1:1f., 14; 1 Cor 8:6; Col 1:16f.; Heb 1:2f.; Rv 3:4. [16]2 Cor 5:17; Gal 6:15; Col 3:10. [17]Rom 5:12,18; 1 Cor 15:21,45. [18]Eph 1:22f.; 2:15; Col 1:18. [19]Eph 2:10; cf. Jn 1:12; Rom 8:14-17; Gal 3:26-28. [20]1 Cor 7:31. [21]Mk 16:15; Col 1:23. [22]Rom 8:18-22; Jas 1:18. [23]Rv 21:1-5.

→ universe—world.

Cretans, Crete

1. Gk. *Krētē.* An island in the Mediterranean, whose Minoan civilization went back to the third millenium. It was attached in 27 B.C. to the Roman senatorial province* of Cyrene.* Jews were poorly regarded there.[1]

[1]Acts 27:7,12f.,21; Ti 1:5 □.

→ Map 3

2. Gk. *Krēs.* There were Cretans in Jerusalem for Pentecost. In its account the N.T. mentions a scarcely flattering citation of the Cretan poet Epimenides of Cnossos (the sixth century B.C.) which had been handed on by Callimachus.[1]

[1]Acts 2:11; Ti 1:12f. □.

crib

→ manger.

cripple

Gk. *chōlos.* An infirmity as common in Palestine as blindness. One such was, according to the Law, unsuited to the priesthood,[1] but he was at the same time the object of solicitude by God,[2] Jesus[3] and the Apostles.[4]

[1]Lv 21:18. [2]Is 35:6; Mt 11:5 (= Lk 7:22). [3]Mt 15:30f.; 18:8 (= Mk 9:45); 21:14; Lk 14:13,21. [4]Acts 3:2; 8:7; 14:8; cf. Jn 5:3; Heb 12:13 □.

criticism

→ historical criticism—literary criticism—textual criticism.

crown Gk. *stephanos.* In the beginning, a band to hold back one's hair, then an emblem to signify the dignity of a person or an object; afterwards, to express the joy of a feast, it was transformed into a garland.[1]

[1]Is 3:20; 61:10; Ez 24:17; Acts 14:13.

1. In ancient Israel it signified the consecration to Yahweh of the entire person of the king*[2] or the High Priest.*[3] Metaphorically, it spoke of moral glory.[4]

[2]2 Kgs 11:12; Ps 21:4. [3]Ex 29:6; 39:30; Lv 8:9. [4]Prv 12:4.

2. In the N.T., the promised reward,[5] incorruptible as gold.*[6]

[5]1 Cor 9:25; Phil 4:1; 1 Thes 2:19; 2 Tim 2:5; 4:8; Heb 2:7,9; Jas 1:12; 1 Pt 5:4; Rv 2:10; 3:11; 6:2; 12:1. [6]Rv 4:4,10; 9:7; 14:14 □.

3. The crown of thorns* imposed on Jesus was a caricature of the royal diadem.[7]

[7]Mt 27:29 (= Mk 15:17); Jn 19:2,5.

cross **1.** Gk. *stauros.* An instrument of punishment (sometimes still referred to by the Gk. *xylon:* "wood, gibbet")[1] on which Jesus of Nazareth died. A symbol of Jesus' voluntary suffering and passion[2] at the same time as it was a breaking with the world of covetousness.*[3]

[1]Acts 5:30; 10:39; 13:29; Gal 3:13; 1 Pt 2:24. [2]Mt 27:40,42 (= Mk 15:30,32); Heb 12:2. [3]Gal 5:24.

2. The cross of Jesus is to be received in its scandalous* horror,[4] but it is also to be understood within God's plan*[5] and to be appreciated according to its effects: a deliverance from the curse* of the Law[6] and from sin,[7] reconciliation* effected with God[8] as well as between Jews and pagans,[9] the re-establishment of peace,* the source of life.[11] It has become a category of Christian thought and preaching.*[12]

[4]1 Cor 1:23; Gal 5:11; 6:12,14. [5]Acts 13:29. [6]Gal 3:13; Col 2:14f. [7]Rom 8:3; 1 Pt 2:21-24. [8]Col 1:20. [9]Eph 2:16. [10]Eph 2:14-18. [11]Jn 3:14f. [12]1 Cor 1:17f., 25; Gal 3:1.

3. The sign of a Christian, who, following Jesus, has to take up and carry his cross[13] in order to proclaim that he has died to the wicked world*[14] and, above all, that this is his greatest title to glory.[15]

[13]Mt 10:38; 16:24 (= Mk 8:34 = Lk 9:23); Lk 14:27. [14]Rom 6:6; Gal 2:19. [15]Jn 12:26; Gal 6:14,17.

→ crucifixion—Jesus Christ—suffer—tree—Trial of Jesus.

crucifixion **1.** Even though it was probably Oriental in its origins, the execution of a criminal by death on a cross was a Roman punishment, "the cruelest and the most shameful," according to Cicero. It was applied to slaves and noncitizens (in the case of a revolt, of theft or murder), sometimes to citizens* (in the case of high treason). Jews had experienced it since 88–83 B.C., when Alexander Janneus crucified 800 Jews, but chiefly beginning with the Roman occupation, especially at times of uprisings in Galilee. The Christians readily likened it to the punishment imposed by Jews: according to the Law, the body of an already executed criminal was suspended (Gk. *kremazō*) on a wooden pole planted outside a city's walls; thus presented as a shameful example, the corpse, which was struck with a curse, had to be removed and buried before nightfall since it was a defilement of the entire nation.[1] Its resemblance, therefore, related less to the punishment than to the shame and curse.[2]

[1]Dt 21:22f.; cf. Heb 13:13. [2]Lk 23:39; Acts 5:30; 10:39; Gal 3:13.

2. For the crucifixion itself the Romans added to the stake a wooden crossbeam (Lat. *patibulum*) that could be attached to the top of the beam (Lat. *crux commissa* T) or, lower down, within a slot (Lat. *crux immissa* †). The one condemned had to carry it himself to the place of punishment after he had undergone the mandatory scourging.* Ordinarily, he wore around his neck an inscription that indicated the reason for the penalty, something which was later fastened above the cross. The convict was attached to the cross with cords binding his hands and feet or, more often, he was nailed to it. The convict's clothes went by right to the executioners. A Jewish custom specified that a narcotic drink be given to him. Death, slow as it was, came about by exhaustion or else through respiratory or circulatory problems. Death by asphyxiation was hastened by the fact that, once the legs had been broken, the condemned man could not straighten himself out to catch his breath; thus the body could be removed before nightfall, in conformity with the Jewish rule (notably so, on the eve of Passover).

3. Through gospel and archaeological data, a certain number of historical assertions about Jesus' crucifixion call for recognition: Pilate's judicial decision; the fact that Roman soldiers carried out the crucifixion after the scourging had been seen to; that it went according to Roman (the soldiers' guard, the sharing out of the clothing) and Jewish customs (the narcotic drink). The motivation for his condemnation was political: Jesus was reckoned to be a seditious person. It is difficult to know whether Jesus' cross was of the *immissa* or *commissa* type, more likely the latter. It is highly probable that, as John maintained, Jesus was crucified on the eve of a Passover, a Friday, 14 Nisan, about noon.

4. The event has never been reported independently of an interpretation of it that revealed its meaning. The past fact was without doubt attributed to the Jews of the period,[3] but straightaway it was situated also within God's plan*[4] and it acquired a supratemporal value which allowed for the event's being made contemporary: in being unfaithful to Christ, one "crucified anew" the Son of God.[5] To be Christ's faithful disciple, one must take up his cross "each day."[6] John depicted his elevation on the cross as his exaltation* in glory; the term *hypsōthēnai* that he used to this end might correspond to a Palestinian Aramaic *izd^{e}qéf,* which could signify "to be crucified" as well as "to be glorified."

[3]Acts 3:13-15; 1 Thes 2:15. [4]Acts 2:23. [5]Heb 6:6. [6]Lk 9:23. [7]Jn 12:33.

→ cross—exaltation—Jesus Christ—Trial of Jesus.

cubit Gk. *pēchys,* Lat. *cubitus:* "elbow." A measurement of length extending from elbow to the fingertip, equal to about 0.45 m. (1.5 ft.) or even 0.52 m. (1.7 ft.).[1]

[1]Mt 6:27 (= Lk 12:25); Jn 21:8; Rv 21:17 □.

→ measures.

cult, cultic

→ worship.

cummin Gk. *kyminon:* Lat. *nigella sativa.* Black aromatic grains which, along with pepper, people freely sprinkled on bread.[1] Pharisees* paid a tithe* on it,[2] although this was not prescribed by the Law.*

[1]Is 28:25,27. [2]Mt 23:23 □.

cup **1.** Gk. *potērion* (related to *potos:* "a drink," *pinō:* "to drink"). A vessel for drinking, made of clay or metal, wide-mouthed and not at all deep.[1] According to mealtime use, the head of the family offered to each diner an already filled cup; also, to drink from the same cup symbolized a communion* among the guests.[2] Hence, as well, the metaphorical use of the cup to designate someone's fate,[3] a trial to go through[4] or a punishment to be undergone.[5]

The "cup of salvation," offered and drunk at the Temple in thanksgiving* for a benefit received, implied community with God;[6] there was an analogous rite in the worship of idols.*[7]

In the course of the paschal meal,* several cups[8] were passed, the third of which was called the "cup of blessing,"* for the final thanksgiving.[9] Finally, the "Lord's cup" designated the Eucharist.*[10]

[1]Mt 23:25f. (= Lk 11:39); Mk 7:4. [2]Ps 16:5; 1 Cor 10:20. [3]Mt 20:22f. (= Mk 10:38f.). [4]Nm 5:12-28; Mt 26:39,42 (= Mk 14:36 = Lk 22:42 = Jn 18:11). [5]Is 51:17,22; Jer 25:15-29; 51:7; Rv 14:10; 16:19; 17:4; 18:6. [6]Ps 116:13. [7]1 Cor 10:21. [8]Lk 22:17,20. [9]1 Cor 10:16. [10]Mt 26:27 (= Mk 14:23 = Lk 22:20 = 1 Cor 11:25); 26:29 (= Mk 14:25 = Lk 22:18); 1 Cor 11:21,26-29 △.

2. Gk. *phialē:* a cup of perfumes,*[11] symbolizing prayer*[12] or the divine wrath.*[13]

[11]Ex 25:29, Nm 7:84,86; 1 Kgs 7:50; Jer 52:18. [12]Ps 141:2; Rv 5:8; 8:3f. [13]Rv 15:7; 16:1-17; 17:1; 21:9 △.

curse **1.** Gk. *kat-araomai* (derived from *ara:* a vow, an imprecation having recourse to a superior power against the cursed object). It was not a case of an official statement about a woeful condition ("woe* to you!"[1]), nor even of the announcement of a misfortune which was the consequence of one's behavior,[2] but was rather the contrary or the inversion of a blessing*: it was a judgment bringing about a separation.[3] Thus, the Law condemned* those who transgressed it.[4] But Jesus bought men back from the curse by taking it on himself.[5]

Jesus never cursed, unless it were, according to an obscure narrative, the barren fig tree.*[6]

[1]Mt 11:21; Lk 6:24ff. [2]Mt 18:7; 24:19. [3]Jer 26:6; Mal 2:2; Mt 25:41; Jn 7:49; Heb 6:8. [4]Dt 11:26-29; 30:1,19; Rom 3:14; Gal 3:10; 2 Pt 2:14. [5]Gal 3:13. [6]Mk 11:21.

2. A Christian ought never to curse, but instead ought to bless those who curse him.[7] In the broad sense, proceeding from other Greek words like *kakologeō,* (contrary to the views of some translators) the issue was rather one of insults* and outrages.

[7]Lk 6:28; Rom 12:14; Jas 3:9f. □.

→ anathema—blaspheme—insult—raca—slander—woe.

custom, duty

→ tax.

custom-house Gk. *telōnion.* The place where taxes (duties, tolls) imposed on merchandise entering or leaving a country were collected. Capernaum* was located on the border between Galilee* and Trachonitis.*[1]

[1]Mt 9:9 (= Mk 2:14 = Lk 5:27) □.

→ Intr. VII.3.—tax—tax collector.

cymbal Gk. *kymbalon.* A percussion type of musical instrument, formed from two discs or two cones of metal that were struck against one another.[1]

[1]1 Cor 13:1 □.

Cypriots, Cyprus Gk. *Kypros.* An island in the eastern Mediterranean,[1] with Salamis* and Paphos as its principal cities;[2] a senatorial Roman province* from 22 B.C. A land of refuge for Christians dispersed after Stephen's martyrdom,[3] it was evangelized by Barnabas and Paul, who welcomed into the faith the first converted proconsul.[4] The native land of the Cypriots Barnabas,* Mnason and several others.[5]

[1]Acts 21:3; 27:4. [2]Acts 13:5f.,13. [3]Acts 11:19. [4]Acts 13:4-12; 15:39 △. [5]Acts 4:36; 11:20; 21:16 △.

→ Map 3.

Cyrene, Cyreneans **1.** Gk. *Kyrēnē.* A city located west of the Nile delta in modern-day Libya. Cyrene, which had first been a Greek colony, became a Roman praetorian province* in 75–74 B.C., then in 67 B.C. a part of Crete,* which became a senatorial province in 27 B.C.[1]

[1]Acts 2:10 □.

→ Map 3.

2. Gk. *Kyrēnaios.* The numerous Jewish population lived in tension with the Greeks of the place. Simon* carried Jesus' cross.[1]

[1]Mt 27:32 (= Mk 15:21 = Lk 23:26); Acts 6:9; 11:20; 13:1; cf. 27:17 □.

Dalmanutha An unknown place, mentioned in Mk 8:10 □, corresponding to the Magadan* in Mt 15:39, itself an unknown locale.

Dalmatia Gk. *Dalmatia.* The name given about A.D. 10 to the Roman province* of Illyricum. Perhaps Titus* visited its Adriatic Coast, while Paul contemplated going there from that side of it which lay on the Macedonian frontier.[1]

[1]2 Tim 4:10 □; cf. Rom 15:19.

→ Illyricum—Map 3.

Damascus Gk. *Damaskos.* An important city northeast of the Sea of Galilee, capital of present-day Syria, incorporated into the Decapolis* after the Roman conquest in 64 B.C., but ruled in Paul's time by Aretas IV.* The arrival point of trade with the Far East, it was in constant communication with Petra (Arabia). It numbered more than 15,000 Jews and numerous proselytes,* some of whom became Christians, the ones Paul intended to persecute. It was at Damascus that Paul received baptism and from Damascus that he fled in highly dramatic fashion.[1]

[1]Acts 9:2-27; 22:5-12; 26:12,20; 2 Cor 11:32; Gal 1:17 □.

→ Map 2.

[Damascus (Document)] Otherwise known as the Zadokite Document. This work was discovered in Cairo in 1897 and published in 1910. Fragments of it were discovered at Qumran.* The booklet describes the "community of the new covenant," which was to be established at "Damascus." We do not know which place was meant thereby; perhaps it was Qumran. In fact, the writing is related to and makes allusions to the Rule of the Community of Qumran.

→ Essenes—Qumran.

dance The dance (Gk. *choros*) accompanied solemn festivals.[1] Dancing (Gk. *orcheomai*) was to show forth one's joy or to delight one's guests.[2]

[1]Lk 15:25 △. [2]Mt 11:17 (= Lk 7:32); 14:6 (= Mk 6:22) △.

→ Intr. IX.7.—song.

[Daniel (The Book of)] The Book of Daniel is listed in the Hebrew Bible* among the "Writings" (between Esther and Ezra), in the Greek Bible among the "Prophets" (after Ezekiel). This work belongs to the apocalyptic* genre, offering revelations of the end of time with the aim of encouraging steadfastness in a difficult time. The author fictionally placed himself in Babylon* in the sixth century B.C., but wrote of the era of Antiochus Epiphanes (168–165 B.C.). The book was written in two languages (Aramaic in the sections from 2:4 to 7:28);

it knew numerous additions (rejected as apocryphal* by Protestants): the prayer of Azariah (3:24–50), the canticle of the three young men in the furnace (3: 51–90), Susanna (13:1–64), Bel (14:1–22), the Dragon (14:23–42). The influence of this work on the N.T. was great, particularly its passage on the Son of Man* (Dn 7:13f.), its faith in the resurrection of the dead (Dn 12:2), its angelology (Gabriel,* Michael*).

→ Intr. XII.—Bible.

darkness Gk. *skotos, skotia.*

1. The absence of light* which typifies night.*[1] It can metaphorically describe what lies hidden.[2]

[1]Jn 6:17; 12:35; 20:1. [2]Mt 10:27; Lk 12:3.

2. The power over which God triumphed at the time of creation* and set in order within night.[3] An image of terror,[4] misfortune,[5] corruption,[6] and death,[7] it describes whatever is wretched.[8]

[3]Gn 1:2; Is 45:7. [4]Am 5:18. [5]Ps 23:4. [6]Ps 88:7. [7]Jb 10:21; 17:13; Ps 88:13. [8]Mt 6:23 (= Lk 11:34-36); 27:45 (= Mk 15:33 = Lk 23:44f.); Lk 22:53.

3. Darkness is the kingdom of Satan* and sin,[9] as well as that of men who are born there in darkness[10] and produce wicked deeds.[11] God is master of the darkness[12] and snatches whomever he wills out of it into the light.[13] Man, for his part, is caught in a combat* between light and darkness (cf. Qumran*), out of which the Christian emerges triumphant in his following of Christ.[14] This victory presupposes faith and brotherly love.[15] As their opposite, exterior darkness is the place of punishment located outside of heaven.*[16]

[9]Acts 26:18; Eph 6:12. [10]Is 9:1; Mt 4:16; Lk 1:79; Rom 1:21; 2:19; Eph 4:18; 5:8. [11]Jn 3:19; Rom 13:12; Eph 5:11. [12]Acts 13:11; 2 Cor 4:6. [13]Col 1:13; 1 Pt 2:9. [14]Jn 1:5; 3:19; 8:12; 12:46; 2 Cor 6:14; 1 Jn 1:5. [15]1 Jn 1:6; 2:9,11. [16]Mt 8:12; 22:13; 25:30; Rv 16:10.

→ light.

darnel Gk. *zizanion,* Lat. *lolium temulentum.* A poisonous weed. In the O.T. it is a collective term used to refer to every noxious plant, the offshoot of culpable sloth and God's punishment consequent upon men's sins.[1] Darnel resembles wheat but grows no higher than one meter (three feet). When burned, it becomes an image of sinners who are victims of Satan.[2]

[1]Prv 24:31; Is 5:6. [2]Mt 13:25-40 □.

→ brambles

David Gk. *Dauid,* Heb. *dâwîd:* "beloved." A native of Bethlehem,*[1] the son of Jesse,[2] king of Israel from about 1010 to 970 B.C.[3] A man according to God's heart,[4] a model of liberty with regard to ritual prescriptions,[5] the one to whom God promised a posterity that would never end,[6] the ancestor of Jesus through Joseph,[7] through his psalms* a prophet of the coming of the Christ[8] and his resurrection.[9] It is the son of David who is the awaited messiah-king:*[10] he is the Lord* even of his very own ancestor David.[11]

[1]Lk 2:4,11; Jn 7:42. [2]Mt 1:5f. (= Lk 3:31); Acts 13:22; Rom 15:12 △. [3]1 Sm 16–1 Kgs 2; Acts 7:45. [4]Acts 13:22. [5]1 Sm 21:1-7; Mt 12:3f. (= Mk 2:25 = Lk 6:3). [6]2 Sm 7:12-16; Ps 2:7-9; 89:4; 110:1f.; Is 9:5f.; 55:3; Lk 1:69; Acts 15:16f.; 2 Tim 2:8. [7]Mt 1:17,20; Lk 1:27,32; 2:4; Rv 5:5; 22:16. [8]Sir 47:8; Acts 1:16; 2:25,34; 4:25; Rom 4:6; 11:9; Heb 4:7. [9]Acts 2:29-36; 13:34-37. [10]Mt 9:27; 12:23; 15:22; 20:3f. (= Mk 10:47f. = Lk 18:38f.); 21:9,15; Mk 11:10; Rom 1:3; Rv 3:7. [11]Mt 22:42-45 (= Mk 12:35-37 = Lk 20:41-44); Acts 2:34 □.

→ Son of David.

day Gk. *hēmera.*

1. As in all civilizations, day extends "from morning till night";[1] it is the opposite of night,* as light* is opposite to darkness.* While its actual length could vary from ten to fourteen hours* according to the season, "twelve hours" were counted in a day.[2] Day followed night;[3] one said that it became day,[4] spoke of the heat of the day[5] and of the day that set.[6] The successive mentioning of day and night indicated some extent of time.[7]

[1]Acts 28:23. [2]Jn 11:9. [3]Lk 21:37; Jn 9:4; Acts 27:33,39. [4]Lk 6:13. [5]Mt 20:12. [6]Lk 9:12; 24:29. [7]Mt 4:2; 12:40; 1 Thes 2:9; 2 Thes 3:8; 1 Tim 5:5; Rv *passim.*

2. While the Romans reckoned the day from midnight to midnight, the Jews in Jesus' time based their computation on a lunar cultic calendar. Day began with the appearance of the moon and lasted until the next evening.[8] The feast of Passover began with the night watch*;[9] the sabbath* "began shining" from Friday night[10] and the beginning of the "morrow of the sabbath" took place on Saturday night.[11] To indicate a whole day one spontaneously used the expression "night and day";[12] to indicate the duration of a night and a day, Greek said *nycht-hēmeron* (night-day).[13]

[8]Dt 23:11; Mk 16:1f. [9]Jn 19:31. [10]Lk 23:54. [11]Mt 28:1. [12]Mk 4:27; 5:5; Lk 2:37; Acts 20:31; 26:7; 1 Thes 3:10; 2 Tim 1:3. [13]2 Cor 11:25.

→ calendar—cockcrow—evening—hour—morning—night—watch.

Day of the Lord **1.** Gk. *hēmera tou Kyriou.* A stereotyped formula used to indicate God's triumph over his enemies.[1] The imagery used to describe this happening remained constant: the warrior God of the earliest traditions,[2] the creator God triumphing over the Beasts* and chaos[3] in the primordial battle, the sudden character of his coming,[4] the radical transformation of the universe.[5] This belief permitted thought about God's Lordship* over all men and all ages, which was inconceivable except by its being placed at the end of the world.*[6] In Jesus' time the biblical tradition had made progress on several fronts. The Day no longer concerned only Israel, but all the nations.*[7] It would not take place at a moment in time, but at history's end.[8] It was the Lord Jesus' Day as much as God's.[9]

[1]Is 13:2-6; Ez 30:3; Zep 1:7; 2 Thes 2:2. [2]Nm 10:35f.; Jos 10:12f.; Is 9:3; 28:21; Hos 2:2; Mt 24:29f. [3]Is 24:1; Ez 38; Mt 24:29; Rv 19:11–21:1. [4]Am 5:18f.; Mt 24:44; 1 Thes 5:2f.; Rv 3:3. [5]Ps 93; 98; Acts 1:6; 3:20; Rom 8:19-22; Phil 3:20f. [6]Ps 96; 97; 1 Cor 15:24-28. [7]Zep 2:4-15; Zec 14:12-20. [8]Dn 8:17; 9:26; 11:35-40; Acts 2:17; 1 Thes 4:16f.; 1 Cor 15:52. [9]Mt 24:30f.; Lk 17:24; 1 Cor 1:8; Phil 1:6,10.

THE DAY AND ITS DIVISION

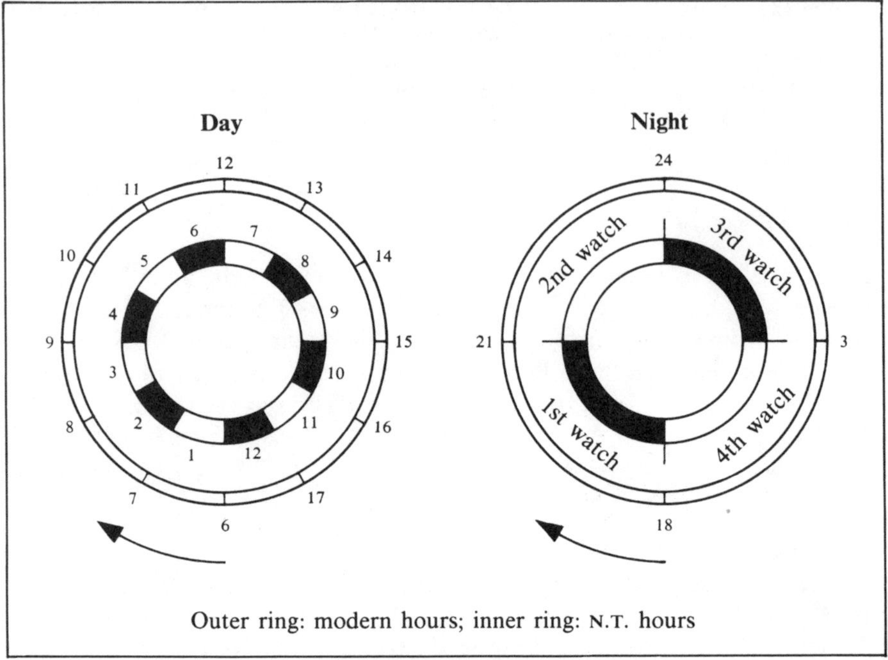

Outer ring: modern hours; inner ring: N.T. hours

2. Jesus' resurrection anticipated in time, on Easter day, God's triumph over Death. Thus the Day is not merely an expected event; it has become interiorized within the believer, who becomes a "son of the Day."[10] Without eliminating the tradition of the last day,[11] John locates the light of Easter and the parousia*[12] within the life of Jesus itself.

[10]1 Thes 5:5. [11]Jn 6:39f., 44,54; 11:24; 12:48; 1 Jn 4:17. [12]Jn 5:24f., 12:31; 14:3,20-23: cf. Mt 28:20.

3. The Lord's Day is also "Sunday," a day especially consecrated to God's worship.[13] It recalls God's great act in raising up Jesus and it foretells Christ's coming again.

[13]Acts 20:7; 1 Cor 16:2; Rv 1:10.

→ hour—judgment—Maranatha—parousia—time.

deacon Gk. *diakonos:* "servant," one who is in the service* of a master.[1] Of a lower order than that of the *episcopoi,** his ministry* was hardly precise, perhaps that of an assistant.[2] One woman is mentioned as a deaconess.[3] Luke assimilated them to the Seven,* without making further qualifications.[4]

[1]Mt 20:26; 22:13. [2]Phil 1:1; 1 Tim 3:8-13. [3]Rom 16:1 □. [4]Acts 6:2-6.

→ episcope—ministry—servant.

deaf Gk. *kōphos*[1]: "dull," a word which can mean "deaf" and "mute,*" from the fact that both infirmities are ordinarily bound together.[2] Deafness, unlike muteness, was not a consequence of demonic possession, except in the case of the epileptic child.[3] In curing it Jesus performed one of the messianic deeds.[4] Deafness can also symbolize a refusal to obey God's Word.* Accordingly, those who so refuse are said to possess "uncircumcised ears."[5]

[1]Mk 7:37. [2]Mk 7:32. [3]Mk 9:25. [4]Is 35:5; Mt 11:5 (= Lk 7:22). [5]Jer 6:10; Acts 7:51.

→ ear—sickness.

death **1.** According to the predominant biblical anthropology, the passage from being-in-existence to being-without-life was not understood as the separation of the soul from the body but as the loss of every vital sign: life* stopped without implying that a shadow of it ceased to exist in Sheol.* The dead person (Gk. *nekros*) was no longer the "living soul," which he had become through creation,[1] because his spirit* had left him to return to God, who alone was immortal.[2] In the N.T., death (Gk. *thanatos*) is viewed in a resurrection context, not in that of immortality.*

[1]1 Cor 15:45. [2]Eccl 12:7; 1 Tim 6:16.

2. In the N.T. era the problem of the individual's death was rigorously considered. Without doubt the image of going "to sleep with one's fathers" (Gk. *koimaomai,* from *keimai:* "to be stretched out")[3] was retained to express the fact that death put an end to a life full of days (Gk. *teleutaō*);[4] but note should also be made of the universal law of death which frequently was brutal (Gk. *apokteinō:* "to kill").[5] As heirs of the wisdom tradition, Paul saw death's origin in sin,*[6] John in Satan.*[7] Death, whose shadow weighed heavily on all of humanity,[8] even became a personified power,[9] keeping sinful man at its mercy.[10]

[3]2 Kgs 14:16; Jb 14:12; Acts 13:36; 1 Cor 11:30; 15:6,18,20,51; 1 Thes 4:13f. [4]Acts 2:29; 7:15. [5]Mt 23:37; Lk 13:4,31; Acts 21:31. [6]Rom 5:12,17; 6:23; 1 Cor 15:21. [7]Jn 8:44; Heb 2:14. [8]Mt 4:16; Lk 1:79. [9]Jb 28:22; 1 Cor 15:56; Rv 20:14. [10]Heb 2:14; Rv 6:8; 8:9; 18:8.

3. Jesus' death was understood from the beginning as a death freely accepted to ransom a multitude of men.[11] Paul tied it to the fact that, since God had "made Christ to be Sin for us,"[12] Jesus suffered the ultimate consequence of Sin (which death is) even to dying on the cross.*[13] But, because Jesus was just, he died for us,[14] reconciling* us to God[15] and stripping Sin of its power.[16] Sin lost its power over him[17] and, through him, its sway over us all as well as over the whole of creation.[18] Death was swallowed up in Christ's victory,[19] a victory which the resurrections* worked by Jesus during his mortal life had prefigured.[20]

[11]Mt 20:28 (= Mk 10:45); Lk 22:27. [12]2 Cor 5:21. [13]Phil 2:8. [14]Rom 5:6-8; 1 Cor 15:3; 1 Thes 5:10. [15]Rom 5:10. [16]Rom 6:10. [17]Rom 6:9. [18]Rom 8:2, 19-22. [19]1 Cor 15:26,54-56. [20]Mt 9:24 (= Mk 5:39 = Lk 8:52f.); Lk 7:12,15; Jn 11:13f.,25f.

4. Through baptism,* every believer has been configured to Christ's death so that Christ's life may be ever increasingly manifest in him:[21] he has "died" in Christ.[22] To believe in Jesus is also to pass from death to life.[23] Bodily death, while remaining sorrowful and detestable because it is the end of life and the loss of that means of self-expression which the body* is, is also the absorption by life of whatever is mortal in us;[24] death becomes a gain and even happiness.[25]

It means that communion with Christ is not broken by the cessation of earthly life,[26] for the Lord Jesus remains the same forever.[27] The believer need fear death no longer,[28] because he is in Christ who lives forever.[29]

[21]Rom 6:3-5. [22]2 Cor 5:14. [23]Jn 5:24; 8:51; 11:25; 1 Jn 3:14. [24]2 Cor 5:1-5; cf. 1 Cor 15:51-53. [25]Phil 1:21; Rev 14:13. [26]2 Cor 5:8; Phil 1:23. [27]Rom 14:8f. [28]1 Cor 15:57f.; Heb 2:14. [29]Jn 11:25f.

→ Intr. VIII.2.D.b.—immortality—life—resurrection.

[death penalty]

→ capital punishment.

debauchery Here we have grouped various Greek words by which the N.T. indicates and condemns disorders in the enjoyment of sensual pleasures. It is difficult to indicate their precise shades of meaning.

1. In the broad sense. The principal term is *porneia* (from *pernēmi:* "to sell"), without doubt a specialized term for prostitution,* but frequently used in the wider sense of lewdness or immorality.[1] Moreover, we find: *a-katharsia* (the negation of *katharos:* "pure"): "impurity";[2] *aselgeia* (of uncertain etymology): "lewdness, dissoluteness, licentiousness";[3] *a-sōtia* (the negation of *sōzō:* "to save"): "loose living, corruption";[4] *a-krasia* ("without vigor, without mastery"): "intemperance, incontinence";[5] *tryphē:* "revelry";[6] *malakos* (literally "soft"): "depraved";[7] *kraipalē:* "debauchery, dissoluteness."[8]

[1]Acts 15:20,29; 21:25; 1 Cor. 5:1,9-11; 6:9; 1 Thes 4:3; 1 Tim 1:10; Heb 13:4; Rv 21:8; 22:15. [2]Rom 1:24; 6:19; 2 Cor 12:21; Gal 5:19; Eph 4:19; 5:3,5; Col 3:5; 1 Thes 2:3; 4:7; Rv 17:4. [3]Mk 7:22; Rom 13:13; 2 Cor 12:21; Gal 5:19; Eph 4:19; 1 Pt 4:3; 2 Pt 2:2,7,18; Jude 4 △. [4]Lk 15:13; Eph 5:18; Ti 1:6; 1 Pt 4:4 △ [5]Mt 23:25; 1 Cor 7:5; 2 Tim 3:3 △. [6](Jas 5:5) 2 Pt 2:13. [7]1 Cor 6:9. [8]Lk 21:34 △.

2. In the sexual area, besides *porneia* (cf. above) in the specific sense of "prostitution,"[9] one reads of *moicheia* (of uncertain etymology): "adultery";[10] *koitē* (from *keimai,* "I lie down"): "sexual intercourse, lewdness";[11] its compound *arseno-koitēs:* "homosexual."[12]

[9]Mt 15:19 (= Mk 7:21); 2 Cor 12:21ff. [10]Mt 15:19 (= Mk 7:22); 1 Cor 6:9ff. [11]Rom 13:13. [12]1 Cor 6:9; 1 Tim 1:10 △.

3. In the area of sustenance: *methē* (related to *methy:* "fermented drink"): "habitual drunkenness, drunken revelry";[13] *kōmos* ("happy group, party, pleasure-trip"): "carousings";[14] *oino-phlygia* (*oinos:* "wine"): "drinking-bout";[15] *potos* (from *pinō:* "to drink"): "drinking-bout."[16]

[13]Mt 24:49 (= Lk 12:45); Lk 21:34; Rom 13:13; 1 Cor 5:11; 6:10; Gal 5:21; Eph 5:18. [14]Rom 13:13; Gal 5:21; 1 Pt 4:3 △. [15]1 Pt 4:3 △. [16]1 Pt 4:3 △.

→ vices.

debt Gk. *opheilē, opheilēma.* A term from legal language designating the obligation one person (the debtor) has towards another (his creditor).[1] Insolvency could entail prison* or slavery.*[2]

[1]Lk 16:5,7; Rom 13:7; Phlm 18f. [2]Mt 18:30,34.

1. In Judaism man's relationship with God ended up by being conceived like that of a debtor towards his creditor; it was through his works that a man could settle his accounts.[3] Jesus retained this image but in two parables* showed that, since the debt could not be paid, man receives from God alone his pardon.* Love reflects the magnitude of the gift received.[5] The pardoning of (others') offenses is the measure of the divine pardon.*[6]

[3]Lk 13:4; Rom 4:4. [4]Mt 18:23-27. [5]Lk 7:41-43. [6]Mt 6:12 (= Lk 11:4).

2. In exhortations, debts are transposed into obligations (Gk. *opheilō*), but without loss of the legal and religious background to the term. This obligation is simply the consequence of being a Christian.[7]

[7]Rom 13:7f.; 1 Cor 11:7,10; 2 Thes 1:3; 2:13; Heb 2:17; 5:3; 1 Jn 2:6.

→ Intr. VI.4.B.d; VI.4.C.c.—pardon—sin.

[decalogue] From the Gk. *deka:* "ten" and *logos:* "word"; the word designates "the ten words of the covenant*"[1] which, unlike other words, Yahweh himself wrote with his finger* on the two stone tablets.[2] Two traditions about it are given.[3] The N.T. makes reference to one or another of these commandments.*[4]

[1]Ex 34:28. [2]Dt 4:13; 9:10; 10:4. [3]Ex 20:1-17; Dt 5:6-21. [4]Mt 19:18f. (= Mk 10:19 = Lk 18:20); Rom 13:9; Jas 2:11; cf. Mt 22:34-40 (= Mk 12:29-33 = Lk 10:27f.)

Decapolis Gk. *Dekapolis* (from *deka:* "ten" and *polis:* "city"). A federation of the ten cities, situated east of the Jordan, except for Scythopolis (modern-day Beth Shean). To mention some, moving from south to north, they were: Philadelphia* (today's Amman) at the same level as Jericho, Gerasa* at the level of Samaria, Pella at the level of Caesarea, Gadara* level with Nazareth, Hippos opposite Tiberias, and finally, at the far north Damascus.* The federation was constituted in 63 B.C. to weaken local powers and to reinforce within the region the Hellenic influence dependent on the Roman province* of Syria* until A.D. 106 when it was dissolved into the province of Arabia.* Jesus had some contact with their inhabitants.[1]

[1]Mt 4:25; Mk 5:20; 7:31 □.

→ Intr. III.2.G; IV.2.C.—Maps 2 and 4.

decree Gk. *dogma.* A public document determining the application of a law. The decree could not be promulgated except by a rightful claimant: the emperor or his delegated chief magistrate,[1] the Law of Moses,[2] or the Council of Jerusalem.[3] On the decree of Lk 2:1 → census.*

[1]Act 17:7; cf. Jn 19:12. [2]Eph 2:15; Col 2:14. [3]Acts 16:4 □.

Dedication Gk. *egkainia:* "renewal," or *phōta:* "lights"; Heb. *hanukkâ:* "consecration." A feast celebrated in winter to commemorate the rededication in December 164 B.C. of the altar that had been desecrated three years earlier by Antiochus Epiphanes.[1] Liturgically it recalled the feast of Booths,*[2] during which the dedication of the Temple by Solomon had taken place: it featured huts, the Hallel,* lights above all. In alluding to it, John could have seen in it a reduplication of the feast of Booths, while at the same time emphasizing the theme of the consecration* on the altar of sacrifice.*[4]

[1]1 Mc 1:54,59; 4:36-59; cf. Nm 7. [2]2 Mc 1:9,18; 10:6. [3]1 Kgs 8:2,62-66. [4]Jn 10:22,36 □.

→ Intr. XIII.3.C.—Abomination of Desolation—feast.

defilement

→ pure.

Demas Gk. *Demas,* perhaps an abbreviation of Demetrius. The fellow worker of Paul at Rome. According to 2 Tim 4:10 he later abandoned him.[1]

[1]Col 4:14; Phlm 24 □.

demoniac

→ possessed.

demons Gk. *daimones* (from the singular *daimōn:* "divine being," in particular the "protector god," from which derives "an interior voice"): inferior gods, evil-minded spirits. Popular belief readily personified the powers hidden behind the ills afflicting humanity, and frequently ended up by divinizing them. The O.T. reflected this view, but stressed God's domination over the demonic powers*: late Judaism developed a veritable demonology, particularly focusing on the host that was at Satan's* disposition and which numbered all kinds of Dominations.*

The N.T. is heir to a part of such beliefs, for example in its manner of describing ills, sometimes by the term demonic possession,* at other times by the demon of the sickness:[1] Jesus "healed*" those possessed or cast out demons.[2] Sickness,[3] idolatry,* untrue teaching,[5] wondrous deeds,[6] all these were attributed to the devil's angels,*[7] to the army of Satan with its leader.[8] But Jesus triumphed over these demons in casting them out,[9] something which his disciples likewise did in their turn.[10]

[1]Comp. Mt 17:15 and 17:18. [2]Mk 1:34,39; Lk 6:18; 7:21. [3]Lk 13:11,16; Acts 10:38; 2 Cor 12:7. [4]1 Cor 10:20f. [5]1 Tim 4:1; Jas 3:15. [6]Acts 8:11; 2 Thes 2:9; Rv 13:13; 16:14. [7]Mt 25:41. [8]Mk 3:22; Eph 2:2. [9]Mt 12:28 (= Lk 11:20). [10]Mk 6:7,13; 16:17; Lk 10:17-20; Acts 8:7; 19:11-17.

→ Intr. IV.6.D.—Dominations—exorcise—possessed—Satan—spirit.

denarius Gk. *dēnarion,* Lat. *denarius.* A unit of the Roman monetary system, made of silver (3.85g., .135 oz.), having the same value as a Greek drachma. It bore the inscription and the head of the emperor Tiberius.*[1] It corresponded to the day's wages of an agricultural laborer[2] or to the average daily cost of living.[3] The worth of wheat or barley,[4] bread,[5] perfume[6] and of debts in general[7] was reckoned in denarii. Jesus was betrayed not for thirty denarii, but for thirty "pieces of silver," that is, thirty shekels,* or one hundred and twenty denarii.

[1]Mt 22:19 (= Mk 12:15 = Lk 20:24). [2]Mt 20:2,9,10,13. [3]Lk 10:35. [4]Rv 6:6. [5]Mk 6:37; Jn 6:7. [6]Mk 14:5; Jn 12:5. [7]Mt 18:28; Lk 7:41 □.

→ coins.

deportation Gk. *metoikesia* (from *metoikos:* "stranger"). Deportations to Babylon* took place on three occasions. The number of those deported is difficult to reckon precisely, for the facts given scarcely agree.[1] In 597 B.C., the number was from 3,000 to 10,000 men from among the wealthy classes, in 586, from 1,000 to 15,000 men with their families, in 581, 745 persons or the "remnant." The return took place in 538.[2] Some Jews remained abroad, constituting the first nucleus of the Diaspora.[3]

[1]2 Kgs 24:10-17; 25:7, 11f.; Jer 52:30. [2]2 Chr 36:22f. [3]Mt 1:11f.,17; Acts 7:43 □.

→ captive—Diaspora—exile—liberate—stranger.

deposit Gk. *para-thēkē,* from *para-tithe-mi:* "to place beside," to put on deposit,[1] to entrust.[2] The body of doctrine which constitutes the teaching of faith received from tradition.[3]

[1]Lk 19:21f. [2]Acts 14:23; 20:32; 2 Tim 2:2. [3]1 Tim 6:20; 2 Tim 1:12,14 □.

→ teach—tradition.

Derbē, Gk. a small city of Lycaonia at the foot of the Taurus mountain chain, visited by Paul on two occasions. Its exact location is still unknown.[1]

[1]Acts 14:6,20; 16:1; 20:4(?) □.

→ Map 2.

desert Gk. *erēmos:* "empty, abandoned place." A quasi-uninhabited region, composed not of sand, but of massive limestone formations, a kind of uncultivated stony wasteland.[1] Springs of water are rare there; vegetation is scanty, except after the spring rains when flowers bloom. The desert of Judea, where John the Baptist lived,[2] corresponds to the eastern slope of the mountains, in the direction of the Jordan Valley and the Dead Sea; its configuration is hollowed out by ravines and grottoes.[3] Paul seems to have dwelt for a time in the desert of Arabia.[4]

[1]Lk 15:4. [2]Mt 3:1 (= Mk 1:4 = Lk 3:2); 11:7 (= Lk 7:24). [3]Intr. II.3-5. [4]Gal 1:17.

1. An arid and dangerous territory,[5] land not blessed* by God,[6] a place without water (Gk. *anhydros*) where evil spirits* go to dwell.[7] A place of Satanic* testing, it acquired meaning from the fact that Jesus sojourned there.[8]

[5]2 Cor 11:26; Heb 11:38. [6]Is 14:17; Mt 12:25 (= Lk 11:17); 23:38; Acts 1:20; Rv 18:19. [7]Mt 12:43 (= Lk 11:24). [8]Mt 4:1 (= Mk 1:12 = Lk 4:1).

2. An era in salvation history during which God trained his people; it was narrated in the book of Exodus.[9]

[9]Ex 15:22-19:2; Nm 10:11-12:16; Jn 3:14; 6:31; Acts 7:30-44; 13:18; 1 Cor 10:1-11; Heb 3:8,17.

3. A place of refuge and solitude for Jesus,[10] as well as for the Church until Christ's coming,[11] all that time during which it has not yet entered into the rest* of God.[12] It was there that Jesus fed the hungry crowds.[13]

[10]Mk 1:35,45 (= Lk 4:42; 5:16); 6:32,35. [11]Rv 12:6, 14. [12]Heb 4:1. [13]Mt 14:13-21 (= Mk 6:32-44 = Lk 9:10-17).

→ temptations—test.

desire **1.** Gk. *epi-thymeō* (from *thymos:* "breath, heart, eagerness, desire"): "to desire strongly" something, for example to satisfy oneself, to find friends, to see God.[1] In the N.T. the verb generally has the pejorative nuance of covetousness.*

[1]Gn 31:30; Prv 10:24; Mt 13:17; Lk 15:16; 16:21; 17:22; 22:15; Phil: 1:23; 1 Thes 2:17; 1 Tim 3:1; Heb 6:11; 1 Pt 1:12; Rv 9:6; 18:14

2. Gk. *epi-potheō,* from *potheō:* "to desire something that is absent" with a note of regret, or "to cherish."[2]

[2]Ps 119:20,131,174; Rom 1:11; 15,23; 2 Cor 5:2; 7:7,11; 9:14; Phil 1:8; 2:26; 4:1; 1 Thes 3:6; 2 Tim 1:4; Jas 4:5; 1 Pt 2:2 △.

3. Other terms are: *homeiromai* (related to *himeros:* "passionate desire"): "to desire ardently";[3] *oregomai:* "to tend towards, to aspire to";[4] *euchomai:* "to pray, to wish."[5]

[3]1 Thes 2:8 △. [4]Wis 16:2f.; Sir 18:30; Rom 1:27; 1 Tim 3:1; 6:10; Heb 11:16 △. [5]Acts 26:29; 27:29; Rom 9:3; 3 Jn 2; cf. 2 Cor 13:7,9 △.

→ covetousness—zeal.

[deuterocanonical writings] From the Gk. *deuteros:* "second" and *kanōn:* "rule [of faith]." Inspired books that belong to the canon* of the Scriptures, but were only placed in it at a late date. In Protestant terminology they are called "apocryphal*" and do not belong to the canon. In the O.T. they are: Judith, Tobit, 1 and 2 Maccabees, Wisdom,* Sirach,* Baruch (chapters 1–5), the Letter of Jeremiah (Baruch 6), additions to Esther and Daniel* (Dn 13 = Susanna, Dn 14 = Bel and the Dragon). Although disputed for quite a long time in Christian antiquity, seven works of the N.T. are recognized as canonical by Protestants as well as by Catholics: the Epistle to the Hebrews, the Epistle of James, the Second Epistle of Peter, the Second and Third Epistles of John, the Epistle of Jude, and Revelation.

→ Intr. XII; XV.—apocryphal writings—Bible—canon.

devil Gk. *diabolos* (from *dia-ballō:* "to divide, accuse, calumniate"): "the slanderer."[1] Another name of Satan's*[2] and of every adversary of the Kingdom of God.*[3] He operates here below[4] and produces a breed.[5] The Christian must resist him.[6] He has the power of death, but will be destroyed.[7]

[1]1 Tim 3:11; 2 Tim 3:3; Ti 2:3. [2]Mt 4:1-11 (= Lk 4:2-13); 25:41; Rv 12:9; 20:2. [3]Jn 6:70; 13:2; 1 Jn 3:8; Jude 9. [4]Mt 13:39; Lk 8:12; Heb 2:14; Rv 2:10; 12:12. [5]Jn 8:44; Acts 10:38;

13:10; 1 Jn 3:10. [6]Eph 4:27; 6:11; 1 Tim 3:7; 2 Tim 2:26; Jas 4:7; 1 Pt 5:8. [7]1 Tim 3:6; Heb 2:14; Rv 20:10 □.

→ demons—Satan—slander.

Diaspora Gk. *diaspora:* "dispersion." The sum of Jewish communities in exile.* The term is used metaphorically to characterize Christians as "pilgrim people," whose fatherland is not on earth but in heaven.[1] Curiously, the Septuagint* never translates the specific Hebrew term *gôlâ, gâlût:* "exile" by *diaspora* but by more expressive words: *aichmalōsia:* "captivity*" and *ap-oikia:* "exile." This reflects the fact that, in the course of centuries, this punishment was not reckoned as anything but the situation willed by God,[2] linked as it was with the spread of the faith among the Gentiles.[3]

[1]Jas 1:1; 1 Pt 1:1; cf. 2:11. [2]Is 60; Zec 8:20-23. [3]Jn 7:35; Acts 8:1,4; 11:19 □.

→ Intr. I.1.A; III.3; IV.6.E.; IV.7.A; VI.—deportation—exile—fatherland.

didrachma Gk. *di-drachmon.* A Greek coin* made of silver (8.60 g, 0.3 oz.), worth two drachmas, corresponding to the wages for two days' work. The amount of the annual tax* to the Temple owed by each Jew.[1]

[1]Mt 17:24 □.

→ coins.

dill Gk. *anēthon* (from which we get "anise"), Lat. *feniculum:* "little hay." One of the spices, along with mint and cummin, on which the Pharisees* put themselves under compulsion to pay the tithe,* even though the Law did not mention it.[1]

[1]Mt 23:23; Lk 11:42 □.

discern

1. Gk. *dokimazō:* "to put to the test, examine, reckon."[1] The word suggests the idea of "weighing," to verify in that action the quality and worth of something, from which comes the associated aspect of "testing" someone or something.

[1]Lk 12:56 (cf. Mt 16:3); Rom 2:18; 12:2; 1 Cor 3:13; 11:28; Gal 6:4; Phil 1:10; 1 Thes 5:21; 1 Jn 4:1.

2. Gk. *diakrinō* (from *krinō:* "to separate, to choose, to cut"): "to distinguish, to discern."[2] The word underlines the discursive aspect of knowledge and judgment: it also corresponds to interpretation.

[2]Mt 16:3 (cf. Lk 12:56); 1 Cor 6:5; 11:29,31; 12:10; 14:29; Heb 5:14 △.

→ judgment—spirit—test.

disciple

1. Gk. *mathētēs* (from *manthanō:* "to learn, to accustom oneself to something, to become familiar with."[1] In the O.T. only one text[2] from the Jewish period shows knowledge of the word "disciple," undoubtedly because the relationship of the individual to God was always conceived within the bosom of the assembly of Israel. Those who accompanied Moses, Elijah, Elisha, or Jeremiah were not disciples but servants* (Heb. *meshârét*).[3] It was in Judaism,* and probably under the influence of Hellenism,* that there developed the idea of the *talmîd* related to his rabbi, of one who inherits divine authority in the interpretation of the Scriptures.

[1]Ez 19:3,6; Mi 4:3; Mt 9:13; 11:29. [2]1 Chr 25:8. [3]Ex 24:13; 1 Kgs 19:21; 2 Kgs 4:12; Jer 32:12f.

2. In the N.T., the word does not appear except in the gospels and in Acts. It is never a case of the "pupil" who receives instruction from a master, but always of someone who shares a close and definitive relationship with one person.[4] More precisely, the disciple is the one who, at Jesus' call,[5] follows* after him;[6] he must observe the will of God[7] and even, binding himself unreservedly to the person of Jesus, go as far as death and the gift of his life out of love.[8] This disposition presupposes humility,* poverty*[9] and even conversion* after a possible fall.[10] There has been a tendency to identify the disciples with the Twelve* and the Seventy-two,[11] but, according to Acts, a disciple is any believer.[12]

[4]Mt 9:14 (= Mk 2:18 = Lk 5:33); 11:2 (= Lk 7:18); Jn 1:35; 9:28. [5]Mk 3:13; Lk 6:13; 10:1. [6]Lk 9:57-62 (= Mt 8:19-22). [7]Mt 10:29. [8]Mt 10:25,37; 16:24 (= Mk 8:34f.; Lk 14:25f.; Jn 13:35; 15:13. [9]Mt 18:1-4; 19:23f.; 23:7. [10]Lk 22:32. [11]Mt 10:1; 11:1; Lk 12:1. [12]Acts 6:1; 9:19.

3. The "beloved disciple" is a personality proper to the Fourth Gospel, whom we cannot designate further, other than to indicate that he belonged to the Twelve; he is sometimes designated as "the other disciple,"[13] at other times as "the disciple whom Jesus loved."[14] The one and the other are the same person,[15] a historical person whose symbolic significance is undeniable, but difficult to define precisely. Explicitly set over against Peter by John, this disciple always takes the better part by his intelligent presence and by the fact of his "being loved" in a special way. He might symbolize the function of the disciple who is able to perceive, understand and speak, because he knows that he is loved by Jesus.

[13]Jn 18:15f.; 20:3f.,8. [14]Jn 13:23-26; 19:25-27; 20:2; 21:7,20-23,24. [15]Jn 20:2.

→ follow—master—teacher.

Dispersion

→ Diaspora.

divorce Gk. *apo-stasion* (from *aph-istēmi:* "to place apart from, separate"), a juridical term designating every liberation from a bond; Gk. *apo-lyō:* "to loose from, liberate, set free."

1. Although disapproved of by the prophets,[1] the rupture of the bond of marriage,* solely on the initiative of the husband, was permitted by the Law,* although not without reservation. The motive could be "something shameful" on the woman's part.[2] In the time of Jesus, the Jewish legislators discussed the interpretation of this defect: any fault at all or loose living only? The procedure demanded a "writ of separation" which attested the repudiation and gave the woman,* as well, the freedom to remarry.[3]

[1]Mal 2:13-16. [2]Dt 22:19,29; 24:1; Mt 5:31; 19:7f. (= Mk 10:4). [3]Mt 1:19; 19:3 (= Mk 10:2).

2. In contrast, Jesus proclaimed the indissolubility of marriage.[4] The exception "in the case of lewd conduct"[5] is variously interpreted by Christian denominations (as an illegitimate or adulterous union). After having recalled the Lord's command,[6] Paul declared that a separation was permitted in the case of the conversion of one of two pagan spouses.[7]

[4]Mk 10:11f.; Lk 16:18. [5]Mt 5:32; 19:9. [6]1 Cor 7:10f. [7]1 Cor 7:12-15 □.

→ Intr. VIII.2.B.d.—adultery—marriage—prostitution.

[Docetism] From the Gk. *dokeō:* "to appear." A Christological conception according to which Jesus was God, who had only the appearance of a man; thus Jesus would not really have suffered and the cross would cease to be a scandal. Docetism was combatted in the Epistle to the Colossians* as well as in the Gospel and Epistles of John.*

doctor Gk. *iatros,* Heb. *rophé.* In the beginning the doctor was likened to the magician* or identified with the priest*:[1] he seemed to compete with God, the only healer.*[2] Later on, his role was honored and, in the Roman era, there were numerous professionals: bleeders, surgeons, bathers, all of whom were highly regarded even if criticized.[3]

[1]Lv 13. [2]Ex 15:26; 2 Kgs 20:8; 2 Chr 16:12. [3]Cf. Sir 38:1-15; Mt 9:12 (= Mk 2:17 = Lk 5:31); Mk 5:26 (= Lk 8:43); Lk 4:23; Col 4:14 □.

doctor (of the Law) Gk. *didaskalos* (from *didaskō:* "to teach").

1. A scribe* considered particularly in his function of teacher.*[1] A term sometimes specified as *nomo-didaskalos:* "doctor of the Law."[2]

[1]Lk 2:46; Jn 3:10; Rom 2:20 △. [2]Lk 5:17; Acts 5:34; 1 Tim 1:7 △.

2. A Christian who had received the charism* or office of teacher.[3] It would be more appropriate not to translate the word as "doctor," for there is only one Doctor, one Teacher.*[4]

[3]Acts 13:1; 1 Cor 12:28f.; Eph 4:11; 1 Tim 2:7; 2 Tim 1:11; 4:3; Heb 5:12; Jas 3:1 △.

→ Intr. XII.1.C.—chair of Moses—rabbi—scribe—teach.

dog Gk. *kyōn, kynarion.* Besides the familiar domestic animal[1] there was also the dreaded wild mongrel.[2] A harmful, scornful term.[3]

[1]Ex 11:7; Tb 6:1; 11:4; Mt 15:26f. (= Mk 7:27f.). [2]1 Kgs 14:11; Ps 22:17; 59:7; Lk 16:21. [3]Dt 23:19; 1 Sm 17:43; 24:15; Mt 7:6; Phil 3:2; 2 Pt 2:22; Rv 22:15 □.

Dominations Under this word we have grouped numerous related Greek terms translated in quite diverse ways in various bibles. *Archai*[1] (from *archē:* "beginning, head"): "authorities, dominations, principalities"; *dynameis*[2] (forces): "powers"; *exousiai:*[3] "authorities, dominations, powers"; *kyriotētes*[4] (from *kyrios:* "lord"): "lordships, sovereignties"; *thronoi*[5] (literally "seats"): "thrones." Other N.T. expressions are the equivalents of these, such as *archontes tou aiōnos, kosmokratores:*[6] "rulers of the world," *pneumatika tēs ponērias,*[7] "spirits of evil."

[1]Rom 8:38; 1 Cor 15:24; Eph 1:21; 3:10; 6:12; Col 1:16; 2:10,15 △. [2]Rom 8:38; 1 Cor 15:24; Eph 1:21; 1 Pt 3:22. [3]1 Cor 15:24; Eph 1:21; 3:10; 6:12; Col 1:16; 2:10,15; 1 Pt 3:22 △. [7]Eph 1:21; Col 1:16 △. [5]Col 1:16 △. [6]1 Cor 2:6,8 △; Eph 6:12 △. [7]Eph 6:12 △.

1. The variety of this vocabulary and its interchangeability depict in supraterrestrial, even though not divine, beings the multifarious manifestations of power that have been attributed to Satan,* the prince of this world. These are not "wicked angels,*" but rather cosmic powers which, having been led astray, need to be reconciled, subjected. Often placed after the general term for angels,[8] these names come, most often at least, in pairs, as if to suggest the totality and intensity of the forces opposed to the salvation of men, exercising a hold on people,[9] political institutions,[10] the course of events,[11] nature,[12] and, above all, believers.[13] We cannot establish their hierarchy (even if tradition has occasionally regrouped them into classes of angels), nor the characteristics specific to each entity. According to some observers, the representation of these "dominations" derives from that Jewish belief according to which supraterrestrial beings held stewardship over each human authority, man or institution, or had played a role in the promulgation of the ancient Law.

[8]Rom 8:38; 1 Pt 3:22. [9]Mk 1:23; Acts 5:16; 10:38; Jn 8:44; Jas 3:14f.; Rv 2:10f. [10]Cf. Rv 13, particularly 13:4. [11]1 Thes 2:18; cf. Rom 8:35. [12]Gal 4:8-10; Col 2:16,18. [13]1 Tim 4:1; Eph 6:10-12.

2. Alien to every kind of dualism,* the N.T. declares that the initial state of these "dominations" was that of creatures,[14] their sovereignty was one that had been usurped. They had disregarded the divine plan.[15] By his victory Christ despoiled them and they are, henceforth, subject to him.[17] Nonetheless, the believer is still confronted with their hostility,[18] without it being possible for them to separate him from Christ.[19]

[14]Col 1:16. [15]Eph 3:10. [16]1 Cor 15:24; Col 2:15. [17]Eph 1:21; Col 2:10; 1 Pt 3:22. [18]Eph 6:12. [19]Rom 8:38.

→ angels—demons—elements of the world—power—Satan—spirit.

Dominions

→ Dominations.

door **1.** Gk. *thyra.* An opening permitting entry into a building or exit from it: a house,[1] the Temple (hence the "Beautiful Gate"),[2] a hall[3] or a room;[4] occasionally the word means the swing-door that closes the opening.[5] Another word, Gk. *pylē, pylōn,* refers more particularly to a large door, a portal;[6] in the plural *(pylai),* the term takes on a Semitic coloring and means a large space in front of the city gate and often corresponds to the public square,* the place where city life was concentrated.[7]

[1]Mk 1:33; 2:2; 11:4; Lk 11:7; 13:24f.; Jn 18:16f. [2]Acts 3:2; 21:30. [3]Mt 25:10; Jn 20:19,26; Acts 5:9,19,23; 12:6; 16:26f. [4]Mt 6:6; 27:60. [5]Acts 12:13. [6]Mt 26:71; (Lk 7:12); 16:20; Acts 3:10; 10:17; 12:13; 14:13. [7](Lk 7:12); Acts 9:24; (12:10); (14:13); 16:13; Heb 13:12; Rv 22:14.

2. The N.T. is cognizant of the metaphorical use of terms, such as an opening for apostolic labor,[8] the danger at the gates,[9] a way into the Kingdom and to heaven.[10] Heaven* and the netherworld,* conceived as enclosed places, also have doors, synonymous with the places themselves, ones to which God holds the key.[11]

[8]Acts 14:27; 1 Cor 16:9; 2 Cor 2:12; Col 4:3. [9]Mt 24:33 (= Mk 13:29); Jas 5:9. [10]Comp. Mt 7:13f. and Lk 13:24; Mt 25:10; Rv 4:1. [11]Mt 16:18; Rv 9:1f.

3. Jesus is himself, from this very moment, the door through whom the believer enters into the fullness of life.[12] The heavenly Jerusalem has twelve gates, always open, facing the four cardinal directions, to symbolize the invitation addressed to all peoples.[13]

[12]Jn 10:7,9. [13]Rv 21:12-25.

→ city—public square—street.

dot

→ stroke (of the law).

[doublet] A term of literary criticism* indicating maxims read twice in the same gospel. Such are the sayings on divorce,[1] on the lamp,[2] and on the sending out of the disciples.[3]

[1]Mt 5:29f. = 18:8f. [2]Lk 8:16 = 11:33. [3]Lk 9:1-6 = 10:1-11.

dove Gk. *peristera.* A common name for several birds: the rock-pigeon, ring-dove, pigeon, and turtledove. The dove, found widely in Palestine, was the bird most often mentioned in the Bible. It was the offering of poor people, especially in purification* rites.[1] Hence, the presence in the Temple of dove sellers.[2] The dove, to which the Holy Spirit descending from heaven on Jesus at his baptism was likened, is of uncertain interpretation: it may be meant to evoke God's love[4] or, following the line of some Jewish interpretations, a new creation.[5] The simplicity—or naïveté—of the dove was proverbial.[6]

[1]Lv 5:7; 12:8; Lk 2:24. [2]Mt 21:12 (= Mk 11:15); Jn 2:14,16. [3]Mt 3:16 (= Mk 1:10 = Lk 3:22); Jn 1:32. [4]Cf. Sg 2:14; 5:2. [5]Cf. Gn 1:2. Hos 7:11; Mt 10:16 □.

down-payment

→ pledge.

doxology From the Gk. *doxa:* "opinion, reputation, honor, glory." A formula of liturgical prayer celebrating the glory of God or of Christ. An acclamation of the type: "To God be glory, honor, power, praise, salvation, dominion." Or else: "Thanks be to God, God be praised."[2] Or: "He is worthy of. . . ."[3] These doxologies focus on God, who is extolled under various aspects of his inexhaustible divinity,[4] or on Jesus Christ, through whom or in whom salvation is given.[5]

[1]Lk 2:14; Rom 16:27; 1 Tim 1:17; 6:16; 1 Pt 4:11; Rv 5:13; 7:12; 12:10; 14:7; 19:7. [2]Rom 6:17; 7:25; 9:5; 1 Cor 15:57; 2 Cor 1:3; 2:14; 11:31; Eph 1:3-14; 1 Pt 1:3. [3]Rv 4:11; 5:12; 19:5. [4]Rom 16:27; 1 Tim 1:17; 6:16; Jude 25. [5]Rom 7:25; 16:27; Eph 3:21; Jude 25; Rv 7:10; 11:15; 12:10.

→ hymn—psalm—song.

drachma Gk. *drachmē.* A unit of the Greek monetary system, made of silver (3.5 grams, .12 oz.), the equivalent of a Roman denarius* and corresponding to the wages for a day's labor.[1]

[1]Lk 15:8f. □.

→ coins.

dragon Gk. *drakōn,* sometimes a serpent, at other times a fish. Legendary animal, symbolizing the original chaos of Babylonian* mythology, and, according to the Greek myth, the persecutor Python killed by Apollo.[2] One of the names of Satan.*[3]

[1]Ps 74:13; Is 51:9. [2]Rv 12; 13:2,4; 16:13. [3]Rv 12:9; 20:2; cf. 13:11 □.

→ Antichrist—beasts, the Beast—Satan—serpent.

dream Gk. *kat'onar:* "in a dream." The continuations of psychic phenomena manifest themselves during sleep,* what we would call dreaming and wherein we are inclined to see a deep expression of the personality; among earlier men these were interpreted in some instances as communication with the invisible world. Inferior in kind to prophetic speech, revelations in a dream (Gk. *enhypnion*) were promised[1] or took place, either to enlighten individuals[2] or to make clear God's plan.[3] The N.T. reports not one dream of Jesus. These are not to be confused with appearances,* theophanies* or visions.

[1]Acts 2:17. [2]Mt 27:19; Acts 18:9. [3]Mt 1:20; 2:12f.,19,22 □.

dress The usual translation of the Gk. *stolē* (from *stellō:* "to outfit"). Outer clothing* and not exactly dress in its modern sense. Except in Revelation,[1] where it is the equivalent of *himation* ("cloak*"), the term stresses the social condition of the one who wears the garment.[2] The wedding dress (Gk. *endyma gamou*) is sometimes translated as a "nuptial robe"; it was a ceremonial outfit.[3]

[1]Comp. Rv 6:11; 7:9,13 and 3:5,18; 4:4; as well as 7:14; 22:14 and 19:13. [2]Gn 41:14,42; Ex 28:2; 40:13; Nm 20:26; Sir 6:29,31; 45:7; 50:11; Mk 12:38 (= Lk 20:46); 16:5; Lk 15:22; cf. 1 Tim 2:9. [3]Mt 22:12f. △.

→ Intr. VIII.1.B.—clothing.

dropsy Gk. *hydropikos,* from *hydrōps:* "accumulation of water." A discharge of fluid into a cavity of the body or between elements of connective tissue.[1]

[1]Lk 14:2 □.

→ Intr. VIII.2.D.—heal—sickness.

Drusilla Gk. *Drousilla.* The youngest daughter of Herod Agrippa I,* the sister of Berenice* and of Agrippa II,* the wife of the king of Emesa (Syria), then of Felix,* the governor of Judea.[1]

[1]Acts 24:24 □.

[dualism] **1.** From the Gk. *dyo:* "two." A doctrine according to which reality derives from two irreducible and antagonistic principles. Cosmological dualism explains the world with the help of two absolutes, Good and Evil, principles which have been set against each other from all eternity: so Gnosticism* or Manichaeism.* Theological dualism attributes these two principles to two divine beings. Anthropological dualism explains man as originating in two opposed realities, soul and body, spirit and flesh. Ethical dualism explains the presence of good and bad people in humanity by a divine predestination* to good and to evil.

2. For the Bible, God is the sole creator of all: light and darkness, life and death, salvation and perdition;[1] in addition, he has triumphed over adverse powers.[2] Nonetheless, under Iranian influence, Hellenistic Judaism integrated certain elements of cosmological dualism, but this was in applying them to the end* of time: so we may also speak of an eschatological dualism, for example in the case of teaching about the two aeons,* the terrestrial and the celestial. We may draw attention to a certain ethical dualism, admitting of predestination,*[3] at Qumran.* The N.T. does not retain a true dualism, for Jesus Christ has come into time to save all men; but we may discern certain dualistic modes of thought, for example, the doctrine of the "two ways*"[4] or, most of all, in the Fourth Gospel: the opposed pairs of light/darkness, truth/falsehood, spirit/flesh are attested,[5] though they are transformed by the fullness of Christ's glory[6] and by his appeal to man's decision.[7]

[1]Is 45:7. [2]Rom 8:37-39; 1 Cor 15:24 [3]*The Rule of the Community* 3:13–4:6; *The Damascus Document* 2:7f. [4]Mt 7:13f. (= Lk 13:24). [5]Jn 1:5; 8:41-45. [6]Jn 1:3,16. [7]Jn 3:19-21.

→ Dominations—evil—predestine—soul.

duty

→ custom.

dwelling-place

→ abide.

eagle Gk. *aetos.* Bird of prey, difficult to distinguish, in texts, from the vulture.* It nests in inaccessible rocky crags,[1] in high places, which makes it the symbol of heavenly beings.[2] Its swift flight is proverbial.[3] Mention of its bald head and search for carrion leads one to think more of the vulture.[4]

[1]Jb 39:27-29. [2]Ez 1:10; 10:14; 17:3,7; Rv 4:7; 8:13 [3]Dt 28:49; Jb 9:26; Rv 12:14. [4]Jb 39:30; Mi 1:16; Mt 24:28 (= Lk 17:37) □.

ear Gk. *ous.* That part of the body we call the ear[1] symbolizes understanding, along with that nuance which properly distinguishes it from the eye,* namely: to hear* is to obey.* "To have ears"[2] is to be apt for understanding but it also implies the power to block them off and to "render them uncircumcised"[3] so as not to hear and understand.[4] To attract someone's attention one invites him to "put words into his ears" (Gk. *en-ōtizomai*)[5] or one tries to "introduce" them there.[6] When Jesus "opened the ears" of the deaf*[7] it was to signify the action of God who "awakens the ear"[8] in a way that the words might be "fulfilled in the ears":[9] the word becomes a realized happening. These ears can be "blessed*" and, when linked with the eyes,[10] point to a being in its totality. In contrast with proclamation from the housetops one may speak or hear in the hollow of the ear, in secret.[11] Always it is a case of revelation* and of wisdom*: the ear is even identified with the heart.*[12]

[1]1 Cor 12:16. [2]Mt 11:15; 13:9; Mk 7:16; Rv 2:7. [3]Jer 6:10; Acts 7:51. [4]Is 6:10; Mt 13:15; Acts 28:27. [5]Is 28:23; Acts 2:14 △. [6]Jer 9:19; Lk 9:44. [7]Is 35:5f.; Mt 11:5 (= Lk 7:22); Mk 7:34f. [8]Ps 40:7; Is 50:4f.; cf. Heb 10:5. [9]Lk 4:21; cf. 1:44. [10]Mt 13:16. [11]Mt 10:27 (= Lk 12:3). [12]1 Kgs 3:9; Prv 23:12.

→ hear—obey.

earth Gk. *gē:* "soil, earth, land," *epigeios:* "terrestrial, earthly."

1. God's is the heaven,*[1] as well as the earth,[2] which he has given to men. The couplet heaven/earth can be used as a binomial expressing totality,[3] for example to proclaim Jesus Christ's lordship over the universe.*[4] It may also be used in the manner of opposition:[5] the couplet earthly/heavenly describing the origin, conduct and destiny of men.[6] A creation of God, the earth is good, but it is in turmoil until it be transformed.[7]

[1]Ps 115:16; Mt 5:35; 11:25. [2]Ps 24:1; 1 Cor 10:26. [3]Mk 13:27; Lk 21:35. [4]Mt 5:18; 28:18. [5]Mt 16:19. [6]Jn 3:12; 1 Cor 15:47-49; 2 Cor 5:1f.; Phil 3:19; Jas 3:15. [7]Rom 8:19-22.

2. The country of Judah or Israel is without doubt the portion of land which had been promised to Abraham;[8] but the promise* pointed to something beyond it: to the new earth,[9] the true land of definitive rest.*[10] Hence, the symbolic use of earthly values to speak about heaven.[11] Jesus declared blest the gentle* ones who would possess the earth as their inheritance.[12]

[8]Mt 2:6,20; 27:45; Acts 7:3f.,29; Heb 11:9. [9]2 Pt 3:13; Rv 21:1. [10]Heb 3:7–4:11. [11]Ps 63:2; Is 28:23f.; Hos 10:12f.; Mt 6:26-28; 22:2-10; Jn 2:1-11. [12]Mt 5:4.

→ Intr. V.1.—heaven—universe—work—world.

earthquake Gk. *seismos* (from *seiō:* "to shake"). Palestine experienced earthquakes, such as those in the eighth century B.C.[1] or in 31 B.C. The Bible saw therein a manifestation of the Creator's omnipotence as he came to help or judge his people,[2] such as the earthquakes at the death and resurrection of Jesus,[3] at the time of Paul and Silas' escape from Prison,[4] at the end of time.[5] The same word *seismos* was also used to describe a violent commotion.[6]

[1]Am 1:1; Zec 14:5. [2]Ex 19:18; Jgs 5:4; 1 Kgs 19:11; Ps 99:1; Is 13:13; Heb 12:26. [3]Mt 27:51,54; 28:2. [4]Acts 16:26. [5]Mt 24:7 (= Mk 13:8 = Lk 21:11); Rv 6:12; 8:5; 11:13,19; 16:18. [6]Mt 8:24; Rv 6:13 □.

east

→ Orient.

edict

→ decree.

edify

→ build up.

education

→ Intr. VIII.2.C;IX.2.

Egypt Gk. *Aigyptos,* Heb. *Miṣrayim.* For a Jew in N.T. times, Egypt was not only a great neighboring power renowned for wisdom,[1] where one might go for refuge,[2] it also preserved the traits of a country which had oppressed the Hebrews and from whom the Lord had set his people free;[3] it symbolized enemy power.[4] Its leading city: Alexandria.

[1]Acts 2:10; 7:22; Heb 11:26. [2]Mt 2:13-19; cf. 1 Kgs 11:40. [3]Ez 29–32; Acts 7:6-40; 13:17; Heb 3:16; 8:9; 11:26-29; Jude 5. [4]Rv 11:8 □.

→ Apollos—Philo—Map 3.

Elamite Gk. *Elamitēs.* The inhabitants of Elam, a country situated between Babylon, Media, Persia and the Persian Gulf, with Susa for its capital, were non-Semites; nonetheless they numbered Jews in their midst.[1]

[1]Jer 49:34-39; Acts 2:9 □.

elder Gk. *presbyteros:* "older [rather than younger]"; from which derive the English words "priest,*" "presbyter," even though these also translate the Gk. *hiereus.*

1. A kind of lay aristocracy, the elders for centuries exercised a type of collegial religious and civil authority over Israel,[1] as well as over the business of Palestinian cities.[2] Members of the sanhedrin,* they watched over the preservation of traditions.*[3] The term can also refer to rabbis* of the past.[4]

[1]Ex 3:16; 12:21; Nm 11:16. [2]Dt 21:2; Jgs 11:5; 1 Kgs 21:8. [3]Mt 21:23; 26:3,47; 27:1; Acts 4:5; 22:5; 24:1; 25:15. [4]Mk 7:3,5.

2. Following the Jewish model, Christian churches had at their head a college of elders who extended the action of the Apostles in order to govern the community.[5] These elders—the equivalent, it would appear, of *episcopoi**[6]—were recruited according to precise rules and were established in their functions through the laying on of hands.*[7] Occasionally one elder would be singled out from the group, doubtlessly because of his venerable authority.[8]

[5]Acts 11:30; 14:23; 15:2-23; 16:4; 20:17; 21:18; Jas 5:14; 1 Pt 5:5. [6]Ti 1:5,7. [7]1 Tim 4:14; 5:17,19. [8]1 Pt 5:1; 2 Jn 1; 3 Jn 1 △.

3. The "old men*" of Revelation[9] constitute a type of celestial senate whose number, twenty-four, remains unclarified.

[9]Rv 4:4–19:4 △.

→ Intr. XII.1.B.—episcope—presbyter.

election Gk. *eklogē* (from *ek-legomai:* "to gather together from"). Set apart for a determined goal. Not to be confused with the call which is addressed to all men. Through a free initiative of his love,[1] God chooses for himself a people,[2] some individuals (Abraham,[3] Moses,[4] David,[5] the prophets,[6] the kings,[7] priests[8]), Zion,[9] the Temple.[10] Correlative to this are the theme of the faithfulness* required by the chosen people[11] and that of its eventual rejection, which places it among "the others."[12] Out of the midst of the unfaithful people God is to raise up for himself a new Israel,[13] the Servant of God.[14] Jesus is this chosen one,[15] the one on whom God has set all his love,[16] the chosen stone* which makes the building hold together.[17] In his turn, Jesus freely chooses the Twelve.*[18] In him, those who were chosen from before the foundation of the world[19] constitute a new race,[20] the chosen ones,[21] the first fruits of a universal salvation;[22] but only faith ratifies election.[23]

[1]Ex 19:5; Dt 7:6-8; 1 Jn 4:19. [2]Nm 23:8f.; Jos 24:3; Ps 106:5. [3]Gn 12:3. [4]Ex 3; Ps 106:23. [5]2 Sm 7:8-16; Ps 89:4. [6]Is 8:11; Jer 20:7; Am 7:15. [7]1 Sm 16:1. [8]Ex 19:6; Dt 10:8; 18:5. [9]1 Kgs 8:16. [10]Ps 78:68; Dt 12:5. [11]Dt 28; Am 3:2. [12]Jer 14:19; 31:37; Rom 9:13. [13]Is 41:8. [14]Is 42:1; 49:3; 52:13. [15]Lk 9:35; Jn 1:34. [16]Mt 3:17. [17]1 Pt 2:4-6. [18]Mk 3:13-15; Jn 13:18; 15:16,19. [19]Eph 1:4. [20]1 Pt 2:9. [21]Mt 24:22; Rom 8:33; 16:13; Col 3:12; 2 Tim 2:10; Ti 1:1; 1 Pt 1:1. [22]Eph 3:11. [23]Jn 6:64-70; 15:16-19; Rom 9–11.

→ beloved—covenant—love—predestine.

elements of the world 1. Gk *stoicheia* (related to *stichos:* "line, row"): "elements, foundation, fundamental principle."[1] According to ancient peoples, the four constitutive principles of the universe,[2] on which all beings, including man, depend, were: water, earth, air and fire. The Stoics* taught that these elements would become fire.[3]

[1]Heb 5:12. [2]Wis 7:17-19; 19:8. [3]2 Pt 3:10,12.

2. The expression could also designate the stars,* which exert a certain influence on the movement of the world and, by extension, the heavenly spirits* who, in ancient cosmologies, governed the motions of the stars. The Christian has been freed by Christ from these powers, which he reckons to be weak and fragile, as well as from the Law which they serve.[4]

[4]Ga 4:3,9; Col 2:8,20 □.

→ Dominations—fire—world.

Elijah Gk. *Ēlias,* Heb. *éliyyâhû:* "Yahweh is God." A prophet* of the ninth century B.C.[1] A figure popular in Judaism because of his intransigence in the faith and because of the efficacity of his prayer.[2] Since he had been carried up into heaven instead of dying, his return as the precursor of the Messiah was awaited;[3] also it was believed he could be recognized in Jesus[4] or in John the Baptist,[5] even if, according to John, the latter denied this identification.[6] Elijah was at the side of Jesus when he was transfigured.[7]

[1]1 Kgs 17:1–2 Kgs 2:18. [2]Sir 48:1-11; Mt 27:47,49 (= Mk 15:35f.); Lk 4:25f.; 9:54; Rom 11:2; Jas 5:16-18. [3]Mal 3:23; Lk 1:17. [4]Mt 16:14; Mk 6:15; 8:28; Lk 9:8,19. [5]Mt 11:14; 17:10-12 (= Mk 9:11-13). [6]Jn 1:21,25. [7]Mt 17:3f. (= Mk 9:4f. = Lk 9:30,33) □.

→ Intr. XII.2.A.a.

Elisha Heb. *èlishâᶜ:* "God helps." A prophet* from the end of the ninth century B.C. The successor of Elijah. Numerous traditions made him popular, particularly because of his miracles.[1]

[1]1 Kgs 19:16-21; 2 Kgs 2–13; Lk 4:27 □.

Elizabeth Heb. *èlishèba':* "My God is fullness." A female offspring of "the daughters of Aaron," the wife of Zechariah* and mother of John the Baptist,* a relative of Mary.*[1]

[1]Ex 6:23; Lk 1:5,7,13,24,36,40,41,57 □.

emancipation

→ freedman.

Emmanuel Heb. *'immânû'él:* "God with us." A symbolic name given to Jesus*[2] and to the son to come to King Ahaz.[1]

[1]Mt 1:23; cf. 28:20 [2]Is 7:14; 8:8,10. □.

Emmaus Gk. *Emmaous.* A village situated some 12 km. (8 mi.) from Jerusalem; there the Risen One appeared to two disciples.[1] Its location is difficult to establish; Amwas which has the same corresponding sounds is 30 km. (19 mi.) away; according to an old tradition, it might be el-Qubeibé or Latroun.

[1]Lk 24:13 □.

→ Map 4.

[emperor] 1. From the Lat. *imperator:* "the one who commands"; originally the title bestowed, on the occasion of a "triumph," to a victorious general on his return from a military campaign; then, beginning with the initiative of Octavian in 27 B.C., the title of the first (Lat. *princeps*) Roman citizen. Octavian authorized emperor worship in the provinces,* against which practice the book of Revelation* seems to rebel.

2. The following emperors lived in succession during the N.T. era:

Octavian (Augustus*) 31 B.C.–A.D. 14
Tiberius* (14–37)
Caligula (37–41)
Claudius* (41–54)
Nero (54–68)
Galba (68–69)
Otho (1/15/–4/16/69)
Vitellius (4/17–12/21/69)
Vespasian (7/1/69–6/24/79)
Titus* (79–81)
Domitian (81–96)
Nerva (96–98)
Trajan (98–117)

→ Intr. IV.2.A.—Augustus—Caesar—Chart, p. 31.

end of the world Gk. *synteleia tou aiōnos,* from *telos:* "end," to which is added the idea of fulfillment, of recapitulation (Gk. *syn*).

1. The present world,* the one we know, has to come to an end,[1] that is, it will be subject to judgment,*[2] will be renewed,[3] will give way to the "world to come."[4] No date can be assigned to this end,[5] except the coming of Jesus, his parousia*: this will be the Day of the Lord,* "the end" (Gk. *to telos*).[6] The end of the world signifies a break, but this does not mean that all the values of the world will disappear: merely the sinful "structure of this world, this will pass away."[7]

[1]Mt 13:39f.; 49; 24:3; 28:20. [2]Jn 3:17; 12:31; Rom 3:6; 1 Cor 6:2. [3]Acts 3:21. [4]Eph 1:21. [5]Mk 13:33. [6]Mt 10:22 (= Mt 24:13 = Mk 13:13); 24:6 (= Mk 13:7 = Lk 21:9); 1 Cor 1:8; 15:24; Heb 3:14; 1 Pt 4:7; Rv 2:26. [7]1 Cor 7:31.

2. Today such language is startling; nonetheless, it is full of meaning. If the Bible speaks of a beginning and of an end of the world, it is to be able to embrace history and the life of all humanity; it takes God's point of view, the one who alone rules over the succession of time, days and ages.* This language also tells of man's communitarian aspect, for no one can make himself indifferent to those who have preceded him or those who will come after him.

→ Intr. XII.2.A.—aeon—age—Day of the Lord—eschatology—fulfill—time—world.

enemy Gk. *echthros* (in the feminine, *echthra:* "hatred"). The term designated more than the accuser (Gk. *anti-dikos*)[1] and the adversary* (Gk. *anti-keimenos:* "the one who keeps himself against"),[2] for it seems to have not an act, but a state, in view. The presence of enemies is a constant given of the Bible;[3] the devil* is the enemy *par excellence.*[4] Jesus sets himself against his enemies,[5] of which death* is the last.[6] When demanding love towards their enemies from his disciples,[7] he sets himself in opposition not to the O.T. but, very probably, to injunctions toward hatred,* like those which the Qumran* documents reveal.[8]

[1]Mt 5:25; Lk 12:58; 18:3; 1 Pt 5:8 △. [2]Lk 13:17; 21:15; 1 Cor 16:9; Phil 1:28; 2 Thes 2:4; 1 Tim 5:14; cf. Ti 2:8; Heb 10:27 △. [3]Lk 23:12; Rom 12:20; Gal 4:16. [4]Mt 13:25,28,39; Lk 10:19. [5]Ps 110:1; Mt 22:44 (= Mk 12:36 = Lk 20:43); Acts 2:35; 1 Cor 15:25; Heb 1:13; 10:13. [6]1 Cor 15:26. [7]Mt 5:43f. (= Lk 6:27,35). [8]*The Rule of the Community* 1:3f.; 1:9f.; cf. Ps 139:21f.

→ adversary—hatred.

engaged

→ betrothed.

[Enoch (The Books of)] The Enochian literature is comprised of a collection of exhortations, parables and prophecies, belonging to the apocalyptic* genre and attributed to the patriarch Enoch.[1]

[1]Gn 5:3-18; 1 Chr 1:1-3; Lk 3:37; Heb 11:5.

1. The *Book of Enoch (1 En)* contains 108 chapters grouped in five parts and belonging to different eras. The core, chapters 1–36 and 83–104, was written before the first century B.C., with the visions (chap. 83–90) being dated even earlier than 150. It is a key text for understanding the eschatology* of the N.T. The parables (chap. 37–71) might stem from the third century A.D. They make mention of the "Son of Man" to designate the Messiah, a pre-existent person who is more than a man. The text was not found at Qumran*: by chance or because reproved? Finally, it contains an astronomical section (chap. 72–82) and an account of the flood (chap. 106–108). The book is quoted by the N.T. in Jude 14f.

2. The *Secrets of Enoch* (*2 En,* Slavonic Enoch), originally written in Greek and preserved in two Slavonic editions; the shorter and less novelistic dates from the tenth century A.D. The original probably predated A.D. 70.

3. The *Hebrew Enoch (3 En)* is later than the two preceding ones. It has been influenced by gnosticism and rabbinism. It dates from the third or fourth century A.D.

→ apocryphal writings.

envy Gk. *phthonos:* "a feeling experienced in seeing others enjoying a good which one would like to have," without thereby desiring to possess it exclusively (which would be jealousy*). One of the vices castigated in the N.T.,[1] and which might be confined to jealousy in certain cases.[2]

[1]Rom 1:29; Gal 5:21,23; 1 Tim 6:4; Ti 3:3; 1 Pt 2:1. [2]Mt 27:18 (= Mk 15:10); Phil 1:15; Jas 4:5 □.

→ jealousy—vices.

Epaphras Gk. *Epaphras,* a contraction of *Epaphroditos.* The founder of the Church of Colossae,* a companion of Paul's in captivity at Rome.[1] It is difficult to identify him with Epaphroditus.*

[1]Col 1:7; 4:12; Phlm 23 □.

Epaphroditus The envoy of the Church of Philippi,* he became the highly regarded fellow worker of Paul.[1]

[1]Phil 2:25-30; 4:18 □.

[Ephesians (Epistle to the)] A kind of circular letter directed toward the churches of Asia.* According to some, it is a resumption of the Epistle to the Colossians by Paul himself, or by a secretary, during his captivity at Rome (62–63). According to others, this letter, deriving from a Pauline milieu, dates from post-apostolic times.

→ Intr. XV.—Epistles.

Ephesus Gk. *Ephesos.* A pre-Hellenistic port city, the most prominent of Asia Minor (modern-day Turkey), a communications center between East and West, the capital (with Pergamum*) of the Roman province* of Asia* from 133 B.C. The home of culture (Heraclitus), art (the temple of Artemis,* one of the seven wonders of the ancient world) and of various cults. Its magicians* were famous. In its population of half a million residents, Jews were both numerous and influential. Evangelized by Paul, Ephesus became the Christian metropolis of Asia.[1] The fourth gospel was probably composed there.

[1]Acts 18:19,21,24; 19; 20:16f.; 21:29; 1 Cor 15:32; 16:8; Eph 1:1; 1 Tim 1:3; 2 Tim 1:18; 4:12; Rv 1:11; 2:1 □.

→ Intr. IV.2.C; IV.3.C.—Ephesians (Epistle to the)—Map 2.

Ephraim Heb. *èphrayim,* perhaps signifying "double fruitfulness."

1. The eponymous* ancestor of one of the twelve tribes* of Israel; this one is named after his father, Joseph.*[1]

[1]Rv 7:8; cf. Gn 49:22-26 □.

2. A place to which Jesus retreated and which is perhaps the modern-day village of et-Taiyebeh, to the northeast of Jerusalem, near the desert.[1]

[1]Jn 11:54; cf. Jos 16:5-9 □.

→ Map 4.

[Epictetus] A Stoic* philosopher (A.D. 60–140), born at Hierapolis,* in a region evangelized by Paul. His moral teaching is related to that of the N.T., but elaborated in another spirit.

Epicureans The disciples of Epicurus, a Greek philosopher (341–270 B.C.), who identified the world and its beings (according to an explanation he inherited from Democritus) with the interplay of a multitude of moving atoms, an interplay to which the gods were strangers. According to him, it is chance that governs the world; also, the way to happiness consists in pursuing pleasure in a well-regulated manner which avoids trouble. In a period of agitation it is better to abstain from public affairs by a "hidden life." His moral teaching ought not to be confused with popular epicureanism, the simple search for pleasures.

Epicureanism was in vogue in Athens* at the time that Paul went there to proclaim Jesus.[1]

[1]Acts 17:18 □.

epileptic

→ lunatic.

episcope

1. In the communities, the function of presiding (Gk. *pro-istēmi:* "to place in front of")[1] or of "over-sight" (Gk. *epi-skopeō*),[2] belonged to deacons,* to presbyters* (elders) or to the "episcopoi," without any appreciable difference.[3] According to the Pastoral Epistles,* wherein mention is made of the deacons in the plural, there existed but one inspector (Heb. *mebaqqér*); without enjoying the fullness of power but having received the gift of government,[5] this "guardian" had to shepherd the flock of God by watching over its unity and its proclamation of the Gospel.[6] The term does not have the modern meaning of bishop.

[1]Rom 12:8; 1 Thes 5:12; 1 Tim 3:4f., 12; 5:17 △. [2]Acts 20:28; Phil 1:1; 1 Tim 3:1f.; Ti 1:7; 1 Pt 5:2 △. [3]Comp. Acts 20:17 and 20:28; Ti 1:5 and 1:7. [4]1 Tim 3:1f. and 3:8. [5]1 Cor 12:28. [6]1 Tim 3:1-5,12; 5:17; Ti 1:7; 1 Pt 5:2.

2. The term is also applied to Christ the Shepherd.[7]

[7]1 Pt 2:25; 5:4.

→ deacon—elder—presbyter.

epistle

1. Gk. *epistolē.* A term designating a solemn kind of letter.[1]

[1]Acts 9:2; 15:30; 22:5ff.

→ Intr. IX.3.

2. Captivity Epistles. An expression referring to the Pauline letters wherein an allusion is made to an imprisonment of Paul. According to Acts,* Paul was in prison at Philippi* about in the year 50, but remained there for but one night. He was in captivity at Caesarea (58–60), then at Rome (61–63).

According to Paul himself, he was, even prior to 57, several times in prison (2 Cor 11:23). From this comes the hypothesis of a captivity around 56 at Ephesus where he suffered great danger (1 Cor 15:32; 2 Cor 1:8). From this latter captivity the Epistle to the Philippians* would derive, while the epistles to the Colossians* and to Philemon* would date from the Roman captivity, as would the Epistle to the Ephesians.* As far as Second Timothy is concerned, it is not listed with this group.

3. The Catholic Epistles. Applied to seven epistles ranked in order of their length and their attribution (James,* First and Second Peter,* First, Second and Third John,* Jude*), the term *katholikos* (universal) has been used to qualify these writings by distinguishing them from those of Paul or from the Epistle to the Hebrews and by grouping them around their respective authors; their recipients were not one particular church (except Second and Third John) but the Church as a whole.

4. The Pastoral Epistles. The two letters to Timothy* and the letter to Titus* constitute a homogeneous grouping; they are kinds of handbooks for use by ministers of the Church. Modern criticism contests the traditional affirmation of their Pauline authenticity* without being able to remove all the worth of the arguments advanced by those who, even today, maintain their attribution to Paul.

→ Intr. XV.

[eponym] A hero or god who gives his name to a tribe, a family, a city: thus, Ephraim,* Esau,* Israel.*

error Gk. *planē* (whence *planaō:* "to cause to err, stray"): "an errant course, deviation." In conformity with the biblical notion of truth,* error is not simply ignorance or misapprehension due to appearances, but a rejection of the truth, infidelity, deception. The biblical image of sheep* who are lost because they are without a shepherd is taken up in the N.T.[1] Satan* and false prophets* will cause men to wander haphazardly (erringly)[2] and mislead them from the right path (Gk. *meth-ōdeia*)[3] in seducing (Gk. *apataō:* "to dupe, deceive") them[4] by their guile and their imposture (Gk. *dolos*).[5]

[1]1 Kgs 22:17; Ps 119:176; Is 53:6; Ez 34; Mt 18:12f.; 1 Pt 2:25. [2]Mt 24:5,11,24 (= Mk 13:5f.,22 = Lk 21:8); Eph 4:14; 2 Thes 1:11; 1 Tim 4:1; 2 Pt 2:15; 2 Jn 7; Rv 2:20; 12:9; 19:20; 20:3,8. [3]Eph 4:14; 6:11. [4]Rom 7:11; 16:18; 2 Cor 11:3; Eph 4:22; 1 Tim 2:14; Ti 1:10; Jas 1:26. [5]2 Cor 4:2; 11:3; Eph 4:14.

→ lie—seduce—truth.

Esau **1.** The elder son of Isaac* and Rebecca,* the twin brother of Jacob, who sold his birthright and did not receive his father's principal blessing.*[1]

[1]Gn 25; 27; Heb 11:20; 12:16f. □.

2. The eponymous* ancestor of the Edomites or Idumeans, whence his second name: Edom.* In this case God is said to hate* Esau, or to put it another way, to love him less than Jacob.[2]

[2]Mal 1:2f.; Rom 9:13 □.

[eschatology] **1.** A discourse on the last things (from the Gk. *eschata:* "last things," *logos:* "discourse"). It shares in language that tells of the end of the world* and thereby also of the last times,*[1] the last days,[2] the last day,*[3] the last hour,*[4] the last moment.[5]

[1]Jude 18. [2]2 Tim 3:1; Jas 5:3. [3]Jn 6:39f.,44,54; 11:24; 12:48. [4]1 Jn 2:18. [5]1 Pt 1:5.

2. For the Christian overtaken by the end of the ages,[6] the last times describe the period which elapses between the coming of Jesus and his return at the parousia.*[7] The temporal condition of the believer can and thus ought to be described as eschatological.

[6]1 Cor 10:11. [7]Acts 2:17; Heb 1:2; 2 Pt 3:3.

→ Intr. XII.2.A.—time.

[Essenes] Gk. *essēnoi, essaioi,* a term probably deriving from the Aram. *hasîn* and signifying "the pious ones" (Heb. *hasîdim*). A Jewish sect* not mentioned by the Bible but by Josephus* and Philo*; it was probably this sect which settled at Qumran.*

→ Intr. XI.3.—Damascus Document—Qumran.

eternal **1.** Like every man, the Semite comes to the concept of eternity by first of all denying those aspects of his temporal condition that, beginning with his experience of death, he considers to be decaying. Moreover, God is for him the Living One who does not die: there is no degree of change in him;[1] he is without beginning, or end, or becoming.[2] Unlike the Greeks, the Semite does not move from this experience to an abstract definition which denies time*; as a matter of fact, in his eyes eternity is not an empty framework, but rather it is already filled with lived experiences. The eternal God also brings time under control; he is the king of the ages.*[3] Eternity is grasped, not by excluding time, but by the integration of time: it is the fullness of being, the absolute.

[1]Jas 1:17. [2]1 Cor 2:7; Col 1:26; Heb 1:12. [3]Rom 16:26; 1 Tim 1:17; cf. Is 40:28; Wis 4:2.

2. The epithet *eternal* ordinarily translates the Gk. *aiōnios* (cf. aeon*) in order to describe not only God but everything that participates in his absolute plenitude: life,[4] the ages,[5] the Good News,[6] the inheritance,[7] the glory,[8] the heavenly world.[9] It is only by virtue of the antithetical style of Semites (love/hate, reward/punishment) that opposing realities are sometimes said to be eternal, in order to indicate that the decision against God is not properly speaking "without end" (a spatio-temporal category), but absolute, "definitive" (a qualitative category): such are sin,[10] the consuming fire,[11] damnation,[12] punishment.[13]

[4]Mt 19:16,29; Jn 3:15f.,36; 17:2f. [5]Rom 16:25; 2 Tim 1:9; Ti 1:2. [6]Rv 14:6. [7]Heb 9:15. [8]2 Cor 4:17; 2 Tim 2:10. [9]2 Cor 5:1. [10]Mk 3:29 △. [11]Mt 18:8; 25:41; Jude 7 △. [12]2 Thes 1:9 △. [13]Mt 25:46 △.

→ aeon—time.

Ethiopian Gk. *aithiops:* "with the burnt face" (cf. Gk. *aithō:* "to burn"), a resident of "Ethiopia," the kingdom of Nubia of the southwest, in modern-day Sudan, whose queen was called Candace.*[1]

[1]Acts 8:27 □.

ethnarch Gk. *ethnarchēs.* In the Orient, a kind of grand duke, but not a king; a title accorded to "customary" leaders governing populations most often of a tribal background. Such a one was Archelaus.*[1]

[1]1 Mc 14:47; 15:1; 2 Cor 11:32; cf. Mt 2:22 □.

Eucharist From the Gk. *eucharistia* (*eu:* "well" and *charizomai:* "to please, give a grace"): "thanksgiving." As a result of the thanksgivings pronounced over the bread and the cup by Jesus, then by Christians, at the end of the second century people came to call the Lord's Supper[1] "the eucharist," the thanksgiving par excellence.

[1]Mt 26:26f. (= Mk 14:22f.); Lk 22:19 (= 1 Cor 11:24).

→ cup—Last Supper—Lord's Supper—thanksgiving.

eunuch The Gk. *eunouchos:* "guardian (Gk. *echō*) of the bed (Gk. *eunē*)" might designate someone castrated or, metaphorically, a chamberlain or a high functionary. The context (or other sources) permit more precision in the matter: Potiphar was married;[1] the administrator-general of the treasury of Queen Candace* was castrated.[2] The fact of being castrated rendered one unfit for worship,[3] an obstacle removed at the end of time.[4] Jesus made use of the term to describe men whom the kingdom of God invites to renounce marriage.[5]

[1]Gn 39:1,7. [2]Acts 8:27,34,36,38f. [3]Dt 23:2. [4]Is 56:3-5; Wis 3:14. [5]Mt 19:12 □.

Euphrates The longest river of Asia (2,270 km., 1,419 mi.), it has its source in Armenia and flows into the Tigris. In the eyes of the Romans it constituted a natural border which would have been difficult for the terrific cavalry of the Parthians* and Medes* to cross. With the Tigris, it was one of the four rivers of Paradise.*[1]

[1]Rv 9:14; 16:12; cf. Gn 2:14 □.

evangelize

→ gospel.

Eve Heb. *hawwâ,* the name of the first woman,* which popular etymology linked to the verb "to live" (Heb. hâyâ): "the Living Woman, the mother of the living." Of her the N.T. retains mention only of the seduction of which she was the victim.[1]

[1]Gn 3:20; 2 Cor 11:3; 1 Tim 2:13f. □.

evening Gk. *hespera,*[1] *opsia (hōra):* late (hour) (from *opse:*[2] "late"). The beginning of night or even the end of the first watch (nine o'clock).

[1]Lk 24:29; Acts 4:3; 28:23 △. [2]Mt 28:1; Mk 11:19; 13:35 △.

→ day—hour—night—watch.

evil A reality opposed to what is well or good, what we call wicked (inadequate, of lesser worth) or wretched (morally or religiously destructive). It was expressed in Hebrew by *ra' (ra'ah),* in Greek by two almost equivalent words: *kakos (K)* and *ponēros (P)* (from *ponos:* "work, fatigue, trouble"); *ponēros* was used, moreover, to indicate a certain responsibility in evil, a perversity, or in order to personify Evil.

1. The fact of evil is established in the N.T., as in the O.T.: wicked things undergone in the physical order[1] or produced in the moral order,[2] wicked men,[3] evil spirits,[4] evil as such,[5] personified Evil, identified with Satan.*[6] Evil divided from God and from men;[7] one had to avoid it at all costs[8] and to pray for this avoidance.[9]

[1]Mt 15:22; Lk 16:25; Acts 28:5. [2]Mt 22:18(*P*); Acts 23:9; Rom 14:20; Col 1:21(*P*). [3]Mt 21:41; 24:48; 2 Tim 3:13(*P*). [4](*P*): Mt 12:45; Lk 7:21; 8:2; 11:26; Acts 19:12f.,15f.; Eph 6:12. [5]Mt 5:11(*P*); Rom 7:19,21(*K*); Rom 12:9(*P*); 12:21(*K*). [6](*P*): Mt 5:37; 13:19,38; Jn 17:15; Eph 6:12,16; 2 Thes 3:3; 1 Jn 2:13f.; 3:12; 5:18f.; probably Mt 6:13; 13:38. [7]Rom 1:29; Ti 3:3. [8]Rom 12:9(*P*); 12:17,21; Col 3:8; Eph 4:31; 1 Pt 3:9. [9]Mt 6:13; Acts 8:22.

2. The problem of evil is not directly treated: the N.T. does not trouble itself to acquit God of the charge of being the author of evil. Evil is either the result of a merited divine punishment inviting one to convert,* lest something worse happen,[10] or else it is a trial* to be endured by experiencing God's love.[11] Evil is not a metaphysical principle, nor a constitutive principle of the world (Zoroaster), not even the product of a "spirit of darkness" opposed to the "spirit of light" (Qumranian dualism*). It does not come from God,[12] but from man's heart, which has been wicked from the beginning:[13] man lets himself be carried along by evil because of the wicked powers,[14] concupiscence,[15] or a bad use of his liberty or his tongue.[16] Evil is not caused by ignorance, but by sin.* Also, it is only Jesus Christ who has overcome it,[17] and who sets free from evil and its powers.

[10]Lk 13:1-5. [11]Rom 5:5; 8:20-22,35f.,38f. [12]Jas 1:13. [13]Gn 6:5; 1 Sm 17:28; 1 Kgs 2:44; Jer 3:5; (*P*):Mt 9:4; 12:34; 22:18; Mk 7:22; Lk 11:39; Rom 1:29; 1 Cor 5:8; Heb 3:12. [14]Eph 6:12. [15]1 Tim 6:10. [16]1 Cor 14:20; Jas 3:8; 1 Pt 2:1; 3:10. [17]Mt 12:28; Jn 17:15; Acts 3:26; Gal 1:4; Col 2:15; 1 Jn 2:14.

→ liberate, liberty—Satan—sin.

Exaltation of Christ

1. To state that Jesus Christ is the Lord in glory, forever alive after his death, there exists a primitive vocabulary other than that of the Resurrection*: it is the vocabulary of Exaltation. It belonged to a Jewish tradition, one according to which God raises up the one who has been humbled[1] and preserves the just* man from death (the descent to the netherworld*) by lifting him up to heaven: Enoch,* Elijah, the Servant.*[2] This terminology presupposes a theology worked out on the basis of a three-stage cosmology:[3] heaven (above, where the Most High is throned), earth (below, where men live), the underworld (underneath, where the dead are).

Jesus was raised up (Gk. *hypsoō*), taken up (Gk. *ana-lambanō,*[5] *ep-airō*[6]), carried up *(ana-pherō*[7]) to heaven. God made him sit (Gk. *kathizō*,[8] *kathēmai*[9]) at his right* hand. He is above (Gk. *epi, hyper, hyper-anō*[10]) all. He is the Lord* of the universe.

[1]1 Sm 2:7; Ez 21:31; Mt 23:13; Lk 1:52; 14:11; 18:14; Jas 1:9; 4:10; 1 Pt 5:6. [2]2 Kgs 2:11; Sir 48:9-12; 49:14; Is 52:13. [3]Intr. V.1; Rv 5:3-13. [4]Acts 2:33; 5:31; Phil 2:9; Heb 7:26. [5]Mk 16:19; Lk 9:51; Acts 1:2(9); 11:22; 1 Tim 3:16. [6]Acts 1:9. [7]Lk 24:51. [8]Mt 25:31; Mk 16:19; Acts 2:30; Eph 1:20; 2:6; Heb 1:3; 8:1; 10:12; 12:2; Rv 3:21. [9]Ps 110:1; Mt 22:44 (= Mk 12:36 = Lk 20:42); 26:64 (= Mk 14:62 = Lk 22:69); Acts 2:34; Col 3:1; Heb 1:13. [10]Rom 9:5; Eph 1:21f.; 4:6,10; Phil 2:9.

2. Other texts do not preserve the image of his going-up: Jesus has gone into heaven,[11] he is gone from here.[12] John has retained the traditional language, but he has also been inspired by the Greek scheme of the descent from heaven/

ascent back to heaven,[13] such that his being lifted up on the cross inaugurates his exaltation into heaven in glory.[14]

[11]Heb 9:24. [12]Acts 1:10f.; 1 Pt 3:19,22. [13]Jn 3:31. [14]Jn 3:14; 8:28; 12:32,34.

3. Christian life can be viewed in terms of the exaltation of Christ: raised up, seated in the heavens, the believer seeks the things that are above,[15] for his city is found in the heavens.[16]

[15]Eph 2:6; Col 2:3-5. [16]Phil 3:20.

→ appearances of Christ—Ascension—heaven.

example Gk. *(hypo)deigma* (from *deiknymi:* "to show,") *typos* (from *typtō:* "to strike"): "impress."

1. Christian existence is penetrated by the tradition left by the fathers in the faith, as well as by solidarity in the way it is lived. Elders, prophets,[1] a crowd of witnesses to God[2] exist as models to follow, while others are to be shunned.[3] Paul,[4] the responsible authorities,[5] the communities themselves,[6] all ought to encourage their descendants or their contemporaries to imitate (Gk. *mimeomai,* whence "mime") their conduct.[7]

[1]Jas 5:10. [2]Heb 12:1. [3]Heb 4:11; 1 Pt 2:6; Jude 7. [4]Gal 4:12; 2 Thes 3:9; 1 Tim 1:16. [5]1 Tim 4:12; Ti 2:7; Heb 13:7; 1 Pt 5:3. [6]1 Thes 1:7. [7]1 Cor 4:16; Phil 3:17; 1 Thes 2:14; 2 Thes 3:7,9; Heb 6:12; 13:7.

2. To act as an example does not mean an invitation to copy in human fashion. It proceeds like a game played with mirrors: imitating Paul is imitating the Christ whom he imitates,[8] finally it is imitating God the Father, whose perfect reflection the Son is.[9] Thus does the commandment "Do as . . . I do" find its true basis.[10] John is more explicit: Jesus is not simply a channel through which the influence of the Father flows, but he in his turn does the works which the Father gives him to bring to their fulfillment;*[11] similarly, in their turn, men accomplish the works God has prepared beforehand.[12]

[8]1 Cor 11:1; 1 Thes 1:6. [9]Rom 8:29; Eph 5:1; Col 1:15. [10]Mt 5:48; Lk 6:36; Jn 13:15,34; 15:12; 1 Pt 1:15f. [11]Jn 5:36; 17:4. [12]Eph 2:10.

→ disciple—figure—follow—image—typology.

excommunicate The N.T. shows acquaintance with two of the three degrees of excommunication specified by the rabbis*: (a) radical excommunication (Heb. *hérèm*) consists in laying down an anathema*[1] or in a deliverance to Satan*;[2] (b) setting apart from the life of the community (Heb. *neziphâ*) and temporary exclusion (Heb. *nidduy. . .*) are reflected in the following expressions: to be exiled from the synagogue* (Gk. *apo-synagōgos*),[3] to separate (Gk. *aphorizō*),[4] to cut off from the group *(ekballō),*[5] to treat as a Gentile,[6] to bind and loose.[7]

[1]Rom 9:3; 1 Cor 16:22; Gal 1:8f. [2]1 Cor 5:5; 1 Tim 1:20. [3]Jn 9:22; 12:42; 16:2. [4]Lk 6:22. [5]3 Jn 10. [6]Mt 18:17. [7]Mt 16:19.

→ anathema—bind and loose—Church.

[exegesis] Gk. *exēgeomai:* "to lead, guide from end to end, expose in detail, explain, interpret." The science of interpretation, striving to establish the meaning of a text or of a literary work. It makes use of the classical methods of reading the text: textual, literary, historical criticism*; it is to issue a "telling" of the text in a contemporary way of speaking.

exile The place and living conditions of a deported people. The origin of this depiction is found in the image of the deportation* to Babylon,* which the Jews interpreted as a punishment for sin and as a fruitful test,* an experience of death and resurrection. Two Greek terms take a bead on this image: *par-oikeō:* "to dwell *(oikeō)* beside *(para)* the people of the country," "to be a resident* alien," "an immigrant." Like Abraham and his descendants, like Moses,[1] the Christian reckons himself to be a foreigner in exile on this earth.[2] The other word *ek-dēmeō,* to be outside of *(ek)* one's people *(dēmos)* is applied only to man's mortal state.[3]

[1]Acts 7:6,29; 13:17; Heb 11:9f. [2]1 Pt 1:17; 2:11. [3]2 Cor 5:6-9.

→ Intr. I.1.A.—deportation—Diaspora—fatherland—stranger.

exodus Gk. *exodos,* meaning "the way leading out," whence "the action of going out" (Lk 9:31). The name of the second book of the Pentateuch,* called in Hebrew *weélle shemôt* ("And these are the names").

1. In the strict sense, the going out of the Hebrews from Egypt or, more broadly speaking, the long journey in the desert which led them to the promised land, probably in the thirteenth to the twelfth centuries B.C.[1]

[1]Acts 7; 13:17f.; Heb 3:8,16f.; 8:5,9; 11:22,29; 12:20.

2. Following Isaiah, who interpreted the return from the deportation* as a new exodus,[2] the N.T. describes the redemption* wrought by Jesus Christ with the help of figures* taken from the Exodus tradition: the passage through the Red Sea,[3] the gift of manna[4] and of living water,[5] the lifting up of the serpent in the desert,[6] the formation of a new people of God[7] entrusted with a new worship,[8] the renewal of the Covenant,[9] on the mountain,[10] finally, Jesus the immolated Paschal lamb.[11]

[2]Is 35; 40–45. [3]1 Cor 10:1-16; Rv 15:3; cf. Ex 14–15; Wis 18–19. [4]Jn 6:31-49; cf. Ex 16. [5]Jn 7:37f.; 19:34; cf. Ex 17. [6]Jn 3:14. [7]1 Pt 2:9f. Rv 5:9f.; cf. Ex 19:6; Is 43:20. [8]1 Pt 2:5; cf. Ex 4:23. [9]Rv 11:19; cf. Ex 25:9. [10]Acts 7:37f.; Gal 4:24f.; Heb 8:5; 12:20; cf. Ex 24. [11]Jn 1:29; 19:36; 1 Cor 5:7; 1 Pt 1:18f.; Rv 5:9; cf. Ex 12:5.

→ desert—manna.

exorcize **1.** Three Greek verbs designate the action by which a demon is cast out of a possessed person in the name of the deity or in virtue of oaths or formulas of a more or less magical kind: "to adjure, conjure up (Gk. *horkizō, ex-, en-*) the demon to come out." Their use is rare in the N.T., which places this word only in the very mouth of the demon whom Jesus exorcized[1] or in that of Jewish exorcists,[2] or, finally, uses it in the metaphorical sense.[3] To drive out, expel (Gk. *ek-ballō*). To go out (Gk. *ex-erchomai*).

[1]Mk 5:7. [2]Acts 19:13. [3]Mt 26:63; 1 Thes 5:27.

2. The Jews were acquainted with these practices.[4] At the same time as he revealed himself an exorcist,[5] Jesus ordinarily was satisfied to command without declaiming an oath,[6] and his disciples did the same in the name of the authority given them.[7] The casting out of demons signified that the kingdom* of God triumphs over Satan,[8] at least when it is effected by the just.*[9]

[4]Mt 12:27; Mk 9:38f. (= Lk 9:49f.); Acts 19:13-19. [5]Mk 7:33f.; 8:23-25. [6]Mk 1:25 (= Lk 4:35); 5:8 (= Lk 8:29); 9:25 (= Lk 9:42). [7]Mt 10:1,8 (= Mk 3:15; 6:7 = Lk 9:1); 17:19; Mk 16:17; Acts 5:16; 8:7. [8]Mt 12:24-28 (= Mk 3:22-27 = Lk 11:14-20); Lk 13:32. [9]Mt 7:22; Lk 10:20.

→ demons—magic—possessed—Satan—spirit.

expiate, expiation From the Lat. *expiare:* "to purify by erasing the fault which separates from the gods," "to render pleasing" to the gods a person, place, or thing. Gk. *hilasmos:* "expiation," deriving from *hilaskomai:* "to show oneself to be favorable, to agree with,"[1] *hileōs:* "propitious,[2] benevolent." Heb. *kippèr:* "to cover, pardon." While Greek religion saw in the rite of purification the reparation which rendered the gods favorable, the O.T. centered its attention on Yahweh who, through the cultic act of the High Priest,* acted alone and pardoned sins.[3] To expiate sins is not—despite the evolution of the English language—to undergo punishment, even if it be accepted as proportionate to the transgression, but it is, through a faith which is active, to allow oneself to be reconciled* by God. In Jesus Christ, who by his blood* made expiation for our sins,[4] cultic activity finds its true meaning: Jesus Christ is the only intercessor* (Gk. *hilasmos*) through whom God becomes propitious and man pleasing to God.[5]

[1]Lk 18:13; Heb 2:17 △. [2]Mt 16:22; Heb 8:12 △. [3]Ex 29:36f.; Lv 1:4; 4:20,26. [4]Heb 2:17. [5]1 Jn 2:2; 4:10 △.

→ Atonement (Feast of the)—pardon—propitiatory—reconcile—sin.

eye Gk. *opthalmos* (cf. *opsomai:* "I will see," *pros-ōpon:* "face, visage"), Heb. *'ayin:* "source, eye," the source of tears.[1] This organ of vision is a member of the body;[2] the eye and the ear* can signify the totality of human action.[3] It is one of man's most precious possessions, as is indicated by the word "pupil" which in Greek is translated *korē:* "daughter of the eye"[4] and in Heb. by *ishôn:* "little man of the eye."[5] Among expressions in which the eye is prominent are these: "To open the eyes" means to give sight,[6] to deliver from spiritual darkness;[7] to have one's eyes open is to recognize someone.[8] The eye is identified with the heart* in order to point to the spirit* which lays hold of something.[9] The eye gives away the inner man, it is the "lamp of the body"[10] which, in letting in the divine light, forestalls a fall[11] and lets one marvel at God's wondrous deeds.[12] Moreover, there is mention of a good eye[13] and an evil eye,[14] as well as the covetousness of eyes.[15] "To lift up one's eyes" means to become aware of something[16] or to enter upon a dialogue with someone, even with God himself.[17] Jesus opened the eyes of the blind* to symbolize the reception of the Good News.[18] Happy were those eyes![19]

[1]Jer 8:23; Rv 21:4. [2]1 Cor 12:16f. [3]Is 6:11; Mt 13:14f.; Mk 8:18. [4]Ps 17:8; Lam 2:18. [5]Dt 32:10. [6]Mt 9:30; Jn 9:10,14. [7]Is 42:7; Acts 26:18. [8]Lk 24:31. [9]Sir 17:8; Lk 19:42; Gal 3:1; Eph 1:18. [10]Mt 6:22f. [11]Mt 15:14. [12]Ps 118:23; Mt 21:42 (= Mk 12:11). [13]Lk 11:34. [14]Mt 20:15. [15]Mt 5:29; 18:9; 2 Pt 2:14; 1 Jn 2:16. [16]Mt 17:8; Lk 16:23; Jn 4:35; 6:5. [17]Lk 6:20; 18:13; Jn 11:41; 17:1. [18]Mt 9:29f.; Mk 8:18,23,25; Jn 9. [19]Mt 13:16 (= Lk 10:23).

→ blind—face—see.

[Ezra] **1.** A Jewish reformer after the exile,* he lived under Artaxerxes II toward 400 B.C. (rather than under Artaxerxes I, toward 458 B.C.). This important scribe,* responsible for Jewish questions at the court of the King of Persia, was, with Nehemiah, the founder of the Jewish community, whose protection he ensured by means of the Law, as a "hedge" surrounding it.[1]

[1]Neh 8.

2. The canonical* books of *Ezra/Nehemiah* were originally joined together in the Hebrew Bible and preceded Chronicles; much later they were separated. Ezra includes some passages written in Aramaic.*[1]

[1]4:8–6:18; 7:12-26.

3. The *Third Book of Ezra* is an apocryphal* variant of Chronicles. It bears the number three from the fact that, in the Vulgate, it followed Nehemiah, which in turn was reckoned as Second Ezra.

4. The *Fourth Book of Ezra* (also called the *Apocalypse of Ezra,* or *Second Ezra*) is an apocryphal* writing of the O.T., edited in Aramaic toward the end of the first century A.D. and known through the Latin translation of a Greek version. A work of the apocalyptic genre, it is related to the Apocalypse of Baruch.* The Requiem derives from this work. Chapters 1–2 and 15–16 are Christian interpolations.

fabrics The N.T. mentions several kinds of fabrics (in the generic sense, Gk. *rhakos*) which can be made of flax* or wool,* dyed purple* or scarlet*: namely linen* wrappings, cloths,* shrouds,* linens* (handkerchief, napkin or apron), tablecloths,* facecloths,* veils.*[1]

[1]Mt 9:16 (= Mk 2:21) □.

→ *Intr.* VIII.1.B.

face Gk. *prosōpon* (derived from *ōps:* "sight"): "in front of the sight."

1. The face should reflect the heart's* sentiments;[1] otherwise, man risks being partial in judging others on appearances,*[2] something which neither God nor Jesus ever does.[3]

[1]Prv 27:19; Sir 13:25; Mt 6:16f. [2]Col 3:25; Jas 2:1-9; Jude 16. [3]1 Sm 16:7; Sir 35:22; Jer 11:20; Mt 22:16 (= Mk 12:14 = Lk 20:21); Acts 10:34; Rom 2:11; Gal 2:6; Eph 6:9; 1 Pt 1:17.

2. God's face, contemplated by the angels,*[4] but which no man has even seen,*[5] is God himself as he turns toward man.[6] It was actualized in this world in Jesus, in whom the Father can be seen;[7] it was anticipated in Jesus' glorious transfiguration,*[8] but also jeered at, veiled, disfigured here below.[9]

[4]Mt 18:10. [5]Ex 33:18-23; Is 6:5; Jn 1:18; 5:37. [6]Ps 4:7; 80:4; 104:29; Is 54:8; Acts 2:28; 1 Pt 3:12; cf. Nm 6:25; Ps 22:25. [7]Jn 14:9. [8]Mt 17:2 (= Lk 9:29). [9]Mk 14:65.

3. The believer, with uncovered face, reflects the glory* of God which is on the face of Christ,[10] while he waits to see God directly, face to face.[11]

[10]2 Cor 3:18; 4:6. [11]1 Cor 13:12; Rv 22:3f.; cf. Mt 5:8; Heb 9:24; 12:14; 1 Jn 3:2.

→ glory—see.

facecloth Gk. *soudarion* (borrowed from the Lat. *sudarium*). A kind of scarf or handkerchief,[1] meant for wiping off sweat. It could also be used to hide money in the ground[2] or to wrap up a dead person's head.[3]

[1]Acts 19:12. [2]Lk 19:20. [3]Jn 11:44; 20:7 □.

→ Intr. VIII.2.D.b.

faith Gk. *pistis* (from *pith-ti-s:* "the act of giving one's trust," with which *peithomai:* "to believe in, trust in, entrust oneself to" is also related): "trust." The verb *pisteuō* has the same sense. These Greek words enabled the Septuagint* to render the Hebrew *emûnâ, hè'èmîn* (derived from the root *'mn:* "to be stable"), adding to the Greek the nuance of firmness and the aspect of truth* (Heb. *emèt*) which is not something discovered, but rather is that living relationship established between two beings. Another Semitic substrate, the root *bâtâh:*

"to depend on, entrust oneself to" agrees even more with the Greek sense of trust.* Finally, the N.T. adds to the O.T. usage the expression *pisteuein eis:* "to believe in" and *pisteuein hoti:* "to believe that." A correct understanding of faith in the biblical sense must lay hold of the aspects of trust and of the truth relationship. John makes use only of the verb.

1. Abraham* is the type and the father of believers. To God, who took the initiative and promised him a land* and a posterity, he replied in obedience* to his word, supplying belief in God despite appearances to the contrary.[1] When Abraham received a son he was invited to offer him in sacrifice, but that was in order that he might receive him back alive. Through this test he came to understand the promise* of God, not the God of promises.[2] Therefore, he became the father of a multitude of peoples.[3]

[1]Gn 12:1-3; 15:1-6; Rom 4:18-22; Heb 11:8-10. [2]Gn 22; Heb 11:17-19. [3]Lk 1:54f.; Rom 4:17.

2. It is by faith that man lives: without it he cannot continue to exist.[4] Faith is man's profound response to God's initiative recognized in his word and in his saving interventions.[5] It is not the result of human reflection, but is freely brought about in us by the power of God, by the Holy Spirit.[6] To welcome the Word is to commit oneself totally in a relationship with God; indeed, the object of faith is not a certain number of truths but the personal and subsisting truth* from which these truths receive their worth. Faith is knowledge* in the biblical sense of this term: it grasps one's whole being, is intelligent adherence and not a leap in the dark; it is absolute trust in the living and true God, a dependence exclusively on him and a loving obedience.[7]

[4]Is 7:9; Hab 2:3f.; Rom 1:17. [5]Rom 10:14f.; Gal 1:11f. [6]Acts 5:11; Rom 3:27; 4:2-5; 1 Cor 12:3; Eph 2:8f.; 2 Thes 2:13. [7]Rom 1:5; 6:17; 2 Cor 10:4; 1 Thes 1:6; 2 Thes 1:8.

3. The faith which Jesus demanded during his earthly life and which his miracles sought to elicit was a faith in the almighty power of God.[8] But he himself demanded the equivalent when he required men to accept his own word[9] and when he blessed the one who heard the Word of God and kept it.[10]

[8]Mk 11:22. [9]Mt 18:6; Jn 14:1. [10]Lk 11:28; cf. 1:45.

4. Christian faith has as its proper object the mystery of Jesus Christ, whom God raised from the dead[11] and made Savior of all men.[12] Occasionally the term contains an "objective" sense, thereby designating the apostolic message;[13] a prophet* must remain in agreement with the faith of the Church (*kata tēn analogian tēs pisteōs:* "in accord with the faith").[14]

[11]Rom 4:24; 10:9; 1 Cor 12:3; 15:3-5; Phil 2:8-11. [12]Acts 4:12; Rom 3:23-26; 1 Cor 1:30f.; Gal 2:16; Eph 1:3-11. [13]Rom 10:8; Gal 1:23; 3:2,5; 6:10; Eph 4:5; 1 Tim 3:9; 4:1,6; Ti 1:4. [14]Rom 12:6.

5. Faith alone justifies and not works* of the law.[15] But faith is active through love and produces the delightful fruits* of charity.[16] Hence, the sense of a "rule" of faith, succeeding the rule of Law.*[17]

[15]Rom 3:21-26; 10:6; Gal 3:16. [16]Rom 8:14; 1 Cor 6:9-11; Gal 5:25; 6:8; 1 Thes 1:3; Jas 2:17-26. [17]Rom 1:17; Gal 3:6-29.

6. As the adherence of one's whole being, faith is fidelity* in the midst of tests*[18] and continual progress in knowledge of God which flowers in wisdom.*[19] Bound intimately to hope and love,* faith manifests two characteristics: not seeing (which will end in heaven)[20] and acceptance of the Word (which will continue in heaven).[21]

[18]1 Cor 16:13; Phil 1:29; Eph 6:16; Col 1:23; 2:5-7; 1 Thes 3:2f.; 2 Thes 1:4. [19]1 Cor 1:19f.; 2 Cor 10:15; Eph 3:16-19; Phil 3:8-10; 1 Thes 3:10; 2 Thes 1:3. [20]1 Cor 13:12; Heb 2:8; Rv 22:4. [21]Jn 17:14,17; 1 Cor 13:13; 1 Thes 1:6; 1 Jn 2:5.

→ Intr. X.—amen—faithful—see—trust—truth—unbelief.

faithful, fidelity The Greek of the N.T. does not distinguish between faith and fidelity *(pistis),* between believing and faithful *(pistos).* In fact, this term translates the single Heb. word *emûnâ,* which came from the word truth* *(emèt).* The word's content was made precise: faith* did not signify only the knowledge and affirmation of some truth, but also and above all a trusting commitment to one person, God or man, who was the sought after "truth" and who was discovered in dialogue. Hence, that aspect of permanence which was characteristic of truth in the Hebraic sense of the term. Consequently, the English language allows for some shading of the literary data. Someone is faithful who, through the test of time, holds fast in the faith[1] and who thereby expresses God's fidelity to his promises[2] and Jesus Christ's fidelity to God himself.[3]

[1]Mt 24:45; 25:21 (= Lk 19:17); Lk 12:42,46; 16:10-12; Rom 3:3; 1 Cor 4:2,17; Col 1:7; 4:7,9; 1 Tim 1:12; 3:11; 2 Tim 2:2,13; Ti 2:10; Heb 3:5; 1 Pt 5:12; 3 Jn 5; Rv 2:10,13; 17:14; 21:8. [2]Rom 3:3; 1 Cor 1:9; 10:13; 2 Cor 1:18; 1 Thes 5:24; 2 Thes 3:3; 2 Tim 2:13; Heb 10:23; 11:11; 1 Pt 4:19; 1 Jn 1:9. [3]Heb 2:17; 3:2; Rv 1:5; 3:14; 19:11.

→ faith—trust—truth.

fall Two terms, occasionally joined for more descriptive purposes,[1] delineate the fact or the cause of a believer's fall. One can stumble (Gk. *proskoptō*) against a stone,*[2] which then becomes a stumbling block (Gk. *proskomma*):[3] this expression stands for any obstacle one can run up against and as a result of which one falls down.[4] Reckoning this obstacle as something actually active, one can then speak of a *skandalon:* a person,[5] word,[6] deed,[7] organ,[8] event,[9] something[10] which becomes a snare.[11] The cross* of Jesus is the obstacle above all others.[12]

[1]Is 8:14; Rom 9:33; 14:21; 1 Cor 8:9,13; 1 Pt 2:8. [2]Mt 4:6; Lk 4:11; Jn 11:9f. [3]Rom 9:32f.; 1 Pt 2:8. [4]Acts 24:16; Rom 14:13,20f.; 1 Cor 8:9; 10:32; 2 Cor 6:3; Phil 1:10 △. [5]Mt 11:6; 13:57; 18:6; 26:31,33; Mk 6:3; 9:42; 14:27,29; Lk 7:23; 17:2; Rom 16:17. [6]Mt 15:12; Jn 6:61. [7]Mt 17:27; Rom 14:13,21; 1 Cor 8:13. [8]Mt 5:29f.; 18:8f.; Mk 9:43,45,47. [9]Mt 13:21; 24:10; Mk 4:17; Jn 16:1; 2 Cor 11:29. [10]Mt 13:41; 18:7; Lk 17:1; Rom 9:33; 11:9; 1 Pt 2:8. [11]Ps 124:7; Rv 2:14. [12]1 Cor 1:23; Gal 5:11 △.

→ scandal.

[farewell discourse] A literary genre* universally characteristic of literature, attested in the O.T.[1] and Judaism (Testaments of the Twelve Patriarchs, Jubilees, etc.), usually containing four phases: the dying subject summons his family (frequently in the context of a meal), encourages and advises his children, rehearses his past (which he offers as a model) and foretells the future. The N.T. reproduces Paul's farewell discourse at Miletus[2] or in the Pastoral Epistles*;[3] it also presents several traditions of farewell discourses by Jesus who, in them, confers meaning upon his death: there is only a trace of such a discourse in Matthew and Mark,[4] but it is developed in Luke[5] and prominent in John.[6]

[1]Gn 49; Dt 33; 1 Kgs 2; Tb 14; 1 Mc 2:49-70. [2]Acts 20:17-38. [3]1 Tim 4:1f.; 2 Tim 3–4. [4]Mt 26:29 (= Mk 14:25). [5]Lk 22:15-18,21-38. [6]Jn 13–17.

fast, fasting Gk. *nēsteia.*

1. In Judaism, unlike in other religions, fasting was not an ascetical exploit: is not food a gift of God?[1] It was the equivalent of "humbling one's soul," an attitude of dependence on God.[2] Thus, it was practiced to prepare to meet God,[3] to make lamentation[4] or to implore some favor or other[5] (pardon for a group or for an individual,[6] divine light,[7]) as well as before fulfilling a mission.[8] Inseparable from almsgiving* and prayer,*[9] it further implied abstention from baths,* perfumes* and sexual relations; above all, it necessitated love of the poor.*[10]

[1]Dt 8:3; Mt 15:32; Mk 8:3. [2]Lv 16:29-31. [3]Ex 34:28; Dn 9:3. [4]1 Sm 31:13. [5]2 Sm 12:16,22; Jl 2:12-17. [6]1 Kgs 21:27; Jon 3:5,7f. [7]Dn 10:3,12. [8]Jgs 20:26; Acts 14:23. [9]Mt 6:2-4,5-8,16-18; 17:21 (= Mk 9:29); Lk 2:37; Acts 13:3. [10]Is 58:3-7; Jl 2:16.

2. In Jesus' time, it was prescribed on certain occasions and notably on the day of atonement* called: "the Fast."[11] Out of devotion John the Baptist's disciples and the Pharisees* practiced it regularly, not without running a risk of ostentation.[12]

[11]Lv 23:29; Acts 27:9. [12]Jer 14:12; Mt 6:16f.; 9:14 (= Mk 2:18 = Lk 5:33); Lk 18:12.

3. Jesus' fast in the wilderness was an act of abandonment, of trust in the Father alone, at the moment when he began his mission.[13]

[13]Mt 4:2; cf. Ex 34:28; 1 Kgs 19:8.

4. It remained a normal practice of the Christian Church, in which it revealed its expectation of the Lord's return.[14]

[14]Acts 13:2; 2 Cor 6:5; 11:27; cf. Mt 9:14f. (= Mk 2:19f. = Lk 5:34f.) □.

father Gk. *patēr,* Heb. *âb.* Heb. *abînû:* to say "our father."

1. In the proper sense. The father as well as the mother were to be honored,[1] but this obligation was not an absolute.[2] They had to keep themselves from arbitrariness and brutality.[3]

[1]Intr. VIII.2.A; Ex 20:12; Mt 15:4-6 (= Mk 7:10-12); 19:5,19 (= Mk 10:7,19 = Lk 18:20); Eph 5:31; 6:2. [2]Mt 4:22 (= Mk 1:20); 8:21 (= Lk 9:59); 10:35,37 (= Lk 12:53; 14:26); 19:29 (= Mk 10:29); Lk 2:48f. [3]Eph 6:4; Col 3:21; Heb 12:7.

2. In the broad sense. The ancestors (in the plural), and more particularly Abraham, Isaac, Jacob, David.[4] In Judaism, the rabbi* was called "father"; Jesus condemned excess in this usage,[5] while Paul considered himself the father of Christians whom he had guided to the faith.[6]

[4]Mt 3:9 (= Lk 3:8); 23:30,32 (= Lk 11:47f.); Mk 11:10; Jn 4:1,12,20; 6:31; 8:56; Acts 3:13; Rom 4; Jas 2:21; 2 Pt 3:4. [5]Mt 23:9. [6]1 Cor 4:15; Gal 4:19; 1 Thes 2:11; Ti 1:4; Phlm 10.

3. God, in the O.T., was said to be Israel's father[7] or king but rarely an individual's father;[9] this was in virtue of a paternity that had nothing to do with mythology or biology, but which derived from their election* and redemption* by God.[10] This fatherhood moreover had nothing in it of the Roman *paterfamilias* idea, but instead brimmed over with tenderness.[11] Confronted by downcast spirits, Jesus revealed the breadth and depth of the divine fatherhood towards all men, even sinners.[12] He never called God the father of Israel, but either "my father" (abba!*)[13] or "your father";[14] or, equivalently, in the prayer of the disciples: "our Father"; all believers are sons of God, children* of God.[15]

[7]Ex 4:22; Dt 32:6; Is 63:16; Jer 31:9. [8]2 Sm 7:14; Ps 89:27. [9]Sir 4:10; 23:1-4; 51:10; Mal 2:10. [10]Dt 14:1f.; Hos 11. [11]Hos 11:3f. [12]Mt 5:45; 6:32; Lk 15. [13]Mt 7:21; 10:32; 11:27; Mk 14:36; Lk 2:49; Jn. [14]Mt 5:16; Mk 11:25f.; Jn 20:17. [15]Lk 11:2; Jn 1:12,18; Rom 8:15,29; Gal 4:6; 1 Pt 1:17; 1 Jn 3:1.

→ abba—child—God—mother.

fatherland

Gk. *patris.* This word means either the land of the fathers in its entirety[1] or the place of origin, the city or town where the family settled down.[2] While Jesus wept over Jerusalem, he had no earthly dwelling-place,[3] like the patriarchs who were searching for a better fatherland.[4]

[1]2 Mc 8:21; Jn 4:44. [2]Mt 13:54 (= Mk 6:1), 57 (= Mk 6:4 = Lk 4:24). [3]Cf. Mt 8:20; Lk 19:41; Jn 1:38. [4]Heb 11:14-16; cf. Phil 3:20; 1 Pt 1:1 □.

Fathers of the Church

→ Church Fathers.

fathom

→ span.

fear

Gk. *phobeomai.*

1. In the face of certain dangers, death,[1] a demon,[2] God's judgment,[3] the catastrophes of the end of time,*[4] the hardness of a demanding master,[5] man experiences a feeling which causes him to be apprehensive about a harmful outcome. The believer must overcome this fear in Christ.[6]

[1]Heb 2:15. [2]Mt 10:28 (= Lk 12:5). [3]Heb 10:27. [4]Lk 21:11. [5]Mt 25:25. [6]Mt 10:28; Heb 2:15.

2. The fear of God has nothing to do with such fright. It is a feeling of reverence before God who reveals himself, either personally or through his angels; through hearing "Don't be afraid!" a man transforms his fear into adoration* and into a filial trust* which puts aside every fear;[7] he becomes a man who is pious* (Gk. *eulabēs*).[8] In reverse fashion, the hardened* sinner can tremble.[9] Love drives out fear.[10]

[7]Mt 14:27; 17:6f.; 28:5,10; Lk 1:12f.,30; 2:9f.; 5:10; cf. 2 Cor 7:15. [8]Heb 5:7; 11:7. [9]Heb 10:27,31. [10]1 Jn 4:18; 5:3.

→ adore—piety—sacred.

feast **1.** From the Lat. *festus:* "joyful, rejoicing"; Gk. *heortē.* Ordinarily, the term is specified by a proper noun: Unleavened Bread, Passover,[1] Booths,[2] or by the context.[3] Used absolutely, it refers to the Jewish Passover.[4] In the plural it has a general meaning.[5] Once, also, we find the word *panēgyris* (from *pas:* "all" and *ageirō:* "to assemble," *agora:** "assembly"): "festal gathering, reunion."[6]

[1]Lk 2:41; 22:1; Jn 2:23; 6:4; 13:1. [2]Jn 7:2; cf. 5:1. [3]Mt 26:5 (= Mk 14:2); 27:15 (= Mk 15:6 = Lk 23:17); Lk 2:42; Jn 7:8,10f.,14,37; 13:29. [4]Jn 4:45; 11:56; 12:12,20; 1 Cor 5:8. [5]Col 2:16 △. [6]Heb 12:22. △.

2. A celebration of a cultic and communitarian nature, lived out by the whole people and linked with the events of nature (the lunar and solar cycles), of work (sowing, harvest, seasons, vintaging) and of its history (the exodus from Egypt, the consecration of the Temple). Thanksgiving and jubilation before God the Creator and Savior typified the Jewish feasts, one of them being set aside to ask for forgiveness and for reconciliation with God.[7]

[7]Intr. XIII.3.

3. The meaning of the feast was not restricted to recalling the past; it was also a calling out for God's fidelity in the present, and most of all asking that he bring hope to reality and salvation to completion.

4. Jesus fulfilled his sacrifice in the setting of Passover (liberation from the bondage of Egypt),[8] foretold the gift of the Spirit on the Feast of Booths,[9] a gift that was given on Pentecost.[10] In keeping with his role in the prophetic tradition, Jesus powerfully recalled that worship is not worth a thing without the exercise of justice.[11]

[8]Jn 19:36. [9]Jn 7:37f.; Rv 7:9. [10]Acts 2:33. [11]Is 1:13; Hos 2:11-13; Am 5:21-24; Mt 12:1-8 (= Mk 2:23-28 = Lk 6:1-5).

5. With Jesus' action the ancient forms of worship* became out-of-date, for believers are no longer subject to the cycle of nature[12] and the events formerly celebrated were but figures* of the reality which is the Covenant in Christ's Passover.[13] Furthermore, celebration of the paschal mystery is the Christian feast par excellence, of which each Sunday is a reflection.

[12]Gal 4:10; Col 2:16. [13]1 Cor 5:7f.; 10:11.

→ Intr. XIII.3.—Atonement—Booths—Dedication—joy—Lord's Day—Passover—Pentecost—pilgrimage—sabbath—Unleavened Bread—worship.

Felix A Latin name meaning: "fruitful, happy" (related to *fecundus*). The brother of Pallas (a favorite of Claudius*), a freedman* of the empress Antonia, the (uncircumcised) husband of Drusilla* (the daughter of Agrippa I), procurator* of Judea from 52 to 59/60. Contrary to what Tertullus says in Acts 24:2f., with great cruelty Felix put down the Zealot* movement which developed under his rule. In spite of the juridical practice which permitted him to set Paul free, he kept him in prison to please the Jews and in order to obtain money from him.[1]

[1]Acts 23:24–24:27; 25:14 □.

fertility

→ fruitfulness.

Festus A Latin name signifying: "festive, merry, joyous, amusing." Porcius F. Festus, named procurator* of Judea by Nero in 60. He submitted to Caesar (that is, to Rome) the case of Paul, whom Felix* had kept prisoner.[1] He died suddenly in 62.

[1]Acts 24:27–26:32 □.

fever Gk. *pyretos.* For the ancient world a fever was not a symptom but an illness. The word, derived from *pyr:* "fire," meant "the fire's heat"; for the rabbis it was "the fire of the bones." Fever, which designated a malady that was occasionally fatal, was one of the punishments that Yahweh had reserved for his unfaithful people.[1] As with other illnesses, a demonic*[2] origin was readily assigned to fevers, something which only prayer and a miracle could overcome.[3]

[1]Lv 26:16. [2]Comp. Lk 4:39 and Mt 8:15 (= Mk 1:31). [3]Jn 4:52; Acts 28:8 □.

→ heal—sickness.

fidelity

→ faithful, fidelity.

fiery pool Gk. *limnē tou pyros:* "lake of fire," "pool of fire." One of the apocalyptic* terms to designate hell,* the place of definitive punishment. It is the equivalent of fiery Gehenna.* In this there might well be a reflection of that conception according to which the Dead Sea underwent the punishment of Sodom through fire* and sulphur.*[1]

[1]Rv 19:20; 20:10,14f. □; cf. Lk 17:29; Rv 21:8.

→ fire—hell—sea.

fig tree Gk. *sykē: ficus carica.* Found widely in Palestine, where its shade was appreciated, the fig tree flourished even in rocky terrain when there was sufficient moisture. After the harvest of mid-summer, it remained weighted down with the little green figs which had been unable to ripen; but these furnished the first of the fruit at the onset of the following June. Frequent mention is made of it and its fruits.[1]

[1]Is 28:4; Jer 8:13; Hos 9:10; Mt 7:16 (= Lk 6:44); 21:19-21 (= Mk 11:13,20f.); 24:32 (= Mk 13:28 = Lk 21:29); Lk 13:6f.; Jn 1:48,50; Jas 3:12; Rv 6:13 □.

→ Intr II.5; VII.1.A.

figure From the Lat. *figura,* translating the Gk. *typos.* This word can also mean "imprint,"[1] "idol image,"[2] "rule of doctrine."[3] It ought not to be confused with the Gk. *schēma,* which is translated "structure*" (1 Cor 7:31) or "aspect" (Phil 2:7). Here it is taken in a particular sense which goes off in two directions.

[1]Jn 20:25; 2 Cor 3:7. [2]Acts 7:43. [3]Rom 6:17.

1. First of all, it allows for the expression of a parallel that unites the N.T. with the O.T., deriving out of that specific conception of God's plan* which sees the O.T. as the "figurative" proclamation and the N.T. as its fulfillment.* Situated at the end* of time, the believer comprehends what had been a "figure" in past history. So, Adam* was a figure of the Adam who had to come;[4] the events of the Exodus* happened in figures for us whom the end of time has brought together;[5] baptism* is an "antitype" of the flood;[6] Abraham's* faith had us equally in view.[7]

[4]Rom 5:14. [5]1 Cor 10:6,11. [6]1 Pt 3:21. [7]Rom 4:24.

2. According to another orientation, one related to Platonic exemplarism, the happenings which we live through today possess a "model" in the heavens from all eternity.[8] Thus, in the Epistle to the Hebrews, the former sanctuary is but an image of the reality;[9] Isaac on the sacrificial pyre is a symbol* (Gk. *parabolē*) of Christ put to death and raised;[10] rest in the Promised Land prefigures the heavenly rest.[11] Beginning with these few explicit instances, the reader can take a chance on finding implicit correspondences such as the twelve apostles and the twelve tribes of Israel, Jesus' last meal and the paschal sacrifice, the Eucharist and the manna in the desert.

[8]Ex 25:40; 1 Chr 28:11; Wis 9:8. [9]Heb 9:24. [10]Heb 11:19. [11]Heb 4:9-11.

→ example—form—parable—time—typology.

finger of God Gk. *daktylos tou Theou.* A symbol of the power* of God and of his Spirit.*[1]

[1]Ex 8:15; 31:18; Ps 8:4; Lk 11:20 □.

→ arm—decalogue.

fire Gk. *pyr.* (cf. *pyroō, kaiō:* "to burn"; *phlogizō:* "to inflame"; *haptō:* "to light"): "fire, oven, furnace, charcoal fire, smoke, vapor."

1. One of the four elements,* along with earth, water and air, which, according to the ancients, were constitutive of every body. One of the symbols that speaks of an aspect of divinity,[1] and of heavenly[2] or glorified[3] beings, often associated with contrary symbols like water* or wind.*[4]

[1]Gn 15:17; Ex 3:2-6; 13:21; 19:18; 24:17; Dt 4:24; Jgs 13:20; Heb 12:29. [2]Rv 10:1. [3]Dn 10:6; Rv 1:14; 2:18. [4]1 Kgs 18:38; 19:12.

2. The eschatological* fire is, before all else, purifying;[5] that of Gehenna* and of the fiery pool*[6] is to devour everything.[7] Nonetheless, when anticipated in the present age, this fire is a theophany.*[8]

[5]Gn 19:24; Ex 9:24; Is 66:15; Am 1:4,7; Mal 3:19; Mt 3:10-12; 7:19; 13:42,50; 1 Cor 3:15; 1 Pt 1:7; 4:12-17. [6]Mt 5:22; Rv 20:10,14f. [7]Dt 9:3; Is 33:14; Heb 10:27; 12:29; Jas 5:3. [8]Dn 7:10; Acts 7:30; Rv 1:14; 15:2; 19:12.

3. In Jesus the fire is present, not in the form of vengeance*[9] but under the aspect of baptism* in the Spirit and fire.[10] At Pentecost,* the fire is that of the Spirit* who makes himself heard by all nations.[11] God, finally, consumes the holocaust* of our lives in a worship* that is pleasing to him and in unfailing radiance.[12]

[9]Lk 9:54f. [10]Lk 3:16; 12:49f. [11]Acts 2:3. [12]Heb 12:28.

→ fiery pool—Gehenna—hell—salt—sulphur.

firstborn Gk. *prōtotokos,* Heb. *bekôr:* "what breaks open the womb." The offering of firstborn males, the first fruits* of men, to Yahweh who preserved the sons of the Hebrews in the night in which the firstborn of Egypt perished,[1] was brought about by a substitute gift to the Temple.[2] As the first fruits of a humanity reunited with the Father, Christ is said to be firstborn, a term suggesting priority and excellence,[3] the one who broke through the womb of Sheol,* the firstborn from among the dead.[4] In their turn, believers, the first fruits of the Church, comprise an assembly of the firstborn.[5]

[1]Ex 22:28f.; 34:19; Heb 11:28. [2]Ex 13:13; Lk 2:7,22f.; cf. Gn 22. [3]Rom 8:29; Col 1:15; Heb 1:6. [4]Col 1:18; Rv 1:5. [5]Heb 12:23; cf. Jas 1:18 □.

→ first fruits.

first fruits Gk. *aparchē.* A sacrificial term: a setting apart levied on the "first" fruits of the earth, to be offered to God, the source of every good.[1] Since the part held good for the whole lot,[2] the entire harvest was sanctified by this rite for the sanctified people, who were themselves "the first fruits of God's harvest."[3] The metaphor* is applicable to the risen Christ,[4] to the gift of the Spirit given to believers,[5] to the first converts,[6] to virgins.[7]

[1]Dt 26:1-11. [2]Rom 11:16. [3]Jer 2:3. [4]1 Cor 15:20,23. [5]Rom 8:23. [6]Rom 16:5; 1 Cor 6:15; Jas 1:18. [7]Rv 14:4 □.

→ Intr. VI.3.B.b.—sacrifice—tithe.

fish Gk. *ichthys.* A common foodstuff of economic value.[1] Dietary laws proscribed fish without fins or scales.[2] Dried fish (Gk. *opsarion*) was known.[3] The first Christians spontaneously represented Christ by the emblem of the fish, whose letters stood for *Iēsous Christos Theou Yios Sōtēr* (Jesus Christ, God's Son, Savior).

[1]Mt 7:10 (= Lk 11:11); 14:17,19 (= Mk 6:38,41,43 = Lk 9:13,16); 15:34,36 (= Mk 8:7); 17:27; Lk 5:6,9; 24:42; Jn 21:6,8,11. [2]Lv 11:9-12; 1 Cor 15:39 △; cf. Mt 13:47f. [3]Jn 6:9,11; 21:9f.,13 △.

→ Intr. II.6; VIII.1.D.a.—dragon—fishing.

fishing **1.** On the Lake of Gennesaret corporations, which grouped together employers and workers,[1] practiced the fishing trade (Gk. *halieuō:* "to live on the sea, fish," from *hals:* "sea, salt"; or *agreuō:* "to take with a snare, to fish"), most of all at night with lanterns,[3] with one or several boats.[4] In addition to lines with fish hooks[5] (and spears[6]), they chiefly used nets (Gk. *diktyon*). This was either a kind of sweepnet (Gk. *amphiblēstron,* from *amphi:* "around" and *ballō:* "to cast") weighted on the edges, used mostly for deep-water fishing,[7] or a kind of dragnet (Gk. *sagēnē*), weighted on one end, and with floats on the other, used mostly for surface fishing or for fishing from the shore.[8]

[1]Intr. VII.1. B; Mk 1:20; Lk 5:7. [2]Mk 12:13; 2 Tim 2:26. [3]Lk 5:5; Jn 21:3. [4]Mk 4:36; Lk 5:11. [5]Mt 17:27. [6]Jb 40:26; Am 4:2. [7]Mt 4:18 (= Mk 1:16). [8]Mt 13:47

2. The expression "fishers of men" (Gk. *haleeis anthrōpōn*)[9] or "you will catch men" (Gk. *anthrōpous esēi zōgrōn*)[10] is difficult to interpret. It contains the notions of capturing and snatching, as if with a snare. Possibly it depends on the biblical symbolism of the infernal waters* of death[11] out of which men are snatched; more probably, it seeks to describe the gathering together of men for the final judgment.*[12]

[9]Mt 4:19 (= Mk 1:17). [10]Lk 5:10; cf. 2 Tim 2:26 □. [11]Ps 18:17; 144:7. [12]Mt 13:47–50.

→ fish.

flesh Gk. *sarx,* Heb. *bâsâr.*

1. The creaturely condition. Man *was* flesh more than he *had* flesh. This fact described man's state as exterior, corporeal, earthly; flesh was not so much "matter" (the body) as it was "form" (the soul) molded into a human being. As he did with the word "soul,*" the Semite used the word "flesh" to point to the person,[1] to kinship.[2] The sign of recognition between spouses was not that they were one spirit, but truly one flesh:[3] the core itself of the person was corporeally determined. "All flesh" refered to the totality of creation that was alive.

Flesh was characteristic of the fragile, terrestrial state, in contrast with that of the spirit,* which pointed to a divine or heavenly origin:[5] except for God, all else was flesh.[6] Here below man existed "according to the flesh";[7] he lived "in the flesh."[8] Through the flesh he was visible, present;[9] he suffered,[10] survived.[11] In this sense, the Word* become flesh was truly human, subject to the limitations of this world,[12] but without seeing corruption.[13] "Flesh and blood*" described man in his earthly fragility.[14] "To eat the flesh and drink the blood" of Jesus was to eat him, that is to unite oneself very profoundly to him through the Spirit who gives life; for the flesh by itself had no worth.[15]

At times, under the influence of Hellenism,* flesh could designate man's dullness and his propensity to evil and to sin.[16]

[1]Ps 63:2; 84:3; Acts 2:26. [2]Rom 11:14; Heb 12:9. [3]Gn 2:24; Mt 19:5 (= Mk 10:8); 1 Cor 6:16; Eph 5:31. [4]Jb 34:15; Ps 56:5; Is 66:23; Mt 24:22 (= Mk 13:20); Lk 3:6; Jn 17:2; Rom 3:20; 1 Cor 1:29; Gal 2:16; 1 Pt 1:24 △. [5]Jn 3:6; Rm 1:3f; Phlm 16; Heb 7:16; 1 Pt 4:6. [6]Is 40:6,8; Jer 17:5; Ez 10:12; Jn 1:13; 1 Pt 1:24. [7]Rom 4:1; 9:3,5; 1 Cor 1:26; 10:18; Eph 6:5; Col 3:22. [8]2 Cor 10:3; Gal 2:20; Phil 1:22-24; 1 Pt 4:1f. [9]Col 2:1,5. [10]2 Cor 7:5; 12:7; Gal 4:13f. [11]Eph 5:29. [12]Jn 1:14; Heb 2:14; 5:7; 1 Jn 4:2; 2 Jn 7. [13]Acts 2:31. [14]Mt 16:17; Jn 6:51-56; 1 Cor 15:50; Gal 1:16; Eph 6:12; Heb 2:14 △. [15]Jn 6:53-58,63; cf. 3:6. [16]Mt 26:41 (= Mk 14:38); 2 Pt 2:10.

2. The sinner before God. Following the thought of later Judaism* in readily linking flesh and sin (without thereby making flesh out to be the source of sin), Paul stressed in his teaching a train of thought that was unknown in the O.T.

Good in itself because created by God, the flesh became the source of sin* in that extent to which it "boasted before God."[17] The flesh might designate the rule of the Law* which had lapsed.[18] Though Paul still lived *in* the flesh, he could no longer live *according* to the flesh, for this would involve becoming carnal.[19] Paul systematized this aspect of his thought with his flesh/spirit antithesis:[20] this opposition did not correspond to the one so often made between body and soul, between pure and impure. Rather it played upon the opposition between the earthly and heavenly, alluding thereby to the twofold experience of the Holy Spirit, given to the Christian, and of sin, which reigned in the flesh.[21] But the believer emerged victorious from this combat, through Christ, who, in taking on this "body of flesh,"[22] came in the sinful condition of the flesh and condemned sin in the flesh itself.[23] Living in Christ, the Christian has crucified* his flesh.[24]

[17]Jer 17:5f.; 1 Cor 1:29. [18]Rom 7:5; Gal 3:3; 6:8; Phil 3:3f. [19]Rom 8:12f.; 1 Cor 3:3; 2 Cor 1:12; 10:2-4; 11:18; 1 Pt 2:11. [20]Rom 8:4-9; Gal 4:23,29; 5:16,17,19. [21]Rom 7–8; Gal 4:21-31. [22]Col 1:22. [23]Rom 8:3; 1 Pt 4:1. [24]Gal 5:24; 1 Jn 2:16.

→ body—bone—man—soul—spirit.

flock Gk. *poimnē, poimnion* (which is associated with *poimanō:* "to pasture").[1]

[1]Mt 26:31 (= Mk 14:27); Lk 2:8; 12:32; Jn 10:16; Acts 20:28f.; 1 Cor 9:7; 1 Pt 5:2f. □.

→ Intr. VII.1.B.—goat—sheep—shepherd.

flood Gk. *kataklysmos.* The catastrophic inundation from which only Noah* and his family escaped in the ark.*[1] A type of the judgment* that surprises those unprepared,[2] but spares the just* ones.[3] A prefiguration of salvation* which comes by water baptism.*[4]

[1]Gn 6:5–9:19. [2]Mt 24:38f. (= Lk 17:27). [3]Wis 10:4; 14:6; Sir 44:17f.; Is 54:9; 1 Pt 3:20f. [4]2 Pt 2:5; 3:6 □.

flute Gk. *aulos.* A musical instrument made, in the first instance, from a reed (then from wood, bone or metal) having one or two pipes and with a range of sounds that was probably limited. The melodies of a flute accompanied dancing[1] or mourning.[2] The accompaniment of at least two flutes was the rule for funeral corteges.

[1]Is 5:12; 30:29; Mt 11:17 (= Lk 7:32); 1 Cor 14:7; Rv 18:22. [2]Jer 48:36; Mt 9:23 □.

→ Intr. IX.6.

follow **1.** Gk. *akoloutheō,* from *akolouthos* (the copulative *a* and *keleuthos:* "path"): "companion," which translates the Heb. "to go behind," "to go after" (Gk. *erchomai opisō*), without a significantly different shade of meaning. Two features are worthy of note: the phrase and the verb are hardly ever found except in the gospels[1] and, in their metaphorical meaning, concern the earthly Jesus.[2] The O.T. scarcely uses them at all in reference to God, but regularly uses them to refer to idolatry;*[3] Judaism uses them, in addition, to describe the attitude of a disciple* and of a rabbi's* servant.

[1]In addition 1 Pt 2:21; Rv 14:4. [2]In addition Jn 21:19-22; Acts 5:37; 20:30; 1 Tim 5:15; 2 Pt 2:10; Jude 7; Rv 13:3; 19:14. [3]Dt 4:3; 13:5; Jgs 2:12; 1 Kgs 18:21; Hos 2:7.

2. Jesus called men to his following.[4] As in the O.T., this signifies not "to imitate," nor "to learn behavior," but rather "to attach oneself to, to obey,*"[5] something which, according to John, is the same as "believing."[6] To follow Jesus was to enter the Kingdom of God, which was present; it was to bind oneself to his lot and, more especially, to his cross and his glory.[7] After Easter, it is no longer a case of following Jesus,[8] but of "being in Christ."[9]

[4]Mt 4:19 (= Mk 1:17,20); 9:9 (= Mk 2:14 = Lk 5:27); 19:21 (= Mk 10:21 = Lk 18:22); Jn 1:43. [5]Dt 13:5; 1 Kgs 14:8. [6]Jn 8:12; 10:4f.,27. [7]Mt 8:19,22 (= Lk 9:57,59); 10:38; 16:24 (= Mk 8:34 = Lk 9:23); Jn 12:26. [8]Except in Jn 21:19-22; Rv 14:4. [9]Gal 3:28.

folly **1.** Strange behavior, attributed to various causes and manifested in various ways. Gk. *mania:*[1] "delirium, rambling," admitting of the idea of being in a rage, troubled with violent outbursts, (often attributed to a spirit); insane, Gk. *mōros:*[2] "dazed, dull," *a-phrōn*[3] (from *phrēn*): "disspirited, thoughtless"; out of one's mind (Gk. *ex-istamai:*[4] "to be out of"; unintelligent, Gk. *a-noētos*[5] (from *nous*): "without intelligence"; *a-synetos*[6] (from *syniēmi*): "unable to understand"; without discretion or wisdom, Gk. *a-sophos*[7] (from *sophia*): "without wisdom"; stupid, without reactions, unconscious, inert (Gk. *ap-algeō:*[8] "outside of feeling"). These ways of acting are often set in opposition to a prudence which has been advised (Gk. *phronimos*),[9] with wisdom (Gk. *sophia*).[10]

[1]Jn 10:20; Acts 12:15; 26:11,24f.; 1 Cor 14:23 △. [2]Mt 5:22; 1 Cor 1:18–2:14. [3]Mk 7:22; 2 Cor 11:1–12:11; Eph 5:17ff. [4]Mk 3:21; 2 Cor 5:13 △. [5]Lk 24:25; Rom 1:14; Gal 3:1,3ff [6]Mt 15:16; Mk 7:18; Rom 1:21,31; 10:19 △. [7]Eph 5:15 △. [8]Eph 4:19 △. [9]Mt 7:24,26; 25:2-8; Acts 26:25; 1 Cor 4:10; 2 Cor 5:13; 11:19. [10]Rom 1:22; 1 Cor 1:20f.,25,27; 2:13f.; 3:19; Eph 5:15.

2. According to the Bible, mad conduct often originates in a failure to take account of God.[11] From this, through a paradoxical reversal of perspective, the term designates the ways of God, which paradoxically run counter to the ordinary wisdom of men or, in God's eyes, human ways.[12]

[11]Ps 14:1f.; Jer 4:22; Mt 7:26; 25:2f. [12]Is 29:16; 1 Cor 1:18-25.

→ raca—wisdom.

foot **1.** The foot (Gk. *pous*) refers to someone's power or authority: ancient conquerors set a foot on a conquered one's neck. "To put under" someone's feet meant to submit that to his power: thus Christ's enemies and all things will be put "under" him,[1] or the elements of the universe in the visions of Revelation.[2] "To cast oneself at" someone's feet or "to clasp them" meant to recognize his superiority, to beseech him, to thank him, to adore him;[3] "to be seated at" his feet meant to be submissive, a disciple;[4] "to set down at" someone's feet, either someone or something, meant to entrust that to him.[5]

[1]Dt 2:5; 1 Kgs 5:17; Ps 8:7; 110:1; cf. Mt 22:44 (= Mk 12:36 = Lk 20:43); Acts 2:35; 1 Cor 15:25,27; Eph 1:22; Heb 1:13; 2:8. [2]Rv 10:2; 12:1. [3]Mt 18:29; 28:9; Lk 17:16; Jn 11:32; Acts 10:25; Rv 3:9; 19:10. [4]Lk 8:35; Acts 22:3. [5]Mt 15:30; Acts 4:35; 7:58.

2. To remove a guest's shoes was a slave's function.[6]

[6]Cf. Mk 1:7.

3. To wipe off the dust from one's feet was a gesture of breaking off relations.[7]

[7]Mt 10:14 (= Mk 6:11 = Lk 9:5); Acts 13:51.

→ shoe—wash.

forehead Gk. *met-ōpon* (from *ōps:* "sight, face"). The part of the face exposed to view on which a mark (Gk. *charagma*), a seal (Gk. *sphragis*) may be imprinted. Attested in the O.T.,[1] the custom is linked to tattoos inscribed in the Orient to honor a god or to show off the fact of belonging to a master. In Revelation, the names of God, Christ or the Beast[2] are etched on foreheads.

[1]Ex 12:13; Ez 9:4. [2]Rv 7:3; 9:4; 13:16; 14:1,9; 17:5; 20:4; 22:4 □.

foreskin Gk. *akrobystia.* A fold of skin that covers the tip (Gk. *akros*) of the penis (Gk. *peos, posthē*); Jews perhaps felt it shared some similarity of sound with the word *bôshet:* "shame, shameful member." After having been drawn back slightly, it was cut off by circumcision.*

1. In the strict sense, the "uncircumcised" are those who have kept their foreskin[1] or those who, like the Jews who acted out of shame in the Maccabean period, have had it surgically restored.[2]

[1]Gn 34:14; Acts 11:3. [2]1 Mc 1:15; 1 Cor 7:18.

2. In the metaphorical sense, the "uncircumcised" describes the pagans,* who do not indeed belong to the Covenant of which circumcision is the sign,[3] or even to paganism itself.[4]

[3]Rom 2:25-27; Gal 5:6; 6:15; Col 2:13. [4]Rom 3:30; 4:9-12; Gal 2:7; Eph 2:11; Col 3:11 □.

→ circumcision.

forever

→ age.

forgive, forgiveness Gk. *aphiēmi:* "to let go, set free," Heb. *kippèr:* "to cover," *nâsâ:* "to suppress," *sâlah:* "to pardon." To re-establish that relationship between two beings which had been broken through some offense.

1. Beginning with the O.T. period God is above all the God of pardon, forgiveness;[1] his heart is not like that of man;[2] from the sinner he seeks conversion.*[3] Once God has forgiven, sin* is removed, destroyed, cast behind[4]—it no longer exists, even if man continues to remember that he was a sinner. Here, then, is what God has accomplished in Jesus Christ.[5]

[1]Neh 9:17. [2]Hos 11:8f. [3]Ez 18:23. [4]Ex 32:32; Is 1:18; 6:7; 38:17. [5]Rom 3:21-26; 2 Cor 5:19.

2. Jesus was not content merely to proclaim the forgiveness of the merciful Father; he remitted sins from the time of his earthly ministry.[6] Sent by God to expiate* sins, he gave his life and poured out his blood.* Thus he effected the reconciliation* between God and men.[9] Raised to life, he entrusted to his disciples the mission of proclaiming forgiveness[10] and the power to pardon, forgive in his name.[11]

[6]Mt 9:1-8 (= Mk 2:1-12 = Lk 5:17-26); Lk 7:36-50. [7]Heb 2:17; 1 Jn 4:10. [8]Mt 26:28; Mk 10:45; Lk 22:20; 1 Pt 2:24; 1 Jn 1:7. [9]Rom 5:10f.; 2 Cor 5:18-20; Eph 2:16. [10]Lk 24:47; Acts 5:31; 10:43; 13:38f. [11]Jn 20:23; cf. Mt 16:19; 18:18.

3. To be a son of the heavenly Father, the believer must imitate God and ceaselessly forgive.[12]

[12]Mt 5:23f.,43-48; 6:12-15 (= Mk 11:25 = Lk 11:4); 18:21-35.

→ conversion—debt—expiate—reconcile—sin.

form Two Greek words correspond to that which, without however giving it its true sense, we designate by the word "form." *Morphē* (=M), from an obscure etymology: "mode of being, shape" and *schēma* (=S), from *echō:* "to hold, remain": "bearing; posture; shape; clothing." Each of these has its compound: conform *(syn-);* transform, transfigure *(meta-).*

1. Contrary to that usage which clearly opposes form and essence as if they were the equivalents of appearance and reality, it is advisable to recognize in the "form" not something superimposed on an essence (as clothing is on a body), but rather the being itself which gives expression to itself, lets itself be seen, manifests itself.

2. In this way, the Law manifests a form, one expressive of knowledge and truth.[1] What is in the process of disappearing along with "the form of this world" is not the world's appearance but the world itself, fraught with sin.[2] Of the two ways in which he might have presented himself, Jesus chose the traits not of a lord but of a slave.*[3] During his Easter appearances, he revealed himself with characteristics other than those by which he might have been recognized as Jesus of Nazareth.[4]

[1]Rom 2:20 (*M*). [2]1 Cor 7:31 (*S*). [3]Is 52:14 (*M*); Phil 2:6 (*MS*). [4]Mk 16:12 (*M*).

3. Accordingly, in the N.T. "to conform oneself" means not to imitate a model, but to be handed over from within to a power, to the world,* to covetousness,* or to be invaded by the efficacious power of the death* of Christ[7] and to allow the image* of the Son[8] to be reproduced in oneself. To be transformed or transfigured* is not merely to be changed in one aspect only, but rather it is to allow a power to work in the depth of one's being, namely that glory* which shines on the face of Christ*[9] or that new principle of being, Jesus Christ himself, who will make our mortal body as glorious as his own.[10]

[5]Rom 12:2 (*S*). [6]1 Pt 1:14 (*S*). [7]Phil 3:10 (*M*). [8]Rom 8:29 (*M*); Gal 4:19 (*M*); cf. 2 Cor 3:18. [9]Mt 17:2 (*M*). [10]Phil 3:21 (*SM*).

4. The pseudo-apostles do not disguise themselves as apostles, nor does Satan disguise himself as an angel of light; rather they appear as such.[11] In the the last days some will appear to be pious, but their piety* does not come from Christ.[12]

In addressing the Corinthians, Paul does not offer himself as "an example,*" but rather gives form to his teaching by applying it to Apollos and himself.[13]

[11]2 Cor 11:13-15 (*S*). [12]2 Tim 3:5 (*M*). [13]1 Cor 4:6 (*S*) □.

5. In the literary sense, form is that which gives structure and stability to collected materials. By convention the term designates small literary units; as such, its extent is less than that of the "literary genre.*"

→ appearance—figure—image—structure.

form criticism

→ *Formgeschichte.*

[Formgeschichte] A German word signifying the history *(Geschichte)* of the form *(Form)* which a text has evolved. A method of literary criticism* that attempts to describe the history of a text's formation. In the case of the gospels, the successive strata of this history are determined, starting from the setting in life* in which diverse forms* have given expression to the gospel tradition. Here, "to form" does not mean to invent, but "to give a stable form" to pre-existent material. Today some critics want to replace the word *Formgeschichte* with the English term form criticism, which is less closely connected than the former to diachrony; in this, however, they fail to appreciate the complementary relationships which should unite diachrony and synchrony.

→ Intr. XV.3.—literary genre—*Redaktionsgeschichte*—setting in life.

forty Gk. *tesserakonta.* A number conventional in antiquity, designating in more particular fashion the time necessary for life's maturity. In the O.T., a sufficiently long period,[1] the age for marrying,[2] the length of a generation.[3] In the N.T.: a round number[4] or one of archetypal* significance: the years of Israel in the desert,[5] the periods of Moses' life,[6] the time of Jesus' fast[7] or temptation,[8] the span of time of the Risen One's appearances.[9]

[1]Gn 7:4; Ex 24:18; Lv 12:4; Dt 25:3; 1 Sm 17:16; Ez 4:6; Jon 3:4. [2]Gn 25:20. [3]Ex 16:35; Nm 14:33f.; Jgs 3:11,30; 2 Sm 5:4f.; 1 Kgs 11:42. [4]Acts 4:22; 23:13,21; 2 Cor 11:24. [5]Acts 7:42; 13:18,21; Heb 3:10,17. [6]Acts 7:23,30,36. [7]Mt 4:2 (= Mk 1:13 = Lk 4:2); cf. Dt 9:9. [8]Mk 1:13; cf. Dt 8:2. [9]Acts 1:3 □.

→ numbers.

free, freedom

→ liberate, liberty.

freedman 1. Gk. *ap-eleutheros* (from *ap-eleutheroō:* "to set free in separating oneself"), a former slave who has become free. Among Jews, slaves* had to be set free in the seventh year.[1] Among the Romans, emancipation was effected through two distinct procedures. Either the slave paid out a sum required for his ransom at a sanctuary (thereby he became the exclusive property of the deity), or else his master, for an inspired motive, especially that of Stoic* morality, spontaneously let his slave go free either by taking the step of making a witnessed deposit or else through an audible proclamation. In every case a sum of money was owed to the freedman. From fear of aggravating poverty, collective emancipation was forbidden.

[1]Ex 21:2; Dt 15:12; cf. Acts 6:9.

2. According to Paul, the Christian is the Lord's freedman.[2] The verb *eleutheroō:* "to make free" was also used to signify that the believer had been set free from sin[3] and that he was freed by the truth,[4] by Christ.[5]

[2]1 Cor 7:22 △. [3]Rom 6:18,22; 8:2,21. [4]Jn 8:32f. [5]Jn 8:36; Gal 5:1 △.

→ Intr. IV.4.C.—liberate, liberty—slave.

fringe Gk. *kraspedon,* the translation of the Heb. *ṣîṣit:* "tassel." Every pious Israelite wore on the four corners of his garments a cloth strip which called for a heavenly blue (or violet) thread in order to remind him of God's commandments.[1] It served to express his piety,[2] and even to draw attention to itself.[3]

[1]Nm 15:38f; cf. Ez 8:3. [2]Mt 9:20 (= Lk 8:44); 14:36 (= Mk 6:56). [3]Mt 23:5 □.

→ clothing—phylactery.

fruit Gk. *karpos.* The obligation to bear fruit, constantly emphasized in the O.T., is taken up with insistence in the N.T.: the grain sown in the earth,[2] the vine,[3] the fig tree,[4] the entrusted talents.[5] Very simply, one must bear fruit which testifies to conversion,[6] something which is impossible unless the believer remains grafted onto Christ;[7] accordingly, through the Holy Spirit, the unique fruit of love will be delightful[8] and the tree of life will ceaselessly give forth its fruit.[9]

[1]Gn 1:22,28; Is 5:4; 37:30. [2]Mt 13:8,23 (= Mk 4:8,20 = Lk 8:8,15); Mk 4:29. [3]Mt 21:34,41,43; Mk 12:2; Lk 20:10. [4]Mt 21:19 (= Mk 11:14); Lk 13:6-9. [5]Cf. Mt 25:26; Lk 19:13. [6]Mt 3:10 (= Lk 3:8). [7]Jn 12:24; 15:2-8,16. [8]Rom 7:4; Gal 5:22; Col 1:10. [9]Rv 22:2.

→ fruitfulness—grow, growth—sterility.

fruitfulness The N.T. does not have a proper word for fruitfulness, except "fruit of the womb" and "fruit of the loins*";[1] in the figurative sense, it means the capacity to "bear fruit."

[1]Lk 1:42 △; Acts 2:30 △.

→ fruit.

fulfill From the biblical viewpoint, "fulfilling" means more than "doing." It means "to bring to completion" (Gk. *teleō*), a concept reserved especially for the Word of God or the Scriptures[1] or, more particularly, for the Passion of Jesus.[2] Above all, it means "to fill up" (Gk. *plēroō*) in the sense of "to meet an expectation," from which derive the notions of conformity with, fidelity to, or the exact agreement of what was expected to happen with what actually came about: the fulfillment is like the prophecy.* To fulfill also means "to bring to perfection": what was contained in the fulfillment is seen to reflect something more than what had to be fulfilled. The occurrence surpasses the prediction as reality surpasses a shadow. The same verb proclaims that persons are filled with the Spirit[3] or with Satan,[4] by virtues[5] or vices.[6]

[1]Lk 1:45; 18:31; 22:37; Acts 13:29; Rom 9:28; Rv 17:17. [2]Lk 12:50; Jn 19:28. [3]Lk 1:15,41,67; 4:1; Acts 2:4; 4:8; 6:3,5; 7:55; 9:17; 11:24; 13:9; Eph 5:18. [4]Acts 5:3. [5]Lk 2:40; 5:26; Acts 2:28; 3:10; 6:5,8; 9:36; 13:52; Rom 15:13f.; 2 Cor 7:4; Phil 1:11; Col 1:9; 2:10; 4:12; 2 Tim 1:4. [6]Lk 4:28; 6:11; Acts 5:17; 13:10; 19:28; Rom 1:29.

1. To fulfill the Scriptures. The first Christians read in the O.T. prophecies of the events they had recently experienced with Jesus and in the Holy Spirit. Hence, the frequent occurrence of the formula, "this happened to fulfill" the Scriptures, or a speech, or what had been said by a prophet.[7] In retrospect, realized happenings cast definitive light on texts, showing how God was at work in the history of Israel.[8]

[7]Mt 1:22. [8]Acts 3:18; 13:27.

2. The time* has been fulfilled. The ordinary sense of time as something gone by or completed (duty, birth . . .)[9] is theologically transformed by the idea of God's plan* which is being fulfilled.[10] From this view there comes the rich expression, "the fullness of time."[11]

[9]Lk 1:23,57; 2:6,21f.; Acts 7:23,30. [10]Lk 9:51; 21:24; Acts 2:1. [11]Gal 4:4; Eph 1:10.

3. To fulfill the will of God*, his justice and, most especially, the Law in love[13]—such is Jesus' plan. In "fulfilling" the Law he causes it to reach its full scope.[14]

[12]Mt 3:15; Rom 8:4. [13]Rom 13:8,10; Gal 5:14; 6:2. [14]Mt 5:17.

→ perfect—plenitude.

fuller Gk. *gnapheus.* A craftsman who stiffened fabrics and cleaned garments; he made use of large vats in which he trampled down the fabrics* with his feet or else immersed the materials in a type of potash.[1]

[1]Mal 3:2; Mt 9:16 (= Mk 2:21); Mk 9:3 □.

fullness

→ plenitude.

furnace Gk. *kaminos.* The potter's oven,[1] the blacksmith's forge,[2] the furnace of punishment.[3]

[1]Sir 27:5; 38:30. [2]Is 48:10; Ez 22:18-22; Rv 1:15. [3]Dn 3:6,20-23; Mt 13:42,50; Rv 9:2 □.

→ hell.

Gabriel Heb. *gabrî'ēl:* "man of God" or "God has shown himself strong." The angel* charged with revealing the meaning of visions and of the unfolding of history, in particular with announcing God's intervention for man's salvation, most especially the coming of Messiah.*[1]

[1]Dn 8:16; 9:21-27; Lk 1:11-38 □.

Gadarenes (Territory of the) From the Gk. *gadarēnos,* the territory of Gadara. A Hellenistic city of the Decapolis,* some 10 km. (6.25 mi.) southeast of the Sea of Galilee. Matthew identified it, wrongly it would seem, with the Gerasene* region.[1]

[1]Mt 8:28; cf. Lk 8:26,37 □.

→ Map 4.

Galatia Gk. *Galatēs, Galatia.* The northern region of central Turkey, including modern-day Ankara, so designated from the name of its inhabitants, the Celtic invaders (Gauls) of the third century B.C. A territory only lightly Hellenized. A Roman province* dating from 25 B.C. that, in N.T. times, also included some southern regions: a part of Phrygia,* Pisidia, Lycaonia,* Isauria.[1] A very few scholars think that Paul evangelized the Galatia of the south.

[1]Acts 16:6; 18:23; 1 Cor 16:1; Gal 1:2; 3:1; 2 Tim 4:10; 1 Pt 1:1 □.

→ Galatians (Epistle to the)—Map 3.

[Galatians (Epistle to the)] A letter written from Ephesus,* about 54 or 56, by Paul to the Galatians of the north, whom he himself had evangelized, to put them on guard against the doctrine and wrangling of his opponents, the Judaizers* (not merely the Judeo-Christians*).

→ Intr. XV.

Galilee Gk. *Galilaia,* from the Heb. *ha(g)-gâlîl:* "the circle." A region to the north of Palestine. From 4 B.C. to A.D. 37 part of Herod* Antipas's tetrarchy*; from 39–44 part of Herod* Agrippa I's kingdom. After 44, it was governed by a Roman procurator.* Called "Galilee of the Nations,"[1] in memory of the Assyrian* and Chaldean* invasions which brought in their wakes a mingling of the populations and, hence, the presence of numerous pagans. Thereafter, the Galileans, recognizable by their accent,[2] were looked down upon by other Jews.[3] Matthew systematically located Jesus' activity in Galilee.[4]

[1]Is 8:23; Mt 4:15f. [2]Mt 26:73. [3]Jn 7:52. [4]Mt 10:5.

→ Intr. II; III.2.D.—Map 4.

Galilee (Sea of) The lake of Galilee which the O.T. called the lake of Chinneret[1] or of Gennesaret.[2] Some 21 km. [13 mi.] in length, by 12 km. [7.5 mi.] wide, with a depth of 42–48 m. [137–157 ft.], it is located some 208–210 m. [682–689 ft.] below sea level. Waters abounding with fish and sudden storms typify it. The greatest part of Jesus' ministry in Galilee took part on its banks or in its environs. It was called the "Sea of Galilee,"[3] the "Lake of Gennesaret"[4] or the "Sea of Tiberias,"[5] more generally "the sea," rarely "the lake."[6]

[1]Nm 34:11; Jos 13:27. [2]1 Mc 11:67. [3]Mt 4:18; 15:29; Mk 1:16; 7:31; Jn 6:1 △. [4]Lk 5:1 △. [5]Jn 6:1; 21:1 △. [6]Lk 5:2; 8:22f.,33 △.

→ Map 4.

Gallio The brother of the philosopher Seneca, proconsul of Achaia* in 51–52 or 52–53, according to the chronology* established through the Delphic inscription. His behavior shows that he considered the Christian faith to be a "licit religion."[1]

[1]Acts 18:12-14,17 □.

Gamaliel Heb. *Gamalî'ēl:* "God has done good to me." Rabbi Gamaliel I, or the Elder, probably the grandson of Hillel,* a Pharisee,* an illustrious doctor of the Law.* He was Saul's* teacher and showed himself to be understanding in regard to the new faith.[1]

[1]Acts 5:34-39; 22:3 □.

garment

→ clothe, clothing.

Gehenna Heb. *gé-Hinnûm,* Gk. *gehenna:* a valley to the south of Jerusalem. Cursed from the time when humans were sacrificed there, corpses and garbage were permanently burning in it.[1] Hence, a metaphoric use of the term: the place of punishment by fire,[2] the eschatological* punishment and a power already at work.[4] The apocryphal* writings underlined this doctrine.

[1]2 Kgs 23:10; Jer 7:31f. [2]Mt 18:8f. (= Mk 9:43,45,47). [3]Is 66:24; Mt 5:22, 29f.; 10:28 (= Lk 12:5); 23:33. [4]Mt 23:15; Jas 3:6 □.

→ fiery pool—hell—Map 1.

[genealogy] **1.** Semites readily produced a list of the ancestors of a historical person. The verb to beget* does not exclusively bear upon someone's immediate or even physical descent. Joram could "beget" Ozias, his great-grandson[1] or a people.[2] According to various traditions, a single person might have two genealogies.[3]

[1]Mt 1:8. [2]Gn 10. [3]1 Chr 2:3–3:4; 4:1-23; 7:6-12; 8:1-40.

2. Two genealogies are reported of Jesus,[4] each ending with Joseph, the father of Jesus, but quite different in the number of ancestors and the names. It is not enough to say that one is Joseph's genealogy, the other Mary's, nor to imagine the double marriage of two brothers-in-law. Matthew wanted to show Jesus' Davidic sonship, Luke his universal descent from Adam.*

[4]Mt 1:1-17; Lk 3:23-38.

3. It does little good to have recourse to an unlikely and unverifiable interpretation of the three times fourteen generations mentioned by Matthew[5] through appeal to a gematria (cf. numbers*) on the name David (D + V + D = 4 + 6 + 4). This ignores the true orthography of David (perhaps DVYD), and Matthew's genealogy has Abraham as much in view as David. More worthwhile are recollections of the apocalyptic* calculations of that time. According to Fourth Ezra,* the world was divided into twelve periods of seven weeks; according to Luke, Jesus came at the beginning of the twelfth and last week of the world, since in his account there are 11 × 7 = 77 ancestors' names. According to the Book of Enoch,* Israel's time had been divided into seven weeks: two from Israel to Solomon, two from Solomon to the Exile, two from the Exile to the "time of the sword"; according to Matthew, Jesus would have come at the beginning of the seventh and last week, since in his account there are 6 × 7 ancestors—the only difficulty coming from the fact that Matthew speaks of 3 × 14. Also, it would be simpler to state that Matthew has dressed up the traditional genealogy of David[6] by mentioning the three patriarchs, a fact which establishes a sequence of fourteen names; by adverting to the three classical benchmarks (Abraham, David, Exile), he completed the list by reconstructing two other series of fourteen.

[5]Mt 1:17. [6]Ru 4:18-22 (= 1 Chr 2:10-13).

Gennesaret **1.** From the Gk. *Gennēsaret,* rendering the Heb. *Ginnôsar.* A place (or territory) situated on the right bank of the lake of Tiberias, between Magdala and Capernaum.[1]

[1]Mt 14:34; Mk 6:53 □.

2. Only Luke calls the lake by this name.[2]

[2]Lk 5:1 □.

→ Galilee (Sea of)—Map 4.

genre (literary)

→ literary genre.

Gentiles From the Lat. *gentes:* "nations," Heb. *gôyîm,* Gk. *ethnikoi.* The name given to non-Jews by the Jews, then to non-Christians by the Christians. This name, in disuse today, attempted to describe the nations in their non-Christian religious dimension.[1]

[1]Mt 5:47; 6:7; 18:17; Gal 2:14; 3 Jn 7 □.

→ nation(s)—pagan.

gentle, gentleness **1.** Gk. *praytēs, praus.* Not the resignation of the "humiliated,"[1] but rather a positive welcoming disposition directed toward God and everyone.[2]

[1]Ps 37:11. [2]1 Cor 4:21; 2 Tim 2:25; Ti 3:2; Jas 1:21; 1 Pt 3:4,16.

2. Jesus, "gentle and humble of heart,"[3] neither cried out nor contended in the streets; he did not extinguish the still smoldering wick but, and above all else, proclaimed and administered the mercy of God.*[4] Finally, in conformity with what was prophesied, he entered Jerusalem in modest "array."[5]

[3]Mt 11:29. [4]2 Cor 10:1; cf. Mt 9:13; 12:7,19f. [5]Mt 21:5.

3. A fruit of the Holy Spirit,[6] gentleness is an aspect of goodness and humility, virtues with which we often find it associated.[7] The freedom of the Christian, who knows himself to be loved of God, radiates a share of this prevenient love; such is the gentleness which Jesus declared to be blessed and which the epistles recommended.[8]

[6]Gal 5:23. [7]Gal 6:1; Eph 4:2; Col 3:12 (= 1 Tim 3:12). [8]Mt 5:5; 1 Tim 6:11; Jas 3:13 □.

→ humility—poor—virtue.

Gerasenes (Territory of the) From the Gk. *gerasēnos,* the territory of Gerasa, a city of the Decapolis* near Yabboq, some 55 km. (34 mi.) southeast of the lake of Tiberias, identified with modern-day Jerash. The expulsion of the demon from the herd of pigs seems to have taken place at El Kursi, to the south of the Wadi-es-Semah, on the east bank of the lake.[1]

[1]Mk 5:1; Lk 8:26,37 □.

→ Map 4.

Gethsemane Gk. *Gethsēmani* (from the Heb. *gat:* "press: [or *géy':* "valley"] and *sh'emâny:* "olive"): "oil press." An estate located at the foot of the Mount of Olives,* a "garden" to the east of Kedron* which was a witness to Jesus in his agony.*[1]

[1]Mt 26:36; Mk 14:32 □.

→ Map 1.

gift Gk. *dōron, dōrea* (from *didōmi:* "to give"). The term doubtlessly designated what was given, but it also implied the donor's intention: free, motivated and concerned.

1. God gave his Son,[1] his justifying grace,*[2] all kinds of gifts,[3] essentially the Holy Spirit*[4] and, with him, charisms.*[5] God gave Jesus the Spirit, judgment,* tasks to be fulfilled, disciples.[6]

[1]Jn 3:16; 4:10. [2]Rom 3:24; 5:15-17; 2 Cor 9:15. [3]Mt 7:11; Jn 6:32; Jas 1:17. [4]Lk 11:13; Jn 14:16; Acts 2:38; 5:32; 8:20; 10:45; 15:8; 2 Cor 1:22; 5:5; 1 Thes 4:8; 1 Jn 3:24. [5]1 Cor 12:7. [6]Jn 3:34; 5:22,36; 10:29; 17:6,9; 18:9.

2. Jesus Christ gave loaves of bread and the cup,*[7] his life;[8] he handed himself over (Gk. *para-didōmi*)[9] for us; he conferred authority and power,[10] divine sonship, the water of life, life, peace, glory,[11] and lastly, various gifts.[12]

[7]Mt 26:26f. (= Mk 14:22f. = Lk 22:19); Jn 6:51. [8]Mt 20:28 (= Mk 10:45); Lk 22:19; Gal 1:4; 1 Tim 2:6; Ti 2:14; cf. Jn 10:11,15,17f.; 1 Jn 3:16. [9]Gal 2:20; Eph 5:2,25. [10]Mt 10:1 (= Mk 6:7 = Lk 9:1); 16:19; Lk 10:19. [11]Jn 1:12; 4:14f.; 6:33; 10:28; 14:27; 17:22. [12]Eph 4:8.

3. The disciple, who has freely (Gk. *dōrean*) received, must in his turn freely give[13] and offer God worshipful* offerings.[14]

[13]Mt 10:8; Rom 3:24; 2 Cor 11:7; 2 Thes 3:8; Rv 21:6; 22:17. [14]Mt 5:23f.; 8:4; Rom 11:35; cf. Jn 13:37; Rom 12:1f.

→ charism—grace—tradition.

girdle

→ loincloth.

glory Gk. *doxa,* translating the Heb. *kâbôd.* In the N.T. the word never conveys the usage current in Greek: "opinion"; sometimes it means brilliancy, fame, generally what renown is based on, what gives weight (the Heb. root *kbd* implies the idea of weight[1]): wealth,[2] social importance.[3]

[1]2 Sm 14:26. [2]Gn 13:2; 31:1; Mt 4:8; 6:29. [3]Gn 45:13; 1 Kgs 3:13.

1. The God of glory[4] is this rich and powerful being of such plentitude* that it overflows and diffuses its wealth throughout creation.[5] Present in theophanies,* his glory is ordinarily accompanied by a cloud* which veils it and yet simultaneously reveals it.[6] Already discernible in the angels, this plenitude was concentrated in Jesus Christ;[7] it is to be spread anew in the glorious bodies,* through which it will inexhaustibly gush forth.[8] God's glory is God as he is revealed, it is Jesus Christ, it is man alive.[9]

[4]Acts 7:2; Eph 1:17. [5]Ps 19:2; Wis 13:1-9; Is 6:3; Rom 1:20f. [6]Ex 16:10; 33:20; Lk 9:31f., 34f.; 2 Pt 1:17. [7]Jn 1:14; Ti 2:13. [8]Rom 8:17; Phil 3:21; Col 3:4. [9]Ps 8:6; 2 Cor 3:18; 4:6.

2. To give glory to God is to recognize that God is the one in whom what has just been said fits perfectly.[10]

[10]Ps 3:4; Is 42:8,12; Lk 2:14; 19:38; Rv 4:9.

3. "The Glories" refer to celestial angels.*[11]

[11]2 Pt 2:10; Jude 8.

→ cloud—confidence—doxology—light—transfiguration—white.

[glossolalia] From the Gk. *glōssa:* "tongue, language" and *lalia:* "speech": "to speak in tongue(s).*"

[gnosis] From the Gk. *gnōsis:* "understanding," ordinarily translated in the N.T. as "knowledge."

1. In its broad sense, gnosis indicates those religious movements which tend to situate salvation* solely within a knowledge of divine secrets and fail to appreciate earthly values.

2. In its narrow sense, gnosticism indicates an orientation in religious thinking (Jewish, Greek, or Christian) which was manifest between the first century B.C. and the fourth century A.D. It revealed itself through the dualistic* systems

which separated creation and redemption, speculations on emanations of the divine in the world, theories of redemption which sought to set human spirits free from the matter in which they were trapped so that they might return to their original homeland, the deity.

go astray

→ error—seduce.

goat (he-goat) **1.** Gk. *tragos.* An animal traditionally offered in sacrifice, above all for expiation.*[1]

[1]Lv 4:23; Heb 9:12f.,19; 10:4 □.

2. The Gk. term *eriphos:* "kid" means a "she-goat.*"[1]

[1]Mt 25:32f.; Lk 15:29 □.

goat (she-goat), kid Gk. *eriphos:* "he-goat kid, she-goat, kid" (papyri speak of them in the plural, alongside sheep, to designate not he-goats* but she-goats). Mixed in pasture with the white sheep, the black she-goats were separated in the stable.[1] The kid (Gk. *eriphion*) was a feast-time meal.[2]

[1]Ex 12:5; Lv 1:10; Mt 25:32. [2]Gn 27:9; Lk 15:29; cf. Mt 25:33 □.

God **1.** The Gk. *Theos* ordinarily corresponds to the Heb. *El,* a common Semitic* name for the deity and a proper name (the plural *Elohim* deriving from the fact that the divinity was regarded as a plurality of powers), the name that the patriarchs inherited from the surrounding culture,[1] the one in which Yahweh revealed his true name.[2] The God of the N.T. is the same as in the O.T., but he has revealed himself fully in Jesus Christ.*

[1]Gn 14:18-22. [2]Ex 3:14.

2. God is unique, one. Through this fundamental affirmation Jews and Christians set themselves in opposition to the neighboring religions.[3] He is the God of the fathers, the God of Abraham, Isaac and Jacob.[4] No other God could be tolerated alongside him.[5] Only in him could one believe[6] and hope,[7] for he alone is living and true.[8]

[3]Dt 6:4f.; Mk 12:29f.; Rom 3:30; 1 Cor 8:4-6; Eph 4:6; Jas 2:19. [4]Ex 3:6; Mt 22:32 (= Mk 12:26 = Lk 20:37); Acts 3:13; 5:30; 22:14. [5]Ex 20:3; 1 Kgs 19:18; Is 42:8; 43:10f.; Jer 2:11; Mt 6:24; Acts 14:15; 17:24f.; Gal 4:8; Phil 3:19. [6]Is 7:9; Jn 14:1; Rom 4:3; Gal 3:6; Jas 2:23; 1 Pt 1:21. [7]Is 8:17; Acts 24:15; Rom 4:18. [8]Jgs 8:19; 1 Kgs 17:1; Ps 36:10; 1 Thes 1:9; 1 Tim 1:17.

3. God is the Lord of all, the Creator* of heaven and earth,[9] he who sits enthroned in heaven,*[10] the Most High,[11] the first and the last, the master of the ages and of history,[12] for whom nothing is impossible.[13] Man's fundamental task is to re-cognize his Creator,[14] and his basic attitude must be one of total trust.[15]

[9]Gn 1:1; Acts 17:24; Heb 3:4; Rv 10:6. [10]Ps 11:4; Is 66:1; Mt 5:34. [11]Ps 91:1; 92:2; Is 57:15; Lk 1:32. [12]Is 44:6; 48:12; Rv 1:8; 21:6. [13]Gn 18:14; Jb 42:2; Mt 19:26; Lk 1:37; Acts 5:39. [14]Rom 1:19,21f. [15]Mt 6:8,30.

4. God is not an impersonal force spread throughout the world. Anthropomorphisms speak of his personality: he speaks, acts, gives orders, wishes to establish an everlasting covenant with man, and so forth. The revelation proper to Jesus and already sketched in the O.T.[16] is that God's proper name is not merely "our God, my God,"[17] but "Father.*"[18] It is to him that we are to pray in secret;[19] it is in him that we are to trust,[20] for we are his children,[21] begotten by him.[22]

[16]Ex 4:22f.; Dt 32:6; Is 63:16; Jer 31:9; Hos 11:9. [17]Ex 15:2; Jos 24:18; Ps 31:15; 48:15; Acts 2:39; Rom 1:8; 2 Cor 12:21; Phil 1:3; Rv 7:12; 19:5. [18]Mt 11:25f. (= Lk 10:21f.); Mk 14:36; Lk 23:34,46; Jn 11:41; 17:1,5,11. [19]Mt 6:4,18. [20]Mt 6:26-32; 10:29-31; Lk 15. [21]Rom 8:16; Gal 4:6. [22]1 Jn 3:9; 4:4.

5. The designations qualifying God are countless. Holy* and jealous,* faithful* to his promises, omnipresent, just,* Savior,* full of mercy*. . . . Two features, however, are especially noteworthy. No one has ever seen* God, and men search for him gropingly;[23] the only Son who dwells in the bosom of the Father has made him known*[24]—above all it is in the filial disposition of Jesus that the believer can contemplate God and know him.[25] God has revealed himself as Spirit[26] and above all that he is love,* the source of love on earth.[27]

[23]Acts 17:23-27. [24]Jn 1:18. [25]Jn 5:19f.,30; 14:9. [26]Jn 4:24. [27]Jn 3:16; 1 Jn 4:8,10.

6. Jesus Christ came from God; he is Emmanuel,* "God with us."[28] Sent by God, he is the Son of God.*[29] He is the image* of the invisible God,[30] in him dwells the plenitude* of the divinity.[31] He is one with God,[32] his words and his deeds are those of God himself.[33] Still, he is but the mediator* of salvation[34] and he is never identical to God the Father.[35] Nonetheless, with qualifications which should be noted, some texts declare him to be God.[36]

[28]Is 7:14; Mt 1:23; Rv 21:3. [29]Rom 1:3f. [30]Col 1:15. [31]Col 2:9. [32]Jn 10:30; 14:10; 17:11,21. [33]Jn 9:4; 17:4. [34]2 Cor 5:19; Col 1:20. [35]Eph 1:20; Phil 2:9f.; 1 Pt 3:22. [36]Jn 1:1,18; 20:28; Rom 9:4f.; Ti 2:13; 1 Jn 5:20.

7. What seems to be appropriate only to Jesus is also predicated of God: thus there are the designations, the Church of God,[37] the temple of God.[38] Finally, there are several formulas which point to the trinitarian dogma (Father, Son, Spirit), which was elaborated after the N.T.;[39] but the binary formulas (Father, Son) are more numerous.[40]

[37]Acts 20:28; 1 Cor 1:2; 1 Thes 2:14. [38]1 Cor 3:16; 2 Cor 6:16; Eph 2:21f. [39]1 Cor 12:4-6; 2 Cor 13:13. [40]Jn 16:14; 1 Cor 8:6; 2 Cor 3:17; 1 Tim 2:5; 1 Jn 2:1.

→ Intr. X.2.—abba—God's plan—God's will—gods—idolatry—Lord—Son of God—Spirit of God—Yahweh.

God's plan With this English phrase we translate several Greek words whose shades of meaning are hard to pinpoint exactly. The closest to our own phrase would be *boulē* (from *boulomai:* "to wish," which, in contemporary N.T. Greek, tends to be supplanted by *thelō*)[1]; one also reads of *thelēma*[2] (which principally indicated a desire rather than a plan), *prothesis* (the equivalent of predestination*),[3] *eudokia* (underlining the divine pleasure),[4] or *oikonomia* (which links up with the idea of a divine allotment).[5] All of these terms attempt to express the will* that God has for the totality of his creation, namely salvation* for all in Jesus Christ.[6]

[1]Lk 7:30; Acts 2:23; 4:28; 13:36; 20:27; Eph 1:11; Heb 6:17. [2]Rom 2:18; 1 Cor 1:1; 2 Cor 1:1; Gal 1:4; Eph 1:1,5,9-11; 2 Tim 1:1. [3]Rom 8:28; 9:11; Eph 1:9,11; 3:11; 2 Tim 1:9. [4]Mt 11:26; Lk 12:32; 1 Cor 1:21; 10:5. [5]1 Tim 1:4. [6]Eph 1:9f.; 1 Tim 2:4.

1. Fixed from all eternity in the divine predestination, the divine plan was sketched out in the course of the O.T. in cultic confessions* of faith, in prophets'* interventions which revealed the meaning of events, in syntheses of history, in the reflections of the wisdom or apocalyptic* writers. The arrangement of the O.T. books in the canon* (from Genesis to Maccabees) was itself an outline of God's plan.

2. Jesus claimed to have come in the fullness* of time,*[7] his destiny signifying that of the people of God.[8]

[7]Mt 12:28; 1 Cor 10:11; Gal 4:4. [8]Mt 21:33-44; 22:1-11.

3. The primitive Church, notably Luke, situated some happenings within the general plan of salvation,*[9] particularly the scandal* of Jesus' crucifixion[10] as well as the proclamation of salvation to all men, not only to Israel.[11]

[9]Lk 7:30. [10]Acts 2:23; 4:28; 13:36; 20:27. [11]Acts 10:35f.

4. Paul, in his turn, offered in the epistles to the Romans and to the Ephesians a synthesis of the godly design; more particularly, he attempted to comprehend Israel's situation when it refused Christ, for in this rejection there lay a scandal to faith.[12]

[12]Rom 3:1-8; 9–11; Eph 2:14-22.

→ election—God's will—predestine.

God's Spirit, Holy Spirit

→ Spirit of God, Holy Spirit

God's will Gk. *thelēma tou Theou.* Unlike God's plan,* the will of God can take account of this or that particular event and enter into a relationship with the will of a man who senses himself to be more or less in agreement with it. Here, then, our concern is not with the global sense of the terms predestination,* election,* vocation,* promise,* plan.

1. Jesus came to fulfill the will of his Father;[1] this was his food.[2] At the moment of death he felt his flesh to be in a state of fundamental disagreement, but he abandoned* himself with trust to the Father's benevolent will[3] and, in this abandonment, he was heard when he received back life in its fullness.[4]

[1]Heb 10:7,9; cf. Acts 13:22. [2]Jn 4:34; 5:30; 6:38-40. [3]Mk 14:36; Lk 22:42. [4]Heb 5:7.

2. The believer must pray to the Father that his will be done on earth;[5] and he must endeavor to discern what precisely the divine will is for him[6] through the Holy Spirit, who reveals to him the secrets of the Lord's plan (Gk. *nous:* "thought").[7] Man recognizes that it is God who "works to will and to act"[8] to fulfill this will since, in man's activity, all comes from himself and yet all is from God: the tasks are not split up between the two, but the roles are diverse within a community of action. God gives, man receives.

[5]Mt 6:10. [6]Rom 12:2; Eph 5:17. [7]1 Cor 2:16. [8]Phil 2:13.

→ commandment—God's plan—test.

God-fearer Gk. *ton theon phoboumenos* (from *phobeomai:* "to fear") or *sebomenos* (from *sebomai:* "to offer worship"). In this way were the numerous non-Jews in the Diaspora* referred to, attracted as they were by the monotheistic faith of the Jews and observing only one or another of their practices: the sabbath,* dietary regulations, temple tribute,* pilgrimages.* Unlike proselytes,* they remained uncircumcised and so legally were pagans.* It was possible to call them "worshippers."[1]

[1]2 Chr 5:6; Acts 10:2,22; 13:16,26,43,50; 16:14; 17:4,17; 18:7 □.

→ Intr. IV.6.E; IV.7.A.—adore—piety—proselyte.

gods Gk. *theoi,* the plural of *theos:* "God."

1. The N.T. presents an account of the polytheistic mentality of this period. Here we find mentioned: Artemis,* the Great Goddess,[1] and the unknown god of the Athenians;[2] in it Herod Agrippa,[3] Paul and Barnabas,[4] Paul alone,[5] are all acclaimed as "gods"; but each time, these attempts are brought to faith in the only God.*[6] Paul vigorously criticized polytheism,[7] those gods which were nothing but nonentities[8] and whose worship was blasphemy.[9]

[1]Acts 9:24-37. [2]Acts 17:23. [3]Acts 12:22; cf. Dn 11:36f.; 2 Thes 2:4. [4]Acts 14:11. [5]Acts 28:6. [6]Acts 14:15; 17:24-27; 19:26. [7]Gal 4:8f.; 1 Thes 1:9; 4:5. [8]1 Cor 8:4-6. [9]Acts 7:40,42; 1 Cor 10:20.

2. Nonetheless, the N.T. also is aware of the metaphorical use of this term which is found in the O.T.: thus, the king[10] and judges[11] are like gods, are gods in the sense that they are lords* over their subjects and in that they enter people's hearts. In addition, the powers of this earth, the demons,* can be called "gods": "there are many gods";[12] "the god of this world"[13] exists; the powers from which one breaks away, such as the belly or dietary laws, can be reckoned "gods."[14]

[10]2 Sm 14:17; Ps 45:7. [11]Ps 58:2; 82:6; Jn 10:34f. [12]1 Cor 8:5. [13]2 Cor 4:4. [14]Phil 3:19.

→ God—idolatry.

[go'ël] A Hebrew term designating the near relative on whom was incumbent the obligation of buying back goods and persons which had become a stranger's property. He was the redeemer, defender, protector of the interests of the individual and of the group, especially in questions of patrimony, sterility or vengeance.[1]

[1]Lv 25:25-55; Nm 35:19; Dt 25:5.

→ Intr. VIII.2.A.a.—redemption.

Gog and Magog According to Ezekiel, *Gôg* is the king of the region called *Magôg.*[1] In Jewish and Christian apocalypses,* these are two nations that are to attack Israel (the Church) during the messianic era; they will be conquered.[2]

[1]Ez 38:2–39:15. [2]Rv 20:8 □.

gold Gk. *chrysos.* Known from antiquity in Israel, which imported it chiefly from southern Arabia, this precious metal served as coinage; not at all indispensable, it was judged to be perishable.[1] Still, it stood for what was beautiful, rich, glorious, valuable and durable.[2]

[1]Eccl 12:6; Mt 10:9; Acts 3:6; 20:33; 1 Cor 3:12; 1 Tim 2:9; Jas 2:2; 5:3; 1 Pt 1:7,18; 3:3. [2]Mt 2:11; 23:16f.; Acts 17:29; 2 Tim 2:20; Heb 9:4; Rv 1:12f.; 3:18.

→ riches—silver.

Golgotha From the Aram. *gulgoltâ,* corresponding to the Heb. *gulgôlet:* "skull." An area of gardens and tombs outside of the city, to the northwest of Jerusalem. Perhaps it included a slight elevation which suggested a skull's shape; hence the English "calvary" (derived from Lat. *calvaria:* "skull"). The place where Jesus was crucified.*[1]

[1]Mt 27:23; Mk 15:22; Jn 19:17 □.

→ Map 1.

gospel From the Gk. *eu-aggelion* (*eu:* "well" and *aggellō:* "to announce"): "good news," Heb. *besôrâ,* above all a victory proclamation.[1] The term took on a religious meaning in the sixth to fifth centuries B.C., beginning with Second Isaiah.*[2] In the N.T., it is not used except by Mark and Paul; Matthew cited the term only with the complementary qualifier: "of the Kingdom."[3] The verb *eu-aggelizomai:* "to proclaim good news," unknown in Mark and Matthew,[4] is common in Luke and Paul.

[1]2 Sm 18:20-22. [2]Is 40:9; 52:7; cf. Ps 96:2. [3]Mt 4:23; 9:35; 24:14; 26:13 △. [4]Except Mt 11:5 △.

1. In Jesus prophecy was fulfilled. Jesus proclaimed the Good News of the Kingdom of God;[5] in "evangelizing the poor" he gave notice that the Kingdom was very near.[6] It was through his life, death, and resurrection that salvation was made available, so much so that Jesus come in person was the Gospel.[7]

[5]Mt 4:23; 9:35; Mk 1:15; Lk 8:1. [6]Mt 11:4f. (= Lk 7:22); Lk 4:18. [7]Mk 1:1; Acts 5:42; 17:3,18.

2. Paul thought out the notion systematically: corresponding to the promise (Gk. *ep-aggelia*) there was the Gospel,[8] the salvific action of God wrought through his Son Jesus. Furthermore, Paul spoke interchangeably of the Gospel,[9] the Gospel of God[10] or the Gospel of Christ.[11]

[8]Rom 1:2-4. [9]Rom 1:15f.; 10:16; 11:28; 1 Cor 1:17ff. [10]Rom 15:16; 2 Cor 11:7ff. [11]Rom 15:19; Gal 1:7ff.

3. The Gospel must be proclaimed to all the earth.[12] Its preachers are "evangelists"[13] charged with announcing the inbreaking of the Rule[14] and, above all, the Easter victory of Christ:[15] therein lay the only true Gospel.[16] Their proclamation of it was efficacious: with God's concurrence it stirred up faith and brought about salvation.[17] It was only in the second century that the word ended up designating the written accounts of the life of Jesus, that is, books.

[12]Mk 16:15; Rom 9:17. [13]Acts 21:8; Rom 10:15; Eph 4:11; 2 Tim 4:5 △. [14]Mt 24:14. [15]Rom 1:16. [16]Gal 1:8f. [17]Rom 1:16f.; Phil 1:27.

4. The booklets called *gospels* constitute a unique literary genre.* They belong to a historical type in that they collect various traditions that circulated in the Church over a span of thirty or forty years before being brought together in a book. Despite this, they cannot be reckoned as given accounts of past events. In reality, like the traditions of which they are echoes, they themselves attempt in their own way to answer problems in one community or another and thereby to arouse or nourish faith. Hence, the very many variants that we can recognize within the Synoptics,* or between them and John. But all of these concentrate on the life and teaching of Jesus of Nazareth, the one whom believers knew to be alive after his death. The four gospels of Matthew,* Mark,* Luke* and John* are known as canonical* gospels.

→ Intr. XV.—kerygma—preach—promise.

governor Gk. *hēgemōn.* In the N.T., this term designates the Roman official who administered a province.* He was either a proconsul, whose title was made more precise (for senatorial provinces), or a legate,* prefect* or procurator* (for imperial provinces); such were Quirinius,* Pilate,* Felix,* Festus.*[1]

[1]Mt 10:18 (= Mk 13:9 = Lk 21:12); 27:2–28:14; Lk 2:2; 3:1; 20:20; Acts 23:24-33; 24:1-27; 26:30.

→ Intr. IV.2.B; IV.3.

grace Gk. *charis* (related to *chara:* "joy"), Lat. *gratia,* translating the Heb. *hén* (the idea of "inclining oneself" favorably towards someone) and *hèsèd* (adding the motif of fidelity within the Covenant). The term, absent from the lips of Jesus, belongs above all to the theological language of Paul (100 times out of 155).

1. God is grace, the inexhaustible source of the favor he evidenced towards man[1] and which reached its culmination in Jesus Christ.[2] In this way was the rule of grace inaugurated (succeeding that of the Law*[3]), one in which man gratuitously[4] received—in contrast with any notion of a retribution* that was owed.[5] Such was the Good News,[6] such was the favor wished at the opening[7] and closing of the Pauline letters.[8]

[1]Ex 34:6f.; Ps 36:8-10; Eph 2:7; Col 1:6; Heb 4:16; cf. 1 Cor 16:3; 2 Cor 8:6-9,19. [2]Jn 1:14,16; Eph 1:6f. [3]Jn 1:17; Rom 5:2,17; 6:14; 2 Thes 1:12; 1 Tim 1:14. [4]Rom 3:24; 11:5; Gal 1:15; Eph 2:5,8; 2 Thes 2:16. [5]Rom 4:4,16; 6:1,15; 11:6. [6]Acts 14:3; 20:24,32; 1 Pt 5:12. [7]Rom 1:7; 1 Cor 1:3ff.; 1 Pt 1:2; 2 Pt 1:2. [8]Rom 16:20; 1 Cor 16:23f.; Heb 13:25; cf. Rv 22:21.

2. The riches of a multiform grace were revealed in God's favorable disposition,[10] in the remission of faults (forgiveness*),[11] in the gift* of eternal life, in the superabundance of spiritual gifts (Gk. *charisma*).[13]

[9]Rom 5:17,20; 2 Cor 4:15; 9:8,14; Eph 1:7; 2:7; 1 Tim 1:14; 1 Pt 5:10. [10]Lk 2:40; Acts 14:26; 15:40; cf. Acts 24:27; 25:9. [11]Rom 5:15,20f.; Eph 1:7; Col 2:13; 3:13; 2 Tim 1:9; Ti 2:11; 3:7; Heb 2:9; cf. Lk 7:42f.; Acts 3:14; 25:11,16; Eph 4:32. [12]Rom 6:23. [13]Rom 1:11; 11:29; 12:6; 1 Cor 1:7; 7:7; 12:4; Eph 4:7; 1 Pt 4:10.

3. From the point of view of the one who receives we say: to enjoy the favor of, to be full of grace, to have found favor in God's presence,[14] in men's presence,[15] or, effectively, to court favor as a recompense or an act of recognition.[16] To this last aspect we may add the meaning of "thanks" ("thanks to . . .").[17]

[14]Gn 6:8; Lk 1:28,30; 2:52; Jn 1:14; Acts 6:8; 7:46. [15]Gn 39:4; Acts 2:47; 4:33; 7:10. [16]Lk 6:32-34; 17:9 (cf. 17:16). [17]Rom 6:17; 7:25; 2 Cor 9:15; Col 3:16; 1 Tim 1:12; 2 Tim 1:3.

4. In its commmonplace or basic sense: graciousness in speech.[18]

[18]Prv 22:11; Sir 21:16; 37:21; Lk 4:22; Col 4:6.

→ charism—gift—greet—justice—justification—mercy—thanksgiving.

graft, grafting The image of Rom 11:17–24 reverses the normal method of grafting. The text could simply have intended to stress the graft's vital dependence on the tree or, supposing that the wild olive* tree was likened to the pagan, the paradox of a salvation received first by pagans.

grasshopper Gk. *akris.* A food of the poor.[1] The invasion of grasshoppers, which was a punishment[2] and a curse,[3] was an image of the judgment*[4] or symbolized the assault of forces hostile to the Kingdom.[5]

[1]Lv 11:22; Mt 3:4 (= Mk 1:6). [2]Ex 10. [3]Dt 28:38. [4]Jl 1:4. [5]Rv 9:3,7 □.

→ Intr. II.6; VIII.1.D.

Greece Gk. *Hellas.* The Greek name of the Roman province of Achaia.*[1]

[1]Acts 20:2 □.

greed Gk. *pleonexia* (from *pleon,* "in addition," *echō,* "I hold"). A will to power* which expresses itself by oppression and violence to another's detriment,[1] by taking advantage of him or by tricking him.[2] Covetousness,*[3] associated with impurity*[4] and, above all, money.*[5] It was the proof of a life without God[6] and so could be called idolatry.*[7]

[1]Jer 22:17; Ez 22:27. [2]2 Cor 2:11; 7:2 [3]Mk 7:22. [4]1 Cor 5:10f.; Eph 4:19; 5:3; Col 3:5; 1 Thes 4:6. [5]Lk 12:15; 2 Cor 9:5; 12:17f.; 1 Thes 2:5; 2 Pt 2:3,14. [6]Rom 1:29; 1 Cor 6:10. [7]Eph 5:5; Col 3:5 □.

→ covetousness—jealousy—money—vices—violence.

Greek In Gk. *Hellēn.*

1. In general the term designated every man of Greek language and culture, whatever his origin might have been.[1] As a result of the Jewish Diaspora,* some were sympathetic to Israel's religion.[2]

[1]Rom 1:14; Gal 2:3. [2]Jn 12:20.

2. When contrasted with the Jew,* the term refers to non-Jews, that is to the pagans.[3] Even if there is an order for coming to faith, one that locates the Greek after the Jew,[4] in Christ every such distinction has been abolished.[5]

[3]2 Mc 4:36; Mk 7:26; Jn 7:35; Acts 11:20ff.; 1 Cor 1:24. [4]Rom 1:16; 2:9f. [5]Rom 3:9; 10:12; 1 Cor 12:13; Gal 3:28; Col 3:11.

3. The Greeks properly so-called were characterized in Paul by their search for wisdom* with the aid of human reason.[6]

[6]1 Cor 1:22.

4. The "common" (Gk. *koinē*) language in the Hellenistic and Roman worlds from the time of Alexander the Great's conquest (from 333 B.C. to A.D. 500) was a Greek quite different from the classical, Attic language because of its acceptance of elements from Ionian or various dialects; however, it ought not to be simply identified with the vulgar speech of the Egyptian papyri. The Septuagint* and the N.T. used it for phonetics and syntax; but the style and meanings of words ordinarily were dependent on biblical language (such was the case with glory,* blessing,* etc.). The Greek of the N.T. was not uniform. Its Semitic* base made itself felt particularly in the words of Jesus. Mark was more popular and offered numerous "Latinisms." Matthew often offered Hebraisms, all the while preserving good Greek. Luke, who was capable of Atticizing (e.g., Lk 1:1–4), freely imitated the speech patterns of the Septuagint. Paul had his own personal style, issuing from a man who spoke two languages. John wrote in a normal Greek, but in a surprising style. The Pastoral Epistles, those of James and of Peter, were close to a good *Koinē*. The Epistle to the Hebrews was the writing that was nearest to literary language.

→ Intr. IV.5; V.3.C; IX.9.—barbarian—God-fearer—Hellenism—pagan—proselyte.

greet, greeting **1.** Gk. *aspazomai:* "to greet with eagerness, with joy, to hail." The word manifests classical usage in the N.T., without our being able to introduce into it an idea of "salvation" in the sense of "to save."[1]

[1]Mt 5:47; 10:12; 23:7; Mk 15:18; Lk 1:29,40f.; Acts 18:22; 20:1; Rom 16.

2. Gk. *chaire* (the imperative of *chairō:* "to rejoice, to be happy"): "rejoice! joy to you! hello to you! God protects you!" a Greek greeting of welcome in encounters, often transformed in the Bible by the wish for peace* (Heb. *shalôm*) and grace* (Gk. *charis*).[2]

[2]Mt 26:49; 27:29 (= Mk 15:18 = Jn 19:3; 28:9); Lk 1:28; Acts 15:23; 23:26; Jas 1:1; 2 Jn 10f. △.

grow, growth **1.** Gk. *prokoptō* (from *koptō:* "to strike, to cut," with *pro:* "in advance"): "to draw out, whence to progress, to grow." Hence, the night is far advanced.[1] One can make progress in wisdom[2] or in Jewish doctrine.[3] The Gospel,[4] the Christian,[5] or the impious;[6] they, too, are progressing.

[1]Rom 13:12. [2]Lk 2:52. [3]Gal 1:14. [4]Phil 1:12. [5]Phil 1:25. [6]2 Tim 2:16; 3:9,13 △.

2. Gk. *auxō, auxanō:* "to increase, to enlarge." Hence, lilies[7] or wheat[8] grow. Jesus or John increases;[9] the Lord's word spreads;[10] the people grow numerous;[11] it is God who gives the growth,[12] just as he made Jesus grow in relation to John.[13] In this way the body of Christ* is to grow,[14] and, likewise, every believer.[15]

[7]Mt 6:28 (= Lk 12:27). [8]Mt 13:30,32; Mk 4:8; Lk 13:19. [9]Lk 1:80; 2:40. [10]Acts 6:7; 12:24; 19:20; Col 1:6. [11]Acts 7:17. [12]1 Cor 3:6; 2 Cor 9:10. [13]Jn 3:30. [14]Eph 2:21; 4:15; Col 2:19. [15]Col 1:10; 1 Pt 2:2; 2 Pt 3:18 △.

3. Gk. *pleonazō:* "to exceed the number." In this way grace, sin, transgressions[16] multiply; but so, too, do faith and love.[17]

[16]Rom 5:20; 6:1; 2 Cor 4:15; 1 Tim 1:14. [17]1 Thes 3:12; 2 Thes 1:3.

4. Gk. *perisseuō:* "to abound." Once again, the idea of surpassing,[18] of outstripping what is ordinary,[19] of outdoing oneself[20] is applied to the churches,[21] or to grace triumphing over sin, which had abounded,[22] or also to hope.[23]

[18]Mt 5:20. [19]Mt 5:47. [20]1 Cor 15:58. [21]Acts 16:5. [22]Rom 5:20. [23]Rom 15:13.

→ fruit.

guardian

→ pedagogue.

Hades The Greek name *Haidēs* (popular etymology *a-eidēs:* "invisible"), from the God of the netherworld (according to Greek mythology), then the netherworld* itself, the dwelling-place of the dead. In the N.T., it is also the lower regions, the underworld[1] where the dead[2] are located; it even comes to mean the Kingdom of Death* personified.[3] Jesus was liberated from it and holds its keys;[4] he has promised his Church that she will hold fast when faced with death's power.[5] On the last day, Hades will be cast into the fiery pool.[6]

[1]Mt 11:23 (= Lk 10:15). [2]Lk 16:23; Rv 20:13. [3]Jb 38:17; Is 28:15; Rv 6:8. [4]Acts 2: 24,27,31; Rv 1:18. [5]Mt 16:18. [6]Rv 20:14 □.

→ fiery pool—netherworld—Sheol.

Hagar Heb. *hâgâr.* Sarah's* Egyptian servant who, by Abraham, bore a son, then was put to flight with him.[1] In the eyes of Paul she was a figure* of the ancient Covenant*; she seems thus to have served, under a supposed etymology (*ha-hâr* signifying in Hebrew "the mountain*") as a type for Sinai,* "the mountain*" par excellence.[2]

[1]Gn 16:1-16; 21:9-21. [2]Gal 4:24f. □.

hair Even though, according to the O.T., men readily wore long hair (so Absalom, who cut his once a year, had hair that weighed 2.3 kg. [5 pounds]),[1] Paul castigated this custom.[2] On the other hand, it was shaved off as a sign of mourning[3] or at the expiration of a vow,*[4] (in the latter case for burning[5]). Women considered their hair as clothing,[6] but they were not to care for it excessively.[7] All of this was advice that indicated the customs of their times, nothing more.

[1]2 Sm 14:26. [2]1 Cor 11:14. [3]Is 3:24; Jer 7:29; Am 8:10. [4]Jgs 5:2; 13:5; Acts 18:18; 21:23f. [5]Nm 6:18. [6]1 Cor 11:15. [7]Is 3:16f.; 1 Tim 2:9; 1 Pt 3:3.

→ Intr. VIII.1.C.c.

Hakeldama Gk. *Hakeldamach,* from Aram. *haqêl* (field) and *demâ* (blood): "the field of blood." According to Acts 1:19, the blood might have been that of Judas. According to Mt 27:6–10, the blood was that of Jesus and the estate became the "potter's field" because of the prophecy of Zec 11:12f., which was inserted within those of Jer 18:2f.; 19:1f.; 32:7–9. Beginning in the fourth century, Christian tradition located this field in the Valley of Hinnon where, long ago, potters had previously labored.

→ Map 1.

Hallel

→ Alleluia—psalms.

hand **1.** Gk. *cheir,* Heb. *yâd* (*kaph:* "palm"). God's hand symbolized his sovereign power.* Strong and terrible,[1] it governed the people's history;[2] one could trust in it.[3] The Father put all into Jesus' hands;[4] he has made them all-powerful.[5] When the Lord's hand is with someone,[6] his hands also become powerful.[7]

[1]Dt 3:24; 4:34; Jb 19:21; Heb 10:31; 1 Pt 5:6. [2]Ex 13:3,14; 1 Sm 5:9; Ps 8:7; Acts 4:28,30. [3]Dt 33:3; Ps 31:6; 73:23; Wis 3:1; Mt 4:6 (= Lk 4:11); Lk 23:46; Jn 10:29. [4]Mt 3:12 (= Lk 3:17); Jn 3:35; 13:3. [5]Jn 10:28f.; cf. Mt 11:27. [6]Ps 89:22; 139:5; Jer 1:9; Ez 1:3; Lk 1:66; Acts 7:25; 11:21; 14:3; 19:11. [7]Mk 6:2; Acts 5:12.

2. Hence, the gesture of the laying on of hands with its various O.T. meanings: blessing,*[8] sacrificial rites,[9] scapegoat,[10] rite of initiation,[11] gesture of substitution.[12] Thus, Jesus blessed[13] or healed;*[14] similarly did the disciples.[15] This gesture became a rite that signified the transmission of a power or an office and, perhaps, the gift of the Holy Spirit after baptism.*[17]

[8]Gn 48:14. [9]Lv 3; Nm 8. [10]Lv 16:21. [11] Nm 27:18,23. [12]Lv 24:14; Dn 13:34. [13] Mt 19:13,15 (= Mk 10:16); Lk 24:50; Rv 1:17. [14] Mk 6:5; 8:23,25; Lk 4:40; 13:13. [15]Mt 9:18; Mk 7:32; 16:18; Acts 9:12,17; 28:8. [16]Acts 6:6; 13:3; 1 Tim 4:14; 5:22; 2 Tim 1:6. [17]Acts 8:17f.; 19:6; Heb 6:2.

happy Gk. *makarios.* The beatitude is a wisdom expression, known in secular writings and in the O.T.[1] In the present tense, it represented the attribution of happiness to someone because of a gift received or a state of blessedness experienced.[2] In the future tense, it proclaimed a coming joy.[3] Beatitudes should not be confused with blessings.*

[1]Ps 1:1; 32:1f.; Sir 25:7-11. [2]Mt 5:3-11; 13:16; 16:17; Lk 6:20; 1 Pt 4:14; Rv 14:13ff. [3]Mt 11:6; Lk 11:28; 12:37f.,43; Jn 20:29ff.

harden Gk. *sklērynō:* "to render hard, inflexible," *pōroō:* "to make callous," *pachynō:* "to fatten," *typhloō:* "to blind." In a celebrated text which was capitalized on by the N.T., Isaiah described how people who separate themselves from God gradually become hardened:[1] blindness,*[2] blocked ears,*[3] stiffened necks,*[4] hearts* of stone, such were the effects of this "sclerosis." When it is maintained that God hardens,[6] this reflects Semitic thought which readily disregards consideration of secondary causes. Nonetheless, to harden does not mean to reject but rather to let sin come to its fruition in death or to ratify the sin for which someone does not repent. Man bears full responsibility for this condition: he is brought to a state of no longer being able to believe.[7] Only some action of God can triumph over it.[8]

[1]Is 6:10; Mt 13:14f.; Mal 4:12; Jn 12:40; Acts 28:26f. [2]Is 29:9; Mt 23:16f.; Lk 6:39; 2 Cor 3:14; 4:4; 1 Jn 2:11; Rv 3:17. [3]Zec 7:11. [4]Ex 32:9; Dt 9:6; Is 7:26; Acts 7:51. [5]Ex 4:21; 7:3,13; 8:11; 1 Sm 6:6; Mt 19:8; Mk 3:5; 6:52; Rom 2:5; Eph 4:18; Heb 3:8; 4:7. [6]Rom 9:18. [7]Jer 13:23; Jn 3:19-21; 9:38-41; Heb 3:13,15. [8]Jer 31:33; Ez 11:19; 36:26f.; Hos 13:2; Mi 7:18; Rom 11:32.

→ blind—deaf—sin—wrath.

harp Strictly speaking, the N.T. never alludes to the *psaltērion* (from *psallō:* "to cause the string of a musical instrument to vibrate"); in Heb. *nébèl,* a ten-string musical instrument known from ancient times, limited to use with sacred music, more particularly to accompany singing. It was differentiated from a *kinnôr* (Gk. *kithara:* "zither") by the resonating board. In translating the Gk. *kithara* by harp, we should keep in mind what a zither was, namely an instrument with no resemblance to the guitar.[1]

[1]1 Sm 10:5; 2 Sm 6:5; Ps 33:2; 92:4; 144:9; Is 5:12; 14:11; Am 5:23; 6:5.

→ Intr. IX.6.—zither.

harvest Gk. *therismos,* Heb. *qâṣîr.* The gathering in of cereal plants took place in April-May. This time was one of joy[1] and reward.[2] Hence, it was an image of God's final judgment.* Anticipated in the era of the Church,[3] God's harvest will definitively take place on the Day of the Lord.*[4]

[1]Ps 126:5; Is 9:2; Jn 4:36. [2]2 Cor 9:6; Gal 6:7-9. [3]Mt 9:37f. (= Lk 10:2); Jn 4:35-38. [4]Mt 13:24-30,36-43; Mk 4:29; Rv 14:14-19.

→ Day of the Lord—feasts—fruit—joy—judgment—Pentecost—vintage.

hatred Gk. *misos.*

1. Love's* opposite, hatred was murder.[1] The fruit of sin, it was Satanic[2] in its origins. From this fact, it was the violent alternative placed before man when God manifested to him his truth and his love; he had to choose one or the other.[3] In giving his life Jesus put hatred to death.[4] Henceforward, only evil* has to be hated, never the sinner.[5]

[1]Gn 4:2-8. [2]Wis 2:24; 1 Jn 2:9,11; 3:10,12,15. [3]Ps 26:4f.; 119:113; Prv 8:13; Am 5:15; Mt 6:24 (= Lk 16:13); Rom 8:7; Jas 4:4; 1 Jn 2:15. [4]Eph 2:14,16. [5]Lk 6:27.

2. Moreover, since the Semitic mind commonly associated opposing pairs, without distinguishing intermediate shades of meaning, "to hate" could signify "to love less."[6] Such is the case in one's dealings with God[7] or in an attitude towards one's relatives or even towards one's own life when faced with God's call[8] or, finally, what was told to Jews in Jesus' time,[9] "you shall not love your enemies.*"

[6]Gn 29:31; Dt 21:15f. [7]Mal 1:2-4; Rom 9:13. [8]Lk 14:26; cf. Mt 10:37; Jn 12:25. [9]Mt 5:43.

→ Cain—combat—enemy—vengeance.

head Gk. *kephalē.* A part of the body. The term has several metaphorical meanings.

1. What is at the top, as in a man's body; such, probably, is the capstone,* which crowns a building.[1]

[1]Mt 21:42 (= Mk 12:10f. = Lk 20:17); Acts 4:11; 1 Pt 2:7.

2. What is in front, as in the case of animals' heads,[2] such as the leader who exercises primacy, leading the others.[3] So Christ is in relation to the universe[4] and in relation to the Church.[5]

[2]Is 9:13. [3]Ex 6:14. [4]1 Cor 11:3; Eph 1:10,22; Col 2:10. [5]Eph 5:23; cf. 1 Cor 11:3-5.

3. What is the principle of life, in conformity with ancient physiology, the source of cohesion and of growth: so, Christ in relation to the Church.[6]

[6]Eph 4:15f.; Col 2:19.

→ body—Body of Christ—Church.

heal **1.** In addition to the classical Greek verbs *therapeuō:* "to give one's care to, to make oneself the servant of,"[1] *iaomai:* "to cause a sickness to cease,"[2] or *hygiainō:* "to restore health,"[3] the N.T. uses the following verbs in this same sense: *katharizō:* "to purify from leprosy,"[4] *sōzō:* "to save"[5] and, once, *apolyō:* "to loose."[6]

[1]Mt 4:23; 8:7; Lk 4:23ff. [2]Mt 8:8ff. [3]Jn 5:4-15; Acts 4:10. [4]Mt 8:2f. (= Mk 1:40-44 = Lk 5:12-14); 10:8; 11:5 (= Lk 7:22); Lk 4:27; 17:14-17 △. [5]Mt 9:21f.; Mk 10:52; Lk 17:19ff. [6]Lk 13:12.

2. Jesus healed numerous sick people, generally with a mere word (except Mk 7:33; 8:23; Jn 9:6),[7] often linked to a sabbath occurrence;[8] thereby he indicated that the reign* of God had drawn near.[9]

[7]Mk 1:25; 2:11; 9:25. [8]Mt 12:10-12; Mk 3:2,4; Lk 6:7,9; 13:14-16; 14:3; Jn 5:16,18; 9:14. [9]Mt 11:4f. (= Lk 7:22); Lk 6:19; Acts 10:38.

3. The power to heal the sick was given to the Twelve*[10] and even to the seventy-two disciples.[11] This activity was carried on in Jesus' name.[12] There even was a gift* of healing.[13]

[10]Mt 10:1,8; Mk 6:13; 16:18; Lk 9:1,6. [11]Lk 10:9. [12]Acts 3:6; 19:13. [13]1 Cor 12:9,28; cf. Jas 5:14f.

→ anointing—sickness.

hear Gk. *akouō:* "to hear, listen to," with its compounds *eis-akouō:* "to give ear to, grant" and *hyp-akouō:* "to obey," *par-akouō:* "to disobey." Biblical existence meant "hearing God," while seeing* was put off until the end of time. "To see and hear" was to fulfill and authenticate earthly seeing through a type of hearing which issued in an act of obedience.*[1] "To hear and do," to hold fast to words, was to put them into practice; the word "listen to" did not necessarily convey this.[2] "Hearing and understanding," in contrast with hardening,* was the same as welcoming the Word, believing.*[3]

[1]Mt 11:4; 13:16f. (= Lk 10:24); 17:5 (= Mk 9:7 = Lk 9:35); Lk 2:20; Acts 2:33; 4:20; 1 Jn 1:3,5; Rv 1:10; 5:11; 22:8. [2]Mt 7:24,26 (= Lk 6:47,49); Lk 11:28; Jn 10:16,27; 12:47; Rom 2:13; Heb 4:7; Jas 1:22f., 25. [3]Ps 40:7f.; Is 50:5; Mt 11:15; 13:15,19,23; 15:10; Mk 4:16; Jn 5:37; 6:45; 8:43,47; Acts 16:14; Rv 2:7.

→ ear—obey—see—voice—word.

heart Gk. *kardia,* Heb. *lêb.* In the N.T., the word sometimes indicates the locus of vital forces;[1] ordinarily, it had a metaphorical meaning. It did not signify the affective life exclusively,[2] but focused on a man's varied self-manifestations: the hidden place (in contrast with the face* or lips*[3]), the source of one's inmost intellectual intentions[4] (very close to "spirit*": Gk. *nous*[5]), of faith,[6] understanding,[7] hardening.* It was the center of decisive choices,[9] the moral conscience,* the unwritten law*[10] and of an encounter with God[11] who alone touched it;[13] the spirit of the Son which dwells in it[14] revealed God's love to man[15] and made him cry out: "Abba,* Father."[16] The believer's heart was no longer afraid,*[17] it had been purified by Christ's blood,*[18] becoming a heart that was pure,[19] strong,[20] at peace.[21]

[1]Lk 21:34; Acts 14:17; Jas 5:5. [2]Jn 16:6,22; Acts 2:26,37. [3]Mt 15:8 (= Mk 7:6); 2 Cor 5:12; 1 Thes 2:17; 1 Pt 3:4. [4]Mk 2:6,8; Lk 3:15. [5]Lk 9:47; Acts 16:14; 2 Cor 3:14f; Phil 4:7; Rv 2:23. [6]Mk 11:23; Rom 10:8f. [7]Lk 24:25; Eph 1:18. [8]Mk 6:52. [9]Mt 22:37 (= Mk 12:30 = Lk 10:27); 1 Cor 7:37; 2 Cor 9:7. [10]Mt 15:18f. (= Mk 7:19,21); Rom 2:15. [11]Mt 13:19 (= Lk 8:12,15). [12]Lk 16:15; Acts 15:8; Rom 8:27; 1 Cor 4:5; 1 Thes 2:4. [13]Lk 24:32. [14]2 Cor 1:22; Eph 3:17. [15]Rom 5:5. [16]Gal 4:6. [17]1 Jn 3:19-21. [18]Heb 10:22. [19]Mt 5:8; 1 Tim 1:5. [20]2 Thes 2:17; Heb 13:9. [21]Jn 14:1,27; Col 3:15.

→ conscience—hardening—soul—spirit.

heaven Gk. *ouranos,* Heb. *shâmayîm.*

1. A part of the universe that was always named before the earth, together with which it constituted the universe.

2. According to ancient cosmology, heaven meant, first of all, an inaccessible region,[1] situated "above." A solid vault (the firmament) separated the heaven above (celestial) from that below (terrestrial); it opened up to let down divine riches: rain,*[2] manna,*[3] the Spirit.*[4] Above the visible heaven, and above the waters* on high, was the invisible heaven, "the heaven of heavens."[5] God sat in heaven; earth was the domain of men.[6] In this sense, the heaven/earth distinction expressed the radical God/man distinction, namely God's transcendence.

[1]Dt 30:12f.; Jn 3:13; Rom 10:6. [2]Lk 4:25; Acts 14:17; Jas 5:17f.; Rv 11:6. [3]Ex 16:14; Ps 78:24; Jn 6:31. [4]Mt 3:16f. (= Mk 1:10 = Jn 1:32); Acts 2:2; 1 Pt 1:12. [5]2 Cor 12:2; Eph 4:10. [6]Ps 2:4; Mt 5:34; Acts 7:49.

3. On the other hand, heaven was the place that ruled the earth, whence God's sovereignty was exercised. God was the God of heaven, the Lord,* the earth's master.[7] Heaven was less a place than a point of departure for the divine lordship. It was from heaven that God sent out his angels,[8] from which he revealed himself and made his voice* heard,[9] from which he sent forth fire* and his wrath,*[10] it was thence that he made Jesus ascend[11] and "seated" believers.[12] In this sense, as late Judaism expressed it, Heaven was one of God's names.[13] To lift up one's eyes to heaven, was to lift them up to God.[14]

[7]Rv 11:13; 16:11. [8]Mt 24:31; Lk 22:43; Gal 1:8. [9]Mt 3:17 (= Mk 1:11 = Lk 3:22); Jn 12:28; 2 Pt 1:18. [10]Lk 9:54; 17:29f.; Rom 1:18; Rv 20:9. [11]Acts 1:11; Eph 4:10; 1 Thes 1:10; Heb 7:26. [12]Eph 2:6. [13]Mt 5:10; 6:20; 21:25 (= Mk 11:30); Lk 10:20; 15:18,21; Jn 3:27. [14]Mt 14:19 (= Mk 6:41 = Lk 9:16); Mk 7:34; Lk 18:13; Jn 17:1; Acts 7:55.

4. Jews were not deluded by the preceding language, and they knew that heaven was not a place, but was God himself. The Lord of all, present to all, the one whom heaven and even the heaven of heavens could not contain,[15] "the Father of heaven" watched over his children.[16] In this sense, heaven is not above us, it is within us, all the while remaining distinct from us. Finally, in Jesus, heaven had been present on earth, and angels from his time on "go up" from heaven to earth.[17] "To enter heaven" is to discover God.

[15]1 Kgs 8:17; cf. 8:13. [16]Mt 6:26,32. [17]Jn 1:51; cf. Gn 28:12.

5. According to apocalyptic* traditions, the earth had its destiny written in heaven. To pray that everything be fulfilled "on earth as in heaven," "on earth according to the image of heaven"[18] was to beseech God that earth be what it ought to be, in accordance with the divine plan.

[18]Mt 6:10.

→ Intr. V.1.—earth—paradise—universe.

Hebrew From the Heb. *'ibrî,* Gk. *hebraios.*

1. The people. An ethnic designation which stressed the Palestinian origin of some members of the chosen people.[1]

[1]Acts 6:1; 2 Cor 11:22; Phil 3:5 △.

2. The language. A Canaanite dialect, related (like Syriac) to the Northwest Semitic language group, taken over by the Hebrews once they had settled in Canaan. Related to Aramaic,* after the Exile* it was replaced by the latter as the basis for everyday speech, but it continued to be the sacred language and a powerful unifying factor for the Jewish people. The language of the inspired* text and of prayer, it was certainly known by Jesus.[2]

[2]Lk 23:38; Jn 5:2; 19:13,17,20; 20:16; Acts 21:40; 22:2; 26:14; Rv 9:11; 16:16 △.

→ Intr. III.2.A; V.3.B.—Israelite—Jew.

[Hebrews (Epistle to the)] This is not a letter, but a kind of exhortation to which an epistolary note (13:22–25) has been attached. The exhortation is phrased in a language and style that betray the hand of a writer other than Paul, who remains unknown; nonetheless, its thought is close to Paul's, a fact that explains the epistle's association with the Pauline corpus. The author was writing to unidentified Christian communities, already well-established, who were under the influence of Judeo-Christian* elements. Its date, though uncertain, should be set between 65 and 70. A deuterocanonical* epistle.

→ Intr. XV.

hell A place to be distinguished from the netherworld,* the dwelling-place of the dead. This word did not exist as such in the Bible, but it brings within our purview the lot reserved for sinners. The N.T. describes it, menacingly, with the help of a large number of images originating in diverse mythologies*; the Abyss,* exterior darkness,* the fiery pool,* the blazing furnace,* fire* that never goes out, the torment of fire, Gehenna,* the worm,* corruption, the definitive punishment, the penalty, perdition, ruin, the place of weeping and gnashing of teeth, the situation of no longer being known and no longer knowing,* lastly the very power of death* itself.

This very enumeration shows at one and the same time the richness of the experience and the halting quality of language itself. All these expressions attempt to pictorially depict the fact that the sinner would find himself definitively "far off from" God and his Christ, that is "separated," cut off, far away from the source of life.[1]

[1]Ps 6:6; 88:11; Mt 7:23; 25:41.

→ punishment—wrath.

[Hellenism] 1. The period between Alexander the Great (†323 B.C.) and Augustus (†A.D. 14).

2. It also refers to the spread of Greek* culture, made possible by Alexander's conquests, and its intermingling with the thought world of the East.

→ Intr. IV.5.

3. The Hellenism which influenced Jewish thought in the Diaspora* (Wisdom,* Sibylline Oracles*) penetrated some formulations of the Christian faith; not only in vocabulary (gnosis, epiphany . . .) and in reasoning processes (the Stoic* diatribe), but also in its very thinking (wisdom,* logos,* figure* and reality . . .).

[Hellenist] Gk. *Hellēnistēs:* "someone who speaks Greek* or who lives in the Greek fashion": such as Stephen* or Saul.* In the Acts of the Apostles, a Jew of the Diaspora* who was Greek-speaking.[1]

[1]Acts 6:1; 9:29; 11:20 □.

→ Intr. I.3.A, III.3.—Greek.

hem

→ fringe.

heritage, inheritance Gk. *klēronomia* (from *klēros:* "the lot which falls, lot in life"[1] and *nemō:* "to share"). The *kleronomoi* receive a share, they take possession *(nemontai)* of a lot.

[1]Mt 27:35; Acts 1:26.

1. In the Bible, heritage designates that inalienable possession of a good[2] in some way other than through the fruit of one's labor, by gift,[3] conquest,[4] inheritance,[5] distribution.[6] When used of the relations existing between God and man, this terminology emphasizes the aspect of gratuity: man merits nothing; he receives into his possession.

[2]1 Kgs 21:3f. [3]Gn 15:7. [4]Ex 23:30. [5]Gn 21:10. [6]Jos 13:7,14.

2. The heir (Gk. *klēronomos*) of God's promises* was Jesus Christ in whom descent from Abraham[7] was concentrated. Moreover, he was the Son who, by his birth, held title to inheriting all things;[8] in fact, by accepting his death out of obedience he has inherited the Name.*[9] In him believers become adoptive sons* and coheirs;[10] Jews and Gentiles, all are sharers of the same inheritance.[11]

[7]Gal 3:16. [8]Mt 21:38f.;Heb 1:2. [9]Heb 1:4. [10]Rom 8:14-17; Gal 4:1-7; Heb 9:15. [11]Acts 26:18; Eph 3:6.

3. The inheritance, which had already been spiritualized in the O.T.,[12] was no longer Canaan,[13] but the divine blessing,[14] the heavenly city,[15] the true Promised Land,*[16] the Kingdom of God,*[17] which is eternal life,[18] given in hope;[19] in its definitive form, it was God himself.[20] Such was the promise made first of all to the poor*[21] and then to all adoptive children who prove faithful.[22] This is not merely a hope, but by faith it is already present, for it is the very gift of which the Holy Spirit is the pledge.[23]

[12]Dt 10:9; Ps 16:5; 73:26; Jer 10:16. [13]Dt 7:1; Acts 13:19. [14]1 Pt 3:9. [15]Heb 11:8-10. [16]Ps 37:9; Mt 5:5. [17]Mt 25:34. [18]Mt 19:29; Mk 10:17 (= Lk 18:18). [19]Ti 3:7. [20]Rv 21:7. [21]Jas 2:5. [22]1 Cor 6:9f.; 15:50; Gal 5:21; Eph 5:5. [23]Eph 1:14.

→ Intr. VI.4.B.c.—promise—remnant—testament.

[hermeneutic] Gk. *hermēneuein:* "to express, to interpret, to translate." Limited in the first instance to the theory of explaining a text, this method today tends to designate the interpretative act which, in attempting to be a "translation" or "transposition" also strives to understand and express the text in contemporary terms.

→ discern—exegesis.

Herod Gk. *Hērōdēs,* from *hērōs* "nobleman, a divinized hero." The N.T. refers to three persons by this name→ *Herod the Great* → *Herod Antipas* → *Herod Agrippa I.* Others include Herod Boethos (called Philip* in Mt 14:3 = Mk 6:17) and *Agrippa II.

Herod Agrippa I A grandson of Herod the Great* (by Mariamne I and Aristobulus), born in 10–9 B.C. The friend of Caligula (from whom in 37 he received the tetrarchy* of Philip* along with Abilene, and then, in 39, Galilee and Perea) and of Claudius* (who, in giving him Judea* and Samaria* in 41, presented him with the entire kingdom of his grandfather). After a reign of six years (37–44), he died suddenly at Caesarea. In order to curry favor with his people, he persecuted the early Christian community.[1]

[1]Acts 12:1-23 □.

→ Intr. I.1.D.—Herod.

Herod Antipas Gk. *Antipas,* an abbreviation of *Anti-patros:* "in place of his father." A son of Herod the Great* and Malthake, the younger brother of Archelaus,* born in 22 B.C. Tetrarch* of Galilee and of Perea in 4 B.C. He dismissed his wife, the daughter of Aretas IV,* to form a liaison, contrary to Jewish law, with Herodias,* the wife of his half-brother. He established or fortified several cities, one of which, Tiberias,* became his residence. In 39 he was exiled by the Romans to Lugdunum Convenarum (which may be St. Bertrand-of-Comminges).[1]

HEROD THE GREAT (37–4 B.C.)

married ten wives among whom were

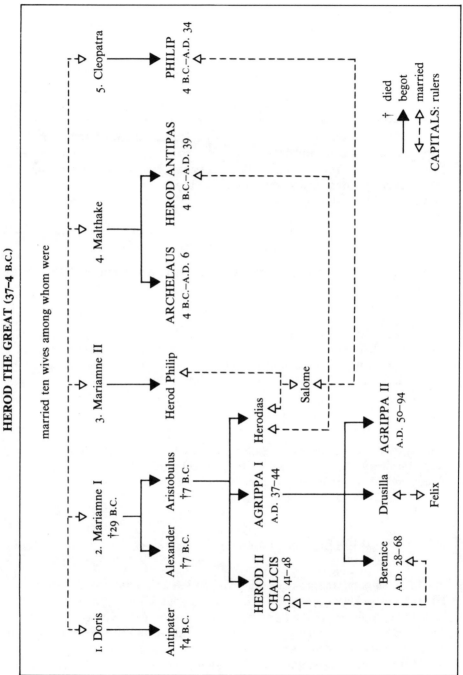

1. Doris
2. Mariamne I †29 B.C.
3. Mariamne II
4. Malthake
5. Cleopatra

Antipater †4 B.C.

Alexander †7 B.C.

Aristobulus †7 B.C.

Herod Philip

ARCHELAUS 4 B.C.–A.D. 6

HEROD ANTIPAS 4 B.C.–A.D. 39

PHILIP 4 B.C.–A.D. 34

HEROD II CHALCIS A.D. 41–48

AGRIPPA I A.D. 37–44

Herodias

Salome

Berenice A.D. 28–68

Drusilla

AGRIPPA II A.D. 50–94

Felix

† died

⟶ begot

⇠ ⇢ married

CAPITALS: rulers

[1]Mt 14:1,3,6; Mk 6:14,17,21,26; 8:15; Lk 3:1; 8:3; 13:31; 23:7,15; Acts 4:27; 13:1 □.

→ Intr. I.1.D.—Herod.

Herod the Great Born about 73 B.C. to an Idumean, Antipater, and an Arab princess. He had ten wives (of whom five are known: Doris, Mariamne I, Mariamne II, Malthake and Cleopatra) and seven sons (Antipater, Alexander, Aristobulus, Herod Boethos Philip, Archelaus, Herod Antipas and Philip). He succeeded in winning and extending his power with the help of Rome, whose friend he proclaimed himself to be from the time of Julius Caesar* up to Augustus.* Governor* of Galilee in 47 B.C., tetrarch,* then King of Judea in 41–40, lord of Jerusalem in 37, then of Samaria and several cities, including Jericho, until his death in 4 B.C. A great builder, he endowed Jerusalem with numerous monuments and founded or restored Hellenistic cities on which he bestowed the emperor's name, notably Caesarea.* His bloody dictatorship and the murder of three of his sons confer some weight to the narrative of his massacre of the children of Bethlehem.[1]

[1]Mt 2:1-22; Lk 1:5; Acts 23:35 □.

→ Intr. I.1.D.—Herod.

Herodians Supporters of Herod Antipas* (perhaps Sadducees*), hostile to Jesus.[1]

[1]Mt 22:16; Mk 3:6; 12:13 □.

Herodias The granddaughter of Herod the Great by Mariamne I and Aristobulus; she left her uncle and husband, Herod Philip I, to enter upon an illegal marital union with another uncle, Herod Antipas,* whom she followed into exile at Lugdunum Convenarum (St. Bertrand-of-Comminges?) in the year 39.[1]

[1]Mt 14:3,6; Mk 6:17,19,22; Lk 3:19 □.

→ Herod.

Hierapolis Gk. *Hierapolis*: "holy city." A city of Phrygia,* founded in the second century B.C., several kilometers (miles) north of the confluence of the Lycus and Meander Rivers. It became prosperous on account of its thermal waters and its wool trade. The birth place of Epictetus.*[1]

[1]Col 4:13 □.

High Priest, high priests Gk. *archi-hiereus,* from *archō:* "to be first" and *hiereus:* "priest."

1. In the singular: the supreme pontiff of the Jews; the offspring of the sacerdotal aristocracy. He enjoyed great civic and religious authority, so that he represented the people before the Romans. He presided over the Sanhedrin,*[1] but his privileges and duties chiefly concerned worship.* Consecrated with a special anointing,* and invested with a unique holiness, he offered the daily sacrifice,*[2] presided over great ceremonies and, he alone, entered the Holy of Holies* on the feast of the Atonement.*[3] He was appointed and deposed by the Romans, but even out of office maintained his pesonal prestige, as Annas* did.[4] According to the Epistle to the Hebrews,* Christ, having entered heaven, is the High Priest forever according to the manner, not of Aaron,* but of Melchizedek.*[5] He brought the office of High Priest to its term by himself being both priest* and victim, becoming the unique mediator* of the new covenant.*[6]

[1]Cf. Mt 26:57. [2]Ex 29:42. [3]Heb 9:25. [4]Lk 3:2; Jn 18:13,24. [5]Heb 4:14–5:10; 6:20. [6]Heb 9:1-28.

2. In the plural: members of the priestly aristocracy of Jerusalem, admitted to the Sanhedrin,[7] entrusted with the finances[8] and policing of the Temple.[9] Along with the elders* and scribes,* they designated the ensemble of the authorities of the Jewish people.[10]

[7]Mt 26:59. [8]Mt 27:3. [9]Mk 14:1,10. [10]Mt 26:3; Mk 15:31.

→ Aaron—mediator—priest—sacrifice—worship—Chart, p. 31.

[Hillel] The great Hillel was a contemporary of Herod the Great*; he lived from 30 B.C. to A.D. 10. A learned Pharisee,* he favored a broad interpretation of the texts of the Law.*

[historical criticism] A science which tries to determine the historicity of the account of an event in terms such as: "This happened," or the authenticity* of a saying: "This was said by so-and-so."

[historical tradition] **1.** The memory handed on about an event. **2.** The transmission of the memory of an event.

holocaust The sacrifice* offered at the Temple each morning and evening, as well as on numerous other occasions. As the sign of an irrevocable gift and of a "perfect sacrifice" (Heb. *kâlîl*), the animal was wholly (Gk. *holos*) burned by fire (Gk. *kaiō*), whence the name holocaust derives (Gk. *holokautōma*). The smoke from the sacrifice went up (Heb. *'âlâ*) towards God, from which the Hebrew designation of the rite *('ôlâ)* derives. Incapable of effecting a purification of sins, it was voided by Christ's offering, which alone was efficacious.[1]

[1]Lv 1:3-17; Dt 33:10; Dn 8:11; Mk 12:33; Heb 10:6,8 □.

→ Intr. XIII.2.A.—altar—sacrifice.

holy "Holy" must not be confused with sacred* (Gk. *hieros*), which refers to a reality of this world that has been set aside from secular use to be dedicated to the godhead. In the Bible, holiness, which is proper to God, can be the characteristic of a being (a person or thing); it signifies that a new relationship has been established between God and this being, either by stressing the presence in him of the holy God (Gk. *hagios*) or in recalling this man's fidelity to the Covenant,* required by this new relationship (Gk. *hosios*).

1. The Greek term *hagios* ordinarily translates the Heb. *gâdôsh,* of uncertain etymology, meaning "to separate" and "to belong to the deity." As in the O.T., the N.T. proclaims that God alone is holy,[1] that his name* must be made holy, that is, God must be recognized as God by all men.[2] In fact, the divine holiness is radiant and communicates itself to its entourage: the angels,[3] the prophets,[4] the elect,[5] the Temple,[6] the Law,[7] the Scriptures.[8] What is new in the N.T. is that the call to holiness[9] can be heard only in Jesus, the Holy One of God,[10] who sanctifies himself (and sacrifices himself) so that men may be sanctified.[11] This call cannot be brought about except by the Spirit who is the Holy One above all others:[12] the Spirit given by God at baptism, causing the believer to share in the very holiness of God,[13] leading him to be worthy of the call that has been heard[14] and to pour out around him the Love which is the Holy Spirit.[15]

The verb *hagiazō,* "to make holy," may preserve a note of "consecration" which the word "sacrifice" evokes.[16] It says more than *hagnizō,* which is more related to a properly cultic meaning.[17]

"The Holy" (plural *ta hagia,* except in Heb 9:1)[18] means the holy place at the core of the Temple esplanade. Its entry was protected by a large veil.* Beyond it lay the Holy of Holies.*

[1]Hos 11:9; Jn 17:11; 1 Pt 1:15f.; Rv 4:8; 6:10. [2]Is 6:3; Mt 6:9; Lk 1:49. [3]Mk 8:38; Acts 10:22; Rv 14:10. [4]Lk 1:70. [5]Lv 19:2; 1 Pt 1:15f. [6]Mt 24:15; Acts 6:13. [7]Rom 7:12. [8]Rom 1:2. [9]1 Thes 4:7; 2 Tim 1:9. [10]Mk 1:24; Lk 1:35; Jn 6:69; Acts 4:27; Rv 3:7. [11]Jn 17:17,19. [12]Lk 3:16; 1 Cor 3:16f.; *passim*. [13]Eph 2:21; 1 Pt 2:9. [14]1 Thes 3:13; Rv 22:11. [15]Rom 5:5; 15:30; Eph 4:16; 2 Tim 1:7. [16]Jn 17:19. [17]Jas 4:8; 1 Pt 1:22. [18]Heb 8:2; 9:2-25; 10:19; 13:11.

2. The term *hosios* describes a characteristic of man's faithful disposition toward God or the correspondence of things to the divine law. The Septuagint* linked it, among other terms, to the notion of piety* in the biblical sense of the term, that is, to *hassidim* (the "pious ones") fidelity to the Covenant proposed by God. The N.T. does not make use of *hosioi,* the current designation, to indicate the Christian members of the chosen community; it replaces that term with *hagioi* or by "the elect."[19] Nonetheless, God was still said to be holy;[20] Jesus was the faithful one who would never see corruption,[21] the being who was innocent and without sin.[22] A believer's behavior could be "religious," "pious"[23] or their opposite, a sacrilege.[24]

[19]Acts 9:13; Rom 1:7ff. [20]Rv 15:3f. (Ps 145:17); 16:5 (Dt 32:4). [21]Acts 2:27; 13:34f. (Ps 16:10). [22]Heb 7:26. [23]Lk 1:75; Eph 4:24; 1 Thes 2:10; 1 Tim 2:8; Ti 1:8. [24]1 Tim 1:9; 2 Tim 3:2 △.

→ anathema—blessing—justice—love—piety—priest—pure—sacred—sacrifice—sin.

Holy of Holies Gk. *Hagia tōn Hagiōn.* The description of Heb 9:3–5 makes reference to Ex 26:33. In the N.T. era it was a cubical room, 4.40 m. (14.4 ft.) on each side, located in the Temple* of Jerusalem, behind the Holy Place.* Totally dark and empty, it was the place above all others of the divine presence, accessible once each year only to the High Priest.*[1]

[1]Heb 9:3; cf. Lv 16 □.

→ holy—temple.

Holy Spirit

→ Spirit of God, Holy Spirit.

homeland

→ fatherland.

honey Gk. *meli.* Honey abounded in the desert of Judea, deposited there in rocky hollows by wild bees.[1] According to some, it may have been more truly a vegetable honey, a syrup deriving from grapes, dates or figs.[2]

[1]Jgs 14:8f., 18; Mt 3:4; Mk 1:6. [2]Ez 3:3; Rv 10:9f. □.

hope Gk. *elpis, elpizō.*

1. The noun is unknown in the gospels, while the verb appears but once in Matthew in an O.T. quotation, once with its theological meaning in Luke, and once in John.[1] Conversely, these same terms appear frequently outside the gospels, especially in Paul. To hope is to wait for the object of one's desire (from the root *vel-:* "to wish") to be realized. This feeling relates to an object which one does not yet possess, thereby implying perserverance.* The O.T. introduced a change in stating that Yahweh himself was Israel's hope[2] and this so much so that, by faith,* hope became a certitude based on God's very own fidelity.*[3] With the coming of the N.T., the believer's state was radically transformed, for he was now seen as suspended between the present *already come* (which justification, sonship, and the Holy Spirit, who had been given, together constituted) and the future *not yet come* (which heaven, eternal life and seeing face to face made up).

[1]Mt 12:21; Lk 6:34; 23:8; 24:21; Jn 5:45. [2]Ps 71:5; Jer 14:18; 17:13. [3]Is 8:17; Mi 7:7.

2. As a subjective disposition, hope is never an anxious waiting, like that of pagans;[4] through faith which is its substance[5] and which gives it steadfastness in the face of death,[6] it is self-assured. It is God's gift[7] at the very moment of the gospel message,[8] through the Holy Spirit's power, the first fruits* of glory.[9] Hope tenaciously withstands (Gk. *hypomenō*) trials* which typify the tension between the already and the not yet,[10] even amid tribulations,[11] so that occasionally hope is called perseverance (Gk. *hypomonē*).[12]

[4]Eph 2:12; 1 Thes 4:13. [5]Heb 11:1. [6]Rom 4:18; 8:20f., 38. [7]2 Thes 2:16. [8]Col 1:23. [9]Rom 8:23; 15:13. [10]Rom 5:4; 8:25. [11]Rom 12:12; 2 Cor 1:6; 6:4; Heb 10:36; Rv 2:3. [12]1 Thes 1:3; 2 Thes 1:4; Ti 2:2.

3. Objectively speaking, hope, which is alive,[13] looks forward to salvation,[14] the resurrection,[15] eternal life,[16] the vision of God[17] and his glory.[18] It is not, then, an earthly state of well-being, but the advent of the kingdom of the God who will transform our bodies and the entire world;[19] it is God alone and his Son Jesus.[20]

[13]1 Pt 1:3. [14]1 Thes 5:8. [15]Acts 23:6; 24:15; 1 Cor 15:19. [16]Ti 1:2; 3:7. [17]1 Jn 3:2f. [18]Rom 5:2; 2 Cor 3:12; Col 1:27. [19]Rom 8:20f.; Phil 1:20. [20]Mt 12:21; 1 Tim 1:1.

4. Of itself the waiting (Gk. *ekdechomai, prosdechomai*) may indicate no more than an aspect of hope and could signify no more than an attitude of welcome that is completed by "hope."[21] In spite of this, in context it may occasionally be equated with hope: such as in expectation of the Messiah, the Kingdom of God, the Consolation of Israel, the resurrection, the redemption of the body, new heavens and a new earth.[22] It may also describe a lively tension within it, not unlike that of an animal holding up its head in front of something which comes upon it unexpectedly (Gk. *apokaradokia,* from *to kara:* "the head").[23]

[21]Gal 5:5; Phil 1:20; Ti 2:13. [22]Mt 11:3 (= Lk 7:19f.); Mk 15:43 (= Lk 23:51); Lk 2:25,38; Acts 24:15; Rom 8:23; 2 Pt 3:13. [23]Rom 8:19; Phil 1:20.

→ Intr. XII.2.A.—faith—patience—perseverance—trust.

horn Gk. *keras,* Heb. *qèrèn.* A weapon of the ram or the bull, signifying power and confidence amid shepherd people.[1] Hence, the symbol of the power* of Messiah* and of the Lamb.*[2] The horns of the Dragon* and the Beast* might represent the vassal powers of Rome.[3] Discussion still continues on the meaning of the four horns of the altar* (outgrowths at the four corners),[4] perhaps they are to be linked with stones which had been erected in former times (Heb. *maṣṣéba*).

[1]1 Sm 2:10; Jb 16:15; Ez 29:21; Lk 1:69. [2]Ps 132:17; Dn 7:7f.; Rv 5:6. [3]Rv 12:3; 13:1,11; 17:3,7,12,16. [4]Ex 27:2; 29:12; 1 Kgs 1:50; Rv 9:13 □.

horse Gk. *hippos.* A draft and saddle animal used in battles.[1] As a sign of human power[2] it was criticized in the Bible[3] or had been transformed within the literature of apocalyptic.*[4]

[1]Jer 6:23; Jas 3:3. [2]1 Kgs 9:19,22; 10:28. [3]Dt 17:16; Ps 20:8; Is 2:7; Mi 5:9; Zec 9:10. [4]Zec 1:8; Rv 6:2-8; 19:11-21.

Hosanna From the Heb. *hôshia'nâ:* "help!" (from the Heb. root *hôshîa':* "to save").[1] A popular acclamation,[2] the equivalent of our hurrahs, used at the feast of Booths* and for processions.[3] The expression might also come from the Aramaic *'ushenâ:* "power," and signify "praise to."[4]

[1]Ps 118:25. [2]2 Sm 14:4; Ps 12:2. [3]Lv 23:40; Mk 11:9; Jn 12:13. [4]Mt 21:9,15; Mk 11:10 □.

Hosea Heb. *hôshéa'* (a contraction of *yehôshua':* "Yahweh saves." An eighth century B.C. prophet* during the period of decadence in the Northern Kingdom. Although its author is named only once in the N.T.,[1] the book of Hosea belongs to that Bible* which the Church freely consulted for its own self-understanding. Not only has its admirable saying on the superiority of mercy* over sacrifice[2] been retained, but it also allowed for recollection of the threat that weighs on sinners,[3] for understanding that the Church is composed of two peoples,[4] and for proclamation of trust in God who is the conqueror of death.[5]

[1]Rom 9:25. [2]Mt 9:13; 12:7 (= Hos 6:6). [3]Lk 23:30 (= Hos 10:8); cf. Rv 6:16. [4]Rom 9:25f. (= Hos 2:1,25); 1 Pt 2:10 (= Hos 1:6,9; 2:3,25). [5]Mt 2:15 (= Hos 11:1); 1 Cor 15:55 (= Hos 13:14) □.

→ Intr. XII.—Bible—prophet—Chart, p. 67.

hospitality Gk. *philo-xenia:* "love of the stranger." The verbs *xenizō:* "to shelter, lodge" and *dechomai* or *lambanō:* "to welcome, receive" describe this activity. A sacred law of the ancient world, which was extolled by the O.T.,[1] hospitality is highly regarded in the N.T. Its refusal stirred up indignation,[2] instances of its neglect were mentioned,[3] a disinterested type of it was demanded.[4] Jesus made known the mystery at its core: in the stranger it was Christ himself who was being welcomed or rejected.[5] The fervent practice of hospitality was held to be one of the criteria of Christian life.[6]

[1]Gn 18:1-8; 19:8; Jgs 4:17-22; 19:3-9; Jb 31:32; Wis 19:13-17; Sir 31:23. [2]Lk 9:53f.; cf. Mt 10:14f.; 22:7. [3]Lk 7:44-46. [4]Lk 14:13f.; cf. 10:34f. [5]Mt 10:40; 25:35,43; Jn 1:11; Heb 13:2. [6]Rom 12:13; 1 Tim 3:2; 5:10; Ti 1:8; 1 Pet 4:9.

→ inn—stranger.

hour Gk. *hōra.*

1. A division of the day.* Twelve of them were enumerated from the rising to the setting of the sun;[1] they varied in length according to the seasons and could be lengthened or shortened by as many as eleven minutes. The first hour or early morning* corresponded to our six o'clock;[2] then came the third hour (or nine o'clock),[3] the sixth hour (noon),[4] the ninth hour (three o'clock in the afternoon),[5] and finally, evening.*[6] The N.T. also preserves references to the seventh hour (one o'clock in the afternoon),[7] the tenth hour (four o'clock),[8] the eleventh hour (five o'clock).[9]

[1]Jn 11:9. [2]Mt 20:1; Lk 24:1; Jn 8:2. [3]Mt 20:3; Mk 15:25; Acts 2:15. [4]Mt 20:5; 27:45 (= Mk 15:33 = Lk 23:44); Jn 4:6; 19:14; Acts 10:9. [5]Mt 27:46 (= Mk 15:34); Acts 3:1; 10:30. [6]Mt 8:16 (= Mk 1:32). [7]Jn 4:52. [8]Jn 1:39. [9]Mt 20:9.

2. A short period of time.[10]

[10]Jn 5:35; 2 Cor 7:8; Gal 2:5; 1 Thes 2:17; Phlm 15; Rv 17:12; 18:10,17,19.

3. A time determined by an event[11] or by some thing;[12] more particularly, the hour at the end* of the ages (which no one knows except the Father), that of the Lord's final intervention[13] and the messianic hour (which refers to the moment fixed by the Father for the glorifying of his own Son through his works and the cross[14]).

[11]Mt 8:13; 9:22; Jn 4:21,23. [12]Lk 1:10; 14:17; Jn 16:21; Rv 3:10; 14:15. [13]Mt 24:36,44,50 (= Lk 12:39,46); 25:13; Jn 5:25,28; 1 Jn 2:18; Rv 3:3,10; 14:7,15. [14]Mt 26:45; Mk 14:35,41; Jn 2:4; 7:30; 8:20; 12:23,27; 13:1; 17:1.

→ day—midnight—time.

house Gk. *oikos, oikia,* Heb. *bayît* (*béit* in compound words like Beth-el: "the house of God"). As in the majority of languages, a house means a building as well as a family.[1] In Hebrew the analogy is based on the fact that the same root *bânâ* means to build a house and a family.[2]

[1]Gn 12:1; Lk 1:69; 1 Cor 3:9; 1 Tim 3:15. [2]2 Sm 7:5,13.

→ Intr. VIII.1.A.—build up.

humility From the Latin *humilis:* "low, near the ground *(humus).*" From the Heb. *'ânâh,* related to *'any:* "poor," which ordinarily is translated in Greek by *tapeinos:* "humble," from which derives *tapeinoō:* "to lower oneself."

1. The word is understood by way of an opposition to terms of exaltation (Gk. *hypsoō*) and pride.* Above all, through Jesus' words, the N.T. makes its own that divine law which states God's preference for the humble and the lowly.[1]

[1] 1 Sm 2:7; Jb 5:11; Ps 147:6; Ez 17:24; Mt 23:12; Lk 1:52; 14:11; 18:14; Jas 1:9f.; 4:6; 1 Pt 5:5f.

2. Jesus was said to be "gentle and lowly of heart,"[2] the characteristics of a humble condition and one given expression by Mary[3] and Paul.[4] This state was not the outcome of penitential practices,[5] but rather a constant feature of one's being: one was blessed in possessing nothing, for then one was aware that it is God who comforts the humble.[6]

[2] Mt 11:29. [3] Lk 1:48. [4] Acts 20:19; Rom 12:16; 2 Cor 10:1. [5] Col 2:18,23. [6] 2 Cor 7:6; Phil 3:21; 4:12; Jas 4:10.

3. Jesus' being humble was a result of his having humbled himself and having emptied himself of everything (kenosis*),[7] the condition of his pointing out to his disciples the necessary path of self-abasement.[8] God desired that hills be levelled,[9] and he knew how to keep his apostles humble.[10]

[7] Phil 2:8; cf. Acts 8:33. [8] Mt 18:4; Eph 4:2; Phil 2:3; Col 3:12; 1 Pt 3:8; 5:5. [9] Lk 3:5. [10] 2 Cor 11:7; 12:21 □.

→ gentleness—poor—pride.

hymn Gk. *hymnos* (from *hymneō:* "to sing a solemn song," whether religious or epic). These pieces, ones which originated in the liturgy and in which Jesus was joyfully acclaimed to be the Lord glorified by God, must have borne resemblances to biblical psalms.*[1] Critical study claims to have found Christian hymns[2] as well as doxologies* underlying N.T. texts.

[1] Acts 16:25; Eph 5:19; Col 3:16; Heb 2:12 □. [2] Lk 1:46-55; 68-75; 2:29-32; Jn 1:1,3-4,9-11,14*a,b,e,* 16,17; Rom 10:5-8; Eph 4:7-10; 5:14; Phil 2:6-11; Col 1:5-20; 1 Tim 3:16; Heb 1:3f.; 1 Pt 1:19f.; 2:23f.; 3:18-22; 4:6; Rv *passim.*

→ doxology—psalm—song.

hypocrite Gk. *hypokritēs* (from *hypo-krinomai:* "to explain by causing the answer to surface from the depths of oneself," in particular with regard to dreams; whence "to replay, interpret [a text], declaim"): "one who plays a role.[1]" The term not only points out the person whose speech and acts disagree with his thoughts,[2] but also adds a further nuance, one which probably derives from the Aramaic word *hanefâ* and which, in the O.T., generally meant "perverse or impious." By force of habit a hypocrite becomes unfaithful[3] and, occasionally, blind:[4] his judgment is twisted or perverted.[5] Hypocrisy is the opposite of a sincerity that is without pretense or deviance.[6]

[1]Lk 20:20; Gal 2:13. [2]Mt 6:2,5,16; 15:7; 22:18; 23:13. [3]Mt 24:51; cf. Lk 12:46. [4]Mt 7:5. [5]Lk 6:42; 12:56; 13:15. [6]Rom 12:9; 2 Cor 6:6; 1 Tim 1:5; 1 Pt 1:22.

→ lie—vices.

hyssop Gk. *hysōppos* (from the Heb. *'ezôb*). An aromatic shrub tree with blue or red flowers, it grew in the cracks of walls and could reach 1 meter (3 ft.) in height. It resembled the caprier. Its stalks, quite fragile, served as sprinklers in ritual aspersions.*[1]

[1]Ex 12:22; Lv 14:4; 1 Kgs 4:33; Ps 51:9; Jn 19:29; Heb 9:19 □.

I

Iconium Gk. *Ikonion.* A city of Lycaonia* on the high plateaus of Asia Minor, it was evangelized on several occasions by Paul.[1] Modern-day Konya.

[1]Acts 13:51; 14:1,19,21; 16:2; 2 Tim 3:11 □.

→ Map 2.

idolatry, idols Gk. *eidōlo-latria* (from *eidōlon:* "image" and *latreia:* "worship"). Faced with the only God,* who could not be represented,[1] Israel often was attracted to pagan worship and its sacred images.[2] From the time of the Exile* and even before, Judaism did not see in these mute images anything but emptiness.[3] They were deceitful and their worship was directed to demons.[4] In being converted from them, the pagan abandoned the idols of his city and homeland in order to serve the living God,[5] and he had to guard himself against greed* which was idolatry.[6]

[1]Ex 20:2-5; Dt 4:15-24; Acts 17:29; Rom 1:23. [2]Jgs 8:24-27; 17:1–18:31; 1 Kgs 12:28f.; 15:13; Acts 7:41-43; 15:20; 17:16; Rom 2:22; 1 Cor 5:10f.; 6:9; 10:7. [3]Ps 115; Wis 15; Is 44; Bar 6; 1 Cor 8:4; 10:19-21; 12:2. [4]Rv 9:20. [5]1 Thes 1:9. [6]Eph 5:5; Col 3:5.

→ Intr. VI.4.C.2—gods—image—meats (of sacrifice)—money—prostitution—worship.

[Ignatius of Antioch] A bishop of Syrian Antioch. One of the first of the Apostolic Fathers,* several of whose letters, written around the year 110, we possess (to the churches of Ephesus, Magnesia, Philadelphia, Rome, Smyrna, Tralles, as well as to Polycarp).

Illyricum Gk. *Illyrikon.* The mountainous country of northwestern Macedonia, corresponding today to Albania and Yugoslavia. Occupied from 167 B.C. by the Romans, Illyricum became an imperial province* in 27 B.C. In the first century A.D., it was often called Dalmatia,* although this corresponded more to the Adriatic coast, while Illyricum designated the region near the Macedonian frontier.[1]

[1]Rom 15:19 □; cf. 2 Tim 4:10.

→ Map 3.

image Gk. *eikōn.* What more or less exactly reproduces and represents (renders present) a reality.[1]

[1]Mt 22:20 (= Mk 12:16 = Lk 20:24).

1. Of the invisible God,* no image had any value,[2] except man,* the very image of God.[3]

[2](Acts 17:29;) Rom 1:23. [3]Gn 1:26; Wis 2:23; Rom 8:29; 1 Cor 11:7.

2. Christ was the image surpassing all others of the invisible God.[4]

[4]Wis 7:26; Jn 1:18; 14:9; Col 1:15; (Heb 1:3).

3. The entire universe* has been stamped with the unique imprint of Christ[5] and every person is created in the image of the heavenly Adam which Christ has become.[6]

[5]Col 1:15-20. [6]1 Cor 15:49; 2 Cor 3:18–4:4; Col 3:10.

→ Intr. IX.5.A.—form—idolatry—see.

Immanuel

→ Emmanuel.

immolate

→ meat sacrificed to idols—sacrifice.

immortality **1.** Gk. *a-thanasia.* According to Hellenistic anthropology, the soul, as an emanation of the deity, was itself incorruptible and immortal. According to the Bible, only God possessed immortality;[1] man, who was himself mortal, still had to be clothed with immortality.[2] Since the victory over death was a fundamental presupposition of biblical faith, the term immortality appears only three times in the N.T.

[1]Dt 32:40; Wis 15:3; 1 Tim 6:16. [2]Wis 1:15; 3:4; 8:13,17; Sir 17:30; 1 Cor 15:53f. △.

2. Incorruptibility (Gk. *a-phtharsia*) was also one of God's proper attributes,[3] while men, who were created for incorruptibility, had become bound by sin* to corruption;[4] but, through Christ, who had been preserved from it,[5] man will one day be able, through the living God's word,[6] to inherit incorruptibility.

[3]Wis 12:1; Rom 1:23; 1 Tim 1:17. [4]Wis 2:23f.; Rom 1:23; 8:21; 1 Cor 15:42-54; 2 Cor 4:16; Gal 6:8; Eph 4:22; 2 Pt 1:4; 2:12. [5]Acts 2:27,31; 13:34-37. [6]Wis 6:19; 1 Pt 1:18,23; cf. 3:4. [7]Rom 2:7; 1 Cor 9:25; 15:42-54; Eph 6:24; 2 Tim 1:10; 1 Pt 1:4 △.

→ Intr. IV.6.C.—death—life—resurrection.

impious

→ Antichrist—piety.

imposition of hands

→ hand.

impure

→ pure.

incense Gk. *libanos.* A resinous substance obtained from cutting into the bark of a fir (or pine) tree (Heb. *lebonâ*) indigenous to India, Somalia or Arabia of the South ("the country of Saba"),[1] the Orient of the N.T.[2] Incense went into the confecting of perfumes* and aromatics,* and was likened to the perfume of the offering (Gk. *thymiama*).[3] It was burned in the Temple at the time of certain sacrifices as a sign of adoration of the godhead.[4] Because of its smoke, which rose up to heaven and spread everywhere, it could symbolize the prayer of messianic times.[5]

[1]1 Kgs 10:1-10; Jer 6:20. [2]Mt 2:11; Rv 18:13 △. [3]Lk 1:9-11; Heb 9:4; Rv 18:13. [4]Lv 2:1,15; 24:7; Lk 1:9-11. [5]Ps 141:2; Is 60:6; Rv 5:8; 8:3-5; 18:13 △.

→ altar—perfume.

incorruptibility

→ immortality.

infirmity Gk. *astheneia* (from *sthenos:* "power, vigor" and *a* privative): "without power," Gk. *arrōstos* (from *rhōnnymai:* "to be vigorous, strong"): "feeble, ill."

→ sickness.

inheritance

→ heritage, inheritance.

iniquity This word does not mean the various sins which a man can commit, but rather that opposition to God which is at the root of all sins committed, particularly the sin which leads to unbelief. The Greek *anomia* (from *nomos:* "law" with the *a* privative) better expresses this eschatological* power hostile to God about which the Judaism of Christ's time readily spoke.[1] The Greek *adikia* (from *dikē:* "rule, justice" with *a* privative): "injustice" may also be translated in this sense, and this to such an extent that the biblical sense of justice* is seen to underlie it and, where the context warrants it, that it is more an instance of a power at work than of a result brought about.[2]

[1]Mt 7:23; 13:41; 23:28; 24:12; Rom 4:7; 6:19; 2 Cor 6:14; 2 Thes 2:3,7; Ti 2:14; Heb 1:9; 10:17; 1 Jn 3:4 △. [2]Rom 1:18; 2:8; 9:14; 1 Cor 13:6; 2 Thes 2:10,12; 2 Tim 2:19; 1 Jn 1:9; 5:17.

→ justice—law—sin.

injure Gk. *blasphēmeō* (from *blas,* related to *blabē:* "damage, wrong" and *phēmi:* "to speak"): "to speak ill of, injure, insult." In the N.T. the context demands a degree of deliberation and attack which suggests that "insult" is to be preferred as its translation.

→ blaspheme—insult.

inn Gk. *pan-docheion:* "welcome for all."[1] To be distinguished from *katalyma* (from *kata-lyō:* "to unharness"): "room for guests," whether in a house or a caravan enclosure, where one sojourns temporarily.[2] It differs also from *xenia:* "resting-place, dwelling."[3]

[1]Lk 10:34f. △. [2]Mk 14:14 (= Lk 22:11); Lk 2:7; cf. 9:12; 19:7 △. [3]Acts 28:23; Phlm 22 △.

inspired 1. Gk. *theopneustos* (from *theos:* "God" and *pneō:* "to breathe"). "Every Scripture is inspired by God."[1] In accordance with Jewish belief, the writings of the Law and the Prophets were "words of God."[2] One could not do away with them;[3] in them one discovered eternal life.[4]

[1]2 Tim 3:16 △. [2]Rom 3:2. [3]Jn 10:35. [4]Jn 5:39.

2. In an extended sense, one may say that the authors of the sacred writings were "inspired": they were "impelled by the Holy Spirit"[5] so that one may say indiscriminately: "God spoke through so-and-so" or "So-and-so said."[6]

[5]2 Pt 1:21. [6]Mt 1:22; Acts 3:21; 4:25; cf. 2 Pt 3:16.

→ Intr. XII.—Bible—Scripture—spirit.

insult Various Greek terms refer to the ways of acting that lead one to attack others through words or gestures (such as spitting on someone), injuring that person's dignity or honor. According to Jewish law, verbal abuse was a very serious fault.[1]

[1]Mt 5:22.

1. *Blasphēmeō* meant—and in this it differed from its English equivalent—not only an outrage against the diety but an injury* or outrage directed against men. Accordingly, its meaning was "to insult, outrage, launch out into abuses." Such were those against Jesus,[2] God's messengers,[3] Christians,[4] other people in general.[5] Believers have to shun such a vice.[6]

[2]Mt 27:39 (= Mk 15:29); Lk 23:39. [3]Acts 13:45; 18:6; Rom 3:8. [4]Rom 14:16; 1 Cor 10:30; 1 Pt 4:4; Rv 2:9. [5]Mt 15:19 (= Mk 7:23); 1 Tim 6:4; 2 Tim 3:2. [6]Eph 4:31; Col 3:8; Ti 3:2.

2. *Kako-logeō* (from *kakos:* "evil," *legō:* "to speak"): not to curse, but, for example, to insult one's parents[7] or to speak ill of a leader, such as the High Priest.[8]

[7]Ex 21:17; Ez 22:7; Mt 15:4 (= Mk 7:10). [8]Ex 22:27; Acts 23:5.

3. *Loidoreō* (cf. Lat. *ludus,* game): "to mock" in some outrageous manner. Thus, this kind of treatment of Jesus[9] or believers.[10] A vice to be shunned.[11] Christians are to reply to it with the opposite disposition, that of Jesus.[12]

[9]1 Pt 2:23. [10]Acts 23:4; 1 Cor 4:12; cf. Jn 9:28. [11]1 Cor 5:11; 6:10; cf. 1 Tim 5:14. [12]1 Cor 5:11; 1 Pt 3:9 △.

4. *Oneidizō* (from a root meaning "banter, scoffing," or else "reproach"): "to accuse, inveigh against, discredit."[13] A term used above all to refer to the opprobrium undergone by Jesus[14] and by his disciples following him. Hence, it becomes an honor for them.[15] Another word: *chleuazō* (from *chleuē:* "to laugh*"): "jeer at, make fun of."[16]

[13]Lk 1:25; 1 Tim 3:7. [14](Ps 69:10;) Mt 27:44 (= Mk 15:32); Rom 15:3; Heb 11:26; 13:13. [15]Mt 5:11; Heb 10:33; 1 Pt 4:14. [16]Acts 2:13; 17:32 △.

5. *Empaizō* (from *paizō:* "to act like a child [*pais*], amuse oneself"): "to make fun of someone,[17] bring into derision, scoff at."[18] A term chiefly used of Jesus in his Passion.[19] An equivalent word: *(ek-)mykterizō* (from *myktēr:* "nose"): "to thumb one's nose at, ridicule."[20]

[17]Mt 2:16. [18]Lk 14:29; 2 Pt 3:3; Jude 18. [19]Mt 20:19 (= Mk 10:34 = Lk 18:32); 27:29,31 (= Mk 15:20), 41 (= Mk 15:31); Lk 23:11; Heb 11:36 △. [20]Lk 16:14; 23:35; Gal 6:7 △.

→ blaspheme—injure—laugh—raca—slander—tongue—vices.

intercession Every prayer* of petition made on behalf of others is an intercession for them. Abraham,*[1] Moses,* the Servant* of Yahweh[3] were famous intercessors who foreshadowed the mediator* above all others, Jesus Christ. Intercession was prayer (Gk. *deomai:* "to lack, need, pray") for someone other than oneself.[4] Another way of expressing it is that of dealing with someone with the aim of soliciting on someone else's behalf or for some thing (Gk. *entygchanō*): this is the case with Jesus Christ[5] or the Holy Spirit[6] or with believers generally.[7] The notion of intercession presupposes another, that of a solidarity among beings.

[1]Gn 18:16-33; 19:29. [2]Ex 32:11-14. [3]Is 53:12. [4]Acts 8:24; Phil 1:4,19; Eph 6:18. [5]Rom 8:34; Heb 7:25. [6]Rom 8:26. [7]1 Tim 2:1.

→ mediator—pray.

iota Gk. *iōta:* the ninth letter of the Greek alphabet, corresponding to the tenth letter of the Hebrew alphabet, *yôd.* In the N.T. period, both were the tiniest letters of their respective alphabets.[1]

[1]Mt 5:18 □.

Isaac Gk. *Isaak,* from the Heb. *yiṣḥâq,* the abbreviation of *yiṣḥaq-'ēl:* "May God smile [be favorable]!"[1] Abraham's* son and the father of Jacob,*[2] he was the child and the heir of the divine promise.*[3] Offered in sacrifice by his father, but saved from death,[4] he prefigured Christ and foretold the freedom of believers.[5]

[1]Gn 17:17,19; 18:12; 21:6; Gal 4:27. [2]Dt 1:8; Mt 1:2; 8:11; 22:32 (= Mk 12:26 = Lk 20:37); Lk 3:34; 13:28; Acts 3:13; 7:8,32. [3]Gn 17:15-22; 18:9-15; 21:1-7; Rom 9:7,9f.; Gal 4:23,28; Heb 11:20. [4]Gn 22:1-19; Rom 4:19; Heb 11:17f.; Jas 2:21. [5]Gal 4:22-31; Heb 11:9-19; cf. Jn 8:56 □.

Isaiah, Isaias Gk. *Ēsaias,* from the Heb. *yᵉshaʿ-yâhû:* "Yahweh saves." The name of a Jewish prophet* of the eighth century B.C. He gazed on God's glory and foretold the coming of Jesus.[1] The collection of prophecies published under his name is the one most often cited by the N.T. Chapters 1–12; 15–23; and 28–33 are attributed to him. *Deutero-Isaiah* (Second Isaiah) or the "Book of Israel's Consolation," dating from the Exile,* was composed of chapters 40–55 and 34–35; *Trito-Isaiah* (chapters 56–66) originated in the period of the return from exile; the *Apocalypse* (chapters 24–27) was later than the fifth century. The following are texts explicitly cited in the N.T., with or without a reference to Isaiah:

[1]Is 6:1-5; Jn 12:41.

1. Beginning with the "Book of Emmanuel"[2] and several related texts, the N.T. illumines the Church's reality as the New Israel. Therein are found: the call to conversion,[3] a hardening of the chosen people,[4] a proclamation of salvation to the nations,[5] the birth of Emmanuel[6] who would be filled with trust,[7] and the stumbling block which also served as the cornerstone.[8]

[2]Is 6:1–9:6. [3]Is 40:3f. (= Mt 3:3 = Mk 1:2f. = Lk 3:4f. = Jn 1:23); 52:11 (= 2 Cor 6:17). [4]Is 6:9f. (= Mt 13:14f. = Jn 12:39f. = Acts 28:25-27; cf. Mk 4:12; Lk 8:10); 29:13 (= Mt 15:7-9 = Mk 7:6f.). [5]Is 8:23–9:1 (= Mt 4:14-16); 11:10 (= Rom 15:12); 40:5 (= Lk 3:6); 52:7 (= Rom 10:15). [6]Is 7:14 (= Mt 1:22f.). [7]Is 8:17f. (= Heb 2:13). [8]Is 8:14f. (= 1 Pt 2:8); 28:16 (= Rom 9:33 = 10:11 = 1 Pt 2:6).

2. From the "Servant Songs" and kindred material the N.T. appropriated several proclamations: the saving mission of the Messiah, whom God chose for his purpose,[9] whose bearing was lowly,[10] and whose destiny was a glory consequent upon misunderstanding and an ignominious death.[11] His apostles, sent out to the nations,* would apparently suffer a similar reversal.[12]

[9]Is 61:1f. (= Lk 4:17-19). [10]Is 42:1-4 (= Mt 12:17-21). [11]Is 53:1 (= Jn 12:38); 53:4 (Mt 8:17); 53:7f. (= Acts 8:32f.; 53:9 (= 1 Pt 2:22); 53:12 (= Lk 22:37). [12]Is 49:6 (= Acts 13:47); 53:1 (= Rom 10:16).

3. From other quotations the following notions converge: God had always yearned for a Temple that would be a true house of prayer,[13] rather than a building made of stone.[14] All men have sinned,[15] but sin will be definitively removed;[16] a remnant will be saved[17] and everyone will be taught by God.[18] Moreover, through Jesus, the holy one promised to David,[19] the pagans themselves will enter into Israel's inheritance.[20]

[13]Is 56:7 (= Mt 21:13 = Mk 11:17 = Lk 19:46). [14]Is 66:1f. (= Acts 7:48-50). [15]Is 59:7f. (= Rom 3:15-17). [16]Is 59:20f. (= Rom 11:26f.) [17]Is 1:9 (= Rom 9:29); 10:22f. (= Rom 9:27f). [18]Is 54:13 (= Jn 6:45). [19]Is 55:3 (= Acts 13:34). [20]Is 65:1f. (= Rom 10:20f.).

→ Intr. XII.2.A.b.—Chart, p. 67.

[Isaiah (Ascension of)] An apocryphal* writing which contained a Jewish legend on the martyrdom of Isaiah, dating from the first century B.C.,[1] along with two Christian fragments of an apocalypse,* dated between A.D. 100 and 150.[2]

[1]Asc. Is. 1:1–3:12; 5:12-16. [2]Asc. Is. 3:13–5:1; 6:1–11:43.

Iscariot

→ Judas Iscariot—Simon Iscariot.

Israel Heb. *Yisrâ'él,* a word composed of a subject and a verb, both of which possess a controverted etymology. The subject *él* means "goal, territory, leader," whence also "God." The verb derives from the root *srr:* to shine, illuminate, save, subdue, or from the root *srh:* to fight, wrestle. Hence the meaning: "May God rule [over us] or fight [for us]."

1. Jacob's* name; according to popular etymology: "strong against God."[1]

[1]Gn 32:29; 35:10; Rom 9,6 △.

2. An ethnic designation of the northern part of David's* kingdom,[2] then of the totality of the country.[3]

[2]Intr. III.2; 2 Sm 5:3; 1 Kgs 12:19. [3]Mt 2:20f.; 10:23.

3. The sacred name given to the people of the promises, after Judah* had taken over the first place;[4] it embraced twelve tribes*[5] whose history was full of meaning.[6]

[4]Dt 5:1; Is 41:8; Mt 2:6; Acts 2:36; 4:10. [5]Ex 24:4; Mt 19:28 (= Lk 22:30). [6]Acts 7:2–53; Rom 1:26f.

4. A political, religious community of the descendants of the Judeans*; the term was the equivalent of the name Jews*: the sons of Israel, Israel itself.[7]

[7]Neh 9:1f.; Jn 3:10; Rom 9:4; Phil 3:5.

5. In line with the prophets who proclaimed that "only a remnant* would be saved,"[8] Christians distinguished between the Israel of God[9] and Israel according to the flesh.[10] In their view, the community of those who believed in Jesus fulfilled the Jewish hope constituting them as a new Israel, the new people of God.[11]

[8]Is 10:20f.; 46,3; Rom 9:27,29. [9]Gal 6:16. [10]1 Cor 10:18. [11]Jer 31:31-33; Ez 36:22-30; Rom 9:6; Heb 8:8-10; Rv 7:4; 21:12.

→ Intr. III.2.B.—Israelite—people of God.

Israelite Gk. *Israēlitēs.* A term indicating the Jews,* primarily in their religious aspect.[1]

[1]Jn 1:47; Acts 2:22; 3:12; 5:35; 13:16; 21:28; Rom 9:4; 11:1; 2 Cor 11:22 □.

Italy The term, which originally meant southern Calabria, from Caesar's* time on referred to what is modern-day Italy. The country included important Jewish communities at Rome and Puteoli, a fact which partly explains Christianity's quick successes in these regions.[1]

[1]Acts 18:2; 27:1,6; Heb 13:24 □.

Iturea Gk. *Itouraia.* A pagan territory northeast of Palestine. One of the three regions of Philip II's* tetrachy,* whose capital was Chalcis.[1]

[1]Lk 3:1 □.

J

Jacob Gk. *Iacōb,* from the Heb. *ya'aqôb,* an abbreviation for *ya'qôb-él:* "God protects(?)," a name interpreted from *'âqab:* "he was mistaken."[1]

[1]Gn 27:36; Jer 9:3.

1. The grandson of Abraham,* a son of Isaac,*[2] the one who was preferred over Esau his brother,[3] the father of the twelve patriarchs[4] who gave his name (which was also Israel*) to the chosen people.[5] The N.T. alludes to several episodes from his life.[6]

[2]Gn 25–50; Mt 1:2 (= Lk 3:34); 8:11 (= Lk 13:28); 22:32 (= Mk 12:26= Lk 20:37); Acts 3:13; 7:8,12,14f., 32; Heb 11:9. [3]Rom 9:13; Heb 11:20; 12:16. [4]Mt 1:2; Acts 7:8. [5]Lk 1:33; Acts 7:46; Rom 11:26. [6]Jn 4:5f., 12; Acts 7:8,12,14-16; Heb 11:21 □.

2. The father of Joseph,* Mary's husband.[7]

[7]Mt 1:15f. □.

James Gk. *Iakōbos,* from the Heb. *ya'aqôb.*

1. *James "the Greater,"* son of Zebedee* and perhaps of Salome,*[1] the elder brother of John,* with whom he was a "son of thunder,"[2] one of the Twelve.*[3] With Peter and John, one of the three privileged witnesses of the great moments in Jesus' life: the raising of Jairus' daughter, the Transfiguration, the Agony.[4] He died by decapitation under the reign of Herod Agrippa I,* between 41 and 44.[5]

[1]Mt 4:21 (= Mk 1:19f. = Lk 5:10); 27:56; cf. Mk 15:40; Mk 10:35,41; cf. Mt 20:20. [2]Mk 3:17 (cf. Lk 9:54). [3]Mt 10:2 (= Mk 3,17 = Lk 6:14); Acts 1:13. [4]Mt 17:1 (= Mk 9:2 = Lk 9:28); cf. Mk 1:29; 5:37 (= Lk 8:51); 13:3; Jn 21:2. [5]Acts 12:2 □.

2. *James, the son of Alphaeus,* one of the Twelve.[6] Sometimes confused with James the Little through the (incorrect) identification of Alphaeus with Clopas.[7]

[6]Mt 10:3 (= Mk 3:18 = Lk 6:15 = Acts 1:13). [7]Mk 15:40; Jn 19:25 □.

3. *James the Little* (called *the Less*); the son of Clopas and Mary, the brother of Joses[8] and Jude.[9] Often confused with James, the son of Alphaeus. Though he was not a disciple of Jesus of Nazareth, James saw the Risen Lord.[10] Probably because he was "the brother* of the Lord,"[11] he played a key role in the Church of Jerusalem; the Judeo-Christians* appealed to him.[12] Tradition makes him out to be the author of the Epistle of James.*[13] According to Josephus,* he was stoned to death in 62.

[8]Mk 15:40; cf. 6:3; 15:47. [9]Jude 1. [10]1 Cor 5:7. [11]Gal 1:19; cf. Mt 13:55 (= Mk 6:3). [12]Acts 12:17; 15:13; 21:18; Gal 2:9,12. [13]Jas 1:1 □.

4. The father of Jude.[14]

[14]Lk 6:16; Acts 1:13 □.

[James (Epistle of)] An exhortation addressed in good Greek by a Christian of Jewish background to Judeo-Christians. It takes up again the tradition of the words of James the Little,* not the apostle but the brother of the Lord.* It may date from 57–62 or, more likely, from 80–90. A deuterocanonical* epistle.

→ Intr. XV.—Epistles (Catholic).

Jannes and Jambres Names given by 2 Tim 3:8 to the magicians* of Egypt mentioned by Ex 7:11f., 22; 8:3, 14f.; 9:11□.

jar

→ pitcher.

jealousy 1. The N.T. speaks of the pangs and ill will that a person can experience when seeing others enjoy a good which he would like to have ("envy*" which generally translates the Gk. *phthonos*)[1] or possess exclusively ("jealousy" properly speaking, which, along with "zeal," translates the Gk. *zēlos:* "competition, rivalry," from which come "envy, ambition, fervor, zeal").[2] One of the meanings of the "evil eye.*"[3]

[1]Mt 27:18 (= Mk 15:10); Rom 1:29; Gal 5:21,26; Phil 1:15; 1 Tim 6:4; Ti 3:3; Jas 4:5; 1 Pt 2:1 △. [2]Acts 7:9; Rom 13:13; 1 Cor 3:3; 13:4; 2 Cor 12:20; Gal 4:17f.; 5:20; Jas 3:14,16; 4:2. [3]Dt 15:9; Sir 31:13; Mt 20:15; Mk 7:22.

2. The word *zēlos* often had a religious meaning; it was for God's sake that one was jealous, whether in good or evil.[4] When emptied of all traces of egocentrism and applied to God, the term has to be related to the fact that God, being unique, is jealous of all that touches on his holiness* (God does not tolerate idols*)[5] and on his love (God does not tolerate adultery*).[6] It is the equivalent of God's wrath,* another aspect of his "holiness."

[4]Nm 25:11; 1 Kgs 19:10; 1 Mc 2:24-27; Ps 69:10; Jn 2:17 Acts 5:17; 13:45; 17:5; 21:20; 22:3; Rom 10:2,19; 11:11,14; Gal 1:14; Phil 3:6; Ti 2:14; 1 Pt 3:13; Rv 3:19 △. [5]Ex 20:5; 34:14; Dt 4:24; Jos 24:19f.; 1 Kgs 14:22; 1 Cor 10:22; Heb 10:27. [6]Ez 16:38; 23:25; 2 Cor 11:2 △.

→ adultery—envy—holiness—vices—wrath—zeal.

Jeremiah Gk. *Ieremias,* from the Heb. *Yirmeyâhû:* probably "Yahweh raises up." This great prophet* of the seventh–sixth centuries B.C. lived through the destruction of Jerusalem and the deportation into exile. Jesus' contemporaries awaited his return.[1] Above all, the N.T. keeps hold of chapter 31 and its references to a new covenant[2] and alludes to Rachel, who wept over her departed children.[3] For his part, Paul took up from it his appeal to true pride[4] and Matthew attributed to Jeremiah a prophecy of Zechariah.*[5]

[1]Mt 16:14. [2]Heb 8:8-12; 10:16f. (= Jer 31:31-34). [3]Mt 2:17f. (= Jer 31:15). [4]1 Cor 1:31 (= Jer 9:22f.). [5]Mt 27:9 (= Zec 11:12f.; cf. Jer 32:6-9) □.

→ Intr. XII.2.A.b.—Chart, p. 67.

Jericho Gk. *Ierichō,* from the Heb. *yerîhô.* A neolithic site. Also called the "city of palms," it had been magnificently reconstructed by Herod the Great* next to the ruins of a Canaanite city of the same name, in a very fertile oasis of the deep Jordan trench. It was linked to Jerusalem across the desert of Judah by a precipitous 37 km. (23 mi.) roadway that afforded ideal conditions to highway robbers.[1]

[1]Dt 34:3; Jos 5:13–6:26; Mt 20:29 (= Mk 10:46 = Lk 18:35); Lk 10:30; 19:1; Heb 11:30 □.

→ Map 4.

Jerusalem Gk. *Ierosolyma, Ierousalēm,* Heb. *Yerûshâlém, Yerûshâlaim.*

1. From the time of its conquest by David[1] (tenth century), the Canaanite city of *Urushalim* ("the god of Salem's foundation") was the heart of Jewish national unity. The biblical tradition located there Melchizedek's* city and identified the site with Mount Moriah, the place where Abraham* had offered his sacrifice. The dwelling-place of Yahweh from the time of the transfer of the ark* and the construction of the Temple,*[2] it was the Holy City, the people's spiritual center, to such an extent that its history represented Israel's destiny. Once having become idolatrous,* it suffered God's judgment:[3] it was taken and burnt (sixth century); after the Exile* it became once more, through the rebuilt Temple, the place of the divine presence, prefiguring, according to the prophet, the city of peace (*Yerûshâlaim,* from *shâlôm:* "peace") where the eschatological* judgment would take place and where joy would be offered to all peoples.[4]

[1]2 Sm 5. [2]2 Sm 6–7; 1 Kgs 6–8. [3]Cf. Ez 9:1–10:7. [4]Is 25:6-10; Jl 4:9-17.

2. In Jesus' time the city was endowed by Herod the Great with magnificent works: murals, the two palace-fortresses (the Antonia and the Palace), the new Temple esplanade and the Temple* itself, numerous residences, a theater, an amphitheater, and a hippodrome. It was surrounded by gardens to the north and west. It was also the center of religious activity and the seat of the Great Sanhedrin.* On festival occasions, people went up there from everywhere on pilgrimage* to the Temple. Out of respect for Jewish sensitivities, the Roman authorities resided at Caesarea* and did not come into Jerusalem except at times of mass gatherings of the people.

3. Jesus often went up to Jerusalem;[5] it was there that one last time he confronted the people with his message and his person. There he died, after having been crucified. It was at Jerusalem that the first Christian community was shaped and, beginning there, the preaching of the gospel radiated out into the world.[6] It was also there that the Judeo-Christians* established themselves under the leadership of James.* Upset by pagan acceptance of the Good News, they claimed a right to impose circumcision.*[7] A compromise was worked out at the Council* of Jerusalem.[8] But, little by little, with the spreading of the Christian faith to Antioch, Ephesus and Rome, the holy city no longer figured as the center of Christianity.[9] Its role in the realization of salvation had come to an end, but this was so that a transfer might be made to the Jerusalem given in heaven,* of which the earthly one was but a figure.* The new Jerusalem is, since the conclusion of Christ's mission, the definitive fatherland* of all who have been ransomed.[10]

[5]Lk 13:34f.; Jn 2:13. [6]Acts 1:8; 2:1-11. [7]Acts 15:1. [8]Acts 15:23-29. [9]Rom 15:19. [10]Heb 12:22; Rv 21:1–22:5.

→ Intr. I.1.C; I.3.C; II.3.B; II.4.B; VI.2.A.—Barnabas—Council of Jerusalem—Judeo-Christians —Map 1.

Jesus Christ

1. Gk. *Iēsous,* from the Heb. *Yéshûa', Yehôshûa':* "Yahweh saves." A name borne before Jesus of Nazareth by Joshua*[1] and, probably, by Barabbas.*[2] It is through the name* of Jesus of Nazareth that man is to be saved.[3] The compound name "Jesus Christ" extols the name of a person (Jesus) as well as a functional title (Gk. *Christos:* "the Anointed* One"), thereby inseparably uniting the historic person and the object of faith; frequent in the Acts of the Apostles, the designation is rare in the gospels.[4]

[1]Nm 27:18-23. [2]Mt 27:16f. [3]Acts 4:12; Phil 2:9-11. [4]Mt 1:1,18; 16:21; Mk 1:1; Jn 1:17; 17:3 □.

2. As is the case with the majority of the founders of religions (Moses, Buddha or Mohammed), the life of Jesus was scarcely mentioned by nonbelieving writers. Nonetheless, we may cite Josephus* towards the year 93, Pliny* in 112, Tacitus about 116, Suetonius about 120, and non-canonical* documents such as the Gospel of Thomas.* With reference to N.T. documents which are not gospels, their focal point is without doubt the person of Jesus, even when they do not give particulars about his earthly life. The four gospels (Matthew, Mark, Luke and John) constitute the principal historical source for the life and work of Jesus. Through their testimony of faith the historian can reconstruct, in the broad sense and insofar as the essential points are concerned, what his existence was like.

3. Jesus lived in Palestine, particularly in Galilee, at Capernaum,* by the lake, as well as in Jerusalem,* the capital of Judea. His existence can be situated through a definite reference point, his baptism by John,* who came preaching and baptizing at the Jordan* during the year which followed October 1, 27, or the month of August, 28. His life ended on a Friday, the fourteenth of Nisan,* on the eve of the Jewish Passover,* a fact that permits two very probable datings: April 7, 30 and April 3, 33. His other dates are more approximate: Jesus was born at Bethlehem* in 7 or 6 before our era; his public activity, between his baptism by John (27–28) and his death (30 or 33) lasted about two years and several months, give or take a year.

4. On this historical canvas we can trace a probable itinerary. At Nazareth* Jesus practiced the trade of a carpenter* until the days when he withdrew into the solitude of the Judean desert and was baptized by John. Thereafter, he conducted a baptizing ministry like John before returning to Galilee, proclaiming the Good News of the Kingdom of God, healing the sick and driving out demons. His preferred company was the "poor," children, women, the disinherited, those despised by the religiously observant. He challenged the rigorism and narrowness of certain Pharisees,* but he refused to encourage the revolutionary aspirations of the Zealots* and the people. In order to extend his activity, he gathered around himself an itinerant band of disciples,* choosing from them twelve* privileged ones who were to evoke memories of the tribes* of Israel and were to prefigure the new Israel.* Jesus ran up against the incomprehension of the crowds, the jealous suspicion of the religious leaders, the political astuteness of Herod Antipas* (who had had John beheaded). So, he broke away from Galilee and went up one last time to Jerusalem, a city which he entered triumphantly on the day of palms; there he drove the merchants from the Temple, an act of violence that embroiled him in an unyielding conflict with the Sadduceean* and Pharisaic* authorities: a decision was made then to put an end to his activity and to use the offices of Judas,* the traitor, to accomplish this. Several days later, after a meal* in the course of which he expressed his farewell wishes to his disciples and symbolically announced his death through words and in an act of thanksgiving, Jesus was arrested, probably by Roman troops, and was questioned by Jewish leaders who thought him deserving of death for having blasphemed* and for claiming a divine dignity; he was handed over to the prefect Pilate* who judged him to be an agitator who had disturbed public order by claiming to be the king of the Jews. After scourging* him, he condemned him to be crucified.* Jesus died on the cross* and was buried.* When the sabbath was over the disciples discovered his tomb was empty and went forth proclaiming that Jesus had risen* and had appeared* to them. Then, the history of Jesus gave way to the history of the Christian Church.

5. The message of Jesus can be reconstructed with some accuracy from behind the transformations which it necessarily underwent when the faith was being handed down. For Jesus, as for every good Jew who had been converted by John's word, time* had undergone a radical change: God was about to intervene in a decisive way, his kingdom* was near; one had to be ready, watchful and repentant in order to welcome the Lord who was coming. In Jesus' eyes, in contrast with the view of the Jews, the Kingdom of God had already arrived amid his own actions: the finger of God was there;[5] here was someone greater than Solomon, someone greater than Jonah;[6] one had to discover the hidden treasure;[7] one had to abandon all to follow Jesus.[8]

If God was acting in this way, it was to tell men that they were his children, without any distinction between races, national boundaries or merits: my neighbor* is the one to whom I draw near.[9] While valuing the personal worth of each child* of God, who was to have complete trust* in him,[10] Jesus did not scatter God's people,* but instead established them forever on the foundation of his own sacrifice,* everlastingly sealing with his own blood* a covenant* between God and man.[11] Jesus did not abolish, but brought to fulfillment* both the Law and Israel.[12] The believers who gathered around him did not constitute a "church" alongside Israel, but were a band whose sole cohesive bond was their attachment to his word and person.[13]

Behind the faith of the evangelists, who explained the meaning of Christ's words and deeds, the historian may grasp what Jesus truly said and did on earth. The following is what can be recovered from within a welter of exegetical opinions. Without doubt Jesus never explicitly proclaimed himself as "Messiah,*" except on the eve of his death. Doubtless too, Jesus never called himself the "Son of God*"; but we can attribute to him certain words which lead us to ask questions about his true personal identity. Jesus thought of himself as possessing a unique relationship with God his Father: he was "the Son" above all others,[14] calling God "Abba*"[15] and maintaining a singular union with him.[16] Furthermore, he claimed that all men had to go through him in order to obtain eternal life.[17] His conduct was the basis for his words: he claimed to forgive sins,*[18] he took his meals* with sinners to reveal the renewal of God's covenant with all men;[19] finally and above all, he acted out among his disciples the role of the one who "serves.*"[20] Although the historian cannot attribute to Jesus of Nazareth the christological titles which faith conferred on him, he does run up against his own extraordinary claims and hears anew the question put long ago to others: "And you, who do you say that I am?"[21]

[5]Lk 11:20. [6]Lk 11:31f. [7]Mt 13:44. [8]Mt 16:24-26. [9]Lk 10:29-37. [10]Lk 12:22-32. [11]Lk 22:20. [12]Mt 5:17. [13]Mt 12:30. [14]Mk 12:6; 13:32. [15]Mk 14:36. [16]Mt 11:27. [17]Mt 7:24-27. [18]Mk 2:10. [19]Mk 2:16f. [20]Mk 10:45; Lk 22:27. [21]Mt 16:15 (= Mk 8:27).

6. To this question, believers have unanimously answered: "You are the Christ and the Lord." This answer is important for the historian, who cannot be content merely with questioning the texts to uncover a kernel (what Jesus said and did on earth), but who obliges himself to question them in order to grasp the diverse understandings which they offer of the facts. Generally speaking, we can distinguish four stages in the Jesus tradition. Jesus, raised to heaven, fulfilled the hopes of Israel and became the Lord of all ages.*[22] The death* of Jesus, understood in the light of prophecies, is the source of salvation.*[23] The man Jesus bequeathed teachings and a style of life which gave order to Christian conduct.[24] Finally, faith delves more and more into the mystery of Jesus of Nazareth, searching it out for the human and divine origins of the one whom it proclaims to be alive forever.[25]

[22]Acts 2:36; Rom 10:9; 1 Thes 1:10. [23]Acts 3:13,26; 1 Cor 15:3f. [21]Heb 10:7; 1 Pt 2:21-24. [25]Mt 1–2; Lk 1–2; Jn 1:1,18; Rom 1:3f.; 5:12-21; 1 Cor 15:15; Phil 2:6-11; Col 1:15; 2:9; Heb 1:2f.

→ appearances of Christ—Body of Christ—Christ—cross—God—Lamb of God—Lord—Messiah—pre-existence—resurrection—Son of God—Son of Man—Word.

Jew Gk. *Ioudaios,* from the Heb. *yehûdî* (→ Judah). The book of the Acts of the Apostles* presents us with all the shades of the word's meaning.

1. The neutral meaning. In the beginning, a member of the kingdom of Judah*;[1] in Jesus' time, a member of the people of Israel, containing within it a racial connotation,[2] for example in the Synoptic* expression: "king of the Jews"—with its exclusion of the Samaritans.*[3]

[1]2 Kgs 16:6; Jer 32:12. [2]Jn 3:1. [3]Mt 2:2; 27:11 (= Mk 15:2 = Lk 23:3); Jn 4:9,22.

2. The religious meaning*—(a) Observers of the Law and the Mosaic traditions.[4] Typically, Paul associated them with the Greeks, both to recall their priority within the order of salvation and to rank them along with the pagans within the sphere of God's mercy.[5]—(b) Distinguished from Christians, sometimes without any pejorative note,[6] at other times with a connotation of their unbelief directed at Jesus or a note of hostility with regard to Christians.[7] In John, the word generally ceases to have an ethnic meaning, in order that it might designate a category of unbelievers.[8]

[4]Mk 7:3; Jn 2:6,13; 5:1; 6:4; 7:2; 11:55; 12:9,11; Rom 2:17,28f.; Rv 2:9; 3:9. [5]Rom 2:9; Gal 3:28. [6]Mt 28:15; Jn 8:31. [7]Jn 9:22; 2 Cor 11:24. [8]Jn 2:18-20; 6:41; 10:31.

→ Intr. III,2.C; IV.6.E.

jewel

→ precious stone.

Jezebel Gk. *Iezabel,* Heb. *izèbèl,* of unknown meaning: perhaps "not lifted up" (cf. *I-kâbôd:* 1 Sm 4:21). The name of King Ahab's pagan wife, the enemy of the prophet Elijah.* In Rv 2:20, it is either the name of a false prophetess, or a name symbolically designating this prophetess or even the Nicolaitan* heresy itself.[1]

[1]1 Kgs 16:31; 19:1-3; 21:5-15,23; 2 Kgs 9:10,22,30-37 □.

Job Gk. *Iōb,* Heb. *iyyôb* = *Ayya-âbû:* "Where is the father (God)?" The hero of the book bearing his name. An example of justice and patience.[1]

[1]Ez 14:14-20; Jas 5:11 □.

→ Bible—Chart, p. 67.

[Johannine Comma] Gk. *komma:* "an interpolated clause, part of a phrase." The name given to an inauthentic gloss interpolated in the fourth century between verses 7 and 8 of 1 Jn 5. Its origin lay in Spain or North Africa; it may go back as far as St. Cyprian. Its content: "[7] for there are three who witness *in heaven: the Father, the Word and the Holy Spirit; and these three are one; and there are three who witness on earth:* the Spirit,[8] the water and the blood, and these three are one."

John Gk. *Iōannēs,* from the Heb. *yehôhânân, yôhânân:* "Yahweh is gracious."

1. The son of Zebedee* and perhaps of Salomé*; the younger brother of James "the Greater,"* who was, along with him, a "son of thunder,"[2] one of the Twelve.*[3] One of three privileged disciples, generally in company with Peter and James.[4] One of the pillars of the Church.[5] Tradition identified him with the disciple* whom Jesus loved and attributed to him the Fourth Gospel, three epistles and the Book of Revelation.[6] He is said to have lived at Ephesus and been martyred under Trajan at the beginning of the second century.

[1]Mt 4:21 (= Mk 1:19f. = Lk 5:10); 27:56; cf. Mk 15:40. [2]Mk 3:17; cf. Lk 9:54. [3]Mt 10:2 (= Mk 3:17 = Lk 6:14); Acts 1:13. [4]Mt 17:1 (= Mk 9:2 = Lk 9:28); Mk 1:29; 5:37 (= Lk

8:51); 9:38 (= Lk 9:49); 10:35,41; 13:3; 14:33; Lk 9:54; 22:8; Jn 21:2. [5]Acts 3:1,3f., 11; 4:13,19; 8:14; Gal 2:9. [6]Rv 1:1,4,9; 22:8 □.

2. The father of Simon Peter, also called Jonah.[7]

[7]Mt 16:17; Jn 1:42; 21:15-17 □.

3. John Mark. → Mark.

4. A Jew of the high priestly family.[8]

[8]Acts 4:6 □.

[John (Epistles of)] Three letters, probably composed by the same author, who called himself the "Elder," whom we may identify with the apostle John —at least for the first, the one which is dated the latest. This one and the second epistle are a kind of exhortation addressed to a group of churches to help them remain faithful in the faith. The third epistle is more personal.

→ Intr. XV.—deuterocanonical writings—Epistles (Catholic).

[John (Gospel of)] Written towards the end of the first century, this booklet comes across quite differently from the Synoptics,* but it, too, is a gospel.* It recounts the ministry of Jesus in order to elicit faith. The thread of this ministry's character is no longer that of the sequence of two periods (Galilee, then Jerusalem), but instead it depicts the predominance of Judea, with several episodes only located in Galilee. John omits many details handed down by the Synoptics; but he reports numerous other details, of a historical and topographical order, which are worth a great deal to the historian. What distinguishes the Fourth Gospel above all else is the perspective within which it is set. The Holy Spirit is the one who makes possible an understanding of Jesus' history. So much is this the case that the Gospel of John has been called "the spiritual gospel." He methodically proclaims the import of the Good News for the present age by recounting the past history of Jesus of Nazareth. Another characteristic of John is its realized eschatology,* one which allows for a determination of the very gift of eternal life in one's encounter with Jesus. The origin of the work lies with the Apostle John, even if it is to a Johannine school that we are in debt for what is most characteristic in it, and though it was these last editors who brought about its publication.

→ Intr. XV.

John the Baptist John, the son of Zechariah* and Elizabeth,*[1] whose activity was also mentioned by the Jewish historian Josephus,* made his appearance as a prophet*[2] in the desert around the year 28 (or perhaps beginning in 27). His preaching presents some resemblances with several aspects of the writings found at Qumran.* His ministry had a great impact on crowds, but he lasted scarcely any length of time because Herod Antipas* had him beheaded one or two years later.[3] "John's baptism," which is a stereotyped formula,[4] was an innovation on earlier practices of baptism*: first of all it was for Jews (and not for proselytes) and it could be administered only once (not daily as was the case with Essenes*); it required each person's conversion* (thereby specifying the nature of the eschatological* purification proclaimed by the prophets).[5] John's historical connections with Jesus are hard to tie down. Jesus carried on a baptism analogous to John's[6] and proclaimed his own admiration for God's eschatological messenger.[7] For his part, John wondered whether Jesus was the one who was to come.[8] A kind of sect, the "Johannites," the heirs of John's disciples, continued to exist parallel to the Christian movement and mention is made of them at Ephesus about the year 54.[9] Moreover, Paul tended to subordinate John to Jesus,[10] and the gospel tradition tended to reduce his role as baptizer in order to stress his role as the precursor and an unsullied witness.[11]

[1]Lk 1. [2]Mt 3:1,4 (= Mk 1:4,6); Lk 3:1f.; 20:6. [3]Mt 14:1-10 (= Mk 6:14-27); Lk 3:20. [4]Mt 21:25f. (= Mk 11:30,32 = Lk 20:4); Acts 1:22; 18:25; 19:3. [5]Ez 36:25; Zec 13:1. [6]Jn 3:22. [7]Mt 11:7-14; 17:11-13. [8]Mt 11:2f. (= Lk 7:18f.). [9]Acts 18:25; 19:3f. [10]Acts 13:24f. [11]Mt 3:11-15 (= Mk 1:7f. = Lk 3:15-18); Jn 1:15,19-36; 3:27-30; 5:35f.; 10:40f.

→ Intr. I.2.—baptism.

Jonah

1. Gk. *Iōnas,* Heb. *yônâ:* "dove." A prophet* of the Northern Kingdom in the eighth century B.C.[1] The hero of the book (fifth century) that bears this name, the one whose person, preaching and sojourn in the belly of a sea monster were in the eyes of the Ninevites a sign of his mission; such also was the case with Jesus.[2]

[1]2 Kgs 14:25. [2]Jon 1:1; 3:2-5; Mt 12:39-41; 16:4; Lk 11:29f. □.

→ Intr. XII.—Chart, p. 67.

2. Simon Peter's father.[1]

[1]Mt 16:17 □.

→ John.

Jonathan Gk. *Iōnathas.* A Jew of the high priestly family.[1]

[1]Acts 4:6 □.

→ John.

Joppa Gk. *Ioppē,* Heb. *yâphô:* "beauty." A very ancient and important port, but one that was supplanted by that of Caesarea* in Palestine. Peter raised up Tabitha there; there also, at the house of Simon* the tanner, where he was staying, Peter had a vision that involved him in a mission to the house of the centurion Cornelius.* Modern-day Jaffa.[1]

[1]Acts 9:36-43; 10:1–11:13 □.

→ Map 4.

Jordan

1. Gk. *Iordanēs,* Heb. *yardén* (from *yârad:* "to descend"). This river followed a course determined by a fault which, from the end of the tertiary period, extended from Syria in the north to eastern Africa; from its source, 520 meters above sea level (1,706 ft.), it travelled 220 km. (138 mi.) to the Dead Sea (392 m. [1,286 ft.] below sea level).[1]

[1]Mt 3:6,13; Mk 1:5,9; Lk 4:1△

→ Intr. II.3.C.—Map 4.

2. The N.T. distinguishes the Jordan region[2] from the region "across the Jordan."[3] The latter designated the east side of the river, whose inhabitants were longtime strangers to, if not enemies of, the Israelites.

[2]Mt 3:5 (= Lk 3:3). [3]Mt 4:15 (= Mk 3:8); 19:1 (= Mk 10:1); Jn 1:28; 3:26; 10:40 △

Joseph Gk. *Jōsēph,* Heb. *yôséph,* the abbreviation of *yôséph'él:* "May God add [other children to the one just born]!"

1. Jacob* and Rachel's first son.[1] His personal history[2] seems to have foretold that of Jesus.[3] The eponym* of a tribe* of Israel, which later on was divided between his two sons, Ephraim and Manasseh.[4] It also designated the Kingdom of the North[5] or of Israel.[6]

[1]Gn 30:23–25. [2]Gn 37–50; Jn 4:5; Heb 11:21f. [3]Acts 7:9–18 △. [4]Nm 13:11; Rv 7:8△. [5]Ez 37:16. [6]Ps 77:16.

2. The spouse of Mary, the mother of Jesus,[1] a descendant of David,*[2] resident of Nazareth,[3] a carpenter*—that is a tradesman[4]—reckoned to be the father of Jesus.[5]

[1]Mt 1:16,18–24; 2:13,19; Lk 1:27; 2:4,16. [2]Mt 1:20; Lk 1:27. [3]Mt 2:23; Lk 2:4,39,51. [4]Mt 13:55. [5]Lk 3:23; 4:22; Jn 1:45; 6:42 □.

3. Joses (Joset), the son of Mary (3),* the brother of James the Little, one of the brothers of Jesus.*[1]

[1]Mt 13:55 (= Mk 6:3); Mt 27:56 (= Mk 15:40,47) □.

4. A prominent Jew of Arimathea.[1]

[1]Mt 27:57–59 (= Mk 15:43–45 = Lk 23:50); Jn 19:38 □.

5. Joseph, called Barsabbas, who was put forward as a candidate to replace Judas.[1]

[1]Acts 1:23 □.

Josephus A Jew born at Jerusalem in A.D. 37, who died at Rome around 98. He took part, first on the Jewish side then on the Roman side, in the Jewish war whose history he wrote up: *The Jewish War* (75–79); he edited the *Jewish Antiquities* (about 95), a history extending from the world's creation up to the year 66, and the treatise *Against Apion* (about 96), a defense of the former book against those who regarded it as fable and legend. The information which he furnished has great historical value (even if some features—such as the census* of Quirinius—can be contested), particularly about Pilate, John the Baptist, James of Jerusalem and the brief note on Jesus' disciples. He lets an apologetic note shine through, writing as he did to the glory of Israel's people and in favor of himself as well as of his patrons.

→ Intr. I.2.

Joshua Gk. *Iēsous,* Heb. *Yehôshua':* "Yahweh saves." The successor to Moses who brought the Hebrews through to the conquest of the promised land. His history is recounted in the book of Joshua.[1]

[1]Ex 17:8-13; Nm 11:28; 13:16; Sir 46:1; Acts 7:45; Heb 4:8 □.

joy The feeling of satisfaction and fullness of well-being, which we call joy, is expressed in the N.T. by means of three terms possessing different connotations.

1. Gk. *euphrainō, euphrosynē* (from *eu:* "well" and *phrēn:* "place of the feelings and passions, heart"): "to rejoice, delight in." This term, the predominant one in the O.T., is infrequent in the N.T.; it is found chiefly in Luke, used to designate collective joy rather than an individual's feelings, and this particularly so in the presence of creation in general[1] or in festivals of good cheer.[2] It is a feeling of being happy in one's place and with others. This term, which in the O.T. can mean eschatological* joy,[3] hardly appears in the N.T. with this meaning, except in citations and allusions to the O.T.[4] Two other uses should be noted.[5]

[1]Acts 14:17. [2]Lk 12:19; 15:23f.,29,32; 16:19. [3]Ps 96:11; 97:1; Is 65:19. [4]Acts 2:26,28; 7:41; Rom 15:10; Gal 4:27; Rv 12:12; 18:20. [5]2 Cor 2:2; Rv 11:10 △.

2. Gk. *chara, chairō* (with the same consonants as *charis:* "grace") is the preferred N.T. word for joy. Its secular meaning was also found in epistolary contexts[6] or to indicate a "greeting*" in an encounter between two beings.[7] Joy comes chiefly from the fulfillment of the O.T. expectation: the presence of salvation in the person of Jesus.[8] Luke systematized this reaction to the Good News: conversion, an experience of the Risen One.[9] John revealed that joy was the result of the new condition inaugurated by Christ,[10] while Paul stressed, especially in 2 Corinthians and Philippians, the paradox of joy in the midst of sadness and suffering.[11] These same features are found in other N.T. writings too.[12]

[6]Acts 15:23; 23:26; Jas 1:1. [7]Mt 26:49; 27:29 (= Mk 15:8 = Jn 19:3); 28:9; Lk 1:28; Acts 15:23; 23:26; 2 Jn 10f. △. [8]Mt 2:10; 13:20 (= Mk 4:16 = Lk 8:13); 25:21,23; 28:8. [9]Lk 1:14,58; 2:10; 10:17,20; 15:5-10; 19:6,37; 24:52. [10]Jn 3:29; 4:36; 8:56; 16:20-22; 17:13; 20:20. [11]2 Cor 6:10; 7:4; 13:9; Phil 1:18; 2:17. [12]Mt 5:12 (= Lk 6:23); Acts 5:41; Jas 1:2; 1 Pt 4:13.

3. Gk. *agalliasis, aggalliaomai:* "to be jubilant, exult, be glad." This often came as a reinforcement of the word *chara,* to manifest its explosion into the exterior;[13] in continuity with the O.T., which depicts the universe exulting in Yahweh's great deeds,[14] the N.T. centers the theme of jubilation upon Jesus Christ, particularly in worship:[15] gladness characterizes the believer who has recognized in Jesus the definitive gift.

[13]Mt 5:12; Lk 1:14; Jn 8:56; Acts 2:26; 1 Pt 1:8; 4:13. [14]Ps 9:15; 19:6; 89:13; 96:11; Is 25:9; 61:1; 65:19. [15]Lk 1:44,47; 10:21; Acts 2:46; 16:34; Heb 1:9; 1 Pt 1:6,8; 4:13; Jude 24; Rv 19:7; cf. Jn 5:35 △.

→ Alleluia—happy—laugh—sadness.

[Jubilees] Or "Little Genesis." An O.T. apocryphal* work which recounted the history of the world's creation up to Moses' time in fifty "jubilees" (from the Heb. *yôbél:* "a horn announcing the feast, jubilee year") or forty-nine-year periods, the final year of which was that of the settlement in the Holy Land. The work was composed around 125 B.C. It manifested a priestly and legal bent. The Hebrew text of chapters 1–2, 21–22, 25 and 32–40 has been discovered at Qumran,* thereby authenticating the worth of the Latin and Ethiopic translations in our possession.

Judah Gk. *Ioudas,* from the Heb. *Yehûdâ,* the abbreviation of *Yehud-'el:* "El be praised" [?].[1] The son of Jacob* and Leah,[2] the ancestor of the principal tribe* of Israel,[3] the one from which Jesus was a descendant.[4]

The territory which devolved to this tribe bore his name: it was Judea.*[5]

[1]Gn 29:35. [2]Mt 1:2f.; Lk 3:33 △. [3]Gn 49:8-12; Mt 1:2f.; Lk 3:33; Heb 8:8; Rv 7:5. [4]Heb 7:14; Rv 5:5 △. [5]Jos 15; Mt 2:6; Lk 1:39 △.

Judaism Gk. *ioudaismos.* "Late Judaism" designated the post-exilic religion of Israel (after 538 B.C.). The development of O.T. thinking, particularly under the influence of Hellenism.[1]

[1]Gal 1:13f. □.

→ Intr. I.1.B; XI.—Hellenism.

Judaizer From the Gk. *ioudaizō:* "to behave like a Jew." A name given historically only to the Judeo-Christians* who, despite the decision of the Council of Jerusalem,* wanted to impose the Jewish Law,* which they themselves continued to observe,[1] on converts from paganism. They were violently opposed to Paul, for whom their attitude was an implicit denial of the salvific power of faith in Christ.[2] Not to be confused with false teachers of Jewish origin.[3]

[1]Gal 2:14 □; cf. Acts 11:2; 15:5; 21:20. [2]Gal 2:21. [3]1 Tim 1:3-7; Ti 1:10-16.

Judas, Jude Gk. Ioudas, from the Heb. *yehûdâ* (→ Judah).

1. Iscariot. Gk. *Iskariōtēs,* occasionally *Iskariōth,*[1] of uncertain meaning; from the Heb. *ish kariôt:* "the man from Carioth" or from the Aram. *ishqaryâ:* "the false one," or from the Gk. *sikarios:* "the hired assassin." The son of Simon,* one of the Twelve,*[2] always cited last on the list and with a note that he betrayed Jesus.[3] Two reasons were given for his betrayal: his love of money[4] and Satan's activity.[5] Various traditions recounted his death.[6]

[1]Mk 3:19; 14:40; Lk 6:16. [2]Mt 26:14,47 (= Mk 14:10,43 = Lk 22:47f.); Lk 22:3; Jn 6:71; Acts 1:25f. [3]Mt 10:4 (= Mk 3:19 = Lk 6:16); 26:25; 27:3; Jn 6:71; 12:4; 13:2; 18:2,3,5; Acts 1:16. [4]Mt 27:15f.; Jn 12:6; cf. 13:29. [5]Lk 22:3; Jn 6:70f.; 13:2,26f. [6]Mt 27:5; Acts 1:18,25f. □.

2. The Galilean, born in Gaulanitis. He stirred up an insurrection, probably at the time of Quirinius' census* (A.D. 6–7), struggling as he did for liberation from the Roman yoke and the reestablishment of a theocracy with the slogan: "No king but God!" He was the originator of the Zealot* party.[7]

[7]Acts 5:37 □.

3. A resident of Damascus, probably a Judeo-Christian.*[8]

[8]Acts 9:11 □.

4. Jude (the son) of James, one of the Twelve.* In the parallel listings, he corresponds to Lebbaeus in Matthew and Thaddaeus in Mark.[9]

[9]Lk 6:16; Jn 14:22; Acts 1:13 □.

5. One of the brothers of Jesus.*[10]

[10]Mt 13:55 (= Mk 6:3) □.

6. The author, perhaps pseudonymous, of an epistle* that bears his name.*[11] The brother of James, whom some identify with (5) above.

[11]Jude □.

7. Barsabbas, a Christian of Jerusalem delegated for a mission to Antioch.[12]

[12]Acts 15:22,27,32 □.

Jude (Epistle of) A kind of homily, with a heavy Jewish accent, attributed to Jude,* not the apostle but the brother of the Lord.* It dates probably from 80–90.

→ Intr. XV.—deuterocanonical writings—Epistles (Catholic).

Judea Gk. *Ioudaia.*

1. In the Hellenistic* period, the term indicated that southern part of Palestine,* the ancient kingdom of Judah,* with Jerusalem as its capital.[1] A part of Herod the Great's* kingdom,[2] then of the ethnarch Archelaus,*[3] it had become integrated within the Roman province* of Syria from 6 B.C.,[4] except from 41 to 44 when it was subject to Herod Agrippa I.*[5] The birthplace of John and Jesus;[6] the privileged locale of the preaching of the Baptist,[7] Jesus[8] and the first Christian communities.[9]

[1]Mt 3:5 (= Mk 1:5); 4:25 (= Mk 3:7 = Lk 6:17); Acts 1:8; Rom 15:31; 2 Cor 1:16. [2]Lk 1:5. [3]Mt 2:22. [4]Lk 3:1. [5]Acts 12:19. [6]Mt 2:1,5; Lk 1:65; 2:4. [7]Mt 3:1. [8]Mt 19:1 (= Mk 10:1); Jn 3:22; 4:3,47,54; 7:1,3; 11:7. [9]Acts 2:9; 8:1; 9:31; 11:1,29; 12:19; 15:1; 21:10; 28:21; Gal 1:22; 1 Thes 2:14 △.

2. The term can also designate the totality of Palestine.*[10]

[10]Lk 4:44; Acts 10:37 △.

→ Intr. II.1.—Map 4.

[Judeo-Christians] A name given historically to Christians, Hebrews[1] or Hellenists, who originated in Judaism, not in paganism. Their Jerusalem community had James, "the brother* of the Lord,"[2] as its leader and continued to observe the Law and certain Jewish customs,[3] without thereby leaning towards the excesses of the Judaizers.*[4] It was dispersed following the destruction of Jerusalem in A.D. 70.

[1]Acts 6:1. [2]Gal 1:19; 2:9-12. [3]Acts 2:46; 10:14; 13:2f.; 18:4,18; 20:6,16; 21:21-23. [4]Acts 11:2; Gal 2:14-16.

→ Intr. I.3.A.

judgment

1. Gk. *krisis.* In addition to the meaning (original in the Greek) of: "to try, to sift, to separate, to discern,[1] to appraise,[2] to examine,"[3] the words *krinō, krisis* ordinarily possessed a juridical dimension as well: a right to be established according to law,[4] injuries to be redressed, justice to be restored by a judge,[5] decisions taken.[6] Such judicatory activity was characteristic of God and Christ's work.

[1]Mt 16:3; Lk 12:57; 1 Cor 11:29-32; 12:10; Heb 5:14. [2]Lk 7:43; 19:22; Jn 7:24; 8:15f.; Acts 4:19; 16:15; 26:8; Rom 14:1,3-5; 1 Cor 14:24,29. [3]1 Cor 11:31. [4]Lk 23:24; Jn 18:31; Acts 23:3; 24:6. [5]Mt 5:25; Lk 12:14. [6]Acts 3:13; 16:4; 20:16; 21:25; 25:25; 1 Cor 7:37; Ti 3:12.

2. God was the judge of the living and the dead.[7] This conviction rested on two pieces of evidence. To do justice* was to enforce and to establish it.[8] Just and merciful as he was, God knew man's heart.[9] The judgment was not dependent on men, accordingly,[10] but had been entrusted by God to his Son, Jesus, who would render it at the end* of time.[11]

[7]1 Sm 2:10; Ps 67:5; 75:8; Jer 25:31; Acts 17:31; Rom 3:6; 1 Cor 4:4; 5:13; Heb 12:23; 1 Pt 4:5. [8]Gn 16:5; Ex 5:21; Ps 72:1; Is 11:3f.; Jer 23:5; Mt 12:18,20; 23:23; Acts 8:33; 1 Pt 2:23. [9]Ps 7:10; Jer 11:20; 17:10; Lk 18:6; Heb 4:12. [10]Mt 7:1f. (= Lk 6:37); 1 Cor 4:3,5; 10:29; Jas 4:12. [11]Jn 5:22-27; Acts 10:42; 2 Tim 4:1.

3. The imagery used was traditional: the final assizes,[12] a trial,[13] retribution according to one's behavior,[14] on the last "Day,*"[15] at the "Judgment."[16] Above all, this judgment would be conducted on the criterion of love of one's neighbor[17] and one's welcome of the gospel message;[18] in instances of contempt of court, the same word *krinō* came to have the meaning "to condemn."[19]

[12]Mt 19:28 (= Lk 22:30); 25:31-46; 2 Tim 4:8; Heb 6:2; 9:27; 10:27; Rv 20:4. [13]Is 41:21-24; Jer 2:9; Hos 4:1; 1 Cor 6:1-7. [14]Mt 16:27; Rom 2:2,12,16; 5:16; Heb 13:4; Jas 2:13; 1 Pt 1:17; Rv 20:12f. [15]Mt 10:15; 11:22,24; 12:36; Rom 2:5,16; 2 Pt 2:9; 3:7; 1 Jn 4:17; Jude 6. [16]Mt 12:41f.; Lk 10:14; 11:31f. [17]Mt 25:31-46; 1 Jn 3:14. [18]Jn 12:48; 2 Thes 2:12. [19]Mt 23:33; Mk 12:40 (= Lk 20:47); Lk 11:32; 24:30; Jn 5:29.

4. John showed how this judgment at the last day[20] was already at work in history. Having come into the world and having received the power of judgment from the Father,[21] Jesus doubtlessly did not come for judgment/condemnation, but rather wrought a discernment, a sorting-out, a judgment among men who had been set in the presence of the light.*[22] Already now, the prince of this world* has been judged and condemned, because God has rendered judgment in saving Jesus from death, and the Paraclete* convinces believers of the justice of Christ's cause.[23]

[20]Jn 12:48. [21]Jn 5:22,27. [22]Jn 3:17,18-21; 9:39; 12:31,47. [23]Jn 16:8-11.

→ condemn—discern—justice—Trial of Jesus.

justice, justification Gk. *dikaiosynē, dikaios:* "just, conformed to the law"; *dikaiōsis:* "justification"; *dikaioō:* "to justify"; *dikē:* "right, punishment, venegeance"; all of these terms derive from the root *dik-,* which signified direction (as in *deiknymi:* "to indicate"). They translated the Heb. *ṣèdèq (ṣᵉdâqâ), ṣaddîq,* which describe an attitude that undergirds and sustains a communion covenant existing between two parties.

1. The justice of God was salvific justice at its best: faithful to the Covenant,* the just God fulfills his promises* of salvation.[1] It fought for the establishment of right and happiness, without thereby becoming identified with commutative justice (the equalizing of obligations and charges).[2] Rarely, the term was used to speak of forensic justice (Gk. *dikaiōma*): "verdict, decisions"[3] or distributive justice (retribution*),[4] but never for punitive justice. The wrath* and justice of God were not two successive, temporal moments in history; they expressed the faithful activity of God who was reconciling the sinner to himself or removing the sinner from his presence.[5] In its definitive form, it was Jesus in person.[6]

[1]Ps 40:10f.; Is 45:21; 46:13; Mt 3:15; 21:32; Rom 3:21-26. [2]2 Sm 8:15; Ps 45:4-8; Is 41:2; cf. Mt 20:4. [3]Lk 1:6; Rom 1:32; 2:26; 8:4; Heb 9:1,10; Rv 15:4. [4]2 Thes 1:5f.; Heb 2:2; cf. Lk 23:41. [5]Ps 85:4-6; Mi 7:7-9; Rom 1:17f.; 10:3; Phil 3:9; Jas 1:20. [6]1 Cor 1:30; cf. 2 Cor 5:21.

2. God justifies: he considers (or renders) just, makes right, sets free.[7] Man cannot justify himself; it is God alone who justifies;[8] he pardons the impious one not in virtue of his works or observance of the Law,*[9] but in virtue of the grace* in Jesus Christ, the Just One who has been raised up, to whom the believer is united by faith.[10] In the justified one Christ inaugurates the life of the sanctifying Spirit,* who is the source of works of charity.[11]

[7]Gn 44:16; Sir 23:11. [8]Is 50:8; Rom 4:5f.; 8:33; cf. Lk 10:29. [9]Jb 4:17; Ps 143:1f.; Gal 2:15-21; 3:6-29. [10]Hos 2:21f.; Mt 9:13 (= Mk 2:17 = Lk 5:32); Rom 1:17; 3:21-26; 3:27 4:25; 9:30-32; 10:3-10; Phil 3:8f.; Ti 3:5-7. [11]Mt 12:37; Rom 2:13; 5:1; 1 Cor 1:30; Heb 11:7; Jas 2:14-26.

3. The justice of man consists in being "just," what God wants him to be in the Covenant,[12] through a life in conformity with the divine will.*[13] Luke preserved a vocabulary that echoed that of Judaism: Jesus, the parents of John, Simeon, Cornelius—all were just,[14] while others appeared to be so.[15] Matthew also echoed this theme,[16] but he espoused a new, Christian justice.[17]

[12]Ps 7:9; 17:1-5; 18:22-24; 26:1-6. [13]Mi 6:8; Lk 1:75; Eph 6:14; 2 Tim 2:22; 1 Jn 2:29; 3:10; Rv 19:8. [14]Lk 1:6; 2:25; 23:47-50; Acts 3:14; 7:52; 10:22; 22:14; cf. Mk 6:20; Jas 5:6; 1 Jn 3:7. [15]Lk 10:29; 16:15 (= Mt 23:28); 20:20. [16]Mt 1:19; 10:41; 13:17,43,49; 23:35; 25:37,46; 27:19. [17]Mt 5:6-10,20; 6:1,33.

→ Intr. VI.4—faith—fidelity—iniquity—wages.

Kedron Gk. *Kedrōn,* Heb. *qidrôn* (from *qâdar:* "to be dark, cloudy"). The bed of a brook, which ordinarily was dried out, to the east of Jerusalem, the only pathway toward the Mount of Olives* or Gethsemane.*[1]

[1]2 Sm 15:23; 1 Kgs 2:37; Jn 18:1 □.

→ Map 1.

keep watch

→ watch, keep watch.

kenosis **1.** Gk. *kenōsis:* "the action of emptying out, of being deprived of everything." A specialized term of theological language used to speak about the self-abasement under discussion in a passage from the Epistle to the Philippians: "He emptied himself, taking on the form of a slave . . ." (Phil 2:7) → 3.

2. The Greek adjective *kenos* describes a reality (faith, the cross, confidence, glory, doctrine) that is vain,[1] sterile,[2] of no significance,[3] hollow.[4] The Greek verb *kenoō* describes an action that produces such a result.[5]

[1]Acts 4:25; 1 Cor 15:58; 2 Cor 6:1; Gal 2:2; Phil 2:16; 1 Thes 2:1; 3:5; Jas 4:5. [2]1 Cor 15:10. [3]1 Cor 15:14; Eph 5:6; Col 2:8. [4]1 Tim 6:20; 2 Tim 2:16; Jas 2:20. [5]Rom 4:14; 1 Cor 1:17; 9:15; 2 Cor 9:3.

3. The meaning of the expression "he emptied himself" depends on the interpretation given to the Greek word *morphē:* "form" (does it pertain to a "nature" that is divine and human, to the appearance only, or to the "traits" under which "he" revealed himself?) as well as to the subject of the sentence (does it pertain to the Word becoming incarnate or to the existing Christ?). According to the common opinion of scholars, what is not at issue is the incarnation of the Word* (which would mean its taking on human "nature"), for in abasing himself he would be despoiled of the divine nature and, in being glorified, he would have abandoned this human nature. Rather, the topic of discussion is Christ, who, instead of preserving his traits of divine glory, preferred to be deprived of them all in his assuming of the traits of a slave.* The text says nothing of some kind of "annihilation" of the deity; it describes the phases of Jesus Christ's stripping of himself, even to his death* on the cross.

kerygma A technical term, from the Gk. *kērygma:* "proclamation, preaching."[1] The verb *kēryssō* is used more frequently.

[1]Mt 12:41 (= Lk 11:32); Rom 16:25; 1 Cor 1:21; 2:4; 15:14; 2 Tim 4:17; Ti 1:3 □.

1. The proclamation of Jesus, who, by his resurrection, has become Christ, Lord, Savior.

2. In the broad sense, it embodies catechesis*: this is the response (like an echo) to the experience of the living Lord which the Church brings about.

→ preach.

key Gk. *kleis* (from *kleiō:* "to close"). Permitting the opening and closing of a door,*[1] the key symbolized the one who possessed authority and dominion over the kingdom* of heaven, knowledge, Death,* Hades* or the Abyss.*[2]

[1]1 Sm 23:7; Rv 3:7. [2]Is 22:22; Mt 16:19; Lk 11:52; Rv 1:18; 9:1; 20:1 □.

→ Intr. VIII.1.A.—bind and loose—door.

kid

→ goat (she-goat).

king, kingdom

→ reign.

kiss Gk. *(kata-) phileō, philēma.* A mark of affection and tenderness.[1] A sign of respect, pretended or real.[2] From its uses in worship, the N.T. preserves no traces of the kissing of idols;*[3] but this same gesture was put forward as a means of signifying the community's unity.[4]

[1]Gn 29:13; Ex 4:27; Lk 15:20; Acts 20:37; cf. Mk 9:36; 10:16. [2]2 Sm 20:9f.; Mt 26:48f. (= Mk 14:44f. = Lk 22:47f.); Lk 7:38,45. [3]1 Kgs 19:18; Hos 13:2. [4]Rom 16:16; 1 Cor 16:20; 2 Cor 13:12; 1 Thes 5:26; 1 Pt 5:14 □.

→ adore.

know, knowledge Gk. *ginōskō:* "to be acquainted with; to recognize"; in the perfect tense, "to know."

1. According to the Bible, knowledge was not reducible to an act of the intellect that apprehended an object. The word preserves an experiential dimension that is characteristic of it: to observe, to experience, to know,[1] to discern, to appraise,[2] to establish an intimate relationship between two persons,[3] whence to choose, to elect,[4] to enter a sexual union,[5] finally, to recognize.[6] In conformity with this notion of truth,* to know was to encounter someone; not to know was to thrust him aside from oneself.[7] Knowledge of God was possible because this meant a "re-cognition" of the one who, through his creation, was already there.[8] To know was to be disposed to obey.*[9]

[1]Gn 3:7; 41:31; Is 47:8; Jn 4:1; Phil 1:12. [2]2 Sm 19:36; Is 7:16; Mt 7:16,20; 12:33; Jn 5:42; 10:27; Rom 2:18; 1 Cor 16:18; 1 Jn 2:29; 3:16; 4:2,13. [3]Dt 34:10; Is 54:13; Jer 31:34; Mt 11:27 (= Lk 10:22); 17:12; Jn 10:14f.; 1 Cor 2:12; 8:2f. [4]Jer 1:5; Am 3:2; 1 Cor 13:12; Gal 4:9; 2 Tim 2:19; 1 Pt 1:2,20; 1 Jn 3:20. [5]Gn 4:1,17; 19:8; Mt 1:25; Lk 1:34. [6]Ez 6:7,13f.; Hos 4:1f.; Acts 22:14; Rom 2:4; Gal 2:9; Rv 3:9. [7]Mt 7:23; 25:12; Lk 13:25-27; Rom 7:7; 10:3; 2 Cor 5:16,21. [8]Rom 1:19-21,28; 1 Cor 1:21; cf. Wis 13:1-9. [9]Jn 7:49; Rom 1:28; 2:18,20; 2 Cor 10:5.

2. The N.T. also speaks of "knowledge" (Gk. *gnōsis*) of God in the O.T. sense;[10] but the term ordinarily crops up in battles with the gnosis* of the era. Paul struggled against it by stressing that it was God who knew us (chose us) and that knowledge is subordinate to love.*[11] John rejected all gnosis when he affirmed that God is not known, except through his Son come in the flesh (and eternal life* consists in this)[12] as well as in proportion to one's brotherly love.[13]

[10]Rom 11:33; Eph 4:13; Phil 1:9; 3:8; Col 1:9; 3:10; Phlm 6. [11]1 Cor 8:1,10f. 13:2,12; Eph 3:19. [12]Jn 14:7; 17:3; 1 Jn 4:2. [13]Jn 13:35; 1 Jn 2:3f.; 3:19.

→ election—mystery—revelation—taste—truth—wisdom.

[koinē] A Greek adjective meaning: "common." It designated the Greek* language commonly spoken *(koinē dialektos)* in the Roman Empire of N.T. times.

→ Greek.

kor Gk. *koros,* Heb. *kor.* A Hebraic measure of capacity, equalling about 360 liters (324 dry quarts).[1]

[1]Lk 16:7 □.

→ measures.

korban Gk. *korban,* from the Heb. *qorbân:* an offering brought to the Temple* treasury (Gk. *korbanas*). A consecratory* formula whereby the thing so dedicated could not be put to a secular use.[1]

[1]Lv 1:2; Nm 7:3; Mk 7:11 □; cf. Mt 15:5.

→ anathema.

Kyrios

→ Lord—teacher.

L

Lamb of God **1.** In the book of Revelation,* the Risen Christ is depicted with the attributes of a slain lamb (Gk. *arnion*),[1] who is also living and glorious.[2] He leads the combat* and liberates the people of God with the might of a lion.*[3] This image comes from apocalyptic* literature (Enoch) which places at the head of the flock not a strong beast,* but a lamb. The Lamb is the lord of history[4] and invites men to follow him[5] until the day of his wedding feast.[6]

[1]Rv 5:6,12; 13:8; cf. 7:14; 12:11. [2]Rv 5:8,13; 7:9f.; 14:1. [3]Rv 5:5; 17:14. [4]Rv 6:1,16f.; 14:10. [5]Rv 7:17; 14:4; 15:3. [6]Rv 19:7,9; 21:9.

2. Christ was sometimes considered as the Paschal Lamb (Gk. *amnos*) who purchased men at the price of his blood,*[7] at other times as fulfilling the role of the prophetic Servant* of Yahweh, the mute lamb who goes to the sacrifice.[8]

[7]Ex 12:5,13; 1 Pt 1:19; cf. Jn 19:36; 1 Cor 5:7. [8]Is 53:7; Acts 8:32.

3. According to John, John the Baptist* presents Jesus as the Lamb (Gk. *amnos*) who takes away the sin of the world;[9] this presentation is tied to the apocalyptic tradition of the conquering lamb and to the Essene* tradition of the Messiah* who purifies the world of its sin.[10] The Precursor's language can be perceived in another way by a believer, as descriptive of the Paschal Lamb and of the Servant of God.

[9]Jn 1:29. [10]Cf. 1 Jn 3:4f.

lamentation Gk. *odyrmos*:[1] "groan, lamentation," *thrēneō*:[2] "to lament with a mourning song, with a funereal song," translating the Heb. *qînâ.*

[1]Mt 2:18; 2 Cor 7:7 △. [2]Mt 11:17 (= Lk 7:32); Lk 23:27; Jn 16:20 △.

→ mourning—sadness.

lamp **1.** Gk. *lampas,* Heb. *lapîd.* It seems to refer rather to a torch or a lantern.[1]

[1]Gn 15:17; Ex 20:18; Jgs 7:16; 15:4; Jdt 10:22; Jb 41:11; Sir 48:1; Is 62:1; Ez 1:13; Dn 10:6; Mt 25:1-8; Jn 18:3; Acts 20:8; Rv 4:5; 8:10 △.

2. Gk. *lychnos, lychnia,* Heb. *nér, m*ᵉ*nôrâ.* In Jesus' time it was made of clay, was round and flat, had a pinching on one side to contain the wick, was fueled with oil* and was set on a stand.[2] It remained lit day and night, a source of fire* and light* in the dark house.*[3] Once it was extinguished, life ceased.[4] Made for the purpose of enlightening,[5] it could symbolize vigilance,*[6] the radiance of the churches,[7] lastly, the prophetic word[8] and the presence of God[9] or the Lamb.[10] In those instances in which it stands for the churches,[11] it might be better to translate it as a candelabra or a lampstand.*

[1]Mt 5:15 (= Mk 4:21 = Lk 8:16 = 11:33). [2]Lk 15:8. [3]Jb 18:5f.; Prv 13:9; Jer 25:10; Rv 18:23. [4]Mt 6:22; Mk 4:21; Lk 11:33f.,36. [5]Ex 27:20f.; 2 Chr 29:7; Lk 12:35. [6]Mt 5:15; Phil 2:15;

Rv 11:4. [7]Jn 5:35; 2 Pt 1:19. [8]2 Sm 22:29; Ps 119:105; Prv 20:27; Rv 22:5. [9]Rv 21:23. [10]Rv 1:12f.,20; 2:1,5; cf. Heb 9:2 △.

lampstand Gk. *lychnia.*

1. A domestic utensil used to support lamps.[1]

[1]Mt 5:15 (= Mk 4:21 = Lk 8:16 = 11:33).

2. A cultic object: a golden lampstand with seven branches had been set up in the interior of the Holy Place*;[2] removed by the Romans and depicted on Titus'* arch of triumph at Rome, it symbolized Israel's hope. In the book of Revelation, the term refers to the churches.[3]

[2]Heb 9:2. [3]Zec 4:1-14; Rv 1:12f.,20; 2:1,5; 11:4 □.

→ lamp.

land

→ earth.

Laodicea Gk. *Laodikeia.* A city of Phrygia* in Asia Minor. Its textile industry had eclipsed that of Colossae.*[1] Its Christian community, established perhaps by Epaphras,*[2] was an object of Paul's solicitude; one of the letters lost to us today[3] had been addressed to it, as had one of the seven messages of the book of Revelation.[4]

[1]Cf. Rv 3:17f. [2]Col 1:7; 4:12f.,15. [3]Col 2:1; 4:16. [4]Rv 1:11; 3:14 □.

→ Map 2.

Last Supper Was Jesus' last meal the Jewish Passover meal? Critical opinions are divided due to the fact that, according to the Synoptics,* Jesus celebrated the paschal meal on Thursday night, the eve of his death,[1] while, according to John, Jesus died just before the Jewish paschal meal.[2] Three hypotheses have been proposed: (a) a paschal meal voluntarily anticipated by Jesus; (b) a paschal meal according to an unofficial calendar*; (c) a fraternal meal to which Jesus gave a paschal coloring. According to this last hypothesis, Jesus fulfilled the Jewish rite of Passover, not by another rite, but by the deed of his sacrificial death which took place at the moment of Passover.

[1]Mt 26:17,20 (= Mk 14:12,17); Lk 22:15f. [2]Jn 18:28; 19:14,31.

→ Lord's Supper—Passover.

last will

→ testament.

laugh Gk. *gelaō:* "to laugh, to laugh at, to mock."

1. In keeping with the biblical law of eschatological* reversal, the laugh of those who have been satisfied will be changed into weeping and mourning,*[1] while the tears of the unfortunate will become a joyous laughter of joy that will not end,[2] the laughter of a richly blessed soul.[3]

[1]Lk 6:25; Jas 4:9. [2]Lk 6:21. [3]Jb 8:21; Ps 126:2.

2. The mocker's laugh, particularly in front of a suffering just man,[4] indicated his unbelief in the presence of an unexpected happening.[5] Such joking and mockery (Gk. *chleuazō, mykterizō, empaizō*), which verged on insults,* were provoked by the sufferings of Jesus,[6] by the announcement of the Resurrection,[7] by the manifestations of the Holy Spirit;[8] they will break out anew at the end of time.[9]

[4]Ps 22:8. [5]Mt 9:24 (= Mk 5:40 = Lk 8:53). [6]Mt 27:29,31,41; Mk 15:20,31; Lk 22:63; 23:11,35f. [7]Acts 17:32. [8]Acts 2:13. [9]2 Pt 3:3; Jude 18.

→ insult—joy—sadness.

law Gk. *nomos* (from *nemō:* "to share, to attribute, to possess"): "usage, custom, law," Heb. *tôrâ:* "teaching, law." A word frequent in Paul, rare in the gospels and absent from Mark, the Catholic Epistles* (except James), and the book of Revelation.

1. In the broad sense, the term sometimes stood as the equivalent of the whole O.T.[1] Ordinarily, it designated the five first books of the Bible,* which were attributed to Moses,* the trustee of Yahweh's will for his own people:[2] in short, it was the Torah* or the Pentateuch.*

[1]Jn 10:34; Rom 3:19f.; 1 Cor 14:21. [2]Mt 7:12; 12:5; Lk 2:27; 16:17; 24:44; Rom 3:21; Gal 4:21; Intr. XII.

2. In its strict sense, the Law was the revelation* taught by God to Israel[3] in order to govern its conduct. It should never be isolated from God, who alone gave value to it by his word. When the decalogue* did not become dialogue, it became hardened into a catalogue.

[3]Intr. VIII.2.C.d; XII.1; XIV.

3. Jesus did not abolish the Law of the O.T., understood in the sense of a living revelation; he brought it to its fulfillment.*[4] Totally submitting to it,[5] he located its precepts in conjunction with the need for interior conversion, and he set himself in opposition to a contemporary legalism which overrated them without distinctions.[6] Above all, he concentrated it into the double commandment of love for God and one's neighbor;[7] he radicalized it by identifying it with an absolute obligation to love[8] and personalized it when he proclaimed: "But I say unto you. . . ."[9]

[4]Mt 5:17. [5]Mt 5:18; Lk 2:22-24,27,39; 16:17. [6]Mt 12:5; 15:6; 23:23. [7]Mt 22:36,40 (= Lk 10:26). [8]Mt 5:43f.; Lk 6:27f. [9]Mt 5:22,28,32,34.

4. John used the word "law" exclusively in the sense of the ancient Law.[10] While in other respects allowing it to have totally diverse meanings, Paul also used it to refer to the O.T. governance of God's relationships with Israel. This "economy" had lapsed because Christ had put an end to it;[11] he was the one in whom the rule of grace had been inaugurated.[12]

[10]Jn 1:17; 8:17; 10:34. [11]Rom 10:4. [12]Rom 5:20; 6:14.

5. Hence, in his polemic against those who found the source of justification in the Law, Paul reduced the Law to nothing but a simple indication of a good to be done, even if, in its origin, it had been divine;[13] its indications were, in themselves, powerless to transform human conduct, just as the prophets had declared.[14]

[13]Rom 7:7-25. [14]Jer 31:33; Intr. I.4.

6. Finally, the word may be applied to the two poles of God's* plan of salvation. On one side, there was talk of a law inscribed upon the conscience* which was "naturally" accomplished without an awareness of its divine origin: this was to indicate not a regime wherein God was absent, but rather the condition in which those who did not possess the Jewish or Christian faith* found themselves. On the other end, Paul spoke of the "law of Christ"[15] not to assert that the new covenant was still a legalistic regime, but instead to show that, once having died with Christ on the cross, the Law had in some sense risen through the power of the Spirit who makes the words of Jesus of Nazareth intelligible.[17] In the same way, the Epistle of James* could speak of a "royal law of freedom."[18] With regard to John, who identified the law with the law of Moses, all that had been positive in the Law had now passed over into the "commandment."[19]

[15]Rom 2:14f. [16]Gal 6:2; cf. 1 Cor 9:21. [17]Rom 8:1-17. [18]Jas 1:25; 2:8,12. [19]Jn 13:34f.; 15:12,17; 1 Jn 3:23.

→ commandment—doctor of the Law—lawyer.

lawyer Gk. *nomikos:* literally "one concerned with the Law,"[1] "jurist."[2] A term used chiefly by Luke to indicate the scribe* as a specialist in applications of the Law,[3] a "doctor* of the Law" (Gk. *nomodidaskalos*).[4]

[1]Ti 3:9. [2]Ti 3:13. [3](Mt 22:35); Lk 7:30; 10:25; 11:45f.,52; 14:3 △. [4]Lk 5:17; Acts 5:34; 1 Tim 1:7 △.

→ Intr. XII.1.C.—doctor (of the Law)—scribe.

laying on of hands

→ hand.

Lazarus Gk. *Lazaros,* from the Heb. *èl'âzâr:* "God helps."

1. A resident of Bethany,* the brother of Martha and Mary, restored to life by Jesus.[1]

[1]Jn 11:1,2,5,11,14,43; 12:1,2,9,10,17 □.

2. The name of a poor man in a parable*; the only case in which a fictional character has received a name, perhaps chosen because of its meaning.[2]

[1]Lk 16:20,23,24,25 □.

leaven Gk. *zymē.* A bit of the dough for making bread,* that was left to ferment and which was incorporated into the fresh dough to make it rise. Thus, leaven had the power to raise up the entire mass.[1] Since the ancients believed that the process involved an alteration of the substance, the Law did not permit its use in cultic offerings;[2] so also, the image of leaven ordinarily had a pejorative meaning and signified a hidden cause of corruption.[3]

[1]Hos 7:4; Mt 13:33 (= Lk 13:20f.). [2]Ex 23:18; Lv 2:11. [3]Mt 16:6 (= Mk 8:15 = Lk 12:1); 16:11f.; 1 Cor 5:6-8; Gal 5:9 □.

→ unleavened bread.

[legate] Lat. *legatus Augusti pro praetore:* the general of a legion* delegated by the emperor with his full authority; he had the rank of governor* of a province. The legate of Syria* had three legions at his disposal, somewhere between eighteen and thirty thousand legionaries.

legion Gk. *legiōn,* from the Lat. *legio.* Composed of ten cohorts,* of some six to ten thousand men, it was the most important unit of the Roman army. In the N.T. it is a synonym for a multitude.[1]

[1]Mt 26:53; Mk 5:9,15; Lk 8:30 □.

leper Gk. *lepra.* In addition to the sickness of this name, the term designated various skin infections that entailed a cultic impurity that excluded those affected from the community. To be able to re-enter when healed, a person had to be ritually purified* by a priest.*[1]

[1]Lv 13–14; 2 Kgs 5:7; Mt 8:2f. (= Mk 1:40,42 = Lk 5:12f.); 10:8; 11:5 (= Lk 7:22); 26:6 (= Mk 14:3); Lk 4:27; 17:12 □.

lepton Gk. *lepton,* from *leptos:* "thin" (*lepō:* "to remove the wrapping, peel"), understanding *nomisma:* "what is established by usage, coin." The smallest of Greek and Roman coins, made of copper (about 1.55 grams), of infinitesimal worth (one-eighth of an as*). Occasionally synonymous with the obol* or the copper piece. Some translators suggest it be translated as a "penny."[1]

[1]Mk 12:42; Lk 12:59; 21:2 □.

→ coins.

letter **1.** Gk. *gramma* (from *graphō:* "to dig, to engrave, to write"). The word indicated "a writing character,"[1] "an inscription,"[2] "a note,"[3] "the Holy Letters,"[4] the letter in contrast to the spirit.[5]

[1]2 Cor 3:7; Gal 6:11. [2]Lk 23:38. [3]Lk 16:6f.; Acts 28:21. [4]2 Tim 3:15. [5]Rom 2:27,29; 7:6; 2 Cor 3:6 △.

2. Gk. *epistolē* (from *epistellō:* "to send a letter, to send news")[6]. The word ordinarily designated correspondence,[7] occasionally official letters.[8]

[6]Acts 15:20; 21:25; Heb 13:22 △. [7]Acts 23:25,33; Rom 16:22; 1 Thes 5:27. [8]Acts 9:2; 15:30; 22:5.

→ Intr. IX.3.B.—epistle—Scripture.

Levi Gk. *Leyi, Leyei,* Heb. *Lēwî,* of obscure meaning; according to popular etymology: "to join with others, to attach oneself to."

1. The son of Jacob* and Leah, and the eponymous* ancestor of the priestly tribe* of Levites.*[1]

[1]Gn 29:34; Dt 33:8-11; Heb 7:5,9; Rv 7:7 □.

2. A publican* named Matthew in Matthew 9:9.[2]

[1]Mk 2:14; Lk 5:27,29 □.

[levirate] From the Lat. *levir,* "brother-in-law." A prescription of the law to ensure the perpetuation of a name and to secure the sustenance of a family's well-being: the eldest brother of a man who had died without descendants had to marry his brother's widow.*[1] An exception to the law concerning the degrees of affinity in marriage.[2] A custom illustrated by the story of Tamar,[3] Ruth[4] and by the case of conscience presented by the Sadducees* who tried to make Jesus look foolish.[5]

[1]Dt 25:5-10. [2]Lv 18:16; 20:21. [3]Gn 38. [4]Ru 2:20; 3:12. [5]Mt 22:23-33 (= Mk 12:18-27 = Lk 20:27-38).

→ Intr. VIII.2.B.e.—marriage.

Levites Gk. *leyitēs,* Heb. *lēwî.* The descendants of the priestly tribe of Levi,[1] the ancient priests of the rural high places who became a kind of low-ranking clergy unable to have access to the altar*[2] but charged with tasks ancillary to worship*: execution of music, preparation of sacrifices, collection of tithes;[3] the Levites also looked after the policing of the Temple.

[1]Dt 33:8-11; Lk 10:32; Jn 1:19; Acts 4:36; Heb 7:11. [2]2 Kgs 23:9; Ez 44:10-16. [3]Heb 7:5,9 □.

→ Intr. VIII.2.C; XIII.1.A.b.—Aaron—High Priest—Levi—priest—priesthood—tithe.

lewdness

→ prostitution—vices.

libation This indicated a rite which was complementary to the sacrifice,* one in which oil,[1] water[2] or wine[3] was poured out around or on the altar.* Evoking blood which had been poured out (Gk. *ekchynnō*),[4] the Gk. term *spendomai* was used in a figurative sense by Paul.[5]

[1]Gn 35:14. [2]2 Sm 23:16. [3]Dt 32:38; Sir 50:15. [4]Ex 29:12; Lv 8:15; Mt 23:35 (= Lk 11:50); 26:28 (= Mk 14:24 = Lk 22:20); Acts 22:20; Heb 9:22; Rv 16:6. [5]Phil 2:17; 2 Tim 4:6 □.

→ blood—sacrifice—sprinkling.

[Liber Antiquitatum Biblicarum] An O.T. apocryphal* writing. An edifying book about biblical antiquities, that is, about the history of salvation from Adam to Saul. The original Hebrew has come down to us in a Latin translation that shows traces of a Greek version. No Christian interpolation has been discerned in it. The work has been dated to before A.D. 70. It had been falsely attributed to Philo, hence its name "Pseudo-Philo."

liberate, liberty 1. Gk. *eleutheroō:* an action by which an individual or a people has been snatched from slavery* and become free. While the O.T. was full of the experienced reality (deliverance from Egypt,* the return from Babylon*), the N.T. never considers quite specifically political and temporal aspects of liberation. There are even other preferred terms which it uses: save,* buy back.* Clearly, Jesus' disciples were exempt (free) of the Temple tax,*[1] and men were in fact divided into "slaves and free,"[2] but this vocabulary was not used except in a single passage in John[3] and in three passages in Paul.[4]

[1]Mt 17:26; cf. Rom 7:3; 1 Cor 7:39. [2]1 Cor 12:13; Eph 6:8; Col 3:11; 1 Pt 2:16; 2 Pt 2:19; Rv 6:5; 13:16; 19:18. [3]Jn 8:32-36. [4]Rom 6–8; 1 Cor 7–10; Gal 2–5.

2. Liberty (Gk. *eleutheria*), which in the N.T. never means civil liberty (the Roman foundation of human dignity), is not defined as independence nor even as self-control, but rather consists in the fact that we are children* of God.[5] This spiritual freedom had been acquired by Christ[6] and communicated by the Spirit;[7] it made one free of another person's judgment.[8] This was the believer's royal law of liberty, namely God's word which had been planted within him.[9]

[5]Rom 8:21. [6]Gal 2:4; 5:1,13. [7]2 Cor 3:17. [8]1 Cor 10:29. [9]Jas 1:21,25; 2:8,12 □.

3. In the N.T., as in other places generally, the condition of a free man (Gk. *eleutheros*) is defined through contrast with the slave's* condition. But contrary to the political or Stoic* mentality, man was not held to be born free but instead was seen as a slave to corruption.[10] He could not make himself free through knowledge* or through any initiation into a mystery* religion or through any myth.* He was in bondage to evil powers, to sin* and death,* he could not free himself; indeed, without the Spirit, he was being led fatally to death.[11] It is only Christ who sets people free,[12] and not in a way that they become independent of the Liberator, but so that, free from the Law,[13] sin and death,[14] they might become instead "slaves" of Jesus Christ[15] and of his brothers,[16] thus obtaining access to justice and holiness.[17]

[10]Jn 8:39; 2 Pt 2:19. [11]Rom 7:7-25. [12]Jn 8:32-36; Rom 6:18-22; Gal 5:1. [13]Rom 7:3-6; 8:3. [14]Rom 8:2. [15]1 Cor 7:21f.,39; Gal 3:28; 5:1. [16]1 Cor 9:19. [17]Rom 6:20,22.

4. The free will is solicited by those opposing powers, the flesh* and the spirit*; it does not suffer violence from God's all-powerful grace* nor from Satan's activity; but, though formerly a slave of sin, it can resist such a tendency and it can respond to the incessant appeal of God, who invites it to conversion.*[18]

[18]Jn 6:44; Rom 3:5-8; 9:19f.; Gal 5:13; Jas 1:13-15; 1 Pt 2:16; 2 Pt 2:19.

→ Intr. XIV.2.A.—freedman—redemption—save—slave.

Libya A country situated to the west of Egypt,* neighboring upon Cyrene.*[1]

[1]Acts 2:10 □.

lie Gk. *pseudomai.* To lie was not only to deceive by appearances or words that were not in accord with one's being and thought,[1] but it was also to break a bond that linked oneself to other men[2] and to the God who does not lie.[3] In fact, truth* was an interpersonal relationship; to lie was to lead someone to perdition, to destroy one's solidarity, to kill the other.[4]

[1]Ex 20:16; Jn 8:55; Rom 9:1; 2 Cor 11:31; 1 Tim 2:7; 4:2; Ti 1:12; Jas 3:14; Rv 3:9. [2]Ps 78:36; 101:7; Prv 6:19; 30:8; Jer 9:4f.; 13:25; Mt 5:11; Rom 1:25; 3:4,7; Eph 4:25; Col 3:9; 1 Tim 1:10; 1 Jn 1:6; 2:4,21f.; 4:20; Rv 14:5; 21:8,27; 22:15. [3]Ps 89; Ti 1:2; Heb 6:18; 1 Jn 1:10; 2:27. [4]Jn 8:40-44; 2 Thes 2:9.

→ error—hypocrite—truth—vices.

life Gk. *zōē,* corresponding to *zēn:* "to live."

1. Life included the idea of a power which manifested itself particularly through the breath (the soul*) and the blood.*[1] What moved was said to be "living"; so spring water was "living water."[2] The primordial given of the Bible was that God (the Father) was the Living One above all others, the only living source, while all created life was fragile and perishable, however precious it might be in God's eyes.[3]

[1]Lv 17:14. [2]Jn 4:10f.; 7:38. [3]1 Kgs 17:1; Jb 7:7; Ps 36:10; Is 40:7f.; Mt 6:25-34; 16:16; 26:63; Jn 6:57; Acts 14:15; 1 Thes 1:9; Heb 10:31; Rv 4:9f.

2. Except in the writings of Paul and John, in the N.T. life is presented as an extension of the O.T. conception. Earthly life was the good exceeding all others, the one that was identified with the "soul" (Gk. *psychē*);[4] but it could not be secured by the good things a man disposed of,[5] it was received rather as the gift of the Living One.[6] To be far from God was to be as if dead;[7] to live was to be fed on his Word,[8] to trust totally in him for one's "soul."[9] Also, Jesus, who lived this way on earth, became, in a surpassing manner, "the Living One";[10] "eternal life" was simply "life."[11]

[4]Mt 10:39 (= Lk 17:33); 16:25f. (= Mk 8:35-37 = Lk 9:24). [5]Lk 12:15. [6]Acts 17:25. [7]Lk 15:24,32. [8]Mt 4:4 (= Lk 4:4). [9]Mt 6:25 (= Lk 12:22f.). [10]Lk 24:5; Rv 1:18; cf. Acts 1:3; 3:15; 25:19; Heb 7:25; cf. Dt 30:19. [11]Mt 18:8f. (= Mk 9:43,45).

3. Paul reinterpreted life as a function of that life which Jesus received after his death through the resurrection.[12] In its definitive form, living was Christ in person;[13] thus, it meant allowing oneself to be taken over by faith in the Living One,[14] not living for oneself but always belonging to the Lord.[15] This new life, already begun here below, will not, however, be fully realized until the destruction of the last enemy, Death.[16]

[12]Rom 14:9; 2 Cor 13:4. [13]Gal 2:20. [14]Rom 14:7f.; 2 Cor 5:15. [15]Phil 1:21. [16]1 Cor 15:22,26; Gal 5:25; Col 3:3f.

4. John laid hold of life in the pre-existent Word, the divine creative force.[17] Jesus not only brought authentic life,[18] he was life itself,[19] a life which also was pure light.[20] This very life he surrendered out of love for the Father and men;[21] but it was in order that he might receive it back anew[22] and communicate it abundantly.[23] For a man to be entrusted with life, he had to believe;[24] he also had to love his brothers under pain of abiding in death.[25]

[17]Jn 1:4; 1 Jn 1:1f. [18]Jn 6:58; 10:28. [19]Jn 6:35,57; 11:25f. [20]Jn 8:12. [21]Jn 10:15f.; 15:13; 1 Jn 3:18. [22]Jn 10:17f. [23]Jn 4:14; 5:26; 6:35,47,51,57; 10:10; 1 Jn 5:12. [24]Jn 3:15f.; 6:40,47. [25]1 Jn 3:14f.

→ death—eternal—soul.

light Gk. *phōs,* Heb. *ôr.*

1. One of God's creatures, characterized by that brightness[1] which the sun,[2] fire*[3] and lamps*[4] radiate.

[1]Gn 1:3,5; Jn 11:9f. [2]Rv 22:5. [3]Mk 14:54 (= Lk 22:56). [4]Lk 8:16; 11:33; 15:8; Acts 16:29; 2 Pt 1:19; Rv 18:23; 22:5.

2. A symbol of happiness, prosperity and joy,[5] it came from God who is light[6] and who is accompanied by it in his glorious manifestations,[7] such as during Jesus' Transfiguration*[8] or in the appearance to Paul,[9] or even to clothe* his angels.[10] Jesus' disciples had to bring their light to the world[11] and to speak it in broad daylight.[12] The morning star* was already shining in their hearts while they awaited the light of the heavenly Jerusalem.*[13]

[5]Ps 27:1; Is 58:8; Am 5:20; Mt 4:16; Lk 1:79; 2:32. [6]Ps 36:10; 1 Tim 6:16; 1 Jn 1:5. [7]Ps 104:2; Ez 43:2. [8]Mt 17:2,5. [9]Acts 9:3; 22:6,9,11; 26:13. [10]Acts 12:7. [11]Mt 5:14,16; Lk 12:35. [12]Mt 10:27; Lk 12:3. [13]2 Pt 1:19; Rv 21:23f.; 22:5.

3. According to Paul, through the mediation* of Christ, who was the reflection of God's glory, the light shines in our hearts,*[14] so that it can never be in accord with darkness.*[15] The believer has become a "son of the light,"[16] a fact which engenders irreproachable conduct[17] and an obligation to shine forth.[18] In combat* one needs to take up weapons of light[19] against Satan* who disguises himself as an angel* of light.[20] The Father of lights will bring everything into clear light.[21]

[14]2 Cor 4:4,6; Col 1:12; 2 Tim 1:10. [15]2 Cor 6:14. [16]Eph 5:8; 1 Thes 5:5; cf. Lk 16:8. [17]Eph 5:9. [18]Phil 2:15. [19]Rom 13:12. [20]2 Cor 11:14. [21]1 Cor 4:5; cf. Jas 1:17.

4. In John's writings, Jesus Christ is the true light[22] who transforms believers into sons of light.[23] The light commits itself to a combat* with darkness,[24] and man has to choose between these options, that is, he has to believe in Jesus and love the brethren.*[25]

[22]Jn 1:4; 8:12; 9:5; 12:35,46. [23]Jn 12:36. [24]Jn 1:9; 1 Jn 2:8. [25]Jn 3:19-21; 1 Jn 2:10.

→ darkness—day—glory.

lily Gk. *krinon,* Heb. *shûshan.* A collective term designating various wild flowers of the fields (lilies, crocuses, irises, tulips, narcissuses) with brilliant colors. In Mt 6:28 (= Lk 12:27), the reference may be to anemones, whose red color might have suggested Solomon's royal clothing.[1]

[1]Cf. Sg 2:1f.,16; 4:5; 6:2f.; Hos 14:6 □.

linen A plant cultivated in Egypt and in Palestine,[1] it was useful for weaving deluxe fabrics* (Heb. *bad,* Gk. *linon*) destined above all for use as cultic vestments.*[2] The Hebrew term *shésh, bûṣ,* (Gk. *byssos*) seems to have referred to a superior quality linen used by the priests and rich people.[3] Out of linen were made shrouds* and linen wrappings* used for burial.*

[1]Ex 9:31; Jos 2:6. [2]Lv 6:3; 16:4,23; 2 Sm 6:14; Dn 10:5; 12:6f.; Rv 15:6. [3]Gn 41:42; Ex 39:28; 2 Chr 5:12; Prv 31:22; Lk 16:19; Rv 18:12,16; 19:8,14 □.

linen cloth Gk. *sindōn.* Material woven out of linen or wool which could serve as a garment or a veil.[1]

[1]Mk 14:51 □.

→ shroud.

linen wrapping Gk. *keiria:* "strap, bandage, band"[1] and *othonion:* "a piece of linen" (from *othonē:* "fine linen"[2]). In the plural, bands of linen cloth used at the time of burial to bind the hands and feet of the corpse.

[1]Jn 11:44 △. [2]Lk 24:12; Jn 19:40; 20:5-7 △.

→ Intr. VIII.2.D.b.—bury.

lion Gk. *leōn*. A wild beast which could come up from the desert regions of the Jordan right into the pasture lands of Judea.[1] Because of its strength, it described a brutal enemy,[2] God's powerful word,[3] the victory of a hero, the lion of Judah.[4]

[1]Jer 49:19; Mi 5:7. [2]2 Kgs 17:25; Dn 6:4-24; 2 Tim 4:17; Heb 11:33; 1 Pt 5:8; Rv 9:8,17; 10:3; 13:2. [3]Jer 25:30; Rv 4:7; 10:3. [4]Gn 49:9f.; Nm 23:24; 1 Sm 7:34; Rv 5:5 □.

→ beasts.

lips Gk. *cheilos.* Employed in the heart's* service, they revealed its designs.[1] The word, the "fruit of the lips," was meant to confess* God's name*[2] and to proclaim it.[3]

[1]Ps 141:3; Prv 10:32; 26:23; Is 29:13; Mt 15:8 (= Mk 7:6); Rom 3:13; 1 Pt 3:10. [2]Ps 51:17; Is 6:5; 57:19; Zep 3:9; Heb 13:15. [3]1 Cor 14:21 □.

[literary criticism] That science which seeks to establish the earlier history, the structure* and the meaning of a text, particularly through source criticism.*

[literary genre] **1.** A means of expressing oneself according to a fixed form. Thus, the epistolary genre: out of 13,500 letters from antiquity, some 4,500 present the same introduction ("protocol") and even the same conclusion, and this despite a span of some 1,000 years.

2. The literary genre implies the assumption, within one's personal vision, of a stable way of living, acting, thinking and writing. So, Paul transformed the epistolary genre by substituting grace (Gk. *charis*) for the joy *(chara)* which was ordinarily wished.

3. In addition to the diverse genres concerning the words attributed to Jesus (*logia,* * rules of life, parables,* etc.), the gospels present his deeds under the forms of miracle narratives, framed utterances, dialogues, tales about Jesus, summary statements, etc.

4. The determination of a literary genre depends on literary criticism* and does not immediately imply a critical judgment of a historical kind on the reality of what has been recounted.

→ allegory—apocalypse—form—*Formgeschichte*—parable—*Redaktionsgeschichte*—setting in life.

[literary tradition] A succession of writings concerning the same subject, moving from the original manuscripts to the present-day text.

[literary unit] A pericope* or sequence of organized pericopes.

Living Ones Gk. *zōa* (the plural of *zōon,* tied to *zēn:* "to live"): "animals"[1] or, in the book of Revelation, strange beings conceived according to the vision of the Cherubim* in Ez 1:5–14 and of the Seraphim of Is 6:2f.[2] According to some ancient writers, they depicted in figurative form the four evangelists according to the beginnings of their narratives: Matthew by the man (whose genealogy he presented), Mark by the lion (of the desert where John preached), Luke by the bull (offered in sacrifice at the Temple by Zechariah), John by the eagle (who plumbed the depths of the Word).

[1]Heb 13:11; 2 Pt 2:12; Jude 10 △. [2]Rv 4:6-9; 5:6,8,11,14; 6:1,3,5,6,7; 7:11; 14:3; 15:7; 19:4 △.

loaves of offering Gk. *artoi tēs protheseōs:* "loaves of bread set before" the face of Yahweh, twelve in number, placed on a table (not the altar,* but in the Holy Place*) and renewed each sabbath* by priests who consumed them. The origin of the "bread of offering" rite is very ancient and remains in dispute.[1]

[1]Lv 24:5-8; Mt 12:4 (= Mk 2:26 = Lk 6:4); Heb 9:2 □.

locust

→ grasshopper.

lodge, lodging

→ inn.

[logia] The plural of the Greek word *logion:* "the reply of an oracle, a word, a sentence."

1. A sentence that does not necessarily belong to the context in which it is found: for example, Mt 5:13; 5:15.

2. Following the lead of Papias (A.D. 100–130), who edited an *Exegesis of the Logia of the Lord,* scholars think that, as one of the sources of the synoptic gospels,* there was a collection of the sayings of Jesus, often referred to by the abbreviation Q.*

→ agrapha—exegesis—literary genre—Q—setting in life—Thomas (Gospel of).

Logos A Greek word, meaning "word." It translated the Heb. *dâbâr* which both designated a spoken word*[1] as well as a deed that was done, a transaction.[2] In the Johannine literature, it refers to the personified Word, the Verbum.*[3]

[1]Mt 7:24,28; 8:8; 15:12; Lk 4:32,36. [2]Mt 21:24 (= Mk 11:29 = Lk 20:3); Acts 8:21; 15:6. [3]Jn 1:1,14; 1 Jn 1:1; Rv 19:13 △.

→ word.

loincloth Gk. *zōnē.* A kind of kilt made of woven material or an apron made of skins and varying in length, which was hung about the loins. The ancient dress of the Canaanites,* it had become an undergarment, corresponding to underwear. In John the Baptist's case, it could have been either a belt tying his cloak* or a prophet's style of dress, that is, one that served as both a loincloth and a cloak.[1]

[1]1 Sm 2:18; Jer 13:1f.; Mt 3:4 (= Mk 1:6); cf. 2 Kgs 1:8; Zec 13:4 □.

→ belt—clothing.

loins 1. Gk. *nephroi.* Like God, the Risen One "probes the loins and hearts,"[1] that is, a man's secret regions where his hidden designs are formed and his violent passions are roused.

[1]Jer 11:20; 17:10; Rv 2:23 △; cf. Ps 139:12f.; Jn 2:25.

2. Gk. *osphys.* The loins refer to the area wherein a man's vigor is concentrated;[2] he must gird them to be ready for combat.[3] In them is concentrated the power of generation.[4]

[2]Jb 40:16. [3]Lk 12:35; Eph 6:14; 1 Pt 1:13; cf. Mt 3:4; Mk 1:6. [4]Gn 35:11; Acts 2:30; Heb 7:5,10 △.

loose Gk. *lyō* (and its compounds): "to untie, to destroy." One untied an ass,[1] undid a sandal's straps,[2] burial wrappings,[3] a prisoner's chains,[4] a seal,[5] the ties of a marriage,[6] loosened those of an illness (just like an ox from its manger*),[7] those of the Law and the Scripture[8] or of the sabbath,[9] lastly those of sin[10] and death.[11] The meaning "to destroy" was unclear, except in reference to the Temple,[12] God's work or the devil's,[13] a barrier,[14] the human body[15] and the elements of the universe.[16] Is there any link between these two meanings? One is not forestalled from seeing therein an image of bonds (understood of the sabbath* law or of sin,* both of which could make man a slave*) from which the Church could loose someone.[17] Concretely, the term was the equivalent of "freeing oneself from something." Finally, it occasionally referred to the work of redemption.*[18]

[1]Mk 11:2-5. [2]Mk 1:7 (= Lk 3:16); Acts 7:33; 13:25. [3]Jn 11:44. [4]Acts 22:30; cf. Rv 9:14f.; 20:3,7. [5]Rv 5:2. [6]1 Cor 7:27. [7]Mk 7:35; Lk 13:12,15f. [8]Mt 5:17,19; Jn 7:23; 10:35. [9]Jn 5:18. [10]1 Jn 3:8. [11]Acts 2:24. [12]Mt 24:2 (= Mk 13:2 = Lk 21:6); 26:61 (= Mk 14:58); 27:40 (= Mk 15:29); Jn 2:19; Acts 6:14. [13]Acts 5:38f.; Rom 14:20; Gal 2:18; 1 Jn 3:8. [14]Eph 2:14. [15]2 Cor 5:1. [16]2 Pt 3:10-12. [17]Mt 16:19; 18:18; cf. Lk 6:37. [18]Rv 1:5.

→ bind and loose—liberate—pardon.

lord Gk. *Kyrios,* translating the Heb. *âdôn,* the Aram. *mâra:* "master," one who disposes of someone or something.

1. The royal title of Yahweh,* whose name, expressed by the sacred tetragrammaton, had been transposed into *Adonai:* "My Lord."[1] It signified the trust which his servants had in his absolute sovereignty. This title had become God's proper name and was translated in Greek by *Kyrios* which sometimes meant his lordship, at other times God's incommunicable name.

[1]Gn 15:2,8.

2. Beginning with Psalm 110, Jesus showed that the Messiah was "lord," and so superior to David whose son he was.[2] The first Christians saw in Jesus the Lord,[3] a designation which took account not of the nature but of the power of Jesus Christ: to him was attributed the same sovereignty as had been attributed to Yahweh.[4]

[2]Mt 22:43-45 (= Mk 12:35-37 = Lk 20:41-44). [3]Acts 2:36; Rom 10:9; 1 Cor 12:3; 16:22; Rv 22:20f. [4]Phil 2:9,11; Jn 20:28.

3. This title could have been a way of protesting against the pretensions of emperors.[5]

[5]1 Cor 8:5f.; Rv 17:14; 19:16.

→ Ascension—Exaltation of Christ—master—Maranatha.

Lord's Day Gk. *kyriakē hēmera*[1] (Lat. *dies dominica*): "lordly day." A Christian designation which derived neither from the Jewish week,* nor from the Essene* calendar,* from the cult of Mithra* or from Mandeanism.* Sunday, the English equivalent of the Lord's Day, corresponds to the first day of the week,[2] which is the day after the sabbath;*[3] this day commemorates the resurrection* of Jesus[4] and his appearances* to the disciples during a meal.[5]

[1]Rv 1:10 □. [2]Mt 28:1 (= Mk 16:2 = Lk 24:1); Mk 16:9; Jn 20:1,19. [3]Mt 28:1 (= Mk 16:1). [4]Acts 20:7; 1 Cor 16:2. [5]Lk 24:36-49; Jn 20:19-23; Acts 1:4.

→ Day of the Lord.

Lord's Supper Gk. *kyriakon deipnon* (1 Cor 11:20). This is the oldest name (along with the breaking of bread*) for the sacrificial thanksgiving meal of Christians. It includes three complementary aspects.

1. The proclamation of Jesus' sacrificial death through a memorial of his last meal (the "Last Supper"). Two traditions (Luke/Paul and Mark/Matthew) situated this meal within a context which indicated its meaning: by showing how Jesus understood his death. The first tradition related it to the sacrifice of the Isaianic Suffering Servant;*[1] the second saw in it the fulfillment of the Mosaic Covenant* on Sinai.[2] Both emphasized the redemptive* value for the many (multitude*) of Jesus' death. John saw it similarly.[3] Only the Luke/Paul tradition reported the command of its commemoration,[4] Mark/Matthew concerning themselves only with showing the voluntary aspect of Jesus' sacrifice.

[1]Is 53:12; Lk 22:19f.; 1 Cor 11:25. [2]Ex 24:4-8; Mt 26:28; Mk 14:24. [3]Jn 6:51. [4]Lk 22:19; 1 Cor 11:24f.

2. Communion* with the living Savior. Retaining an ancient depiction of the sacrificial meal, Paul described the unity that those who took part (Gk. *metechō*) and communed (Gk. *koinōneō*) in the body and blood of Christ actually shared.[5] The paschal coloring of the account stressed the real nature of the Risen Lord's presence, a feature Paul underlined through the analogy he saw between the eucharistic meal and idolatrous* meals.[6] Along with the synoptic tradition which eucharistically colored the narratives of Jesus' feeding of the crowds in the wilderness,[7] John showed that in the eucharistic meal the gift of manna* found its fulfillment in the manna of eternal life.[8]

[5]1 Cor 10:16f. [6]Mt 26:30 (= Mk 14:26); 1 Cor 10:18-21; 11:27. [7]Mt 14:19 (= Mk 6:41 = Lk 9:16); 15:36 (= Mk 8:6f). [8]Jn 6:26-58.

3. In anticipation of Christ's return, Jesus' saving death was proclaimed. According to another tradition contained in the institution accounts, Jesus himself looked forward to the eschatological* banquet,[10] the Last Supper preserving his thanksgiving meal during the time of his absence.

[9]1 Cor 11:26. [10]Mt 26:29; Mk 14:25; Lk 22:16-18.

→ breaking of bread—communion—cup—Eucharist—Last Supper—Maranatha—meal—sacrifice.

lordships Gk. *kyriotētes* (plural of *kyriotēs:* "sovereignty"): heavenly beings inferior to Christ.[1] In the singular, the term may designate Christ.[2]

[1]Eph 1:21; Col 1:16. [2]2 Pt 2:10; Jude 8 □.

→ Dominations.

Lot Gk. *Lōt,* Heb. *Lôth,* of uncertain etymology. Abraham's* nephew, he emigrated with him to Canaan.[1] Having remained "just" in the midst of the sinners of Sodom, Lot was delivered by God.[2] The punishment of his fellow citizens suggested the "Day* of the Son of Man*"; that of his wife ought to urge one not to turn back "on that day."[3]

[1]Gn 11:27,31; 13:1-13. [2]Gn 19. [3]Wis 10:6f.; Sir 16:8; Lk 17:28f., 32; 2 Pt 2:6-8 □.

love The Heb. word *ahâbâ* was translated in the Bible by the Gk. *agapē.* The noun was practically unknown in secular language, but not so the verb *agapaō*—"to welcome with affection," particularly a child, a guest. This term tended to tell of the deliberate character of a tender "inclination towards" someone (Gk. *phileō, philia*). One never finds the term *erōs* ("passionate love"). What characterized the O.T. conception of love was its essential connection to election*: before Deuteronomy systematized this thinking, the first biblical authors showed that the God who chooses men or a people acts in their favor, etc. Justice,* Law,* grace,* inheritance,* all these were manifestations of the God who took the initiative.[1] The prophetic tradition, beginning with Hosea, presented God's love under the traits of a conjugal love that was passionate because it was faithful.[2] All vied to show that man's response was to love God, something which was verified in obedience* and fidelity.*[3] The Law commanded one to love his neighbor as oneself,[4] namely like one's own life which one cannot hate.

[1]Dt 6:5; 7:6-11. [2]Is 54:4-8; Jer 2; 3:6-10; 31:3f.; Hos 1–3; 11. [3]Ex 20:6; Dt 10:12f. [4]Lv 19:18.

2. The synoptic tradition, which presents Jesus as the beloved son* (Gk. *agapētos*),[5] does not, however, explicitly speak of God's love for man, but rather of his mercy;*[6] it was not in his words but by his behavior and his teaching that Jesus revealed the divine love.[7] Moreover, he made an innovation on the O.T. by linking and basing the commandment* of love of one's neighbor on one's love for God;[8] he radically surpassed the Jewish tradition in requiring love of one's enemies.*[9]

[5]Mt 3:17 (= Mk 1:11 = Lk 3:22); 12:18; 17:5 (= Mk 9:7 = Lk 9:35); Mk 12:6 (= Lk 20:13). [6]Mt 9:13 (= 12:7). [7]Mt 18:33; Lk 15. [8]Mt 22:37,39 (= Mk 12:30f.,33 = Lk 10:27). [9]Mt 5:43-46; Lk 6:27,32,35.

3. As an heir of the O.T., Paul ordinarily bound love and election* together:[10] the "ones called" were "beloved" (Gk. *agapētoi*).[11] Love's initiative manifested itself in the act of salvation,*[12] so that it was Jesus himself, who, by surrendering himself, showed his love.[13] Love snatched wrath* away and reconciled* men with God; for love is stronger than death.[14] God and love are in some sense interchangeable terms.[15] Finally, Christ's love was presented with the traits of marital love, not to make an erotic symbol out of it, but to stress the love of election and its fidelity.[16]

Through the Spirit, the justified believer knows himself to be loved of God.[17] In response he proclaims his (re)cognition and gives his faith (bound in with love[18]), quite rarely, love itself.[19] The believer has to love his neighbor.[20] It is faith that grounds brotherly love,[21] but it is love which gives authenticity to a faith existence.[22] Love alone creates the community of believers, Christ's body.*[23]

[10]Rom 9:13,25; 11:28. [11]Rom 1:7; Col 3:12. [12]Rom 5:8; 8:35. [13]2 Cor 5:14f.; Gal 2:20; 2 Thes 2:13; Eph 3:19; 5:2. [14]Rom 8:37; 1 Cor 15:55; 2 Cor 5:1; 1 Thes 1:10. [15]2 Cor 13:11,13. [16]Eph 5:25. [17]Rom 5:5; 15:30. [18]Eph 6:23; 1 Thes 1:3; 3:6; 5:8; 1 Tim 1:14. [19]Rom 8:28; 1 Cor 2:9; 8:3. [20]Rom 13:8-10; Gal 5:14. [21]Gal 5:6. [22]1 Cor 13:1-8. [23]1 Cor 8:1; 14:1; 16:14; Eph 1:15; 3:17; 4:16; Phil 2:1; Col 2:2; 2 Thes 1:3.

4. John went so far as to identify God and love (Gk. *agapē*):[24] God first loved us in sending us his Son.[25] Man's response has to be love, the kind the Son showed the Father:[26] believers have been inserted into this relationship of love[27] and have to love the Father and the Son with the same love.[28] It is this love which grounds brotherly love,[29] this being necessary to authenticate faith,[30] as Paul also maintained.

[24]1 Jn 4:8,16. [25]1 Jn 3:1,16. [26]Jn 14:31; 1 Jn 4:19. [27]Jn 17:26. [28]Jn 14:21. [29]Jn 13:34; 1 Jn 4:21. [30]1 Jn 3:10; 4,7f.,20f.

5. The verb *phileō* designates more of an inclination towards someone or something.[31] It was rarely used to mean God's love,[32] but rather was used to manifest the love of friendship which Jesus showed[33] and which he demanded of the faithful. Sometimes it served to indicate love for God or for Jesus,[34] without our being able to detect in this a nuance different from that found in the verb *agapaō.*[35] Above all, it served to designate that brotherly love which we might call charity.[36] The love of affection was sometimes indicated by words deriving from the Gk. *stergō,*[37] camaraderie by *hetairos.*[38]

[31]Mt 6:5; 23:6; Lk 7:6; 11:5-8; 14:10,12; 15:6-9,29; 16:9; 21:16; 20:46; 23:12; Jn 19:12; Acts 10:24; 19:31; 27:3; 28:2,7; Ti 1:8; Jas 4:4; 3 Jn 9:15; Rv 22:15. [32]Jn 5:20; 16:27; Ti 3:4; Jas 2:23. [33]Mt 11:19 (= Lk 7:34); Lk 12:4; Jn 3:29; 11:3,11,36; 15:13-15; 20:2; Rv 3:19. [34]Mt 10:37; Jn 16:27; 1 Cor 16:22; 2 Tim 3:4. [35]Jn 21:15-17. [36]Rom 12:10; 1 Thes 4:9; Ti 2:4; 3:15; Heb 13:1; 1 Pt 1:22; 3:8; 2 Pt 1:7. [37]Rom 1:31; 12:10; 2 Tim 3:3 △. [38]Mt 11:16; 20:13; 22:12; 26:50 △.

→ beloved—God—election—mercy—Spirit of God.

lowliness, lowly

→ gentle, gentleness.

Luke Gk. *Loukas,* probably a diminutive of the Lat. *Lucanus.* Of pagan birth, a doctor, Paul's travel companion (as the first person plural passages [the "we narratives"][1] of the Acts of the Apostles suggest), Luke was the author of the third gospel and of the Acts of the Apostles.*[2]

[1]Acts 16:10-17; 20:5-15; 21:1-18; 27:1–28:16. [2]Col 4:14; 2 Tim 4:11; Phlm 24 □.

[Luke (Gospel of)] Written probably after 70 (the destruction of Jerusalem) and before 80–90 by a Greek whom tradition identified with Paul's doctor companion (Col 4:14). Echoing numerous traditions, this gospel, composed for Christians of Greek culture, constituted the first volume of a work which, with the Acts of the Apostles,* depicted God's salvific plan.*

→ Intr. XV.

lunatic From the Lat. *lunaticus,* Gk. *selēniakos* (from *selēniazomai:* "to be under the moon's sway"). A sick person influenced, it was believed, by the phases of the moon* and temporarily "seized" by convulsions attributed to an evil spirit.* Perhaps it is to be identified with epilepsy. Its healing resembled the freeing of possessed persons.*[1]

[1]Mt 4:24; 17:15 □.

Lycaonia Gk. *Lykaonia.* A region of the high plateaus of modern-day Turkey, to the north of Cilicia,* annexed since 25 B.C. to the Roman province* of Galatia.* People spoke Greek* there, as well as the native language. Paul evangelized its cities of Iconium,* Lystra* and Derbe.*[1]

[1]Acts 14:6 □.

→ Map 3.

Lydda Gk. *Lydda,* Heb. *Lod,* between Tel Aviv and Jerusalem. An ancient city where Peter healed Aeneas and where there was established towards the end of the first century B.C. an important center of Talmudic* studies, where the two great rabbis* Eleazar ben Hyrcanus and Aqiba taught.[1]

[1]1 Chr 8:12; Acts 9:32,35,38 □.

→ Map 4.

Lysias Gk. *Lysias.* A tribune* of Greek and oriental parentage. Having acquired the status of a Roman citizen,* he was charged with maintaining order at Jerusalem. He intervened on the occasion of a riot against Paul;[1] his name is mentioned only twice.[2]

[1]Acts 21:31–23:30. [2]Acts 23:26 (and 24:7); 24:22 □.

Lystra Gk. *Lystra, Lystroi.* A small city of Lycaonia,* to the northwest of Iconium.* It became a Roman colony* in 6 B.C.[1]

[1]Acts 14:6,8,21f.; 16:1f.; 2 Tim 3:11 □.

→ Map 2.

[Maccabees] 1. Heb. *maqqabi,* the surname of Judas, the third son of Mattathias, who organized the Jewish resistance to the oppressor Antiochus Epiphanes (166–161 B.C.). The surname given to the seven brothers who were martyrs. The term may derive from *maqqèbèt:* "hammer," a surname analogous to that of Charles Martel.

2. *The First Book of Maccabees* recounted Jewish history from 175–135 B.C. It had been written in Hebrew at the beginning of the first century B.C. under Alexander Janneus (103–76), but we possess only the Greek version. It is a deuterocanonical* writing.

3. *The Second Book of Maccabees* recounted the same history in a manner that pretended to be more edifying. It was written in Greek, about the year 120 B.C. It is a deuterocanonical* writing.

4. *The Third Book of Maccabees* is an apocryphal* Greek writing, dated between the first century B.C. and the first century A.D. It has nothing in common with the preceding canonical books. It described in romantic fashion the triumph of Jews over their enemies.

5. *The Fourth Book of Maccabees* is an apocryphal* Greek writing, dating from the first century A.D. A discourse in the Stoic style, it was elaborated by beginning with the account of the courageous martyrdom of the Maccabees.

Macedonia A territory of North Greece. A Roman province* from 146 B.C., it was often crossed or visited by Paul.[1]

[1]Acts 16:9f.; 12; 18:5; 19:21f.,29; 20:1,3; 27:2; Rom 15:26; 1 Cor 16:5; 2 Cor 1:16; 2:13; 7:5; 8:1; 9:2,4; 11:9; Phil 4:15; 1 Thes 1:8; 4:10; 1 Tim 1:3 □.

→ Intr. IV.3.C.—Philippi—Thessalonica—Map 3.

madness

→ folly.

Magadan An unknown site on the edge of the lake of Gennesaret*; Mk 8:10 called it Dalmanutha.*[1]

[1]Mt 15:39 □.

Magdalene A native of Magdala (cf. Heb. *migdol:* "tower"), a city located on the sea of Galilee,* north of Tiberias.* It was sometimes identified with Magadan and Dalmanutha.* A designation of Mary Magdalene.

Magi Gk. *magos.* Originally, according to Herodotus, the name of a Persian tribe with priestly functions, skilled in the interpretation of heavenly phenomena.[1] Those whom Matthew mentions were wise men, aliens to the

Jewish world,[2] of whom we cannot state that they were "kings" nor that they were "three" in number. In a Greek milieu: sorcerers.[3]

[1]Jer 39:3,13; Dn 1:20; 2:2,10,27; 4:4; 5:7,11,15. [2]Mt 2:1,7,16. [3]Acts 8:9,11; 13:6,8 □.

magic Gk. *mageia.* Pretension to occult power over the diety through various means: magical knots, consultation of spirits, the dead or stars,* enchantments, charms, divinations, sorcery (Gk. *pharmakeia*). Practiced generally in the ancient world,[1] it penetrated into Israel, despite the Law's interdictions of it.[2] The N.T. thrusts it aside with horror.[3]

[1]Ex 7:11; Is 47:9; Acts 8:9,11; 13:6,8; 19:19; Rv 9:21; 18:23. [2]Ex 22:17; Lv 19:26,31; Nm 23:23; Dt 18:10f.; 1 Sm 28; 2 Kgs 9:22; 17:13; Mi 5:11. [3]Gal 5:20; Rv 21:8; 22:15.

→ Intr. IV.6.D; VI.4.C.b.—idolatry—oracle—vices.

malediction

→ curse.

Mammon Gk. *mamōnas,* Aram. *mâmôn:* "riches," a word to be set in relation with the root *'mn:* "what is sure, what one can count on, what endures." A term of late literature, biblical and rabbinical,* with the meaning of wicked riches. Thus is it used in the N.T.[1]

[1]Sir 31:8; Mt 6:24; Lk 16:9,11,13 □.

→ money—riches.

man Gk. *anthrōpos,* Heb. *âdâm, enôsh.*

1. Unlike Western views, Jews did not consider man apart from his religious setting. Man was not simply a permanent composite of body* and soul,* but a being dependent on God for breath itself, for his spirit.*[1] The image* of God, man was to increase and fill the earth.[2] He was not an individual who could be reckoned with in isolation; rather through his flesh* he was a social being. Recognizing in the woman* whom God gave him the very expression of himself with her own distinct differences, man learned to go out of himself in love.[3] Every encounter with a neighbor* variously made manifest that relationship on which society was founded. Finally, man reflected the divine lordship* and had to bring the earth under his dominion.[4]

[1]Gn 2:7. [2]Gn 1:26-28. [3]Gn 2:23f. [4]Gn 1:28f.

2. But how was this ideal to be reached? Sin divided the human family,[5] rendered the universe hostile,[6] delivered man up to death*[7] and to a split in his conscience.*[8] Only Jesus Christ achieved it in his role as the Servant* of God, who was faithful unto death,[9] reconciling* men with God and with each other.[10]

[5]Gn 3–11. [6]Rom 8:20. [7]Gn 3:19; Wis 2:24; Rom 5:12. [8]Rom 7:7-24. [9]Is 52:13 53:12; Phil 2:6-11. [10]2 Cor 5:18-21.

3. Jesus Christ, who identified himself as the Son of Man,* was the new and last Adam*[11] the new Man*[12] above every other, the one with whom everyone can be rid of the old man by crucifying him,[13] can have a renewed understanding[14] which is the very mind of Christ himself[15] and can clothe himself as the new man.[16] The interior person thus becomes a new creature.[17] The entire humanity has in Jesus Christ its principle of unity, allowing all to encounter one another, because he has absorbed in himself every difference of sex, race or social standing.[18]

[11]1 Cor 15:45. [12]Eph 2:15. [13]Rom 6:6; Col 3:9. [14]Rom 12:2. [15]1 Cor 2:16. [16]Eph 4:22-24. [17]2 Cor 4:16; 5:17. [18]Gal 3:28.

→ Intr. V.2.—Adam—Son of Man.

[Mandaeanism] Beliefs and rites of a gnostic* and baptist sect established in the south of Mesopotamia. The term derives from the Aramaic *manda:* "knowledge." These sectarians were also called Nazoreans* (probably from the root *nṣr:* "observer") and Sabeans (from the root *sb':* "baths"). Through texts that are quite late, we may recognize gnostic dualism* (light/darkness), influences that are Babylonian, Iranian, Manichaean, and even Muslim. There are in it several striking resemblances to the N.T., in particular to John's gospel, but it is difficult to assert mutual dependence. The Mandean language was Oriental Aramaic.*

manger Gk. *phatnē.* The feeding trough of stable animals; by extension, the stable itself.[1]

[1]Lk 2:7,12,16; 13:15 □.

[Manichaeism] The doctrine inspired by Mani, a Persian of the third century A.D., according to which Good and Evil were the two originating principles of existence, independent of one another and locked in combat with each other.

manna Gk. *manna:* "a grain of incense," taking up the Gk. *man,* which, in the Septuagint,* translated the Heb. *mân.* A popular etymology (Heb. *mâ hû:* "What's that?"[1]) tells of the mysterious origin of the nourishment given by God to his people during their crossing of the desert.*[2] An event variously interpreted in the course of biblical tradition: the sustenance and the trial* of Israel,[3] spiritual food,[4] a type of Christ's gift,*[5] eschatological* nourishment.[6]

[1]Ex 16:15. [2]Ex 16; Nm 11:7-9; Heb 9:4. [3]Dt 8:1-6; Mt 4:1-4 (= Lk 4:1-4). [4]Wis 16:20-29; 1 Cor 10:3. [5]Jn 6:31,49. [6]Ps 78:23-25; Rv 2:17 □.

Maranatha An Aramaic* expression, perhaps liturgical in origin, which can be translated: "The Lord* comes" *(mâran-atâ)* or "Our Lord, come!" *(mâranâ-tâ).*[1] An expression translated into Greek as: "Come, Lord Jesus."[2]

[1]1 Cor 16:22. [2]Rv 22:20 □.

Mark Gk. *Markos,* a name of Roman origin, meaning: "hammer." John, surnamed Mark, the son of Mary of Jerusalem, a cousin of Barnabas,* the companion of Paul's first journey;[1] perhaps identical to the one who enjoyed a relationship with Paul and Peter.[2] According to tradition, the author of the second gospel in the canonical* collection.

[1]Acts 12:12,25; 13:5,13; 15:37,39. [2]Col 4:10; 2 Tim 4:11; Phlm 24; 1 Pt 5:13 □.

[Mark (The Gospel of)] The oldest gospel,* written at Rome before 70 (the destruction of the Temple), seemingly after 64 (Nero's persecution), beginning with numerous written or oral traditions some of which may go back to the apostle Peter. Probably addressed to non-Jews, it invited belief in Jesus Christ. One recognizes at its source the voice of a witness and also that of a community that handed on its catechism of faith. The "ending of Mark" (16:9–20) is canonical,* but not authentic*; it may date from the end of the first century.

→ Intr. XV.

marriage Gk. *gamos.* On the institution of marriage→ Intr. VI.4.B.b; VIII.2.B.

1. The conjugal union complies with a twofold objective: mutual support[1] and a fruitfulness whereby the couple procreates.[2] Despite the authorizations of the Law[3] and some practices reported in the O.T.,[4] Jesus affirmed that marriage was to be stable, monogamous, and that legislation on divorce* was merely a concession to men's "hardness of heart."[5]

[1]Gn 2:18; 1 Cor 7:3-5. [2]Gn 1:28; 3:20; Dt 25:5; Mt 22:24-28 (= Mk 12:19-23 = Lk 20:28-33). [3]Ex 21:10; Dt 21:15-17; 22:22,28. [4]Gn 29:15-30; Jgs 8:30; 2 Sm 3:2-5; 1 Kgs 11:3. [5]Ps 128; Sir 25:1,8; 26:1,13; Mt 19:8.

2. Marriage was man's normal state during his mortal life.[6] But Jesus, who was not married, revealed the value of celibacy for the sake of the kingdom of heaven:[7] it was a special gift[8] signifying the new situation brought by the end of time inaugurated in Jesus. From this point of view, "there is no man or woman, for all of you are but one in Christ Jesus":[9] to the former opposites of man/woman there is added now that of married/virgin. These two forms are necessary to constitute and to express in complementary fashion the fullness of the kingdom of heaven.

[6]Rom 7:2f.; Eph 5:22; Col 3:18. [7]Mt 19:12; Lk 18:29. [8]1 Cor 7:7. [9]Gal 3:28.

3. According to the order of creation, marriage was not the object of a specifically religious institution; nonetheless, the Covenant* between Yahweh and Israel was often expressed with the help of the matrimonial metaphor.[10] In founding the new covenant in his blood,[11] Jesus became the Church's Spouse; henceforth, the unifying symbol* of marriage is no longer only the ideal union of a man and a woman, but also the union of Christ and the Church: This is the "great mystery*" that Paul speaks about.[12]

[10]Is 54:5-7; Jer 2:2; Ez 16:6-14; Hos 2:21f. [11]Lk 22:20. [12]Eph 5:32; cf. Mk 2:19; Jn 3:29; 2 Cor 11:2; Rv 19:7; 21:2,9.

→ adultery—betrothed—covenant—divorce—fruitfulness—spouse—virginity—wedding—widow—woman.

Martha Gk. *Martha,* the sister of Mary of Bethany* and Lazarus.*[1]

[1]Lk 10:38-41; Jn 11:1-39; 12:2 □.

martyr Gk. *martys,* "witness." Beginning with the text of the O.T.,[1] apocryphal* narratives about martyrs[2] and the words of Jesus,[3] the term ended up referring to one who gave his life in fidelity to an act of witnessing* rendered to Jesus.[4]

[1]2 Mc 6–7; Dn 3:24-26. [2]Cf. Heb 11:35-39. [3]Mt 10:18 (= Mk 13:9), 10:32f. (= Lk 12:8f.); Jn 15:13. [4]Acts 22:20 (?); Rv 2:13; 6:9; 17:6; 20:4.

Mary Gk. *Maria(m),* Heb. *Miryâm.*

1. *Mary, the mother of Jesus,* a native of Nazareth, the wife of Joseph,* a cousin of Elizabeth.*[1] According to the gospels she was the Daughter of Zion,* the Virgin who begot the Messiah, the believer above all others, whose motherhood tells of faith and perfect obedience.[2] Jesus' mother was present at the beginning[3] and at the end of the public life of her son.[4] Tradition saw in her the "new Eve,*" the mother of believers.[5]

[1]Mt 1–2; 13:55 (= Mk 6:3); Lk 1–2; Acts 1:14.[2]Lk 1:38,45; 11:27f. [3]Jn 2:1-12; [4]Jn 19:25f. [5]Jn 19:27; Rv 12; cf. Gn 3:15,20.

→ mother—virgin—woman.

2. *Mary, the mother of James the Less and Joseph (Josēs).* Some identify her with Mary of Clopas,* the sister of Jesus' mother. Generally she is mentioned with Mary Magdalene.[6]

[6]Mt 27:56,61; 28:1; Mk 15:40,47; 16:1; Lk 24:10; Jn 19:25 □.

3. *Mary of Bethany, the sister of Martha* and Lazarus*.*[7] She has been identified by John with the woman who poured the perfume over Jesus' head[8] and also, but incorrectly by some writers, with the sinner of Lk 7:37–50.

[7]Lk 10:39,42. [8]Jn 11:1 12:3 □.

4. *Mary, the mother of Mark.*[9]

[9]Act 12:12 □.

5. *A Christian of Rome.*[10]

[10]Rom 16:6 □.

Mary Magdalene Gk. *Maria hē Magdalēnē:* "Mary the Magdalene.*" A former possessed* woman healed by Jesus, who was present at his death and burial, the first woman to have been met by the Risen One. Not to be identified with Mary of Bethany* nor with the sinner of Lk 7:37–50.[1]

[1]Mt 27:56,61; 28:1; Mk 15:40,47; 16:1,9; Lk 8:2; 24:10; Jn 19:25; 20:1,11,16,18 □.

master As in English, the word presents various shades of meaning, such as "the one who rules" or "the one who knows."

1. *Oikodespotēs:* "the master of the house";[1] *despotēs:* "the owner,"[2] applied to God or to Christ.[3]

[1]Mt 10:25; 13:27. [2]1 Tim 6:1f.; Ti 2:9; 1 Pt 2:18; Intr. VIII.2.A. [3]Lk 2:29; Acts 4:24; 2 Tim 2:21; 2 Pt 2:1; Jude 4; Rv 6:10 △.

2. *Kyrios,* from which *kyrieuō:* "to have soverignty, to rule" derives; ordinarily translated by "Lord," except in several instances in which it is applied to others and not to God or to Jesus.[4]

[4]Mt 6:24 (= Lk 16:13); 18:25; 20:8; 21:30; 24:45-50; Jn 20:15.

3. *Epistatēs:* "the one who holds himself above";[5] in Luke, the Greek translation of rabbi.*

[5]Lk 5:5; 8:24,45; 9:33,49; 17:13 △.

4. *Didaskalos* (Heb. *rabbi**): "the one who teaches," often used as a title of address to Jesus.[6]

[6]Mt 8:19; Mk 4:38; Lk 7:40; Jn 1:38.

→ teach.

Matthias Gk. *Matthias,* an abbreviated form of *Mattathias.* The disciple who replaced Judas Iscariot and thus become one of the Twelve Apostles.*[1]

[1]Acts 1:23,26 □.

Matthew Gk. *Maththaios.* A publican,* a collector of taxes and duties, identified by Matthew's gospel with Levi. One of the Twelve.* According to tradition, the author of the first gospel.[1]

[1]Mt 9:9; 10:3; Mk 3:18; Lk 6:15; Acts 1:13; cf. Mk 2:14 (= Lk 5:27,29) □.

[Matthew (The Gospel of)] The first of the collection of four gospels.* Attributed by an ancient tradition to the apostle of this name. An echo of Palestinian traditions, it is not, however, the translation of some Aramaic original, but is a work edited in Greek. Probably composed in Syria, at the latest around 80–90, it is addressed, according to some, to believers come from Judaism; according to others, to Christian Hellenists.* This gospel, written out of faith for faith, is characterized by the importance given to Jesus' teachings, but it presents Christ's message in the form of a way of life that has doctrinal implications. The Gospel of the Church par excellence.

→ Intr. XV.

meal **1.** Like the Greek, the Jew was familiar with two meals after the breakfast which preceded work:[1] one, fairly light, in the late morning or towards noon (*ariston*[2]), and the other, the main meal, at night (*deipnon*[3]). One sat or stretched out on the floor[4] or on couches,[5] leaning on the left elbow, eating with one's hands from the surface of a flat piece of bread. Generally one was satisfied with bread, water, fruit, and, in the evening, with some hot dish. Meat and wine, as luxurious commodities, were reserved for special occasions, which, one might add, were not lacking;[6] hence, references to feasting and carousals.[7]

[1]Lk 14:2. [2]Jn 21:12. [3]Lk 17:8. [4]Mt 14:19. [5]Am 2:8; 6:4; Jn 13:23. [6]Mt 14:6; 22:2; Lk 15:22-32; Jn 2:1. [7]Gal 5:21.

2. Occasionally, a meal sealed a covenant.*[8] It always told of the brotherhood in the act which sustained life; this table fellowship presupposed a sense of hospitality*[9] and a union of hearts, under threat of its becoming a Satanic betrayal.[10] Jesus expressed in this way his love for "sinners."[11] Following the prophets,[12] he depicted the joy of heaven as a joyous banquet[13] and longed for the eschatological* meal.[14]

[8]Gn 26:30; 31:46,54. [9]Lk 7:36-50. [10]Ps 41:10; Jer 41:1f.; Jn 13:18,26f. [11]Lk 15:1f.; 19:2-10. [12]Is 25:6. [13]Mt 8:11; Lk 13:29; cf. Rv 3:20. [14]Mt 26:29; Lk 22:30.

3. A meal was held to crown ritual sacrifices,* signifying communion* with the godhead;[15] such was also the case with the Lord's Supper.*[16] The "breaking of bread,"*[17] by contrast, could not be anything but an ordinary meal, requiring fraternal charity; but it could become the Lord's Supper.[18]

[15]Ex 18:12; 24:11; 1 Cor 10:18,20f. [16]1 Cor 10:16f. [17]Acts 2:42,46. [18]1 Cor 11:20-34.

4. Jesus' last meal → Last Supper.

5. The Risen One's meals with his disciples[19] commemorated the earthly meals Jesus shared with his own, and, at the same time, anticipated the eschatological meal.

[19]Lk 24:30; Jn 21:13; Acts 1:4; 10:41.

→ Intr. VIII.1.D.—agape—bread—breaking of bread—feast—wine.

measure **1.** Gk. *metrētēs.* A Greek measurement of liquid capacity. This term corresponded to the Hebraic measure, the *éyphâ* or else the *bath.* It was equal to one-tenth of a *kor,* that is, 36.44 liters (38.6 quarts).[1]

[1]Jn 2:6 □.

2. The same word "measure" translated the Gk. *saton,* a Greek version of the Heb. *se'â.* An ancient measurement of solid capacity, equal to one-third of an *éphâ,* or 12.13 liters (10.9 dry quarts).[1]

[1]Mt 13:33; Lk 13:21 □.

3. Occasionally also, a "measure" meant the *koros,* the Greek version of the Heb. *kor,* the ancient measurement of the capacity of solids and liquids, the equal of 364 liters (327.6 dry quarts or 385.8 liquid quarts),[1] or ten ephahs. The Heb. *homèr,* which corresponded equally to it, meant what an ass could carry.[1]

[1]Lk 16:7 □.

4. Finally, the *choinix,* a Greek measurement of solid capacity, equal to about 1.21 liters (1.09 dry quarts), or one-tenth of a *se'â.* [1]

[1]Rv 6:6 □.

→ measures

[measures] The measurements of length or capacity which the N.T. mentions are difficult to estimate, due to the fact that the base units vary with the civilizations (Babylonian, Hellenistic, Roman, Syrian, Palestinian) and to the fact that diverse estimates of them have interfered with one another. This explains the differences offered in the tables set out in dictionaries or in Bibles. At least one element seems to be constant—one carefully indicated in the following tables—the proportionate relationships among the different measures. Though the base unit (the *cubit* and the *ephah*) varied, the relationship each had with the other units did not: the *span* equalled four *cubits*, the *stadion* was equal to 400; the *seah* was equal to one-third of an *ephah*, the *kor* equalled ten. Estimates, therefore, definitely depend on the choice of the base unit's equivalent worth.

Linear measures. These were taken as a function of the human body: the cubit went from the elbow to the extremity of the fingertips, the span (half-cubit) measured the open hand from the thumb to the little finger, the palm (a third of a span) corresponded to a hand's breadth, the finger (or thumb, a quarter of a palm). For distances, Jews were acquainted with the "sabbath day's journey" (between 1,100 and 1,250 meters or between 1,203 and 1,367 yards). The reed,* or cane, equalled six cubits.

LINEAR MEASURES

						Syria	*Palestine*	*Greco-Roman*
mile	1					1,572.7 m.	1,537.5 m.	1,478.9 m.
stadion	7.5	1				213.0	205.0	185.0
span	750	100	1			2.13	2.05	1.85
pace	1,500	200	2	1		1.065	1.025	0.925
cubit	3,000	400	4	2	1	0.5328	0.525	0.462
foot	4,500	600	6	3	1.5	0.3552	0.341	0.308

Measures of capacity. These were of two kinds, according to whether they concerned solid content (wheat, barley, etc.) or liquid content (oil, wine, etc.). In the case of solids, the N.T. mentions two Hebraic measurements, designated by Greek terms: the *seah* and the *kor,* as well as a Greek measurement, the *choinix,* and a Roman measurement, the measure (Gk. *modios*) or bushel. In Palestine, for liquids use was made of the Greek *xestēs:* "jar, pitcher" (0.46 liter, 0.41 quart) (a term which appears in its current meaning at Mk 7:4), the Hebraic *bath* and the Gk. *metrētēs,* one equal to the other.

MEASURES OF CAPACITY

kor/koros	1				364.00 liters
ephah-metrētēs-bath-jar	10	1			36.44
seah-saton	30	3	1		12.13
choinix	300	30	10	1	1.21

meat **1.** The meat of animals which had not been slaughtered. Gk. *pniktos:* "choked." Since the Law forebade the consumption of the blood,* which contained the life, it was forbidden to eat the meat of animals whose blood had not been poured out.[1]

[1]Lv 7:26f.; 17:10-14; Acts 15:20,29; 21:25 △.

→ Intr. XIV.1.A.

2. Meat sacrificed to idols. Gk. *eidōlothyton* (from *eidōlon:* "image," *thyō:* "to sacrifice"); this designation came from a Jewish polemic directed against paganism: it described this meat as "immolated in sacrifice" (Gk. *hiero-thyton*).[2] The leftovers of the flesh of animals, immolated, with their blood, to idols, meat that was sold in the markets[3] or eaten in the outer buildings of temples.[4] The Council of Jerusalem* required abstention from such meats,[5] while Paul spelled out the conditions for their consumption.[6]

[2]1 Cor 10:28 △. [3]1 Cor 10:25. [4]1 Cor 8:10. [5]Acts 15:28f.; 21:25; cf. Rv 2:14,20. [6]Rom 14:1–15:13; 1 Cor 8:1-13; 10:14-33 △.

→ idolatry—sacrifice—worship.

Medes Gk. *Mēdoi.* The inhabitants of the region south of the Caspian Sea, Iranian in origin but politically reunited with Persia about 550 B.C. Some Israelites had been deported among them from Samaria* around 720 B.C.[1]

[1]Gn 10:2; 2 Kgs 17:6; 18:11; Tb 1:14; Acts 2:9 □.

mediator. Gk. *mesitēs.*

1. In the common meaning of the term, he was an intermediary between two separated parties who sought reconciliation. The majority of religions has sought to make up the distance experienced between God and man. Magicians, priests, kings, heavenly heroes, incarnations of Vishnu or Mithra, all kinds of beings were charged with establishing a bond between divinity and humanity. Among the Jews, angels,* kings, prophets, priests, the Servant of Yahweh,* all played this role; but it was Moses* who was represented as the definitive mediator of the Covenant by means of the Law and of worship.

2. But Paul declared that the mediation sought after had not been obtained. The Law,* having been materialized in the letter, became a ministry of condemnation[1] and, in bringing the sinner's state to his awareness,[2] brought with it a curse* in its wake.[3] Victims offered in worship* did not really cause one to enter into communion* with God.[4] Law and worship accentuated the separation without effecting harmony.

[1]2 Cor 3:6-9. [2]Rom 7:7-15. [3]Gal 3:10f. [4]Heb 10:1-11.

3. Jesus was presented as the unique mediator.[5] How? Not because from the moment of his incarnation he, according to some theologians, united in his person the two natures—divine and human—but by virtue of his sacrifice of reconciliation.* The cross brought about in him the most extreme kind of separation from men and from God,[6] but simultaneously it effected both perfect obedience* to God and complete solidarity with men.[7]

[5]1 Tim 2:5; Heb 8:6; 9:14f. [6]Mk 15:34; Gal 3:13. [7]Heb 5:7-9.

4. Jesus, the mediator, is not merely a third party, a means by which, through his intercession,* he "mediates" a relationship between men and God; he is the one in whom communion* between God and men is forever being effected.[8]

[8]Jn 14:6.

meekness

→ gentle, gentleness.

Melchizedek Heb. *malki-ṣèdèq:* "my king is justice." A king-priest,[1] the founder of a royal priesthood[2] superior to that of Aaron,[3] he appeared without beginning or end; he prefigured the Christ.[4]

[1]Gn 14:18-20. [2]Ps 110:4. [3]Heb 7:1-17. [4]Heb 5:6,10; 6:20 □.

→ Aaron—priesthood.

memory Gk. *mimnēskomai:* "to recall, remember." The Hebrew *zâkar* is the root of a family of words by which the Jew revealed himself to be a man of tradition,* profoundly rooted in his people. In the same way that God remembers his Covenant and his promises,[1] the believer delights in recalling the great deeds God has done, so that he might keep himself in a disposition of authentic belief.[2] So, in God, he comes to master time itself. The Christian shows his difference from O.T. traditions by the fact that in the Eucharist he makes present the saving event of the redeeming cross. He brings Jesus to memory *(eis tēn anamnēsin).* [3] According to John, this remembering is made possible by the activity of the Holy Spirit, who, in recalling Jesus to mind, makes us understand and actualize his very presence.[4]

[1]Gn 9:15f.; 30:22; Ex 2:24; 32:13; 1 Sm 1:20; Ps 98:3; 105:8,42; Jer 15:15; 18:20; 31:34; Heb 8:12; 10:17. [2]Ex 20:8; Dt 5:15; 8:2; 26:3-10; Ps 103:18; 105:5; Mal 3:22. [3]Lk 22:19; Acts 20:35; 1 Cor 11:24f.; 2 Tim 2:8. [4]Jn 14:26.

merchants

→ money-changers—Temple.

mercy Among the related words: goodness, compassion, grace, mercy, pity —all of which signify an attitude favorable to the one who is in misery—two thrusts which enable us to gauge the breadth of the biblical term are discernible.

1. One side stresses the disposition which seeks to relieve another's distress. Ordinarily, it is the Greek word *eleos* which indicates this *(Kyrie eleison);*[1] this is not identical with a feeling of compassion but it implies the twofold nuance of an "inclination toward" (Heb. *hén*) and covenant fidelity (Heb. *hèsèd*). Faithful to himself and to his Covenant, God enters into solidarity with the wretched and the sinner, doing him a favor, namely offering clemency and "misericord" (from the Lat. *miseri-cordia:* "a heart" sensitive to "misery").[2]

[1]Cf. Mt 9:27; 15:22; 17:15; 20:30f. (= Mk 10:47 = Lk 18:38f.); Lk 17:13. [2]Nm 14:17-19; Ps 103:7-10; Is 54:7f.; 55:7; Lk 1:54,72; Mt 5:7; 23:23.

2. The other thrust takes into account the place, source and depth of the feeling which inclines to an act of pity: the compassion (Heb. *rahamim:* "the bowels") corresponding to Gk. *oiktirmos:*[3] "compassion shown" or *splagchna:*[4] "entrails, maternal womb," heart, tenderness, goodness.

[3]Rom 12:1; 2 Cor 1:3; Heb 10:28. [4]Mt 9:36; 14:14 (= Mk 6:34); 15:32 (= Mk 8:2); 20:34; Mk 9:22; Lk 10:33; 7:13; 15:20; 2 Cor 6:12; Eph 4:32; Phil 1:8; Phlm 7; 1 Jn 3:17.

3. Only the context indicates a passage's shade of meaning. Besides, the Greek, like the Hebrew, often juxtaposed different terms as if intending to describe at the same time the reality and its source, the deed and its feeling.[5] The verbs seem to contain both nuances, while the nouns favor the distinction. Mercy is proper to God,[6] and it ought also to be a characteristic of the Christian.[7]

[5]Ex 34:6f.; Lk 1:78; Rom 9:15; Phil 2:1; Col 3:12; Jas 5:11. [6]Ex 33:19; Lk 1:50; Rom 9:15f.,18,23; 11:32; 15:9; 1 Pt 1:3. [7]Ps 112:5; Mi 6:8; Mt 9:13; 12:7; 18:23-35; Lk 6:36; 10:37; Rom 12:8; Jas 2:13.

→ almsgiving—grace.

Mesopotamia

Mesopotamia Gk. *Mesopotamia.* In the broad sense, the territory "between the rivers": the Tigris and the Euphrates.* Abraham's* fatherland.[1]

[1]Acts 2:9; 7:2 □.

Messiah

Messiah Gk. *Messias,* translating the Heb. *Mâshiah,* the Aram. *meshihâ:* the "Anointed One.*"

1. In the O.T. the term was applied, first of all, to the king, then to priests consecrated by anointing, finally, and to an eminent degree, to the promised liberator, ordinarily the Son of David.[1]

[1]Intr. XII.2.C; Ex 28:41; 1 Sm 9:16; 2 Sm 7:12-16; Ps 132:17.

2. In Jesus' time, the title Messiah connoted an idea of temporal kingship.[2] Jesus, himself, did not want it to be bestowed on him[3] even though, at his life's end, he let himself be acclaimed by an equivalent title: Son of David.*[4] On the other hand, in proclaiming his fate, he situated himself within the transcendent world of the Son of Man,*[5] all the while linking it with the suffering which awaited him.[6]

[2]Jn 6:15. [3]Mt 16:20 (= Mk 8:30 = Lk 9:21); Lk 4:41. [4]Mt 20:30 (= Mk 10:47f. = Lk 18:38f.). [5]Mt 26:63f. (= Mk 14:61f. = Lk 22:69). [6]Mt 16:21f. (= Mk 8:31f. = Lk 9:22); 17:22f. (= Mk 9:31f. = Lk 9:44); 20:18f. (= Mk 10:33f. = Lk 18:31,33).

3. Normally, the N.T. uses it in its Greek equivalent: "Christ."[7] The first Christians proclaimed that the Risen One was the Christ, in a way that fulfilled* and surpassed the Jewish hopes, and they readily linked this title to that of Lord.[8]

[7]Except Jn 1:41; 4:25 △. [8]Acts 2:36.

→ Christ—Jesus Christ—Lord—Son of David.

[metaphor] Gk. *metaphora* (from *pherō:* "to carry" and *meta:* "between, from one side to the other"): a "transposition of meaning." A procedure of language by which, in basing ourselves implicitly on a comparison ("Achilles lunged forward like a lion"), we specify one object with a term which properly belongs to another ("The lion lunged forward"). The Bible is in the habit of speaking metaphorically, something which then comes to acquire a traditional value: thus, the "owner of the vineyard" is God himself, the "servants" are the prophets, etc. (Mt 20:8; 21:33–44).

→ allegory—literary genre—parable.

Michael Gk. *Michaēl,* Heb. *Mykâ'ēl:* "Who is like God?" The archangel who triumphs over the Dragon.*[1]

[1]Dn 10:13,21; 12:1; Jude 9; Rv 12:7 □.

midnight Gk. *mesonyktion*[1] or "in the middle of the night,"[2] the end of the second watch.

[1]Ex 12:29; Mk 13:35; Lk 11:5; Acts 16:25; 20:7 △. [2]Mt 25:6; Acts 27:27 △.

→ day—hour—night—watch.

[midrash] A Hebrew word (from the Heb. *dârash:* "to search into") meaning "inquiry," joining together nuances of study and explanation.

1. This term characterized synagogal* exegesis,* a work of tradition and reflection (not one of revelation as in apocalyptic*). A procedure whereby a passage of Scripture was explained and illustrated in its relation to the present and with a view to an exhortation to live better; it should not be likened to fables or to legendary storytelling. This method extended the biblical procedure of reflecting on past Scriptures: for example, Ez 16, Is 60–62, Ps 78, Wisdom or the apocryphal* writings such as Jubilees* or the Testaments of the Twelve Patriarchs,* or even Mt 21:2–7 on Zec 9:9.

2. A writing (in the plural: *midrashîm*) gathering together traditional exegeses. Applied to the legislative parts of the Torah,* it elaborated new rules of conduct; this was *halakah* (Heb. *hâlak:* "to walk, to drive"): these were, for Exodus, *Mekhilta* ("measure"), for Leviticus, *Sifra* ("book"), for Numbers and Deuteronomy, *Sifre* ("books").

Applied to the narrative parts of the Torah, midrash strove to disengage the significance of narratives and events. This was *haggadah* (Aram. *aggadtâ*), "presentation"—thus the *Genesis Rabba,* the *Song of Songs Rabba,* the *Lamentations Rabba.* (*Rabba* comes either from the name of the first author, Rabbi Ochaya Rabba, or from the Hebrew *rab,* whence "Genesis Developed").

→ Intr. XII.1.C.

mile Gk. *milion,* Lat. *mille passus:* "a thousand (double-) paces," a Roman measure of distance, equal to 7.5 stadia,* or about 1.5 km (0.94 mile). Boundary markers indicated its distance along the length of Roman highways.[1]

[1]Mt 5:41 □.

→ measures.

Miletus Gk. *Milētos.* A port on the west coast of Asia Minor.[1]

[1]Acts 20:15,17; 2 Tim 4:20 □.

→ Map 2.

military cloak Gk. *chlamys.* A kind of military jacket without sleeves, Greek in origin. A large piece of cloth fastened at the left shoulder, with the two ends taken up on the right side.[1]

[1]Mt 27:28-31 □.

→ clothing.

milk Gk. *gala.* From the ewe, she-goat or cows, milk was the basic nourishment of the Hebrews* who, first of all, had been nomads, then settled in Canaan, a country of pasture lands.[1] Along with honey and wine, milk was an image of well-being and of messianic happiness.[2] As a metaphor,* it described Christ's word[3] or the rudiments of Christian teaching.[4]

[1]Dt 32:14; Prv 27:27; 1 Cor 9:7. [2]Ex 3:8; Sir 39:26; 46:8; Jer 11:5; Ez 20:6,15; Jl 4:18. [3]1 Pt 2:2. [4]1 Cor 3:2; Heb 5,12f. □.

[millenarianism (millennialism)] In its narrow sense, the doctrine interpreting Rv 20:1–6 literally: the last judgment and the establishment of the Kingdom of God will be preceded by a period of a thousand years, in the course of which the glorious Christ will reign over the earth in company with the saints who will have experienced the "first resurrection."

In the broad sense, every conception which expects the world to come under the image of a promised land or an earthly paradise, linking it up with the myth of an original golden age or an earthly messianism.

millstone Gk. *mylos.* Two superimposed millstones, of which the upper one kept on turning, served to grind the cornmeal needed each day. Laborious work, reserved to the womenfolk,[1] but one whose stopping signified the cessation of life.[2] Larger mills were driven by donkeys.[3]

[1]Ex 11:5; Mt 24:41. [2]Eccl 12:3f.; Jer 25:10; Rv 18:21f. [3]Mt 18:6; Mk 9:42 □.

mina Gk. *mna.* A Greek reckoning coin, made of silver (436 grams, 15.38 oz.), the equivalent of the wages for some fifteen years' work.[1]

[1]Lk 19:13-25 □.

→ coins.

ministry **1.** From the Lat. *ministerium:* "service." An office received by delegation and exercised with authority.* The generic term can designate civil authorities,[1] Jewish liturgical services,*[2] Jesus Christ's sacerdotal dignity,[3] his authority itself[4] or, finally, various services entrusted to believers. The principal Greek words corresponding to Christian ministry are *diakonia,* "service,"[5] *exousia,* "authority,"[6] *oikonomia,* "administration,"[7] *charis/charisma,* "gracious gift,"[8] *pempō, apostellō,* "to send,"[9] *presbeia,* "embassy."[10]

[1]Lk 12:11; 20:20; Ti 3:1. [2]Lk 1:23; Heb 9:21. [3]Heb 5:4. [4]Mt 7:29. [5]Acts 6:1,4; Rom 12:7. [6]2 Cor 10:8; 13:10. [7]Col 1:25. [8]Rom 1:5; 1 Cor 12:4. [9]Jn 4:34,38; Acts 1:25; 15:25; 1 Cor 4:17. [10]2 Cor 5:20; Eph 6:20.

2. The one who stands at the source of ministries is the envoy above all others,[11] Jesus Christ, who entrusts them[12] and who confers on each their respective authority.[13] The Holy Spirit coordinates the divers ministries, which he adapts to each person, and whose exercise he ensures.[14]

[11]Heb 3:1f.; 13:20; 1 Pt 2:25. [12]Acts 20:24; Rom 1:5; 1 Cor 4:1-5; 5,4f.; 12:5. [13]Mt 10:40 (= Lk 10:16); Jn 13:20; 2 Cor 5:20. [14]1 Cor 12:4,11,18; 14:26; Eph 4:7,16.

3. The Church is structured according to the some/all distinction: *some* are at the service of *all.* The two principal ministries are the service of the Word[15] and the service of fraternal communion.[16] Beginning there, there is a great diversity of ministries which are established as a function of circumstances: oversight (episcope,* presbyter,* deacon*), aid (thus the collection*), the gift of healing,* etc., not to mention the apostolate,* prophecy.*[17] When any were celebrated, the graces necessary for their administration were communicated through the laying on of hands.* All Christians, men and women, can exercise ministries, although no woman has been mentioned as an episcope or as a presbyter.

[15]Rom 12:6-8; 1 Cor 12:8; 1 Tim 3:2; Heb 13:7; 1 Pt 4:11. [16]Rom 12:8,13; 1 Cor 12:28; 1 Thes 5:12. [17]Acts 20:28; Rom 12:4-7; 1 Cor 12:9f.,28-30; 1 Thes 5:12; 1 Tim 3:1; 5:17; 1 Pt 2:5f.

→ apostles—Church—deacon—episcope—presbyter—serve.

mint Gk. *hēdyosmon,* Lat. *mentha piperita.* An aromatic herb in abundance which was used as a spice. The Pharisees* obliged themselves to pay the tithe* on it, even though the Law did not prescribe this.[1]

[1]Mt 23:23; Lk 11:42 □.

miracle From the Lat. *mirari:* "to be astonished at." An act of power (Gk. *dynamis,* generally in the plural: "powers"), a marvel (Gk. *teras:* always in the plural: "extraordinary, shocking things") through which God gives a sign (Gk. *sēmeion*) to men who are amazed at it *(thaumazō).* These words express various aspects of the one reality: its extraordinary nature, its source (someone's power), its significant bearing or its surprising effect. Although Jesus performed many miracles, one never finds the term *dynameis* except in three instances within his sayings,[1] while it spontaneously comes to the lips of spectators[2] or from the pen of narrators.[3] The word "marvel" is never used except when joined with that of "sign" in the stereotyped formula, *sēmeia kai terata;*[4] without doubt these were marvels, but there is no interest in them except for their sign value: seeing, hearing, walking, living.

[1]Mt 7:22; 11:21,23 (= Lk 10:13); Mk 9:39 △. [2]Mt 13:54 (= Mk 6:2); 14:2 (= Mk 6:14). [3]Mt 11:20; 13:58; Mk 6:5; Lk 19:37. [4]Mt 24:24 (= Mk 13:22); Jn 4:48; Acts 2:19,22,43; 4:30; 5:12; 6:8; 7:36; 14:3; 15:12; Rom 15:19; 2 Cor 12:12; 2 Thes 2:9; Heb 2:4 △.

2. Besides phenomena of an eschatological* kind which are foretold of the future (like the moon* turned into blood or stars* which fall from the sky) and which took over apocalyptic* language,[5] along with miracles concerning Jesus which belong to the sphere of theological language,[6] the N.T. tells of some miracles performed after Easter: speaking in tongues* on the day of Pentecost, glossolalia,* and the other miracles performed by the Apostles (multiple healings, the raising of Tabitha, exorcisms[7]). Chief among the miracles worked by Jesus, some twenty-five accounts of healings stand out: fever,*[8] leprosy,*[9] paralysis,[10] deaf*-mutes,*[11] blindness,[12] epilepsy,[13] rheumatisms,[14] hemorrhages,[15] a wound;[16] three exorcisms* properly speaking,[17] three raisings* of the dead,[18] eight or nine natural miracles: a storm calming,[19] loaves multiplied,[20] walking on water,[21] a didrachma in a fish's mouth,[22] miraculous catches,[23] water changed into wine,[24] and a withered fig tree.[25] This number is hardly high when one compares contemporary literature on the topic or if one brings criticism to bear on some narratives which make up doublets.[26]

[5]Mt 24:29; Rv 6:12. [6]Lk 1:34f.; 9:29ff. [7]Acts 2:6-8; 3:6; 8:13; 9:32-42; 19:11; 2 Cor 12:12. [8]Mt 8:14f. (= Mk 1:29-31 = Lk 4:38f.). [9]Mt 8:1-4 (= Mk 1:40-44 = Lk 5:12-16); Lk 17:11-19. [10]Mt 8:5-13 (= Lk 7:1-10); 9:1-8 (= Mk 2:1-12 = Lk 5:17-26); 12:9-14 (= Mk 3:1-6 = Lk 6:6-11); Jn 4:46-54; 5:1-9. [11]Mt 9:32-34; Mk 7:31-37. [12]Mt 9:27-31; 20:29-34 (= Mk 10:46-52 = Lk 18:35-43); Mk 8:22-26; Jn 9. [13]Mt 17:14-21 (= Mk 9:14-29 = Lk 9:37-43). [14]Lk 13:10-17. [15]Mt 9:20-22 (= Mk 5:25-34 = Lk 8:43-48); Lk 14:1-6. [16]Lk 22:50f. [17]Mt 8:28-34 (= Mk 5:1-20 = Lk 8:26-39); 15:21-28 (= Mk 7:24-30); Mk 1:21-28 (= Lk 4:31-37). [18]Mt 9:18-26 (= Mk 5:21-43 = Lk 8:40-56); Lk 7:11-17; Jn 11. [19]Mt 8:18,23-27 (= Mk 4:35-41 = Lk 8:22-25). [20]Mt 14:13-21 (= Mk 6:31-44 = Lk 9:10-17); 15:32-39 (= Mk 8:1-9); Jn 6:1-15. [21]Mt 14:22-33 (= Mk 6:45-52). [22]Mt 17:24-27. [23]Lk 5:1-11; Jn 21:1-14. [24]Jn 2:1-11. [25]Mt 21:18-22 (= Mk 11:12-14,20-24). [26]Thus for Mt 9:27-31,32-34; 15:32-39.

3. Though Jesus took the initiative to perform miracles, that was not to satisfy the curiosity of someone who came into the healer's presence,[27] nor to rebut ill will,[28] but rather to show forth God's power at work, as prophecy had foretold,[29] and to overcome Satan by the finger of God.[30] These miracles did not automatically convert their witnesses;[31] Jesus allowed them to be drawn out of himself according to that measure of faith which earnestly requested them.[32] If, occasionally, they were described as having been produced out of Jesus' compassion,[33] more generally they were seen as divine approbation of the Messiah and the symbol of his victory over the devil.[34] Finally, God continued to effect miracles through believers, so much so that one may speak of the "gift of miracles."[35]

[27]Lk 23:8. [28]Mt 12:38f. (= Lk 11:29f.); 16:3f. (= Mk 8:11f.). [29]Is 29:18f.; 35:4-6; 61:1f.; Mt 11:2-6 (= Lk 7:18-23). [30]Mt 12:28 (= Lk 11:20). [31]Mt 11:21 (= Lk 10:13). [32]Mt 13:58; Mk 6:5. [33]Mt 9:36; 14:14 (= Mk 6:34); 15:32 (= Mk 8:2); 20:34. [34]Acts 2:22; 10:38. [35]Mk 16:17,20; Rom 15:19; 1 Cor 12:10; 2 Cor 12:12; Gal 3:5; 1 Thes 1:5; Heb 2:4.

→ blind—ear—heal—power—sign.

mirror Gk. *esoptron* (from *eis:* "toward" and the root *op* meaning: "to see"; cf. *eis-oraō:* "to have one's eyes directed toward, to contemplate"). While, in the time of the Romans, mirrors made of glass already existed, the majority were made of polished metal, for example, out of bronze.* The mirror of ancient man reflected a faithful, although still slightly blurred, image of a man's face.[1] The Christian was a mirror of the divine glory* which had flooded into him.[2]

[1]Ex 38:8; Jb 37:18; Sir 12:11; 1 Cor 13:12; Jas 1:23f. □. [2]Wis 7:26; 2 Cor 3:18.

[Mishnah] **1.** A Hebrew word (from the Heb. *shânah:* "to repeat"): "teaching." In the beginning, oral repetition of the Law.*

2. A collection edited by Judah the Holy (135–200), with Tannaitic traditions (from the Aram. *tannain:* "repeaters" who lived from A.D. 10–200), oral then written. This collection of jurisprudence contained six parts or "ranks" (Heb. *sedârîm*), sixty-three treatises (Heb. *massektôt*) and 523 chapters (Heb. *perakîm*), which gathered together the various *mishnayôt.* It was the basis of the Talmud.*

→ Intr. XII.1.B.—Law—Torah.

mission

→ send.

[Mithra] An ancient Indo-European deity. This "mystery* religion" did not really penetrate the Roman Empire until the second century A.D., in particular under the emblem of the triumphant sun god *(sol invictus).*

Molech Gk. *Moloch.* A Greek transcription of the Heb. *molèk.* A word gotten perhaps through an intentional corruption of *mèlèk,* "king," or, more probably, from the technical term indicating child sacrifice. A Canaanite* deity who demanded human sacrifices.[1]

[1]Lv 20:5; 2 Kgs 16:3; 23:10; Am 5:26; Acts 7:43 □.

→ Gehenna.

money-changers Gk. *kollybistēs, kermatistēs.* In order to be able to pay the Temple tax in Jewish coinage, money-changers were permitted in the sanctuary. They made the exchange against foreign currency, at the rate of one silver obol* to a half-shekel.*[1]

[1]Mt 21:12 (= Mk 11:15 = Jn 2:15); Jn 2:14. □.

→ bank—Temple.

money Gk. *argyrion:* "silver coin" (from *argyros:* "the brilliant metal"). Imported from Arabia and Egypt, this metal served as silver plate,[1] as payment,[2] in the manufacture of coins measured by weight (the shekel*),[3] coins for tribute,[4] for capital.[5] Money was not to be condemned,[6] but was poorly regarded because of the Pharisees'* or the walking preachers' traffic in it.[7] Because of the covetousness* of those who loved it,[8] it was not an estimable value, but was perishable.[9]

[1]Gn 24:53; Acts 17:29; 19:24; 2 Tim 2:20; Rv 9:20; 18:12. [2]Gn 23:9; Acts 7:16; 19:19. [3]Gn 23:16; Ezr 8:27; 1 Mc 15:6; Mt 26:15 (= Mk 14:11 = Lk 22:5); 27:3-9: 28:12,15. [4]2 Kgs 18:14f.

[5]Ex 21:21; Mt 25:18,27; Lk 19:15,23; 1 Cor 3:12; Jas 4:13; cf. Rv 18:3. [6]Cf. Mt 22:19-21 (= Mk 12:15-17 = Lk 20:24f.). [7]Lk 3:13; 2 Cor 2:17. [8]Lk 16:14; Acts 20:33; 1 Tim 3:3; 6:10; 2 Tim 3:2; Heb 13:5. [9]Mt 10:9 (= Lk 9:3); Acts 3:6; 8:20; Jas 5:3; 1 Pt 1:18 □.

→ coins—gold—Mammon—riches—shekel.

money-changers' table

→ bank.

monitor

→ pedagogue.

month **1.** The month (Gk. *mēn*) was tied to lunar phases, something suggested by the etymology: month *(yèrah, mèn)* and moon *(yâréah, mènè)* derive from the same root. The month was alternatively of 29 and 30 days (according to astronomy, its average length was 29 days, 12 hours, 44 minutes, 2.8 seconds). The months bore names (not mentioned in the N.T.) and ordinal numbers, the first being the month of Nisan* (March-April).

2. Because of the tie-in between the calendar* and worship, the word "month" could take on the meaning of religious feast.[1] "Neo-meny" can mean "new month" or "new moon";[2] it was solemnly celebrated with sacrifices.[3]

[1]Gal 4:10. [2]Col 2:16. [3]Nm 28:11–15; Ez 46:6f.

→ calendar—moon—Nisan.

moon Gk. *selēnē.* Without being the object of some worship,* the new moon (Gk. *neomēnia*) determined the calendar of feasts*[2] and exercised a real influence over humans.[3] On the last day, according to apocalyptic* imagery, it will lose its white* color and its brightness.[4]

[1]Dt 4:19; 17:3; Jer 8:2; 2 Kgs 23:5. [2]Gn 1:14; Lv 23; Nm 10:10; Ps 81:4; Is 1:13; Hos 2:13; Col 2:16. [3]Ps 121:6; Mt 4:24; 17:15. [4]Is 24:23; 30:26; Jl 3:4; Mt 24:29 (= Mk 13:24); Lk 21:25; Acts 2:20; 1 Cor 15:41; Rv 6:12; 8:12; 12:1; 21:23 □.

→ Intr. V.1; XIII.3.A.

moon (new)

→ new moon.

morning Gk. *prōi.* Not the morning, but the fourth watch* of the night (3–6 o'clock), when the day began to dawn.[1] The Gk. *orthros* is precise: "the dawn, day-break."[2]

[1]Mt 16:3; 20:1; 21:18; 27:1; Mk 1:35; 11:20; 13:35; 15:1; 16:2,9; Jn 18:28; 20:1; 21:4; Acts 28:23; Rv 2:28; 22:16 □. [2]Lk 21:38; 24:1,22; Jn 8:2; Acts 5:21 □.

Moses Gk. *Mō(y)sēs,* Heb. *Môshé* (a name of Egyptian origin: *mos* = son, hence, for example, Thutmoses).

1. The liberator and legislator of Israel. In Jesus' time, Hellenistic Judaism had made of him a hero, "a superman"; Palestinian Judaism saw in him the inspired author of the five books of the Torah,*[1] the Law's supreme mediator between God and the people,[2] the definitive teacher,[3] finally, the prophet* above all others whose return was to be awaited.[4] Such an authority could have hindered the Jews from recognizing what was being affirmed in the deeds and sayings of Jesus.[5]

[1]Mt 22:24 (= Mk 10:3f. = Lk 20:28); Mk 7:10; 10:3f. [2]Jn 7:19,22; Rom 9:15; 10:5; cf. Gal 3:19. [3]Mt 8:4 (= Mk 1:44 = Lk 5:14); 23:2; Jn 7:22f. [4]Acts 3:22; 7:37. [5]Jn 5:45f.; 7:28f.; 2 Cor 3:15.

2. In the eyes of Christians, Jesus was superior to Moses, who prefigured him as the head and redeemer, legislator and prophet.[6]

[6]Mt 17:3; Jn 1:17,45; Acts 7:35; 13:38; 26:22; Heb 3:2f.

→ Aaron—covenant—law—mediator—prophet.

[Moses (Assumption, Apocalypse of)]

1. The *Assumption of Moses* is an O.T. apocryphal* writing, dating from shortly after Herod's death (4 B.C.).

2. The *Apocalypse of Moses* is an O.T. apocryphal* writing, dated between 20 B.C. and A.D. 50. It is identical with The *Life of Adam and Eve,* a title that describes more exactly its content.

moth

Gk. *sēs.* A larva that reduced fabrics,* which were some of the riches of the day,[1] to dust.

[1]Mt 6:19f.; Lk 12:33; Jas 5:2 □.

→ worm.

mother

Gk. *mētēr.*

1. The N.T. is aware of the joys and tribulations of a woman* who conceived,[1] was pregnant,[2] gave birth in pain,[3] suckled her infant at the breast,[4] cared about her children's future[5] or wept over those that were no more.[6] Motherhood was a good and wholesome thing.[7] Like the father, the mother was entitled to filial devotion.[8]

[1]Lk 1:24,31,36; 2:21. [2]Mt 1:18,23; Lk 2:5. [3]Lk 1:13,57; 23:29; Jn 16:21; Rv 12:2,4f. [4]Mt 24:19 (= Mk 13:17 = Lk 21:23); Lk 11:27. [5]Mt 20:20. [6]Mt 2:18. [7]1 Tim 2:15; 5:14. [8]Mt 15:4-6 (= Mk 7:10-12); 19:19 (= Mk 10:19 = Lk 18:20).

2. In the N.T. a mother's dignity derived from the fact that Jesus was born of a woman[9] and that he was inseparable from "his mother."[10] Moreover, in her Jesus admired merely the one who had heard the Word of God[11] and was not afraid of losing it during the time of his public life[12] or even on the very day of his death;[13] "his mother" was whoever did the will of "his Father."[14] So, the call to follow Jesus can take precedence over filial devotion.[15]

[9]Gal 4:4. [10]Mt 2:11,13f.,20. [11]Lk 11:27f. [12]Lk 2:48; Jn 2:4. [13]Jn 19:27. [14]Mt 12:46-50 (= Mk 3:31-35 = Lk 8:19-21). [15]Mt 10:35,37 (= Lk 12:53; 14:26); 19:29 (= Mk 10:29f.).

3. The maternal task was applied metaphorically to the heavenly Jerusalem, which supplanted the Jerusalem below,[16] thereby becoming the Woman above all others.[17] In God's own image himself,[18] Jesus acted like a mother who gathered her children together.[19] Paul likened his ministry* to giving birth[20] and to the tender concerns of a mother.[21]

[16]Gal 4:26; Rv 21:2. [17]Rv 12. [18]Is 49:15; 66:13. [19]Lk 19:41-44. [20]Gal 4:19. [21]1 Thes 2:7f.

→ child—father—woman.

mountain Gk. *oros,* Heb. *har.*

1. In the majority of religions, the mountain was considered as the point where the sky met the earth. It was the place of the gods' assembly,[1] the place of the world's creation.[2] It could symbolize man's pride.[3] It constituted a privileged place for worship, such as the high places of Israel or Mount Zion;[4] but with the coming of Jesus Christ, it was neither on this or that mountain, but in spirit and truth, that man was to adore God.[5]

[1]Is 14:13. [2]Ez 28:14,16. [3]Is 2:12-15; Ez 6:3; Lk 3:5. [4]Ps 2:6; Jer 2:20. [5]Jn 4:20f.

2. The mountainous region of Israel and Judah[6] was a solitary, almost desert place[7] where it was good to pray[8] or even to take refuge in time of distress.[9]

[6]Lk 1:39,65. [7]Comp. Mt 18:12 and Lk 15:4; Mt 14:23; Mk 5:5,11 (= Lk 8:32f); Jn 6:3. [8]Mk 6:46; Lk 6:12; Jn 6:15. [9]Mt 24:16 (= Mk 13:14 = Lk 21:21); Lk 23:30; Heb 11:38; Rv 6:14-16.

3. Five mountains are explicitly mentioned: the Mount of Olives,* Sinai,*[10] Zion,*[11] Gerizim[12] and that of Nazareth.[13] However, it is difficult to be sure what mountain is meant in the following cases: the Temptation,[14] the Transfiguration,[15] the locale of the "Sermon on the Mount"[16] or the call of the disciples,[17] the mountains of Revelation,[18] a mountain where Jesus sat down,[19] the mountains referred to by Jesus in his teaching,[20] the mountain where Jesus held a rendez-vous.[21]

[10]Heb 8:55; 12:20. [11]Rv 21:10. [12]Jn 4:20f. [13]Lk 4:29. [14]Mt 4:8; cf. Lk 4:5. [15]Mt 17:1,9 (= Mk 9:2,9 = Lk 9:28,37); 2 Pt 1:18. [16]Mt 5:1; 8:1; cf. Lk 6:17. [17]Mk 3:13; Lk 6:12. [18]Rv 8:8; 16:20; 17:9. [19]Mt 15:29; Jn 6:3. [20]Mt 5:14; 17:20; 21:21; Mk 11:23; 1 Cor 13:2. [21]Mt 28:16.

→ Intr. II.3.—Armageddon—Hagar.

Mount of Olives Gk. *to oros tōn Elaiōn* or also *oros kaloumenon Elaiōn:* "the mountain called Olive":[1] *(Eleona).* A ridge some 3 km. (1.6 miles) east of Jerusalem, at least 1 km. (.62 mile) from the walls of the city, beyond the Kedron Valley.* It offered a splendid panorama of the city and onto the Temple parade. Near Kedron was found Gethsemane*; on the southern summit, Bethphage* (812 m. [2,664 ft.]); on the opposite slope, to the east, was Bethany.* The Roman road from Jericho to Jerusalem passed by the Mount of Olives. In Jesus' time, the hillock was covered with a thick forest of olive trees, quite suitable for solitary withdrawal.[2]

[1]Mt 21:1 (= Mk 11:1); 24:3 (= Mk 13:3); 26:30 (= Mk 14:26 = Lk 22:39); Jn 8:1. [2]Lk 19:29; 21:37; Acts 1:12 □.

→ Map 1.

mourning 1. Gk. *penthos:* "affliction." A show of sorrow which Jews extended for seven days,[1] the rites of mourning were also acts intended to ensure the peace of the dead, as they were among the neighboring peoples (although Israel excluded every kind of worship of the dead). In the first instance, mourning consisted in fasting*[2] as well as the tearing open of the neck of one's clothing,* in shaving one's head, wearing sackcloth,* sprinkling oneself with ashes,* beating one's breast,* weeping. At the family's cries, neighbors would come to join in prolonged lamentation* over the deceased[3] and to console those weeping.[4] As with everything associated with the dead, mourning was completed by a rite of purification.*[5] Exaggerated affliction does not become the Christian, who is not without hope,* since Jesus has conquered death.[6]

[1]Cf. Jn 11:39. [2]1 Sm 31:13; Mt 9:15. [3]Mt 2:18; Mk 5:38; Jn 16:20. [4]Mt 11:17 (= Lk 7:32); Lk 23:27; Jn 11:19; Acts 9:39; Rom 12:15. [5]Nm 31:19. [6]1 Thes 4:13.

2. In crucial circumstances,[7] similar rites indicated an act of collective penance.*

[7]Mt 11:21 (= Lk 10:13).

→ Intr. VIII.2.D.b.—bury—death—fast—lamentation—sackcloth—sadness.

multitude This word ordinarily translates the pronominal adjective, with or without the article, *(hoi) polloi,* corresponding to the Heb. *(ha)rabbim.* The Greek comparative meaning ("in contrast with others," "less numerous") is not acceptable except in two cases;[1] ordinarily, in keeping with O.T.[2] usage as well as that of Qumran,* the meaning is positive and refers to a totality.[3] Some translators, nonetheless, continue to hold out for a restrictive meaning ("many") in some cases, especially when the term is an adjective.[4]

[1]Mt 24:12; 2 Cor 2:17. [2]Is 52:14; 53:11f. [3]Mt 20:28; 26:28; Rom 5:15; 12:4f.; 1 Cor 12:12; Heb 9:28. [4]Mt 22:14; Lk 7:47; Rom 5:16.

mustard A plant common to Palestine, also called mustard seed (Gk. *kokkos sinapeōs*). It could grow to 3 m. (9.8 ft.) in height and even 4 m. (12.8 ft.) near the Lake of Gennesaret. Its grains, from which one drew the condiment of the same name, were so tiny that they proverbially indicated whatever was very small.[1]

[1]Mt 13:31 (= Mk 4:31 = Lk 13:19); 17:20 (= Lk 17:6) □.

mustard seed Gk. *sinapi.*[1]

[1]Mt 13:31 (= Mk 4:31 = Lk 13:19); 17:20 (= Lk 17:6) □.

→ mustard.

mute Gk. *a-lalos:* "one who does not speak,"[1] a handicapped person who was generally deaf* (Gk. *kōphos*) as well, as may be indicated by the context.[2]

Muteness could be a punishment, as it was inflicted on John the Baptist's father, or else the result of demonic possession.[4] Also without voice (Gk. *a-phōnos*) were the lamb* of Isaiah's prophecy, idols* and Balaam's ass.[5] Matthew did not highlight the healings of mutes as a messianic sign.[6]

[1]Mk 7:37; 9:17,25 △. [2]Mt 9:32f.; 12:22; 15:30f.; Lk 1:22; 11:14. [3]Lk 1:20,22,64. [4]Mt 9:33; Lk 11:14. [5]Acts 8:32; 1 Cor 12:2; 2 Pt 2:16. [6]Is 35:6; Mt 11:5.

→ deaf—voice—word.

myrrh Gk. *smyrna,* Heb. *môr* (from a root meaning: "bitter"). A precious balsam, made with a red resin imported from Arabia and used for wedding perfumes,*[1] for burials;*[2] as a component of the consecration oil, it could serve as an offering.[3] Mixed with wine* and bitter to the taste, myrrh increased heady courage; according to a Jewish custom, this drink was sometimes given to executed criminals.[4]

[1]Ps 45:8f.; Prv 7:17; Sg 1:13; 4:14; 5:5,13. [2]Jn 19:39. [3]Ex 30:23-35; Mt 2:11. [4]Mk 15:23.

→ perfume—vinegar.

Mysia Gk. *Mysia.* A region northwest of modern-day Turkey, integrated since 129 B.C. within the Roman province* of Asia.*[1]

[1]Acts 16:7f.; cf. 20:6 □.

→ Pergamum—Troas—Map 3.

mystery Gk. *mystērion* (from *myō:* "to close [the mouth]"; *myeō:* "to introduce" into cultic ceremonies, such as those of Eleusis, Isis, Mithra*; *mystēs:* "initiated"). Worship or knowledge restricted to initiates.

1. In the broad sense: "something hidden, obscure; a secret."[1] It corresponded to the Heb. *sôd*[2] and to the Aram. *râz.*[3] In the O.T. (Daniel,*[4] Wisdom*[5]) and apocryphal* literature (Enoch,* Qumran*), divine secrets concerning the eternal plan* of salvation; what was stressed was not so much the aspect of what was unfathomable to the reason, but the aspect of revelation.* Similarly, in the N.T., the term, which is ordinarily tied to a verb of revelation or of announcing, has nothing in common with the Greek mystery cults[6] nor with Oriental religions.

[1]Tb 12:7,11; Sir 27:16,21. [2]Am 3:7. [3]Dn 2. [4]Dn 2:28; 4:6. [5]Wis 2:22; 6:22; 12:5. [6]1 Cor 12:2; cf. Wis 14:23.

2. Three principal meanings can be disengaged from the N.T. data: God's great deeds, his interventions in the establishing of his reign,*[7] his hidden wisdom* revealed in Jesus Christ—the mystery above all others;[8] secret revelations;[9] the deep meaning of certain realities, such as Israel's destiny,[10] the activity of Antichrist,*[11] marriage.[12]

[7]Mt 13:11; 13:35; Rv 10:7. [8]Rom 16:25; 1 Cor 2:7f.; Eph 1:9; 3:3; 6:19; Col 1:25-27; 1 Tim 3:16. [9]Rv 1:20; 17:7. [10]Rom 11:25. [11]2 Thes 2:7. [12]Eph 5:32.

→ Intr. IV.6.B.C.

myth Gk. *mythos* (not deriving from *myeō:* "to initiate," but perhaps from an Indo-European root meaning "thought, consideration"): "word, narrative, fable."

1. In language contemporary with the N.T. (and in a degraded sense), the term was equivalent to "legend,"[1] in contrast to the true statements of eyewitnesses.[2]

[1] 1 Tim 1:4; 4:7; Ti 1:14. [2] 2 Tim 4:4; 2 Pt 1:16 □.

2. In the modern sense, myth is that discursive form given to what cannot, in truth, be handed on in a definition—a narrative in which the divine world conditions and clarifies the origin, nature and end of the world of men. Hence, myth must not be identified with imaginary accounts produced by human naïveté nor with the literary coating of some reality. According to its formal structure, myth is the present-day enactment of an event that belongs to the beginning, whether that event be considered historical or not.

3. Israel inherited these first expressions of religious existence; it took them up again within the perspective of an absolute monotheism. Thus, one can rightly speak of myth with regard to some narratives: Adam's sin, the flood, the wars of the nations and Antichrist,* the new Adam.* One can also recognize mythic motifs (extracts of mythical narratives) in some traditions, especially the apocalyptic.*

→ symbol—truth.

Naaman Gk. *Naiman.* A general of the Syrian army and a native of Damascus,* he was healed of leprosy by Elisha.*[1]

[1]2 Kgs 5; Lk 4:27 □.

[Nabatean] The Nabatean kingdom, which flourished from the first century B.C. to the first century A.D., extended from the Red Sea to Damascus, skirting the Holy Land. Its capital was Petra. In A.D. 106 it became the Roman province* of Arabia.* Its language was Aramaic.*

→ Arabia—Aretas IV.

[Nag Hammadi] A village of Upper Egypt, not far from Chenoboskion, the place where Pacomius founded some monasteries in the fourth century. Around 1947, thirteen books dating from the fourth century were found there; they constituted a library of some thousand pages, works for the most part translated from Greek into Coptic (the language of the Christians of Egypt, with a Greek alphabet and seven other letters deriving from the "demotic," the everyday writing of the ancient Egyptians). Among these books we note the following: *The Apocryphon* (the Secret Book of John), the *Wisdom of Jesus,* the *Gospel of Truth* (a homily intending to unveil the truth of the Gospel), the *Gospel of Thomas** and the *Gospel of Philip** (a florid collection of gnostic* utterances and thoughts).

→ apocryphal writings—gnosis.

name Gk. *onoma,* Heb. *shém.*

1. On the eighth day after birth, a man received from his parents (or from God himself) a name that expressed his role in the world;[1] this name was sometimes changed in the course of his lifetime.[2] In the Greco-Roman era, the Jews of the Diaspora* also had a second name, either Greek or Latin.[3]

[1]Gn 3:20; 1 Sm 25:25; Mt 1:21,23; Lk 1:13,63. [2]Gn 17:5; 32:28-30; 2 Kgs 23:34; Mt 16:18. [3]Acts 13:9.

2. According to a well-known conviction, the name told something about the person in the depth of his being. It spoke simultaneously of someone's active presence and of his distance, just as when Yahweh caused his Name to dwell on the earth.[4] Also, to know someone's name was to have access to the mystery of his being[5] and even to control him to some extent.[6]

[4]Dt 12:5; 2 Sm 7:13; 1 Kgs 3:2; 8:16. [5]Jn 10:3; Rv 19:12. [6]Gn 2:19f.; 2 Sm 5:9; 12:28; Ps 49:12.

3. "The Name" designated Yahweh* himself.[7] To know him was to discover oneself in his presence.[8] To call on him was to enter into communion with him;[9] to sanctify him was to recognize that he was God himself;[10] to pronounce his name in vain was to improperly dispose of his person.[11] Jesus revealed that "Father" was God's true name.[12]

[7]Lv 24:11-16; Dt 12:5; Ps 54:3; 89:25; Jn 12:28. [8]Ex 3:13-16; Jn 17:26. [9]Acts 2:36. [10]Is 29:23; Mt 6:9. [11]Ex 20:7; Rom 2:24; Rv 13:6. [12]Jn 17:6; Rom 8:15; Gal 4:6.

4. Jesus received the names Emmanuel,* Lord,* Christ,* Son of God.* He even inherited the Name that belonged to God alone.[13] As well, the believer was to pray and act in Jesus' name, that is to say, in intimate union with his power,[14] while awaiting the bestowal of a new name,[15] perhaps the one which is above every other name,[16] or else the name of the Son on whose name one called.[17]

[13]Acts 5:41; Phil 2:10f.; 3 Jn 7. [14]Mt 7:22; 18:20; Mk 9:38; 16:17; Lk 10:17; Jn 14:13f; 15:16; Acts 3:6; 10:43. [15]Is 62:2; Rv 2:17; 3:12; 14:1. [16]Phil 2:9. [17]Mt 5:9; 1 Jn 3:1.

→ blaspheme—vocation.

nard Gk. *nardos.* The perfumed oil of a Himalayan plant; extremely rare, it was often counterfeited. According to late Judaism, nard was one of the things that Adam* took with him from Paradise.*[1]

[1]Mk 14:3; Jn 12:3 □.

→ perfume.

Nathanael Heb. *nᵉhan'ēl:* "God has given." According to John, a native of Cana, one of Jesus' first disciples, a type of the Israelite who is capable of faith. Beginning in the ninth century, some people identified him with Bartholomew* who, like him, was named along with Philip.*[1]

[1]Jn 1:45-50; 21:2; cf. Mt 10:3 □.

nation, nations **1.** In the singular, the Gk. *ethnos* (Heb. *gôy*) signified a nation in the political sense of that term,[1] the Jewish nation,[2] or the Christian people as well, the new generation,[3] the holy nation.[4]

[1]Mt 24:7; Acts 7:7; 8:9. [2]Lk 7:5; 23:2; Jn 11:48,50-52; 18:35; Acts 10:22; 24:2,10,17; 26:4; 28:19 △. [3]Mt 21:43; cf. Jer 7:28f. [4]1 Pt 2:9; cf. Ex 19:6.

2. In the plural, the Gk. *ethnē* (Heb. *gôyîm*) designated in a shorthand way, the pagan* nations, or, exceptionally, Christians of pagan background,[5] ordinarily, all those who did not yet constitute a part of the chosen people,[6] in some sense "the others," those who possessed neither Jewish nor Christian faith.[7] English translations seem not to preserve the term "nations" except within O.T. quotations.[8] More rarely, the context reveals that the meaning remains a political one. In several cases, however, this distinction is uncertain.[9]

[5]Rom 11:25; Gal 2:12; Eph 3:1. [6]Gn 10:5; Dt 7:6; Jer 10:25; Mt 4:15; 10:5; 20:25; Lk 21:24; Acts 4:25. [7]Mt 6:32; 1 Cor 5:1; 12:2; 1 Pt 2:12. [8]For example: Mt 12:18. [9]Lk 21:25; 24:47.

→ Gentiles—pagan—people.

natural man

→ spirit 4.

navigate Gk. *pleō.* A term maintained, chiefly by Luke, to describe various tasks: to embark,[1] to set sail,[2] to sail,[3] to disembark.[4]

[1]Acts 15:39; 18:18; 20:6. [2]Acts 13:4; 14:26; 20:15; 27:1. [3]Acts 20:16; 21:7; 27:2,4-10,24; Rv 18:17. [4]Lk 8:26 □.

→ Intr. IV.3.B.

Nazara, Nazareth Gk. *Nazaret*(h)[1] or *Nazara;*[2] in Aram. perhaps *naṣerat* or *naṣerâ.* An insignificant large village of Galilee, not mentioned by the O.T., by Josephus* or by the Talmud.* It was situated at an elevation of some 350 m. [1,148 ft.] and was located 4.5 km. [2.8 mi.] from Sepphoris, the place where Judas the Galilean led his revolt in A.D. 6.[3] Through Nazareth there ran a highway which connected Sepphoris to a secondary road joining Damascus to Egypt.

[1]Mt 2:23; 21:11; Mk 1:9; Lk 1:26; 2:4,39,51; Jn 1:45f.; Acts 10:38 △. [2]Mt 4:13; Lk 4:16 △. [3]Intr. II.3.B; XI.4.

→ Map 4.

Nazarene, Nazorean **1.** Gk. *Nazarēnos,* to be translated by "Nazarenean" or "from Nazareth": a citizen of Nazareth.*[1]

[1]Mk 1:24; 10:47; 14:67; 16:6; Lk 4:34; 24:19 △.

2. Gk. *Nazāraios,* translated by Nazorean or Nazarene: a term designating Jesus,[1] the Galilean,[2] and once designating Christians.[3] The term poses an unresolved etymological problem. It has sometimes been made to derive from the Heb. *nâzîr:* "consecrated, holy,"[4] at other times from *néṣèr:* "scion"[5] or at still others from *neṣûrîm:* "the remnant."[6]

[1]Mt 2:23; Lk 18:37; Jn 18:5,7; 19:19; Acts 2:22; 3:6; 4:10; 6:14; 22:8; 26:9. [2]Comp. Mt 26:71 and 26:69. [3]Acts 24:5 △. [4]Jgs 13:5; cf. 16:17; Mk 1:24. [5]Is 11:1. [6]Is 49:6.

[Nazareth Inscription] An inscription, said to be from Nazareth, was discovered in 1878; a slab of marble measuring 0.6 m. × 0.375 m. (23.6 in. × 14.8 in.) on which there was discovered, written in Greek, an ordinance against the desecration of burial places. Specialists today are agreed that it is recognizable as the translation of a Latin text from the emperor Augustus' edict, published by the procurator Coponius in the year 8, at the time of an act of Temple profanation by the Samaritans. They had strewn the bones of corpses there. This edict ought not to be associated with the narrative of the alleged removal of Jesus' corpse by his disciples (Mt 27:62–66; 28:11–15). The following is a translation of the *Diatagma Kaisaros:* "Caesar's Ordinance: It pleases me that the burial places and tombs which people have religiously erected for their elders or children or near relations should remain unalterable in perpetuity. If, however, an accuser should bring charges against someone, either of having destroyed them or of having exhumed in some other manner the bodies which had been buried, whether by having transferred them elsewhere by some fraudulent maneuver and with injurious consequences or, finally, by having changed the location (or wording) of the tablets or tombstones, I decree that the guilty party should be condemned (or put under judgment) for an outrage against religion in regard to men, with the same rigor as for an outrage against filial devotion in reference to the gods (or as in a matter of outrage against the deity through the dereliction of the obligations which men have toward the gods). For, one must honor the dead much more (than has been done). It is absolutely forbidden to anyone to change (the tombs) (or to displace the bodies). Otherwise, I desire that the guilty one, as the leader of the burial place desecration, be condemned to death" (trans. J. Schmitt).

Nazirite From the Heb. *nâzîr:* "set apart, consecrated." A person performing a religious practice deriving from a vow,* occasionally permanent,[1] sometimes limited to thirty days;[2] in the latter case, it concluded with a Temple sacrifice.[3] In virtue of this vow, one was held to not cut one's hair, to not drink fermented liquor, and to not contract legal impurities.[4]

[1]Jgs 13:4f.; 1 Sm 1:11,28; Lk 1:15; cf. Am 2:11. [2]Nm 6:2. [3]1 Mc 3:49; Acts 21:23. [4]Nm 6:1-21.

→ vow.

neck Gk. *trachēlos:* "neck."[1] That part of a beast's body that grew stiff under the yoke; hence, "stiff-necked" (Gk. *sklēro-trachēlos*), a symbol of obstinacy.[2]

[1]Mt 18:6 (= Mk 9:42 = Lk 17:2); Lk 15:20; Acts 15:10; 20:37; Rom 16:4 △. [2]Acts 7:51; cf. Is 48:4 △.

neighbor Gk. *plēsion:* "near to," the Septuagint's* paradoxical translation of the Heb. *réa':* "the other," the one who is not my brother by blood, but whose associate or companion one wishes to become. The opposite of the brother* to whom one is bound by a blood relationship, the neighbor does not belong to the parental home but is the one who draws near. On this subject two traits differentiate the N.T. from the Hebrew O.T. My neighbor, to whom justice is due, is not only the Israelite brother,[1] not even the resident alien* alone,[2] but rather every person who draws near to me, even though he be an enemy.[3] Moreover, through the Good Samaritan parable[4] Jesus summoned me no longer to ask "Who is my neighbor?" but instead "Am I not a neighbor to this man who is in difficulty?"; I am no longer at the center of things, but he/she is.

[1]Lv 17:3; 19:11,13,16-18. [2]Lv 17:8,10,13; 19:34. [3]Mt 5:43-48. [4]Lk 10:29-37.

→ Intr. VIII.2.A; XIV.1.B.—brother—love—stranger.

netherworld **1.** Literally "the infernal regions," from the Lat. *inferi, inferni* (the plural of *infer, infernus:* "beneath, lower"). The dwelling-place of the dead,* distinct from what we call hell.* The English word embraces diverse Greek designations: Sheol,* Hades,* the Abyss,* Tartarus,* the depths of the earth.[1] Two images sustain this depiction: a) the "underneath" (of the earth), the part below, the place to which one goes down, into which one is cast down;[2] b) the "enclosed" place, like a city with gates* and keys.* God, and not Satan,* is its master.[3] For a time the dead lead a diminished existence there, without a real relationship with God.[4]

[1]Ps 18:5f.; 42:8; 63:10; 69:2f.; 95:4; Mt 12:40; Acts 2:24; Rom 8:39; Eph 4:9; Rv 5:3,13. [2]Mt 11:23 (= Lk 10:15). [3]Jb 26:6; Ps 9:14; Wis 16:13; Is 26:19; 38:10; Mt 16:18; Acts 2:27,31. [4]Jb 10:21f.; 26:5; Ps 6:6; 30:10; 88:6,12; 115:17; Prv 1:12; 27:20; Is 5:14; 14:9.

2. Late Judaism assigned the dead to places that either anticipated the eternal punishment of the wicked or the happiness (Paradise*) of the just: such was the case with the rich man and Lazarus.[5]

[5]Lk 16:22-26.

3. In descending to the nether regions at his death, Christ went to proclaim his triumph to the angelic powers and the just ones who were waiting for it there.[6] With belief in the resurrection, the underworld yielded its place to a hell for the wicked and a heaven* for the just, that is to say, yielded to Christ.[7]

[6]1 Pt 3:19-21; 4:6. [7]2 Cor 5:18; Phil 1:23; 1 Pt 3:19.

→ Intr. V.1.—abyss—Hades—hell—paradise—Sheol—Tartarus.

new Two Greek words depict newness. *Kainos* (K), the more frequent, described what had never yet been used,[1] what was unexpected,[2] discovered, totally other, what was an innovation. *Neos* (N) told of what was new with respect to what had been past, to what was young rather than old: hence, the youngest[3] or unaged wine.[4] Sometimes, one term or the other was coupled with the word "old" (Gk. *palaios*) to express totality[5] or opposites: the Spirit and the letter,[6] the new man and the old man,[7] the new being and the old,[8] the two covenants,[9] the new commandment,[10] the new yeast,[11] a renewed judgement.[12]

[1]Mt 9:17 (Mk 2:21f. = Lk 5:38); 27:60 (= Jn 19:41). [2]Mk 16:17. [3](N) Lk 15:12f.; 22:26; Jn 21:18. [4](N) Mt 9:17 (= Mk 2:22 = Lk 5:37-39). [5]Mt 13:52. [6]Rom 7:6. [7]Eph 4:24; Col 3:10 (K and N). [8]2 Cor 5:17. [9]Heb 8:13; 12:24 (N). [10]1 Jn 2:7. [11]1 Cor 5:7. [12]Eph 4:23.

1. Before all else, it was the Covenant* that, fulfilling prophecy,[13] was new;[14] with it all creation[15] and life[16] had been renewed[17] through a spirit of newness.[18]

[13]Jer 31:31; Ez 36:26. [14]Lk 22:20; 1 Cor 11:25; 2 Cor 3:6; Heb 8:8,13; 9:15; Heb 12:24 (N). [15]Rv 21:5. [16]2 Cor 5:17; Gal 6:15. [17]Rom 6:4. [18]Rom 7:6; Ti 3:5.

2. With his coming, Jesus brought a new teaching[19] and gave his commandment, new in the sense that he himself linked it to the New Covenant.[20]

[19]Mk 1:27; Acts 17:19,21. [20]Jn 13:34; 1 Jn 2:7f.; 2 Jn 2:5.

3. Christ,[21] the New Man,* made believers to be new men,[22] who, through the Spirit were ceaselessly to renew their judgments,[23] their inner selves;[24] they had received a new name.*[25]

[21]Eph 2:15. [22]Eph 4:24; Col 3:10 (K and N); cf. Heb 6:6. [23]Rom 12:2; Eph 4:23 (N). [24]2 Cor 4:16; Col 3:10 (N). [25]Rv 2:27; 3:12.

4. The Church strained towards new heavens and a new earth,[26] the heavenly Jerusalem,[27] where Jesus, with his disciples, would drink the new wine,[28] and where the chosen ones would sing a new song.[29]

[26]2 Pt 3:13; Rv 21:1. [27]Rv 3:12; 21:2. [28]Mt 26:29 (= Mk 14:25). [29]Rv 5:9; 14:3.

→ dedication—old man.

new moon Gk. *neomēnia,* from *neos:* "new" and *mēnē:* "moon": "new moon, new month, first day of the month."[1]

[1]Gal 4:10; Col 2:16 □.

→ calendar—month—moon—year.

New Testament Gk. *hē kainē diathēkē:* "the new covenant."* The collection of twenty-seven books received by the Church as canonical.*

→ Intr. XV.—Bible—canon—testament.

Nicodemus Gk. *Nikodēmos* ("victorious people"), a name frequent among the Greeks and in Jewish tradition. A Pharisee,* an eminent Jew, a "doctor of Israel," perhaps a member of the Sanhedrin.* John depicted him as an upright man, faithful but timorous and even obtuse when he encountered Jesus.[1]

[1]Jn 3:1,4,9; 7:50; 19:39 □.

Nicolaitans Gk. *Nikolaitai.* According to Rv 2:6, 15 □, a sect, probably a Christian one, perhaps of gnostic* or libertine leanings. We do not know the identity of the Nicolas from whom they took their name.

night Gk. *nyx.*

1. In the Roman era, the period extending from the setting to the rising of the sun was divided into four watches,* the length of which was not constant.

2. The symbolism of creation saw in night both mortal darkness and hope for the day.[1] It was reinterpreted as an aspect of the paschal night in which salvation had been effected.[2] Henceforward, a believer, even if still *in* the night, was no longer *of* the night, right up until that day* on which there will be light without fail.[3] God spontaneously revealed himself during the night,[4] a privileged time of prayer.[5]

[1]Gn 1:5; Ps 130:6; Is 21:11; Jn 11:10; Rom 13:12. [2]Ex 11:4; 12:12,29; Wis 18:14f.; 1 Cor 11:23. [3]Thes 5:5; Rv 21:25; 22:5. [4]Acts 5:19; 16:9; 18:9; 23:11; 27:23; 1 Thes 5:2. [5]Mk 1:35; Lk 6:12.

→ darkness—day—light—watch.

[Nisan] A Babylonian name for the month* which began at the first new moon following the spring equinox (March/April). In the time of Jesus, this month was the first of the year.

→ calendar.

Noah Gk. *Nōe,* from the Heb. *Noah* (*nwh:* "to rest").[1] In keeping with the priestly,[2] sapiential[3] and apocalyptic (Book of Enoch*)[4] traditions, the N.T. saw in him a type of that just and vigilant man who escaped imminent punishment and was the beneficiary of salvation.[5]

[1]Gn 5:29–9:28; Lk 3:36. [2]Gn 6:9. [3]Wis 10:4; Sir 44:17. [4]*Book of Enoch* 6:1–11:2; 60:1-25; 65:1–69:25; 106:1–107:3. [5]Mt 24:37-39 (= Lk 17:26f.); Heb 11:7; 1 Pt 3:20; 2 Pt 2:5.

→ flood.

noon **1.** The hour. The middle of the day (Gk. *mesēmbria, hēmeras mesēs*), the sixth hour.*[1]

[1]Acts 22:6; 26:13 □.

2. The territory. The countries of the south (Gk. *mesēmbria*).[2] The ordinary term was *notos,* which properly speaking meant "the south wind."[3]

[2]Gn 24:62; Acts 8:26 □. [3]Sg 4:16; Mt 12:42 (= Lk 11:31); Lk 12:55; 13:29; Acts 27:13; Rv 21:13 □.

→ day—hour.

numbers **1.** In addition to numbers of exact or approximate arithmetical value, there also were numbers with symbolic* meanings that were not always easy to decipher. Clearly, the Bible did not depend on Pythagorean speculations (in which 1 and 3 were masculine, 2 and 4 were feminine, 7 was virginal), but it did present sufficiently clear cases of symbolic values: 4—cosmic totality; 7—a complete series, like the week,* a number whose perfection was divisible (3+4 or 3½) or not reached (7−1=6); 10—the mnemonic value of the ten fingers; 12—a perfect figure of the 12 lunar cycles, the ancient base of Sumero-Akkadian computations and the number of the 12 tribes*; 40—the years of a generation.

2. Numbers designated as triangular resulted from calculations dear to the ancients: it was possible to represent them by an equilateral triangle wherein the units out of which they had been composed were written out horizontally (∴̇). They constituted the arithmetical sum of the n first numbers ($1+2+3+4+\ldots n$) a sum which is equal to

$$n\,\frac{n+1}{2}.$$

Thus, for the 120 people in the Upper Room (Acts 1:15) $n=15$, for the 153 large fish (Jn 21:11) $n=17$, for 666, the number of the Beast* (Rv 13:18), $n=36$ (itself a number obtained from $n=8$, corresponding to the eighth king of Rv 17:11, or the square of 6 as well, the imperfect number par excellence).

3. Gematrias allowed for the interpretation of some numbers that represented the addition of a numerical value that had been assigned to the different letters of the alphabet. Thus, 666=NRWN QSR (Nero Caesar)=50+200+6+50+100+60+200; or LATEINOS = 30+1+300+5+10+50+70+200: that is, the Roman Empire. Without doubt it is difficult to demonstrate the exactness of this hypothesis, and 666 could simply, through its repetition of 6 (7−1), designate the imperfection above all others.

O

oath **1.** Gk. *horkos, horkizō.* Oaths hold a large position in the O.T.,[1] not in order to take God as the witness for what one proposed but in order to call upon God so that he might act on the one who spoke: such was the meaning of "to take God's Name."[2] Also, oaths were readily advised against.[3] It came to be agreed upon that one was "to swear" (Gk. *omnyō*) by substitutes for the Name*; Jesus denounced not only the inherent risk of perjury in this, but further declared that in fact one ought not swear at all.[4] Jesus even added a positive injunction which has been variously interpreted. According to Matthew,[5] "let your word be 'Yes, yes,' 'No, no'; all else comes from the Evil One," that is: Your speech ought to be absolutely true. According to James:[6] "Let your yes be a yes and your no be a no," that is: Your lips ought to utter what is in your heart. Man cannot swear by the God who does not belong to him; the sole guarantee of one's language is to be fraternal sincerity.

[1]Lv 5:4f. [2]Ex 20:7. [3]Sir 23:9f. [4]Mt 5:33-35. [5]Mt 5:36f. [6]Jas 5:12.

2. Jesus introduced his most solemn pronouncements with "Amen,* I say to you," which might have been akin to his response to an interior revelation of the Father. He agreed to reply to the High Priest who administered an oath to him.[7] God had undertaken to engage himself by a promise or an oath,[8] while men, Herod[9] or Peter,[10] undertook one to their condemnation.

[7]Mt 26:63f. [8]Lk 1:73; Acts 2:30; Heb 3:11,18; 4:3; 6:13,17; 7:20f,28. [9]Mt 14:7,9 (= Mk 6:23,26). [10]Mt 26:72,74 (= Mk 14:71).

obedience, obey Generally, obedience and disobedience translate the Greek *hyp-akoē, par-akoē*, which describe something heard (Gk. *akoē,* from *akouō:* "to listen, to hear"): this means to hear* the voice by putting oneself under it *(hypo)* or to refuse to hear it by putting oneself off to the side of it *(para):* hence, an attitude of clinging to the faith*[1] or a refusal of it by the estrangement of oneself from it.[2] Sometimes, these words translate the terms *peithomai, apeitheō*, which mean "to let oneself be persuaded" or "to rebel," "to trust" or "to distrust," to be docile or to be intractable, to submit oneself to or to resist.[3]

[1]Gn 22:18; Ex 5:2; 1 Sm 15:22; Mt 8:27 (= Mk 4:41); Rom 1:5; 5:19; 10:16; 2 Cor 10:5; Phil 2:8; Heb 11:8. [2]Mt 18:17; Mk 5:36; Rom 5:19; 2 Cor 10:6; Heb 2:2. [3]Lk 1:17; Acts 5:29,32; 26:19; 27:21; Rom 1:30; 2:8; 10:21; 11:30-32; Gal 5:7; Eph 2:2; 5:6; Heb 3:18; 4:6,11; Jas 3:3.

→ covenant—ear—fidelity—God's will—hear—sin—trust.

[obol] Gk. *obolos.* A small Greek coin, worth one-sixth of a drachma,* or copper piece (Gk. *chalkos*).

→ coins.

offering Gk. *prosphora,* from *pros-pherō:* "to bring."

→ present—sacrifice—worship.

oil Gk. *elaion, elaia:* "olive tree"; in Heb. *shèmèn:* "fatty," *yiṣehâr:* "bursting, sparkling." Except for pure oil,[1] it was obtained by pressure on crushed olives.[2] A vital foodstuff[3] and a sign of blessing.*[4] Oil had various uses: it was a source of light*;[5] it could also alleviate wounds,[6] strengthen the sick,[7] give a glow to one's complexion[8] and gladden one's heart.[9] Mixed in with perfumes, it was a mark of respect given to one's guests.[10]

[1]Ex 27:20. [2]Jb 24:11. [3]Sir 39:26. [4]Dt 7:13; 28:40. [5]Mt 25:3f. [6]Is 1:6; Lk 10:34. [7]Mk 6:13; Jas 5:14. [8]Ps 104:15; Mt 6:17. [9]Ps 45:8; Is 61:3; Heb 1:9. [10]Ps 23:5; Lk 7:46.

→ anoint—perfume.

old age, old man The old man (Gk. *gerōn, presbytēs*) was worthy of respect and of submission[1] because of his great age and his experience. So, the Ancient of Days in Dn 7:9, became visible to the Son of Man with white hair.[2] The leading citizens, among Jews and Christians[3] alike, bore the name of elders (Gk *presbyteroi*). The old men of the book of Revelation are suggestive of the responsible officials of Israel or of the churches, or else they symbolize the everlasting nature of God's court.[4]

In other respects, riches acquired from experience can result in a closing in on the past or a rejection of the newness brought by Jesus.[5] In such cases we have instances of culpable aging (Gk. *palaiotēs*), that of the old man which has to give way to the new man.[6]

[1]1 Tim 5:1f. [2]Rv 1:14. [3]Mt 21:23; Acts 11:30; 15:4. [4]Rv 4:4ff. [5]Mt 15:2; 27:1,41. [6]Rom 6:6; 7:6; Eph 4:22; Col 3:9f.; Heb 8:13.

→ Intr. VIII.2.C.e.—elder.

olive tree Gk. *elaia.* With the fig tree and the vine, one of the three plants that are characteristic of Israel.[1] Always green, it spontaneously symbolized the just person[2] and the Wisdom that reveals the path of justice.[3]

[1]Intr. II,5; VII.1.A; Rom 11:17,24; Jas 3:12. [2]Ps 52:10; Rv 11:4. [3]Sir 24:14,19-23.

→ Intr. II.5; VII.1.A.—graft—oil.

Olives (Mount of)

→ Mount of Olives.

Omega

→ Alpha and Omega.

Onesimus Gk. *Onēsimos:* "useful, profitable, advantageous." A slave on whose behalf Paul interceded in the note sent to Philemon,* who was probably his master.[1]

[1]Col 4:9; Phlm 10 □.

→ Archippus—Philemon.

oracle The deity's response to a man who consulted it. The N.T. mentions this practice of divination (Gk. *manteuomai*),[1] but does not use the proper term *chrēmatismos* except with the meaning of a revelation* given by God;[2] with the verb *chrēmatizō* this revelation sometimes takes on the aspect of a warning, which leads to the frequent translation: "divinely warned by . . . ," but there it is simply a case of an instruction: God reveals his will to Joseph, to Simeon, to Cornelius, to Moses, to Noah or to men, without their having prayed for it.[3] Outside of these cases, the English translation "oracle" adds a dimension which the N.T. itself seems to have attempted to avoid, particularly since the Septuagint,* which it ordinarily follows, did not in that instance take up the term *chrēmatizō* but preserved instead the verb "to speak" (Gk. *legō,* Heb. *dibbèr*). Without doubt, in one instance the context (with its use of the Gk. *logia*) can suggest this very interpretation,[4] but it serves no purpose to confer upon biblical simplicity a magical overtone which it had shaken off.[5]

[1]Acts16:16△. [2]Rom 11:4 △. [3]Mt 2:12,22; Lk 2:26; Acts 10:22; Heb 8:5; 11:7; 12:25 △. [4]Acts 7:38. [5]Mt 2:17; 12:17; 13:35; 21:4; 22:31; 27:9; Rom 3:2; Heb 5:12.

→ dream—magic—revelation.

order **1.** For the N.T. as for the O.T., God created the universe "with measure and number and weight."[1] When addressing the pagans, Paul revealed this arrangement, noting how God had established set times, seasons, etc.[2]

[1]Wis 11:20. [2]Acts 14:17; 17:24-27.

2. Gk. *taxis, tagma.* The assembly of Christians, even when numbering *charismatics, had to keep itself decently in order.[3]

[3]1 Cor 14:40; 15:23; cf. Col 2:5.

3. "According to the order of Melchizedek*" meant "according to Melchizedek's manner," to distinguish the two kinds of priesthood.*[4] This expression has nothing in common with the "power of order."

[4]Heb 5:6,10; 6:20; 7:11,17 △; cf. Ps 110:4.

Orient Lat. *oriens* (present participle of *oriri:* "to rise"), Gk. *anatolē* (from *ana-tellō:* "to cause to rise"): "the rising sun, the east."

1. One of the four cardinal points. "To orient oneself" was to face the rising sun[1] (just as the Magi* faced the star),[2] it was to have the south (the Negev) on one's right hand, the west (the Sea*) in back and the north (the hidden region) at one's left.

[1]Ez 43:1; Rv 21:13. [2]Mt 2:2,9.

2. A territory situated east of the Jordan,[3] that place in which one found "the sons of the Orient,"[4] or even still farther away.[5] Exceptionally, misfortune[6] could come from this region; generally, however, it was happiness, like the glory of Israel's God, that came.[7]

[3]Nm 32:19. [4]Jgs 6:3. [5]Mt 2:1; 8:11 (= Lk 13:29); 24:27. [6]Rv 16:12. [7]Ez 43:2; Rv 7:2; cf. 2 Pt 1:19.

3. It was used metaphorically to indicate that light which followed upon darkness,[8] the star or the sun of justice.[9]

[8]Is 8:23; 9:1; Mt 4:16. [9]Lk 1:78. [10]Mal 3:20.

→ morning—noon—stars—sun.

orphan Gk. *orphanos.* According to the O.T., succor of orphans, the most unprovided for of individuals—along with widows* and resident aliens*—was an act of piety* prescribed by the Law,[1] a sign of the justice*[2] which can be characteristic of sincere religion.[3] The metaphoric meaning, "to be deprived of one's leader," is taken up with a note of tenderness in the Last Supper discourse.[4]

[1]Dt 14:29. [2]Jb 29:12. [3]Jas 1:27. [4]Jn 14:18 □; cf. Lam 5:3.

outer court Gk. *hē aulē hē exōthen tou naou:* "the court outside the sanctuary." A walkway surrounding the sanctuary* inside the Temple.*[1]

[1]Rv 11:2 □.

oven

→ furnace.

P

pagan From the Lat. *paganus:* "rustic," a name for non-Christians who had to retire into a rural district *(pagus)* after Christianity's expansion in the Roman world. The Gk. term *ethnikos* (derived from *ethnē:* "nations") meant the non-Jew.[1] The pagans (Gk. *hoi ex ethnōn*) were distinguished from the chosen people* in that they did not know God,[2] but they could still be used as examples:[3] they themselves were also called by God[4] and even were called to faith.[5] The Jews/pagans distinction has survived throughout the existence of the Church, which has anticipated their reconciliation.[6]

[1]Is 8:23; Mt 5:47; 6:7; 18:17; 3 Jn 7; cf. Gal 2:14 □. [2]Gal 2:15; Eph 2:11f. 1 Thes 4:5. [3]Mt 5:47; Rom 15:9-12. [4]Is 45; Mt 8:10; Acts 14:16. [5]Lk 13:28; Acts 11:1,18; Rv 12:5; 15:4; 21:24. [6]Rom 9–11; Eph 2:11-21.

→ Intr. I.3.C; III.2.G; IV.6–7; VI.1.B.—Gentiles—nations.

[Palestine] Gk. *hē Palestinē (Syria),* Heb. *peleshèt.* Originally, the country of the Philistines (who nonetheless had occupied but a small part of it); then, a region integrated into the Roman province of Syria* in A.D. 65; finally, beginning in A.D. 139, the Roman province of Judea.

→ Intr. I.1; II; III.1–2.—Map 4.

palm tree Once abundant in the Jordan Valley, the date palm (Gk. *phoinix,* Heb. *tâmâr*) was held to be sacred and its motif was depicted on the Temple and on certain synagogues.[1] A metaphor of the just man, of beauty and of wisdom.[2] People gathered its branches (Gk. *baion*) as a joyous sign at the Feast of Booths*[3] or for triumphs of victorious leaders.[4]

[1]Jgs 4:5; 1 Kgs 6:29-35; Ez 40:16. [2]Ps 92:13; Sg 7:8; Sir 24:14. [3]Lv 23:40. [4]1 Mc 13:37,51; Jn 12:13; Rv 7:9 □.

→ Intr. II.5.

Paphos

→ Cyprus, Cypriots.

parable **1.** Several terms were used to describe the literary form that operated by way of simile and riddle. The Greek words were *parabolē* (*para* and *ballō:* "to set side by side") and *paroimia,* corresponding to the Hebrew *mâshâl* and *hîddâ,* and had a more extensive reach. In fact, these referred not only to the developed simile, but also to the riddle, the allegorizing simile, whose goal was not merely to provide an illustration, but also to elicit a search for its meaning.

2. The Synoptics* occasionally designate a saying or a proverb[1] as a parable, but more generally use it for an extended simile or a story that was a delight to hear: such were the parables of the Kingdom, of the murderous vinedressers, of the wedding banquet, of the fig tree, of Satan casting out Satan, of the speck and the beam, of the rich man, of the vigilant servant, of the barren fig tree, of the invitation to the supper, of the lost sheep, of the wicked judge and the widow, of the Pharisee and the publican, of the talents.[2] Apart from their contexts, the different elements of these parables are without meaning; they converge to shape a single teaching.

[1]Mt 15:15 (= Mk 7:17); Lk 4:23; 5:36. [2]Mt 13 (= Mk 4 = Lk 8); 21:33-45 (= Mk 12:1-11 = Lk 20:9-18); 22:1-14 (= Lk 14:15-24); 24:32 (= Mk 13:28 = Lk 21:29); Mk 3:23; Lk 6:39; 12:16; 12:41; 13:6; 14:7; 15:3; 18:1; 18:9; 19:11.

3. John preferred the Greek term *paroimia,* which he spontaneously contrasted with *parrēsia:* "freedom of speech,"[3] conferring on the word a meaning that was more enigmatic than "parable." Moreover, one must observe that *paroimia* was used, additionally, in the sense of a proverb.[4] Because of their content one is brought to the point of associating Johannine parables with allegories,* in which, contrary to parables, the various details each have a specific meaning: the good shepherd, the true vine.[5]

[3]Jn 16:25,29. [4]2 Pt 2:22. [5]Jn 10:6; 15:1-6.

4. The word *parabolē* was also used in the sense of a symbol* or a figure.*[6]

[6]Heb 9:9; 11:19.

→ allegory—mystery—revelation—teach—wisdom.

Paraclete Gk. *paraklētos,* a Johannine word related to *paraklēsis:* "consolation," but with a different meaning; it was tied to *parakaleō* taken in the sense of "to call near to oneself," a juridical term referring to the one who was "called to the side of" (the Gk. passive of *parakaleō,* Lat. *ad-vocatus*) an accused, to defend him or help him. This function was carried out by the Holy Spirit on Christ's behalf within the hearts of his disciples[1] or by Christ before his Father on behalf of the disciples.[2] The Paraclete indicated three aspects of the Holy Spirit's activity: Jesus' presence,[3] Jesus' defense,[4] the Church's living memory which allowed her to bring about what Jesus said.[5]

[1]Jn 14:16. [2]1 Jn 2:1. [3]Jn 14:15-17. [4]Jn 15:26; 16:7. [5]Jn 14:26 □.

Paradise The Gk. *paradeisos* (derived from the Persian, cf. Heb. *pardés:* "park") translated the Heb. *gân:* "garden." In keeping with those who imagined the existence of the gods to be like the happy life of fortunate folk here below, Eden was characterized as the original Paradise,[1] the Paradise of delights,[2] the Paradise of God,[3] the one wherein one hoped to live with God "in the highest heavens."[4] Judaism saw in it the hidden place where the dead waited for the resurrection, a sojourn which was transformed for Luke's good thief by an awareness of his being "with Jesus."[5]

[1]Gn 2:8. [2]Gn 3:23f.; Ez 31:9; Jl 2:3. [3]Ez 28:13; Rv 2:7. [4]2 Cor 12:4. [5]Lk 23:43 □.

→ heaven—netherworld.

[parallel] A literary critical term referring to a gospel passage closely resembling a passage in another gospel, generally one of the Synoptics. Parallel texts are indicated by the abbreviation =.

→ doublet—synoptic.

parapet of the Temple

→ pinnacle.

Parasceve From the Gk. *Paraskeuē,* from *para-skeuazō:* "to put in good order, to prepare."[1]

[1]Mt 27:62; Mk 15:42; Lk 23:54; Jn 19:14,31,42 □.

→ Preparation Day.

pardon

→ forgive, forgiveness.

parousia From a Greek word *parousia* (from the participle of *par-eimi:* "to be there"), generally meaning presence[1] or "coming."[2] Used in the Greco-Roman world to refer to official visits by emperors, additionally it got attached to the O.T. apocalyptic* tradition of the coming of the Lord.[3] Essentially, it referred to the Lord's coming, to the arrival of his Day.*[4] When longed for with love, it effected changes in Christian behavior.[5]

[1]1 Cor 16:17; 2 Cor 10:10; Phil 1:26; 2:12. [2]2 Cor 7:6f. [3]Zec 9:9. [4]Mt 24:3,27,37,39; 1 Cor 15:23; 1 Thes 2:19; 3:13; 4:15; 2 Thes 2:1,8f.; 2 Pt 1:16. [5]1 Thes 5:23; Jas 5:7f.; 2 Pt 3:4,12; 1 Jn 2:28 □.

→ Day of the Lord—judgment.

Parthians Gk. *Parthoi.* Residents of the region southeast of the Caspian Sea, of Iranian origin. From 248 B.C. to A.D. 224, they were an independent kingdom constantly at war with the Romans. There were Jews numbered among them.[1]

[1]Acts 2:9 □.

[paschal] **1.** Of or relating to the time of Passover.

2. More particularly, something that has been brought about by the first Christians' belief in the resurrection of Jesus.

[Passion of Christ] From the Lat. *pati:* "to support, suffer,"* Gk. *paschō.* A term which sums up the sufferings that Jesus foretold and underwent, and which Christians have interpreted as having redemptive* worth for the liberation of men.

→ cross—crucifixion—scourging—suffer—Trial of Jesus.

passions

→ covetousness.

Passover Gk. *pascha,* Heb. *pèsah,* Aram. *pashâ* (of disputed etymology: "appeasement," a "blow" striking the firstborn, "to leap over" the houses of the Hebrews). It also designated the feast of the sacrificial lamb.

1. Jewish Passover. The principal solemnity of Israel began in April on the night of 14 Nisan (the last day before the full moon following the spring equinox) and lasted seven days, the week of Unleavened Bread.*[1] The ancient nomadic feast of springtime (the shepherds offered the first fruits of the flock) had become transformed in commemoration of the foundational event of the people: Yahweh's causing the Hebrews to leave Egypt across the Sea of Reeds.[2] In principle, every Jew had to go on pilgrimage* to Jerusalem to celebrate the feast* above all others, the Passover, something which Jesus did.

According to the ritual that probably was in effect in Jesus' time, the paschal meal was prepared at the end of the afternoon of 14 Nisan. One could not eat leavened bread during the seven following days. Each family had to sacrifice at the Temple a lamb (or a kid*); it had to be a male, one year old, without blemish. Its blood* was carefully collected; then, with a hyssop* branch, it was used to mark the posts and the lintel of the door to the house. Next, the entire lamb was roasted, care being taken that not one of its bones be broken.[3] Then, in sufficient numbers, the banqueters gathered together, preferably in an upper room decorated with carpets for the occasion. The meal was introduced by a cup* of wine over which the host pronounced two blessings and which he then passed around the table. A basin of water was passed from hand to hand to allow the participants to purify* themselves before eating the Passover. While the second cup made its round, the host explained to the youngest diner the meaning of the different rites. The lamb was the one which turned aside the destroying angel from the Hebrew homes before the departure from Egypt; the unleavened bread was that which the Hebrews brought with them as they fled in haste from Egypt, before it had had time to be leavened.[4] Then, after singing the beginning of the Hallel,*[5] the meal's host took loaves, broke them and distributed them to those at table. The paschal lamb was eaten with bitter herbs and pieces of unleavened bread dipped in *harosèt* (a mixture of figs and raisins cooked in wine which symbolized the bricks made by the Hebrews during their bondage in Egypt). The paschal lamb had to be eaten in its entirety and any scraps burned before daybreak. At this point the cup of blessing was drunk and the conclusion of the Hallel intoned.[6] A final cup of wine closed out the meal. People went their separate ways then, but without departing from the house, for no one was allowed to leave it at any time during the night of Passover.

[1]Ex 12:15-20. [2]Ex 12:11-14,23; Heb 11:27. [3]Jn 19:33. [4]Ex 12:17-20. [5]Ps 113–114. [6]Ps 115–118; Mk 14:26.

2. The Christian Passover celebrated the resurrection of Jesus, which took place on the first day of the week after 14 Nisan, that is on Sunday.*[7] In addition, it was the commemoration of Jesus' sacrificial action and the anticipation of the eschatological* feast.[8] Paul identified Christ with the paschal victim and drew out of the ritual of Unleavened Bread implications for a Christian paschal life of holiness and purity.[9]

[7]Lk 24:1; Acts 20:7; 1 Cor 16:2; Rv 1:10. [8]1 Cor 11:26. [9]1 Cor 5:6-8; cf. Rv 5:6; 13:8.

→ Intr. VI.4.C.b; XIII.3.B.—Eucharist—feast—Last Supper—meal—memory—resurrection—sacrifice—unleavened bread—upper room.

pastor

→ shepherd.

Pastoral Epistles

→ Epistles (Pastoral).

patience 1. Gk. *makrothymia* (from *makros:* "long" and *thymos:* "heart, courage, ardor, wrath"): "lengthy courage, patience, endurance." The Septuagint* and the N.T. use this word to render the Heb. *èrèk appayîm:* "to keep back wrath [to have the nose outstretched]," whence "forbearance": "to possess length of breath." Patience was a characteristic of the covenant God,[1] who did not forget his suffering chosen ones[2] and who knew how to bide his time to allow the sinner to repent.[3] In turn, through the power of the Spirit, man must show himself patient with his neighbor,[4] long-suffering by way of his charity[5] and, like the plowman, patiently await his Lord's arrival.[6]

[1]Ex 34:6; Nm 14:18; Ps 103:8; Sir 2:11; Rom 2:4. [2]Lk 18:7. [3]Rom 9:22; 1 Tim 1:16; 1 Pt 3:20; 2 Pt 3:9,15. [4]Mt 18:26,29; Eph 4:2; Col 1:11; 3:12; 1 Thes 5:14. [5]1 Cor 13:4; 2 Cor 6:6; Gal 5:22. [6]Jas 5:7f.

2. Gk. *anochē/anechomai* (from *ana:* "on high" and *echomai:* "to hold"): "to keep up, hold straight, firm, sup-port." The term indicates less the interior disposition than it does the exterior bearing that was its result: to let something evil pass by. Thus, God postpones his wrath without renouncing the establishment of his justice.[7] Jesus patiently endured his contemporaries' lack of understanding;[8] the believer, in his turn, has to be patient in tests and persecution, or, quite simply, in his life with others.[9] Patience tends to become perseverance (Gk. *hypomonē*).[10]

[7]Rom 2:4; 3:26. [8]Mt 17:17 (= Mk 9:19 = Lk 9:41). [9]1 Cor 4:12; Eph 4:2; Col 3:13; 2 Tim 2:24. [10]2 Thes 1:4.

→ hope—mercy—perseverance.

Patmos A small rocky island in the Aegean Sea, south of Samos, to the west of Miletus.* The author of the book of Revelation* found himself there "because of the Word of God and his witness to Jesus." Even though these phrases do not require the interpretation that he had been deported there or was a prisoner, tradition later on interpreted this passage as describing the effects of a persecution, either in Domitian's time (around 94), or perhaps in Nero's time (around 70).[1]

[1]Rv 1:9 □.

→ Map 2.

Paul Gk. *Paulos.* A Jew of Tarsus, of the tribe of Benjamin, a Pharisee,* by birth a Roman citizen.*[1] Once the persecutor of Christians, he had been converted to Christ who appeared* to him;[2] he became the Apostle to the Gentiles, whom he visited in the course of three great missionary journeys.[3] He was arrested at Jerusalem and, after two years of captivity at Caesarea, was transported to Rome.[4] He was the author of numerous epistles* not all of which have been preserved for us: two to the Thessalonians, one to the Philippians, four to the Corinthians, one to the Galatians, one to the Romans, one to Philemon, one to the Colossians. The following epistles are also attributed to him: one to the Ephesians, two to Timothy, one to Titus. He is no longer reckoned to be the author of the Epistle to the Hebrews.

It is impossible to condense into one simple formula Paul's theological thought, whether that be justification by faith or life in Christ Jesus. One can delineate three major stages marking the evolution of his highly complex thought. In the first stage (the epistles to the Thessalonians*), a perspective of the imminent parousia* dominated his reactions: the Easter event experienced in the past counterbalanced a teaching which could have become exceedingly polarized by the coming end of time. In the second stage (the epistles to the Philippians,* Galatians,* Corinthians* and Romans*), Paul revealed the depth of the present Christian experience: it was not only an instant set between the past and the future, but rather, through baptism, it actualized the past Easter event and, through the gift of the Spirit, anticipated the coming parousia; the letter to the Romans appears to be a veritable synthesis of Paul's thought at this stage. In the third stage (the epistles to the Colossians,* to Philemon,* and to the Ephesians*), he rediscovered the earlier viewpoint of the Exaltation* and considered Christ and the Christian to be "in the heavens." From this summit, the epistle to the Ephesians painted a synthesis of God's plan. With regard to the Pastoral Epistles,* they interpreted the Pauline message as a function of the church which was caught in the grip of new doctrinal threats.

The influence of Pauline doctrine has been considerable, so much so that, in the latest of the N.T. writing, praise was given to the wisdom he had given at the same time as a warning was issued, to be on one's guard against possible errors of interpretation; for there were some difficult passages to be found in his writings.[5]

[1]Acts 16:21,37f.; 22:25-29; 23:27; Phil 3:5. [2]Acts 9:1-30; 22:3-21; 26:9-20; 1 Cor 9:1; Gal 1:13-17; Phil 3:12. [3]Acts 13:1–14:28; 15:36–18:22; 18:23–21:14. [4]Acts 21:17–28:31. [5]2 Pt 3:15f.

→ Intr. I.4.—chronology—Maps 2,3.

peace Gk. *eirēnē,* Heb. *shâlôm.* The tranquil possession of good things,[1] happiness[2] and, above all, health.[3] Not only an absence of war[4] and disorder,[5] but a cordial understanding[6] made possible by the God of peace who, in it, inaugurates his rule*[7] and heralds the Messiah,* the Prince of Peace.[8] By shedding his blood, Jesus Christ reconciled* men with God and with one another.[9] The peace he gave was not the world's,*[10] but one which went along with the gift of the Holy Spirit[11] and one which held firm even in persecutions.*[12] Also, the Christian, who was a fashioner of peace,[13] loved to wish others peace, especially in his greetings.[14]

[1]Lk 11:21; Acts 24:2. [2]Jgs 19:20; Ps 73:3. [3]2 Sm 18:32; Ps 38:4; Is 57:19. [4]Eccl 3:8; Lk 14:32; Acts 12:20; Rv 6:4. [5]1 Cor 14:33. [6]1 Kgs 5:26; Mk 9:50; Acts 7:26; Rom 12:18; Eph 4:3; Jas 3:18. [7]Ps 85:9-14; Rom 14:17; 2 Cor 13:11. [8]Is 9:5f.; Lk 1:79; 2:14; 19:42; Acts 10:36; Eph 2:17; 6:15. [9]Eph 2:14-22; Col 1:20; Rv 1:4; cf. 2 Cor 5:18-20. [10]Jer 6:14; 8:11; Mt 10:34 (= Lk 12:51); Jn 14:27. [11]Jn 20:19-23; Gal 5:22. [12]Jn 16:33. [13]Mt 5:9. [14]Lk 7:50; 10:5; Rom 1:7; 1 Cor 1:3; 2 Cor 1:2; Gal 1:3; Eph 1:2; Col 3:15; 1 Pt 1:2; 5:14.

→ reconcile—rest—salvation.

pearl Gk. *margaritēs.* A jewel highly regarded and of great worth,[1] it could serve as a woman's adornment;[2] metaphorically, it expressed the inestimable worth of the Kingdom of God[3] and the splendor of the heavenly Jerusalem.[4]

[1]Rv 18:12. [2]1 Tim 2:9; Rv 17:4; 18:16. [3]Mt 7:6; 13:45f. [4]Rv 21:21 □.

pebble (white)

→ white pebble.

pedagogue Gk. *paidagōgos:* "children's guide." A slave* entrusted with the task, not of educating (which was the father's role), but of leading the child to school, until he reached the age of his majority.[1]

[1]1 Cor 4:15; Gal 3:24 □.

→ Intr. IX.2.

penance From the Lat. *poenitentia* (from *poenitere:* "to repent," with a notion of punishment and, for us, the penitent's image). A sense of punishment or of penalty began to be prevalent about A.D. 1220. It seems regrettable that this word should have been used by translators to render the Greek term *metanoia* which means "conversion, repentance."

In itself, penance implied confession* of sins and practices of austerity (to fast,* to cloth oneself in sackcloth* and ashes*) to which it was all too often reduced. Its "works" were the totality of Christian behavior, which only find their meaning in total and radical conversion,* in reconciliation* with God and the Church, and in the restoration of one's spiritual building.*

→ confess—conversion—expiate—repent.

[Pentateuch] From the Gk. *hē pentateuchos biblos,* "the book* in five [books]": the five books (Genesis, Exodus, Leviticus, Numbers, Deuteronomy) that constitute the Torah* in the strict sense. This division was not originally made, but already existed at the time of the Septuagint* translation. In the N.T., it was known as the Law* (Gk. *ho nomos*).

Pentecost **1.** A Jewish feast which at a late date (the second century B.C.) received this name from the fact that it was celebrated on the fiftieth day (Gk. *hē pentēkostē*) after Passover. It coincided with the harvest feast,* a day of thanksgiving* on which, after the "seven weeks" that the harvest on average lasted, the first fruits* of the produce of the earth were offered:[1] it was the feast of the "first fruits," the Feast of Weeks.*[2] It was the occasion for a pilgrimage* to Jerusalem,[3] an echo and a culmination of the paschal pilgrimage. The rabbis later saw in it the annual memorial of the Covenant,* when the Law was given on Sinai.*[4]

[1]Ex 23:16. [2]Ex 34:22; Lv 23:15; Dt 16:9. [3]Acts 2:9; 20:16; 1 Cor 16:8 □. [4]Cf. Ex 19:1–16.

2. The Christian feast commemorated the Pentecost following the death of Jesus; it was marked by the eschatological* gift of the Holy Spirit which inaugurated the period of a church open to all peoples.[5]

[5]Jl 3:1-5; Acts 2:1-11.

→ Intr. XIII.3.B.—feast.

people **1.** The people of God was ordinarily designated by *laos,*[1] on two occasions by *ethnos.*[2] The people, which God had acquired as his very own possession,[3] reconciled* in one same faith in Jesus Christ both the Israel* of the ancient Covenant and the pagan nations*;[4] thereby it had become God's sanctuary,* where the Covenant* was fulfilled.[5] Remaining rooted in history, it was on the road to its completion, the heavenly fatherland.*[6]

[1]Acts 4:10; 13:17. [2]Mt 21:43; 1 Pt 2:9. [3]Ex 19:5f.; Ti 2:14. [4]Acts 15:14; Rom 9:24. [5]2 Cor 6:14-16. [6]Heb 4:9; 11:13.

2. In a diminished sense: a crowd, occasionally *laos,*[7] generally *ochlos.*[8] Not to be confused with an assembly *(ekklēsia),* a mob *(dēmos),* nor with the nations *(ethnē).*

[7]Mt 4:23; Lk 1:10; 7:1; 20:1,9; Acts 2:47. [8]Mt 4:25; 9:33; 13:34; 14:5; Mk 15:15; Lk 3:7,10; Jn 12:9; Acts 1:15; Rv 7:9.

→ Intr. X.3.—Church—covenant—election—Israel—nations—priesthood.

perfect Gk. *teleios* (from *telos:* "end, goal"). Etymologically, this epithet was applied to those limited beings about whom one could say they were complete, finished, without fault and enjoyed physical and moral integrity.[1] While the Bible declared that God's works were perfect,[2] it never said (unlike the Greeks) that God was perfect, except in Mt 5:48 where Jesus invited men "to be perfect as God is perfect." Some critics ascribe to Matthew this Hellenization of the adjective "merciful*" which Luke has preserved in a parallel text.[3] Others read in it an anthropomorphism derived from the O.T. commandment: "Be holy because I am holy."[4] Matthew situated in God the ideal of perfection which he proposed to believers: not to be satisfied with the practice of the Law, but to love all men,[5] to give one's goods to the poor.[6] Even when one is no longer a beginner, a "baby,"[7] the new perfection[8] not only loomed ahead, but referred to a state which was not to be acquired except in heaven, in the perfect Man.*[9] Moreover, through Jesus, who has been made perfect,[10] the believer too has to strain forward toward perfection.[11] The same ideal was kept in view through the rejection of impurity (Gk. *a-mōmos:* "without blemish")[12] or reproachable behavior (Gk. *a-memptos:* "without reproach").[13]

[1]Gn 17:1; Lv 22:22; Dt 18:13. [2]Dt 32:4; 2 Sm 22:31; Ps 19:8; Rom 12:2; Jas 1:17,25; 1 Jn 4:12. [3]Lk 6:36. [4]Lv 19:2; 1 Pt 1:15f. [5]Mt 5:20,48. [6]Mt 19:21. [7]1 Cor 3:1; Heb 5:14. [8]1 Cor 2:6; 14:20; Phil 3:15; Col 4:12. [9]Eph 4:13; Phil 3:12. [10]Heb 2:10; 5:9; 7:28; 12:2. [11]Col 1:28; Heb 6:1; 10:14; Jas 1:4; 3:2; 1 Jn 4:18. [12]Eph 1:4; 5:27; Phil 2:15; Col 1:22; Heb 9:14; 1 Pt 1:19; 2 Pt 3:14; Jude 24; Rv 14:5 △. [13]Lk 1:6; Phil 2:15; 3:6; 1 Thes 3:13; 5:23; Heb 8:7f. △.

→ fulfill—holy—love—plenitude—pure.

perfume Gk. *osmē:* "odor," *euōdia:* "good odor," *thymiama, myron:* "perfume."

1. Indispensable for social and religious life in Israel, as they were through all the ancient East,[1] perfumes were made of resins imported chiefly from Arabia and eastern Africa, plain (spices) or mixed with oil. Of the thirty or so perfumes mentioned in the O.T., the N.T. mentions aloes,* amomum, spices,* cinnamon, incense,* myrrh,* nard.*

[1]Rv 18:13.

2. To anoint a guest's* head with perfume was a traditional gesture of welcome;[2] in burials* the anointing* was an act of respect bestowed on the dead.[3]

[2]Lk 7:46. [3]Mt 26:7,12 (= Mk 14:3,8 = Jn 12:3,7); Mk 16:1.

3. In worship* perfume, which gave forth smoke as it burned, symbolized prayer.*[4] From this came the ancient expression a "sweet-smelling sacrifice"[5] to refer to Christ's oblation[6] or to the believer's generosity.[7] From this, too, derived the radiance of those who had been anointed in baptism.[8]

[4]Lk 1:9; Heb 9:4; Rv 5:8. [5]Gn 8:21. [6]Eph 5:2. [7]Phil 4:18. [8]2 Cor 2:15.

→ Intr. VIII.1.C.b.—altar—anoint—fast—incense—joy—oil—spice.

Pergamum Gk. *Pergamos.* Modern-day Bergama (Turkey). The ancient capital of Mysia,* celebrated in the time of the Attalides; then, around 170 B.C., there spread the use of parchment, "the skin of Pergamum" (*hē pergamēnē diphthera).* The renowned center for healings by the god Aesculapius (Gk. *Asklēpios*). From 129 B.C., the capital (with Ephesus*) of the Roman province* of Asia. There was a temple there in honor of Augustus and Rome.[1]

[1]Rv 1:11; 2:12 □.

→ Map 2.

[pericope] A passage within a collection which, when cut off (Gk. *perikoptō*), can stand alone: such as the healing of the leper.[1]

[1]Mk 1:40-44.

persecution Gk. *diōgmos* (from *diōkō:* "to pursue,[1] persecute"): "persecution."

[1]Phil 3:12,14.

1. The fact is there, God's messengers are persecuted: prophets*[2] and disciples,*[3] Paul,* who had been a persecutor,[4] all were persecuted, just as Jesus had been.[5] Far from fleeing persecution, one has to endure it courageously[6] and to pray for one's persecutors.[7]

[2]Mt 5:12; Acts 7:52. [3]Intr. I.3:B; Mt 5:11; 10:23. [4]1 Cor 15:9; Gal 1:13,23; 5:11; Phil 3:6; 1 Tim 1:13; 2 Tim 3:11f. [5]Jn 5:16; 15:20. [6]Gal 6:12. [7]Mt 5:44; Rom 12:14.

2. Persecution has meaning. It derives from the world's hatred for Jesus;[8] it is directed against "the Way*" and the person of Christ.[9] Jesus foretold it to his disciples[10] and told them to be "happy*" because of it.[11] Whoever is persecuted always receives help from Christ and the Spirit.[12]

[8]Jn 15:18-20. [9]Acts 9:4f.; 22:4,7f.; 26:14f. [10]Mk 10:30. [11]Mt 5:10. [12]Mt 10:19f. (= Mk 13:11 = Lk 12:11f.); Lk 21:12-15; Rom 8:35; 2 Cor 12:10; 2 Thes 1:4.

→ suffer—tribulation.

perseverance Gk. *hypomenē* (from *menō:* "to remain" and *hypo:* "below"): "endurance"; one does not flee from it but holds firm under a shock or a weight. This attitude cannot be reckoned as identical with patience: one does not affirm that God perseveres, but one does affirm that he is faithful and patient. The "steadfastness" at issue deals almost exclusively with "trials, sufferings,* persecutions*: the issue there is "to hold fast." Thus, Jesus endured the cross,[1] demonstrating those attitudes which ought to be the possession of a Christian, especially an apostle.[2] Constancy, undergirded by God,[3] is the expression of authentic faith,*[4] is characterized by and produces hope,*[5] one leading to victory.[6] This is the condition of salvation.*[7]

[1]Heb 12:2f. [2]Rom 12:12; 1 Cor 3:7; 2 Cor 1:6; 6:4; 12:12; 1 Tim 6:11; 2 Tim 3:10. [3]Rom 15:4f.; 2 Thes 3:5; Rv 1:9; 3:10. [4]2 Thes 1:4; Jas 1:3; Rv 13:10; 14:12. [5]Rom 5:3f.; 8:25; 1 Thes 1:3. [6]Lk 8:15; Rom 2:7; Col 1:11; 2 Tim 2:12; Jas 1:12; 5:11. [7]Mt 10:22 (= Mt 24:13 = Mk 13:13); Lk 21:19.

→ faithful—hope—patience—persecution.

[Peter (Epistles of)] **1.** The first letter was attributed by tradition to Peter, writing from Rome before 64 (Nero's persecution). The difficulties, raised by scholars against this attribution, at least partially, are not insurmountable.

2. The second belongs to the literary genre* of "testaments" (the farewell discourse* of someone dying); the attribution to Peter (1:1) does not demand its authenticity.* Some authors date it from 70–80, the majority roll back its composition date to about 125. It seems to be addressed to churches threatened by heresy in doctrine and in morals. It is a deuterocanonical* epistle.

→ Intr. XV.—Epistles (Catholic).

Peter (Saint) Gk. *Petros:* "stone,*" the masculine form of *Petra:* "rock," corresponding to his surname *Kēphas,* itself the Greek form of the Aramaic *Képhâ:* "rock."[1] Simon,* the son of Jonah, Andrew's brother, the first of the Twelve.*[2] A fisherman hailing from Bethsaida,* he resided in Capernaum* with his mother-in-law,[3] from which we conclude that he was married. During the lifetime of Jesus and of the primitive Church, he held a place apart among the disciples. According to an excellent tradition, Peter lived for a time in Rome and died there a martyr's* death, crucified under Nero between 64 and 67. Two epistles bear his name.

[1]Mt 16:18; Jn 1:42. [2]Mt 4:18; 10:2 (= Mk 3:16 = Lk 6:14); 16:17. [3]Mk 1:29f. (= Lk 4:38); Jn 1:44.

→ Intr. I.3–4; VI.2.B.—Cephas.

Pharisee Gk. *pharisaios,* from the Aram. *perishayya:* "the separated one." The term, attested to from 132 B.C., is variously interpreted: it means a Jew who has withdrawn from Judas Maccabeus and the Hassidim, or who has withdrawn from sin by his rigorous observances, or, finally, who has become set apart because he sees what is good in the Law. Behind the gospel's systematization we are able to recognize that Jesus condemned not Pharisaianism, but Pharisee-ism, that is, the perduring danger which afflicts every religious spirit by binding its quest for God to observance of the Law. On the other side of the coin, there were Pharisees who not only invited Jesus to dine at their tables, but who also took his part, either to defend him against Herod or to embrace the Christian faith.[1]

[1]Lk 13:31; Acts 5:34; 15:5; 23:9.

→ Intr. XI.2.—Gamaliel—Nicodemus—Paul—Sadducee.

Philadelphia Gk. *Philadelpheia.* A Hellenistic city of Lydia in Asia Minor, founded by Attalus II Philadelphos (159–138 B.C.). After its destruction by an earthquake in A.D. 17, it was rebuilt by Tiberius* under the name of Neo-Caesarea.* Little is known of the origins of the Christian community of the place, which proved faithful in persecution.[1] Not to be confused with Rabbat Ammon[2] (modern-day Amman in Jordan), called Philadelphia by Ptolemy II Philadelphos (285–246 B.C.), and which became one of the cities of the Decapolis* in 63 B.C.

[1]Rv 1:11; 3:7 □. [2]2 Sm 10-12; Jer 49:2; Ez 25:5.

→ Maps 2 and 3.

Philemon Gk. *Philēmōn.* A Christian at whose home the Church at Colossae* gathered, probably the master of the slave Onesimus.* To him was addressed the Epistle to Philemon.[1]

[1]Phlm 1 □.

→ Archippus—Onesimus.

[Philemon (Epistle to)] The shortest of Paul's letters, written during his captivity at Rome (or Caesarea) at the same time as the Epistle to the Colossians.

→ Intr. XV.

Philip Gk. *Philippos:* "lover of horses."

1. *Herod Philip I,* whose real name was Herod Boethos. The son of Herod the Great* and Mariamne II; the husband of Herodias.* Cut off from the royal line

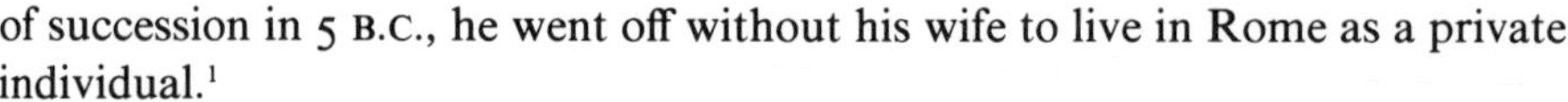

of succession in 5 B.C., he went off without his wife to live in Rome as a private individual.[1]

[1]Mt 14:3; Mk 6:17 □.

→ Herod.

2. *Herod Philip II.* Born about 24 B.C. of Herod the Great* and Cleopatra; the husband of Salome. From 4 B.C. to A.D. 34 the tetrarch* of Iturea,* Trachonitis* and the territory near Lake Gennesaret.[2]

[1]Lk 3:1 □.

→ Intr. I.1.D.—Bethsaida—Caesarea Philippi—Herod.

3. One of the Twelve,* a native of Bethsaida.* To him were attributed two apocryphal works: *The Gospel of Philip* (found at Nag Hammadi*) and the *Acts of Philip.*[3]

[1]Mt 10:3 (= Mk 3:18 = Lk 6:14 = Acts 1:13); Jn 1:43-48; 6:5,7; 12:21f.; 14:8f. □.

4. One of the Seven,* a baptizer, called: "evangelist."*[4]

[1]Acts 6:5; 8:5-40; 21:8 □.

Philippi Gk. *Philippoi.* A city founded in the seventh century B.C., which belonged to the Roman province* of Macedonia* beginning in 146 B.C. Well situated on the Via Egnatia, it was a strategic and commercial city. After the Battle of Actium (31 B.C.), it became a Roman colony, enjoying the *ius italicum,* that is, the same rights and privileges as the citizens* of Italy.* Paul was deeply attached to the Christian community that he had founded there in 51.[1]

[1]Acts 16:12; 20:6; Phil 1:1; 1 Thes 2:2 □.

→ Philippians (Epistle to the)—Map 2.

[Philippians (Epistle to the)] This letter was written by Paul to the community at Philippi,* which he himself had founded and to which he remained particularly attached. Although traditionally dated in 63 during the first Roman captivity, scholars think that it was sent about 56 from Ephesus,* where Paul could have been in prison.[1] Some authors think that the present letter gathers together some originally independent notes: a thanksgiving letter[2] and a warning against the Judaizers.*[3]

[1]Cf. 1 Cor 15:32; 2 Cor 1:8. [2]Phil 1:1–3:1; 4:10-23. [3]Phil 3:1–4:9.

→ Intr. XV.—Epistles.

[Philo of Alexandria] Gk. *Philōn.* A Jewish philosopher (about 13 B.C. to A.D. 45–50). Apollos* was perhaps a disciple of his.[1] Philo's work could have exercised some influence on the N.T. writers. Such would be Paul's identifying of the Exodus* rock with Christ, the wisdom of God,[2] his development of the two Adams* motif,[3] or his calling Christ the image* and firstborn of God.[4] So, also for the Epistle to the Hebrews* or for the Johannine conception of the Logos.* On Pseudo-Philo, → *Liber Antiquitatum Biblicarum.**

[1]Acts 19:1-3; 1 Cor 1:12. [2]1 Cor 10:1-5. [3]1 Cor 15:47-49. [4]Col 1:15.

philosophy Gk. *philo-sophia:* "love of wisdom (or of learning)." In Col. 2:8, it is a case not so much of a system of thought of an Aristotelian, Epicurean or Stoic (Acts 17:18□) type, but of a gnosis* which lays claim to giving salvation.

→ Intr. IV.6.C.—elements of the world—Epicureans—gnosis—know—Stoics—wisdom.

Phrygia Gk. *Phrygia.* A region of high plateaus in modern-day Turkey which was invaded by Indo-Europeans about the twelfth century B.C. and underwent successive dominations by the Babylonians (546 B.C.), the Seleucids (312), Pergamum* (188), and finally the Romans, who joined it to the Roman province* of Asia* (about 120). The native place of the mystery cult of Cybele. Jews had been present there in large numbers since the third century.[1]

[1]Acts 2:10; 16:6; 18:23 □.

→ Colossae—Hierapolis—Laodicea—Map 3.

phylactery Gk. *phylaktērion:* "a place to guard" (a guard corps) and "means of guarding" (amulet), talisman; here perhaps from *phylassō:* "to guard (the Law)"; Heb. *tᵉphillîn,* perhaps derived from *tᵉphillâ:* "prayer" or from *phâla:* "to separate". Two cubic leather cases, each containing four essential passages of the Law inscribed on parchment strips, of which one part, the *Shemaʿ,*[1] had to be tied with bands onto the left arm (facing the heart) and onto the forehead of every adult Jew at the time of morning prayer, except on the sabbath.[2] Out of devotion, some kept them on throughout the day.

This custom, still current today among orthodox Jews, derives from a literal interpretation of Dt 6:8: "You will bind my words to your hand as a sign, on your forehead like a band." Jesus criticized only the ostentation and excess which led to the enlarging of phylacteries.[3]

[1]Ex 13:1-10; 13:11-13; Dt 6:4-9; 11:13-21. [2]Dt 6:8; cf. Ex 13:9,16; Dt 11:18. [3]Mt 23:5 □.

→ Intr. XIII.2.B.a.—fringe.

piety, pious A fundamental religious disposition which welcomes God's sovereign authority. Without reducing itself to the observance of cultic acts, it informs a believer's entire behavior. The word derives from the Lat. *pietas:* "respect for the gods, homeland, family, commitments" and was the foundation of the Roman nation's prosperity; but it summarizes the sense of three Greek words which concur in articulating its true biblical meaning.

1. *Eulabeia:* "circumspection, reverential attention to the divine will, fear of God"; *eulabēs* expresses a reverential submission to God's will,[1] the kind that Jesus exemplified perfectly.[2]

[1]Lk 2:25; Acts 2:5; 8:2; 22:12; Heb 11:7; 12:28. [2]Heb 5:7 △.

2. *Hosiotēs:* "holiness," *hosios:* "holy," from a Greek word meaning what is permitted, authorized by divine law, but with the Hebraic weight of the O.T. *hèsèd:* "a tie uniting parents, friends, allies," designating the fidelity* within the Covenant.* It is equally a characteristic of God[3] and of Christ,[4] as well as of the man concerned about fidelity,[5] such as the Pharisees* who had themselves called the *hassîdîm,* the pious.[6]

[3]Rv 15:4; 16:5. [4]Acts 2:27; 13:34f.; Heb 7:26. [5]Lk 1:75; Eph 4:24; 1 Thes 2:10; 1 Tim 2:8; Ti 1:8; cf. 1 Tim 1:9; 2 Tim 3:2. [6]1 Mc 2:42.

3. *Eusebeia, eusebēs* (from *eu:* "well" and *sebomai:* "to venerate, honor, offer worship* to"): the quality of a man who reverences well; today we might say, perhaps, a good practicing Christian.[7] In the Pastoral Epistles,* the term refers to true religion, which is the mysterious knowledge of Christ.[8] It involves spiritual exercises and the uprightness of an authentic Christian life.[9] Trials* accepted out of the following of Christ are sure evidence of it.[10] Actually God's gift,[11] piety looks forward to final salvation.[12]

[7]Acts 10:2,7. [8]1 Tim 3:16. [9]1 Tim 4:7f.; 2 Tim 3:5; Ti 1:1. [10]2 Tim 3:12. [11]1 Tim 6:6; 2 Pt 1:3. [12]Ti 2:12f.

→ adore—fear—fidelity—justice—worship.

pig Gk. *choiros.* An animal sacred to the non-Semitic religions and occasionally ritually sacrificed,[1] the pig was for Israel the symbol of ritual impurity*[2] and, as such, was forbidden as food and in sacrifices.*[3] Herds were raised in the Hellenized Decapolis.*[4] The task of a swineherd was infamous, more particularly because it implied intercourse with pagans.[5]

[1]Is 65:4; 66:3,17. [2]Mt 7:6. [3]Lv 11:7; Dt 14:8; 2 Mc 6:18-21. [4]Mt 8:30-32 (= Mk 5:11-13 = Lk 8:32f.); Mk 5:16. [5]Lk 15:15f. □.

→ Intr. VIII.1.D.a.

Pilate Pontius Pilatus, a Roman knight, prefect* of Judea under Tiberius* from 26 to 36. Little loved by the Jews because he had taken what they considered several blundering measures toward them, he drew from the Temple treasury* to have an aqueduct built and forcibly suppressed the rebellion this action stirred up. In 36 (or 37), having dealt unjustly and severely with the Samaritans,* Pilate was deprived of his functions by Vitellius, the legate of Syria, and sent back to Rome where all trace of him has been lost. To him is attributed an apocryphal writing, the *Letter of Pilate* to Claudius, which Tertullian may have known (before 197) and a *Correspondence with Tiberius,* which dates from the Middle Ages.[1]

[1]Mt 27 (= Mk 15 = Lk 23); Lk 3:1; 13:1; Jn 18:29–19:38; Acts 3:13; 4:27; 13:28; 1 Tim 6:13; cf. Mt 28:14; Lk 20:20 □.

pilgrimage 1. The journeying of the faithful to a place made holy by a divine revelation or by the presence of a man of God, in order to encounter the Lord. The Bible has no specific term to describe this custom; it uses the expression "to go up to" (Gk. *anabainō*).

2. From the time when worship,* centralized at the Temple,* had supplanted every other sanctuary in order to preserve the people from the contamination of idolatrous surroundings, the Law[1] imposed on every adult Jew or proselyte* the obligation of "going up" to worship at Jerusalem three times yearly: at

Passover,[2] at Pentecost,[3] and at the Feast of Booths.[4] The pilgrims arrived in caravans (Gk. *syn-odia:* "the action of journeying together"),[5] most often on foot; with semi-proselytes[6] and aliens, their number could reach some 125,000, and this was exclusive of Jerusalem's residents. They lodged either in the city or in the environs, under tents or in the market towns. This immense throng, gathering to the singing of psalms* of ascent,[7] prefigured the day of universal salvation.* Jesus' entry into Jerusalem probably took place in the context of a Passover pilgrimage.[8]

[1]Ex 23:27. [2]Lk 2:41f.; Jn 2:13. [3]Acts 2:5; 20:16; 24:11. [4]Jn 7:8. [5]Lk 2:44. [6]Jn 12:20. [7]Ps 120–134. [8]Mt 21:1-9 (= Mk 11:1-10 = Lk 19:28-38); Jn 12:12.

3. The application of the metaphor* of a pilgrimage to man's wandering towards the beyond or towards God was frequent in antiquity. The peregrinations of Abraham and the fathers there gave Israel concrete support.[9] The state of a pilgrim, a traveler passing through, was rendered by the term *par-epi-dēmos,* literally "a non-resident alien." Such were Christians called:[10] under the guidance of Christ, their leader and forerunner,[11] they were on a quest for a true fatherland,*[12] on a journey towards the heavenly Jerusalem;*[13] their life was stretching forth to rejoin the Lord,[14] a fact which did not strip them of their worth but rather conferred a true meaning on worshipful pilgrimages.

[9]Gn 23:4; (Lv 25:23); 1 Chr 29:15; Heb 11:13. [10]1 Pt 1:1; 2:11. [11]Heb 2:10 (*archēgos*); 6:20 (*prodromos*). [12]Heb 11:16; 13:14. [13]Heb 12:22-24. [14]2 Cor 5:6; Phil 3:12-14.

→ Intr. IV.6.A; XIII.3.B.—Diaspora—fatherland—feast—stranger—way.

pinnacle Lat. *pinnaculum* (from *pinna,* wing of a building), Gk. *pterygion* (a diminutive of *pteryx,* wing of a building). Most likely the building's summit, perhaps surmounted by a tower; according to others, the highest point of the southeast wing of the Temple's porticos or the upper cornice of one of the large doors facing the Kedron Valley.*[1]

[1]Mt 4:5 (= Lk 4:9) □.

→ temple.

[Pirké Aboth] "Chapters from the Fathers." A treatise from the Mishnah,* also collected in the book of Jewish prayers and read on the six sabbaths between Passover* and the Feast of Weeks (Pentecost*). By establishing the uninterrupted chain of tradition* from Moses right up to the disciples of Johannan Ben Zakkai (first century A.D.), it grounded the legitimacy of rabbinic orthodoxy (I:1–15; II:8–14). To this has been added a collection of sayings of different fathers from the Jewish tradition (principally from the first century B.C. up to the second century A.D.). A work of high religious and moral worth, it was analogous to the biblical books of Proverbs* and Sirach.*

pitcher A vessel made of clay or stone used to draw, store and serve water at the table. Numerous Greek words describe it: *antlēma,*[1] *hydria,*[2] *keramion,*[3] *xestēs* (→ measures*).[4]

[1]Jn 4:11 △. [2]Jn 2:6f.; 4:28 △. [3]Mk 14:13 (= Lk 22:10) △. [4]Mk 7:4 △.

pity

→ mercy.

plague Gk. *loimos.* Beginning with the O.T., a generic term signifying every fatal epidemic: cholera, the plague properly speaking, typhus, etc. One of God's three great punishments, foretold as a premonitory symptom of the end,[1] sometimes called "death."[2] A contemptuous term.[3]

[1]Lk 21:11. [2]2 Sm 24:13f., Rv 6:8; 18:8. [3]1 Mc 10:61; Acts 24:5 □.

plan of God

→ God's plan.

pledge Gk. *arrabōn* (of Semitic origin). A juridical term from the business world. Unlike security, which was returned to the debtor when he paid off his debt,* pledges were advances on a sum due, an installment that guaranteed the future total payment. Thus, the gift of the Holy Spirit participates in the promised inheritance* and guarantees its full reception at the fullness of time.[1]

[1]2 Cor 1:22; 5:5; Eph 1:14 □.

→ first fruits—heritage.

plenitude, pleroma Gk. *plērōma.* The following interpretations are justified by the uses of this term, although exact translations cannot always be given.

1. What fills something: baskets,[1] the earth;[2] or whatever completes something, for example, a torn garment.[3]

[1]Mk 6:43; 8:20. [2]1 Cor 10:26. [3]Mt 9:16 (= Mk 2:21).

2. What brings a number to its totality, in opposition to a limit or diminution: so, the number of the nations.[4]

[1]Rom 11:12,25.

3. What tells of something else's superabundance: such as a blessing,[5] grace;[6] what tells of an overflowing measure, a state of achievement: such is the case with the Law,[7] with time.[8]

[5]Rom 15:29. [6]Jn 1:16. [7]Rom 13:10. [8]Gal 4:4; Eph 1:10.

4. What expresses the totality, the inexpressible richness of God's being[9] or of Christ's.[10]

[9]Eph 3:19; Col 2:9. [10]Eph 4:13.

5. The term, when used without a determinant complement, may be variously interpreted. More probably, it means the totality of the divinity which dwelt in Christ and which God wanted to communicate.[11] Also, a case difficult to interpret (because the determining complement is that of the plenitude itself) is the following: "the Church which is his body *to plērōma tou panta en pasin*

plēroumenou"; here the Church is not the complement, but the expression of Christ in his plenitude; the universe is perhaps associated with him.[12]

[11]Col 1:19. [12]Eph 1:23.

→ fulfill—perfect.

[Pliny the Younger] C.P. Cecilius Secundus Plinius (born in A.D. 61), nephew of Pliny the Elder (the author of a *Natural History*), he was governor of the Roman province of Pontus/Bithynia* from the year 110. In 112 he wrote a famous letter to Trajan in which he reported that the Christians* of the region spoke their songs to Christ as if to a god *(carmen Christo quasi deo dicere).*

[point] A word, sentence, theme of a literary unit* in which the effect that the writer wishes to convey is concentrated. Thus a single parable* may have as its focal point God who cares about the sheep that is "lost" (Lk 15:4–7), or the community's leaders who are to have a care for the one that has "wandered away" (Mt. 18:10–14).

[Pompey] Gnaeus Pompeius (106–48 B.C.), a great Roman military leader, the rival of Caesar,* who triumphed over him. The conqueror of Mithridates, king of Pontus,* he intervened in the rivalries of the leaders of Judea and took possession of Jerusalem in 63; he entered the Holy of Holies,* but did not loot the Temple, and authorized Jewish worship. He created the Roman province* of Syria and established the Decapolis.*

→ Intr. I.1.C.

Pontus A region to the north of modern Turkey, on the border of Pontus-Euxinus: Gk. *Pontos:* "high, full sea," *euxeinos:* "hospitable" (by its opposite?): the Black Sea. A Roman province* after 65 B.C. It numbered Jews in its midst, including Aquila* and his wife Priscilla, as well as the Christians whom Pliny* mentioned.[1]

[1]Acts 2:9; 18:2; 1 Pt 1:1 □.

→ Bithynia—Map 3.

pool Gk. *kolymbēthra.* On account of the summer dryness, water reservoirs, underground or open to the sky, were dug out of rock and supplied by rain and by springs, occasionally far distant ones whose water was brought in by canals. For public use, to water the flocks and as vats for craftsmen.[1]

[1]2 Sm 2:13; 4:12; 1 Kgs 22:38; 2 Kgs 18:17; 20:20; Neh 2:14; 3:15; Is 7:5; 22:9,11; Na 2:9; Jn 5:2,7; 9:7 □.

→ Bethzatha—Siloam.

pool of fire

→ fiery pool.

poor Gk. *ptōchos* (from *ptēssō:* "to squat"), ordinarily translating several Heb. words: *'ânî, 'ânâw, ebyôn.* The poor man was the one for whom something necessary for survival was lacking. The term encompassed two mutually related meanings.

1. In the economic sense. The poor were part of this world's ordinary condition.[1] The Church herself, despite the efforts of the first Christians, knew the oppression of the poor by the rich;[2] but it struggled in favor of the poor, for their condition was intolerable.[3] Hence, the enterprise of a collection* for the needy of Jerusalem.[4]

[1]Dt 15:11; Mt 26:11 (= Mk 14:5 = Jn 12:8). [2]Acts 6:1; Jas 2:2f. [3]Mt 19:21 (= Mk 10:21 = Lk 18:22); Lk 16:8; Jas 2:15f.; 1 Jn 3:17. [4]Rom 15:26f.; Gal 2:10; 1 Cor 16:1-4; 2 Cor 8–9.

2. In the religious sense. On account of their condition, the poor are open to a special presence of God and they find themselves on a level with the Kingdom of God.[5] God prefers them to the wealthy and makes them his protegés.[1] It was to them that Jesus proclaimed the Good News.[7] Welcomed from the hand of God, poverty can become identical with humility*: to be "poor of heart" in the very depth of one's being,[8] something without which all riches are an allurement.[9] Jesus identified himself with his disciples and, perhaps, even with everyone in need, conferring on them his eminent dignity in the world.[10] Far from taking account of their social condition,[11] one must hear the question ceaselessly posed by the poor and discover in them the face of Christ who made himself poor,[12] who was "gentle and humble of heart" (sometimes retranslated into Aramaic by *'nwânâ,* a composite of *'ânî* and *'ânâw*).[13]

[5]Lk 6:20; 16:19. [6]1 Sm 2:7; Lk 1:47f.,52f. [7]Mt 11:5 (= Lk 7:22); Lk 4:18. [8]Mt 5:3. [9]Rv 3:17. [10]Mt 10:42; 25:40,45. [11]Jas 2:1-4 [12]2 Cor 8:9. [13]Mt 11:29.

→ Intr. VII.4.—collection—gentleness—rich.

portico Gk. *stoa.* An open-air gallery covered with a roof supported by colonnades. The N.T. mentions "Solomon's Porch,"[1] on the east side of the Temple, a meeting place for the residents of Jerusalem; the famous Athenian Areopagus,[2] where the Stoics* strolled; and the five porticos of the Bethzatha Pool.*[3]

[1]Jn 10:23; Acts 3:11; 5:12. [2]Acts 17:22. [3]Jn 5:2 □.

possessed Gk. *daimonizomenos,* from *daimōn:* "demon." A human being taken over by a spirit* which, while being other than him, identifies itself with him. The terms used are: "to have a spirit,"[1] "to be with (in, under the dominion of) a spirit":[2] this was to be "possessed." The possessed person discovered himself endowed with superhuman might,[3] capable of a penetration of beings.[4] Jesus exorcized* the possessed[5] and gave this same power to his disciples, although it was to be exercised with the help of prayer and fasting.[6] While in the O.T. some men were overtaken by the "good spirit," the N.T. knows only of possessions by the evil spirit. Occasionally, it is difficult to distinguish a case of possession from an illness.*[8]

[1]Mk 3:30; 7:25; Acts 8:7. [2]Mk 1:23; 5:2. [3]Mk 5:3,5. [4]Mk 1:24; Lk 4:34,41. [5]Mt 8:16; Mk 1:27; 3:11. [6]Mt 10:1; 17:21 (= Mk 9:29); Mk 16:17; Lk 10:20. [7]Jgs 11:29; 14:6. [8]Cf. Mt 17:16 and 17:19, as well as Mt 17:18.

→ demons—exorcize—spirit.

potter 1. Gk. *kerameus* (from *keramos:* "potter's clay, earthenware jar, tile, roof"). A craftsman who made vases on a wheel, which he then baked in an oven.*[1] In the metaphorical sense, probably through its allusions to the creation narrative,[2] this ancient trade served to illustrate God's sovereign freedom toward his creatures.[3]

[1]Sir 38:29f. [2]Gn 2:7. [3]Wis 15:7; Is 29:16; 45:9; 64:7; Jer 18:2-7; Rom 9:21.

2. The "potter's field," situated in the valley of Gehenna,*[4] was to become the "field of blood" after Judas' treason.[5]

[4]Jer 19:2f.; Zec 11:13. [5]Mt 27:7,10 □.

pound Gk. *litra.* A Roman measure of weight, equal to about 327.5 grams (11.55 oz.).[1]

[1]Jn 12:3; 19:39 □.

→ weights.

power Specifically, the word translates the Gk. *dynamis* which does not imply (like *exousia:* "authority") the ordered framework in which power is exercised, but instead, to the notion of might *(ischys, kratos),* adds the idea of potency (might ready to be wielded): in Jesus, his *dynamis* came from his anointing* by the Spirit, while his *exousia* was rather more closely linked by God to his mission.

1. According to the ancients, the world was inhabited by forces which manifested themselves in various ways: the strong man, the man raised up by his dignity or office, the state, the impersonal forces of chaos, the spirits who were mutually at war. While the neighboring religions ended up in a certain dualism,* the Bible, without calling into question the reality of these "powers," regarded God as the All-Powerful,[2] the creator of all, the one who intervened in history by his mighty deeds[3] and who heightened man's capacities by his Spirit.[4]

[1]Mt 24:29 (= Mk 13:25 = Lk 21:26); Rom 8:38; 1 Cor 15:24; Eph 1:21; 1 Pt 3:22. [2]Mk 14:62; Lk 1:49; [3]Mt 22:29 (= Mk 12:24). [4]Mt 19:26 (= Mk 10:27 = Lk 18:27); Mk 14:36; Jn 3:3.

2. Jesus revealed that the all-powerful God was Father* and thus that love* was the source of his power. Jesus showed this omnipotence at work in surprising acts of goodness, his miracles* (*dynameis:* "powerful deeds"),[5] effected by a power which was in him[6] and which he gave to his disciples.[7] Thus, Jesus rendered his adversary* impotent.[8]

[5]Mt 12:22-30; Lk 19:37. [6]Mk 5:30; Lk 4:14; Acts 10:38. [7]Acts 1:8; 4:7,33; 6:8. [8]Mk 3:26f.; Lk 10:19.

3. Christian reflection declared that everything (including the Dominations* and Powers) was created in and for Christ:[9] the resurrection* sealed in fact the victory of omnipotence[10] over the powers par excellence, namely death* and sin.*[11] Surely, sin and death continue to act in the world, but they will be annihilated when Christ hands back the kingdom to his Father.[12]

[9]Col 1:16. [10]Rom 1:4; 2 Cor 13:4; Phil 3:10. [11]1 Cor 15:56. [12]1 Cor 15:20; Rv 1:18; 20:14.

4. Although our vocabulary supports the cosmology implied by the personification of these powers only with difficulty, it remains a fact that sin and death are at work. Also, it is a useful thing to preserve a vocabulary which speaks of the all-powerful Father. In effect, this says that love is stronger than death and, accordingly, that love also is stronger than sin, the ultimate source of death. Jesus revealed the meaning of this power by exercising it in service and in the devotion to duty which culminated in his giving up his life.

→ authority—Dominations—miracle.

Powers **1.** Gk. *dynameis,* the plural of *dynamis:* "power." Also translated by "Dominations."*[1]

[1]Mt 24:29 (= Mk 13:25 = Lk 21:26); Rom 8:38; 1 Cor 15:24; Eph 1:21; 1 Pt 3:22 □.

2. Gk. *exousiai.* Heavenly beings, often working evil, generally named along with the "Authorities"; they were vanquished by Christ.[2]

[2]1 Pt 3:22.

→ Dominations—power.

praetorium Gk. *praitōrion,* from the Lat. *praetorium.*

1. The residence of the praetor, a Roman magistrate with military powers, who was also responsible for justice.[1]

[1]Mt 27:27; Mk 15:16; Jn 18:28,33; 19:9 □.

2. A palace occupied by a prefect or a procurator,* for example Herod's palace at Caesarea.[2]

[2]Acts 23:35 □.

3. The praetorium also referred to a general staff and to a "guard."[3]

[3]Phil 1:13 □.

pray There are no substantial differences between the Greek words *aiteō:* "to ask," *deomai* (stressing the need revealed), and *erōtaō:* "to solicit" (stressing the donor's freedom); used in the secular as in the religious world, they express the idea of asking insistently, praying, begging, and so forth.

1. The N.T. retains the Jewish *forms* of prayer: at meals,[1] at certain hours,[2] standing,[3] kneeling,[4] prostrate on the ground,[5] with upraised hands,[6] ceaselessly.[7] Nevertheless, it was no longer a case of phylacteries* nor of prayer shawls; no more a case of a sacred place, but now one prayed everywhere, outside,[8] in one's private room[9] or in the assembly place.[10]

[1]Mt 15:36 (= Mk 8:6); Acts 27:35; 1 Cor 10:30. [2]Acts 3:1; 10:30. [3]Mk 11:25; Heb 10:11. [4]Lk 22:41; Acts 7:60; 9:40; 20:36; Phil 2:10. [5]Mk 14:35. [6]1 Tim 2:8. [7]Lk 18:1. [8]Mk 1:35. [9]Mt 6:6. [10]Acts 4:31.

2. Jewish *expressions* of prayer were numerous: alleluia,* hosanna,* amen,* doxologies,* canticles,* hymns,* prayers for needs, prayers of intercession,* of thanksgiving* or of adoration.* What was new was that prayer was for one's enemies;[11] an insistence was placed on thanksgiving[12] and, above all, on the *Our Father.*[13]

[11]Mt 5:44. [12]Phil 4:6; 1 Tim 2:1. [13]Mt 6:9-13 (= Lk 11:2-4).

3. By reason of the eschatological* condition that determined a new relationship with God—that of a son—the one who prayed was sure of being heard,[14] for he could do so with Jesus' very own word: Abba.*[15]

[14]Mt 7:7; Mk 11:23f.; Jn 14:13; 15:16; 16:23-26. [15]Lk 14:36; Mk 11:2; Rom 8:15; Gal 4:6.

→ Intr. XIII.2.B.—adore—blessing—intercession—thanksgiving—watch—worship.

preach From the Lat. *prae-dicare:* "to announce, publish." In Greek, various families of words correspond to the phrase "to proclaim the Good News"; while admitting of specific nuances, they were often equivalents.[1] *Euaggelizomai:* "to announce the Good News," *kat-aggellō:* "to announce," *exhēgeomai:* "to interpret," *homologeō:* "to confess," *didaskō:* "to teach," *laleō:* "to speak," *martyreō:* "to witness" and, above all, *kēryssō:* "to proclaim, to announce as a herald." The action verb had it all over the noun: sometimes it stressed the author of the action (so, *kēryx:* "herald"[2]), at other times the content announced (so, *kērygma:* "announcement, message," generally tied to the word,[3] rarely to the function[4]).

[1]Comp. 1 Thes 2:2 and 2:9; Phil 1:18; as well as Lk 4:43; 9:6 and Mk 1:38; 3:14; 6:12. [2]1 Tim 2:7; 2 Tim 1:11; 2 Pt 2:5. [3]Mt 12:41 (= Lk 11:32); 1 Cor 1:21; 2:4; 15:14. [4]Rom 16:25; 2 Tim 4:17; Ti 1:3.

1. Following the lead of the O.T. prophets, John the Baptist preached conversion and baptism;[5] Jesus preached conversion, the Good News of the Kingdom,[6] and entrusted to his disciples the mission of preaching.[7] These proclaimed the Kingdom, the gospel, the word of faith,[8] and, essentially, the person of Christ crucified and present.[9] Situated in its existential context, the message specified that the Holy Spirit was at work;[10] it was preceded by a call to conversion[11] and referred in twofold fashion to a past event (Christ's Passover) and a future event (the Lord's final coming).[12]

[5]Mt 3:1 (= Mk 1:4,7 = Lk 3:3); Acts 10:37; 13:24. [6]Mt 4:17,23; 9:35; 11:1; Mk 1:14,38f.; Lk 4:18f.,44; 8:1. [7]Mt 10:7; Mk 3:14; 6:12; Lk 9:2. [8]Mk 16:20; Acts 20:25; 28:31; Rom 10:8; Gal 2:2; Col 1:23; 1 Thes 2:9; 2 Tim 4:2. [9]Acts 8:5; 9:20; 10:42; 19:13; 1 Cor 1:23; 15:12,14; 2 Cor 1:19; 4:5; 11:4; Phil 1:15; 1 Tim 3:16. [10]Acts 2:4,11,15f.; 1 Thes 1:5. [11]Acts 2:38; 1 Thes 1:9f. [12]Acts 2:22-36; 3:12-16,21; 2 Thes 1:7.

2. The preacher's action was that of Christ's herald who spoke God's word.[13] The Risen One truly spoke through his mouth[14] and came to live in the one who announced his paschal mystery.[15] Further, the herald of the gospel showed himself to be full of assurance and boldness,*[16] proclaiming the Word when convenient and when inconvenient,[17] always solicitous of not rendering the divine word uninspiring.[18] Without fear he could summon to conversion and stir up faith.[19]

[13]1 Cor 9:27; 1 Thes 2:13. [14]Rom 10:14f.; 17. [15]1 Cor 4:9-13; 2 Cor 1:3-11; 3:4–5:21. [16]2 Cor 2:14-16; 4:13. [17]2 Tim 4:2. [18]1 Cor 3:1-22; 2 Cor 2:17. [19]Rom 1:5.

3. The manner of preaching varied according to the audience and circumstances; it could rely on the fulfillment of the Scriptures,[20] admit of evoking Jesus' life,[21] or invite recognition of God the creator of heaven and earth;[22] always it ended by focusing on the mystery of the cross and resurrection of Jesus.[23] Finally, it issued in catechesis and teaching.

[20]Acts 2:17; 3:24; 13:33; 1 Cor 15:3f. [21]Acts 10:37-42. [22]Acts 14:15-17; 17:22-31; 1 Thes 1:9f. [23]1 Cor 1:21; 2:4.

→ catechize—confess—Gospel—kerygma—teach—witness—word.

precious stone Gk. *lithos timios.* Trading in precious stones was important, extending from India to Arabia.[1] The book of Revelation mentions several stones, some of which are hard to identify exactly: amethyst, beryl, chalcedony, chrysolite, chrysoprase, carnelian, emerald, hyacinth, jasper, sapphire, sardonyx, topaz. They may symbolize a visible glory,[2] God's splendor,[3] or the glorious transformation waiting in the New Jerusalem.[4]

[1]Cf. 1 Cor 3:12; Rv 18:12. [2]Rv 17:4; 18:16. [3]Ex 24:10; Rv 4:3. [4]Rv 21:11, 18–20.

predestine Gk. *proorizō* (from *pro:* "before" and *horizō:* "to delimit, fix"): "to destine beforehand." The noun is never used in the N.T. The verb, with a host of others sharing related senses, describes in human categories the activity of God who governs the times of men. Learning the plan of God as it has been realized, the believer traces it to its origin even before the creation of the world.[1]

[1]Eph 1:4.

1. God predestined Jesus to his redemptive passion;[2] he also predestined the "elect*"[3] to accept salvation, to become adopted sons/children, to receive wisdom in virtue of the pre-established plan.*[4] He "knew them beforehand" (Gk. *pro-ginōskō*), that is, he "chose them beforehand."[5] He "prepared them beforehand" (Gk. *pro-etoimazō*) for glory,[6] to put good deeds into practice;[7] he "prepared" (Gk. *hetoimazō*) a kingdom where there are places foreseen,[8] salvation,[9] and, in a word, all that is needed for those who love him.[10] He "instituted beforehand" (Gk. *pro-cheirizomai*) Christ or the mission of Paul.[11] He "fixed, determined" (Gk. *horizō*) the times and places of the human race,[12] the lot of the Son of Man who will be judge of all as Son of God,[13] and also a new day for believers.[14] God "orders" (Gk. *tassō*) the major moments of creation,[15] as well as eternal life.[16] He "constituted, organized" (Gk. *kat-artizō*) worlds, the body of Jesus.[17] He "sets up for" (Gk. *tithēmi eis*) salvation,[18] so that Jesus is "set for" (Gk. *keimai eis*) the raising up of men, and Paul for the Gospel.[19] In this way the constant presence of the God who presided over everything is described, and all this was for the salvation* of men. Nonetheless, we should observe that the verbs *hetoimazō, keimai* and *tithēmi* can also have a negative outcome as their object: a fall and eternal fire;[20] but these verbs never have the prefix *pro-,* although we must also add that the Semitic mind willingly telescoped secondary causes. This indicates that God's initiative toward salvation will illumine the secrets of hearts: Christ is in the world as a sign of contradiction. Also, despite appearances, biblical language does not strike a blow for freedom: while the elect are said to be "prepared beforehand for glory," the others are simply found "all ready for perdition."[21]

[2]Acts 4:28; cf. 2:23. [3]Rom 8:29; 11:2; 1 Pt 1:2. [4]Rom 8:29f.; 1 Cor 2:7; Eph 1:5,11. [5]1 Pt 1:20. [6]Rom 9:23. [7]Eph 2:10. [8]Mt 20:23 (= Mk 10:40); 25:34; Jn 14:2f. [9]Lk 2:31. [10]1 Cor 2:9. [11]Acts 3:20; 22:14; 26:16. [12]Acts 17:26. [13]Lk 22:22; Acts 2:23; 10:42; 17:31; Rom 1:4. [14]Heb 4:7. [15]Acts 17:26. [16]Acts 13:48. [17]Heb 10:5; 11:3. [18]1 Thes 5:9; 1 Pt 2:8. [19]Lk 2:34; Phil 1:16. [20]Mt 25:41; Lk 2:34. [21]Rom 9:22f.

2. The verbs used possess a temporal dimension, whether derived from the preposition *pro-* (before, going ahead of, from which the idea of initiative stems), or by virtue of their contextual setting. Viewed through the prism of our temporal condition, the divine predilection cannot help but appear as "predestination," implying even the rejection of those who are not elected. But this is nothing less than a case of transposing into spatial and temporal terms a reality which cannot be subjected to such categories. The prefix *pre-* projects into time a priority that belongs to the realm of interpersonal relationships, those between God and men. Consequently, it is in the transposition into personalist terms that temporal terms find their true meaning: "God himself first loved us,"[22] lavishing upon men his invincible attractiveness.[23]

[22]Eph 1:1,3-5; 1 Jn 4:19. [23]Jn 6:44; 10:29; 17:2,6,15,24.

→ election—time.

[pre-existence] In order to pierce the secret of history man has always attempted to return by faith to a time before time itself, a realm belonging to God. Thus, man was a god who had fallen and who remembered the heavens. Among Jews, the divine Wisdom* was conceived as active at the beginning of creation;[1] according to the tradition of Enoch,* the Son of Man pre-existed creation.

[1]Intr. XII.3.C; Jb 28:20-27; Prv 8:22-31.

2. In focusing its faith on Jesus, the N.T., as the heir of this language, proclaims Christ as the image* of the invisible God, the firstborn* of every creature,[2] the Son* of God come into the world to save men;[3] he was God with God.[4] In addition, probably through contacts with Hellenistic representations, he came down from heaven to earth.[5]

[2]Col 1:15. [3]Gal 4:4. [4]Jn 1:1. [5]Jn 3:13; 6:38,62.

3. By means of this terminology, the believer is called, not to identify an affirmation of the faith with some spatial or temporal representation, but through faith to look toward the totality of the mystery of Jesus Christ. Jesus of Nazareth is the unique man through whom and in whom all men receive salvation; having been raised up, he extends his presence to the full extent of time. This is what pre-existence terminology expresses in its locating of Christ before time.

→ election—Jesus Christ—predestine.

prefect

→ Intr. IV.2.B.b.—procurator.

Preparation Day Gk. *Paraskeuē:* "Parasceve,* Preparation Day." The day preceding the sabbath or the Passover,* during which one had to prepare for the feast.[1]

[1]Mt 27:62; Mk 15:42; Lk 23:54; Jn 19:14,31,42 □.

→ Intr. XIII.2.B.b.—feast—sabbath.

presbyter From the Gk. *presbyteros* (a substantival adjective, the comparative of *presbys:* "the older of two," "the elder,[1]" "the old man"[2]) which referred to an elder, Jew[3] or Christian:[4] the leader of a community, corresponding to the "overseer" (episcope) but not to the priest (in the modern sense).

[1]Lk 15:25. [2]Jn 8:9; Acts 2:17; 1 Tim 5:1f., Rv 4:4,10; 5:5-11ff. [3]Mt 15:2; Acts 4:5; Heb 11:2. [4]Acts 14:23; Jas 5:14.

→ Intr. I.4.—elder—episcope—priest.

present, Presentation of Jesus Gk. *paristēmi* (replaced in the present tense by *paristanō*).

1. In its intransitive use: "to keep oneself" before; for a servant it meant to keep himself ready for his master's assignment,[1] just as an angel or a minister of God,[2] or like a prophet[3] or in the manner of a priest who keeps himself before God to "serve" him (Gk. *leitourgeō*).[4] In similar fashion, one may be called to "appear" before Caesar[5] or before God's judgment.[6]

[1]1 Kgs 10:8. [2]Lk 1:19; Rv 8:2; 11:4. [3]1 Kgs 17:1. [4]Dt 10:8; 18:5,7. [5]Acts 27:24. [6]Rom 4:10.

2. In its transitive use: "to present" an offering (Gk. *pros-pherō, prosphora*) to the Lord, in a context of worship. Thus, Jesus was "presented" to the Lord in his temple.[7] In the N.T., worship becomes "spiritual" and the believer must "present himself, offer himself as a living victim."[8] By baptism he has stopped offering (the verb is in the present imperative) his members to sin; he must ceaselessly offer (the verb is in the aorist) his members for justice, that is, at every moment make real this worshipful offering which his life ought to be.[9]

[7]Lk 2:22. [8]Rom 12:1; cf. 1 Cor 8:8. [9]Rom 6:13,16,19.

→ sacrifice—worship.

press Gk. *lēnos:* properly a vat* for making wine. The press was constructed out of two superimposed parts: the first, a tiled surface on which grapes were crushed by feet to the rhythm of songs and to cries of joy,[1] the second, a vat hewn out of rock into which the must flowed.[2] There were also oil presses. The press symbolized an overwhelming trial,[3] God having been identified with the vintager who treads down upon the press,[4] and the vat having become the wrath of God.*[5]

[1]Jgs 6:11; Is 16:10. [2]Nm 18:27. [3]Lam 1:15. [4]Is 63:2f. [5]Rv 14:19f.

→ oil—vat—wine.

pride **1.** A series of Greek terms evoked the image of haughtiness whether directly with the word *hypsoō:* "to lift up" (for example, oneself),[1] to be haughty,[2] or with the help of the prefix *hyper* (above) placed before *airō,* "to lift";[3] before *(ē)phania:* "an affected manner," as contrasted with humility;[4] before *phroneō,* "to esteem";[5] before *ogkos,* "volume."[6]

[1]Mt 23:12; Lk 1:52; 2 Cor 10:5. [2]Rom 11:20. [3]2 Cor 12:7; 2 Thes 2:4 △. [4]Mk 7:22; Lk 1:51; Rom 1:30; 2 Tim 3:2; Jas 4:6; 1 Pt 5:5 △. [5]Rom 12:3 △. [6]2 Pt 2:18; Jude 16 △.

2. Another metaphor was that of inflation brought about through a blowing up, whence to inflate, to puff up, in Gk. *physioō* (related to *physaō*).[7] One might also link with it the verb *typhoō:* "to overrun with smoke," to blind with the smoke of pride.[8]

[7]1 Cor 4:6,18f.; 5:2; 8:1; 13:4; 2 Cor 12:20; Col 2:18 △. [8]1 Tim 3:6; 6:4; 2 Tim 3:4 △.

3. Boasting or bragging (*alazoneia;*[9] cf. Plautus' *miles gloriosus*) was indicated by the word *kauchēsis,* taken in its negative meaning: a man boasted about himself because he established his own self-assurance and trust*[10] in himself, whereas true confidence* has its ground in God alone.[11]

[9]Rom 1:30; 2 Tim 3:2; Jas 4:16; 1 Jn 2:16 △. [10]Ps 49:7. [11]Sir 50:20; Jer 9:22f.; Rom 3:27; 4:2; 11:18; 1 Cor 1:29,31; 3:21; 4:7; 5:6; 2 Cor 10:8-17; 11:10-30; Gal 6:13f.; Eph 2:9; Jas 3:14.

→ confidence—humility—trust.

priest The word derives from the Greek *presbyteros:* "old man," the "elder" entrusted with presiding over the believing community. Today, however, it has inherited some of the meaning of the Greek term *hiereus* (from *hieros:* "sacred"); it is in this latter sense that the word is examined here.

1. It designated every responsible official in the world of the sacred,* among the pagans[1] as well as in the O.T.[2] In Jesus' time the priesthood, reserved by inheritance in Israel to members of the sacerdotal families, was the privilege of Aaron's* descendants. Separated off from among them was the High Priest,* appointed and deposed by the Romans; the leaders of the priests, or the high priests, were members of the priestly aristocracy of Jerusalem. At the prescribed age, the priest was introduced by an ordination to sacrificial* acts,[3] to the carrying out of rites,[4] to service in the Temple[5] (to prepare the sacrifice, to burn the perfumes . . .). He did not have responsibility for the teaching of the Law, a matter which the scribes* afterwards reserved for themselves.[6] Habitually residing in villages where they had "benefices," the priests, who were divided into classes, officiated by turns in Temple duty for the length of a week at a time.[7]

[1]Acts 14:13. [2]Intr. XIII.1 and 2. [3]Heb 10:11. [4]Mt 8:4 (= Mk 1:44 = Lk 5:14); Lk 17:14. [5]Lk 1:5,8f. [6]Mt 7:29. [7]Lk 1:8.

2. The N.T. never applies this priestly vocabulary to the ministers of the New Covenant (except in Rom 15:16) for the ministry of the Gospel. Only Jesus Christ was the High Priest,* and that was in a new sense: having fulfilled the ancient Covenant, he brought about a change from the cultic* to the personal. Cultic sacrifice no longer had any worth except through Jesus' personal sacrifice; when Jesus "consecrated" himself, the Church was "sanctified"[8] and found itself responsible for offering spiritual sacrifice.[9]

[8]Jn 17:19f. [9]1 Pt 2:5-9; Rv 1:6; 5:10; 20:6; cf. Ex 19:6.

→ Aaron—High Priest—Melchizedek—priesthood—sacred—sacrifice.

priesthood The sacerdotal order, a term deriving from the Lat. *sacerdotium,* an abstract word which describes the state of the *sacerdos,* the man who "establishes, does" *(do)* sacred objects or the "sacred" *(sacer),* the one who consecrates *(sacrificium).* This word translated various Greek words: *hierōsynē*[1] (the quality of the priesthood), *hierateia*[2] (the priestly function), *hierateuma*[3] (the priestly body).

[1]Heb 7:11f.,24 △. [2]Lk 1:9; Heb 7:5 △. [3]1 Pt 2:5,9 △; cf. Lk 1:8.

1. The sacerdotal or priestly function underwent a long evolution in the O.T. and Judaism. First of all exercized by the head of the family or by the king, it was entrusted to a specialized tribe,* that of Levi.*[4] Hence, the coming of a hierarchical institution: at the top, the High Priest,* who had two principal tasks, the offering of sacrifice and the service of Torah*; next, the priests,* the sons of Aaron*; and, finally, the Levites.*

[4]Ex 32:25-29; Dt 33:8-11; Heb 7:5.

2. The Christians put an end to the ancient priestly institution, seeing in Jesus the unique and definitive High Priest, according to the order of Melchizedek*:[5] Christ offered himself as the perfect sacrifice.[6]

[5]Heb 7:11-24. [6]Eph 5:2; Heb 9:14.

3. The Christian people was the priestly body enjoined by Jesus Christ to offer spiritual sacrifices* and to spread the Word of Christ.[7] Christian life became in its entirety a spiritual worship.*[8]

[7]1 Pt 2:5,9; Rv 1:6; 5:10; 20:6. [8]Rom 12:1; Phil 2:17; 4:18; Heb 13:15f.

4. Is the priesthood of the people one that is exercised by a number of "representatives" with special rights? The answer in the N.T. is not explicit: it cannot come about through an extension or renewal of the O.T. priestly institution, but it seems to be implied by the Church* and by the rite of the laying on of hands,* which transmits the power of an order, a sharing in Christ's unique priesthood.

→ people—priest—sacrifice—worship.

[primitive] This term describes a tradition, text, or context as the oldest, the one nearest the happenings.

Prince of This World

→ Satan.

Principalities Gk. *archai,* the plural of *archē* (the name of an action): "beginning, initiative," from which there are derived the authorities, the heavenly powers.[1]

[1]Rom 8:38; 1 Cor 15:24; Eph 1:21; 3:10; 6:12; Col 1:16; 2:10,15 □.

→ Dominations.

Priscilla Gk. *Priskilla,* the wife of Aquila.*[1]

[1]Acts 18:2 □.

prison Gk. *desmōtērion* (from *deō:* "to bind" and *desmōtēs:* "prisoner"), *phylakē* (from *phylassō:* "to guard"). Before all else, a preventive penalty while one waited for a judicial decision;[1] also, a repressive penalty, for example, for insolvent debts.*[2] Prisoners were lashed together or chained to soldiers or to a wall by the foot, hand or neck.[3] In a metaphorical* sense, the place where Satan is shut up[4] and where men not yet saved are held,[5] or captives of sin.[6]

[1]Mt 14:3 (= Mk 6:17); Lk 3:20; Acts 4:3; 5:18; 12:4f.; 16:23; 21:33–28:31; 2 Cor 6:5; 11:23; Eph 3:1; Phil 1:7; Heb 11:36. [2]Mt 5:25; 18:30. [3]Jer 29:26; Mt 27:2 (= Mk 15:1); Jn 18:12; Acts 12:6; 16:24; 26:29,31; 2 Tim 2:9. [4]Rv 20:2,7; cf. Jude 6. [5]Lk 4:18; 1 Pt 3:19. [6]Rom 7:6-23.

→ Intr. XIV.1.B.—captive.

Probatica Sheep Gate.

proconsul From the Lat. *proconsul,* Gk. *anthypatos.* A former consul assigned to the government of a senatorial province.*[1] However, the proconsul possessed no military power; his office constituted the honorable end of a career for members of the Roman aristocracy. Sergius Paulus* was intelligent and became a believer.*[2] Gallio showed himself to be wise in his intervention.[3]

[1]Acts 19:38. [2]Acts 13:7-12. [3]Acts 18:12-17.

→ Intr. IV.2.B; IV.4.

procurator From the Lat. *procurator; hēgemōn* in Greek. A subaltern official. Called "prefect" up until 42, he was directly dependent on the emperor. In Judea the procurator was subject in part to the legate* of Syria. He had to take account of Herod's* descendants, whose powers were poorly defined, a factor that caused much friction. The procurator had to ensure the preservation of order amid an agitated populace; also, on Passover feast days he went up from his residence in Caesarea* to Jerusalem.

→ Intr. IV.2; IV.4.—governor—Pilate.

progress

→ grow, growth.

promise Gk. *epaggelia.* This word, which meant an "announcement, order, promise" in secular Greek, was unknown in either the O.T. or the gospels;[1] it was a term characteristic of Paul's writings, the Acts and the Epistle to the Hebrews. It took up again the contemporary biblical feature of hope:* God fulfilled what he had said;[2] God's word and prophecy were recapitulated in the word "promise." When realized, the promise *(ep-aggelia)* became the Good News *(ep-aggelizomai).*[3] The word underlined the radical gratuity of God's gift,*[4] in contrast to the law of works.[5] Ordinarily, it was linked with inheritance*[6] and had for its object the land,[7] rest,[8] the Kingdom,[9] life,[10] the Savior,[11] and the Holy Spirit.[12] In Jesus, the promises find their yes.[13]

[1]Except Lk 24:49. [2]Jos 23:14; Rom 9:4; 15:8; Eph 2:12; 6:2; Heb 6:13; 10:23; 11:33. [3]Acts 13:32; Rom 1:2. [4]Rom 4:13-21. [5]Gal 3:17-22. [6]Gal 3:18-29; Heb 6:17; 9:15. [7]Acts 7:5; Heb 11:9. [8]Heb 4:1. [9]Jas 2:5. [10]1 Tim 4:8; 2 Tim 1:1; Ti 1:12; Jas 1:12; 1 Jn 2:25. [11]Acts 13:23; Gal 3:16. [12]Lk 24:49; Acts 2:33; Gal 3:14; Eph 1:13. [13]2 Cor 1:20; Rv 3:14.

→ hope.

prophet Gk. *prophētēs* (from *phēmi:* "to say" and *pro:* "in advance of," "in place of," "in advance" or "in public"): this spokesman was a man sent on a mission and inspired by God to reveal some secret thing, to deliver an oracle,* to speak and make others grasp the divine thought and will, and, finally, sometimes to foretell the future. The Heb. word *nâbî* (deriving from the Akkadian*: "to call," "to announce") had appreciably the same meaning. Through the biblical prophet, God brought about his design for salvation and spoke his word, setting in motion a modification of the present time and, occasionally, making known the future.

1. The prophets of the O.T., along with the Law* (and the sages), constituted Holy Scripture;[1] sometimes their names were given, like those of Isaiah, or Jeremiah or Samuel.[2] By speaking through their mouths, God made known his plan,* not so that we could test its exactitude when prophecy was accomplished, but so that we could situate happenings which had come to pass and which were scandalous, such as Jesus' cross.[3] "The Prophet like Moses" was one of the figures* under which the Christ revealed himself.[4]

[1]Mt 5:17; Acts 13:15; Rom 3:21. [2]Mt 4:14; 16:14; Acts 3:24. [3]Acts 3:18,21. [4]Dt 18:15; Jn 1:21; 6:14; 7:40; Acts 3:22f.,7:37.

2. Men and women who prophesied clustered around Jesus: Zechariah, Anna[5] and John the Baptist: the latter revealed the contemporary meaning of the Law,[6] proclaimed the imminent judgment,[7] proposed a baptism of repentance[8] and discerned Him who was at hand.[9] Jesus was taken for a prophet,[10] but he did not claim the title; he contented himself with acting as he did: he denounced the excesses of the religious leaders and of the Jews,[11] revealed the content of the signs* of the times[12] and recognized that he was vowed to the tragic fate of the prophets,[13] all the while foretelling his unique destiny.[14] But, he set himself above the prophets,[15] for he procured salvation[16] and pronounced words on his own authority.[17]

[5]Lk 1:67; 2:36. [6]Mt 11:9f., 13; 14:4; Lk 3:11-14. [7]Mt 3:2,8. [8]Mt 3:11 (= Mk 1:7f. = Lk 3:16). [9]Jn 1:26,31. [10]Mt 16:14 (= Mk 8:28 = Lk 9:19); Lk 7:16; Jn 6:14; 7:40; 9:17. [11]Mt 15:7; Mk 11:15-17; Lk 11:52. [12]Mt 16:2f. (= Lk 12:54-56). [13]Mt 23:37 (= Lk 13:34). [14]Mt 21:37 (= Mk 12:6 = Lk 20:13). [15]Mt 12:41 (= Lk 11:32). [16]Lk 10:24; 1 Pt 1:10f. [17]Mt 5:22; 7:29.

3. At Pentecost and during the early period of the Church, the gift of prophecy was renewed by the Holy Spirit[18] to such an extent that a prophetic charism* existed,[19] exercised in fact by all kinds of men and women in the Church.[20] The role of these prophets, doubtlessly distinct from that of the prophets who made up the Church's foundation,[21] was to reveal secrets,[22] to exhort, to console, and to build up;[23] unlike the false prophets (Gk. *pseudo-prophētēs*),[24] they prophesied in accord with apostolic authority.[25]

[18]Nm 11:29; Jl 3:1f.; Acts 2:4,17f.; 19:6. [19]1 Cor 14:1-5; 1 Thes 5:20. [20]Acts 11:27f.; 13:1f.; 21:9f.; Rv 10:11; 18:20. [21]1 Cor 12:28f.; Eph 2:20; 4:11. [22]1 Cor 13:2; Rv 1:3; 22:7,10,18f. [23]1 Cor 14:3; Rv 10:7; 11:3. [24]Mt 7:15; 24:11,24 (= Mk 13:22); Lk 6:26; Acts 13:6; 2 Pt 2:1; 1 Jn 4:1; Rv 2:20; 16:13; 19:20; 20:10 △. [25]1 Cor 14:27,33; 1 Tim 1:18.

→ Intr. XII.2.—Bible—Daniel—Elijah—Elisha—Hosea—Isaiah—Jeremiah—Jonah—Moses—Zechariah.—Chart, p. 67.

propitiatory The Gk. *hilastērion* (from *hilaskomai:* "to seek to make oneself favorable") translated the Heb. *kapporèt,* primitively: "what covers over sins," then "what removes sins." A golden plate, adorned with two Cherubim,* set upon the ark* in the Holy of Holies.* The throne of divine presence and the place above all others of Yahweh's forgiveness,* on condition of the sprinkling* of sacrificial blood by the High Priest* on the Day of Atonement.* In Jesus' time it was no longer found in the Temple.[1]

[1]Ex 25:17-22; Lv 16:14; Rom 3:25; Heb 9:5 □; cf. 1 Jn 2:2; 4:10.

→ ark—Atonement (Feast of the)—expiate—forgive—reconcile.

proselyte Gk. *prosēlytos* (connected with the future *pros-eleusomai* from the verb *pros-erchomai:* "to draw near to"). A pagan converted to Judaism and drawn into the Jewish people by circumcision,* a bath* of purification* and a sacrifice* at the Temple. Although he was not a Jew entirely and, though subject to juridical restrictions, he was spiritually "newborn," according to a rabbinic expression, and was held to observing the totality of the Law.*[1] To be distinguished from God-fearers.*

[1]Mt 23:15; Acts 2:11; 6:5; 13:43 □.

→ On the missionary movement: Intr. IV.6.E; IV.7; cf. XI.2.

prostitution Gk. *porneia* (derived from *pernēmi:* "to sell"), translating the Heb. *zenût,* a term which encompassed the very broad meaning of debauchery* or misconduct. A practice current among the neighboring peoples on the occasion of the sale of slaves,[1] prostitution was reproved by the Law,*[2] especially when it took on a sacred character;[3] it nonetheless existed in Israel since relations with unmarried women did not constitute adultery.* In keeping with the Covenant's conjugal symbolism, the prophets saw in the prostitute a figure* of the Israel which was unfaithful to its God.[4] Thus, we find use of this term to refer to idolatrous* worship,[5] as well as the designation of the city of inquity,[6] the antithesis of Jerusalem, as the Great Prostitute.

[1]Cf. 1 Cor 6:15f. [2]Lv 19:29. [3]Dt 23:18. [4]Ez 16:26; Hos 1–3. [5]Rv 2:14,20f. [6]Rv 17:1–19:2.

→ adultery—vices.

province Lat. *provincia,* Gk. *ep-archia* (from *archō:* "to command"). A region occupied by the Romans and forming a state under the authority of a governor.* When it was pacified, the province was said to be senatorial, under the authority of a proconsul* (such as Achaia*); if the presence of troops was still held to be necessary, it was designated imperial, under the authority of a legate, prefect or procurator* (as was the case with Judea*).[1]

[1]Acts 23:34; 25:1.

→ Intr. IV.2.B.

psalms Gk. *psalmos* (from *psallō:* "to cause the cord of a musical instrument to vibrate"): "a poem accompanying a musical piece."

1. Jewish canticles inspired* by God, which made up one of the O.T. books and constituted the prayer* of the chosen people and that of Jesus. Sometimes attributed to David, they were interpreted in a messianic* sense in relation to Christ.[1] After the paschal meal the Hallel was sung (that is, Psalms 115–118), a custom summarized in the single verb *hymneō* ("to sing the hymn").[2]

[1]Lk 20:42; 24:44; Acts 1:20; 13:33; cf. Rom 15:9. [2]Mt 26:30 (= Mk 14:26).

2. Christian songs inspired by the Holy Spirit.[3]

[3]1 Cor 14:15,26; Eph 5:19; Col 3:16; Jas 5:13 □.

→ Intr. XII; XIII.2.B.—doxology—hymn—song.

public square Gk. *agora:* "assembly, marketplace" (Heb. *shûq:* "souk"). Public squares were found at the entrances to cities and villages, not in the interior. Each was the place of public life,[1] the place where judgments were rendered,[2] where one chatted,[3] played,[4] strutted about.[5] Large streets* cannot be likened to them.

[1]Sg 3:2; Mk 6:56; 7:4; Acts 17:17. [2]Acts 16:19; cf 19:38. [3]Mt 20:3; Acts 17:5. [4]Mt 11:16 (= Lk 7:32). [5]Mt 23:7 (= Mk 12:38 = Lk 20:46) □.

→ agora—door—street.

publican In Lat. *publicanus* (derived from *publicus:* "public"): "a gatherer of public monies"; Gk. *telōnēs* (from *telos:* "tax"). In the N.T., the word refers not to the important official who organized the levying of the tax* (a kind of general contractor), but to a minor Jewish subordinate official, whom we generally ought to call a "collector of taxes." He was despised and equated with public sinners*[1] because of his links with the pagan occupying power[2] and his frequent extortion;[3] based on this, he was kept at a distance by every Jewish observer of the Law, but not by Jesus.[4]

[1]Mt 9:11 (= Mk 2:16 = Lk 5:30). [2]Mt 18:17. [3]Lk 3:12f. [4]Mt 5:46; 11:19 (= Lk 7:34); 21:31; Lk 7:29; 15:1f.; 18:13f.; 19:2-9.

→ Intr. VI.3.A.—custom—Levi—Matthew—tax—Zacchaeus.

punish, punishment **1.** Gk. *kolazō:* to prune, to trim, to cut something off, to contain, hence "to chastise, to punish." The word implied an aspect of education, well in keeping with the tradition of Yahweh training his people to bring it to a state of not sinning: punishment was oriented to the revelation of God's love and to the transformation of a sinful people.[1] In the N.T., besides its ordinary meaning,[2] only one text speaks of a "definitive punishment,"[3] prepared for those who refuse conversion; moreover, the word allowed for the linking of fear* with love.*[4]

[1]Ex 20:5; 34:7; Ez 11:10; 15:7; 18:31; Hos 11:9. [2]Acts 4:21. [3]Mt 25:46; cf. 2 Pt 2:9. [4]1 Jn 4:18 △.

2. Gk. *timōreō* (related to *timē:* "honor"):[5] to protect the honor, to avenge justice (Gk. *dikē*), with the idea of making the one who transgressed pay; the background to this lies in the pattern of social relationships of a vengeful social justice: that of the responsible city authority (Gk. *ek-dikos*).[6] Above all else, it was a case of a punitive sanction deserved by the guilty party.

[5]Acts 22:5; 26:11; 2 Cor 2:6; Heb 10:29 △. [6]Rom 13:4; 1 Pt 2:14; cf. Jude 7 △.

→ hell—justice—vengeance—wrath.

punishment (capital)

→ capital punishment.

pure Purity was a condition required of whatever (person, animal or thing) drew near to the holy* God. It was first of all a cultic* term and only secondarily did it take on a moral or spiritual dimension. There were two principal families of Greek words involved. *Hagnos,* deriving (as well as *hagios*) from the root *hag-:* "holy," put greater stress on the condition that man must acquire in his bond of worship with the Holy God.[1] *Katharos* (a word of uncertain etymology), while it may also have had the meaning of physically clean,[2] especially concerned man's condition, whether that be cultic, moral or spiritual. Something *a-kathartos* might exist in the presence of the God who alone was holy, but the same was not the case with something not *hagnos.* Moreover, numerous terms from the two word families (designated below by the initial letters H and K) attempt to describe (chiefly by the use of *a* privative) a state of purity: without stain *(a-miantōs,* from *miasma);*[3] without blemish *(a-mōmos);*[4] without mixture *(a-keraios);*[5] without spot *(a-spilos)*[6] or wrinkle *(rhytis);*[7] or, positively, with a term like *eilikrinēs:* "sincere"[8] and, negatively, with a term like *koinos:* "profane,"[9] *rhypos:* "filthiness, dirt."[10]

[1]1 Pt 1:15f.,22. [2]Mt 27:59; Rv 15:6; 19:8,14; 21:18,21. [3]Jn 18:28; Ti 1:15; Heb 7:26; 12:15; 13:4; Jas 1:27; 1 Pt 1:4; 2 Pt 2:10,20; Jude 8 △. [4]Eph 1:4; 5:27; Phil 2:15; Col 1:22; Heb 9:14; 1 Pt 1:19; 2 Pt 2:13; 3:14; Jude 24; Rv 14:5 △. [5]Mt 10:16; Rom 16:19; Phil 2:15 △. [6]Eph 5:27; 1 Tim 6:14; Jas 1:27; 3:6; 1 Pt 1:19; 2 Pt 2:13; 3:14; Jude 23 △. [7]Eph 5:27 △. [8]1 Cor 5:8; 2 Cor 1:12; 2:17; Phil 1:10; 2 Pt 3:1 △. [9]Mt 15:11,18,20; Mk 7; Acts 10:14,f.,28; 11:8f.; 21:28; Rom 14:14; Heb 9:13; 10:29; Rv 21:27 △. [10]Jas 1:21; 2:2; 1 Pt 3:21; Rv 22:11 △.

1. Cultic purity. The Jews shared the thinking of their age when they specified in their rites the conditions for access to the sacred territory which the holy God had set aside for himself from the profane world.[11] At the other extreme, the demons were by definition "unclean spirits." Like his contemporaries,[12] Jesus observed the ritual prescriptions,[13] but he castigated excesses in their observance, particularly those concerned with dietary taboos[14] and he even declared these rites to be useless to the extent that they did not express a purity of heart.*[15] Nevertheless, the Church as it came to birth needed a long time to free itself from these taboos;[16] Paul even fought them by comparing them to the "elements of the world,"*[17] for in his words, "to those who are pure, all things are pure."[18]

[11]Ex 19:10; Lv 11–16; Nm 6:3. [12]Lk 2:22; Jn 2:6; 11:55; Acts 21:24-26; 24:18. [13]Mt 8:4 (= Mk 1:44 = Lk 5:14); Lk 17:14(K). [14]Mt 15:1-20 (= Mk 7:1-23); 23:25,27; Lk 11:39. [15]Mt 5:8; Mk 7:19; cf. 1 Tim 1:5; 3:9; 2 Tim 1:3. [16]Acts 10:15; 11:9; 15:9; Gal 2:12. [17]Gal 4:3,9; Col 2:16-23. [18]Rom 14:14,20; 1 Cor 10:23; Ti 1:15.

2. Christian purity. Believers have understood that Jesus, by his word*[19] and the blood* he shed,[20] was discovered as the source of authentic purity. Words of purification or of purity henceforth acquired a moral and spiritual dimension that transformed their meaning. Facing God on the last day (root K) the believer will be irreproachable, innocent;[21] when facing men (root H) he must reveal himself to be chaste, pure, "sincere," loyal;[22] negatively, he must avoid impurity (root K).[23] Such "virtues" find their source in the Holy Spirit.[24]

[19]Mk 7:1-23; Jn 15:3; cf. 1 Pt 1:22. [20]Jn 13:10; Eph 5:26; Ti 2:14; Heb 1:3; 9–10; 1 Jn 1:7,9; 3:3. [21]1 Cor 5:7; 2 Cor 7:1; Col 1:22; 1 Thes 2:3; 2 Tim 2:21f.; Jas 1:27; 4:8. [22]2 Cor 6:6; 7:11; 11:3; Phil 1:17; 1 Tim 4:12; 5:2,22; Ti 2:5; Jas 4:8; 1 Pt 3:2. [23]Rom 1:24; 6:19; Gal 5:19; Eph 4:19; 5:3,5; Col 3:5; 1 Thes 2:3; 4:7; Rv 17:4. [24]Gal 5:22.

→ Intr. XIV.1.A; XIV.2.B.—holy—sacred—sin.

purple Gk. *porphyra.* Colored material, of a dark red color verging on violet, obtained from the liquid secreted by a sea mollusk *(murex trunculus).* A fabric of great value.[1]

[1]Est 8:15; Dn 5:7; Mk 15:17,20; Lk 16:19; Jn 19:2,5; Acts 16:14; Rv 17:4; 18:12,16 □.

purse

→ wallet.

Q

[Q] The initial letter of the German word *Quelle:* "source," designating in literary criticism* the material common to Matthew and Luke not reported by Mark. According to the various critics, this abbreviation sometimes refers to a document whose extent, nature and origin one reckons to be able to delimit, at other times it refers to a mass of materials of diverse origins: in the latter case, it is a simple convention useful for indicating the "double tradition," that is, the tradition underlying Matthew and Luke, independent of Mark.

[Qumran] A place name of the northwest bank of the Dead Sea (13 km. [8 mi.] to the south of Jericho,* near Ain Feshka, which gave its name, by extension, to a kind of "monastery" where, from 150 B.C. to A.D. 68, Jews who had broken with official Judaism lived. Some of their characteristics were rigor in the rules of legal purity (the practice of frequent ablutions*), the observance of the ancient solar calendar* governing the liturgy of feasts, a dualistic* and deterministic conception of the plan of God, rejection of the stone Temple. The sect presents numerous affinities with the Essenes,* as well as with the Damascus Document.* Beginning in 1947, excavations have brought to light a veritable library stashed away in the neighboring grottoes: Hebrew texts of the Bible and of the apocrypha,* Greek translations of the Bible, writings proper to the sect.

In references to these findings, the letter Q indicates the Qumran origin, the number that precedes indicates the number of the cave where the manuscript was found, the letter following describes the work. Thus, 1QS (Heb. *sérèk:* "rule" of the community, or the Manual of Discipline), 1QH (Heb. *hôdayôt:* "Hymns"), 1 QM (Heb. *milhâmâ:* "war" between the sons of light and the sons of darkness), 1 Qp (Heb. *péshèr:* "interpretation" of a text like Habakkuk: 1 Qp Hb). The manuscripts of Qumran cast a new light on the texts of the N.T., particularly on the existence of a religious current different from that of the Pharisees.*

→ Intr. XI.3.—Map 4.

quadrant Gk. *kodrantēs,* Lat. *quadrans.* A small bronze coin (3.10 g.), corresponding to a "quarter" of an as,* or two lepta.*[1]

[1]Mt 5:26; Mk 12:42 □.

→ coins.

Quirinius Gk. *Kyrēnios.* Publius Sulpicius Quirinius, the governor* of Syria beginning in A.D. 6; consul from 12 B.C., he was responsible for Roman political order in the Near East.[1]

[1]Lk 2:2 □.

→ census.

rabbi **1.** A Hebrew term (*rabbî*[1]) and Aramaic term (*rabbounî*[2]), the equivalents of "my teacher." A respectful manner of addressing doctors of the Law.* Jesus protested against this usage.[3]

[1]Mt 26:25; Jn 3:26ff. [2]Mk 10:51; Jn 20:16 △. [3]Mt 23:7f.

2. Beginning in A.D. 70, a name for Jewish specialists in the Scriptures: they formed rabbinical schools.

→ Intr. XII.1.C.—master—teach.

[rabbinism] From the Hebrew *rabbî:* "teacher." A teaching tradition of Judaism that came to birth in the first century and has determined the life of Jewish communities to our day. Rabbinic literature is essentially comprised of the Talmud,* the Midrashim* and the Tosephta (from the Heb. *âsâph:* "to assemble, add": complementary traditions).

raca Gk. *raka.* A rare Aramaic term, probably from the Heb. *réqâ:* "hollow." A head without a brain or a man devoid of morality.[1]

[1]Mt 5:22 □.

→ folly.

race Gk. *genos* (from *gignomai:* "be born"): "race, family." The word may mean someone's birthplace,[1] the type of family of which he is the issue,[2] but most particularly his belonging to Israel,[3] to the chosen race forever;[4] can even refer to the divine origin of man.[5]

[1]Mk 7:26; Acts 4:36; 7:13; 18:2,24. [2]Acts 4:6. [3]Acts 7:19; 13:26; 2 Cor 11:26; Gal 1:14; Phil 3:5; Rv 22:16. [4]1 Pt 2:9. [5]Acts 17:28f. □.

→ beget—born—genealogy.

rain Gk. *brochē, hyetos.* According to his will, God opens the reservoirs of water which, the Hebrews imagined, were situated above heaven.[1] This water from heaven, occasionally catastrophic,[2] was, nonetheless, indispensible for the fruitfulness of the fields. Not able to be produced by men's labor (like irrigation), it symbolized God's gratuitous and fruitful gift.[3] When fiery, it symbolized punishment.[4]

[1]Ps 33:7; Mi 5:6; Rv 11:6. [2]Mt 7:25,27; Acts 28:2. [3]Lv 26:3f.; Is 55:10; Mt 5:45; Acts 14:17; Heb 6:7; Jas 5:17f. [1]Gn 19:24; Lk 17:29 □.

→ Intr. II.4;V.1.

ransom Gk. *lytron,*[1] *antilytron,*[2] deriving from *lyō:* "to untie, loose, liberate." A ransom paid out for the liberation of a prisoner of war, a sum of money paid out to buy back a slave.

[1]Mt 20:28 (= Mk 10:45) □. [2]1 Tim 2:6 □.

→ buy back—liberate—redemption.

Rebecca The daughter of Bethuel and a sister of Laban,[1] she married Isaac,* by whom, after twenty years of barrenness, she bore twin boys.[2] Her preference for Jacob* was interpreted as symbolizing the liberty* of the divine choice.[3]

[1]Gn 24:15. [2]Gn 25:21; Rom 9:10. [3]Gn 25:28; 27:5-17; Mal 1:2f.; Rom 9:11-13 □.

reborn

→ born, reborn.

[recension] **1.** In literary criticism* it is the writing down of a tradition.*

2. In textual criticism,* recension refers to the textual reading proposed by a particular manuscript.

recognize

→ know.

recompense

→ retribution.

reconcile From the Gk. *allassō:* "to make other *(allos),* to exchange," a verb to which has been prefixed a preposition which adds the peculiar shade of meaning it can take: *dia-, kata-, apo-kata-, syn-.* We find it used with its secular meaning.[1] In its religious sense, which is the one that predominates in the N.T., it describes the gratuitous action by which God reintroduces the repentant sinner into grace,*[2] through the merits of Christ's blood which expiates* our sins.[3] By means of this new creation[4] which has been effected, man henceforth lives in peace with God;[5] Jews and pagans compose a single body.* The whole universe has been rendered peaceful.[7] This is the message of the apostolic ministry.[8]

[1]Mt 5:24; Acts 7:26; 1 Cor 7:11. [2]Rom 5:10. [3]Rom 5:11. [4]2 Cor 5:17. [5]Rom 5:1,9. [6]Eph 2:16. [7]Rom 11:15; Col 1:20-22. [8]2 Cor 5:18-20 □.

→ enemy—expiate—pardon—peace—redemption—save—sin.

[redactional] An adjective describing a text whose style has been reworked by an author with a particular aim in view, or a passage added to an earlier framework: for example, the Our Father now located in the midst of three admonitions regarding almsgiving, prayer and fasting.[1]

[1]Mt 6:9-13 in 6:2-18.

→ literary criticism—*Redaktionsgeschichte.*

[Redaktionsgeschichte] A German term referring to a method of literary criticism* that seeks to complement that of *Formgeschichte.** It concerns itself with the way in which previously detected, small literary units* have been joined together by the evangelists. It tries to describe the last stage of the formation of the Gospel, the one found in our actual texts, by delineating the work of the latest editors. In effect, the literary units take on a change in meaning according to the changed context into which they have been inserted.

→ Intr. XV.3.

redemption **1.** From the Lat. *red-emptio:* "the buying back, ransom," translating the Gk. *apo-lytrōsis* (from *lytron:* "means of deliverance, ransom"). In English, the term collects the various meanings referring to God's manner of acquiring a people for himself: liberation* from slavery,* deliverance from captivity,* salvation* from peril. This applies particularly to the account of Israel's experience within the broad outlines of the Covenant* relationship. Understood literally, redemption stresses the aspect of "buying back," which comes from two ancient customs. According to family law, the *go'ël** (from the Heb. *gâ'al:* "to deliver") is the nearest kinsman on whom falls the obligation of buying back* goods and persons that had become the property of some foreigner.[1] Hence, Yahweh is the *Go'ël,* the Redeemer of Israel, a fact underlining the family bond between Yahweh and Israel.[2] According to commercial law, one could buy back (Heb. *pâdâ:* "to hand over an equal amount") the lives of the firstborn* or of slaves* by means of a ransom.[3] In applying such an activity to Yahweh in the buying back of Israel,[4] the Bible avoided mentioning a sum paid out, going so far as to stress that this was not the important point, but rather something much more germane, that the issue was the hopeless situation of the one ransomed.

[1]Lv 25:23-55. [2]Ex 6:6; Is 43:14; 44:6,24; 47:4. [3]Ex 13:13-15; 21:8; Lv 19:20; Nm 3:46-51. [4]Dt 7:8; 13:6.

2. The N.T. sees in Jesus the one who gave his life as a ransom (Gk. *lytron*) for the many,[5] bringing about the deliverence (Gk. *lytroō,* [*apo-*]*lytrōsis*) long-awaited,[6] becoming himself our redemption,[7] so that in him we find our redemption.[8] The verb "to buy" (Gk. *agorazō*) is also used to speak of this same reality, without our thereby being permitted to imagine that God paid a sum of money to anyone.[9]

[5]Mt 20:28 (= Mk 10:45); 1 Tim 2:6; Ti 2:14. [6]Lk 1:68; 2:38; 21:28; 24:21; Heb 11:35. [7]Rom 3:24; 1 Cor 1:30. [8]Rom 8:23; Eph 1:7; Col 1:14; Heb 9:12,15; 1 Pt 1:18. [9]1 Cor 6:20; 7:23; Gal 3:13; 4:5; Eph 1:14; 4:30; 2 Pt 2:1; Rv 5:9; 14:3f.

→ buy back—captive—God's plan—go'ël—liberate—reconciliation—save—sin—slave.

reed Gk. *kalamos.*

1. A kind of rush common in Palestine and the length of the Jordan. It could serve as a measuring instrument,[1] and its stalk, when cut, could serve as a cane,[2] or a pen.[3] Beginning with the O.T., an image of weakness,[4] fragility[5] and of inconstancy.[6]

[1]Ez 40:3-9; Rv 11:1; 21:15f. [2]Mt 27:29f.,48 (= Mk 15:19,36). [3]Ps 45:2; 3 Jn 13. [4]Is 42:3; Mt 12:20. [5]Is 9:13. [6]Mt 11:7 (= Lk 7:24) □.

2. As a measure, the reed equalled 3.15 m. (10.4 ft.).

→ measures.

re-establish

→ restore.

reign (rule), king, kingdom Gk. *basileus, basileia,* translating the Heb. *mèlèk, malkût.* The difference between rule and kingdom is not always easy to discern. In the gospels, one should not translate it by "kingdom" except when the context demands a spatial sense.[1] In preference to the "reign of God" Matthew used the rabbinical term the "reign of heaven," "heaven*" being a roundabout equivalent for saying "God."[2]

[1]Mt 5:20; 7:21; 18:3; 19:23. [2]Comp. Mt 3:2 and Mk 1:15.

1. The chief magistrate in Rome was reckoned by the peoples of the East as king in the Hellensitic sense, a person who had received his power from God[3] in order to establish justice* in his kingdom.

[3]Jn 19:12.

2. In Israel's eyes, from eternity the kingship belonged to God alone, kings of the earth being merely his lieutenants. In Jesus' time, there was neither king nor kingdom in the sense in which Israel had known them from the origins of her political existence. But the Jews had inherited a nostalgic memory and a category of thought from this past. All awaited the time when Yahweh would reign definitively over the entire universe, over Israel and the nations.*[4] This hope knew diverse forms according to whether it bore on hopes of a political restoration set free from Roman servitude or looked forward instead to a transformation in the spiritual order. In fact, the rule of God is not properly speaking a place, but a particular relationship between God and man, most especially a relationship with the poor.*

[4]Ps 47; 96.

3. In this latter sense, Jesus proclaimed that God's rule was very near: such was the nature of the Good News.[5] Moreover, Jesus told his detractors that "God's reign has come upon you,"[6] it is truly present, it is now at work. But this is so, not in a startling way, but in the manner announced by John, mysteriously, like a seed, enjoying irresistible power, planted by God in man's heart.[7]

[5]Mt 3:2; 4:17; 10:7; Mk 1:15. [6]Mt 12:28 (= Lk 11:20). [7]Mt 13:24-30,31-33,36-50.

4. Although towards the end of his life Jesus allowed himself to be acclaimed as king,[8] it was only as a peaceful king without earthly ambitions: his kingship was not of this world.[9] In fact, it was by his resurrection* alone that Jesus was enthroned as King by God; henceforth, he extends his sway over all men until he hands over the kingdom to his Father.[10]

[8]Mt 21:5; Lk 19:38; Jn 12:13,15. [9]Jn 18:36. [10]1 Cor 15:24.

→ Intr. XII.2.B.

reins

→ loins.

remain

→ abide.

remission of sins

→ forgive—sin.

remnant Gk. *leimma,*[1] *hypo-leimma:*[2] "that part of a whole which remains;" such was the experience of the Israel which survived various catastrophes. Still, the expression "holy remnant" did not describe a historical remnant[3] but that community which will be saved on the last day: that is, the eschatological* remnant.[4] Another designation of the "holy remnant" referred to the faithful* part of the chosen people, for example that part which God reserved for himself in the time of Elijah.[5]

The Pharisees* and the Qumran* sects wanted to establish themselves as the community of the New Covenant; John the Baptist also readied a holy remnant, but one that was open to any Jew who came to do penance.[6] Jesus summoned to himself anyone who accepted God's grace: all were invited to the banquet.[7] Only a small core of Jews answered his call and this was sufficient to justify God's fidelity to his promises.[8] In a more extended sense, the Church henceforth constituted this Israel* of God, the pledge of the final conversion* of all God's people.[9]

[1]Rom 11:5 △. [2]Rom 9:27 △. [3]Jer 6:9; Ez 9:8; Am 5:15. [4]Is 4:4; 10:22; Jer 23:3; Mi 5:6-8; Zep 3:12. [5]Rom 11:3-5. [6]Mt 3:9,12. [7]Mt 22:14. [8]Rom 11:7. [9]Rom 11:11-24.

→ Intr III.1.—election.

repent Under this word we range the various meanings of the Gk. *metamelomai* which implied a change *(meta)* with respect to what one had set one's heart on (*melei*[1]). It differed from conversion* (Gk. *metanoia*) in that it did not signify a radical transformation of one's being and judgment (Gk. *nous*), but rather the simple possibility of a transformation which God alone could bring about. The change came in what had been established as an error or a fault,[2] but it was not efficacious and could well result either in the barren remorse found in Judas[3] or in an eventual change of one's behavior.[4] Although the O.T. freely made use of anthropomorphisms[5] in God's own case, he never goes back on his decisions and his promises.

[1]Mt 22:16 (= Mk 12:14); Mk 4:38; Lk 10:40; Jn 10:13; 12:6; 1 Cor 7:21. [2]Ex 13:17; Jb 42:6. [3]Mt 27:3. [4]Mt 21:29.32; 2 Cor 7:8-10. [5]Jgs 2:18; 1 Sm 15:11. [6]Ps 110:4; Jer 4:28; Rom 11:29; Heb 7:21.

→ conversion—penance—pardon—sin.

resident alien

→ stranger.

rest Outside of the cases where the term meant relaxation (Gk. *anesis*),[1] refreshment *(anapsyxis)*[2] or dwelling-place (*epi-* or *kata-skēnoō,* words connected with *skēnoō:* "to pitch one's tent,"[3] something opposed to a journey), rest was the cessation of a movement or of a work *(ana-* or *kata-pauomai)*.[4] The Epistle to the Hebrews elaborated a theology of God's rest, that of the promised land into which all are invited to enter:[5] such too, was the sabbath rest *(sabbatismos)* reserved for God's people.[6] Jesus gives rest to those who come to him.[7]

[1]2 Cor 2:13; 7:5; 8:13; 2 Thes 1:7 △. [2]Acts 3:20; Phil 2:19; 2 Tim 1:16 △. [3]Acts 2:26; 2 Cor 12:9. [4]Mt 12:43 (= Lk 11:24); 26:45 (= Mk 14:41); Mk 6:31; Lk 10:6; 12:19; Acts 7:49; Rom 2:17; 1 Pt 4:14; Rv 4:8; 6:11; 14:11. [5]Heb 3:7–4:11. [6]Heb 4:9. [7]Mt 11:28f.; Rv 14:13.

→ sabbath—sleep.

restore, re-establish Gk. *apo-kath-istēmi* (composed of *apo:* "beginning with," *histēmi:* "to establish," *kata:* "below, solidly"). This term did not signify to save* or to buy back,* but to cause to recover a lost former state,[1] to cause to go back to a primitive condition, such as in the reassembling in the Holy Land of dispersed Jews[2] or restoration to health.[3] More often, the verb was used to signify the return to a state of royalty[4] or to that of the first creation.[5]

[1]Gn 41:13; cf. Heb 13:19. [2]Jer 16:15; 23:8; 24:6. [3]Mt 12:13; Mk 3:5; 8:25; Lk 6:10. [4]Acts 1:6. [5]Mal 3:24; Mt 17:11; Mk 9:12; Acts 3:21 □.

→ reconcile—save.

resurrection 1. The principal metaphor through which Jews and Christians described what happens to man after death.* It told not merely of an ordinary return to earthly life (as was the case with Lazarus*), but of an entry into a life* that was full and definitive. The words used for resurrection suggested an act of standing up after having lain down (Gk. *anistamai*)[1] or after sleep (Gk. *egeiromai*):[2] it meant the rising up again after death.

[1]Mt 26:62; Lk 11:7f. [2]Mt 8:26; 9:19; Mk 1:31; Acts 3:7.

2. In Israel, faith in the resurrection became common about the turn of the second century B.C., at the time of the martyrdom of the Maccabees.*[3] Since God was just,* he could not abandon to an eternal Sheol* those who had given their lives to affirm that Yahweh was the true God. From the outset, in keeping with Jewish anthropology, the whole being was conceived as rising or coming back from Sheol. Unlike many of their neighbors, people such as the Egyptians or the Greeks, the Jews did not first believe in the immortality* of the soul* and afterwards come to a belief in the resurrection of the body.* Resurrection did not amount to the immortal soul's taking up its body again, but in the act of a just God who gave man a share in his own, eternal life.

[3]2 Mc 7:14; Dn 12:1-3.

3. The first Christians used two modes of speech to affirm that Jesus had been restored to life after his death: terminology of exaltation* and terminology of resurrection. In the latter, through confessions* of faith,[4] they proclaimed that Jesus was Lord,* Christ,* the Firstborn* from the dead.[5] In the Risen One they

saw the first fruits* of the general resurrection as well as the pledge of our future hope.[6]

[4]Rom 10:9; 1 Cor 15:3-5; 1 Thes 1:9f.; 4:14. [5]Acts 2:36; Rom 8:29; Col 1:18. [6]1 Cor 15:12-28.

4. Jesus rose bodily. This affirmation, which was not deduced from the narrative of the women's discovery of the empty tomb,[7] specified what was implicit in the resurrection terminology itself, namely that the personal being of Jesus had been transformed in its entirety. The Risen One was *the same* as the Jesus of Nazareth, but a Jesus now fully established in glory.* Since the body* was the means by which one was present to others and to the universe in general, the risen body of Jesus could not be described in harsh terms such as a "resuscitated corpse," but rather had to be regarded, in the words of St. Paul, as a "spiritual body."[8] In their own way, the evangelists described the Risen One's new mode of being present through their versions of his appearances.* When someone "touched" his body, it was to adore the presence of the Living One and not to be sure of his corporeal state, a fact which was self-evident.[9] Through his glorified body Jesus was able to be with his disciples no matter what the obstacles.[10] The risen body of Jesus was united with the ecclesial body (called the Church) and the universe, both of which it was the glorious first fruits.*[11]

[7]Mt 28:1-8 (= Mk 16:1-8 = Lk 24:1-10); Jn 20:1.11f. [8]1 Cor 15:44,46. [9]Mt 28:9; Jn 20:17. [10]Lk 24:36; Jn 20:19,26. [11]1 Cor 15:20-28.

5. The general resurrection will take place at the end* of time. In exceptional instances, Paul said that we have been raised with Christ already;[12] and yet, in spite of this, we cannot pretend that the resurrection has already taken place.[13] Ordinarily, "life*" was the term which described the effect on believers of Jesus' resurrection: they had passed from death to life.[14] The glorified bodies* of the future are never described in the N.T.; Paul was content to refer to them as "spiritual bodies," contrasting them with earthly, perishable bodies.[15] One can imagine them along the lines which characterize Jesus' body in the appearance accounts, namely as having an ability to be with others in a way that is not limited by ordinary earthly conditions.

[12]Col 3:1-3. [13]2 Tim 2:18. [14]1 Jn 3:14. [15]1 Cor 15:35-53.

→ Intr. IV.6.B.C, XII.2.A.a.—appearances of Christ—Body of Christ—death—exaltation—glory—immortality—life.

retribution Gk. *(ant-)apo-didōmi:* "to give in return."

1. Retribution is not wages owed for works* in virtue of a contract. It is the normal fruit given by God, at judgment time, to his good servants.[1]

[1]Mt 16:27; 25:46; Rom 2:6; 2 Cor 5:10.

2. Retribution touches every individual as a function of the works which his faith gives expression to, but not as a function of his fate, heredity or his belonging to the chosen people.[2]

[2]Ez 18:2f.,32; Lk 13:2f.; Jn 5:45; 6:29; 9:2f.; 2 Tim 4:14; Heb 10:26-30; Rv 2:23; 22:12.

3. Retribution does not consist in earthly advantages, riches or glory, but in God alone and in his Christ;[3] in them the faithful person rediscovers a hundred times over the realities of this world here below: joy, happiness; no more death or sorrow, but rather love and light.[4]

[3]Mt 6:4-18; Phil 1:21-26; Col 3:24. [4]Rv 2:3f.; 22:1-5.

→ Intr. XIV.2.A.—crown—judgment—justice—wages.

revelation From the Lat. *revelare* (from *velum:* "veil"): "to make one know, to remove the veil," translating the Gk. *apo-kalyptō.* More precisely, the manifestation of the God who is invisible, mysterious, whom man cannot attain on his own, but who gives himself to be known and loved. Synonyms of this reality are: to manifest (from the Gk. *phainō, phaneroō*), to cause to know, to put into the light, "to explain" (Gk. *exēgeomai*), to show, to say, to proclaim, to teach.

1. God reveals himself through his creation, not to give a first-time knowledge of himself, but rather to make himself "re-cognized": in this way, then, God engages himself in dialogue with his creatures;[1] God reveals himself also through theophanies* or through mediators*: angels, words, visions, signs.*

[1]Rom 1:19-21; cf. Wis 13:3-5.

2. Jesus came to crown the revelation which had been sketched in the O.T.[2] Through his parables,* he handed on the mystery of God's plan,*[3] since only he had known the Father.*[4] Special revelations are accorded by God to his privileged ones.[5] Everything will end by being revealed,[6] but the full revelation will only be brought about at the parousia.*[7]

[2]Jn 1:18; Heb 1:1f. [3]Mt 13:35; Mk 4:11. [4]Mt 11:25-27 (= Lk 10:21f.). [5]Mt 16:17; Gal 1:16; 1 Cor 2:10. [6]Mk 4:22. [7]1 Cor 1:7; 2 Thes 1:7.

→ apocalypse—know—truth.

Revelation (Book of)

→ apocalypse 3.

Rhodes Gk. *Rhodos.* An island in the Aegean Sea, facing the southwest coast of Turkey, and including a Jewish colony.[1]

[1]Acts 21:1 □.

→ Map 2

rich, riches **1.** Gk. *ploutos* (related to *polys:* "much" and to *plēthos,* Lat. *plenus:* "large quantity"): "plenitude [of the goods of life]," and, more especially, of material goods. In the Bible, the term often corresponded to the Heb. *kâbôd:* "glory."[1] In revealing the eschatological* dimension of existence, the N.T. (chiefly Luke and Matthew) does not condemn riches, which can still signify God's blessing,*[2] but it denounces its dangers and manifests the meaning of the state of poverty.

[1]1 Kgs 3:13; Rom 9:23; Eph 1:18; 3:16; Col 1:27. [2]Gn 49:25; Dt 28:1-4.

2. Only God is rich[3] and only he enriches.[4] On his side, man must not seek to enrich himself on his own,[5] but he must use money to help the poor,*[6] for example through the collection.*[7]

[3]Rom 2:4; 9:23; 10:12; 11:33; Eph 1:7; 2:4,7; Phil 4:19; Ti 3:6. [4]2 Cor 8:9; Jas 2:5. [5]Lk 12:21. [6]Lk 12:33. [7]2 Cor 8–9; Gal 2:10.

3. The rich themselves are also assuredly called to the Kingdom[8] and some do enter it, going so far as to give up their goods,[9] but this is something very difficult;[10] so much so that Jesus declared them to be "wretched."[11] For, they are given over to the temptation of (self-) sufficiency,[12] forgetting their creaturely condition[13] and ignoring the poor.[14] Hence, the terrible exhortations given by James.[15]

[8]Lk 19:2. [9]Mt 27:57; Lk 19:8; Acts 4:37. [10]Mt 19:23-26 (= Mk 10:23-27 = Lk 18:24-27). [11]Lk 6:24. [12]Mt 13:22 (= Mk 4:19 = Lk 8:14); 1 Tim 6:9. [13]Lk 12:16-21; 1 Tim 6:17f. [14]Lk 16:19-22; Jas 2:6. [15]Jas 5:1-6.

4. In the sense of possessions, riches were designated by other terms: *chrēma:* "what one disposed of,"[16] *ktēmata:* "what one has acquired,"[17] *hyparchonta, hyparxis:* "what is, in the beginning (Gk. *archē*), under *(hypo)* one's hand, the goods of which one disposes,"[18] *ousia:* "existence and its goods,"[19] and, in a pejorative sense, *mamōnas:* "that on which one makes one's base," the unique riches[20] which one is not to amass in treasure chests (Gk. *thesauros*).[21]

[16]2 Chr 1:11; Mk 10:23f. (= Lk 18:24); Acts 4:37; 8:18,20; 24:26 △. [17]Mt 10:9; 19:22 (= Mk 10:22); Lk 18:12; 21:19; Acts 1:18; 2:45; 4:34; 5:1; 8:20; 22:28; Thes 4:4 △. [18]Prv 6:31; Mt 19:21; 24:47 (= Lk 12:44); 25:14; Lk 8:3; 11:21; 12:15,33; 14:33; 16:1; 19:8; Acts 2:45; 3:6; 4:32,37; 1 Cor 13:3; Heb 10:34; 2 Pt 1:8 △. [19]Lk 11:41; 15:12f. △. [20]Mt 6:24; Lk 16:9,11,13 △; cf. Prv 18:10f.; Sir 31:5f. [21]Mt 6:19-21 (= Lk 12:33f.); 19:21 (= Mk 10:21 = Lk 18:22); Jas 5:3ff.

→ Intr. VII.4.—almsgiving—greed—Mammon—money—poor.

right

Gk. *dexios,* Heb. *yâmîn:* "what is on the right."

1. A qualification denoting the nobler side of a man (his hand, his cheek).[1] It also designated the divine power.[2]

[1]Mt 5:29f.,39. [2]Ps 73:23; Is 62:8; Acts 2:33; 5:31.

2. The right-hand side, in contrast with the left,[3] was the more favorable side. The Son of Man* is to sit at the right hand of the Power.*[8]

[3]Gn 48:13f.; Eccl 10:2; Mt 25:33. [4]Ps 110:1; Mt 22:44 (= Mk 12:36 = Lk 20:42); 26:64 (= Mk 14:62 = Lk 22:69); Mk 16:19; Acts 2:34; Eph 1:20; Col 3:1; Heb 1:3,13; 8:1; 10:12; 12:2; cf. Acts 7:55f.

road

→ way.

rock Two related terms can be considered as equivalents of one another: Gk. *petra,* rock, and Gk. *lithos,* stone. In fact, the latter was the more prevalent term.

1. *Petra,* in fact, aside from those cases where it was employed to mean the rock on which one built, on which seed happened to fall or into which one dug,[1] or lastly to refer to nature's rocky crags,[2] is not found except in two extraordinary uses. One refers to Christ, the spiritual rock out of which life flows as once upon a time water flowed from the rock struck by Moses;[3] another refers to Cephas*-Peter, the rock on which Jesus wished to build his Church.*[4] Otherwise, particularly in the prophecy concerning the stumbling stone,* rock gives way to stone.[5] If one must find a special nuance, perhaps this may be found in the fact of the rock's strength and in its oneness, similar to the oneness of God, Israel's rock and refuge.[5]

[1]Mt 7:24f. (= Lk 6:48); 13:5,20 (= Mk 4:5,16 = Lk 8:6,13); 27:60 (= Mk 15:46). [2]Mt 27:51; Rv 6:15f. [3]1 Cor 10:4. [4]Mt 16:18. [5]Is 8:14; Rom 9:33; 1 Pt 2:8. [6]Dt 32:4.

2. Jesus Christ was the cornerstone *(lithos)* on which one built, or which crowned a building's summit; beyond an apparent setback, it guaranteed the cohesion of the holy[7] temple,* into which Christians are being integrated, as it were, like living stones.[8] But, as Yahweh had formerly been, Jesus was simultaneously a stone of scandal*; unbelievers fell upon it,[10] but, in the end, it will crush them.[11] The stone which sealed Jesus' tomb was rolled away by the angel of the Lord.[12]

[7]Mt 21:42 (= Mk 12:10 = Lk 20:17); 1 Pt 2:4,7. [8]Eph 2:20; 1 Pt 2:5f. [9]Is 8:14; 28:16. [10]Rom 9:33; 1 Pt 2:8. [11]Lk 20:18. [12]Mt 27:60,66; 28:2.

3. Formerly graven on stone, a feature which was to signify the Covenant's perennial nature, henceforth the Law is inscribed by the Spirit on hearts of flesh.*[13]

[13]2 Cor 3:3,7.

→ build up—Cephas—stoning—white pebble.

[Romans (Epistle to the)] A letter of Paul sent from Corinth* to the church in Rome, about 57–58. On the verge of bringing to Jerusalem the fruits of his collection* taken up in the churches of Asia,* Paul turned toward the west: in his letter he painted a magisterial fresco of God's plan.

→ Intr. XV.

Rome Gk. *Rōmē.* The capital of the Empire which dominated Judea from 63 B.C. A dreaded power[1] and one confident of its superiority;[2] to be a Roman citizen* was a privilege.[3] In Augustus's* time several thousand Jews were settled in Rome;[4] in A.D. 19, 4,000 were expelled to Sardinia. In 32, Tiberius* published a decree favorable to the Jews, but in 49–50 a new expulsion took place.[5] We are left uninformed about the origins of the Christian community to which Paul wrote his letter.[6] He himself arrived there in chains and stayed there two years under surveillance.[7] Rome was branded as Babylon.*[8]

[1]Jn 11:48; Acts 28:17. [2]Acts 16:21. [3]Acts 22:25-29. [4]Acts 2:10. [5]Acts 18:2. [6]Rom 1:7,15; cf. Acts 19:21; 23:11. [7]Acts 28:14-16,30; 2 Tim 1:17. [8]1 Pt 5:13; Rv 17:5; 18:2 □.

→ Intr. III.2.G; IV.1–2; IV.4.D; VI.2.—Map 3.

roof **1.** Gk. *stegē:* in the proper sense[1] and, metaphorically, for a dwelling.

[1]Mk 2:4. [2]Mt 8:8 (= Lk 7:6) △.

2. Gk. *dōma:* "terraced garden" on the roof, simultaneously a private[3] and a public place.[4]

[3]Mt 24:17 (= Mk 13:15 = Lk 17:31); Acts 10:9. [4]Mt 10:27 (= Lk 12:3); Lk 5:19 △.

→ Intr. VIII.1.A.

room (upper)

→ upper room.

rule

→ reign (rule).

run Gk. *trechō:* "to run" and Gk. *"diōkō:* "to pursue, to hunt, hence, to persecute." Terms employed in both a proper sense and in a figurative sense. The Word of God runs rapidly and fulfills its course.[1] Human existence, frequently compared to a walk,[2] becomes a race when one wishes to evoke the notions of a hurried obedience or an urgent mission.[3] Finally, under the influence of sporting combats,* there is the model of a race run in a stadium,*[4] a race in which we are preceded by the leader of our faith, our "precursor" (Gk. *prodromos,* from *edramon,* the aorist of *trechō*).[5] One's all is, not to run in vain, but, instead, to complete the race.[6]

[1]Ps 147:15; Wis 18:15; 2 Thes 3:1. [2]Jn 8:12; 1 Jn 1:6-7. [3]Ps 119:32; Is 40:31; Acts 13:24f.; 20:24. [4]1 Cor 9:24-27; Phil 3:12-14. [5]Heb 6:20 △; 12:1f. [6]1 Cor 9:26; Gal 2:2; Phil 2:16; 2 Tim 4:7; cf. Rom 9:16.

S

Sabaoth Heb. *s^eba'ôt.* Often associated with the name of Yahweh, the term (a Hebrew plural: "an organized multitude") possessed a meaning that evolved with time: first of all it referred to Israel's armies, then to the world of the stars* and of the heavenly powers. The latter realm was, for the ancients, a world of living beings and, for the pagan religions, a world of gods. In the N.T., this divine title is equivalent to that of the sovereign God, who disposed of all the universe's powers.[1]

[1]Cf. 1 Sm 1:3; 17:45; Is 1:9; Zep 2:10; Rom 9:29; Jas 5:4 □.

sabbath **1.** Gk. *sabbaton.* The etymology of this word is uncertain, but is reminiscent of the Heb. *shabât:* "to stop, to cease, to be unemployed" (or *shib^e'at:* "seventh"). Hence, the word came to be interpreted as "to rest" or, by deduction, "to stop in order to praise (God)."

2. A particular feature of Israel's, pre-Mosaic in origin, the commandment to rest* on the seventh day was tied in with the sacred rhythm of the week* and of the moon.* There were two principal motives for it: the humanitarian aspect of rest, especially for slaves[1] or imitation of the God who rested on the seventh day after the work of his creation.[2] To observe it was to reveal oneself as faithful.

[1]Ex 23:12; Dt 5:14; cf. 5:15. [2]Gn 2:2f.; Ex 20:11; 31:17.

3. The sabbath legislation became increasingly minute, demanding innumerable prohibitions: against preparing meals, the lighting of fires, the collecting of wood,[3] the practice of gathering, tendering help to an animal or to a man in danger, of carrying of burdens, of walking further than 1,250 m. (1,367 yds.)[4] and even of untying a knot or tracing more than a letter of the alphabet. Also, casuists were divided on the extension of, and the obligations to, these various practices.

[3]Ex 16:23; 35:3; Nm 15:32. [4]Mt 12:2,11; Jn 5:10; Acts 1:12.

4. Jesus observed the sabbath,[5] but he harshly criticized the formalism of the doctors* of the Law, not only in his words,[6] but also by his deeds.[7] Master of the sabbath, he restored its true aim[8] and gave it meaning by referring it to the Father who was ceaselessly at work in bestowing life.[9]

[5]Mk 1:21; Lk 4:16. [6]Mt 12:12. [7]Mk 3:2-5; Lk 13:10-16; 14:1-6; Jn 5:8f.; 9:14. [8]Mk 2:27f. [9]Jn 5:16f.

5. Jesus' disciples first of all kept on observing the sabbath[10] and made use of it to proclaim the Gospel.[11] But, very rapidly, the day after sabbath, the first day of the week, Sunday, became "the Lord's Day." With regard to the sabbath—our Saturday—it conserves only a figurative* value, that of the heavenly rest.[12]

[10]Mt 28:1; Jn 19:42. [11]E.g., Acts 13:14; 16:13. [12]Heb 4:1-11; cf. Rv 14:13.

→ Intr.XIII.2.B.b.—rest—Sunday.

sackcloth Gk. *sakkos,* Heb. *saq:* "coarse material," made of hair from the she-goat or the camel. The Latin term *cilicium,* which refers to the same cloth, indicates that it was commonly made in the Cilicia*; Paul carried on the trade of tent maker.[1]

[1]Acts 18:3.

2. A girdle or tunic roughly cut and of rough material,[2] undecorated, covering the body from neck to ankles, as if for burial; the clothing* for penance and mourning,* one which was worn night and day about the loins.[3] The survival of scant primitive clothing, sackcloth made from skin or leather[4] could also be a prophet's garb.[5]

[2]Is 3:24; 50:3; Rv 6:12. [3]Neh 9:1; Is 15:3; Jon 3:5,8; Mt 11:21 (= Lk 10:13). [4]Mt 3:4. [5]Is 20:2; Rv 11:3.

3. In the sense of a "double bag," cf. wallet* (and other Gk. words).

sacred **1.** Gk. *hieros.* According to an ancient convention, the sacred described a reality (a place, person, or thing) that had been withdrawn from the world of the secular (Lat. *pro:* "in front of, out of" and *fanum:* "temple"; Gk. *bebēlos:* "where one may walk" to which was opposed *abaton:* "a place where one might not walk," "sacred place") and the world of the common (Gk. *koinos*) resulting from its contact with the deity and, occasionally, in view of a use that had been foreseen. The distinction between the sacred and the profane derived from the spirit of man who, to encounter the divinity, located it in specific places in the world; but it was nothing more than a projection of the true distinction which exists between the saint* and the sinner.*

2. The O.T. considered as sacred, places (hence, the *hieron:* "temple*"), people (so, the *hiereus:* "priest"), times (the sabbath*) or foods which were declared to be pure.* Jesus respected the sacred insofar as it did not hinder the pursuit of holiness (the love of God and one's neighbor) of which it was a projection here on earth. Neither the sabbath occurrence nor food laws, neither the (natural) "sin" of the Samaritans* nor those of tax collectors, nothing at all separated Jesus from the ordinary world.

3. Except in rare cases, the N.T. did not preserve terms derived from the family of words related to *hieros:* meat* sacrificed to idols,[1] sacriligious actions[2] and, exceptionally, the Scriptures,[3] Gospel service,[4] or some person vowed to a holy life.[5] Through the presence of the Spirit, there was now no longer anything sacred or secular, just as there was no longer any distinction between Jew and Greek: all believers were saints in Christ Jesus and, so, all could become holy (Gk. *hagios*). The former sacred/secular distinction became the saint/sinner distinction.

[1]1 Cor 10:28. [2]Acts 19:37; Rom 2:22. [3]2 Tim 3:15. [4]Rom 15:16; 1 Cor 9:13. [5]Ti 2:3.

→ holy—pure—sacrifice—worship.

sacrifice Gk. *thysia:* "sacrifice," *prosphora:* "offering," *holokautōma:* "holocaust," *spendō:* "to offer as a libation."

1. Israelite ritual presented several kinds of sacrifices: the holocaust, the communion sacrifice, the sacrifice for sin, vegetable offerings, loaves of offering, incense offerings. Also, in general, we may define a sacrifice as every offering, whether animal or vegetable, presented to God on the altar and withdrawn, by its partial or total destruction, from all secular use.

2. A rite of offering* was common to all sacrifices: the believer imposed his hands* on the gifts which were accepted by the priest; doubtless, he thereby indicated that, in offering the gift, he was offering himself. Then, the sacrifice was sometimes consumed by fire,* while at other times it was divided between the priest and the one making the offering. In the case of an animal sacrifice, the symbolism was made more precise through the biblical significance attributed to blood, which was the life itself[1] and something which could not be consumed along with the flesh* (meats* that had been sacrificed).[2] After the immolation (which did not have a peculiar meaning of its own), the flesh was portioned out or burnt, while the blood was sprinkled on the altar,[3] which symbolized God himself.

[1]Lv 17:11,14; Dt 12:23. [2]Dt 12:16. [3]Lv 1:5,11.

3. The exact meaning of the rite is difficult to define. But, let us try to do so. A believer (or the people) was in search of intimacy with God through sharing in an irrevocable gift. In this way, he wanted to close the gap which a sin or a violated prohibition had created between himself and God. He symbolized his desire through an offering and he drew near to God through the mediation of the blood poured out on the altar,* thus reestablishing contact. Through this "expiation*" he once more became pleasing to God. The holocaust,* when it took place, told of the irrevocable nature of the gift, the rising up of a perfume* signified entry into the invisible. Thus, there was effected a passage from the secular to the sacred.* Once the covenant* had been symbolically renewed, communion* was rediscovered.

4. The rite was poorly interpreted whenever it emphasized aspects of destruction and suffering. The rite was falsified when it became separated from its meaning, a mere formalism. The prophets, and Jesus after them, protested the regarding of offering as magic.[4]

[4]Mt 5:23f.; 9:13; 12:7.

5. Jesus did not condemn sacrifice; he is the paschal sacrifice. But since the ancient sacrifices in themselves had been powerless to obtain the definitive forgiveness,* he fulfilled for all time the perfect sacrifice, offering himself once and for all as a unique oblation for our sanctification.[5] The sacrificial character of the Eucharist* was attested to by Paul who situated it in relationship to pagan sacrifices.[6] The rites did not have meaning except when they expressed a gift of self, when they were a reasonable worship:[7] such were the spiritual sacrifices offered by the Church, the priestly* body.[8] The name of sacrifice, therefore, was

applied not only to the offering made to God, but also to that offering which one makes to another person in order to give him succor.[9]

[5]Lv 4:26; Heb 7:27; 9:12; 10:1. [6]1 Cor 10:16-21. [7]Rom 12:1. [8]1 Pt 2:5. [9]Phil 4:18; Heb 13:16.

→ Intr. XIII.2.A.—altar—blood—covenant—Eucharist—expiate—fire—first fruits—forgive—holocaust—holy—perfume—present—redemption—temple—worship.

Sadducee Gk. *saddoukaios,* from the Aram. *zaddûqâyâ,* deriving from the proper name of the High Priest who had been Abiathar's rival, Zadok (Gk. *Sadōk*) whose own name had come from the Heb. *ṣaddîq:* "just." Zadok's descendants exercised a great influence on the clergy of Jerusalem, to such an extent that one came to speak not of "Aaron's sons" but of the "sons of Zadok."[2] In Matthew, they are ordinarily in the company of Pharisees,*[3] but they are clearly distinguished from them by their beliefs,[4] by their political outlook[5] and by their attitude toward Jesus and the first Christians.[6]

[1]2 Sm 8:17; 1 Kgs 1:8. [2]2 Kgs 15:33; Ez 40:46. [3]Mt 3:7; 16:1,6,11f.; 22:34. [4]Mt 22:23 (= Mk 12:18 = Lk 20:27); Acts 23:6-8. [5]Intr. XI.1. [6]Acts 4:1; 5:17 □; cf. Mt 26:57 (= Mk 14:53).

→ Intr.VI.4.A; XI.1.—Pharisee.

sadness **1.** The manifestations of sadness were numerous: weeping (Gk. *dakryō, klaiō*),[1] heaving sighs of grief,[2] choral lamentation* in more or less traditional rhythms,[3] putting on sad airs,[4] fasting,[5] beating one's breast,[6] covering one's head with dust.[7]

[1]Lk 7:13; Jn 11:33,35. [2]Mt 9:23; Jas 5:1. [3]Mt 2:18; Lk 7:32; Rv 18:11 [4]Mt 6:16; Lk 24:17. [5]Mk 2:20. [6]Mt 11:17; Lk 23:27; Acts 8:2. [7]Rv 18:19.

2. Its causes were varied: the conflict between Jesus' summons and the attractions of wealth,[8] the foretelling of evil,[9] the hardening of men and of Jerusalem,[10] the sin of denial,[11] separation from a loved one,[12] above all, a death that was near or approaching.[13] Not all sadness was good: one was from God, another from the world.[14]

[8]Mt 19:22 (= Mk 10:22 = Lk 18:23). [9]Mt 17:23; 26:22 (= Mk 14:19). [10]Mk 3:5; Lk 19:41; Rom 9:2. [11]Mt 26:75 (= Lk 22:62). [12]Mt 9:15; Jn 16:6,20; 20:11,13,15; Phil 2:27f. [13]Mt 26:37f. (= Mk 14:34); Jn 11:35; Heb 5:7. [14]2 Cor 7:10f.; cf. Mt 14:9; 2 Cor 9:7; 1 Thes 4:13.

3. The paradox of Christian life, which was bound up with the conqueror of death, was that out of sadness were born joy* and consolation,[15] while one waited for the definitive disappearance of tears.[16]

[15]Jn 16:22; 17:13; 20:20; 1 Cor 7:30; 2 Cor 6:10. [16]Rv 7:17; 21:4.

→ fasting—lamentation—laugh—mourning.

sail

→ navigate.

Saint

→ holy.

Salamis Gk. *Salamis,* a port on the west coast of Cyprus,* visited by Paul, Barnabas and Mark.[1]

[1]Acts 13:5 □.

→ Map 2.

Salome Gk. *Salōmē.*

1. The daughter of Philip I* and of Herodias, who is not named in the N.T.[1]

[1]Cf. Mt 14:6-11 (= Mk 6:22-28).

→ Chart, p. 227.

2. One of the women, who, after having followed and ministered to Jesus from Galilee, was present at his crucifixion and burial, and then ascertained that Jesus' tomb was empty. Perhaps the sister of Mary and the mother of Zebedee's sons.[1]

[1]Mk 15:40; 16:1; cf. Mt 27:56; Jn 19:25 □.

salt Gk. *halas.* A substance abundant in the region of the Dead Sea or the Sea of Salt.[1] It made foods tasty[2] and preserved them.[3] A condiment that was indispensable for meals[4] and, perhaps, was a purifying complement to sacrificial* offerings.[5] It gave a zest to existence[6] and described fraternal speech.[7]

[1]Gn 14:3. [2]Jb 6:6; Mt 5:13. [3]Bar 6:27. [4]Acts 1:4. [5]Lv 2:13; Ez 43:24; Mk 9:49. [6]Mk 9:50; Lk 14:34. [7]Col 4:6; cf. Jas 3:12 □.

→ Intr. II.2; VIII.1.D.b; VIII.2.C.a.

salvation Gk. *sōtēria,* from *sōzō:* "to save.*"

Samaria, Samaritans Gk. *Samareia.* The capital of the Northern Kingdom, established by Omri about 880.[1] It gave its name to the surrounding environs.[2] After the deportation of 722, its population was a mixture of races.[3] Destroyed in 108 B.C., it was rebuilt in 30 B.C. with the name Sebaste. In the first century, the Samaritans were treated as heretics, legally impure.[4] Jesus' behavior in their regard was especially surprising,[5] as was that of the primitive Church.[6]

[1]1 Kgs 16:24. [2]Lk 17:11; Jn 4:4f.; Acts 8:1-8. [3]2 Kgs 17:3-6,24. [4]Lk 9:52; Jn 4:9; 8:48. [5]Lk 10:33; 17:16; Jn 4:5-40. [6]Mt 10:5; Acts 1:8; 8:5-25; 9:31; 15:3 □.

→ Intr. II; III.2.E; XI.—Map 4.

sanctuary This word ought to be used to translate the Gk. *naos,* which designates the Temple building under its aspect of a holy place.[1]

[1]Mt 23:16f.; 27:40ff.

→ holy—Holy of Holies—temple.

sandal Gk. *sandalion,* a word of Persian origin.

→ shoe.

Sanhedrin Gk. *synedrion* (from *hedra:* "seat" and *syn* "together"), corresponding to the Heb. *sanhedrîn,* a term for which there is evidence from around 65 B.C. This institution seems to have been heir to the "Great Assembly" (Heb. *kenessèt gedôlâ*) of Ezra's* time. The Sanhedrin included 71 members, perhaps in memory of Moses and the 70 elders (Ex 24:1; Nm 11:16). On its role and its competence → Intr. VI.4.A.

Sarah Gk. *Sarra,* Heb. *Sârâ:* "princess." Abraham's wife,[1] the mother of Isaac. By her free status (in contrast with Hagar's* servitude) and by her motherhood, which was tied to a divine promise,[2] she was a figure* of the Jerusalem above, which begets men who are free in relation to the Law and are alive in the Spirit.[3]

[1]Gn 11:29; 1 Pt 3:6. [2]Gn 18:10; Rom 4:19; 9:9; Heb 11:11. [3]Gal 4:22-31 □.

Sardis Gk. *Sardeis.* The ancient capital of Lydia, of which Croesus had been the king in the sixth century B.C., and which had been rebuilt by Tiberius* after an earthquake in A.D. 17. Known for its wool industry.[1]

[1]Rv 1:11; 3:1,4 □.

→ Maps 2 and 3.

Satan 1. Heb. *sathan:* "adversary," a common name, sometimes personified to designate a real power that is opposed to God and the salvation of men (for example, Peter[1]). There were many names corresponding to it: the Accuser, the Adversary,* Beelzebul,* prince of demons, Belial* (the Beast), the Deceiver,* the Devil,* the Dragon,* the Enemy, the Evil One, the Liar, the Murderer, the Serpent,* the Tempter, the Wicked One, the World,* the prince of this world. To him is attributed everything thwarting God's plan,[2] the action of Antichrist,*[3] the origin of Sin, vexations in the apostolate,[4] the betrayal by Judas,*[5] the deception of Ananias,*[6] certain illnesses,[7] the empire of death,[8] the breed of liars and murderers,[9] temptation to sin.[10] He is at work in the world to turn men away from God.[11]

[1]Mt 16:23; cf. 1 Pt 5:8. [2]Mt 13:39; Mk 4:15. [3]2 Thes 2:3f. [4]2 Cor 12:7; 1 Thes 2:18. [5]Lk 22:3; Jn 13:27; 14:30. [6]Acts 5:3. [7]Lk 13:16. [8]Heb 2:14. [9]Jn 8:44. [10]1 Cor 7:5; 1 Thes 3:5. [11]1 Chr 21:1; Jb 1:6-12; Zec 3:1; Lk 22:31; Jn 12:31; 16:11.

2. The N.T. variously depicts Satan's defeat. The account of the temptation*[12] recapitulated in a mysterious scene, in which Satan was the protagonist, the principal temptations launched against Jesus by men.[13] But Jesus conquered Satan.[14] The believer who has chosen Christ[15] triumphs over Satan by undoing the ruses, snares, deceptions and maneuvers[16] of the one who disguises himself as an angel of light.[17] The book of Revelation[18] describes the defeat of the Adversary in symbolic depictions that are hard to decipher.

[12]Mt 4:1-11 (= Lk 4:1-13). [13]Mt 16:23; 27:42; Jn 6:15; cf. Lk 22:28. [14]Mt 12:28; Lk 10:18; Jn 12:31; 16:11,33; Rv 12:9-13. [15]2 Cor 6:14; 1 Jn 5:18f. [16]2 Cor 2:11; Eph 6:11; 1 Tim 3:7; 6:9. [17]2 Cor 11:14. [18]Rv 12–20.

3. Essentially, God is not the author of the evil* in the world. Insofar as the Satanic personification is concerned, it allows for the assessment of that battle in which man's freedom finds itself engaged before the God who summons it. Among his multiple names, that of "Prince of this World" can help to strip off from this figure the legendary tinsel, which was unknown in the Bible, without thereby doing away with the reality of this power to evil which overtakes us.

→ angel—demons—Dominations—evil.

Saul Gk. *Saoul, Saulos,* from the Heb. *shâ'ul.* Paul's original name, and the Latin form of this same name.[1]

[1]Acts 9:4; 13:9.

→ Paul.

save Gk. *sōzō* (from *saos:* "healthy"): "to keep in good health, conserve, preserve." To this first meaning was added the idea of a danger out of which one is preserved or from which one is pulled. The context or an adjoining preposition helps to indicate the specific meaning that should be chosen.

1. To safeguard, to preserve in danger, to keep safe and sound. In a storm or amid hostile people (ordinarily the Gk. *diasōzō*[1] or *rhyomai apo*[2]). This sense can be taken to mean "to safeguard one's life"[3] or "to pass safe and sound through the hour."[4]

[1]Acts 23:24; 27:31,34,43f.; 28:1,4. [2]Mt 6:13; Rom 15:31; 2 Thes 3:2; 2 Tim 4:18 △. [3]Mt 16:25 (= Mk 8:35 = Lk 9:24). [4]Jn 12:27.

2. To pull out of danger: in addition to *sōzō,* we find the terms "to snatch out of" (Gk. *ex-aireō,* designated below by the letter E): "to extract" or Gk. *rhyesthai ek* (below: R): "to deliver" from the storm,[5] from sickness,[6] persecutions,[7] from the power of evil or death,[8] etc. The outcome of the action is "to heal" (equally a meaning of *sōzō*), so that the healings done by Jesus come to symbolize salvation.[9] Faith maintains a vital relationship through which God brings about healing: "Your faith has saved you";[10] doubt leads to loss,[11] hope guarantees definitive salvation.[12] Jesus did not wish to save himself from death.[13]

[5]Mt 8:25. [6]Mt 9:21f. (= Mk 5:28 = Lk 8:48). [7]Lk 1:71; (with E) : Acts 7:10,34; 12:11; 26:17; (with R) : Lk 1:74; 2 Tim 3:11; 2 Pt 2:9. [8]Mt 1:21; (with R) : Rom 7:24; 2 Cor 1:10; Col 1:13; 1 Thes 1:10; 2 Tim 4:17. [9]Mt 9:22; 14:36; Jn 11:12. [10]Mk 10:52; Lk 17:19; 18:42. [11]Mt 8:26; 14:31. [12]Rom 8:24. [13]Mt 27:40,42 (= Mk 15:30f. = Lk 23:35,37,39); Heb 5:7.

3. The Savior is God, the Living One;[14] also Jesus, whose name (which means "Yahweh saves")[15] brings salvation.[16] When applied to the Messiah, the title seems to be Hellenistic in origin.[17] It emphasized the universal aspect of salvation.[18]

[14]Ps 25:5; Lk 1:47; 1 Tim 1:1; Ti 1:3; 3:4; 2 Tim 1:10. [15]Mt 1:21. [16]Acts 4:12. [17]Lk 2:11; Acts 5:31; 13:23. [18]Jn 4:42; 1 Tim 4:10; 2 Tim 1:10; Ti 1:3; 2:10f.; 3:4-6; 1 Jn 4:14.

→ heal—liberation—redemption—restore.

sayings of Jesus

→ logia.

scandal A translation of the Gk. *skandalon,* this term often led to confusion: it is not a bad example or a revolting deed, but a snare, set in the path, which causes one to fall.

→ fall.

scarlet Gk. *kokkinos* (from *kokkos:* "scarlet dye"). Woven material bright red or carmine (but not crimson) in color. A precious fabric, used in worship and for ceremonial.[1]

[1]Lv 14:4; Is 1:18; Mt 27:28; Heb 9:19; Rv 17:3f.; 18:12,16 □.

scorpion Gk. *skorpios.* Abounding in Palestine (there were ten species) and renowned for its painful sting, this animal was characteristic of a world that was harmful and cruel.[1]

[1]Dt 8:15; 1 Kgs 12:11-14; Sir 26:7; 39:30; Ez 2:6; Lk 10:19; 11:12; Rv 9:3,5,10 □.

scourge Gk. *mastix.* Another Greek word is *plēgē* (related to *plessō:* "to strike"): "blow received,"[1] wound, and, from these, "disaster." Poorly understood as blows of fate[2] or divine punishments on the sinful world, scourges were foretold in the book of Revelation in images taken from the plagues of Egypt.[3]

[1]Lk 12:48. [2]Mk 3:10; 5:29,34; Lk 7:21. [3]Ex 7:14–12:34; 2 Mc 7:37; 9:5,11; Sir 27:25-27; Rv 8:12–21:9; 22:18.

→ harden—vengeance—wrath.

scourging **1.** The whip was made of cords, trimmed with little pieces of bone or with metal balls (Lat. *flagrum*), or with thin (leather?) thongs (Lat. *flagellum*). The culprit was sometimes bound to a column by his hands, at other times bent in two, at still other times stretched out on the ground or on a bench. According to Jewish legislation, he received at most thirty-nine blows, for the Law forbade more than forty[1] (the Code of Hammurabi fixed the number at sixty and the Koran would later set it at eighty or one hundred); thirteen blows were administered to the chest, twenty-six on the back.

[1]Dt 25:3; 2 Cor 11:24.

2. Punishment by whipping was carried out in various fashions. For certain faults, Jewish law knew of a scourging given in the synagogue[2] (Gk. *mastigoō*). Jesus predicted to his disciples that they would be treated thus.[3] The Roman punishment was called *verberatio* (Gk. *phragelloō* [from the Lat. *flagello:* "to whip"] or, by assimilation to the preceding, *mastigoō*). It was applied to slaves and to non-citizens after a sentence of death. This is what Jesus underwent.[4] The torture took place at the time of interrogations which tried to obtain confessions.[5] The police officials administered reproofs with their canes or batons (Gk. *rabdizō*). Paul says that he suffered this punishment on three occasions.[6]

[2]Dt 25:2f. [3]Mt 10:17; 23:34. [4]Mt 20:19 (= Mk 10:34 = Lk 18:33); 27:26 (= Mk 15:15); cf. Lk 23:16. [5]Acts 22:24 [6]2 Cor 11:25; cf. Acts 16:22,37.

→ crucifixion.

scribe Gk. *grammateus* (from *grammata:* "letters, writings, texts," cf. *graphō:* "to write"): "secretary,"[1] Heb. *sôphér* (from *sâphar:* "to count"): "a man of the Book."

[1]Acts 19:35.

1. A specialist in, and official interpreter of, the Holy Scriptures.[2] At the end of long years of study, around the age of forty, one was ordained a scribe, a fact which conferred authority in judicial decisions (another word for him was the Gk. *nomikos:* "lawyer*"), especially in the Sanhedrin* with which he sat by right. Among the renowned scribes were: Hillel* and Shammai (20 B.C.), Gamaliel,*[3] Johannan Ben Zakkai (about A.D. 70). Scribes often were Pharisees.*

[2]1 Mc 2:42; 7:12f.; Sir 38:24-39:11; 1 Cor 1:20. [3]Acts 5:34; 22:3.

2. Neither Jesus nor the Apostles had received this kind of learned training.[4] Jesus reproached them for the excesses due to their learning and for their concern for honors.[5] The term appeared on Jesus' lips as an indication of those who were his own disciples.[6]

[4]Jn 7:15; Acts 4:13. [5]Mt 23:1-22,29-36; Lk 11:45-52; 20:46f.; cf. Mt 5:21-48. [6]Mt 13:52; 23:34 (cf. Lk 11:49).

→ Intr. XII.1.C.—doctor (of the Law)—lawyer.

Scripture Gk. *graphē.* The established expression of what is thought and spoken. On the manner of writing→ Intr. IX.3.

1. Writing establishes the spoken word. Through writing man (or God in person)[1] confers on his word an intangible worth and character.[2] It has as its function that of recalling to memory,*[3] of guaranteeing and of sealing.[4] The first Christians, heirs of the biblical tradition, came in their turn to call the O.T. the "Holy Scriptures"[5] and to refer to them as the Word of God*: whether the reference was to a specific passage[6] or to their totality.[7] By the formula "it is written"[8] they stressed that God's plan* was fulfilled in Jesus Christ[9] and that the promise* had been kept.[10] The epistles of the Apostles constituted "holy writings" at the end of the first century.[11]

[1]Ex 32:16; 32:32. [2]Jer 36:23f.; Jn 10:35; 19:22; Rv 22:18f. [3]Ex 17:14; Dt 6:8f.; 11:20. [4]Ex 39:30; Is 8:16. [5]Rom 1:2; 2 Tim 3:15. [6]Mt 21:42; 22:29; Mk 12:10; Lk 4:21; Jn 2:22; Acts 1:16. [7]Mt 26:54; Lk 24:32,45; Jn 5:39; Acts 17:2; 1 Cor 15:3f. [8]Mt 2:5; 4:4ff. [9]Lk 16:16; 24:25f.; Acts 20:27. [10]Heb 3:7-19; 1 Pt 1:10f. [11]1 Tim 5:18; 2 Pt 3:16.

2. Scripture remains bound to the Word. Although nothing of the Scriptures ought to disappear (not even an iota[12]), it is the Word of God which endures forever[13] and gives meaning to it: so one witnesses the transfer from the Law* written on stone to the Law written in hearts.[14] From this derives the Pauline criticism of the written letter, which is in opposition to the spirit.[15] Outside of controversies* (and so without the customary formulas[16]), Jesus did not quote the Scripture, as the scribes* did to justify their sayings, although the gospel tradition did offer him this mode of expression.[17] John went so far as to put Scripture and the Word of Jesus side by side.

[12]Mt 5:18; Jn 10:35. [13]Ps 119:89. [14]Jer 1:33; Ez 36:27; Jn 6:45. [15]2 Cor 3. [16]Mt 22:43. [17]Cf. Mt 21:13 and Jn 2:16; Mt 26:31 and Jn 16:32. [18]Jn 2:22; 18:9.

→ Intr. IX.5.B; XII.—Bible—book—fulfill—scribe—word.

sea Gk. *thalassa.*

1. With the earth and the sky, one of the three regions that constituted the universe.[1] It also referred equally well to the Mediterranean[2] and to the Red Sea (sometimes Gk. *erythros*[3]) as well as to the Lake of Tiberias.[4] The glassy sea was the celestial ocean whence rain came down.[5]

[1]Acts 4:24; 14:15; Rv 10:6; 14:7. [2]Acts 10:6,32; 17:14; 27:30. [3]Acts 7:36; 1 Cor 10:1f.; Heb 11:29 △. [4]Nm 34:11; Mt 4:13ff. [5]Rv 4:6; 15:2 △.

2. Bound up with the chaotic abyss of the beginning,[6] the sea was the place where demoniacal powers resided and were at work,[7] and where the dead were gathered together;[8] one day it would be destroyed.[9] Like God, Jesus mastered the unfettered waves and, according to need, walked on them, while Peter, through his lack of faith, risked sinking in them.[10]

[6]Gn 1:2,9f.; 7:11; Sir 43:25. [7]Jb 7:12; Is 27:1; 51:9f.; Dn 7; Mt 8:32; Rv 7:2f.; 13:1. [8]Rv 20:13. [9]Rv 21:1. [10]Ps 89:9f.; Jon 1; Na 1:4; Mt 8:24-27 (= Mk 4:37-41 = Lk 8:23-25); 14:24-27 (= Mk 6:47-50; Jn 6:17-20).

→ Intr. V.1.—demons—Galilee (Sea of)—water.

seal Gk. *sphragis.* Just like a signature, the seal attested to a proprietary right to, or to the authenticity* of, a document.

1. By its closure, it juridically ensured the mastery of Jesus' tomb,[1] of the abyss,[2] of history.[3] In a derived sense, to seal was to "make secret."[4]

[1]Mt 27:66; cf. Dn 6:18. [2]Rv 20:3. [3]Rv 5:1-9; 6:1-12; 8:1. [4]Rv 10:4; 22:10.

2. Through the impression of the seal of the living God,[5] which in Ezekiel took the shape of a cross (the ancient form of *taw,* the last letter of the Hebrew alphabet)[6] and which, in the book of Revelation, seems to bear God's name and (or) that of the Lamb,[7] the seal tells of some radical or exclusive adherence, on Jesus' part[8] or on that of the elect[9] or on the part of believers who have received the Holy Spirit.[10] One can see connections between these and the marks (Gk. *stigma*) that Paul bore in his body[11] and also make distinctions between these and the mark (Gk. *charagma*) of the Beast.*[12]

[5]Rv 7:2. [6]Ez 9:4,6. [7]Rv 14:1; 22:4. [8]Jn 6:27. [9]Rv 7:3-8; 9:4. [10]2 Cor 1:22; Eph 1:13; 4:30. [11]Gal 6:17 △. [12]Rv 13:16f.; 14:9,11; 16:2; 19:20; 20:4 △.

3. A seal comes to authenticate God's truthfulness,[13] Abraham's justice,[14] Paul's apostolate[15] as well as the collection.*[16]

[13]Jn 3:33. [14]Rom 4:11. [15]1 Cor 9:2; 2 Tim 2:19. [16]Rom 15:28; cf. Tb 9:5 □.

→ stigmata.

[secondary] Lat. *secundarius,* from *sequor:* "to follow." What follows is not first, or "primitive.*" In literary criticism,* the term is applied to a text that has been altered or to a context that has been modified.

sect Lat. *secta,* from *sequor:* "to follow"; Gk. *hairesis* (related to *haireomai:* "to choose," *diaireō:* "to share out"): "a party" of the Nazarenes* or Christians,[1] of the Pharisees*[2] or the Sadducees.*[3] It also referred to schisms[4] or heretical sects.[5] An abbreviation to indicate the community of Qumran.*

[1]Acts 24:5,14; 28:22. [2]Acts 15:5; 26:5. [3]Acts 5:17. [4]1 Cor 11:19; Gal 5:20; Ti 3:10. [5]2 Pt 2:1 □.

seduce Numerous Greek words can be translated by the verb "to seduce." The closest would be *apataō,* which was used to describe the action of the Tempter who seduced Eve,[1] as well as to describe false doctors or vain philosophers* and the impious,*[2] and finally, riches.*[3] Other words stress various aspects of the seduction. To lead astray (Gk. *planaō*): now this was the function of Satan, the seducer above all others,[4] the master of seducers who raged throughout the world[5] and among those who lead people astray.[6] Others "lure with bait" (Gk. *deleazō*) weaker spirits,[7] misleading them (Gk. *meth-odeia*) into error,[8] abusing and duping them (Gk. *para-logizomai*),[9] carrying on their activity with tricks, deceits (Gk. *dolos*),[10] and with guile (Gk. *panourgia*).[11] Unlike the O.T., which presented God as seducing Israel or a prophet,[12] the N.T. never employs this word in a positive sense.

[1]Rom 7:11; 2 Cor 11:3; 1 Tim 2:14; Heb 3:13. [2]Rom 16:18; Col 2:8; 2 Pt 2:13. [3]Mt 13:22 (= Mk 4:19). [4]2 Jn 7; Rv 12:9; 20:3. [5]Eph 4:14; 1 Tim 4:1; 2 Jn 7. [6]Mt 24:5,11,24; Mk 13:6,22; 1 Jn 2:26; 3:7; Jude 11. [7]Jas 1:14; 2 Pt 2:14,18 △. [8]Eph 4:14; 6:11 △. [9]Col 2:4; Jas 1:22 △. [10]Rom 1:29; 2 Cor 11:13. [11]2 Cor 11:3; Eph 4:14. [12]Jer 20:7; Ez 14:9; Hos 2:16.

→ error.

see Gk. *horaō, blepō, theaomai, theōreō.* Among these different verbs the shades of meaning are less noticeable than they were in classical Greek; it is the context which allows for precision in their meanings: to see, to perceive, to attest, to remark, to pay attention to, to look at, to contemplate, to meet, and so forth.

1. God sees: his watchfulness is a way of speaking about his loving attention, his presence in man's heart.[1] Similarly, Jesus penetrates the thoughts of men.[2]

[1]Ex 3:7; 1 Sm 16:7; Ps 139:3,7,16; Mt 6:4; Lk 1:25,48; Acts 7:34. [2]Mt 9:2,4; Jn 1:48,50; cf. 2:25.

2. To see God, this was the desire that the Greeks so strongly stressed. For its part, the Bible emphasized hearing,* putting off to heaven* the satisfying of the desire:[3] God was invisible, no one had ever seen him.[4] Nonetheless, according to John, the Son had seen God;[5] to see Jesus was to see the Father.[6] More precisely, it was faith* that caused one to see Jesus' glory* in his works and on the cross.[7] Faith had no need to see the Risen One,[8] but it based itself on appearances* granted to the first witnesses* of the living Christ, appearances in which seeing was always subordinate to hearing, obeying to a mission.[9] The believer sees in the Crucified One the glory of Christ.[10]

[3]Mt 5:8; 1 Jn 3:2; Rv 22:4. [4]Jn 1:18; Col 1:15; 1 Tim 1:17; 6:16; Heb 11:27; 1 Jn 4:12,20. [5]Jn 3:11; 6:46. [6]Jn 12:45; 14:7,9f. [7]Jn 2:23; 4:48; 6:36,40. [8]Jn 20:29. [9]Mt 28:7,10,17; Mk 16:7; Lk 24:34,39; Jn 20:18,20,25,27; Acts 1:3; 9:17; 13:31; 26:16; 1 Cor 15:5-8; 1 Tim 3:16. [10]Jn 19:37.

→ appearances of Christ—blind—eye—faith—know—sign.

[Semitic] From Shem, one of Noah's* sons, the eponymous* hero of the tribes of western Asia who spoke related languages: Akkadian,* Canaanite, Phoenician, Hebrew,* Aramaic,* Syriac, finally Arabic and Ethiopic. The term designates expressions or conceptions issuing from this cultural world.

[Semitism] Certain N.T. passages betray Semitic* thought and an Aramaic* style. Not to be confused with Hebraisms which, in the Septuagint,* for example, are texts translated literally from the Hebrew.

send

1. To indicate that one caused someone or something to go somewhere, Greek made use of two verbs, without any appreciable difference in meaning: *apostellō* and *pempō,* the latter being more current in secular language. To indicate a special relationship between the sender and the one sent, conferring on the verb an idea of mission, deputation or embassy, the N.T. makes use of *apostellō.*[1] Nonetheless, John (and Paul once[2]) ordinarily used *pempō* as well, without an appreciable difference in meaning.[3]

[1]Mt 11:10; 15:24; Lk 4:18,43; 10:16; Acts 3:26. [2]Rom 8:3; cf. Gal 4:4. [3]Jn 7:28,29; 8:29,42.

2. A term related to the divine election* and concerning the salvation* of men. After having sent the prophets,[4] God sent his own son,[5] whose identity is defined by that very fact.[6] Jesus sent the Holy Spirit[7] and sent out the disciples. These became his "apostles"[8] and would share the same fate as he did.[9] Paul fulfilled the mission of the Servant to the nations.[10]

[4]Is 61:1; Mt 21:34-37; 23:37 (= Lk 13:34); Lk 4:18; 11:49. [5]Lk 4:17-21; Jn 7:28f.; 8:29,42; Acts 3:20; Rom 8:3; Gal 4:4; 1 Jn 4:9,10,14. [6]Mt 10:40; Jn 4:34. [7]Lk 24:49; Jn 14:26; 15:26; Gal 4:6; 1 Pt 1:12. [8]Mt 10:2,5; Mk 3:14; Lk 6:13. [9]Jn 13:16,20; 20:21. [10]Acts 22:17,21; Rom 1:5.

→ apostle—mediator.

[Septuagint] The first Greek translation of the O.T., the Septuagint was composed, according to the legend of the *Letter of Aristeas,* by 72 Jewish doctors who carried the project off in seventy-two days, on orders from Ptolemy Philadelphos (283–246 B.C.); hence its appellation of Septuagint (seventy). According to history, it was done by numerous authors whose work stretched from 250 to 150 B.C. (the prologue of Sirach* mentioned it in about 116). It was intended for Jews who spoke Greek, particularly at Alexandria in Egypt. In relation to the Hebrew canon,* it included, additionally, the deuterocanonical* works, Judith, Tobit, First and Second Maccabees, Wisdom, Sirach, Baruch, the Letter of Jeremiah, the additions to Esther and Daniel, as well as the *apocryphal works, 1 Esdras, 3 and 4 Maccabees, the Odes and Psalms of Solomon. In addition to some papyri from the second century B.C., the Septuagint is chiefly known through the works of Origen (end of the second century A.D.) and by the fourth century codex called *Vaticanus.* Beginning in 130, the Jew Aquila published a strictly "literal" Greek version; the Christian Symmachus proposed another one about the year 170 and Theodotion offered a corrected version of the Septuagint at the end of the second century. Specialists still discuss the origins of the Septuagint: were there one text or many texts? The Septuagint was the Bible used by Christians from the beginning (thus, Mt 1:23).

→ Intr. III.3; XV.—Bible—deuterocanonical writings—Chart, p. 67.

sepulchre

→ tomb.

[sequence] The order of pericopes* organized to form a whole. Hence the day at Capernaum (Mk 1:21–38) or the three first miracles reported by Matthew (8:1–17).

Sergius Paulus The proconsul* in Cyprus* in 46–47 or 49–50.[1]

[1]Acts 13:7 □.

serpent Gk. *ophis.*

1. Frequent in Israel (thirty species), sometimes fatally venomous.

2. The N.T. does not retain the chthonian symbolism that made it out to be one of the attributes of warrior gods (the emblem of Aesculapius), but it does keep the tradition of the bronze serpent that healed the Hebrews bitten by serpents in the wilderness: it prefigured Jesus lifted up on the cross, saving believers who looked on him with faith.[1]

[1]Nm 21:8f.; Wis 16:5-7; Jn 3:14; cf. 19:37; 1 Cor 10:9.

3. A mythical figure of Satan,* the serpent of the earthly paradise, the seducer.[2]

[2]Gn 3; 2 Cor 11:3; Rv 12:9; 20:2.

4. An impure* animal,[3] feeding on dust,[4] crafty,[5] wicked,[6] a hypocrite[7] with venomous speech.[8] Disciples had received a power to trample it underfoot[9] and believers did not have to fear it: they could even pick it up in their hands.[10] Thus, it symbolized the power of evil which had been conquered.

[3]Lv 11:10,42; cf. Acts 10:12; 11:6. [4]Gn 3:14f.; Is 65:25; Mi 7:17. [5]Mt 10:16. [6]Mt 7:10 (= Lk 11:11); cf. 12:34. [7]Mt 23:33; cf. 3:7 (= Lk 3:7). [8]Jb 20:16; Ps 58:5; Rom 3:13. [9]Ps 91:13; Lk 10:19. [10]Is 11:8; Mk 16:18; Acts 28:3.

→ beasts—dragon.

servant **1.** Gk. *doulos:* "slave," then, in relation (to the king or) to God,[1] a title of honor claimed in the O.T. by God's envoys[2] and in the N.T. by Paul and the Apostles.[3] The Gk. *pais:* "young servant, boy, child" also designated domestics, servant girls,[4] perhaps to soften the connotation implicit in the term "slave." The word indicated perfect allegiance to God: "servants and servant girls of God,"[5] radically different from the dependence of a salaried worker, mercenary, hireling (Gk. *misthios, misthōtos*).[6]

[1]2 Mc 7:33. [2]Rv 10:7; 11:18; 15:3. [3]Rom 1:1; Gal 1:10; Col 4:12; Ti 1:1; Jas 1:1; 2 Pt 1:1; Jude 1. [4]Mt 8:6; 14:2; 26:69 (= Mk 14:66 = Lk 22:56); Lk 12:45; 15:26; Acts 12:13; 16:16; Gal 4:22-31. [5]Lk 1:38,48; 2:29; Acts 2:18; 4:29; 16:17; 2 Tim 2:24; 1 Pt 2:16; Rv 2:20; 7:3; 15:3; 19:2; 22:3,6. [6]Mk 1:20; Lk 15:17,19; Jn 10:12f. △.

2. Jesus, who took on the traits of a *doulos,*[7] was never called by this title, which is an honorific for men. It was the word *pais,* used in the O.T. to refer to some man of God or other,[8] or to the Servant of Yahweh in Isaiah's hymns,[9] which was retained to describe the Servant of Yahweh in Jesus. The primitive Church listed his functions: Jesus proclaimed judgment to the nations, offered his life in sacrifice for the multitude* and was glorified by the Father.[10]

[7]Phil 2:7. [8]Gn 32:11; Nm 12:7f.; 2 Sm 3:18; 2 Kgs 9:7f.; Wis 2:13; 9:4f.; Bar 1:20; 2:20,28; Lk 1:69; Acts 4:25. [9]Is 42:1-4; 49:1-6; 50:4-11; 52:13–53:12; Acts 8:34; 1 Pt 2:22-25. [10]Mt 12:18-21; 20:28 (= Mk 10:45); Acts 3:13,26; 4:27,30; Phil 2:5-11.

→ serve—slave.

serve **1.** Gk. *douleuō:* "to be bound to a master." English supports only with difficulty the likening of "service" to "slavery," preferring to use service to speak of a faithful submission to God,[1] to Christ[2] or to the Law of God,[3] and describing as slavery* any bondage to man[4] or to an evil power.[5] Service of God was exclusive of any other.[6] Christians served God, not in fear* but in freedom, not as slaves but as sons.[7] Being no longer servants, but friends of Jesus,[8] they shared in the service of God which he himself realized for the Gospel's sake;[9] Similarly, they ought to make themselves "slaves" of others.[10]

[1]Rom 6:22; 1 Thes 1:9. [2]Rom 14:18; 1 Cor 7:22; Gal 1:10; Eph 6:6f.; Col 3:24. [3]Rm 7:25. [4]Rom 9:12; 1 Cor 7:15. [5]Rom 6:6; 8:21; Gal 4:3,8. [6]Mt 6:24. [7]Jn 8:33-36; Rom 6–7; Gal 4. [8]Jn 15:15. [9]Jn 15:20; Phil 2:7,22. [10]Mt 20:27 (= Mk 10:44); Gal 5:13.

2. Gk. *diakoneō:* "to serve," the act of waiting on table or some other similar service.[11] In gestures of service done by Jesus,[12] the disciples were invited to discover a reversal of values: they had to become servants like him.[13] Moreover, these gestures symbolized the gift that Jesus had made of his life. Thus, this term was a characteristic of Jesus' fundamental attitude on earth[14] and of the last day.[15] To serve Jesus was to follow* him;[16] to serve others was to serve Jesus himself.[17] In the primitive Church, the term had the specific sense of ensuring the functions of the assistant within the community.[18]

[11]Mt 4:11; 8:15; Lk 10:40; Jn 12:2. [12]Lk 22:27; cf. Jn 13:1-20. [13]Mt 20:26 (= Mk 10:43 = Lk 22:26); 1 Pt 4:10. [14]Mt 20:28 (= Mk 10:45); Rom 15:8. [15]Lk 12:37. [16]Jn 12:26. [17]Mt 25:44. [18]Acts 6:1,4; 12:25; 20:24; 21:19; Rom 11:13; 12:7; 2 Cor 3:3-9; 5:18; Eph 3:7; Col 1:23; 1 Tim 1:12; 1 Pt 1:12.

→ servant—slave.

set free

→ liberate.

[setting in life] An expression translating the technical German term *Sitz im Leben.*

1. In literary criticism,* the setting in which literary traditions were "formed." We may make the following distinctions: according to their characteristic activities, the liturgical, catechetical and missionary functions; according to their faith content, their paschal and pre-paschal settings.

2. Not to be confused with the coordinates of events (places, times); the determination of these latter features derive from principles of historical criticism.*

→ *Formgeschichte*—literary genre.

seven Gk. *hepta.*

1. A number rendered sacred by the seventh day, that of God's rest*[1] and having a function within the calendar,*[2] ritual[3] and objects of worship.*[4]

[1]Ex 20:11; Heb 4:4. [2]Ex 12:15. [3]Lv 4:6. [4]Ex 25:37.

2. It could symbolize plenitude, totality.[5]

[5]Mt 18:21f.; Mk 8:5,20; Rv 1:4,11f.,20; 5:1,6; 8:6; 21:9.

3. Co-workers with the Twelve,* they were chosen at the beginning of the Church.[6]

[6]Acts 6:3-6; 21:8 □.

→ numbers—sabbath—week.

shade, shadow

1. Gk. *skia.* It referred to a twofold experience: insofar as it was the absence of light, it was the equivalent of darkness* and death[1]; insofar as it presupposed light* (all the while preserving the sun's heat[2]), it symbolized God's presence and his power by way of protection.[3] Hence, the verb *episkiazō:* "to cover with his shade."[4]

[1]Is 9:1; Mt 4:16; Lk 1:79. [2]Jb 7:2; Jon 4:5f.; Mk 4:32; cf. Rv 7:15f. [3]Ps 17:8; 91:1; Is 4:5f.; 25:4f.; 49:2; Ez 31:6; Heb 9:5. [4]Ex 40:35; Nm 9:18,22; Wis 19:7; Mt 17:5; Lk 1:35; 9:34; Acts 5:15 △.

2. In another context of thought, the shadow was opposed to the reality *(sōma),* just as the figure was to the thing represented.[5]

[1]Col 2:17; Heb 8:5; 10:1 △.

→ cloud—darkness—death—night.

Sharon Gk. *Sarōn.* The coastal plain between Jaffa and Carmel, proverbial for its fertility.[1]

[1]Jos 12:18; Sg 2:1; Is 35:2; Acts 9:35 □.

→ Intr. II.3.A.—Map 4.

sheep Gk. *probaton,* often designating the "small livestock" (Heb. *sè*). One of the principal resources of Israel (wool, milk, skin, meat). Frequently they were offered in sacrifice.*[1] Like the prophets, Jesus often made mention of them to tell of God's solicitude for men, the opposite of wicked shepherds.[2]

[1]Dt 15:19; 18:4. [2]Nm 27:17; 1 Kgs 22:17; Ps 23:1; Is 53:7; Jer 11:19; Ez 34:5; Mt 7:15; 9:36 (= Mk 6:34); 10:6,16; 18:12; 26:31 (= Mk 14:27); Lk 15:4-6; Jn 10:1-27; 21:16f.; Heb 13:20.

→ Intr. II.6.—Lamb of God—Sheep Gate—shepherd.

Sheep Gate Gk. *probatikē (hē pylē)* (from *probaton:* "sheep"): "the gate of the sheep." One of the gates, to the northeast of the Temple enclosure, through which passed the animals destined for sacrifice.[1] Not far from it was located the pool* of Bethzatha,*[2] where, according to Origen, the sheep in question would have been washed.

[1]Neh 3:1. [2]Jn 5:2 □.

→ Map 1.

shekel Gk. *siklos,* Heb. *shéqèl:* "weight." An ancient measurement of weight (14 grams) which became a Jewish monetary unit, made out of silver, with the value of a Greek stater* or a tetradrachma. It corresponded approximately to the wages of four days' labor (four denarii). To indicate a monetary unit, it was necessary to add the qualification shekel "of silver" (Gk. *argyria*).[1]

[1]Mt 26:15; 27:3-9; 28:12,15; Acts 19:19 △.

→ coins—weights.

[Sheol] Heb. *sh^eôl* (its etymology is obscure, having been attributed to various roots meaning "corruption," "to be humble," "place of interrogation"): the place where the dead sojourned, "the netherworld." It was ordinarily translated by the Gk. *haidēs:* "Hades.*"

→ netherworld.

shepherd Gk. *poimēn.*

1. In early morning, the village shepherd walked ahead of the sheep* and goats* which had been brought to him; in the evening he led them back to quench their thirst at the spring; there, each owner gathered his animals back together again by making himself known to them with a clicking of his tongue. In Jesus' time the shepherds belonged to the humbler people who neither knew nor observed the Law. Nonetheless, it was to these that the Good News of Jesus' birth was announced.[1]

[1]Lk 2:8-20.

2. The shepherd was, in world literature, a traditional figure for the guide, whether political or religious, of a community. Such was also the case in the O.T., although the title was given only exceptionally to Yahweh or to Israel's kings;[2] on the other hand, there was a perennial hope for a Shepherd who would come at the end of time to pasture his people in place of the guides who had been unfaithful to their mission.[3]

[2]Gn 48:15; 49:24; Nm 27:15-20; 2 Sm 7:7f.; Ps 23. [3]Is 40:10f.; Jer 23:1-4; Ez 34:2-10; Mi 4:6f.

3. Like God, whom he described as a Pastor full of solicitude,[4] Jesus was filled with mercy for the sheep who were lost[5] and without a shepherd;[6] he even allowed himself to be struck, for he trusted in God who would enable him to gather the little flock together again.[7] On the last day, the Son of Man* will gather it together for judgment.[8] All these traits were brought together by the Fourth Gospel in the allegory of the Good Shepherd;[9] likewise, believers have seen in Jesus the definitive pastor.[10]

[4]Lk 15:4-7. [5]Mt 10:6; 15:24; Lk 19:10. [6]Mt 9:36 (= Mk 6:34). [7]Mt 26:31f. (= Mk 14:27); Lk 12:32. [8]Mt 25:31f. [9]Jn 10:1-30. [10]Heb 13:20; 1 Pt 2:25; 5:4; Rv 7:17.

4. In their turn, the pastors, of whom Peter was the first,[11] were charged with watching over the Church,[12] with going out to look for the lost sheep,[13] and of preserving the flock against wolves.[14]

[11]Jn 21:16. [12]Eph 4:11. [13]Mt 18:12-14. [14]Acts 20:28-31.

shoe Gk. *hypo-dēma* (from *deō:* "to tie" and *hypo:* "on top"), sometimes particularized in *sandalion.* The usual shoe, worn only out of doors, was the sandal,[1] with a leather sole bound to the foot with thongs.[2] Because of the dust of the roadways, hospitality* made it a duty to wash* the feet of visitors. On trips one readily took along a pair for a change of footwear.[3] Iconography testifies to closed-in shoes for persons of note.[4]

[1]Mk 6:9; Acts 12:8 △. [2]Mt 3:11; Mk 1:7 (= Lk 3:16 = Jn 1:27); Acts 7:33; 13:25; Eph 6:15. [3]Mt 10:10 (= Lk 10:4); Lk 22:35. [4]Cf. Lk 15:22.

→ clothing.

showbread

→ loaves of offering.

shroud Gk. *sindōn.* A large piece of fine linen cloth in which bodies were wrapped for burial.*[1]

[1]Mt 27:59 (= Mk 15:46 = Lk 23:53).

→ Intr. VIII.2.D.b.—linen cloth.

[Sibylline Oracles] A Hellenistic collection of traditions that were Jewish in origin, apologetic in their tendency and possessing Christian interpolations (surely Books VI, VII, VIII, XIII) dating from the fifth and sixth centuries A.D. From Book III, the oldest (second century B.C.), Virgil could have known the prophecy of the Virgin Mother (Is 11:6).

sickness **1.** Sickness (Gk. *nosos*[1]), which various terms described or gave shades of meaning to: infirmity (*arrōstos,*[2] *asthenēs:*[3] "without vigor"), listlessness (*malakia:*[4] "softness"), the fact of having been struck (from *mastix:*[5] "scourge") or of being unwell (*kakōs echein*[6]), was understood not as a simple natural phenomenon, but always in its relationship to sin* and to the powers* of evil.* Nonetheless, neither the prophets nor Jesus attributed it to a kind of collective retribution.*[7]

[1]Mt 4:23f.; 8:17; 9:35; 10:1; Mk 1:34; Lk 4:40; 6:18; 7:21; 9:1; Jn 5:4; Acts 9:12; 1 Tim 6:4 △. [2]Mt 14:14; Mk 6:5,13; 16:18; 1 Cor 11:30 △. [3]Lk 5:15; Jn 11,4; Acts 28:9ff. [4]Mt 4:23; 9:35; 10:1 △. [5]Mk 3:10; 5:29,34; Lk 7:21 △. [6]Mt 4:24; 8:16; 9:12; 14:35; 17:15; Mk 1:32,34; 2:17; 6:55; Lk 5:31; 7:2 △. [7]Sir 38:9f.; Is 53:3-5; Ez 18; Lk 13:1-5; Jn 9:2f.

2. Faced with our sicknesses, Jesus experienced pity and struggled against them by healing* them and "bearing" them.[8] This was because he saw in them a consequence of sin and a sign of Satan's* domination.[9] The setting-back of sickness symbolized the progressive triumph of life* over death*. Henceforth, like all suffering, sickness has been situated within the current of redemption,*[10] while waiting for men to be forever healed by foliage from the tree of life.*[11]

[8]Mt 8:16f.; 20:34; 25:36. [9]Lk 13:16; Jn 5:14. [10]2 Cor 4:10; Col 1:24. [11]Rv 22:2; cf. Ez 47:12.

3. The N.T. mentions numerous sicknesses.[12]

[12]Intr. VIII.2.D.

→ doctor—heal—save.

Sidon Gk. *Sidōn,* from the Heb. *ṣidôn:* "fishing-ground," modern-day Saida (Lebanon). An old Phoenician port on the Mediterranean.[1]

[1]Mt 11:21f.; 15:21; Mk 3:8; 7:31; Lk 4:26; 6:17; Acts 27:3 □.

→ Map 3.

sign Gk. *sēmeion* (the same root as *sēmainō:* "to make a sign, to signify, to cause to understand," hence, "to tell the meaning of").

1. A reality that is a throwback to another reality and, in being such, suggests it. The proclamation of an absent reality or one that makes it present. The sign reveals and conceals at the same time. The N.T. is familiar with this ordinary sense of the term: to give a sign,[1] to signify something.[2]

[1]Mt 26:48 (= Mk 14:44); Lk 2:12; 2 Thes 3:17. [2]Jn 12:33; 18:32; 21:19; Acts 11:28.

2. God, who speaks to men through his creation, also gives them signs in a special way through his actions which arouse astonishment. Thus, according to Jewish tradition, the messianic times were to be inaugurated by marvelous signs, like those of the Exodus or Elijah's* time; the expression *sēmeia kai terata* (signs and wonders) was readily employed. The N.T. evokes expectations of these precursory signs.[3] Faced with Jews who wanted to see signs in order to dispose themselves to believe, Jesus refused to give any such spectacular ones and referred people back to his preaching:[4] here were "signs of the times," that is, signs of "these present times,*" characterized by the presence and activity of Jesus, to be interpreted in the same way one scrutinized the face of heaven in order to discover what the weather would be like.[5]

[3]Mt 24:3; 1 Cor 1:22. [4]Mt 12:38f. (= Lk 11:29-32); 16:1,4 (= Mk 8:11f.); Lk 17:20f. [5]Mt 16:2f. (= Lk 12:54-56).

3. The Fourth Gospel added to the sense classical among the Jews the precise meaning of a "miracle*": the "powerful deeds" *(dynameis)* of Jesus were "signs"; in fact, he enshrined his miracles within speeches of his, which expliciated their meaning,[6] or in a context that helped one to grasp their significance.[7] From another point of view, his signs were the "works*" (Gk. *erga*) of God, who invited people to believe in Jesus and to see his glory.[8]

[6]Jn 5:1-47; 6:5-65; 9:1-41 (cf. 8:12); 11:25. [7]Jn 2:1-11: 4:46-54. [8]Jn 12:37.

4. Just as Jesus had been accredited by prodigious signs,[9] so were the disciples at the Church's foundation.[10] In the Church's time, there will be false signs, in the face of which one will need to exercise discernment.[11] The only sign that will be identical with its reality will be the coming of the Son of Man.*[12]

[9]Acts 2:22. [10]Mk 16:20; Acts 2:43; 4:30; 5:12; Rom 15:19; 2 Cor 12:12; 1 Thes 2:13. [11]Mt 24:24 (= Mk 13:22); 2 Thes 2:9; Rv 13:13f.; 16:14; 19:20. [12]Mt 24:30 (= Mk 13:26 = Lk 21:27).

→ miracle—symbol.

Silas Gk. *Silas,* a Greek adaptation of Saul, or *Silvanos* (from the Lat. *Silvanus*). A Roman citizen and Christian of Jerusalem, a prophet* and an esteemed man. A delegate to Antioch, Paul's companion, and the coauthor of the epistles to the Thessalonians and First Peter.[1]

[1]Acts 15:22,27,32,34,40; 16:19,25,29; 17:4,10,14f.; 18:5; 2 Cor 1:19; 1 Thes 1:1; 2 Thes 1:1; 1 Pt 5:12 □.

Siloam Gk. *Silōam,* Heb. *Shîlôah.*

1. The pool. The mouth of the "canal" (in Heb. *ha shîlôah*) constructed by Hezekiah about 700 B.C. to the southeast of Jerusalem. There flowed the waters of the spring Gihon, intended for the city's supply. In the N.T. period, a pool surrounded by a portico with colonnades, the work of Herod the Great.*[1]

[1]2 Kgs 20:20; Sir 48:17; Is 8:6; 22:11; Jn 9:7,11 □.

→ pool—Map 1.

2. The tower. Doubtless, an elevation in a quarter located within the surroundings of Kedron* and neighboring on the pool that had given its name to it.[1]

[1]Lk 13:4 □.

Silvanus

→ Silas.

silver

→ money.

Simeon

Gk. *Symeōn,* from the Heb. *shîmôn:* "God has heard."

1. The second son of Jacob and Leah, the eponymous* ancestor of one of the twelve tribes* of Israel.[1]

[1]Gn 29:33; Rv 7:7 □.

2. An ancestor of Jesus.[2]

[2]Lk 3:30 □.

3. A "just and pious" Jew of Jerusalem.[3]

[3]Lk 2:25,34 □.

4. A Christian of Antioch, a prophet or doctor.[4]

[4]Acts 13:1 □.

5. A personage most probably identical to Simon Peter in Acts 15:14, and certainly so in 2 Pt 1:1 □.

Simon

Gk. *Simōn,* from the Heb. *shîmôn,* Simeon.*

1. The son of John (Jonah), Peter's* first name.[1]

[1]Mt 16:17; Jn 1:42; 21:15 □.

2. The Cananaean, one of the Twelve,* whose name did not signify that he was a native of Cana or of Canaan, but was "the zealous one," an Aramaic term signifying "zealous, zealot."[2]

[2]Mt 10:4; Mk 3:18; Lk 6:15; Acts 1:13 □.

3. One of the "brothers of the Lord."*[3]

[3]Mt 13:55; Mk 6:3 □.

4. A Pharisee.*[4]

[4]Lk 7:40,43f. □.

5. The leper of Bethany, perhaps to be identified with the preceding one.[5]

[5]Mt 26:6; Mk 14:3 □.

6. Simon of Cyrene,* a passerby pressed into the service of carrying Jesus' cross.[6]

[6]Mt 27:32; Mk 15:21; Lk 23:26 □.

7. Simon Iscariot, the father of Judas Iscariot.*[7]

[7]Jn 6:71; 13:2,26 ☐.

8. A magician of Samaria.

[8]Acts 8:9,13,18,24 ☐.

9. The tanner of Joppa.[9]

[9]Acts 9:43; 10:6,17,32 ☐.

sin Among the constellation of terms signifying a failure or a fault, the family of Greek words with the root *hamart-* is the most frequent (296 instances). *Hamartia* also has a more extensive bearing than *adikia:* "iniquity," which draws attention to juridical terminology (22 times), and *parabasis* (from *parabainō:* "to go aside, transgress") which points to the transgression of divine ordinances (14 times). Unlike the Greek world wherein the verb *hamartanō:* "to miss the mark" did not imply malice but rather error or the influence of fate, the O.T. linked sin (Heb. *héth, 'awôn*) essentially with man's relationship to God: to sin was to be unfaithful to the Covenant*; it was to betray love,* to separate oneself from the community. There was no other remedy for sin than forgiveness* from the holy God, something signified by the feast of the Atonement.*

1. Jesus spoke as a Jew of his time. "A sinner" was one who was not within the Covenant (the pagan*)[1] and who did not observe God's will,* particularly as it was expressed in the Law.*[2] Jesus denounced sin, even that which lay in the secret roots of one's behavior.[3] He recalled the infinite mercy* of God which was always ready to forgive[4] and showed himself to be the friend of sinners;[5] he went so far as to forgive sins,[6] a remission that would be fully efficacious through his blood* poured out, and by virtue of his resurrection*;[7] only blasphemy* against the Spirit was unforgiveable.[8] Finally, the believer, like God himself, had to forgive anyone who had sinned against him.[9]

[1]Mt 26:45 (= Mk 14:41); Lk 6:32-34; 24:7; cf. Mt 9:10f. (= Mk 2:15f. = Lk 5:30); Lk 15:1f.; 19:7; Gal 2:15. [2]Mt 9:13 (= Mk 2:17 = Lk 5:32); 19:17-19 (= Mk 10:19 = Lk 18:20); cf. Mt 15:3; Lk 11:42; 13:2. [3]Mt 5:27f.; 6:22f.; 15:1-20 (= Mk 7:1-23). [4]Lk 11:4; 15:1-32; 18:13. [5]Mt 11:19 (= Lk 7:34); Lk 15:1f.; 19:7. [6]Mt 9:2,5f. (= Mk 2:5,7,9f. = Lk 5:20f.,23f.); Lk 7:37-50; 19:9; Jn 5:14; 8:11. [7]Mt 26:28; Lk 24:47; Acts 2:38; 5:31; 10:43; 13:38; 26:18. [8]Mt 12:31 (= Mk 3:28f.). [9]Mt 18:15,21 (= Lk 17:3f.).

2. By means of a profound grasp of Jesus' death and resurrection, Paul penetrated to the very origin, nature, power and universality of sin and its redemption. Recalling that the Law did not preserve from sin (but the contrary!),[10] he proclaimed that all men had sinned[11] and designated the person of Adam* as the inaugurator of the sinful condition of humanity through the action of personified sin; thus, Adam figured as the negative counterpart of Christ, the savior of all.[12] In fact, Jesus, who had never known sin, died for our sins;[13] God "made him to be Sin for our sakes,"[14] thereby condemning the sin from which he sets us free.[15] By his baptism* the believer is dead to sin, but each day he has to actualize this death.*[16]

[10]Rom 3:20; 1 Cor 15:56; Gal 3:19. [11]Rom 3:23. [12]Rom 5:12-21; 7:8-13; cf. Jas 1:15. [13]Rom 5:8; 1 Cor 15:3; Gal 1:4; Col 1:14; 1 Tim 1:15; Ti 2:14; Heb 9:15; 1 Pt 3:18. [14]2 Cor 5:21; Heb 4:15; 1 Pt 2:22,24. [15]Rom 8:2f.; Heb 1:3; 2:17; 5:1; 7:26f.; 9:26; 1 Pt 4:1. [16]Rom 6:1-22; 8:2.

3. According to John, the sin of the world was the power of a hostility to God which pre-existed man, the devil* who is a murderer and a liar.[17] Jesus removed this sin, for he triumphed over the Prince of this world.*[18] In his origin man was in an undifferentiated state, which we may call darkness*; sin consisted in preferring darkness to the in-breaking of the light.*[19]

[17]Jn 8:44; 1 Jn 3:8. [18]Jn 1:29; 12:31f.; 16:11,33; 1 Jn 1:7-10; 2:12; 3:5; 4:10; cf. Rv 1:5. [19]Jn 1:5; 3:19; 9:41.

→ Intr. XIV.2.A-B.—debt—expiate—forgiveness—justice.

Sinai (Mount) Gk. *Sina,* Heb. *Sînay.* Also called Horeb in the O.T. A mountain* difficult to identify, traditionally located to the south of the Sinaitic peninsula (2,285 m., 7,497 ft.). The place of the burning bush theophany,* of the Covenant* and of the gift of the Law.[1]

[1]Ex 3:1; 19:1-20; Acts 7:30,38; Gal 4:24f.; Heb 8:5; 12:20 □.

Sion

→ zion.

[Sirach] A sapiential writing composed in Greek about 180 B.C. by Jesus Ben Sira. His grandson translated it into Greek at Alexandria about 132 B.C. It is a deuterocanonical* writing. It is still referred to as *Ecclesiasticus.*

→ Intr.XII.3.—Chart, p. 67.

[Sitz im Leben]

→ setting in life.

slander To put another's reputation on trial by one's words. When no foundation for this exists in reality, then slandering becomes calumny.

1. For slandering, one finds in Greek: *psithyrismos* (from *psithyrizō:* "to prattle"): "gossip,[1] defamation";[2] *kako-logeō* (*kakos:* "ill," *legō:* "to speak"): "to speak ill of, to disparage,"[3] in some cases: "to insult";[4] *kata-laleō* (*kata:* "against," *laleō:* "to speak"): in the proper sense "to slander";[5] the context sometimes allows for one to identify them as cases of calumny.

[1]2 Cor 12:20. [2]Rom 1:29 △. [3]Mk 9:39; Acts 19:9. [4]Mt 15:4 (= Mk 7:10); Acts 23:5 △. [5]Acts 6:13; Rom 1:30; 2 Cor 12:20; Jas 4:11; 1 Pt 2:1.

2. For calumny: *dys-phēmeō* (the opposite of *eu-phēmeō:* "to speak well of"): "to calumniate, to defame";[6] *dia-ballō* (cf. *diabolos:* "devil, accuser"), "to criticize (in order to divide), to defame";[7] *kata-laleō* (cf. above), in context: "to calumniate,"[8] *ep-ēreazō:* "to calumniate, to plot against someone."[9] These last two terms tend to signify an insult.*

[6]1 Cor 4:13; 2 Cor 6:8 △. [7]1 Tim 3:11; 2 Tim 3:3; Ti 2:3. [8]1 Pt 2:12; 3:16. [9]Lk 6:28; 1 Pt 3:16 △.

→ blaspheme—curse—insult—vices.

slave Gk. *doulos:* "slave, servant." These two meanings indicate the ambiguity of the Greek term, which an English rendering today divulges. Probably some hint of the meaning of "slave" remained attached to the designation "servant."

1. A slave was someone who belonged to another. The condition of a slave, something which Stoic* consciousness alone was able to overcome, was demeaning and, ordinarily, was held in contempt among the pagans.*[1] Among Jews,[2] who had been slaves in Egypt,[3] one was expected to respect, if not their work, at least the persons of Hebrew slaves,[4] while non-Jewish slaves, as elsewhere, remained contemptible, considered as "things,"[5] until the time of their emancipation.* The close relationship which linked a slave to his master tended to become honorific when this master was the king or Yahweh:[6] the terminology then was more metaphorical than real, not retaining anything from the slave condition except the person's strict dependence on his master.

[1]Intr. IV.4.D. [2]Intr. VI.1.C; VI.4.B.a. [3]Ex 13:3. [4]Ex 21:2-11; Lv 25:39; Dt 15:12. [5]Rv 18:13. [6]2 Sm 9:8; Ps 101:6; 134:1; Mt 18:23; 22:3; 25:14; Lk 1:38; 2:29; Acts 2:18; Rv 7:3; 10:7.

2. The gospels allow us to reconstruct the condition of the Jewish slave: his radical dependence on his master, whose power was absolute, his responsibility and his lack of worth.[7] The counsels given to slaves, who spontaneously became Christians, were obedience and submission,[8] out of a motive that did not indicate approval of this condition but rather was a superior vision of the Christian situation,[9] something which later on would bring about the abolition of slavery.

[7]Mt 8:9; 18:27,34; 24:45; 25:30; Lk 17:7-10; Jn 15:15. [8]Intr. IV.7.A; Eph 6:5; Col 3:22; 1 Tim 6:1f.; Ti 2:9; Phlm 16. [9]1 Cor 7:21f.

3. Jesus took on the traits of a slave,[10] subjugating himself to the Law* and to the curse* which it carried along with it,[11] but thereby he conferred on believers the lordly dignity which was his from his exaltation*: he thereby abolished the significance of any slave/free distinction[12] and brought filial adoption* to men.[13]

[10]Phil 2:7. [11]Rom 8:3; Gal 3:13; 4:4; Heb 2:15. [12]1 Cor 12:13; Gal 3:28; Col 3:11. [13]Jn 8:35; Rom 8:15; Gal 4:7.

4. Metaphorical applications of the master/slave* relationship were numerous. Since one could belong to only one master,[14] who was God and Jesus Christ, one could not remain a slave to sin,[15] to the letter of the Law,[16] to the cosmic powers,[17] to the fear of death,[18] to covetousness,[19] to the belly.[20] In freeing us from this bondage, Christ made us exchange masters, so that we become slaves of the Lord,[21] slaves of justice.[22] In this sense, one may prefer to speak of "service" and of "servant," and even of the Christian as the "slave of his brothers,"[23] having modeled himself on Jesus Christ.[24]

[14]Mt 6:24 (= Lk 16:13). [15]Jn 8:33-35; Rom 6:17. [16]Rom 7:6,25. [17]Gal 4:3,8; Col 2:20. [18]Heb 2:15 [19]Ti 3:3. [20]Rom 16:18. [21]Rom 1:1; 6:22; 12:11; 14:18; 1 Cor 7:22; Gal 1:10; Eph 6:6f.; Col 3:24; 1 Thes 1:9; 1 Pt 2:16. [22]Rom 6:18f. [23]Mt 20:27 (= Mk 10:44); Gal 5:13. [24]Phil 2:5-7.

→ freedman—liberty—master—servant—serve.

sleep Gk. *hypnos.*

1. The rest* that regenerated, sleep was a sign of filial trust*;[1] it was the privileged time of divine visitations.[2]

[1]Ps 4:9; Mk 4:38; 1 Thes 4:14. [2]Gn 15:2,12; 28:16; Mt 1:24; 2:13f.,19-23.

2. Sleep, plunged within the dark nighttime, could signify a state of culpability,[3] when set in contrast with vigilance (Gk. *agr-hypnia*[4]).

[3]1 Kgs 19:4-8; Jon 1:5; Mk 14:34,37,40. [4]Mk 13:33; Lk 21:36; 2 Cor 6:5; 11:27; Eph 6:18; Heb 13:17 △; cf. Rom 13:11.

3. Sleep symbolized death, a state from which resurrection was an awakening.[5]

[5]Dn 12:2; Mk 5:39; 13:36; Jn 11:13; 1 Cor 15:20,51; Eph 5:14; 1 Thes 5:6,10.

Smyrna Gk. *Smyrna:* "myrrh"; modern-day Izmir in Turkey. An ancient Aeolian colony that became, after its reconstruction by Alexander the Great, the most active port city of Asia Minor. Subject to Rome from 133 B.C., it was one of the centers of emperor worship, with a temple having been erected in it in A.D. 26.[1]

[1]Rv 1:11; 2:8 □.

→ Intr. IV.2.C.—Map 2.

Solomon Gk. *Salmōn, Solomōn.* The son of David and Bathsheba,[1] the king of Israel from 970 to 931 B.C., the ancestor of Jesus.[3] Tradition retained mention of his wisdom,[4] the magnificence of his reign[5] and of the Temple that he built.[6] Tradition attributed to him the book of Wisdom.* In Jesus there was a greater than Solomon.[7]

[1]Mt 1:6. [2]1 Kgs 1–11; 2 Chr 1–9. [3]Mt 1:7-16. [4]Mt 12:42; Lk 11:31. [5]Mt 6:29; Lk 12:27. [6]Jn 10:23; Acts 3:11; 5:12; 7:47. [7]Mt 12:42; Lk 11:31 □.

[Solomon (Psalms of)] An apocryphal* collection of eighteen psalms dating from 70 B.C., for the most part Pharisaic* in their orientation, reflecting well the messianic* expectations of Jesus' time. They were originally composed in Hebrew, but have been preserved only in the Greek and Syriac.

son

→ adoption—child.

Son of David A messianic title which recalled God's fidelity to the promises he made to King David.*[1] His contemporaries acclaimed Jesus of Nazareth with this title, something against which he did not protest, though he did protest against the title "Messiah."[2] Likewise the Church confessed* its faith in Jesus

Christ,[3] thereby articulating Jesus' rootedness in Israel,[4] while also proclaiming that he was David's Lord.[5]

[1]2 Sm 7:12-16; Ps 2:7; 110:1f.; Is 9:5f.; 11:1,10; 55:3; Lk 1:32; cf. Rv 21:7. [2]Mt 9:27; 12:23; 15:22; 20:30f. (= Mk 10:47. = Lk 18:38f.); 21:9 (= Mk 11:10); 21:15. [3]Rom 1:3; 2 Tim 2:8. [4]Mt 1:1; Lk 3:31; Jn 7:42. [5]Mt 22:42-45 (= Mk 12:35-37 = Lk 20:41-44); Acts 2:25; 13:36; Rv 3:7; 5:5; 22:16 □.

Son of God

1. A name commonly used in the Orient to indicate a man's adoption* by a god. In the O.T., the expression was applied to angels,[1] to the chosen people,[2] to the king* and, through him, to the messiah,*[3] to the faithful Israelites;[4] in the N.T., to all men.[5] It meant that a special relationship united these beings to God. It is not impossible that the Essenes* at Qumran* used this name as a title descriptive of the expected messianic High Priest*; however, we cannot generalize and prove that this was a messianic* title in Jesus' time.

[1]Jb 1:6. [2]Ex 4:22f.; Jer 31:9. [3]2 Sm 7:14; Ps 2:7; 89:27f.; 110:3. [4]Dt 14:1; Hos 2:1. [5]Mt 5:9,45 (= Lk 6:35); 7:11 (= Lk 11:13).

2. In the N.T., the expression offers quite an extensive gamut of meanings: a being with superhuman power, possessing God's special favor,[6] the messiah[7] and even a divine begetting in the strict sense.[8] These different senses can occasionally be extended to the various levels of a reading of the text.[9]

[6]Mt 4:3 (= Lk 4:3); 8:29 (= Mk 5:7 = Lk 8:28); 14:33; 27:54 (= Mk 15:39). [7]Mt 26:63 (= Mk 14:61); Lk 4:41; Acts 9:20,22. [8]Comp. Lk 1:32 and 1:35; 22:67 and 22:70; Jn 10:24 and 10:36. [9]Mt 16:16; Lk 1:35.

3. Jesus himself did not use the expression, but he readily offered himself as "the Son" above all others,[10] for God was his abba* (father) in a particular way,[11] and he communicated everything to him.[12] Hence, the heavenly proclamation in the gospels: "You are my Son."[13] Along with the primitive community, Paul readily proclaimed that Jesus was the Son of God.[14] John made explicit the intimate relationship that Jesus had with his Father.[15]

[10]Mt 11:27 (= Lk 10:22); 21:37 (= Mk 12:6 = Lk 20:13); 24:36 (= Mk 13:32). [11]Mk 14:36. [12]Mt 11:25-27 (= Lk 10:21f.). [13]Mt 3:17 (= Mk 1:11 = Lk 3:22); 17:5 (= Mk 9:7 = Lk 9:35). [14]Rom 1:3f.; 5:10; 8:29ff. [15]Jn 5:19-30; 10:29,36-38.

4. With the outpouring of the Holy Spirit, believers are, from that moment, adoptive sons (Gk. *hyioi*) of God[16] in the unique Son, children* (Gk. *tekna,* in the sense of begotten) of God,[17] and sharers in the divine nature.[18]

[16]Rom 8:14f.; 19:23; Gal 3:26; 4:5-7; Eph 1:5; Heb 2:10; 12:5-8; Rv 21:7. [17]Jn 1:12; Rom 8:16f.,21; 9:8; Phil 2:15; 1 Jn 3:1f.,10; 5:2. [18]2 Pt 1:4.

→ adoption—child—Messiah.

Son of Man The study of this term is one of the most difficult areas in all of N.T. research, and exegetical opinions on it are quite diverse. The following notes express one point of view.

1. Among the origins of the expression we may discern two traditions. The first of these is Ezekiel's; he treated the Hebrew *bèn-âdâm* (Aram. *bar-nâshâ*): "son of man" as the equivalent of the personal pronoun.[1] The second, best represented in Daniel,*[2] was an apocalyptic tradition. According to Daniel, "one like the son of man," representing the "people of God the most Holy's holy ones" ascends from the earth *with* the clouds of heaven and approaches the throne of the Ancient of Days for his investiture. Most likely reworking Ezekiel's reflections, Daniel celebrated the future exaltation of the ideal Jewish people. This view seems to have influenced the terminology of later Jewish apocalypses like IV Ezra* or the Parables of Enoch.* But other factors interfere at this point, such as the expectation of a savior who would come from heaven. In any case, analogous concepts that are found in gnostic texts (Mandaean, Manichaean, Iranian) may not be reckoned as the source of the Jewish tradition because they are all post-Christian.

[1]Ps 8:5; 80:18; Ez 2:1; Heb 2:6. [2]Dn 7:13; Rv 1:13; 14:14.

2. In a Danielic context the expression "Son of Man" (Gk. *ho hyios tou anthrōpou*) reappears in the Synoptic Apocalypse* and in the trial before the Sanhedrin.*[3] The rich nuances of this expression call for an inquiry into the evolution of the term from the time of Daniel's use. First of all, it is appropriate to note that the N.T. added definite articles to the expression "like a son of man"; he became "*the* son of *the* man." No longer was the issue that of a collectivity which resembled a man, but rather of an individual who was the personification of the people. Another difference may be noted in the diverse recensions* found in the passages under consideration. Some[4] follow the text of Daniel closely: the Son of Man comes *with* the clouds of heaven; he will be exalted or seated at the right hand of the power of God. The same exaltation image may be found in certain texts in John.[5] According to others,[6] undoubtedly under the influence of faith in Jesus' resurrection and the expectation of the heavenly savior's coming, the Son of Man comes *on* (or *in*) the clouds, coming down to render judgment. Accordingly, the Son of Man possesses attributes which surpass those of the Messiah, the Son of David; he comes from the divine, transcendent world. Linked with this conception are several other Johannine texts according to which the Son of Man "is in heaven" and descends thence.[7]

[3]Mt 24:30 (= Mk 13:26 = Lk 21:27); 26:64 (= Mk 14:62 = Lk 22:69). [4]Mk 14:62; Lk 22:69. [5]Jn 1:51; 8:28; Acts 7:56. [6]Mt 24:30 (= Mk 13:26 = Lk 21:27); 26:64. [7]Jn 3:13f.; 6:62.

3. Apart from a Danielic context, the expression "the Son of Man" might correspond to the personal pronoun, as in Ezekiel.[8] In this case it preserved a connotation which, strictly speaking, it had only during the earthly life of Jesus and in anticipation of his return at the end of time. Moreover, it designated not so much who Jesus is, as describe what he accomplished in the lowliness of his human condition[9] or what he must perform, namely the judgment of men.[10] In contrast with the apocalyptic use of the term, Jesus exercised this role from his stay on earth[11] and this was viewed from the perspective of the suffering overcome in him.[12]

[8]Comp. Mt 5:11 and Lk 6:22; Mt 16:13,21 and Mk 8:27,31; Mt 10:32f. and Lk 12:8f. [9]Mt 8:20 (= Lk 9:58); 11:19 (= Lk 7:34). [10]Mt 16:27; 25:31; Lk 12:8f. [11]Mt 9:6 (= Mk 2:10 = Lk 5:24); 12:8 (= Mk 2:28 = Lk 6:5). [12]Mt 17:22f.; 20:18; Mk 8:31; 10:33,45; Lk 9:22,44.

4. Jesus and the Son of Man. There are two striking literary features here. The title does not appear except in the gospels and in Acts 7:56. Jesus spoke of him in the third person, as if it were of someone other than himself. Out of this comes the question whether we may attribute the expression to Jesus himself. Our reply is a qualified one. In certain instances it seems that the early Church community modified an original "I" into a form that highlighted Jesus' role as judge.[13] In other cases, by refusing to see Jesus as the originator of the expression, we noticeably complicate the literary situation since the "Son of Man" is not found except in the gospels (and in Acts 7:56). Then again, Jesus did speak in the third person (as he ordinarily did) because he did not care to identify himself as the Messiah (unless it be at the hour of his death).[14] There would then remain a need to explain how Jesus could use the expression. One might spontaneously suggest that, if it were not a "title" current in his era, it was, nonetheless, an apocalyptic personality sufficiently mysterious that Jesus could thereby suggest, without clearly revealing, the glorious aspect of his existence.

[13]Cf. note 8. [14]Mk 14:62 (but cf. Mt 26:64).

→ Intr.XII.2.C.

song Gk. *ōidē* (from *aidō:* "to sing, to celebrate"): "song, canticle." In the course of the liturgy, Christians expressed their faith in hymns of joy.*[1] With difficulty one can distinguish these canticles from the inspired psalms* that belonged to this liturgical genre.[2] In the year 112 Pliny* reported that the Christians sang their songs to Christ as to a god *(carmen Christo quasi deo dicere).* One can recognize vestiges of them in the book of Revelation.[3]

[1]Eph 5:19; Col 3:16; Rv 5:9; 14:3; 15:3 △. [2]1 Cor 14:15,26; Eph 5:19; Col 3:16; Jas 5:13 △. [3]Rv 5:9f.,12-14; 7:12; 11:15f.; 12:10-12; 15:3f.; 19:1f.,6-8.

→ Intr.IX.6.—doxology—hymn—psalms.

soul The Greek word *psychē,* like the Hebrew *nèphèsh,* may be translated not only by "soul," but also by "life," "person," or even by a pronoun: "I" or "someone." This range of translations suggests something of the fullness of meaning that this word can have. It expressed a more extensive realm than that suggested by popular anthropology when it limits "soul" to but one of the constitutive parts of the human person.

1. In its primitive meaning, the soul designated the breath which dwelt within a living person[1] or left a person when he expired.[2] This breath was not man's property but was God's gift.[3] Man became a "living soul" because God, who alone was the Living One, had breathed into his nostrils the breath of life.[4] This soul was not in itself immortal,* but it was possible that it might not die forever;[5] as a matter of fact, it was solely God's prerogative to resurrect* and save* it.[6]

[1]2 Sm 1:9; 1 Kgs 17:21; Acts 20:10. [2]Gn 35:18; Lk 21:26; Acts 5:5,10; 12:23. [3]Ps 104:29f.; Lk 12:20. [4]Gn 2:7; 1 Cor 15:45. [5]Wis 2:23; Mt 10:28; Rv 6:9; 20:4. [6]2 Mc 7:9,14,23; Wis 16:14; Heb 10:39; 1 Pt 1:9.

2. By extension "soul" meant a living being, a person.[7] A soul was someone, it was "Me."[8] It was my very self, with nuances of interiority and living power,[9] capable of expressing myself in diverse ways and of experiencing various feelings.[10] In a text unique within the N.T.,[11] the expression "soul and body" probably indicates not two components of man, but the human person in its self-expression as Luke understood it. In another text, which is also unique,[12] one mentioning "spirit, soul and body," Paul did not propose a tripartite division of the human person (which was neither Greek nor Semitic), but understood man* as a whole under his various aspects.

[7]Gn 1:20f.; 46:27; Mk 3:4 (= Lk 6:9); Acts 2:41,43; 3:23; 7:14; 27:10,37; Rom 2:9; 13:1; 1 Pt 3:20; Rv 8:9; 16:3; 18:13. [8]1 Sm 18:1,3; Mt 12:18; Heb 10:38. [9]Am 6:8; Mt 22:37 (= Mk 12:30 = Lk 10:27); 2 Cor 1:23; Eph 6:6; Col 3:23. [10]Dt 6:5; Mt 11:29; 26:38 (= Mk 14:34); Lk 1:46; 12:19; Jn 12:27; Phil 2:19f.; Heb 12:3. [11]Mt 10:28 (= Lk 12:4f.). [12]1 Thes 5:23.

3. Finally, like life, which was its ordinary translation, the term "soul" was ambivalent. It could designate mortal life here on earth which we try to preserve,[13] but one for which we ought not to be overly concerned[14] and which we may fittingly learn to dedicate, risk,[15] or even sacrifice[16] by following Jesus' example.[17] The perspective of eternal* life, which God himself is, invites us not to desire to secure a temporal existence by ourselves,[18] but to go even as far as to hate this present life,[19] in order that we might hand it back to God, the one who alone is able to keep it safe.[20]

[13]Mt 2:20; Lk 21:19; Acts 2:27; Rom 11:3. [14]Mt 6:25 (= Lk 12:22f.). [15]Acts 15:26; 20:24; Rom 16:4; Phil 2:30. [16]Jn 13:37f.; 15:13; 1 Thes 2:8; 1 Jn 3:16; Rv 12:11. [17]Mt 20:28 (= Mk 10:45); Jn 10:11,15,17. [18]Mt 10:39; 16:25 (= Mk 8:35-37 = Lk 9:24); Lk 17:33. [19]Lk 14:26; Jn 12:25. [20]Jas 1:21; 5:20.

→ Intr.IV.6.C.—body—life—man—spirit.

[sources] A literary-critical term designating oral and written documents used by N.T. writers. Behind Matthew and Luke, in addition to their own peculiar sources, certain scholars detect two sources, Mark and Q,* from which the "Two Source Theory" derives. According to other critics, the composition of the three Synoptics depends either on multiple sources, which have been transformed in the course of oral transmission within the varied milieus of the early Church, or else on two principal documents: one already tightly structured (encompassing Jesus' ministry in Galilee), the other existing in a rather fluid state (corresponding to Mt 5–13).

→ literary criticism—Q—Synoptics.

Sovereignties A translation of the Gk. *Kyriotētes.*

→ lordships.

Spain Gk. *Spania.* A country situated at the most westerly edge of the biblical world. Judas Maccabeus had heard tell of its invasion by the Romans as early as 202 B.C.[1] There were three Roman provinces* there: Tarraconensis (Catalonia), Baetica (Cordoba), Lusitania (Portugal). Paul made plans to go there;[2] we do not know whether he realized his wish.

[1]1 Mc 8:3. [2]Rom 15:24,28 □.

span Gk. *orgyia:* "the length of two arms stretched out from the extremity of one hand to the other"; a Roman surveying measurement of about 1.85m. (6 ft.). In Israel, it could equal 2.05m. (6.7 feet).[1]

[1]Acts 27:28 □.

→ measures.

spirit

1. In its original meaning, the Greek *pneuma* (Heb. *rûah*) designated breath or wind.[1] Man's respiratory breathing, the proof of his life, comes from God and goes back to God when he expires;[2] but God can restore it to him, for one gives it back to God so that God may gather it to himself.[3]

[1]Gn 3:8; Jn 3:8; 20:22; 2 Thes 2:8; Heb 1:7. [2]Gn 2:7; Mt 27:50; Jn 19:30; Acts 7:59; Jas 2:26. [3]Lk 23:46; Heb 12:23; Rv 11:11; cf. Lk 8:55.

2. Like the soul,* man's spirit described the person himself in an intimacy most secretly his own, or in his totality.[5] This was something distinct from what was visible, his body,[6] and what was weak.[7]

[4]Mk 2:8; 1 Cor 2:11. [5]Gn 6:17; Phil 4:23; 2 Tim 4:22; Phlm 25. [6]1 Cor 5:3; 7:34; 2 Cor 7:1; Col 2:5. [7]Mt 26:41 (= Mk 14:38).

3. The believer's spirit was indwelt by the Spirit of God* which had united itself to him to awaken in him a cry of filial prayer,[8] to unite him with his Lord and, with him, to constitute one single spirit;[9] in this way he was renewed completely.[10] Hence, there frequently is some difficulty in deciding whether the term referred to man or to God:[11] this means that God, who was spirit,[12] could be assimilated to those with whom he had united himself. Accordingly, the believer who had been reborn by the Spirit could offer worship* in spirit and in truth.*[13]

[8]Rom 8:16,26. [9]1 Cor 6:17. [10]Eph 4:23. [11]Rom 12:11; 2 Cor 6:6. [12]Jn 4:24. [13]Jn 3:6; 4:24.

4. Paul set the spirit in opposition to the flesh,* like two powers at work in man.[14] The spiritual man (Gk. *pneumatikos*) could become natural (Gk. *psychikos*)[15] and could even regress to a carnal condition.[16] There are some natural men who do not possess the spirit.[17] On the other hand, the earthly or natural body itself could, in its turn, become spiritual.[18]

[14]Rom 8:4; Gal 5:16-25. [15]1 Cor 2:14f. [16]1 Cor 3:1. [17]Jas 3:15; Jude 19. [18]1 Cor 15:44.

5. The spirit was opposed to the letter, as the power of life was opposed to the power of death;[19] Christ enabled one to cross over in freedom from the letter to the spirit.[20]

[19]2 Cor 3:6. [20]2 Cor 3:17; Gal 5:13-18.

6. Gk. *pneumata* (the plural of *pneuma:* "wind, spirit"). Another name for angels,*[21] good beings,[22] or above all, beings which were wicked[23] and ordinarily were described as unclean:[24] those which had been driven out of the possessed* by Jesus[25] and his disciples.[26] One had to wrestle with them[27] and take action in order to discern them, for they were deceivers.[28]

[21]Acts 23:8f.; Heb 12:9. [22]Heb 1:14; Rv 4:5; 5:6. [23]Mt 12:45 (= Lk 11:26); Lk 7:21; 8:2; Acts 19:16. [24]Mt 12:43 (= Lk 11:24); Mk 1:23; 5:2. [25]Mt 8:16; Mk 1:26f.; 3:11; 5:13; 9:25; Lk 7:21ff. [26]Mt 10:1 (= Mk 6:7 = Lk 9:1); Acts 8:7; 19:12. [27]Eph 2:2; 6:12. [28]1 Cor 12:10; 1 Tim 4:1; 1 Jn 4:1; Rv 16:14.

→ angels—demons—Dominations—flesh—man—possessed—soul—Spirit of God—wind.

Spirit of God, Holy Spirit

1. The N.T. recognizes the Spirit of God in its transitory, charismatic* aspects, those which typify it in the O.T.[1] The Spirit came upon a man, lifted him up and made him capable of exceptional activity: sometimes speaking prophetically,*[2] doing extraordinary deeds,[3] so that some individuals were even said to be filled with the Holy Spirit.[4] From this tradition come references to the wisdom* of spiritual persons[5] and to the charisms produced by the Spirit.[6]

[1]Cf. Jgs 3:10; 11:29; 14:6; 1 Sm 11:6. [2]Lk 1:41,67; Acts 2:4,17; 6:10; 7:55; 11:28. [3]Lk 2:27; 4:1,14; Acts 8:39; 21:11. [4]Lk 2:25; Acts 6:5; 11:24. [5]1 Cor 2:10. [6]1 Cor 12:3-13.

2. On the other hand, the N.T. fulfills O.T. prophecy that promised the Spirit would rest in a permanent way on the Messiah* and would be poured out into every heart,[8] thereby ensuring that there would be a new creation.[9] The Spirit descended and rested on Jesus,[10] revealing that Jesus was holy* from the moment of his conception;[11] he possessed the Spirit beyond all measure,[12] and it is his Spirit which he gives.[13]

[7]Is 11:2; 42:1; 61:1. [8]Ez 36:26. [9]Ez 39:29. [10]Mt 3:16; Mk 1:10; Lk 3:22; Jn 1:33; Acts 2:33; 10:38. [11]Mt 1:20; Lk 1:35. [12]Jn 3:34. [13]Jn 16:14f.; 19:30.

3. Baptism* in the Holy Spirit brings about a participation in this perdurable gift.[14] The Spirit pours love* into our hearts,[15] prays in us,[16] and acts as the pledge of our hope.*[17] So we can say that the reign of the Law* has yielded to the reign of the Spirit. This Spirit consecrates the Temple* which believers henceforth create;[18] through his teaching, the Paraclete* recalls the words of Jesus[19] and helps disciples in their witness.*[20]

[14]Acts 1:5; 2:38; 8:17-19; 10:44-47, 19:6; Rom 8:9. [15]Rom 5:5. [16]Rom 8:26f.; Gal 4:6. [17]2 Cor 5:5. [18]1 Cor 3:16; 2 Cor 1:22. [19]Jn 14:26. [20]Mt 10:20; Jn 16:4-15.

→ Intr. XIV.1.C.—charism—gift—God—love—Paraclete.

spouse Gk. *nymphios:* "fiancé, young married man"; *nymphē:* "financée, wife" (from a Greek root meaning "bound, promised"): this was the promise.

1. One of the names of Yahweh,[1] who treated his people Israel as a bride, with a fidelity and a tenderness that were unfailing.[2] In another perspective, divine Wisdom* was said to be the wise man's spouse.[3]

[1]Is 54:4-8. [2]Sg; Hos 1–3; Is 62:5; Jer 2; Ez 16. [3]Wis 8.

2. The N.T. sees in Christ the Bridegroom to whom the promised virgin was presented (Gk. *harmozō:* "matched"), the one who made his Bride, that is, the Church,[5] holy.

[4]2 Cor 11:2. [5]Mt 9:15 (= Mk 2:19 = Lk 5:34); 25:6; Jn 3:29; Eph 5:23-27.

3. The Church was the wife, free and not a slave,[6] the spouse of the Lamb,*[7] the mother of the children of God.[8]

[6]Gal 4:22-27. [7]Rv 21:9. [8]Rv 12.

→ Intr. VIII.2.B.a.—marriage—wedding.

sprinkling Gk. *rhantismos* (from *rhantizō:* "to sprinkle," *rhainō:* "to water"). A purification rite performed with water,*[1] sometimes with the ashes* of a heifer,[2] ordinarily with the blood of an immolated animal.[3] The expression "the blood of the sprinkling" no longer preserves this motif, for it was used in a comparison with Abel's* blood, which had not been sprinkled.[4] Christ's blood purifies in an incomparable way.[5]

[1]Nm 8:7; 1 Sm 7:6; 2 Sm 23:13-17; Ez 36:25; Mk 7:3f.; Heb 10:22. [2]Nm 19:2-12; Heb 9:13. [3]Ex 24:3-8; Heb 9:19,21. [4]Heb 12:24. [5]1 Pt 1:2□.

→ ablution—blood—pure.

square (public)

→ public square.

stadion Gk. *stadion.*

1. A Greek measure of varying length, as a function of the length of the cubit or the foot as its unit of measurement. The Olympic stadion measured 192.67 m. (632 ft.), the Alexandrian stadion 184.8375 m. (606 ft.), the Delphic stadion 177.55 m. (582.5 ft). Generally, the Alexandrian stadion was used, rounded out to 185 m (607 ft.). This measure equaled that of the stadium's race track. It served to measure distances on land[1] and sea.[2]

[1]Lk 24:13; Jn 11:18; Rv 14:20; 21:16. [2]Mt 14:24; Jn 6:19△.

2. By extension, the place where races took place.[3]

[3]1 Cor 9:24△.

→ measures.

stars **1.** For the Hebrews, stars and planets (Gk. *astēr:* an isolated "star" and *astra,* the plural of *astron:* "a constellation") were animated beings, but were not divine: no worship* could be rendered to them.[1] They were charged with executing God's orders and with proclaiming his glory.*[2] Their brightness helped one to imagine the world to come.[3] Their darkening and their fall took part in the depiction of the end* of time.[4]

[1]2 Kgs 17:16; Wis 13:2-5; Acts 7:42f. [2]Jb 38:7,31f.; Ps 19:2. [3]Dn 12:3; 1 Cor 15:41; Heb 11:12. [4]Is 13:10; Mt 24:29 (= Mk 13:25 = Lk 21:25); Rv 6:13; 8:10-12; 9:1; 12:4; cf. Acts 27:20; Jude 13.

2. The morning star (Gk. *phōsphoros:* "lightbearer"), originating with an ancient messianic symbol, designated the Christ.[5] The star of Bethlehem seems to have been but a sign of the Messiah, linked with the theme of a light being lifted up over the nations.*[6]

[5]2 Pt 1:19 △; cf. Rv 2:28; 22:16. [6]Nm 24:17; Is 9:1; 60:1; Mt 2:2-10; cf. Lk 1:78.

3. A symbol of the angels* of the churches[7] and of the tribes* of Israel.[8]

[7]Rv 1:16,20; 2:1; 3:1. [8]Rv 12:1□.

→ Intr.IV.6.D; V.1.—Dominations—Orient—Sabaoth—sun.

stater Gk. *statēr.* A silver Greek coin (8.6 grams), worth 4 drachmas (one tetradrachma), approximately corresponding to the wages for four days' labor.[1]

[1]Mt 17:27□.

→ coins.

stay

→ abide.

Stephen Gk. *Stephanos:* "crown." A Christian of Jerusalem, doubtlessly from a Hellenistic* background, chosen by the Twelve* to look after the serving of "tables*" and probably the administration of the goods of the community. A vigorous controversialist, he showed himself to be very radically opposed to Jewish traditions* and Jewish institutions. Stoned* under the gaze of Saul,* he prayed, as Jesus did, for his persecutors and had a vision of the Son of Man.*[1]

[1]Acts 6:5; 8f.; 7:59; 8:2; 11:19; 22:20□.

sterility By whatever name it was designated, sterility was an evil.* God triumphed over it, as the O.T.[1] and the N.T.[2] show.

[1]Gn 15:2f.; 16:4f.; 30:1. [2]Rom 4:18-24.

1. Greek *steiros* designated sterility, the fact of being without children, something that was a cause for shame.[3]

[3]Lk 1:7,36; 23:29; Gal 4:27△.

2. Gk. *argos* (from *ergon:* "work" and *a* privative): "inactive, lazy": thus was faith without works* condemned.[4]

[4]Jas 2:20; 2 Pt 1:8; cf. Mt 12:36; Ti 1:12; 2 Pt 2:3△.

3. Gk. *kenos:* "empty, vain, without reality."[5]

[5]1 Cor 15:10.

4. Gk. *akarpos* (from *karpos:* "fruit" and *a* privative): "without fruit." Correlative to the obligation to bear fruit,* a tree's barrenness,[6] that of the fig tree[7] or of what was sown,[8] symbolized the absence of true conversion, faith without works, the sterile works of darkness.[9]

[6]Mt 3:10 (= Lk 3:9); 7:16-20 (= Lk 6:43f.). [7]Mt 21:19 (= Mk 11:14); Lk 13:6-9. [8]Mt 13:22 (= Mk 4:7,19). [9]Eph 5:11; Ti 3:14; 2 Pt 1:8; Jude 12.

→ Intr. VIII.2.B.d.e.—fruit—virgin.

stigmata Gk. *stigmata,* the plural of *stigma:* "the prickling of a red hot iron, the mark made by a master in the body of a slave as a sign of his ownership, a sacred tattoo." Paul made allusion not to some "stigmatization" in the modern sense of the word, but to scars resulting from blows received in the service of Christ.[1]

[1]Gal 6:17□.

→ seal.

Stoics Gk. *stōikoi.* Disciples of Zeno (336–264 B.C.), who taught beneath the Portico of Athens *(Poikilē stoa).* According to them, man possessed a breath of the Universal Reason that ordered and governed the world. He is free who follows this reason in everything; fallen is the one who abandons himself to his passions. Impassibility (Gk. *ataraxia*) was, thus, the condition of every virtue. The gods were myths,* useful to guide people who were incapable of guiding themselves. Consequently, the evidence of evil in the world convinced the Stoic Cleanthes to liken this Universal Reason to an unfathomable providence. Thereafter, wisdom consisted in an unconditional submission to fate. In N.T. times, Seneca caused the ethical side of this doctrine to prevail. Later still, Epictetus* (A.D. 50–130) exalted reason as the sole inalienable good of man: by means of it he remains free in every situation, including slavery. By its demands, Stoicism, while exercising an enormous and durable influence, nonetheless remained the proper sphere of an intellectual elite.[1]

[1]Acts 17:18□.

→ Intr. IV.7.A.

stone

→ rock.

stone (precious)

→ precious stone.

stoning Gk. *lithazō, litho-boleō* (from *lithos:* "stone" and *ballō:* "to cast"): "to stone, to cast rocks."

1. In the proper sense, the capital punishment prescribed by the Law, notably in the case of adultery* and blasphemy*; it was carried out outside the city.[1] The first stones had to be cast by the witnesses to the misdemeanor,[2] the others by the assembled people.

[1]Lv 24:14; 2 Chr 24:20-22; Mt 21:35; 23:37 (= Lk 13:34); Jn 8:5; Acts 7:58f.; Heb 11:37; 12:20. [2]Jn 8:7.

2. In the broad sense, an act of lynching expressive of popular furor against a provocateur.[3]

[3]Ex 17:4; Nm 14:10; 15:35f., Lk 20:6; Jn 8:59; 10:31-33; 11:8; Acts 5:26; 14:5,19; 2 Cor 11:25□.

→ Intr. VI.4.C.c.

stranger **1.** The non-Jew (Gk. *allotrios,* stranger[1]) was considered as a pagan with whom one could not make contact;[2] he was excluded from the freedom of the city in Israel,[3] occasionally even treated as an enemy of the people.[4] This distinction was abolished by Christ.[5]

[1]Dt 14:21; 15:3; 32:16; Mt 17:25f.; Lk 17:18; Acts 7:6; Heb 11:9. [2]Jn 10:5; Acts 10:28. [3]Eph 2:12; 4:18. [4]Col 1:21; Heb 11:34. [5]Eph 2:13-17; Col 1:20-22; cf. Acts 10:45.

2. The stranger on a journey (Heb. *nokri,* Gk. *xenos*) enjoyed no right at all, unless it be that of hospitality.[6]

[6]Ru 2:10; 2 Sm 15:19; Mt 25:35; 27:7; Heb 13:2,9; 3 Jn 5; cf. Gn 18:1-8.

3. The resident alien, or immigrant (Heb. *gér,* Gk. *par-oikos, par-epi-dēmos*) benefited from a legal statute that tended to assimilate him to the Jews;[7] consequently, he could become a proselyte,* one adhering totally to Judaism.[8]

[7]Intr. VI. 1.B; VI.4.B.a; VIII.2.A; Ex 22:20; 23:9; Nm 35:15; Acts 2:10; 7:6,29; 17:21. [8]Acts 2:11; 6:5.

4. Analogously, from the vantage point of the Holy Land, Christians of Gentile background are no longer strangers on a journey nor even immigrants; and, from the vantage point of this perishable earth, all Christians should consider themselves as immigrants having no permanent dwelling,[10] on pilgrimage,[11] just as the patriarchs were.[12]

[9]Eph 2:19. [10]1 Pt 1:17. [11]1 Pt 2:11. [12]Heb 11:13.

→ Diaspora—exile—fatherland—hospitality—pilgrimage.

stray, go astray

→ error—seduce.

street The same Hebrew word *rᵉhov* was translated in the Septuagint* by two Greek terms,[1] between which it is difficult to detect any difference: *rhymē* designated the laneway, doubtless of the kind of spaces set aside from time immemorial between houses to allow people to pass by;[2] *plateia* was a substantival adjective (*platys:* "large") which specified the nature of the *rhymē* (or of the *hodos:* "the way"): it was a large street and more common, beginning with the Hellenistic era. Less indication is given about when to translate this word by "square."[3] What characterized the *plateia* was that, just as in the *agora:* "the market place," one could put up a public notice there: hence the redundancy in Lk 14:21.

[1]Is 15:3; cf. Tb 13:17. [2]Mt 6:2; Lk 14:21; Acts 9:11; 12:10△. [3]Mt 6:5; 12:19; Lk 10:10; 13:26; 14:21; Acts 5:15; Rv 11:8; 21:21; 22:2△.

→ agora—public square.

stroke (of the Law) Gk. *keraia:* "horn." Some small graphic sign or other, more precisely it was in the shape of a horn or a hook, used to differentiate Hebrew letters which were identical in form.[1]

[1]Mt 5:18 (= Lk 16:17)□.

[structure] From the Lat. *structura:* "organization, arrangement, construction." A large totality made up of small literary units.* This term describes the composition, architecture and orientation of an ensemble: the assembled parts have been consciously organized as functions of the whole, so that the displacement of one implies the displacement of others. The word can translate the Greek *schēma* in 1 Cor. 7:31.

→ creation—figure—form—literary criticism.

stumbling stone

→ scandal.

suffer Gk. *paschō:* "to experience a feeling, to suffer."

1. Jesus Christ suffered and died. This fact is ceaselessly affirmed in the N.T.;[1] these sufferings had been foretold by Jesus[2] and were situated by the Risen One and by believers within God's plan.[3] Thus, they manifested a meaning, that of liberation from sin:[4] Christ suffered for us[5] through "compassion" with our weaknesses.[8] This interpretation was rendered possible because Jesus, as the Servant of Yahweh,* died and was exalted to heaven.[7]

[1]Lk 22:15; Acts 1:3; Heb 2:18; 5:8; 13:12; 1 Pt 2:23; 4:1; 5:1. [2]Mt 16:21 (= Mk 8:31 = Lk 9:22); 17:12 (= Mk 9:12); Lk 17:25. [3]Lk 24:26,46; Acts 3:8; 17:3; 26:23; 1 Pt 1:11. [4]1 Pt 3:18. [5]2 Cor 1:5; 1 Pt 2:21. [6]Heb 4:15. [7]Is 53; Phil 2:8-11; Heb 2:9f.

2. Christ's faithful adherent has been called to "commune" with the sufferings of Christ;[8] thus, something which is in itself meaningless may be situated within a greater totality and be reckoned worthwhile:[9] in his turn, the believer completes what is lacking in Christ's sufferings[10] and can "sympathize" with the sufferings of others.[11] Consolation can flood in on him, because the glory* is already at work through the sufferings of the moment.[12] He can therefore grasp the paradox of the beatitude* concerning the persecuted.[13]

[8]Acts 9:16; 2 Cor 1:5; Phil 3:10; 1 Pt 4:1,13; Rv 2:10. [9]Rom 8:17; Jas 5:10. [10]Phil 1:29; Col 1:24; 2 Tim 2:3. [11]1 Thes 2:14; 2 Thes 1:5; 2 Tim 3:11; Heb 10:34; 1 Pt 3:8; 5:9. [12]Rom 8:18; 2 Cor 1:5f.; 1 Pt 5:10. [13]Mt 5:10-12 (= Lk 6:22f.); 1 Pt 3:14.

→ persecuted—test, trial—tribulation.

sulphur Gk. *theion.* A mineral substance abounding in the territory of the Dead Sea, rendering the soil unproductive. The chastisement of Sodom by a rain of fire* and sulphur was typical.[1] This punishment[2] became, in the book of Revelation, a plunge into a pool.[3]

[1]Gn 19:24; Dt 29:22; Ps 11:6; Is 34:9; Ez 38:22; Lk 17:29. [2]Jb 18:15; Is 30:33; Rv 9:17f.; 14:10. [3]Rv 19:20; 20:10; 21:8□.

→ fiery pool—fire.

summer Gk. *theros.* The dry season, from approximately mid-April to mid-October.[1]

[1]Mt 24:32 (= Mk 13:28 = Lk 21:30)□.

→ Intr.II.4.

sun Gk. *hēlios.*

1. Necessary for life, this benefit, an image of his universal good will,[1] is dispensed by God to all. But its ardor could be overwhelming and burn.[2]

[1]Dt 33:13f.; Ps 19:5-7; Mt 5:45. [2]Mt 13:6 (= Mk 4:6); Jas 1:11; Rv 7:16; cf. Is 49:10.

2. Luke mentioned its darkening at Jesus' death.[3] Its transformation into darkness* characterized depictions of the end of time.[4]

[3]Lk 23:45. [4]Jl 2:10; Ha 3:11; Mt 24:29 (= Mk 13:24); Lk 21:25; Acts 2:20; Rv 6:12; 8:12; (9:2;) 16:8; 19:17.

3. An image to evoke the shining forth of the just, of heavenly beings, of the transfigured Jesus and of the Son of Man.*[5]

[5]Jgs 5:31; Mt 13:43; 17:2; Rv 1:16; 10:1; 12:1; cf. Acts 26:13; 1 Cor 15:41.

4. In the heavenly Jerusalem,* its brightness will have no more reason to exist, God and the Lamb being the light of the elect.[6]

[6]Is 60:19f.; Rv 21:23; 22:5.

→ Intr. V.1.—moon—Orient—stars.

Sunday

→ Lord's Day.

Supper (Last)

→ Last Supper.

Supper of the Lord

→ Lord's Supper.

swear

→ oath.

sweat (bloody)

→ bloody sweat.

sycamine In Gk. *sykaminos,* derived from *sykē:* "fig tree." A bush producing succulent fruit and leaves on which the silk worm feeds. Not to be confused with the sycamore.*[1]

[1]Lk 17:6□.

sycamore From the Gk. *syko-morea* (from *sykē:* "fig tree," *moron:* "ripe"). A tree of the lowlands that belongs to the fig tree genus and whose lower branches grow low to the ground. Useful for construction wood.[1]

[1] 1 Chr 27:28; Is 9:9; Am 7:14; Lk 19:4□.

Sychar Gk. *Sychar.* A city of Samaria,* perhaps the site of ancient Shechem, destroyed in 128 B.C. and rebuilt in A.D. 72.[1]

[1] Jn 4:5□.

→ Map 4.

[symbol] **1.** Gk. *symbolon* (from *syn:* "with" and *ballō:* "to place, put"): "sign of recognition." In primitive cultures this referred to an object cut into two pieces and entrusted to two table-fellows who, in turn, handed them on to their children. When, at some later date, these were brought together, the two pieces enabled the bearers to recognize one another and to express the hospitality relationships which united them. By extension from this usage, the symbol came to refer to any sign of recognition and every kind of convention. The word is not found in the Bible except in Wisdom 16:6, where the "symbol of salvation" refers to the bronze serpent which the Hebrew people had to look on to be saved.

2. In general, a symbol is that means which becomes a convention of language, a pledge of mutual recognition among several options available. It is a signifying reality, acting as an introduction to the world of values which it embodies and to which it belongs.

3. Symbol should not be identified with allegory* (for example, scales that stand for justice), for in the case of a symbol the reality is prior to the idea. Nor should it be identified with form* or structure,* for its content is inseparable from its expression. Not even with a sign,* for the symbol participates in that which it represents.

4. We may distinguish two kinds of symbols: the traditional symbol, which is a constitutive element of community (as is the case with language or the Eucharist), and the conventional symbol, which is the product of community (as is the case with the numbers* seven* or twelve*).

→ allegory—figure—sign—typology.

synagogue **1.** Gk. *syn-agōgē:* "meeting," whence "place of gathering," translating the Aram. word *k*e*nishtâ:* "house of prayer."

2. The building was oriented in the direction of Jerusalem, for every Jew turned toward the Temple* to pray.[1] It consisted in a hall, where there was no altar,* but a sacred cupboard (in memory of the ark*) containing the scrolls of the Law* and the Prophets. The presider was not a priest but a layman, the synagogue leader, chosen from among the notables of the village or quarter. He was assisted by a *hazzan,* a kind of sacristan, who also held the office of cantor and even of schoolteacher. The sabbath office* was composed of prayers, readings from the Law and a prophetic passage, the whole straightway translated from Hebrew into Aramaic and, finally, an instruction which most often the Pharisees* took responsibility for, but which could be entrusted to one of those in attendance.[2] The meeting ended with a blessing.[3] During the week, scribes* taught the young people the meaning of the Scriptures. The synagogues thus became rallying points for the Christian proclamation.

[1]Cf. Dn 6:11. [2]Lk 4:16-22; Acts 13:15. [3]Nm 6:24-26. [4]Acts 17:10-12; cf. 16:13; Heb 10:25; Jas 2:2.

→ Intr. I.5; IV.7.A; XIII.1.B.—Church.

[synopsis] Gk. *synopsis:* "the action of seeing whole." A work reproducing the text of the first three gospels not in succession but simultaneously, in columns that allow them to be confronted according to their similarities and their differences. Each gospel is integrally represented both in its proper sequence (without repeating its text several times) and in its synoptic state (its relationship to the two other gospels). Each gospel, then, is printed in its order, but also cut up, as a function of the others. Some writers have broken up the Fourth Gospel in terms of the synoptic gospels, but this is to the detriment of its coherence; it would be better to reproduce it integrally at the end of the volume, along with the indispensable comparisons. Not to be confused with a concordance.*

[synoptic] Gk. *synoptikos,* an adjective corresponding to *syn-opsis:* "the action of seeing whole," allowing several elements to be grasped in a single gaze.

1. The three first gospels (Matthew, Mark, and Luke) are called synoptic because they present, on a common frame, numerous divergences and resemblances.

2. It describes a chart reproducing several related texts, for example a synopsis.*

Syria Gk. *Syria,* an abbreviated form of *Assyria.* The heart of the ancient Greek kingdom that acted as persecutor of the Jews,[1] it became a Roman province* in 65 B.C. It included Palestine,* Lebanon, a part of modern-day Syria and of the southeast part of Turkey, with Antioch* as its capital. Contiguous to Galilee,*[2] it made paganism present on Israel's doorstep.[3] It offered a setting often hostile to, but at the same time used to, contact with Jews, who were numerous there.[4]

[1]1 and 2 Mc [2]Mt 4:24. [3]Mk 7:24,26. [4]Gal 1:21; Acts 11:26; 15:23; 18:18; 20:3; 21:3.

→ Map 3.

T

Tabernacles (Feast of)

→ Booths.

table Gk. *trapeza.*

1. A table to be used for meals,*[1] worship*[2] or for the work of money-changers.*[3] In the N.T. era, tables usually had legs, but Psalm 69 alludes to an ancient custom wherein the table consisted simply in a carpet spread on the ground itself and so was something in which one could become entangled.[4] The table could metaphorically refer to the community at table[5] or to the cultic meal.[6]

[1]Mt 15:27 (= Mk 7:28). [2]Heb 9:2. [3]Mt 21:12 (= Mk 11:15 = Jn 2:15) [4]Rom 11:9. [5]Lk 16:21; 22:21,30; Acts 16:34. [6]1 Cor 10:21.

2. Just as the Italian word *banca:* "bench" ended up indicating a "changer's table," so the Greek word can also designate a bank.*[7]

[7]Lk 19:23; cf. Mt 25:27.

3. "To serve table" does not mean "to serve at table" but to be charged with the task of the provisioning of meals (without supposing that it involved the more extensive general functions of an administrator or bursar).[8]

[8]Acts 6:2□.

tablecloth Gk. *othonē.* What Peter saw was not a linen used to cover a dinner table, but a large sheet of cloth.[1]

[1]Acts 10:11; 11:5□.

talent Gk. *talenton.* The most important Greek coin of reckoning, corresponding to a weight* of silver varying, according to estimates, from between 26 to 34 kg. (57.2 to 74.8 lbs.) and even as many as 41 kg. (90.2 lbs.), with a worth of 6,000 denarii. The annual tax for Galilee, joined to that of Perea, was 200 talents; Herod's annual revenue was 900 talents. This allows for some appreciation of the fabulous sum involved in the mention of 10,000 talents, equal to the wages of 16,000 men over a ten-year period.[1]

[1]Ex 25:39; Mt 18:24; 25:15-28□.

→ coins—weights.

[talion] A word derived from the Lat., related to the adjective *talis:* "such." A specific word to indicate the O.T. law which made punishments proportionate to the offences undergone,[1] a law different from that of excessive vengeance* such as the one Lamech practiced.[2] In place of "an eye for an eye, a tooth for a tooth," Jesus called on his disciples to love their enemies.*[3]

[1]Ex 21:23-25; Lv 24:18-21; Dt 19:21. [2]Gn 4:23f. [3]Mt 5:38; cf. Rom 12:19f.

→ Intr. VI.4.C.b.—enemy—vengeance.

[Talmud] Heb. *talmûd:* "study, doctrine." A collection of the explanations of juridical and haggadic texts (→ Midrash*) of the Torah.*

In addition to the Mishnah* ("teaching") it included the *Gemara:* "teaching" (then "complement") and the *Baraitôt:* "exterior (traditions)." The Talmud was the Torah in its broadest sense.

The Jerusalem or Palestinian Talmud remained incomplete into the fourth century A.D.; the Babylonian Talmud at the end of the fifth century. The latter was some four times longer than the Palestinian one.

The *talmidim* were disciples of the rabbis of rabbinism.*

→ Intr. XII.1.C.—tradition.

tares

→ darnel.

[Targum] Aram. *targûm.* A term of Hittite origin: "to announce, to explain, to translate." An Aramaic paraphrase of the Bible, made necessary for the Jews beginning in the time of the return from the Exile.* On the Pentateuch* the following Targums were known: the Targum of Jerusalem II, the Palestinian Targum (of which a whole manuscript, called Targum Neofiti, has recently been discovered), the officially authoritative Babylonian Targum of Onkelos and that of Pseudo-Jonathan (Palestinian Targum of Jerusalem I), derived from the two preceding ones.

→ Intr. V.3.B.

Tarsus Gk. *Tarsos, Tarseus.* The principal city of Cilicia.* An important Greco-Roman intellectual center. Paul's birthplace.[1]

[1]Acts 9:11,30; 11:25; 21:39; 22:3□.

→ Intr. IV.2.C; IV.3.C.—Map 2.

Tartarus Gk. *Tartaros.* In Greco-Latin mythology, one of the names pointing out the netherworld* as a place of torment for the wicked, in contrast with the Elysian Fields, the place of happiness for the virtuous.[1]

[1]2 Pt 2:4; cf. Jude 6□.

→ netherworld.

tassel

→ fringe.

taste Gk. *geuomai.*

1. In the strict sense, to appreciate the flavor of food,[1] to eat.[2]

[1]1 Sm 14:43; Jb 12:11; Mt 27:34; Jn 2:9. [2]Jon 3:7; Lk 14:24; Acts 10:10; 20:11; 23:14; Col 2:21.

2. In the metaphorical sense, the term adverts to an experiential dimension of knowledge,* one which can issue in wisdom.* As was the case with a newborn child, who liked fresh milk, so could the neophyte experience the Lord[3] as a foretaste of the heavenly gift which God's word was.[4] To taste death was to experience bitterness;[5] Jesus did this to preserve men from it.[6] His experience was such that the believer will never have to taste death.[7]

[3]Ps 34:9; 1 Pt 2:3. [4]Heb 6:4f. [5]1 Sm 15:32; Mt 16:28 (= Mk 9:1 = Lk 9:27). [6]Heb 2:9. [7]Jn 8:52□.

tax Gk. *kēnsos* (tax),[1] *phoros* (tribute),[2] *telos* (duty).[3] In all the countries occupied by Rome, whatever their status, the residents who did not possess Roman citizenship were held to pay the "tribute of the earth" (land tax), the "head tribute" (aimed at personal chattels) and different indirect ones, such as the taxes which the publicans* levied. The Jews of Palestine and the Diaspora,* in addition, had to pay an annual tax to the Temple.

[1]Mt 17:25; 22:17,19; Mk 12:14△. [2]Lk 20:22; 23:2; Rom 13:6f.△. [3]Mt 17:25; Rom 13:7 △.

→ Intr. IV.2.B.b; VI.3.—custom, duty—publican—tithe.

tax collector

→ publican.

teach **1.** Gk. *didaskō,* Heb. *limmad* (whence: Talmud*). In Judaism, to teach was, through a better knowledge of Scripture, to transmit the will of God,* not in an abstract fashion nor in order to develop another's intellectual faculties, but rather to invite from someone a decision to obey God. Like the Jews, who began with their concrete situations, Jesus taught in the synagogues*[1] or in the Temple.*[2] In addition, he taught in the open air.[3] As was also the case in Judaism, he spoke of God, of his kingdom and of his will; what was distinctive was the radical character of his teaching, his unique "authority*" which, except in controversies,* did not quote Scripture[4] and which, according to John, derived from his Father;[5] furthermore, he centered this instruction on one's neighbor and also on one's relationship to his person. In the Church, teaching was a charism,* consisting in the interpretation of the Scriptures and in morally attractive exhortations.[6] The principal teacher was the Holy Spirit* whose anointing* has been bestowed on us.[7]

[1]Mt 9:35; 13:54 (= Mk 6:2 = Lk 4:15); Mk 1:21f. (= Lk 4:3f.). [2]Mt 21:23 (= Mk 12:35 = Lk 20:1); 26:55 (= Mk 14:49); Lk 19:47. [3]Mt 5:2; Mk 6:34; Lk 5:3; 13:26. [4]Mt 7:29; Mk 1:27; 11:28. [5]Jn 7:16f.; 8:28; cf. 6:44f. [6]Rom 12:7; 1 Cor 4:26. [7]1 Jn 2:20,27.

2. As was the case in Judaism, there was a certain kind of teaching (Gk. *didachē*),[8] which could evolve into a function.[9] This teaching function (Gk. *didaskalia*), which had been practiced among Jews,[10] existed among Christians[11] and tended to characterize the apostolic teaching as opposed to that of false doctrines;[12] it was healthy, good and salutary.[13]

[8]Acts 2:42; 5:28; 13:12; 17:19; Rom 6:17; 16:17. [9]2 Tim 4:2f.; Heb 6:2; 2 Jn 9f. [10]Mt 15:9 (= Mk 7:7). [11]1 Cor 12:28f.; Eph 4:11. [13]1 Tim 1:10; 4:6; 6:3; 2 Tim 4:3; Ti 1:9; 2:1. [12]Mt 16:12; Eph 4:14; Col 2:22; 1 Tim 4:1; Rv 2:14f., 24.

3. In the Jewish world, the teacher (Gk. *didaskalos,* Heb. *rabbî,*[14] Gk. *epistatēs*[15]) possessed a great reputation; his authority was typified in the figure of the "Teacher of Righteousness" in Qumran,* who was priest, exegete, interpreter of the Law, revealer of the mysteries of God, father of the community, bearer of the Holy Spirit and the eschatological* prophet charged with guiding to salvation. Jesus allowed himself to be called Teacher* and he was asked to intervene in questions belonging to the juridical order and to resolve controversies;[16] he charged his disciples* to become such teachers in their turn, without, however, appropriating the title reserved to him,[17] and to do this teaching in his name.[18] Accordingly, through the Spirit these teachers became charismatic* catechists.[19]

[14]Jn 1:38; 20:16. [15]Lk 8:24,45; 9:33,49; 17:13. [16]Mt 22:24; Lk 12:13f. [17]Mt 23:8; 28:20; Mk 14:14. [18]Acts 4:18; 5:28. [19]Jn 14:26; Acts 13:1; 1 Cor 12:28; Eph 4:11.

→ Intr. IX.1.2; XII.1; XII.3.B.—catechize—preach—rabbi.

teacher

→ master.

tears

→ sadness.

temple **1.** The Greek *hieron* (from *hieros:* "sacred") designated the building's totality, the "temple"; the Greek *naos* designated that part of the temple where the deity resided, the "sanctuary"; this distinction has not always been respected in translations.

Other, rarer terms were: "the (holy) place" (Gk. *topos hagios*),[1] the "Holy Place" (Gk. *to hagion, ta hagia*).[2] In the N.T., only *naos,* is used to refer to the temple in its spiritual sense.

[1]Mt 24:15; Jn 4:20; 11:48; Acts 6:13f.; 7:49; 21:28. [2]Heb 8:2; 9:1,2,3,8,12,24,25; 10:19; 13:11△.

2. The Temple of Jerusalem was an imposing building, its perimeter being about 1,500 m. (4,920 ft.); it had been rebuilt by Herod the Great, then was destroyed in 70. It was composed of two parts: an enclosure open to anyone, and the sanctuary proper, which was inaccessible to non-Jews.[3] The enclosure, the Courtyard of the Gentiles, was a vast esplanade that doubled as a public square. It was surrounded by porticoes (one of which was Solomon's,[4] on the east with pillars 11 m. [36 ft.] high) under which the crowd strolled about[5] or gathered together to hear instructions in the Law.*[6] Vendors[7] provided animals for the offerings and changers provided Jewish coinage, the only kind allowed for payment of the half-shekel tax.* In the center of the esplanade one entered through the Beautiful Gate,[8] first into the Courtyard of the Women, a square about 65 m. (213 ft.) on each side where, next to the treasury room, were located the collection boxes for obols;[9] from there, one passed into the Courtyard of the

Men, which, in turn, surrounded the Priests' Courtyard, in which the altar* of holocausts held the dominant place. Finally, one came to a building which contained a first room, the Holy Place,[10] in which were found the altar of incense, the golden lampstand and the table for the loaves* of offering; a double curtain separated this room from another room, which was empty in Jesus' time, the Holy of Holies.[11]

[3]Acts 21:28. [4]Jn 10:23. [5]Mt 21:14f.; Mk 11:27. [6]Mt 26:55; Jn 7:14. [7]Mk 11:15. [8]Acts 3:2. [9]Mk 12:41. [10]Lk 1:9. [11]Heb 9:3.

3. The Temple was the heart of Israel's life. Each day holocaust* and incense* sacrifices were offered there; prayers were offered at set times.[12] Three times a year, for Passover* at least (presupposing that the obligation was an absolute one), from everywhere in the country people were obliged to go up to the Temple on pilgrimage* even from the country's farthest reaches;[13] finally, it was there that the paschal lamb, which would be eaten in every household, had to be sacrificed.

[12]Acts 3:1. [13]Lk 2:41.

4. Jesus observed and approved of the cultic practices of the Temple, while condemning the formalisms that came to vitiate them.[14] He wanted it to be respected,[15] while also foretelling its impending destruction.[16] At his death its veil* was torn and the sanctuary lost its sacred character.[17] Believers saw in Jesus the true sanctuary, a sanctuary of flesh that would be rebuilt at his resurrection and in which, henceforth, a new kind of worship would be celebrated.[18]

[14]Mt 5:23f.; 12:2-7 (= Mk 2:24-26 = Lk 6:2-4); 23:16-22; Lk 2:22-50. [15]Mt 21:12-17 (= Mk 11:11-17 = Lk 19:45); Mk 11:16; Jn 2:13-17. [16]Mt 23:38f. (= Lk 13:35); 24:2 (= Mk 13:2 = Lk 21:6); 26:60f. (= Mk 14:58); 27:39f. (= Mk 15:29). [17]Mt 27:51 (= Mk 15:38= Lk 23:45). [18]Jn 2:19-21.

5. After having frequented the Temple for some time,[19] the believers understood that the Church (for example, that of Corinth) was God's sanctuary; its foundation was Christ,[20] and pagans and Jews could have access to it.[21] Each Christian himself was God's temple, the Spirit's sanctuary,[22] a living stone of the sanctuary not made by human hands, the one prophets* had dreamed about.[23]

[19]Acts 2:46; 3:1-11; 21:26. [20]1 Cor 3:16f.; 2 Cor 6:16-18. [21]Eph 2:14-22. [22]1 Cor 3:17; 6:19; 2 Cor 6:16. [23]Is 66:1f.; Acts 7:49-51; 17:24.

6. For the Epistle to the Hebrews,* the heavenly sanctuary had been a model for the earthly sanctuary; into it Jesus Christ, the unique High Priest,* had entered in order to afford us access to God's presence.[24] The book of Revelation described this sanctuary which, in its definitive form, was nothing less than God himself and the Lamb.*[25]

[24]Heb 4:14; 6:19f.; 9:11-14,24; 10:19f. [25]Rv 5:6-14; 7:15; 21:22.

→ Intr. XIII.1.A.—Holy—Holy of Holies—pinnacle—sacrifice—treasury—veil—worship.

Temple treasury Gk. *gazophylakeion* (from the Persian *gaza:* "treasury of the king [of Persia]" and from the Gk. *phylakeion:* "the place where one keeps guard") or *korbanas* (from the Heb. *qorban:* "dedicated to God").

1. A room, inaccessible to the public, which contained the treasury of the Temple.[1]

[1]Neh 10:39; 2 Mc 3:6; Mal 3:10; Mt 27:6△.

2. By extension, the portico adjoining this room.[2]

[2]1 Chr 9:26; Jn 8:20△.

3. The chest, shaped like a horn, for the offerings.[3]

[3]Mk 12:41, 43; Lk 21:1△.

→ korban.

Temple veil In Herod's Temple,* as formerly in the nomadic sanctuary of the Hebrews, a curtain (Gk. *katapetasma*) closed off access to the Holy Place,* and another closed off access to the Holy of Holies.*[1] It was the former one, which, according to the Epistle to the Hebrews, was torn apart at Jesus' death.[2] Its tearing signified abrogation of the ancient worship and, above all, free access to the heavenly sanctuary.

[1]Heb 9:3. [2]Mt 27:51 (= Mk 15:38 = Lk 23:45); Heb 10:19f.△.

tempt, temptation 1. The Greek *peirasmos, peirazō:* ordinarily "to put to the test" could also mean, in a pejorative sense: "to tempt," when it was a case of putting a man's very relationship with God into question. Although God could put someone to the test without tempting him ("God does not tempt"[1]), a man could not put God to the test without also doubting his power and contesting his love and fidelity. In the O.T., Massah (also called Meribah) was the typical place of temptation, that is, a place of contestation.[2] Unlike the Hebrews, Jesus did not tempt God.[3] But he was tempted by men on various occasions in his life: by Peter who was called Satan,*[4] by the satiated crowds who wanted to make him king,[5] and by the Jewish leaders who taunted him to save himself by coming down from the cross;[6] the various temptations have been recapitulated in an imposing desert scene in which Jesus triumphed over Satan,* the Tempter above all others, and he did this in that very place where Israel had succumbed.[7]

[1]Jas 1:13. [2]Dt 6:16; 33:8f.; Ps 95:8f.; 1 Cor 10:9; Heb 3:8f. [3]Mt 4:7 (= Lk 4:12); Acts 15:10. [4]Mt 16:23. [5]Jn 6:15. [6]Mt 27:42 (= Mk 15:30). [7]Cf. 1 Chr 21:1 and 2 Sm 24:1; Mt 4:1 (= Mk 1:13 = Lk 4:2); 4:3; Lk 4:13.

2. Temptation is a snare[8] into which the Tempter tries to make believers fall.[9] So, one must pray, not lest God make us submit to temptation, but that he bring it about that we not enter into temptation and that he keep us safe from the Tempter:[10] one needs to watch* and pray* for this.[11]

[8]1 Tim 6:9. [9]Lk 8:13; 1 Cor 7:5; Gal 6:1; 1 Thes 3:5; Rv 2:10. [10]Mt 6:13 (= Lk 11:4). [11]Mt 26:41 (= Mk 14:38 = Lk 22:40,46).

3. Paul sets personified Sin,* which had produced covetousness,* as temptation's starting point;[12] James made covetousness the origin of both sin and death;[13] John pointed the finger at the world* as the source itself of covetousness.[14] Wherever the origin of temptation may be found—in Satan, sin or covetousness, and whether personified to a greater or lesser degree—all that this language attempts to show in an imaginary way, is that it is not God who turns trial into temptation, and that, in temptation, the stakes are set between God and man's freedom.[15] Man must keep watch and pray with the weapons of faith and under the impulse of the Holy Spirit.[16]

[12]Rom 7:8. [13]Jas 1:14. [14]1 Jn 2:16. [15]Lk 22:31; 1 Cor 7:5; 1 Thes 3:5; Rv 2:10. [16]Mt 6:13; 26:41; Eph 6:16.

→ Intr. XIV.2.A.—test, trial, try.

tent Gk. *skēnē* (*skēnoō:* "to pitch a tent").

1. The dwelling-place of the Hebrews in the nomadic period.[1]

[1]Heb 11:9.

2. "The tent of witness": the portable sanctuary of the desert, containing the Ark of the Covenant, considered to be Yahweh's* dwelling-place among his people, the *shekinah* according to late Judaism. Hence the expression "to establish his tent," used with regard to God, not in the sense of a provisional house but in the sense of a permanent "abode."[1]

[1]Jn 1:14; Acts 7:44,46; Rv 12:12; 13:6; 15:5; 21:3.

3. As a metaphor, the tent referred either to earthly or to heavenly existence.[1]

[1]Lk 16:9; 2 Cor 5:1,4; 2 Pt 1:13f.

→ abide—Booths (Feast of).

Tents (Feast of)

→ Booths (Feast of).

test, trial, try

1. To put to the test (Gk. *peirazō*). Testing is characteristic of the human condition, for each encounter between two beings is a test of their liberty. Of itself, a test is not a temptation,* but instead it is an invitation to a more intense life and to a deeper relationship. God from time to time puts friends of his to the test: Abraham,[1] believers;[2] generally he preserved them in it or delivered them out of it,[3] setting the test according to the strength of the man.[4] Jesus was tested during his life, so he is able to come to the aid of those who are tested[5] and to offer them the crown* of life.[6] The coming of the Messiah brings, along with the constrictions of history, that testing above all others which is the tribulation.*

[1]Gn 22:1; Heb 11:17. [2]Acts 20:19; 2 Cor 13:5; Jas 1:2, 12; 1 Pt 1:6; 4:12; 2:10. [3]2 Pt 2:9; Rv 3:10. [4]1 Cor 10:13. [5]Heb 2:18. [6]Jas 1:12.

2. To confirm an attitude, to estimate the value, to approve (Gk. *dokimazō*). A believer must examine (something which is also a kind of putting of another

to the test) things, feelings, persons, himself.[7] Then this other is "judged apt," "capable of"; he has shown his mettle, he is "proven" in virtue of his spiritual judgment, approved,[8] or, on the contrary, reproved.[9] On occasion, the term has no more than the banal meaning "to try to, to attempt";[10] sometimes the situation is similar with the verb *peirazō.* [11]

[7]Lk 12:56; Rom 2:18; 12:2; 1 Cor 11:28; 2 Cor 8:8; Gal 6:4; Eph 5:10; 1 Tim 3:10; 1 Jn 4:1. [8]Rom 14:18; 1 Cor 11:19; 16:4; Jas 1:12. [9]Rom 1:28; 1 Cor 9:27; 2 Cor 13:5-7. [10]Lk 14:19. [11]Acts 9:26; 16:7; 24:6; 26:21; Heb 11:29.

→ discern—suffer—tempt—tribulation.

testament From the Lat. *testamentum,* translating the Gk. *diathēkē:* "covenant."*

1. The term did not only signify the "clause of a will," a juridical act by which someone "disposed of" (Gk. *dia-tithēmai*) his goods in anticipation of the moment of his death;[1] it also included the meaning of the Hebrew word *berît* (also rendered in Greek by *diathēkē*), a covenant pact by which God committed himself, on certain conditions, to fill with good things the one people that had become his very own. The word tended to tone down the bilateral nature inherent in every covenant in order that it might put into sharper focus the testator's authority.

[1]Lk 22:29; Gal 3:15,17; Heb 9:16.

2. The book of the covenant arranged between God and his people.[2] The "new testament" was thus characterized, with special reference to Jesus' words at the Last Supper,*[3] ones which made allusion to Jeremiah's prophecy.[4] Although it was called "new," this was not a covenant to supplant, but was one to fulfill,* the former covenant, a covenant with which it remained in a living and constant relationship.[5]

[2]2 Cor 3:14. [3]Lk 22:20. [4]Jer 31:31. [5]2 Cor 3:6.

3. A literary genre,* the farewell discourse, whose type is found in the *Testaments of the XII Patriarchs.* *

→ Intr. VI.4.B.c.—covenant—farewell discourse.

[Testaments of the XII Patriarchs] A farewell discourse* attributed to the twelve sons of Jacob. This Jewish apocryphal* writing, composed between 100 B.C. and A.D. 100, offered teaching about moral character, close to the doctrine of Qumran.*

tetrarch Gk. *tetr(a)-archēs* ("four" and "leader"): "one who governed a territory according to the fourth part of a province." A title of governors in the Greek kingdoms of the Orient. Rome conceded this designation to princes too unimportant to be called kings, such as Herod Antipas.*[1]

[1]Mt 14:1; Lk 3:1,19; 9:7; Acts 13:1□.

→ Intr. I.1.D.

[textual criticism] That science which, from the various manuscript recensions,* tries to establish the original texts.

Thaddeus Gk. *Thaddaios.* One of the Twelve,* called Lebbaeus in some manuscripts, replaced by Jude in Luke.[1]

[1]Mt 10:3; Mk 3:18; Lk 6:16; Acts 1:13□.

thanksgiving **1.** Gk. *eucharistia* (from *eu:* "good, very" and *charizomai:* "to cause to delight" or *charis:* "that about/in which one rejoices"): "recognition"; *eucharisteō* and *charin echō:* "to thank." This term was scarcely known in the O.T., which ordinarily spoke of a blessing.* Thus, in a Greek milieu, the blessing before the meal became "thanksgiving."[1] So, too did the prayer of blessing quoted in the gospels,[2] and, possibly so, the liturgy of Revelation.[3] All its other uses are found in Paul.

[1]Mt 15:36 (= Mk 8:6 = Jn 6:11); 26:27 (= Mk 14:23 = Lk 22:17,19 = 1 Cor 11:24); Acts 27:35. [2]Lk 18:11; Jn 11:41; cf. Acts 28:15. [3]Rv 4:9; 7:12; 11:17.

2. The thanksgiving is one of the forms of prayer, a transformation of the ancient custom of the epistolary thanksgiving with which one always began a letter: it is a "thank you" addressed to God. In Paul, such thanks (which varied according to his correspondents) essentially had faith, hope and love as their goal, and also the development of the Christian life; regularly his letters closed with a prayer of petition.[4] A thanksgiving, therefore, was also a doxology,* one through which God was praised for his kindnesses[5] in a manner analogous to what was done in blessings.[6] A thanksgiving also appears as the reaction to a distressing possibility, which is afterwards found out to be untrue,[7] or as a "Thank you, my God!" welling up from the core of one's being.

[4]Rom 1:8; 1 Cor 1:4; 2 Cor 1:11; Eph 1:16; Phil 1:3; Col 1:3; 1 Thes 1:2; 2 Thes 1:3; 1 Tim 1:12; 2 Tim 1:3; Phlm 4. [5]2 Cor 8:16; 9:15. [6]Rom 1:25; 9:5; 2 Cor 1:3; 11:31; Eph 1:3. [7]Rom 6:17; 7:25; 1 Cor 15:57; 2 Cor 2:14. [8]1 Cor 1:14; 14:18.

3. Thanksgiving is the soul of Christian life. Its attitude is essential: in contrast with the *acharistoi,*[9] who malign Paul,[10] one ought to be one of the *eucharistoi,*[11] overflowing with acknowledgments[12] at all times,[13] above all in gratitude for the plea that has been heard and the victory which has been given.[14] Thanksgiving ought to undergird every human activity,[15] something creative of "the Eucharist."*

[9]2 Tim 3:2. [10]Rom 1:21. [11]Col 3:15. [12]2 Cor 4:15; Col 2:7. [13]Rom 14:6; 1 Cor 10:30; Eph 5:20; 1 Thes 5:18. [14]2 Cor 9:15. [15]Col 1:12; 3:15-17.

→ Intr. IX.3.B—blessing—Eucharist—prayer—sacrifice.

[theological tradition] **1.** The handing down of revelation.*

2. Everything that the Apostles transmitted for the life and faith of God's people, and which the Church has kept in the course of centuries.

theophany An appearance (Gk. *phainesthai:* "to appear," *phaneros:* "visible") of God *(Theos),* not simply in the course of a dream* or a vision, but during a perceptible revelation (under human or angelic form) or even within cosmic phenomena. Theophanies are very rare in the N.T.[1]

[1]Cf. Mt 28:3-4; Acts 7:2,30,35.

→ revelation—see.

[Thessalonians (Epistle to the)] **1.** The first letter, the oldest N.T. writing (except in the view of some few scholars who date the Epistle to the Galatians in 49), was sent by Paul from Corinth in the year 50–51 (refer to Acts 15:36–18:17) to the community of Thessalonica, which was established by him a short time earlier amidst persecution.

2. The second letter was addressed by Paul from Corinth, probably around 52, to the same recipients whose troubles had become aggravated. According to some scholars, it is a pseudonymous work written after 70.

→ Intr. XV.

Thessalonica Gk. *Thessalonikē.* Modern-day Thessaloniki. Established around 315 B.C., this city of Macedonia* had been a free city from 42 B.C. Situated at the starting point of the *Via Egnatiana* (the great overland highway to Italy), it was much visited. One of the first churches founded by Paul in Europe.[1]

[1]Acts 17:1,4f.,11,13; 20:4; 27:2; Phil 4:16; 1 Thes 1:1; 2 Tim 4:10□.

→ Intr. XV.—Thessalonians (Epistles to the)—Map 2.

Theudas A rioter who stirred up Palestine against the Romans at the time of Herod's death (4 B.C.).[1] In his account, Josephus located this revolt during the government of Fadus (A.D. 44–46).

[1]Acts 5:36□.

→ Zealot.

thief Gk. *kleptēs.* Theft was considered to be a very serious crime[1] without, however, its being answerable to penal law: the thief had only an obligation to restore stolen goods, with something added. Unlike the O.T., the N.T. is not afraid to compare the thief's deed with the coming Day of the Lord,* the Son of Man who comes suddenly[3] in the night.*

[1]Ex 20:15; Lv 19:11; Dt 5:19; Jer 7:9; Mt 15:19 (= Mk 7:21); 19:18 (= Mk 10:19 = Lk 18:20). [2]1 Thes 5:2,4. [3]Mt 24:43 (= Lk 12:39); Rv 3:3; 16:15.

Thomas Gk. *Thōmas,* a shortened form of a word deriving from the Heb. *tô'âm:* "twin," rendered in Gk. by *Didymos.* One of the Twelve.* According to John, a type of the person who believes after having doubted.[1]

[1]Mt 10:3; Mk 3:18; Lk 6:15; Jn 11:16; 14:5; 20:24-28; 21:2; Acts 1:13□.

[Thomas (Gospel of)] **1.** An apocryphal* Greek gospel recounting Jesus' childhood. The manuscript dates from the sixth century, but the original is from the second century. Manifesting a gnostic orientation, it intended to show the divine power operative in Jesus' childhood.

2. An apocryphal* collection of sayings of the Lord and sayings of gnostic origin. A book written in Coptic, deriving from Nag Hammadi,* and reflecting a Greek original from the second century. Out of the one hundred thirteen logia,* some of which were already known from other apocryphal writings, two of the original ones are agrapha* (numbers 8 and 82). The majority are colored by gnosticism.*

→ apocryphal writings—Nag Hammadi.

thorns

→ brambles—crown.

Thrones

→ Dominations.

Thyatira Gk. *Thyateira.* An important financial center on the highway between Pergamum* and Sardis.* The birthplace of Lydia, the woman purple* dye trader.[1]

[1]Acts 16:14; Rv 1:11; 2:18,24.

→ Map 2.

Tiberias Gk. *Tiberias.* Derived from the name of the emperor Tiberius,* a city established around A.D. 17–22 by Herod Antipas* on the southwest bank of the Lake of Gennesaret, the new capital of Galilee in place of Sepphoris, with a royal palace, stadium and parliament (600 members). The Jews felt repugnance at dwelling in this city built over ancient tombs; a short time after its establishment, the prohibition was lifted. Its warm baths attracted the world and, in the second century, it witnessed the settlement there of the famous rabbinical school of Jude the Holy, the principal editor of the Mishnah.* The gospels never tell of Jesus being present in this city, but John mentions it[1] as well as its lake.[2]

[1]Jn 6:23.

→ Map 4.

Tiberius Gk. *Tiberios.* Tiberius Julius Caesar. The adopted son of Augustus*; the second Roman emperor (A.D. 14–37).[1]

[1]Lk 3:1□; cf. 20:22; 23:2; Jn 19:12.

time Three Greek words are used to indicate time. Although the distinctions are not always clear cut, we can try to show the nuances proper to each.

1. Extent of time. Duration, some notion of which was bound up with a life's continuity from birth to death,[1] was expressed by the word *aiōn* (Heb. *'ôlâm*), which, when used absolutely, could also mean: "world."* Ordinarily, a preposition allowed for some indication whether the duration concerned what was before or after the topic under discussion: "since *(apo, ek, pro)* ever" or else "for (*eis,* literally: "towards") ever." The nature of what was alive specified what its duration might be: that of a tree's life,[2] or of an individual,[3] a group and a generation,[4] or, without any limit being given to its proportions, that of God's salvific work which asserted itself within the ebb and flow of generations, both this side of[5] as well as on the other side[6] of an individual's earthly existence, or that of Jesus Christ,[7] or even that of God himself.[8] In these latter two instances, the plural was readily employed in a Semitic expression: "(for) age upon age."[9] So, that spirit which tried to rule over an extent of time was oriented towards eternity.* This was not construed as an abstraction, but rather as the fullness of those generations which constituted the life lavished by the Creator. To live "for ever" was equivalent to living "eternally."[10]

[1]Cf. 1 Sm 1:22 and 1:11. [2]Mt 21:19 (= Mk 11:14). [3]Jn 13:8; 1 Cor 8:13; Phlm 15. [4]Jn 14:16; Acts 7:51; 2 Cor 4:11; 6:10; Col 1:26; Ti 1:2. [5]Lk 1:70; Jn 9:32; Acts 15:18; 1 Cor 2:7; Eph 3:9; Jude 25. [6]Mk 3:29; Heb 9:26. [7]Heb 5:6; 7:24,28; 13:8,21; 1 Pt 4:11; Rv 1:18. [8]Lk 1:55; 2 Cor 9:9; 11:31; 1 Pt 1:25. [9]Lk 1:33; Rom 1:25,9:5; 11:36; 16:27; 1 Tim 1:17; 6:16; 2 Tim 4:18; Rv *passim.* [10]Cf. Jn 6:51 and 6:54; 8:51f.; 11:26.

2. Succession of time. Ordinarily it was the Greek word *chronos* which indicated a determinate length of time, specified by an adjective (short, long, limited)[11] or by the context;[12] it was also the term for an era, the moment of a happening,[13] but, rarely, that of a brief instant.[14] Occasionally, the Greek *kairos* could not help but have the meaning: "at that time"[15] or the time of the seasons[16] or the moment which had come;[17] but it was more fitting to sense in it already that nuance of a time characterized by faith in the Creator God.

[11]Mt 25:19; Mk 2:19; 9:21; Lk 8:27,29; 20:9; 23:8; Jn 5:6; 7:33; 12:35; 14:9; Acts 14:3,28; 18:20,23; 19:22; Heb 5:12; 11:32. [12]Rom 7:1; 1 Cor 7:39; Gal 4:1. [13]Mt 2:7,16. [14]Lk 4:5. [15]Mt 11:25; 12:1ff. [16]Mt 21:34; Acts 14:17; Gal 4:10. [17]Mk 12:2.

3. Designated time. Faith in God, the Lord of time and of moments,[18] ordinarily conferred a new consistency on every lived moment. The Greek *chronos* was rarely used in this pregnant sense. However, it was found in the following cases, in addition to that time humanly described as the moment of giving birth to a child:[19] the time of ignorance,[20] of promise,[21] of the desert,[22] of exile,[23] the last times,[24] the fullness of time,[25] the everlasting times.[26] Habitually, it was the Greek word *kairos* (properly the just point, which touched on the goal; hence either "the critical point" or "the right time") which was reserved for this meaning. According to God's plan,* every being has his time,[27] a time noted down.[28] The coming of Jesus Christ determined a new time, that of the reign of God which had drawn near,[29] that of a "today" which modified the course of time.[30] Henceforward, there was one "favorable time,"[31] which one had to make use of,[32] not miss.[33] One had to recognize the signs of the times,*[34] during this time of combat,* when one had to encourage oneself to not grow weak.[35] The time for respite,[36] the end of time, remained unknown,[37] but for the believer it was Christ's return,[38] a fact which involved him in watching* and praying.*[39]

Among the times designated above all others were the beginning (Gk. *archē*) and the end (Gk. *telos,* or *hēmera:* "Day") of time: they allowed for the unification, under the twin concepts of God, the creator and judge, of a successive multiplicity of human generations.[40] With Christ "the end of time has joined us together,"[41] so that today (Gk. *sēmeron*) becomes the designated time above all others, making present what was reckoned for Jesus as "the hour*" (Gk. *hōra*): something that was the encapsulating of the eternal within the succession of time.[42]

[18]Acts 1:7; 1 Thes 5:1. [19]Lk 1:57. [20]Acts 17:30. [21]Acts 7:17. [22]Acts 7:23; 13:18. [23]1 Pt 1:17. [24]1 Pt 1:20; Jude 18. [25]Acts 3:21; Gal 4:4. [26]Rom 16:25; 2 Tim 1:9; Ti 1:2. [27]Mt 8:29; 26:18; Jn 7:6,8. [28]Lk 4:13. [29]Mk 1:15. [30]Rom 3:26; 5:6. [31]2 Cor 6:2. [32]Gal 6:10; Eph 5:16; Col 4:5. [33]Lk 19:44. [34]Mt 16:3; Lk 12:56. [35]Lk 8:13; Rom 8:18; Heb 3:12f. [36]Acts 3:20. [37]Mk 13:33; Acts 1:7; 1 Thes 5:1; 1 Pt 1:5. [38]1 Cor 4:5; 1 Tim 6:14; 1 Pt 4:17f.; Rv 11:18. [39]Lk 21:36; Eph 6:18. [40]Mt 19:4; 24:14; 28:20; Jn 1:1; 1 Cor 15:24; Heb 1:10; Rv 21:6. [41]1 Cor 10:11. [42]Heb 3:7-4:11.

→ Intr. XII.2.—aeon—age—calendar—day—Day of the Lord—end of the world—eternal—evening—feast—fulfill—hour—midnight—month—morning—night—noon—watch—week—world—year.

Timothy Gk. *Timotheos* (from *timaō:* "to honor" and *Theos:* "God"). Born at Lystra* of a pagan father and a Jewish mother who had become a Christian.[1] Paul's beloved disciple and fellow worker for some fifteen years,[2] he was entrusted with numerous missions to the Churches;[3] he was the co-author of the bulk of the Pauline letters.[4] The Pastoral Epistles* make him out to be one of the principal episcopoi* of the second generation.[5]

[1]Acts 16:1; 2 Tim 1:5; 3:15. [2]Rom 16:21; 1 Cor 4:17; 16:10; Phil 2:20-22; 1 Thes 3:2; 1 Tim 1:2,18; 2 Tim 1:2; 3:10f. [3]Acts 17:14f.; 18:5; 19:22; 20:4; 1 Cor 4:17; 2 Cor 1:19; Phil 2:19; 1 Tim 3:6. [4]2 Cor, Phil, Col, 1 Thes, 2 Thes, Phlm. [5]1 Tim 6:20; cf. Heb 13:23□.

→ Timothy (Epistles to).

[Timothy (Epistles to)] **1.** The first letter to Timothy would have been written by Paul* after his first Roman captivity, between 63 and 66. But the life of Paul after 62 is lost to the history of the N.T. Some scholars push this letter's composition back to the post-apostolic era, towards 75 or even 110–115.

2. The second letter is the last Paul would have written. Supporters of its authenticity* date it in the second Roman captivity (64–68?), more precisely about 67. Other scholars place it towards the end of the first century.

→ Intr. XV.—Epistles.

tithe From an old English word for a tenth, ten percent; Lat. *decima,* Gk. *hē dekatē:* "the tenth part." A religious tax* indicating the proprietary right which God possessed over certain fruits of the earth[1] and even over livestock;[2] the Pharisees extended this obligation to even the most minimal produce.[3] Distinct from the annual Temple tax,*[4] the tithe was destined for the support of religious personnel.[5] Before the sanctuary existed with its personnel,

Abraham* paid tithes to the king-priest Melchizedek,* thereby recognizing the superiority of this priesthood* to that of Levi.*[6]

[1]Dt 14:22f. [2]Lv 27:32. [3]Mt 23:23 (= Lk 11:42); Lk 18:12. [4]Mt 17:24. [5]Nm 18:21; Heb 7:5. [6]Gn 14:20; Heb 7:2-9.

→ Intr. VI.3.B.—cummin—first fruits—levites—mint.

Titus Gk. *Titos.* The first Christian of pagan birth to become a missionary; Paul's very effective co-worker.[1]

[1]2 Cor 2:13; 7:6,13f.; 8:6, 16,23; 12:18; Gal 2:1,3; 2 Tim 4:10; Ti 1:4□.

→ Titus (Epistle to).

[Titus] Flavius Titus (A.D. 39–81), eldest son of the emperor Vespasian, conducted the first Jewish War (66–70) in the course of which Jerusalem was beseiged and destroyed (April–September 70). Becoming emperor in 79, he showed himself well-disposed to the Jews and afterwards to the Christians. He was not allowed to marry Berenice,* who was eleven years his senior.

[Titus (Epistle to)] According to supporters of Pauline authenticity,* a letter of Paul's written in Macedonia* between 63 and 66 to Titus, one of his assistants, entrusted with maintaining the Church of Crete.* A historian, however, dares not decide in favor of its authenticity, for he possesses no definite facts for Paul's life beyond the year 62.

→ Intr. XV.—Epistles.

tomb In the N.T. era, tombs (Gk. *mnēma, mnēmeion:* "memorial," a monument meant to perpetuate the memory of the deceased) or sepulchres (Gk. *taphos,* from *thaptō:* "to bury") were caves within grottoes or dug out of rock.[1] Each spring their exteriors were whitewashed with lime[2] so that they could be recognized, the passersby avoiding contracting a legal impurity through contact with them.[3] The entry, low down and sometimes decorated,[4] was customarily closed with the aid of a large stone rolled in front, and sometimes sealed.[5] Inside and lower down,[6] the funerary chamber contained stone slabs, or niches dug in the wall partitions, which served as receptacles for the corpses. The tombs were grouped outside of cities, for example at Golgotha.* Resident aliens had a place for burial at Jerusalem apart from that of the Israelites.[7] Not to have a tomb was a terrible punishment,[8] because it meant not being able "to be reunited with one's fathers" and to discover oneself dedicated to oblivion, exposed to all coming by.[9]

[1]Mt 27:60 (= Mk 15:46 = Lk 23:53). [2]Mt 23:27. [3]Lk 11:44. [4]Mt 23:29. [5]Mt 27:66; Mk 15:46; 16:3. [6]Jn 20:5,11. [7]Mt 27:7. [8]Rv 11:9. [9]2 Kgs 9:10,34-37; Jer 22:18f.

→ Intr. VIII.2.D.b—bury—coffin.

tongue **1.** Gk. *dialektos:* the language of a people, of a country.[1] On Pentecost each person heard the Apostles speaking in his mother tongue.[2]

[1]Intr. V.3; Acts 1:19; 21:40; 22:2; 26:14. [2]Acts 2:6,8△.

2. Gk. *glōssa:* "tongue,[3] language."[4]

a) By his tongue a man communicates or conceals the sentiments of his heart.* Thus, it can either praise and bless God,*[5] as well as curse men,[6] or conceal the poverty of one's secret intentions.[7]

[3]Ex 11:7; Ps 22:16; Mk 7:33,35; Lk 1:64; 16:24; Rv 16:10. [4]Is 28:11; 1 Cor 14:21; Rv 5:9; 7:9; 10:11; 11:9; 13:7; 14:6; 17:15. [5]Ps 35:28; Is 50:4; Lk 1:64; Acts 2:26; Rom 14:11; Phil 2:11. [6]Sir 28:13-26; Rom 3:13; Jas 1:26; 3:2-12. [7]Jer 9:2,7; 1 Jn 3:18; 1 Pt 3:10△.

b) To speak in tongue(s). Ecstatic prayer and praise addressed to God and necessitating an interpreter in order to be understood by those present.[8] A charism* promised to believers,[9] inferior to that of prophecy.* At Pentecost the disciples proclaimed God's marvels in tongues which strangers heard.[10]

[8]1 Cor 12:10,28,30; 13:1,8; 14. [9]Mk 16:17. [10]Acts 2:3f.,11; 10:46; 19:6△.

→ Pentecost—word.

[Torah] Heb. *tôrâ* (from *yârâ:* "to show"): "indication, teaching."

1. The five books of Moses* (Pentateuch*), distinguished from the "Prophets,"[1] constituting not only a doctrine or law, but also a practical rule: teaching normative for action. The Torah was, in a most excellent way, the revelation.*

[1]Mt 5:17; 7:12; 22:40; Lk 16:16; 24:44; Jn 1:45; Acts 13:15; 24:14; 28:23; Rom 3:21.

2. In Judaism the word designated not only the Bible* in its entirety,[2] but the oral law whose authority was not to be diminished: it was complete and interpreted the written law,[3] something which led to the shaping of the Talmud.

[2]Jn 10:34. [3]Mt 15:6.

→ Intr. XII.—law—Pentateuch—Talmud—Chart, p. 65.

Trachonitis Gk. *Trachōnitis* (from *trachys:* "rocky"). A pagan territory situated to the northeast, beyond the Jordan*; after Herod the Great's death, it was given to Philip,* along with Iturea,* Gaulanitis, Batanaea and Auranitis.[1]

[1]Lk 3:1□.

→ Map 4.

tradition From the Lat. *traditio:* "transmission," Gk. *paradosis.* First of all, in the active sense "to transmit" (Gk. *para-didōmi,* Heb. *mâsar,* whence the Heb. *mâssorâ:* "Jewish exegesis"); in the passive sense "to receive" (Gk. *paralambanō,* Heb. *qibbél*), "thing transmitted" (Gk. *para-dosis,* Heb. *qabbâlâ:* whence "kabbala").

1. Jewish tradition formed a chain that was held to go back to Moses, and this allowed for the guaranteeing of the truth of proposed affirmations;[1] it was assured by the written tradition of the canonical books and by the oral traditions of the elders.[2] After 70, it tended to let itself be entirely fixed in writing within the successive layers that three generations defined: the *tannaim* (from the Heb. *shânâ:* "to repeat"), the *amoraim* (from the Heb. *âmar:* "to say") and the *rabbis* (from the Heb. *rab:* "teacher"), which constituted the Talmud* (from the Heb. *limmad:* "to teach"). Jesus disputed not tradition in general, but the worth and authority of the tradition of the elders.[3] According to John, it was Jesus himself who transmitted the words and works which he had received from the Father.[4]

[1]Ezr 7:6; Neh 1:7; Sir 24:23; Dn 9:11; Acts 7:38. [2]Mt 15:2f., 6 (= Mk 7:3,5,8f., 13); Acts 6:14; cf. Mt 5:21. [3]Mt 15:1-20 (= Mk 7:1-20). [4]Jn 5:36; 17:4,8,14.

2. The primitive Christian tradition included, in addition to the narrative tradition about Jesus,[5] confessions* of faith and rules of life presented under the form of traditions actively received and communicated.[6] Thus Paul, who freed himself from the traditions of the fathers[7] (and which he caricatured in speaking of "totally human traditions"[8]), handed on the words of the Lord and several ecclesiastical traditions.[9] Doing this, he showed himself to be not the slave of tradition, but the slave of the only *Kyrios** who had encountered him through a revelation.*[10] In the late N.T. writings, teaching tended to be condensed into a fixed, given form,[11] which later would come to be called the "deposit."*

[5]Lk 1:2. [6]Acts 16:4; 1 Cor 11:2,23; 15:3; 2 Thes 2:15; 3:6. [7]Gal 1:14. [8]Col 2:8. [9]1 Cor 7:10; 9:14; Phil 4:8f.; 1 Thes 4:1-3; 2 Thes 2:15. [10]Gal 1:15f. [11]2 Pt 2:21; Jude 3.

→ Intr. IX.1; XII.1.B.—catechize—deposit.

transfiguration From the Gk. *metamorpho-omai* ("to change *morphē*": "form"), *metaschēmatizō* ("to change *schēma*": "aspect, figure").

1. A scene in Jesus' life, located by the Synoptics* as a ray of light during his ascent to Jerusalem.[1]

[1]Mt 17:1-9 (= Mk 9:2-10 = Lk 9:28-36); cf. 2 Pt 1:16-18.

2. The spiritual transformation of believers.[2]

[2]Rom 12:2; 2 Cor 3:18; Phil 3:21.

→ appearance—form—image.

treasury

→ Temple treasury.

tree **1.** Every tree (Gk. *dendron*) must produce fruits, and good ones; otherwise, it will be cut down and cast on the fire.[1]

[1]Mt 3:10 (= Lk 3:9); 7:17f. (= Lk 6:43f.); 12:33.

2. Tying in with the symbolism of the cosmic tree, which represented the universe, the kingdom of God was likened to a tree in whose shade* the peoples nestled.[2]

[2]Ez 17:22f.; 31:1-9; Dn 4:7-9; Mt 13:32 (= Lk 13:19).

3. The wood (Gk. *xylon*) of the cross,* the gibbet for those condemned to death, symbolized the curse* that Christ took upon himself to deliver us.[3]

[3]Acts 5:30; 10:39; 13:29; Gal 3:13; 1 Pt 2:24.

4. The tree (Gk. *xylon*) of life was a symbol from Mesopotamian mythology: its fruit communicated immortality. Access to this tree had been cut off from the time of humanity's origins,[4] but it will be open to Paradise* for all believers.[5]

[4]Gn 3:22-24; Rv 22:19. [5]Ez 47:12; Rv 2:7; 22:2,14.

→ Intr. II.5.—brambles—fig tree—mustard—olive tree—palm tree—sycamine—sycamore—vine.

trial, try

→ test, trial, try.

[Trial of Jesus] 1. The trial of Jesus was handed down in four recensions,*[1] which offer many differences but agree on the essential points. These are not verbal transcripts of sessions, but testimonies of Christian faith manifesting their evident apologetic tendencies. Furthermore, it is difficult to restore the detail of the historical scenes. The other narratives of trials recounted in the N.T. justify several conclusions: we mean not the accounts of the court appearances of Peter and John[2] or of the Twelve,[3] but the accounts of Paul's trial before Gallio,[4] before the Sanhedrin,[5] before Felix,[6] before Festus and Agrippa,[7] and, finally, the stoning of Stephen.[8] Historians agree on this fact: the right of capital punishment was tied to the governor's* decision, at least while he was exercising his authority (as he probably was not in the case of John the Baptist's treatment by Herod[9] or that of James by Agrippa[10]). Stephen's stoning seems to have been a unique instance of a transgression of the *ius gladii* reserved to the governor.

[1]Mt 26:57–27:31; Mk 14:53–15:20; Lk 22:54–23:25; Jn 18:12–19:16. [2]Acts 4:5-22. [3]Acts 5:17-41. [4]Acts 18:12-17. [5]Acts 22:30–23:10. [6]Acts 23:33–24:26. [7]Acts 25:1–26:32. [8]Acts 6:8–7:60. [9]Mt 14:3-11 (= Mk 6:17-29 = Lk 3:19f.); cf. Lk 23:3-11. [10]Acts 12:1-6.

2. The juridical procedures of a trial are unknown to us except through the Mishnaic* legislation, dating from around A.D. 150. Hence, the difficulties which obtain in making these data agree with the gospel narratives. According to the Mishnah, the members of the Sanhedrin sat in tiers in a circle presided over by the High Priest. The defendants, prosecutors and witnesses were all in the middle. Judgement could not be rendered at night nor on feast days, including vigils. The judges could not also take the role of a prosecutor or witness. The accused had a lawyer at his side. Before the judgment, a messenger went about the country calling witnesses for the defense. A single defense witness was sufficient; on the other hand two witnesses were needed for a charge. The judgment of condemnation could not be pronounced until at least 24 hours after the first court appearance. Discussion continues today on what constituted a charge of blasphemy.*

→ Intr. VI.4.C.—Sanhedrin.

tribe Gk. *phylē.* Among the Jews, an ethnic grouping that considered itself to have been descended from the one same ancestor. In the N.T. era, the Jews designated the totality of the people by the stereotyped expression: "the twelve tribes of Israel." In Rv 7:4–8, these bear the names of the sons of Jacob: Judah, Reuben, Gad, Asher, Naphtali (Manasseh), Simeon, Levi, Issachar, Zebulun, Joseph, Benjamin. The order is different from that found in Genesis, and Manasseh (with Ephraim, an offspring of Joseph) was substituted for Dan (out of which some traditions said that the Antichrist* would come; this was because of the serpent* to which Dan was compared in Gn 49:17).[1]

[1]Gn 35:22-26; Mt 19:28; Rv 7:4-8; 21:12.

tribulation This word gathers together some words with an eschatological* flavor, which are often linked in the N.T.,[1] describing as they do a situation of constraint (Gk. *anagkē*), oppression (Gk. *thlipsis*), crushing (Gk. *stenochōria*): distress and testing* unlike any other. The inheritors of the Danielic* tradition, these expressions are characteristic of times* shaped by the Parousia*:[2] salvation,* in effect, "had" to be preceded by an era of catastrophe: hatred, persecution, betrayal, death, and so forth.[3] The churches, and Paul especially, knew at first hand such tribulation[4] so that they might fill up Christ's sufferings.*[5] All believers will be delivered up to such a generalized distress;[6] knowing this, they ought not show themselves surprised about it,[7] but must withstand the test with endurance and perseverance,* even in a spirit of joy, like a woman about to give birth.[8]

[1]Rom 2:9; 8:35; 2 Cor 6:4; cf. Dt 28:55; Is 8:22; 30:6. [2]Dn 12:1; Mt 24:21 (= Mk 13:19). [3]Dn 2:1,28f., 45; Acts 20:23; 1 Thes 3:3; Rv 2:9,22; 7:14. [4]Acts 11:19; 2 Cor 1:4; 8:2; Phil 4:14; 1 Thes 1:6; 3:7; 2 Thes 1:4; Heb 10:33; Rv 1:9; 2:10. [5]Col 1:24; cf. 2 Cor 1:4; 4:8; 7:4f; 1 Thes 3:7. [6]Mt 13:21 (= Mk 4:17); 24:9. [7]Acts 14:22; 1 Thes 3:4; 1 Pt 4:12. [8]Jn 16:21f.; Rom 5:3-5; 8:35; 2 Thes 1:4,7.

→ persecution—suffering—test, trial, try.

tribunal 1. Gk. *kritērion.* The place where justice is meted out.[1]

[1]Jas 2:6△.

2. Gk. *bēma:* "the judge's seat."[2]

[1]Mt 27:19; Jn 19:13; Acts 18:12,16f.; 25:6,10,17; Rom 14:10; 2 Cor 5:10△.

3. Gk. *hēmera:* "the day (assigned for rendering justice)"; cf. "diet," from the Lat. *dies,* day.[3]

[1]1 Cor 4:3△.

→ Intr. VI. 4.A.

tribune Gk. *chiliarchos* (from *chilioi:* "thousand," and *archos:* "leader"): the leader of a cohort,* an officer.[1]

[1]Acts 21:31–24:22△.

tribute Lat. *tributum:* "a tax* shared out among the tribes," Gk. *phoros* (from *pherō:* "to produce" or "to bring" the) "contribution.[1]"

[1]Lk 20:22; 23:2; Rom 13:6f.☐.

→ tax.

Troas Gk. *(Alexandreia hē) Trōas.* A small city founded some 15 km. [10 mi.] from ancient Troy on the northwest coast of modern Turkey, which had become a Roman colony under Augustus.* A port of embarkation for Macedonia, where Paul had a vision.[1]

[1]Acts 16:8,11; 20:5f.; 2 Cor 2:12; 2 Tim 4:13☐.

→ Intr. IV.2.C.—Map 2.

Trogyllium Gk. *Trōgyllion.* A city of Asia Minor not far from Miletus.*[1]

[1]Acts 20:15☐.

trumpet Gk. *salpinx,* Heb. *shôphâr.* A musical instrument,[1] whether of an animal's horn or made out of metal. According to the representation on the arch of Titus,* a trumpet could be as long as 50 cm. [20 inches]. It was used to give the signal for a battle[2] or a holiday celebration;[3] the N.T. does not mention the feasts* of the new moon* (become the New Year festival in Judaism) or of Kippur.[4] Horn and trumpet made up part of the literary conventions of theophanies* that announced a revelation: that of the Law at Sinai,[5] that of the end of time;[6] according to the book of Revelation, the voice of the powerful God (or of the Son of Man) was like a trumpet,[7] while the seven angels blew on trumpets.[8]

[1]Rv 18:22. [2]Nm 10:9; 2 Chr 13:12,14; 1 Mc 4:40; 1 Cor 14:8. [3]Jl 2:15; Mt 6:2. [4]Lv 23:24; 25:8f.; cf. Nm 10:10; 2 Chr 5:12f.; Ps 98:6. [5]Ex 19:16; Heb 12:19. [6]Mt 24:31; 1 Cor 15:52; 1 Thes 4:16. [7]Rv 1:10; 4:1. [8]Rv 8:2–11:15☐.

trust **1.** Gk. *pepoithēsis* (from the perfect tense *pepoitha* of *peithomai:* "to rely on," whence the fact of "being persuaded, convinced"); *pistis* (from *pith-ti-s*): "the act of giving one's trust." That aspect of faith,* which, faced with an uncertain future, leans indefectibly on God, the solid rock,[1] and on the definitive action through which God conquered death in Jesus. In fact, one can place one's trust also in men[2] or in one's own actions.[3] The translations, consequently, are nuanced: "to delude oneself about" sometimes corresponds to "being convinced of" or else "to be proud of" to "to depend on." At the base of the expression there is the intimate conviction that can bloom into confidence* (Gk. *parrēsia*).

[1]Mt 27:43; Heb 2:13. [2]Lk 18:9; 2 Cor 1:9; 2 Thes 3:4; Phlm 21. [3]Mk 10:24; Lk 11:22; 2 Cor 3:4; Eph 3:12; Phil 1:14; 3:3f.

2. Gk. *tharseō:* "to have confidence," not in another, but in oneself, because fear has been overcome: one is comforted, reassured, encouraged.[4]

[4]Mt 9:2,22; 14:27; Jn 16:33; 2 Cor 5:6,8; Heb 13:6.

3. Gk. *hypostasis:* a "solid foundation" on which one can rest.[5]

[5]2 Cor 9:4; 11:17; Heb 3:14△.

→ anguish—care—confidence—faith.

truth The English word is found at the convergence of two currents of thought. According to Hellenistic tradition, the Greek *alētheia* (from *a* privative, *lanthanō:* "to be hidden for") signified the unveiled reality, the subsistent being that could be known, correspondence between the reality and the spirit. According to Semitic tradition, the Hebrew *emèt* (from *âmân:* "to be solid, stable") designated the one in whom (that in which) one could trust. On one side, an objective reality, a timeless truth; on the other, a relationship that proved itself in the course of time. Another difference: for the Bible it was God, Jesus Christ, who was the truth, the one who withstood the wear of time. For the Greek the opposite of the truth was error* or the lie*: for the Semite, it was the breaking of the bond between two persons.

1. The Synoptics* used the word in the Greek sense. There it was a case of speaking or teaching a truth which conformed to a reality, or of attesting to the fact that one spoke in conformity with the reality.[1]

[1]Mt 14:33; 22:16 (= Mk 12:14 = Lk 20:21); 26:73 (= Mk 14:70 = Lk 22:59); 27:54 (= Mk 15:39); Mk 5:33; 12:32; Lk 16:11.

2. Paul offered a certain number of expressions which draw attention to the Greek, like "to say the truth"[2] or "to be truthful."[3] Ordinarily, he echoed Semitic thinking: what merited trust,*[4] fidelity,*[5] the obedience* due to the truth which was the Gospel.[6] To proclaim "the gospel of truth" was to set a man free by revealing to him that he is bound to his Creator and to Jesus Christ.[7]

[2]Rom 9:1; 2 Cor 12:6; Eph 4:25; 1 Tim 2:7; Jas 3:14. [3]2 Cor 6:8; 7:14; Phil 1:18. [4]Rom 15:8. [5]Rom 3:3-7. [6]Rom 2:8; Gal 2:14; 5:7; 1 Pt 1:22. [7]Rom 1:18,25; 2 Cor 4:2; 6:7; Gal 4:16; 5:7; Eph 1:13; 4:21.

3. The Pastoral Epistles* were still more under the influence of an Hellenistic current, for example with regard to "knowledge* of the truth,"[8] which seems to have consisted in "sound doctrine."[9] The Epistle to the Hebrews went in the same direction, though it additionally contrasted the true (heavenly) with its image* (the earthly).[10] In its turn, the book of Revelation remained within the Semitic current, for it also drew together the "true" with the "holy, faithful, just."[11]

[8]1 Tim 2:4; 2 Tim 2:25; 3:7; Ti 1:1. [9]1 Tim 1:10; 2 Tim 4:3f.; Ti 1:9; 2:1. [10]Heb 8:2; 9:24; 10:22,26. [11]Rv 3:7,14; 6:10; 15:3; 16:7; 19:2,9,11; 21:5; 22:6.

4. For John, truth came into existence in Jesus Christ,[12] truth in person,[13] a truth which he spoke and testified to,[14] so that his words and deeds were the very expression of God.[15] Hence, among those who did not want to do the truth, there was the desire to kill him, something incomprehensible except in a Semitic perspective.[16] The Spirit of truth was charged with the task of witnessing to the justice* of Jesus.[17]

[12]Jn 1:17. [13]Jn 1:9,14; 14:6. [14]Jn 8:40,45f.; 16:7; 18:37. [15]Jn 5:19f.,36f.; 8:19,26,28; 12:50. [16]Jn 3:21; 8:44. [17]Jn 4:23f.; 14:17; 15:26; 16:13.

→ amen—know—lie—yes.

tunic Lat. *tunica,* Gk. *chitōn.* The principal clothing which was worn under the cloak,*[1] a kind of long shirt worn next to the body, with sleeves shortened or close fitting at the wrists. Ordinarily white, it was decorated with colored piping and could be, or appear to be, seamless.[2] One kept it on for work, but tucked it up with the aid of a belt.*[3] Some of them, more festive or solemn, extended down to the feet (in Gk. *podērēs*).[4] The rich sometimes wore a second, sleeveless one.[5]

[1]Sg 5:3; Mt 5:40 (= Lk 6:29); Acts 9:39; Jude 23. [2]Jn 19:23. [3]Ex 12:11; 2 Kgs 4:29; Lk 17:8; Acts 12:8. [4]Gn 37:3; Ex 29:5; 2 Sm 13:18; Wis 18:24; Ez 9:3; Rv 1:13. [5]Mt 10:10 (= Mk 6:9 = Lk 9:3); Mk 14:63; Lk 3:11 □.

→ Intr. VIII.1.B—cloak—clothing.

turtledove Gk. *trygōn.* A bird, defenseless before predatory animals,[1] which made "its voice"[2] heard from springtime until the time of its "return"[3] in autumn. The offering of the poor for rites of purification.[4]

[1]Ps 74:19. [2]Sg 2:12. [3]Jer 8:7. [4]Lv 5:7; 12:6,8; Lk 2:24.

→ dove.

tutor

→ pedagogue.

Twelve Gk. *dōdeka.*

1. A round number.[1]

[1]Mt 9:20 (= Mk 5:25 = Lk 8:43); 14:20 (= Mk 6:43 = Lk 9:17 = Jn 6:13); 26:53; Mk 5:42 (= Lk 8:42); 8:19; Lk 2:42; Jn 11:9; Acts 19:7; 24:11.

2. A perfect number deriving its origin from the Zodiac and from the months of the year. In the Bible, it symbolized the totality of God's people, constituted by the tribes* (Israel)[2] or the Apostles* (the Church).[3] Its square, multiplied by 1,000, symbolized infinity.[4]

[2]Mt 19:28 (= Lk 22:30); Acts 7:8; 26:7; Jas 1:1; Rv 21:12. [3]Mt 19:28; Rv 12:1; 21:12,14,20f.; 22:2. [4]Rv 7:4; 14:1,3.

3. The number designating, probably in memory of the tribes of Israel, the body of disciples chosen by Jesus and sent out with his authority.[5] Also called apostles, they were the foundation stones on which the city of God was built.[6] Their number had to remain complete, a fact which led to the official replacement of Judas* by Matthias.*[7]

[5]Mt 10:1,5; 11:1; 20:17 (= Mk 10:32 = Lk 18:31); 26:14 (= Mk 14:10 = Lk 22:3); 26:20 (= Mk 14:17); 26:47 (= Mk 14:43 = Lk 22:47); Mk 3:14,16; 4:10; 6:7; 9:35; 11:11; 14:20; Lk 8:1; 9:1,12; Jn 6:67,70f.; 20:24; Acts 6:2; 1 Cor 15:5. [6]Mt 10:2; Lk 6:13; 22:30 (= Mt 19:28); Rv 21:14. [7]Acts 1:26 □.

→ numbers.

[type, typology] From the Gk. *typos:* "mark, form, figure, example, model."[1]

[1]Rom 5:14; 1 Cor 10:6,11; Heb 9:24; 1 Pt 3:21; cf. Jn 20:25.

→ figure.

Tyre Gk. *Tyros,* modern-day Sur in Lebanon, from the Heb. *ṣor:* "rock." An ancient port of Phoenicia, situated on an island which Alexander the Great linked up to the continent. A city jealous of its independence until 332 B.C., it regained its freedom beginning in 126.[1]

[1] 2 Sm 5:11; 1 Kgs 5:15-26; Is 23; Ez 26–29; Mt 11:21f.; 15:21f.; Mk 3:8; 7:24,31; Lk 6:17; 10:13f.; Acts 12:20; 21:3,7 □.

→ Map 4.

U

unbelief **1.** Gk. *a-pistia:* "non-belief," lack of trust. In the O.T., this concept was lacking, but not the reality which it signified.[1] In the N.T., the term castigates absence of faith[2] and even insufficient faith.[3]

[1]Is 7:9; 53:1; Jer 4:22ff. [2]Mt 13:58 (= Mk 6:6); 17:17 (= Mk 9:19 = Lk 9:41),20; 21:25 (= Mk 11:31 = Lk 20:5),32; Mk 16:11-17; Lk 22:67; 24:11; Jn 20:27; Acts 14:2; 19:9; 26:8; 28:24; Rom 3:3; 11:20,23; 1 Cor 6:6; 7:12-15. [3]Mk 4:40; 6:6; 9:24; Lk 1:20; 24:41; Rom 4:20.

2. Gk. *oligopistia:* "little faith." This "little faith" could even affect believers. It consisted in a misunderstanding of the signs of the Divine Presence, through refusing to believe and to trust.[4]

[4]Mt 6:30 (= Lk 12:28); 8:26; 14:31; 16:8 △.

→ faith—fidelity—trust.

unchastity

→ prostitution—vices.

unclean

→ pure, impure.

understand, understanding

→ know, knowledge.

underworld

→ netherworld.

unit (literary)

→ literary unit.

universe Unlike the Greeks who saw in the *kosmos* a harmonious and self-contained whole which was intelligible to man, who was, in his turn, a "microcosm" of it, the Bible did not conceive of the universe apart from its relationship with the Creator. Moreover, only at a late date did it use the term *kosmos* to speak of the totality of creation, and John even attached a negative qualification to it; it could indicate the present world* insofar as it was dominated by the power of evil.*[1] To speak of the universe, the Bible ordinarily used the couplet "heaven and earth"[2] which, in addition to tying everything together, looked directly toward the Creator, or else the more summary Hebraic formula "all" (Gk. *ta panta,* Heb. *hakkôl*).[3] After these phrases came the words "inhabited earth" (Gk. *oikoumenē*)[4] and *aiōn* (which also means elapsed time*),[5] occasionally in the plural.[6] God was the Lord of heaven and earth, never of the *kosmos.*[7] Like the world, heaven and earth will pass away,[8] but "all" will be taken up into Christ.[9] Then there will be created a new universe, never called a "new cosmos," but new heavens and a new earth, or the Kingdom of God.[10]

[1]Jn 1:10,29; 7:7; 12:31; 14:17; 16:8,11; 17:9; 1 Jn 2:15-17; 5:19. [2]Gn 1:1; 2:4; Ex 20:11; Ps 146:6; Acts 4:24; 17:24; Heb 1:10; Rv 10:6; 14:7. [3]Ps 8:7; Wis 9:1; Is 44:24; Jer 10:16; 1 Cor 8:6; 15:27f.; Eph 1:10; Phil 3:21; Col 1:16f.,20; Heb 1:2f.; 2:8,10; 1 Pt 4:7. [4]Wis 9:9; 1 Cor 3:22. [5]Mt 24:14; Lk 2:1; 4:5; 21:26; Acts 11:28; 17:6,31; 19:27; 24:5; Rom 10:18; Heb 1:6; 2:5; Rv 3:10; 12:9; 16:14. [6]Heb 1:2; 6:5; 11:3. [7]Gn 24:3; Is 66:1; Mt 5:34; 11:25 (= Lk 10:21); 28:18; Mk 13:27; Acts 7:49; 17:24; 1 Cor 7:31; 1 Jn 2:17. [8]Is 13:13; 51:6; Jer 4:23-26; Am 8:9; Mt 5:18 (= Lk 16:17); 24:35 (= Mk 13:31 = Lk 21:33); Lk 21:25f.; Heb 12:26; 2 Pt 3:10,12f.; Rv 20:11; 21:1. [9]1 Cor 8:5f.; Eph 1:10; Col 1:16,20. [10]Is 65:17; 66:22; 2 Pt 3:13; Rv 21:1.

→ Intr. V.1.—aeon—age—earth—exaltation of Christ—heaven—world.

unleavened bread Gk. *a-zymos:* "not leavened," translating the Hebrew *maṣṣot.*

1. Bread without leaven. These were prepared on the eve of Passover in order to commemorate the meal of the Hebrews eaten during the night of the Exodus.*[1] They were thought to be purer than leavened loaves.[2]

[1]Ex 12:34,39; Dt 16:3. [2]Ex 34:25; 1 Cor 5:7f.△.

2. The Feast of Unleavened Bread: an agricultural feast that lasted seven days (an offering of first sheaves of corn, then an offering of bread without leaven).[3] Since its first day coincided with the Passover (at least from the seventh century B.C.), the feast of Unleavened Bread was spontaneously identified with it.[4]

[3]Ex 12:18; 23:15; Lv 23:6. [4]Dt 16:1-8; Mt 26:17; Mk 14:1,12; Lk 22:1,7; Acts 12:3; 20:6 △.

→ Intr. XIII.3.B.—feast—Passover.

unspiritual man

→ spirit 4.

unwritten sayings (of Jesus)

→ agrapha.

upper room Sometimes known as the "cenacle" from the Latin *cenaculum* (from *cena:* "meal, dinner"): "dining room." Since the thirteenth century, the word referred to the three meeting rooms of the disciples, without our being able to prove that they were one and the same.

1. The "upper room" (Gk. *anagaion,* from *ana:* "above" and *gaia:* "earth, soil"),[1] being extensive and strewn with carpets, became the "living room" (Gk. *katalyma*)[2] where Jesus celebrated the Passover with his disciples.

[1]Mk 14:15 (= Lk 22:12) △. [2]Mk 14:14 (= Lk 22:11); cf. Lk 2:7 △.

2. The place where the disciples gathered together after Jesus' death and where the Risen One appeared to them was not designated by a particular Greek word; it was only "there."[3]

[3]Lk 24:33; Jn 20:19,26.

→ Map 1.

3. The "upper chamber" (Gk. *hyperōon,* from *hyper;* "above") witnessed the 12 disciples gathered together after Jesus' departure, for the election of Matthias and for the descent of the Spirit on the day of Pentecost;[4] it was located on the upper floor of the house, a place which ordinarily received people passing through.[5]

[4]Acts 1:13. [5]Acts 9:37,39; 20:8 △.

→ Intr. VIII.1.A.

vat Gk. *lēnos.* An apparatus, dug out of rock on two levels, to produce wine; hence, its meaning of press.* The lower cistern (Gk. *hypolēnion*), where the must from grapes crushed by feet dripped down, was a figure of God's wrath* and punishment, the wine* being suggestive of blood.[1]

[1]Is 5:2; 63:2f.; Jer 25:30; Mt 21:33; Mk 12:1; Rv 14:19f.; 19:15 □.

→ press—wine.

veil In Gk. *kalymma* (from *kalyptō:* "to cover"). A piece of woven material covering the head and often the face.

1. Ordinarily, a Jewish woman wore a head veil in public according to Oriental custom,[1] one which Paul alludes to.[2] Reasons for this custom are still debated: modesty[3] before marriage,[4] a means of not being recognized,[5] a sign of belonging to a husband.[6] Taking a stand against the customs of the pagan mystery* cults, Paul prescribed the veil in liturgical assemblies.[7]

[1]Is 47:2. [2]1 Cor 11:6. [3]Gn 24:65; Sg 4:1,3. [4]Gn 29:23,25. [5]Gn 38:15,19; 1 Pt 2:16. [6]1 Cor 11:9f. [7]1 Cor 11:5f., 13.

2. A veil could serve to hide the face, either to make fun of someone,[8] or to protect the reflected light of God's glory.[9]

[8]Mk 14:65 (= Lk 22:64). [9]Ex 34:33-35; 2 Cor 3:13-18.

→ clothing—woman.

veil (of the Temple)

→ Temple veil.

vengeance Gk. *ekdikēsis. Dikē* is rule, right, objective justice (*dikaiosynē,* designating subjective justice, a sense of justice); *dikēn didonai,* was to give someone satisfaction, reparation, or meant "to be punished"; *dikēn lambanein,* was to have one's right vindicated, from that, *ekdikēō* meant to ask for or demand justice. To avenge oneself, then, was above all to have restored a justice that had been hurt.

Only the just and savior God could legitimately avenge justice,*[1] he being the one who exercised it not only against Israel's enemies,[2] but even against his very own people.[3] Also, a man was not to avenge himself[4] but was to entrust himself to the "God of Vengeance," who would himself reestablish all things on the last day.[5] Forgiveness* signified just such an abandonment to God.[6] An authority who had received delegation from God could, nonetheless, effect his vengeance.[7] Finally, the word meant the punishing of a guilty party, an outcome of the reestablishing of justice.[8]

[1]Jb 19:25; Lk 18:3-9; Acts 28:4; Rom 3:19; 1 Thes 4:6; 2 Thes 1:8; Heb 10:30; Rv 19:2. [2]Is 47:3; Jer 50:15; 51:36. [3]Is 1:24; Jer 5:9; 9:9; Ez 24:8. [4]Lv 19:17f.; Mt 5:38-42. [5]Ps 94:1; Jer

15:15; 20:12; Rv 6:10. [6]Jer 11:20; Rom 12:19-21. [7]Rom 13:4; cf. Acts 7:24. [8]Lk 21:22; 2 Cor 7:11; 10:6; 2 Thes 1:9; 1 Pt 2:14; Jude 7 □.

→ go'ël—justice—liberate—punishment—save.

Verbum From the Lat. *verbum:* "word," translating the Gk. *logos.* A designation of Jesus proper to the Johannine writings.[1]

[1]Jn 1:1,14; 1 Jn 1:1; Rv 19:13 □.

→ word.

vices **1.** The evil faults and inclinations which religion and morality disapproved of are freely stigmatized in the N.T.: ninety-six terms are used, of which some eighty-three are found in the Pauline corpus (thirty of them found solely in the Pastoral Epistles*).

2. As the popular philosophers and the Stoics* did, and as was the case in Judaism (especially Qumran*), in the N.T. vices are often grouped in lists.[1] It is remarkable that, unlike lists of virtues,* the vocabulary of vices was borrowed from the pagan milieu. But the N.T. conception differs profoundly from the others. According to the Greek world, vices were precipitated by ignorance, foolishness or the weakness of men. According to Qumran, every person's actions corresponded to the spirit which ruled him entirely, whether light or darkness. For the N.T., vices issued from a man's heart[2] or from the "flesh";[3] they were the fruit of sin, not of error. They begot death.[4]

[1]Mt 15:19 (= Mk 7:21f.); Rom 1:29-31; 13:13; 1 Cor 5:10f.; 6:9f; 2 Cor 12:20; Gal 5:19-21; Eph 4:31; 5:3-5; Col 3:5,8; 1 Tim 1:9f.; 6:4; 2 Tim 3:2-5; Ti 3:3; 1 Pt 4:3; Rv 21:8; 22:15. [2]Mt 15:19 (= Mk 7:21). [3]Rom 7:5,18,25; 8:8; 13:14; Gal 5:16-19; Eph 2:3; Col 2:18,23; 1 Pt 2:11; 2 Pt 2:10,18; 1 Jn 2:16. [4]Rom 1:29-31; 8:13; Gal 6:8.

3. The most general term to be used was: "what was not fitting" (Gk. *ta mē kathēkonta*)[5] or "evil" (Gk. *ta ponēra*).[6] Since the lists do not suggest principles for arranging them, we will now attempt to group the vices most often cited within three categories.

[5]Rom 1:28; cf. Eph 5:4. [6]Mk 7:23.

4. Against God. Idolatry,* sacred prostitution,* magic,* sorcery, impiety, blasphemy,* opposition to God, pride,* injustice, folly* or senseless conduct.

Against other persons and common life.• Behavior which produced disunion occupied the largest place. In order of their frequency they were: murder, slander, injuries,* flagrant insults, discord, evil intentions; passionate outbursts and wrath*; jealousy* and envy*; covetousness,* detraction, a quarrelsome spirit, divisions, chicanery, ruses, double-dealing and lies*; false witness,* heartlessness, hypocrisy,* hatred.*• Attacks on the property of others: greed,* avarice, avidity, rapaciousness, theft*.

Against purity in the broad sense.• In general: impurity,* immorality, loose living, unchastity, licentiousness, debauchery,* depravity, sensual delight.• Adultery,* prostitution,* sexual intercourse, homosexuality.• Orgies, drinking bouts, carousing of every kind, foul tricks.

vigilance, be vigilant

→ watch, keep watch.

vine **1.** A shrubby tree (Gk. *ampelos*) producing fruit[1] in clusters (Gk. *botrys*[2]) which we call grapes (Gk. *staphylē*[3]); wine* is the "produce" (Gk. *genēma*) of the vine.[4] Jesus is the true vine to which the branches (Gk. *klēmata*) (which believers are) should remain united, so that they may live and bear fruit* (Gk. *karpos*); otherwise, like barren shoots, they become useless wood.[5]

[1]Jas 3:12. [2]Rv 14:18 △. [3]Mt 7:16; Lk 6:44; Rv 14:18 △. [4]Mt 26:29 (= Mk 14:25 = Lk 22:18) △. [5]Jn 15:1,4,5 △.

2. In continuity with the O.T., Jesus freely depicted God with the traits of an owner of a vineyard (Gk. *ampelōn*), which was the object of his loving care, but disappointed him; he will in turn call on faithful vineyard workers (Gk. *ampelourgos*) who will constitute his true people.[6]

[6]Is 5:1-7; Mt 20:1-8; Mt 21:28,33-41; Mk 12:1-9 (= Lk 20:9-16); Lk 13:6; 1 Cor 9:7 △.

→ Intr. II.5; VII. 1.A—press—vintage—wine.

vinegar Gk. *oxos,* Lat. *posca.* Not what we call vinegar today, but a sour wine* mixed with water, a popular beverage that was given to workers[1] and to soldiers;[2] it was forbidden to Nazirites.*[3] Strongly acidic, this drink was reckoned to be of little worth.[4]

[1]Ru 2:14. [2]Mt 27:48 (= Mk 15:36). [3]Nm 6:3. [4]Ps 69:22; Prv 10:26; Lk 23:36 □.

vintage The N.T., which was familiar with the act of harvesting grapes (Gk. *trygaō*),[1] does not preserve references to the fact that this was a time of joy* for the faithful,[2] but only that it was an image of God's judgment.*

[1]Lk 6:44. [2]Jgs 21:19-21; Is 16:10; Am 9:13. [3]Jer 25:15-30; Rv 14:18f.□.

→ Intr. VII.1.A—harvest—press—vat—vine—wine.

violence Gk. *bias, biazomai.* These words, which are rare in the N.T., are used with the sense of force (Gk. *bia*),[1] constraint (Gk. *parabiazomai*)[2] or of violence properly so called (Gk. *biazō, biastēs*). The derivation of violence may be located in the life force which, in order to maintain itself, tends to destroy the life of others. In the N.T., the violent are attackers, the enemy, those who hinder men from entering the Kingdom, which, henceforward, is "assailed with violence."[3] Luke interpreted Jesus' saying in the opposite sense, attributing to the disciples a violence which they manifest in wrestling their way into the Kingdom.*[4] In any case, the in-breaking of God's Kingdom unleashes violence.

[1]Acts 5:26; 21:35. [2]Lk 24:29; Acts 16:15 △. [3]Mt 11:12 △. [4]Lk 16:16; cf. 13:24 △.

→ combat—greed—hatred—power—zeal.

virgin

1. Gk. *parthenos:* "young girl, virgin,"[1] by extension: "a celibate";[2] metaphorically,* the Church, Christ's bride.[3]

[1]Mt 1:23; 25:1-11; Lk 1:27. [2]Acts 21:9; 1 Cor 7:25-38; cf. Lk 2:36. [3]2 Cor 11:2; Rv 14:4 △

2. Matthew and Luke, independently of one another, related that Mary was a virgin[4] when she conceived Jesus through the Holy Spirit's intervention.[5]

[4]Mt 1:23,25; Lk 1:27. [5]Mt 1:20; Lk 1:34f.; cf. Gn 1:2.

3. Christian virginity indicated the state of life of a celibacy which had been freely welcomed in response to a personal summons from God.[6] Different from marriage, which is reckoned within the sphere of creation's extension, it was a charism* proper to the N.T., in no way obligatory for the community's ministries.[7] It should not be confused with sterility, which is an evil; it was justified by the reign* of God which is coming.[8] In its way, it connotes an integral faithfulness to God alone; whence the use of the term virgin in reference to the Church which has been presented to Christ[9] and to the elect who have kept their faith from all contamination with idolatry or its practices.[10] Virginity prefigured the resurrection* state.[11]

[6]Mt 19:11. [7]1 Cor 7:7f. [8]Mt 19:12; 1 Cor 7:7,26-31. [9]2 Cor 11:2; Eph 5:27. [10]Rv 14:4. [11]Lk 20:35; cf. Mt 22:30 = Mk 12:25.

→ marriage—sterility.

virtue Lat. *virtus* (from *vir,* man): "strength of character leading to courageous deeds." Gk. *aretē,* associated with the prefix *ari-,* indicating excellence (Gk. *aristos*); this excellence varied according to the ideal which one had of man: a warrior (Homer), a citizen (Plato). Afterwards, there may be found the notion of a specific quality exactly appropriate to a person or a thing. The Hebrew language knew no such corresponding word. The Septuagint* used this term for God's glorious deeds (Heb. *tehillâ*).[1] Judeo-Hellenistic literature celebrated the courage, virility, fidelity and prudence of the Maccabean* martyrs.[2] We even find mention of the four Platonic virtues (become the cardinal Christian virtues): temperance and prudence, justice and fortitude.[3] The Qumran* writings offer some affinities with Stoicism* and its catalogues of virtues: submission to God, patience, kindness, strength, wisdom, purity. The "sons of truth" thereby manifest their adherence to the realm of light.

Despite certain verbal similarities, the N.T. conception is quite different. Christian virtue does not have its origin in man, but in the renewal of one's being through faith in Christ and through his Spirit.[4] From then on, there was no Aristotelian kind of distinction between practical and theoretical virtues: good actions were but the expression of an interior attitude. It was not a case of "harmony of soul" allowing the wise man an unruffled life (Plato), but rather it was the fruit of the Spirit, gifts* given to the members of a community for whom the new creation had already begun. Qumran thought of a divine action within the faithful man; Christian newness implied the primacy of love, to which all the other virtues were subordinate, as were the demands that flowed from it. Their harvest was eternal life.[5]

[1]Is 42:8,12; 43:21; 63:7 (taken up in 1 Pt 2:9; cf. 2 Pt 1:3). [2]2 Mc 6:31. [3]Wis 8:7. [4]Gal 5:22-24. [5]Gal 6:7ff.

2. Lists of the virtues[6] contained a mere thirty terms: love, faith, hope, peace, joy, goodness, good-will, gentleness, harmony with others, sympathy, forgiveness, availability, faithfulness, truth, justice, hospitality, humility, steadfastness, patience, self-control, sobriety, purity, holiness of life. The viewpoint was more theological than moral. It would be difficult to assign them to neatly divided categories (God, others, individual conduct). Three, however, enjoyed a place apart and were often grouped together: faith,* charity,* hope.*[7] Animated by faith and enlightened by knowledge of Christ, the believer follows the Spirit.[8]

[6]2 Cor 6:6f.; Gal 5:22f.; Eph 4:2f., 32; 5:9; Phil 4:8; Col 3:12; 1 Tim 4:12; 6:11; 2 Tim 2:22,24f.; 3:10; Ti 1:8; 3:1; 1 Pt 3:8; 2 Pt 1:5-7. [7]1 Cor 13:13; Gal 5:5f.; Col 1:4f.; 1 Thes 1:3; 5:8; Heb 10:22f. [8]Gal 5:25.

3. Virtues. A class of angels → Dominations.

→ Intr. XIV—liberty—love—vices.

vocation Lat. *vocatio:* "call," corresponding to the Gk. *kaleō:* "to name, to call," with or without the prefixes *epi-* or *pros-*.

1. God invites all men to the wedding* banquet of his Son,[1] but all do not answer.[2] Jesus called sinners, in an absolute manner as Matthew and Mark saw it, "to repentance" as Luke specified it.[3] Paul worked out a theology of the divine call. According to his eternal plan,* in total freedom and without any change of heart on his part, God called Jews and pagans,[4] with the result that those who answered could be described as "the called" (Gk. *klētoi*),[5] making up a Church (Gk. *ek-klēsia:* "the convocation").[6] This call did not change one's state of life,[7] but was truly the creation of another order.[8] The believer thus saw himself called to communion* with Jesus, to freedom, hope, to Christ's peace; to the Kingdom, holiness, God's light; to eternal life but, as well, to that suffering which leads to glory.[9]

[1]Mt 22:3-9; Lk 14:16-24; Rv 19:9. [2]Mt 22:14. [3]Mt 9:13 (= Mk 2:17 = Lk 5:32). [4]Acts 2:39; Rom 8:28; 9:24; 11:29; 1 Cor 1:24; 1 Thes 5:24. [5]Rom 8:28; 1 Cor 1:2; Jude 1. [6]Cf. Rom 9:24; 1 Cor 11:18. [7]1 Cor 7:17-24. [8]Rom 4:17; cf. 2 Cor 5:17. [9]1 Cor 1:9; Gal 5:13; Eph 1:18; Col 3:15; 1 Thes 2:12; 4:7; 1 Tim 6:12; 1 Pt 2:9,21; 5:10.

2. God also called individuals with a specific mission in mind; as Abraham, Moses and the prophets[10] did formerly, so, too, Jesus called others to follow* him.[11] And God, through Christ, called one or another (most especially the apostle Paul) to specific tasks.[12]

[10]Gn 12:1; Ex 3:10,16; Is 8:11; Jer 1:2ff.; Heb 11:8. [11]Mt 4:21 (= Mk 1:20); Mk 3:13; 6:7; Lk 9:1. [12]Acts 13:2; 16:10; 1 Cor 1:1; Gal 1:6,15; Phil 3:14.

→ election—follow—name—predestine—send.

voice Gk. *phonē,* Heb. *qôl:* the noise of the wind, of waters, of wings, of thunder,[1] the sound of a word or an instrument,[2] a cry,[3] a human or divine voice.[4]

[1]Jn 3:8; Acts 2:6; Rv 1:15; 9:9; 10:3; 14:2; 18:22; 19:6. [2]Mt 2:18; Lk 1:44; 1 Cor 14:10f. [3]Mt 27:46,50 (= Mk 15:34,37); Lk 23:21,23; Acts 12:22; 21:34; 22:24. [4]Lk 11:27; Acts 7:31; 12:14; Heb 12:26.

1. To hear God's voice and Jesus' is to receive salvation.[5]

[5]Jn 5:25,37; 10:3f., 16,27; 18:37; Heb 3:7; 4:7; Rv 3:20.

2. As in the Canaanite and Babylonian religions, the Bible readily associated God's voice and thunder.[6] After the cessation of prophecy, late Judaism called the *bath qôl,* "the daughter of a voice," one of the modes of God's revelation.* We find its transposition into the "voice from heaven" which made itself heard at Jesus' baptism and transfiguration;[7] John does not mention it, because it is the Precursor's voice that declares who Jesus is;[8] he even presents a radical critique of the voice from heaven.[9]

[6]Ex 19:16-20; 20:18-21; Dt 4:12f., 33; 5:22-24; Jb 37:2-5; Ps 18:14; 29:3-6; Rv 4:5; 6:1; 8:5; 10:3f.; 11:19; 14:2; 16:18; 19:6. [7]Mt 3:17 (= Mk 1:11 = Lk 3:22); 17:5 (= Mk 9:7 = Lk 9:35f.); 2 Pt 1:17f. [8]Jn 1:23. [9]Jn 12:28,30.

→ cockcrow—revelation—word.

vow To bind oneself by a vow (Gk. *euchē,* which also signifies "prayer") was a practice current in Israel[1] and generally in the ancient world; a spontaneous religious act to implore a favor or to render thanks, it bound seriously. The Law and the prophets had to limit its excesses and abuses.[2] The temporary Nazirite* vow[3] included, among other penitential practices, that of not cutting one's hair, a sign of manly strength. At its conclusion, one had to offer sacrifices at the Temple, cut one's hair and burn the locks on the altar.

[1]Acts 18:18. [2]Mt 15:5f. (= Mk 7:11-13). [3]Nm 6; Jgs 13:5; Acts 21:23 □.

→ korban—oath—prayer.

[Vulgate] From the Lat. *vulgata (versio):* "translation in general use." The term refers to the Latin translation of the Bible made by Saint Jerome in the fourth century and officially recognized by the Roman Catholic Church at the Council of Trent in 1546.

vulture Gk. *aetos:* "eagle,*[1] vulture." The Bible distinguished only with difficulty between these two birds of prey, just as we are unable to determine exactly whether it was a case of the bearded gypaetus, the great ashy vulture or the percnopterus. It fed on decaying carcasses,[2] and was an unclean animal.[3] When mention is made of its bald neck, it is more assuredly a reference to the vulture.[4]

[1]Probably in Rv 4:7; 8:13; 12:14. [2]Jb 39:30; Mt 24:28 (= Lk 17:37). [3]Lv 11:13; Dt 14:12. [4]Mi 1:16.

wages Gk. *misthos:* "securities, pay, salary, settlement, fees," whence "mercenary" (Gk. *misthōtos*) and "just retribution" (Gk. *misth-apo-dosia*).

1. The N.T. was familiar with strict retribution: "the worker deserves his pay"[1] and one had to come to agreement with those whom one hired,[2] the "wage-earners."[3] It was a grave sin to hold back a worker's pay.[4] In the figurative sense, wages stand for the ineluctable consequences of an act.[5]

[1]Lk 10:7 (cf. Mt 10:10); Jn 4:36; Rom 4:4; 1 Co 3:8,14; 9:17f.; 1 Tim 5:18; Rv 22:12; cf. Mt 20:8. [2]Mt 20:2; Lk 3:14. [3]Mk 1:20; Lk 15:17,19. [4]Lv 19:13; Dt 24:14; Jas 5:4. [5]Rom 1:27; 6:23; Heb 2:2; 10:35; 2 Pt 2:13.

2. When applied to a relationship with God, retribution* ceased to be governed by the administration of a commutative justice.* While a hireling cares only about his pay,[6] the faithful person accepts everything from God not as something owed him, but as a gift.*[7] Only in this sense does one speak of God as a rewarder, or of a recompense[8] which, in its definitive form, is God himself.[9]

[6]Jn 10:12f. [7]Mt 20:14f.; Rom 4:4f. [8]Mt 5:12; 6:1; 10:41f.; Heb 11:6; Rv 11:18. [9]Mt 6:4-18.

→ Intr. XIV.2.A.—justice—retribution.

wallet In addition to the belt, whose folds served as a wallet,[1] the N.T. mentions the traveling-bag for provisions (Gk. *pēra*),[2] the alms-purse (Gk. *ballantion*)[3] and the portable moneybox, in ancient days a case for musical reeds (Gk. *glōsso-komon*).[4]

[1]Mt 10:9. [2]Mt 10:10 (= Mk 6:8 = Lk 9:3); Lk 10:4; 22:35f. △. [3]Lk 10:4; 12:33; 22:35f. △. [4]Jn 12:6; 13:29 △.

wander away

→ error—seduce.

wash Gk. *niptō:* "to wash," *niptomai:* "to wash one's" face,[1] hands, feet; but not used to refer to washing an object, fishing nets or clothes (in the latter case, Gk. *plynō*).[2]

[1]Mt 6:17; Jn 9:7,11,15. [2]Lk 5:2; Rv 7:14; 22:14 △.

1. The washing of feet was a service obligatorily rendered to the guests whom one welcomed[3] and, ordinarily, it was performed by a non-Jewish slave.*[4] A service which disciples* liked to do for their rabbis* and one which Jesus wanted to do for his disciples: it was a unique example and the symbol* of that sacrifice* which was foundational to the community.[5] A "beautiful work," ever to be performed.[6]

[3]Gn 18:4; Lk 7:38,44. [4]1 Sm 25:41. [5]Jn 13:4-15. [6]1 Tim 5:10.

2. Washing one's hands before meals was a ritual of cultic purity* which Jesus criticized to the degree that it did not symbolize an interior purity.[7] By this same gesture, Pilate* protested his innocence.[8]

[7]Mt 15:2,20 (= Mk 7:2f.). [8]Dt 21:6-8; Ps 26:6; Mt 27:24 △.

→ Intr. VIII.1.C.—bath—pure—water.

watch, keep watch Not to sleep (Gk. *grēgoreō*[1]), to have sleep* taken away (Gk. *agr-hypneō,* indicated below by the letter A), metaphorically stood for "keeping oneself ready,"[2] something which fasting* and sobriety[3] promoted. Motives for these were various: to pray,*[4] to wait for the Day of the Lord,[5] to keep on guard against the Adversary* and against temptation.*[6] Hence, the more general sense of "being on one's guard against" (Gk. *blepō, pros-echō*[8]), "to guard against" (Gk. *phylassō*[9]), "to watch over" (Gk. *episkopeō*[10]).

[1]Mt 26:38,40; Mk 14:34,37; Lk 9:32; 1 Thes 5:10. [2]Mt 25:13; Rv 16:15. [3]2 Cor 6:5(A); 11:27(A); 1 Thes 5:6; 1 Pt 5:8. [4]Mt 26:41; Mk 14:38; Lk 21:36(A); Eph 6:18(A); Col 4:2. [5]Mt 24:42f.; Mk 13:33(A),35; Lk 12:37,39; Acts 20:31. [6]Mt 26:41; Mk 14:38; 1 Cor 16:13; 1 Pt 5:8 △. [7]Mt 24:4ff. [8]Mt 7:15ff. [9]Lk 12:15ff. [10]Heb 12:15; 1 Pt 5:2 △.

watch (of the night) Gk. *phylakē* (cf. *phylassō:* "to keep a guard"). Originally a military watch in the night, with three changes of the guard among the Jews, four among the Romans. In Jesus' time, the Roman division of the night had been adopted by the Jews: the first watch (about six to nine o'clock, evening*), the second (nine to twelve o'clock, midnight*), the third (twelve to three o'clock, cockcrow*), the fourth (three to six o'clock, morning*).

→ cockcrow—evening—hour—morning—night—watch, keep watch—Chart, p. 158.

water Gk. *hydōr.* According to the cosmology of ancient peoples, water rose up from the mysterious depths of the earth or else freely descended from heaven.

1. The great waters, rising up from the primordial ocean,[1] could be terrible and threatening,[2] as were those of the flood*[3] or the waters of the sea.*[4] Like God, Jesus calmed the waves of the sea,[5] walked on and enabled another to walk on the waters.[6] In the waters of the Jordan, where once Naaman* had been purified, Jesus allowed himself to be baptized.[7] Baptism* was the bath* of salvation.*[8]

[1]Gn 1:7; 7:11; Rv 1:15; 14:2,7; 19:6. [2]Ez 26:19f.; Rv 12:15. [3]Gn 6–8; Ex 14–15; 1 Cor 10:1; 1 Pt 3:20; 2 Pt 3:5f. [4]Jb 7:12; Dn 7; Mt 8:32; Rv 13:1. [5]Jb 26:12; 38:8-11; Ps 104:6-9; Jer 5:22; Mt 8:26f. (= Mk 4:39-41 = Lk 8:24f.). [6]Mt 14:25f. (= Mk 6:48f. = Jn 6:19f.); 14:28f. [7]2 Kgs 5:10-14; Mt 3:16 (= Mk 1:10). [8]1 Pt 3:20f.

2. Purifying water, familiar to the Jews in their cultic usages,[9] through baptism effected the remission of sins;[10] it was through the blood* of Jesus that it acquired this purifying* power.[11] Baptism was a bath which washed* completely.[12]

[9]Mt 15:2 (= Mk 7:2); Jn 2:6. [10]Mt 3:11 (= Mk 1:8 = Lk 3:16). [11]1 Jn 5:6,8. [12]Jn 3:5; Eph 5:26; Heb 10:22.

3. Life-giving water. With bread* it sustained life*; it quenched thirst.[13] Flowing water was a fountain (Gk. *pēgē*) and river (Gk. *potamos*) of life; it healed.[14] Along with his blood, it gushed forth from the side of the Crucified One.[15] Baptism was a bath of regeneration.[16] Living water symbolized the Word, the Holy Spirit, Christ himself.[17]

[13]Ex 23:25; 1 Sm 30:11f.; Mt 10:42; Mk 9:41; Lk 16:24; Rv 22:17. [14]Nm 21:17; Is 44:3; Jer 2:13; Ez 36:25-27; Zec 13:1; Jn 4:10f.; 7:38; Rv 7:17; 21:6; 22:1f. [15]Jn 19:34; 1 Jn 5:6-8. [16]Ti 3:5. [17]Jn 4:10,14; 7:38.

→ Intr. V.1—baptism—bath—rain—sea—wash.

way Gk. *hodos.* A path formed little by little through the repeated footsteps of those who used it.

1. God, who guided his people during the Exodus, had his style of life, his behavior, his preferences: so one speaks of "God's ways"[1] and, in the same terms, of his will;[2] they lead to life.[3] Jesus is the true way that leads to life, the path that leads to truth and life, or the true way that leads to the Father.[4]

[1]Ps 25:10; 67:3; Is 40:3; 55:8f.; Mt 3:3; Rom 11:33; Heb 3:10; Rv 15:3. [2]Ps 18:22; 27:11; Mt 21:32; 22:16 (= Mk 12:14 = Lk 20:21). [3]Acts 2:28; 13:10. [4]Jn 14:4-6.

2. A man's "conduct" was called his "way," indicating his manner of living.[5] The theme of "two ways," frequent in literature, is found in the N.T. in its dependence on the O.T.[6] Man, accordingly, seeks to "enter into" the kingdom of heaven.[7] This he can do because Jesus has entered into God's sanctuary.[8]

[5]Acts 14:16; Rom 3:16; 1 Cor 4:17; Jas 1:8; 5:20. [6]Dt 30:9; Prv 8:13; Jer 25:5; Mt 7:13f. [7]Mt 5:20; 18:8f.; 25:21,23. [8]Heb 9:8; 10:19f.; 2 Pt 1:11.

3. In the Acts of the Apostles, the expression "the Way," taken absolutely, was a synonym for the new life found in the Christian faith.[9]

[9]Acts 9:2; 18:25f.; 19:9,23; 22:4,14,22 □.

→ God's plan—God's will—street.

wedding **1.** Gk. *gamos.* Jesus took part in the wedding feast of Cana.[1] The N.T. sees in the great feasting that went into a wedding party a figure of the eschatological* banquet,[2] the wedding feast of the Lamb.*[3] All men are invited to join in it,[4] if they possess a wedding garment.*[5]

[1]Jn 2:1-3. [2]Is 25:6. [3]Rv 19:7,9. [4]Mt 22:9. [5]Mt 22:11f.

2. Gk. *nymphōn* designated rather the wedding hall[6] in which the "sons of the wedding chamber," those who had been invited,[7] gathered together. Those newly married were called *nymphios*[8] and *nymphē.*[9]

[6]Mt 22:10. [7]Mt 9:15 (= Mk 2:19 = Lk 5:34). [8]Mt 9:15 (= Mt 2:19f. = Lk 5:34f.); 25:1,5f., 10; Jn 2:9; 3:29; Rv 18:23. [9]Mt 10:35 (= Lk 12:53); 25:1; Jn 3:29; Rv 18:23; 21:2,9; 22:17 △.

→ Intr. VIII.2.B.—betrothed—marriage—spouse.

weeds

→ darnel.

week A period of seven days, designated by the seventh day: Gk. *sabbaton.*[1] The different days were simply numbered, except for the sixth, which, in the Hellenistic era, was called the Preparation* Day (Gk. *para-skeuē*).[2] Their Roman designation according to planets is not attested until the first century A.D. The week had been determined first of all by the division of the months* according to the moon's phases; later, it took on a shape of its own, containing seven fixed days and existing independently of the moon: it was characterized by the seventh day, or Sabbath.*

[1]Mt 28:1; Mk 16:2,9; Lk 18:12; 24:1; Jn 20:1,19; Acts 20:7; 1 Cor 16:2 △. [2]Mt 27:62; Mk 15:42; Lk 23:54; Jn 19:14,31,42 △. [3]Ex 23:12; 34:21.

→ calendar—month—sabbath.

weeping and grinding of teeth An expression signifying the spite and the wrath of the damned when they are faced with the happiness of the just.[1]

[1]Mt 8:12; 13:42,50; 22:13; 24:51; 25:30; Lk 13:28; cf. Ps 112:10; Lam 2:16; Acts 7:54 □.

→ hell—sadness.

[weights] Israel made use of the talent* (34.272 kg., 75.6 lbs.) the mina* (.571 kg., 1.26 lbs.), the shekel* (11.424 gr., 0.403 oz.) and the half-shekel. In the Hellenistic period these measures were made of lead. Later on, the names of the weights became the names of the coins themselves. The N.T. mentions only the talent* (Gk. *talantiaios*) and the Roman pound* (Gk. *litra* [327.45 gr., 11.5 oz.]).[1]

[1]Jn 12:3; 19:39; Rv 16:21.

→ coins—measures.

wheat Gk. *sitos.* Wheat constituted the chief source of Israel's nourishment, along with wine and oil;[1] it was also exported.[2] Sown in the earth[3] in November–December, the grain was harvested in May–June. According to Pliny,* the yield of wheat around the Mediterranean was exceptional: from 100 and even 400 to one. Sifted in the air,[4] it was gathered into barns.[5] It served as a means of payment,[6] being worth three times more than barley.*[7] The grain was ground to make flour, or grilled to be eaten as grains.

[1]Jer 31:12; Rv 18:13. [2]Acts 27:38. [3]Mt 13:25,29f.; Mk 4:28; Jn 12:24; 1 Cor 15:37. [4]Lk 22:31. [5]Mt 3:12 (= Lk 3:17); Lk 12:18. [6]Lk 12:42; 16:7. [7]Rv 6:6 □.

→ Intr. II.5; VII.1.A.

white Gk. *leukos* (from the same origin as the Lat. *lux, lumen*). The color of dazzling light,* white was, in the world of the Bible, set in opposition to night, which suggested darkness.* It could signify purity* and innocence,[2] but more often it was harmonized with the feasts of joy* and triumph:[3] it was also the color of glorious,* heavenly[4] or transfigured*[5] beings.

[1]Mt 17:2. [2]Ps 51:9; Is 1:18; Rv 3:4,18. [3]2 Mc 11:8; Eccl 9:8; Rv 2:17; 6:2,11; 7:9,13f.; 19:11,14. [4]Dn 7:9; Mt 28:3 (= Mk 16:5); Jn 20:12; Acts 1:10; Rv 1:13f.; 4:4; 14:14; 20:11. [5]Mt 17:2 (= Mk 9:3 = Lk 9:29); Rv 3:5; cf. Mt 5:36; Jn 4:35 □.

→ white pebble—wool.

white pebble The white pebble (Gk. *psēphos leukē*) of Rv 2:17 can correspond to divers ancient objects: an admission token, a tribunal's acquittal tablet, a divination instrument or talisman (Ex 28:30). The color white was associated with an idea of happiness (Pliny*: "a happy day marked with a white stone") or victory. That was the meaning of the new name* written on the stone.

widow Gk. *chēra:* "empty, deprived of."

1. Permanent widowhood, truly directed to God's service, was preferable, according to Paul, to remarriage,[1] especially when it was institutionally vowed to the community's service.

[1]1 Cor 7:8, 39f.; cf. Lk 2:36f. [2]1 Tim 5:5-16.

2. According to the Law, to come to the aid of widows—persons who were without support and who were exposed to injustice[3] and misery[4]—was an essential act of piety.[5] The primitive Church practiced this and recommended it.[6]

[3]Lk 20:47. [4]Mk 12:42f. (= Lk 21:2f.). [5]Ex 22:21f.; Is 1:17. [6]Acts 6:1; 1 Tim 5:3f.; Jas 1:27.

→ Intr. VIII.2.B.e.—levirate—woman.

wind Gk. *anemos, pneuma* (from *pneō*: "to blow").

→ Intr. II.4.—spirit.

will

→ testament.

will of God

→ God's will.

wine **1.** Among Jews, wine (Gk. *oinos*) was not in daily use; it was the drink of feast days: it gladdened men's hearts[1] and foretold the eschatological* banquet.[2] One was not to abuse it,[3] while knowing how to use it for one's health.[4]

[1]Jgs 9:13; Ps 104:15; cf. Rv 6:6; 18:13. [2]Is 25:6; Mt 26:29 (= Mk 14:25 = Lk 22:18). [3]Sir 31:25-31; Eph 5:18; 1 Tim 3:3,8; Ti 1:7; 2:3; 1 Pt 4:3. [4]Lk 10:34; 1 Tim 5:23; cf. Mt 27:34 (= Mk 15:23).

2. Unlike John the Baptist,[5] Jesus did not abstain from wine;[6] he knew both the acidity of a wine that was too fresh as well as the excellence of an old wine.[7] At Cana, he himself supplied a wine that was better and in great supply.[8]

[5]Nm 6:3f.; Jgs 13:4; Lk 1:15; 7:33. [6]Mt 11:19 (= Lk 7:34). [7]Mt 9:17 (= Mk 2:22 = Lk 5:37f.); Lk 5:39. [8]Jn 2:3,9,10.

3. In the N.T., wine never appears in a cultic context, except during Jesus' last meal where it was called the "fruit of the vine"[9] and in a context of dietary controversies.[10] Metaphorically, it stood for God's wrath* at the end of time.[11]

[9]Mt 26:29 (= Mk 14:25 = Lk 22:18). [10]Rom 14:21. [11]Is 51:17,22; Ez 23:31ff.; Rv 14:8,10; 16:19; 17:2; 18:3; 19:15 □.

→ Intr. VIII.1.D.—cup—myrrh—vices—vine—vintage.

wineskin Gk. *askos.* A goatskin, sewn in the shape of a pouch, intended to hold, carry or preserve some liquid. A skin that had once contained new wine* could not receive any more, because a second fermentation would cause it to burst.[1]

[1]Jb 32:19; Mt 9:17 (= Mk 2:22 = Lk 5:37f.) □.

winnowing fan Gk. *ptyon.* An agricultural implement used to sort out the heavier grain from the lighter husks and the straw in the chopped-up ears. The term sometimes refers to a fork with several teeth (or a shovel), sometimes to a flat-bottomed basket.[1]

[1]Is 30:24; Jer 15:7; Mt 3:12; Lk 3:17 □.

→ Intr. VII.1.A.

winter The season of rains, lasting from about October 15 to May 15.[1] The Greek word *cheimōn* also means stormy weather or a tempest.[2] The N.T. speaks about wintering.[3]

[1]Mt 24:20 (= Mk 13:18); Jn 10:22; 2 Tim 4:21. [2]Mt 16:3; Acts 27:18,20 □. [3]Acts 27:12; 28:11; 1 Cor 16:6; Ti 3:12 △.

→ Intr. II.4.—summer—year.

wisdom **1.** In Stoic* or popular Hellenism, as in the ancient Orient, wisdom (Gk. *sophia,* Heb. *hôkmâ*) described a behavioral mode that was attributed to a certain knowledge (Gk. *sophos:* "skillful, prudent"). According to the Bible, the sage was a technician of class, a good architect[1] or, also, a man amply endowed with instruction.[2] Above all else, he knew how to conduct himself with the skill to succeed in life.[3] This nuance was also conveyed by the term *phronimos:* "prudent, circumspect."[4] At the source of wisdom was to be found a divine gift, namely fear* of God.[5] Jesus was a wise man, a teacher of wisdom: proverbs, parables, rules for life which shocked his contemporaries;[6] there was even his assertion that "there is here a greater than Solomon."[7]

[1]Ex 35:31; 1 Cor 3:10. [2]1 Kgs 5:9-14; 1 Cor 6:5. [3]Prv 8:12-21. [4]Prv 14:6; Sir 21:21-26; Mt 7:24; 10:16; 24:45 (= Lk 12:42); 25:2-9; Lk 16:8; Rom 11:25. [5]Prv 9:10; Is 11:2; Lk 21:15; Acts 6:3,10; 7:10. [6]Mt 13:54 (= Mk 6:2); Lk 2:40,52. [7]Mt 12:42.

2. The personified Wisdom of the O.T.[8] was discernible within the deeds of Jesus;[9] when Jesus called little ones to himself it was not so that a teacher of wisdom might offer them recipes for life, but rather it was a case of the Son revealing God's secrets,[10] the one who became God's wisdom[11] through his sacrifice.

[8]Prv 8:22-31; Wis 7:25f.; Lk 11:49. [9]Mt 11:19 (= Lk 7:35). [10]Mt 11:25-30; Jn 6:35; cf. Prv 9:5; Sir 24:19-21. [11]1 Cor 1:24-30; Col 2:3.

3. By calling not the wise of this world but the little ones,[12] God condemned the human wisdom which claimed to know everything[13] and offered salvation through the folly* of the cross.[14] Also, the one who receives the Wisdom from above[15] can taste* and communicate spiritual things;[16] he conducts himself with a sense of proportion, level-headedness and good sense.[17]

[12]Mt 11:28-30; cf. Dn 2:28-30. [13]1 Cor 1:19f.; 3:19f. [14]1 Cor 1:17-25; 4:10. [15]Eph 1:8,17; Jas 1:5; 3:13-17. [16]1 Cor 2:6-16; 12:8. [17]Eph 5:15; Col 4:5.

→ Intr. IX.4; XII.3.—cross—folly—know—philosophy.

[Wisdom (Book of)] A sapiential Greek deuterocanonical* writing, fictitiously attributed to Solomon, which was composed at Alexandria about the year 50 B.C. Its doctrine was that of the O.T., presented under a Hellenized cloak for the consideration of Diaspora* Jews; thus, faith in the resurrection of the dead was expressed in terms of a belief in immortality.*

→ Intr. XII.3.—Chart, p. 65.

witness Gk. *martys, martyria.*

1. In a trial* context, someone testifies to the existence of a deed or its meaning to an audience who is unaware of it and cannot verify it by sight. Such was the case in the term's usage by Paul, Matthew or Mark: to witness to God's justice,*[1] Jesus' resurrection,[2] Jesus' messianic activity,[3] the authenticity of Paul's behavior.[4] The Jews required two witnesses to render a statement valid.[5] One also finds a weakened sense of it meaning "to attest."[6]

[1]Rom 3:21. [2]1 Cor 15:15. [3]Mt 8:4 (= Mk 1:44 = Lk 5:14); 10:18 (= Mk 13:9 = Lk 21:13); Mk 6:11. [4]Rom 1:9; 9:1; 2 Cor 1:23; Phil 1:8; 1 Thes 2:5,10, [5]Dt 17:6; 19:15; Mt 18:16; 26:60; Jn 8:17; 1 Tim 5:19; Heb 10:28. [6]Rom 10:2; 2 Cor 8:3; Gal 4:15; Col 4:13.

2. According to Luke, Jesus, faithful to the Isaianic tradition,[7] established out of the college of the Twelve* his own witnesses;[8] witnesses not only to his resurrection, but also, by reason of a special election,[9] to his earthly life as well. The Holy Spirit was with them witnessing.[10] Paul and Stephen were also called witnesses.[11] The Twelve identified the Risen One with Jesus of Nazareth; Paul identified him with the Church, Stephen with the heavenly witness who assists us. The testimony of the disciples relied on the prophets,[12] the Holy Spirit,[13] the Lord Jesus.[14] It concerned the resurrection of Jesus,[15] his messianic status,[16] his public life,[17] his lordship,[18] the kingdom of God.[19] It was brought before the people,[20] the leaders,[21] the nations,[22] to Jerusalem,[23] to Rome,[24] before the little and the great.[25]

[7]Is 43:8-13. [8]Lk 24:48; Acts 1:8; 10:41; 13:31. [9]Acts 1:21-26. [10]Acts 3:15; 5:32; cf. Jn 15:27. [11]Acts 22:20; 26:16. [12]Acts 10:43; 13:22. [13]Acts 5:32; 20:23. [14]Acts 14:3; 15:8. [15]Acts 4:33. [16]Acts 18:5. [17]Acts 10:42. [18]Acts 20:21. [19]Acts 28:23. [20]Acts 2:32,40; 13:31. [21]Acts 3:15; 5:32. [22]Acts 10:39-42. [23]Acts 22:18. [24]Acts 23:11. [25]Acts 26:22.

3. In John, the word acquires a special significance. In a unique sense, Jesus was a witness to the truth,*[26] to what he had seen and heard in the presence of the Father.[27] John the Baptist, the works of Jesus, the Father himself, each grounded its own testimony.[28] One had to accept it, under pain of making God out to be a liar.[29] In the believer's heart the Holy Spirit bore testimony to Jesus,[30] about his divine sonship and about the justice of his cause.[31] John joined together Paul's affirmations,[32] and the book of Revelation resumed it in making Jesus out to be the Faithful Witness.[33]

[26]Jn 18:37. [27]Jn 3:11,32f. [28]Jn 5:19-47. [29]1 Jn 5:9-11. [30]Jn 15:26. [31]Jn 16:8-11. [32]Rom 8:16; Heb 10:15. [33]Rv 1:5; 3:14.

4. The ultimate testimony was that of blood,* which the two witnesses poured out after they had prophesied.[34] In English we even refer to a witness by the same Greek designation "martyr"; a witness is associated with the destiny of the one to whom he witnesses.[35]

[34]Rv 11:3-12. [35]Rv 2:13; 17:6; 22:20.

→ Intr. VI.4.C.a.—confess—martyr.

woe Gk. *ouai,* Heb. *ôy, hôy.* An onomatopoeic word signifying the sad declaration of a woeful state[1] or the foretelling of a misfortune to come.[2] Not to be confused with a curse* (Gk. *ara*) which communicates misfortune.

[1]Mt 11:21 (= Lk 10:13); 23:13-29 (= Lk 11:42-52); Lk 6:24-26; 1 Cor 9:16; Rv 9:12; 11:14. [2]Mt 18:7 (= Lk 17:1); 24:19 (= Mk 13:17 = Lk 21:23); 26:24 (= Mk 14:21 = Lk 22:22); Jude 11; Rv 8:13; 12:12; 18:10,16,19 □.

woman Gk. *gynē:* "woman, wife."

1. On the status of women in Israel, → Intr. VI.1.A.b; VIII.2.A; VIII.2.B.c-e; XIII.2.B.a.

2. Through the liberty of his outlook toward women, Jesus stood out in sharp contrast with his age. He did not fear associating with them in public[1] and restored them to health.[2] He let himself be followed by them,[3] confided a mission to Mary of Magdala,[4] cited women as examples[5] or marveled at their faith;[6] but he also knew them to be capable of adultery.*[7] The Pastorals* remind them of certain evil propensities,[8] while Paul, from his contact with pagans, stigmatized their homosexual relationships.[9]

[1]Mt 26:7 (= Mk 14:3); Lk 7:37-50; 10:38f.; Jn 4:27; 8:3-11. [2]Mt 8:14 (= Mk 1:30f. = Lk 4:38f.); 9:20 (= Mk 5:25 = Lk 8:43); 15:22 (= Mk 7:25); Lk 8:2; 13:11. [3]Lk 8:1-3; 23:55. [4]Jn 20:17. [5]Mt 13:33; 25:1-13; Lk 15:8. [6]Mt 15:28; cf. Lk 1:28. [7]Mk 10:12. [8]1 Tim 4:7; 5:3-16; Ti 2:3-5; 1 Pt 3:1-6. [9]Rom 1:26.

3. The primitive community described the role taken by women in the events of the crucifixion,[10] burial[11] and discovery of the empty tomb,[12] then, especially in the Greek world, within the life of the community[13] (notably by widows*[14] or deaconesses[15]). So, even if no contempt was directed at her, it remains a fact that a woman was not freed of dependence on her father[16] or husband[17] or from the secondary status she occupied in the official teaching of the Church,[18] a feature which may be dependent on the social context of the period. On the other

hand, in the new context established by Jesus, the distinction between the sexes has been overcome[19] and woman becomes man's equal.[20] Moreover, her worth is no longer tied to her physical fruitfulness, as it was in the first creation and according to the enduring O.T. tradition:[21] with Christ's call she may be invited to remain a virgin.*[22] In any case, it is always in a community, either conjugal or ecclesial, that woman plays her part.

[10]Mt 27:55 (= Mk 15:40 = Lk 23:49 = Jn 19:25). [11]Mt 27:61 (= Mk 15:47 = Lk 23:55). [12]Mt 28:1-8 (= Mk 16:1-8 = Lk 24:1-10). [13]Acts 1:14; 5:14; 9:36,41; 12:12; 16:14f.; 18:26; 1 Tim 3:11; 5:1f.; Ti 2:3; 1 Pt 3:1. [14]1 Tim 5:3,9. [15]Rom 16:1. [16]1 Cor 7:36-38. [17]1 Cor 11:3,7; Eph 5:22f.; Col 3:18; Ti 2:5; 1 Pt 3:1. [18]1 Cor 14:35f.; 1 Tim 2:11f. [19]Gal 3:28. [20]1 Tim 2:9f. [21]Cf. Gn 3:20. [22]1 Cor 7:8,25-40.

4. In continuity with the O.T., the book of Revelation dreads the woman like Jezebel,* the Great Prostitute, the representation of idolatry.*[23] But above all, it held up as a figure* of the Church, the Woman above all others,[24] which a common interpretation identified with Mary,* the believer.[25]

[23]1 Kgs 11:1-8; Sir 47:19; Rv 2:20; 17. [24]Rv 12; 19:7f; 21:2,9. [25]Cf. Lk 1:45.

→ Intr. VIII.2.B.—man—mother—sterility—virgin—widow.

wool Gk. *erion.* One of the riches of the Orient.[1] Used for underclothing, dyed[2] or white as snow[3]—hence, a symbol of purity.*[4]

[1]2 Kgs 3:4; Ez 27:18. [2]Heb 9:19. [3]Ps 147:16; Dn 7:9; Rv 1:14. [4]Is 1:18 □.

word Gk. *logos* (occasionally *rhēma*), Heb. *dâbâr.* According to the Bible, which agreed with the Oriental mind, there were two principal notes which characterized the word. Word and reality were indissolubly united, such that *dâbâr* meant equally a word (account, commandment) and a thing (reality, affair). There was no word which was not a reality; there was no reality which was communicable without a word. In addition, word and action were bound together: to speak was to act, something true above all of the God who created by his word.

1. The word of God, which effected what it proclaimed,[1] was living and effective.[2] It revealed the meaning of creation and became a saving commandment*;[3] it promised salvation to those whom it summoned.[4]

[1]Ps 33:9; Wis 9:1; Is 55:10f. [2]Heb 4:12. [3]Ex 20:1-17; Ps 119. [4]Acts 13:26.

2. Jesus, unlike the prophets,* did not introduce his words by alluding to the Word of God;[5] he declared: "But I say to you."[6] With a word, his speech worked miracles,*[7] forgave sins,[8] transmitted his personal power[9] and perpetuated his presence.[10] Like God's, his word summoned those who heard it and people had to decide for or against.[11] Today, as formerly, men are divided as they encounter this word.[12]

[5]Am 1:6; cf. Lk 3:2. [6]Mt 5:22,28ff. [7]Mt 8:8, 16; Jn 4:50-53. [8]Mt 9:1-7 (= Mk 2:3-12 = Lk 5:18-25). [9]Mt 18:18; Jn 20:23. [10]Mt 26:26-29 (= Mk 14:22-25 = Lk 22:15-20). [11]Mt 7:24-27; 13:23. [12]Mk 8:38 (= Lk 9:26); Acts 13:46; 1 Thes 1:6.

3. The Word, without a qualifier, ended up by meaning not exactly Jesus' words,[13] but the gospel message proclaimed in Christian preaching.[4] This word was heir to the prerogatives of the Word of God itself: salvation, effectiveness, life (for, when preached, it was the very word of Jesus[15]). So, too, this word in its turn effects a division among men.[16]

[13]Lk 4:36. [14]Acts 4:29,31; 6:2,4; 8:4,25; Gal 6:6. [15]Rom 10:17. [16]2 Cor 2:14-17.

4. According to John, in keeping with the wisdom tradition[17] and following the Epistle to the Hebrews,*[18] the subsistent Word of God pre-existed the creation which it authored;[19] following upon earlier miscarriages of the Word, in latter days it took on features, became flesh.*[20] Moreover, it longed to invite men to recognize the Father in Jesus and to better comprehend their common word.[21]

[17]Prv 8:22-31; Sir 24:7-19. [18]Heb 1:1-4. [19]Jn 1:1-3. [20]Jn 1:11,14. [21]Jn 3:34; 12:50; 17: 8,14.

5. Men receive numerous suggestions about their language in the wisdom tradition.[22] James follows the same line of approach,[23] while Jesus also had recommended a radical sincerity;[24] out of the abundance of one's heart the mouth speaks.[25]

[22]Ps 39:2; 141:3; Sir 28:13-26. [23]Jas 1:19; 3:2-12. [24]Mt 5:33; 2 Cor 1:17f.; Jas 5:12. [25]Lk 6:45.

→ Intr. XII—preach—revelation—truth—Verbum.

work, working Gk. *ergazomai* (from *ergon:* "work"), *kopiaō:* "to work, to take the trouble, to tire oneself out," derived from *kopos:* "labor."

1. Although the N.T. rarely recommends working,[1] this was because it presupposed the Creator's commandment to have been observed.[2] Jesus had been a carpenter* (Gk. *tektōn*)[3] and he drew his teaching from the world of work;[4] one was not to be "frightened" (Gk. *oknēros*) in one's use of talents,[5] without, however, surrendering oneself to the lure of gain or to excessive cares.*[6] Paul took the trouble to work with his hands[7] and he castigated the behavior of lazy types who passively waited for the end of time.[8] Workers deserved their wages.[9]

[1]Eph 4:28; Col 3:23; 1 Thes 4:11. [2]Gn 1:28; 2:15; Prv 6:6-11; Sir 22:1f.; 38:34. [3]Mk 6:3. [4]Mt 4:19; 20:1-8; 21:28. [5]Mt 25:26. [6]Lk 10:41f.; 12:13-34. [7]Acts 18:3; 1 Cor 4:12; 1 Thes 2:9; 2 Thes 3:8. [8]Eph 4:28; 2 Thes 3:10-12. [9]Rom 4:4; 1 Tim 5:18; Jas 5:4.

2. God's service* and that of the Gospel required laborers[10] who earned their keep[11] and who, like Paul, had to toil without counting the cost.[12]

[10]Mt 9:37f. (= Lk 10:2); Phil 3:2. [11]Mt 10:10 (= Lk 10:7). [12]Acts 20:35; Rom 16:6,12; 1 Cor 3:8; 15:10; 16:16; 2 Cor 6:5; 10:15; 11:23,27; Gal 4:11; Phil 2:16; Col 1:29; 1 Thes 2:9; 3:5; 5:12; 1 Tim 4:10; 5:17; Rv 14:13.

works By working* (Gk. *ergazomai, poieō, prassō*) a man produced "works" (Gk. *erga,* the plural of *ergon*), and he possessed a certain "conduct" (Gk. *praxis*); the word "work" denoted an action that had religious significance.

1. Jesus accomplished his Father's works,[1] which were also his own;[2] only faith perceived them behind the signs* or miracles of Jesus.[3] Jesus' unique work was the salvation of men through the cross.[4] It revealed the Father through his Son.[5]

[1]Jn 5:36. [2]Jn 14:10. [3]Jn 12:37. [4]Jn 17:4. [5]Jn 14:9f.

2. Man accomplishes good works and evil works.[6] Jesus, the world's light, acts as a revealer of good works,[7] so that the unique work to be done is believing in the one whom God has sent.[8] God rewards everyone according to his conduct.[9] According to Paul, one needs to know that it is not works but faith alone which is the source of justification and salvation;[10] but, along with John and James, he knew that one had to add that faith without works is dead;[11] the only good work is charity operative in faith.[12]

[6]Mt 5:16; 23:3; Rom 8:13; Gal 5:19-21; Rv 2:2,5f., 19,22f.; 3:1f.,8,15; 14:13; 18:6. [7]Jn 3:19-21; Eph 5:6-14; 1 Jn 3:12. [8]Jn 6:28f. [9]Mt 16:27; 1 Pt 1:17; Rv 20:12f.; 22:12. [10]Rom 3:27f.; 4:2,6; Gal 2:16; 3:2,5,10. [11]Jas 2:14,17f., 20-26; 1 Jn 3:18. [12]Gal 5:14; 1 Thes 1:3.

→ Intr. XIV.1.B—justification—work.

world Gk. *kosmos* (from *kosmeō:* "to order, arrange") and *aiōn* (A) (Heb. *'ôlâm:* "time which lasts" and "the spatial world").

1. The universe.*[1]

[1]Wis 9:9; Jn 1:10; 17:5; 21:25; Acts 17:24; Rom 8:22; 1 Cor 3:22.

2. The place where men live,[2] into which one comes,[3] one exists,[4] out of which one departs,[5] or, with a temporal shade of meaning, that which is to come.[6]

[2]Mt 4:8 (cf. Lk 4:5); 16:26 (= Mk 8:36 = Lk 9:25); 26:13; Lk 12:30 (cf. Mt 6:32); Acts 1:8; Rom 1:8; 4:13. [3]Jn 1:9; 3:19; 11:27; 12:46; Rom 5:12f.; 1 Tim 1:15; Heb 10:5; 1 Jn 4:1; 2 Jn 7. [4]Jn 1:10; 9:5; 17:11; 1 Cor 5:10; 2 Cor 1:12; 1 Jn 3:17; 4:17. [5]1 Cor 5:10; Jn 13:1. [6](A) Mt 12:32; Mk 10:30; Lk 20:35; Eph 1:21; Heb 6:5.

3. The place in which the redumption of man occurs. Paul and John elaborated a theology of the history of salvation in the world. Through sin* the existing world is evil, because it has fallen into the power of the god of the world, the Evil One, the Prince* of this world.[7] Ambiguous reality that it is, the world still testifies to its Creator,[8] but it is opposed to God by its spirit, its wisdom, its peace;[9] it knows neither God nor Jesus, for it hates them both.[10] But Jesus, sent by the God who loves the world,[11] has saved the world by conquering it;[12] he takes away the sin of the world[13] through giving his flesh* so that it might live.[14] The world, weighed down with sin, is in the process of passing away;[15] it is not on its way to being a "new cosmos," but rather must still be judged and assumed into the Kingdom of God.[16] The believer has also overcome the world by his faith.[17] Doubtless he remains *in* the world, but, like Jesus, he is no longer *of* the world[18] and must keep himself from the Evil One.[19] Accordingly, like a lamp that has been lighted,[20] he learns the proper use of the world and cooperates in its transformation.[21]

[7]Jn 12:31; Rom 3:19; 5:12f.; 1 Cor 2:6,8 (A); 4:4 (A); Gal 1:4 (A); 4:3; 1 Jn 5:19. [8]Jn 1:3; Acts 17:24; Heb 1:2 (A); 11:3 (A). [9]Jn 14:27; 1 Cor 1:20f.; 2:12; 3:19; 2 Cor 7:10; Jas 2:5; 4:4. [10]Jn 1:10; 7:7; 14:17; 15:18f.; 17:25; 1 Jn 3:13. [11]Jn 3:16; 10:36; 17:18,21,23; 1 Jn 4:9. [12]Jn 3:17; 4:42; 12:47; 16:11,33; 1 Jn 4:14. [13]Jn 1:29; 2 Cor 5:19; 1 Jn 2:2. [14]Jn 6:51. [15]1 Cor 7:31; 1 Jn 2:17. [16]Cf. Jn 13:1; 16:28; 1 Cor 6:2. [17]1 Jn 5:4f. [18]Jn 8:23; 9:5; 17:11,15f.; 1 Cor 5:10; 1 Jn 4:5. [19]Jn 17:15; Rom 12:2(A); 1 Jn 2:15; 5:5. [20]Phil 2:15. [21]1 Cor 7:29-31.

→ aeon—age—universe.

worm **1.** Gk. *skōlēx.* An insect which attacks organic matter, whether living or in a state of decomposition. Abdominal pains were attributed to an infection of worms, which, after having been cast out of the body, signified death.[1] A symbol of the total decomposition of the unrighteous on the last day.[2]

[1]2 Mc 9:9; Acts 12:23. [2]Is 14:11; 66:24; Mk 9:48 △.

2. Gk. *brōsis,* a word used in place of *brōma* to speak of "nourishment,"[3] but also of "what eats away": a "worm" or "rust."[4]

[3]Jn 4:32,34. [4]Mt 6:19f. △.

→ moth.

worship **1.** Gk. *latreia/latreuō* (from *latron:* "wages"): "to be a hired servant," "salaried work, hired service, cultic service," with the ambivalence of the Heb. *'abôdâ:* "work, cultic service." In relation to the Septuagint,* the N.T. shows a clear evolution. It agrees with it when it uses this term to refer to worship of false gods[1] or, in various ways, to the worship in Israel,[2] more particularly so in retaining its interior aspect of faith or prayer.[3] On the other hand, when it is applied to Christians, the cultic term has something else in mind: when rendered by the Holy Spirit,[4] it designates the apostolic ministry or Paul's prayer.[5] More generally, the one who was faithful had to offer a "reasonable worship" (Gk. *logikē*),[6] that is, either a worship that was not formal or, better, worship that consisted in offering not animal victims, but a "living victim" (Gk. *thysia zōsa*), namely a life of authentic charity.[7]

[1]Acts 7:42; Rom 1:25. [2]Mt 4:10 (= Lk 4:8 = Dt 6:13); Lk 1:74; 2:37; Acts 7:7 (= Ex 3:12); 26:6f.; Rom 9:4; Heb 8:5; 9:9; 10:2; 13:10. [3]Dt 10:12f.; 11:13; Dn 6:11-16; Acts 24:14. [4]Phil 3:3. [5]Rom 1:9; 2 Tim 1:3. [6]Rom 12:1. [7]Heb 12:28; cf. 13:1-6.

2. Gk. *leitourgia/leitourgeō* (from *laos:* "people" and *ergon:* "work, labor"): "public service,[8] mutual aid, cultic service." Here again, the N.T. does not follow the Septuagint practice, except to speak of the service or the ministers of Israel: that of Moses,[9] and of Zechariah,[10] or that of Christ who sacrificed himself.[11] Only once is the word employed to designate Christian worship;[12] ordinarily, when applied to Christians, it no longer has a properly cultic tone: it describes that service of mutual aid, which the collection* and almsgiving[13] were, thereby conferring on it the status of divine service.

[8]Rom 13:6. [9]Heb 9:21; 10:11. [10]Lk 1:23. [11]Heb 8:2,6. [12]Acts 13:2. [13]Rom 15:27; 2 Cor 9:12; Phil 2:25,30.

3. The same evolution in the use of various other terms shows how, even if they still have cultic significance when they have to do with Israel, these terms signify the personal action of Christ or of Christian life in general. So, there is still talk of a "sacrifice or victim" (Gk. *thysia*) with reference to Abel, to the golden calf or to the prescribed levitical sacrifices;[14] by contrast, Christ's sacrifice was not an instance of a ritual victim, but this meant his very own death and his glorification.[15] As far as Christians were concerned, their sacrifice consisted in their lives, their deaths, their alms.[16] These were the "spiritical sacrifices" offered by a "priestly people": prayer and charity.[17] Similarly with the "offering" (Gk. *prosphora*), a word which had ritual worth in the context of Jewish customs;[18] it signified Christ's freely willed offering[19] and, in the case of Christians, apostolic ministry or charity.[20] Finally, the same was true of priestly* vocabulary (Gk. *hiereus/hiereumata*): there was discussion of Jewish priests and Jesus Christ, the High Priest,*[21] but never of an individual Christian priest; it was the people of God which, having received a royal priesthood,[22] was, in its entirety, the priest.

[14]Mk 12:33; Lk 2:24; Acts 7:41f.; Heb 11:4. [15]Eph 5:2; Heb 9:23,26; 10:12,26. [16]Rom 12:1; Phil 2:17; 4:18. [17]Heb 13:15; 1 Pt 2:5. [18]Acts 21:26; 24:17. [19]Eph 5:2; Heb 10:10,14. [20]Rom 15:16; Phil 2:17; 4:18. [21]Mt 8:4; Heb 2:17. [22]1 Pt 2:5,9; Rv 1:6; 5:10; 20:6 △.

4. In his own way, John showed that Jesus abolished the former sacrifices by becoming himself the Holy Temple*[23] and by making room for worship in spirit and truth.[24]

[23]Jn 2:15,21. [24]Jn 4:20-24.

→ Intr. IV.6.A; XIII.—adore—ministry—pray—present—priesthood—sacrifice—serve.

wrath Gk. *orgē* and *thymos,* both translating the Heb. *aph:* "nose, angry outburst, furor, wrath."

1. Except in the case of "holy wrath,"[1] angry flare-ups and wrath were unreservedly deserving of condemnation.[2]

[1]1 Kgs 18:40; Jer 6:11; Mk 3:5; Acts 17:16. [2]Mt 5:22; 1 Cor 13:5; Col 3:8; 1 Tim 2:8.

2. When attributed to God, wrath said in an anthropomorphic way that the God of holiness could not tolerate sin.*[3] In its origin the divine wrath had nothing in common with that mythology which depicted the gods to be jealous of men. God has no other desire than to enable men to share in his holiness*; he is not a god of wrath, but the God of mercy,*[4] who, in extending the invitation to conversion,* has the last word.[5] But man, perceiving in God's desire a radical opposition to sin, experiences it as wrath; this wrath is revealed to him through the world's disorders: sicknesses, scourges, wars.[6]

[3]Rom 1:18-22. [4]Is 54:7f.; Hos 11:9. [5]Rom 11:32. [6]Ps 88:16; 90:7-12.

3. Jesus let the powers of love and holiness muster themselves together in his person so strongly that, at the instant when wrath swept down upon the one who had "become sin,*"[7] it was love* that remained as victor, allowing us to become in him "God's justice.*" The wrath of the end* of time was anticipated in Jesus, so that believers have been delivered from the wrath which is coming.[8] We do not say the "God of Wrath" but the God of Love.

[7]2 Cor 5:21. [8]Rom 5:9; 1 Thes 1:10.

→ holiness—justice—punishment—vices.

write, writing

→ Scripture.

[Yahweh] Certain translators write Yahve or Iahvé; but only the written form *Yahweh* (which corrects the vocalization of the ancient *Jehovah*) respects the sacred tetragrammaton of Jewish tradition: YHWH. A Hebrew name, deriving from the verb *hâwah* or *hâyah:* "to arrive, become, be," according to the popular etymology furnished in the account of the revelation of the Name* which God gave himself during the apparition at the burning bush. Discussion even now continues in order to discover whether the meaning of the verb is active ("the existing one," as the Septuagint* translated Ex 3:14) or causative ("the one causing to be"): in any case, it is neither a pronoun, nor a substantive, but an action verb describing God's very activity. Far from confining God within a concept, the term shows him to be faithfully present to his people in his activity. According to linguists, the word is related to the form *Yau,* which, at Babylon, meant the God invoked by the one who bore his name; so Moses' mother was called *Yô-kèbèd:* "the glory of Yô."

→ God.

year 1. Gk. *eniautos, etos.* The duration of the year depended on the lunar or solar calendar* adopted. The year was divided into two seasons: winter,* the rainy season from October 15 to May 15, and summer,* the dry season from May 15 to October 15. For the pious Jew the divisions were the feast days* which set off stages of the year.

2. The year served as a running unit to designate someone's age,[1] the length of a sickness,[2] one or another period of history[3] or a specific date.[4] In estimates of lengths of time a fraction of a year counted as a whole; so, the "three years"[5] or the "fourteen years"[6] Paul speaks about might correspond to no more than a year and a half or to twelve years and a few months respectively.

[1]Mk 5:42; Lk 2:37,42; 3:23; 8:42; Jn 8:57; Acts 4:22; 1 Tim 5:9. [2]Mt 9:20; Lk 13:11; Jn 5:5; Acts 9:33. [3]Acts 7:6,30,36,42; 13:20; Gal 3:17; Heb 3:10,17; Rv 20:2-7. [4]Lk 3:1. [5]Gal 1:18. [6]Gal 2:1.

3. The years of an emperor's* reign were reckoned as beginning with his accession. Since Tiberius Caesar was elected August 19 in the year 767 from the establishment of the City of Rome *(ab Urbe condita)* or in the year A.D. 14, then the "fifteenth year" of his reign[7] extended from August 19, 28 to August 18, 29. But Luke, instead of following Roman computations, might have followed the Syrian reckoning that began the year on October 1; in that case, Tiberius' fifteenth year would have begun on October 1, 27. Scholars lean toward this second hypothesis.

[7]Lk 3:1.

→ calendar—chronology—day—feast—month—week.

yes Gk. *nai.* In addition to the numerous cases in which a yes introduces or indicates an affirmative answer to a question,[1] an answer that ought to express the inner despositions,[2] several other uses are noteworthy. Yes sometimes is equivalent to Amen,* ratifying an affirmation with a reference to a secret conviction;[3] this is the sense of the yes given by Jesus to the Father[4] or by the Spirit to the Church.[5] Moreover, in Jesus the divine promises find their yes,[6] in Jesus the yes is based and discovered.[7]

[1]Mt 9:28; 13:51; 17:25; 21:16; Jn 11:27; 21:15ff. [2]Mt 5:37; 2 Cor 1:19; Jas 5:12. [3]Mt 11:9 (= Lk 7:26); Lk 11:51; 12:5; 2 Cor 1:20; Rv 1:7. [4]Mt 11:26 (= Lk 10:21). [5]Rv 14:13. [6]2 Cor 1:20. [7]2 Cor 1:19.

→ amen—oath—truth.

yoke Gk. *zygos.* A piece of wood tying together the heads of a pair of oxen and, by extension, the harness of any draft animals.[1] A traditional metaphor in Israel to designate slavery,[2] bondage under a tyrant.[3] It points also to the "slave's" true relationship with his master,[4] authentic wisdom.[5] But the Law rendered this relationship burdensome; Jesus' yoke, which replaces it, is gentle,* that is, easy to carry, because it is well-fitted.[7]

[1]Nm 19:2. [2]Lv 26:13; Jer 27–28; 1 Tim 6:1. [3]1 Kgs 12:4,9-11:14. [4]Jer 2:20; 5:5; Hos 11:4. [5]Sir 51:26. [6]Acts 15:10; Gal 5:1; cf. Mt 23:4. [7]Mt 11:29f.

→ Law—neck—slave.

Z

Zacchaeus Gk. *Zakchaios,* a Jewish name corresponding to the Heb. *zakkay:* "pure, just." The chief tax collector at Jericho.[1]

[1]Lk 19:1-9 □.

→ tax-collector.

Zachary

→ Zechariah.

zeal **1.** The Greek work *zēlos* (perhaps related to *zēteō:* "to seek") translates the Hebrew *qin'â* (from the root *qâna,* meaning the red blush that rises up into an impassioned man's face). The term implies a jealous intransigence and even one of violence.*

2. In the sense of an eager interest for someone or something we find, in addition to *zēlos,*[1] the Greek term *spoudē,* which includes the idea of haste,[2] intense desire[3] and looks to the application that one puts into doing something.[4]

[1]1 Cor 12:31; 14:1,12,39; 2 Cor 7:7,11 □. [2]Ex 12:11; Lk 1:39ff. [3]Lk 7:4; 1 Thes 2:17ff. [4]Rom 12:8,11; Eph 4:3; Heb 4:11; 6:11ff.

→ care—jealousy—Zealot.

Zealot Gk. *zēlōtēs:* "the zealous one." The surname of Simon the apostle.[1] An adherent of the Law.[2] A fervent man, full of desires.[3] An adherent of a revolutionary movement.[4]

[1]Lk 6:15; Acts 1:13. [2]Acts 21:20; Gal 1:14. [3]Acts 22:3; 1 Cor 14:3; Ti 2:14; 1 Pt 3:13. [4]Intr. XI.4.

Zebedee Gk. *Zebedaios,* from the Heb. *zabdî:* "my gift." A fisherman of the Lake of Galilee, the husband of Salome, the father of James and John.[1]

[1]Mt 4:21 (= Mk 1:20) □.

Zechariah Gk. *Zacharias,* from the Heb. *Zekar-yâ:* "Yahweh remembers."

1. The name of a prophet assassinated in the Temple, perhaps the son of Jehoiada, although called the son of Barachiah.[1]

[1]2 Chr 24:20-22; Mt 23:35 (= Lk 11:51) □.

2. The son of Barachiah, a prophet quoted although not named; one of the twelve minor prophets.*[2]

[1]Zec 1:1; 9:9; Mt 21:4; 27:9 □.

3. A priest of Abijah's class, the husband of Elizabeth, the father of John the Baptist, a resident of a city of Judah.[3]

[1]Lk 1:5-67; 3:2 □.

Zion Gk. *Siōn,* Heb. *ṣiôn.* A hill of Jerusalem situated south of the Temple* and north of the Siloam* quarter. Identified with Jerusalem* in its essentially religious aspect, one which foretells heaven.[1]

[1]2 Sm 5:7; Is 2:2f.; 4:5; Mt 21:5; Jn 12:15; Rom 9:33; 11:26; Heb 12:22; 1 Pt 2:6; Rv 14:1 □.

zither. Gk. *kithara,* Heb. *kinnôr.* A musical instrument, with six or eight chords, to accompany singing. This technical term can rightly be rendered "harp," even if some shades of meaning distinguish these two instruments from one another.[1]

[1]1 Cor 14:7; Rv 5:8; 14:2; 15:2; 18:22 □.

→ Intr. IX.6.—harp.

Index of Greek Words

A list of common Greek words cited in the Dictionary of the New Testament.

(The Greek words are listed according to English orthography. The square brackets enclose words not found in the text of the New Testament. Each Greek word is cross-referenced to the entries in which it is mentioned.)

THE JOURNEYS OF PAUL

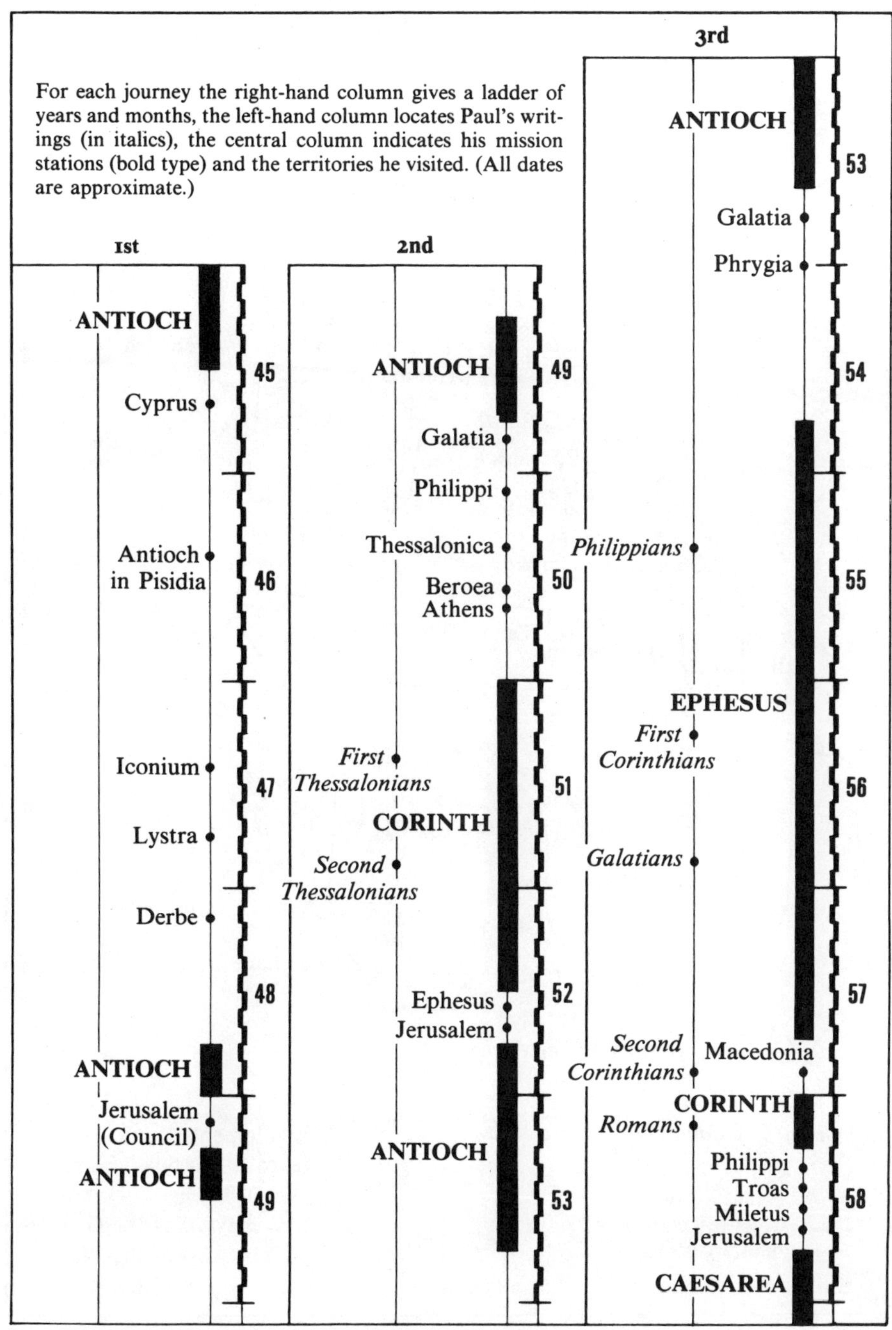
For each journey the right-hand column gives a ladder of years and months, the left-hand column locates Paul's writings (in italics), the central column indicates his mission stations (bold type) and the territories he visited. (All dates are approximate.)
1st
ANTIOCH
45
Cyprus
Antioch in Pisidia
46
Iconium
47
Lystra
Derbe
48
ANTIOCH
Jerusalem (Council)
ANTIOCH
49
2nd
ANTIOCH
49
Galatia
Philippi
Thessalonica
Beroea
50
Athens
First Thessalonians
51
CORINTH
Second Thessalonians
Ephesus
52
Jerusalem
ANTIOCH
53
3rd
ANTIOCH
53
Galatia
Phrygia
54
Philippians
55
EPHESUS
First Corinthians
56
Galatians
57
Second Corinthians
Macedonia
CORINTH
Romans
Philippi
Troas
58
Miletus
Jerusalem
CAESAREA

MAP OF JERUSALEM

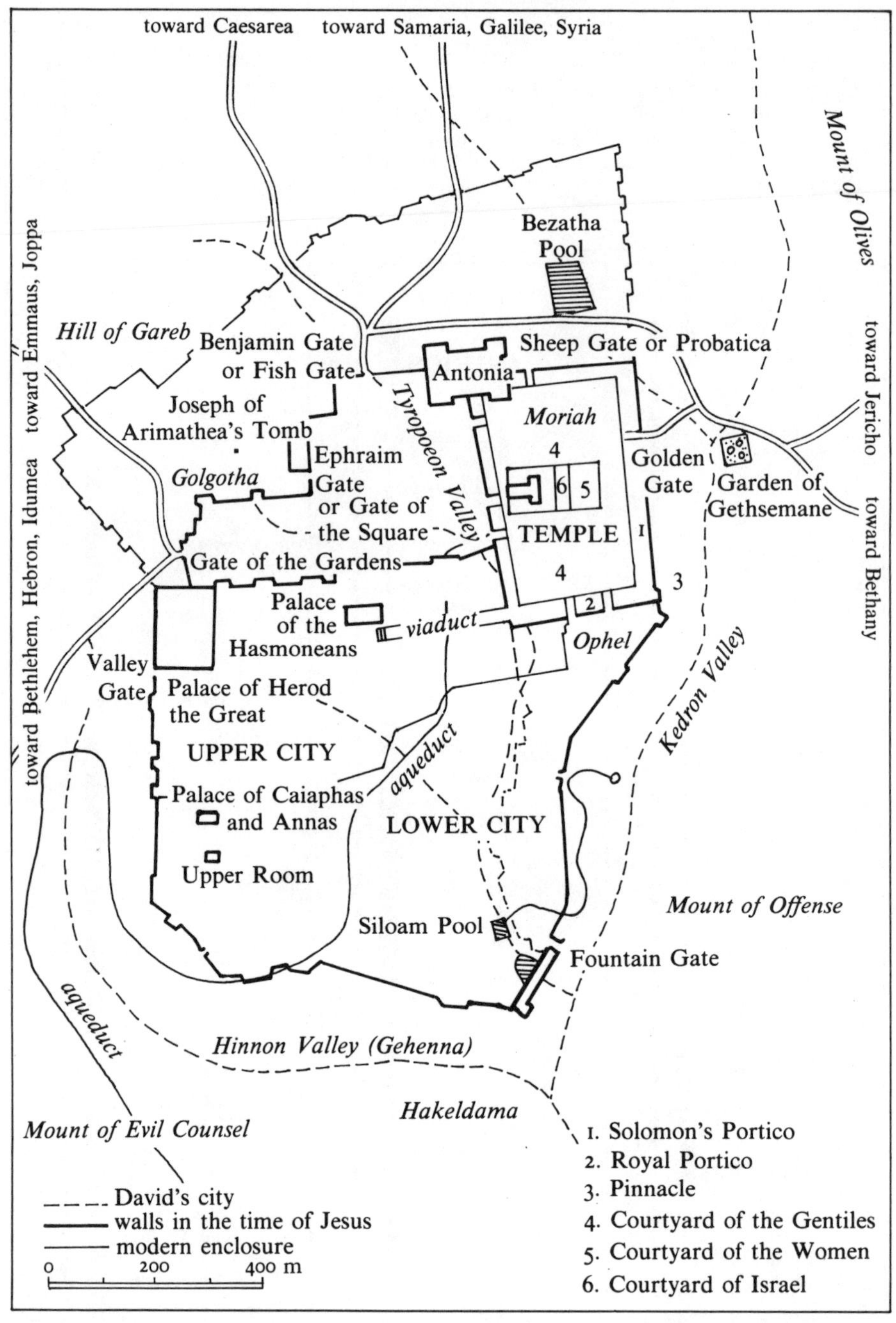
toward Caesarea
toward Samaria, Galilee, Syria
Mount of Olives
Bezatha
Pool
toward Emmaus, Joppa
Hill of Gareb
Benjamin Gate
or Fish Gate
Sheep Gate or Probatica
toward Jericho
Antonia
Tyropoeon Valley
Joseph of
Arimathea's Tomb
Moriah
Ephraim
Gate
or Gate of
the Square
Golgotha
Golden
Gate
Garden of
Gethsemane
TEMPLE
toward Bethany
Gate of the Gardens
toward Bethlehem, Hebron, Idumea
Palace
of the
Hasmoneans
viaduct
Ophel
Valley
Gate
Palace of Herod
the Great
Kedron Valley
UPPER CITY
aqueduct
Palace of Caiaphas
and Annas
LOWER CITY
Upper Room
Mount of Offense
Siloam Pool
Fountain Gate
aqueduct
Hinnon Valley (Gehenna)
Hakeldama
Mount of Evil Counsel
David's city
walls in the time of Jesus
modern enclosure
0 200 400 m
1. Solomon's Portico
2. Royal Portico
3. Pinnacle
4. Courtyard of the Gentiles
5. Courtyard of the Women
6. Courtyard of Israel

PAUL'S MISSIONARY JOURNEYS

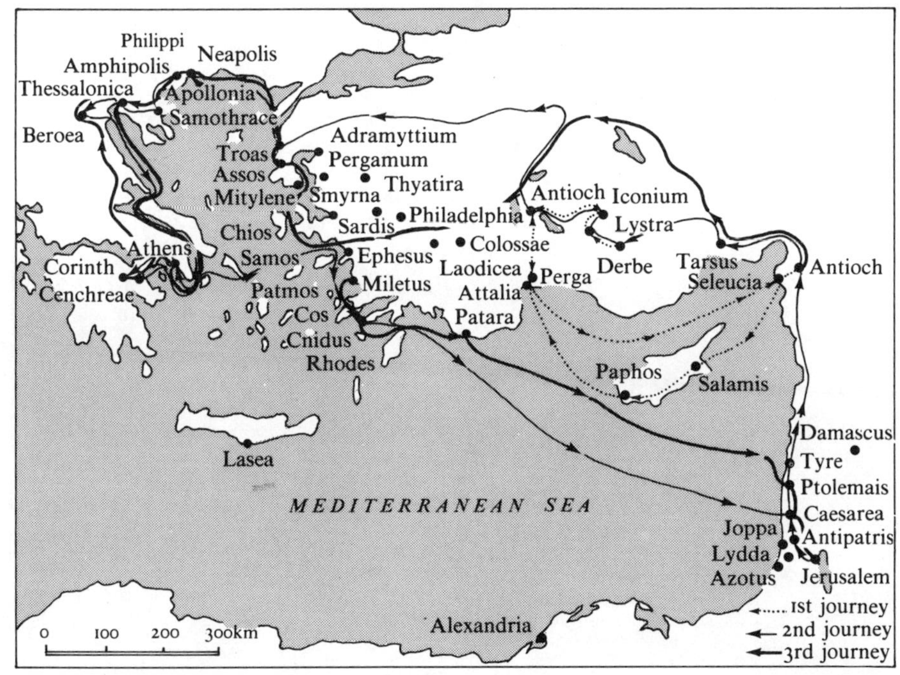

PAUL'S CAPTIVITY JOURNEY

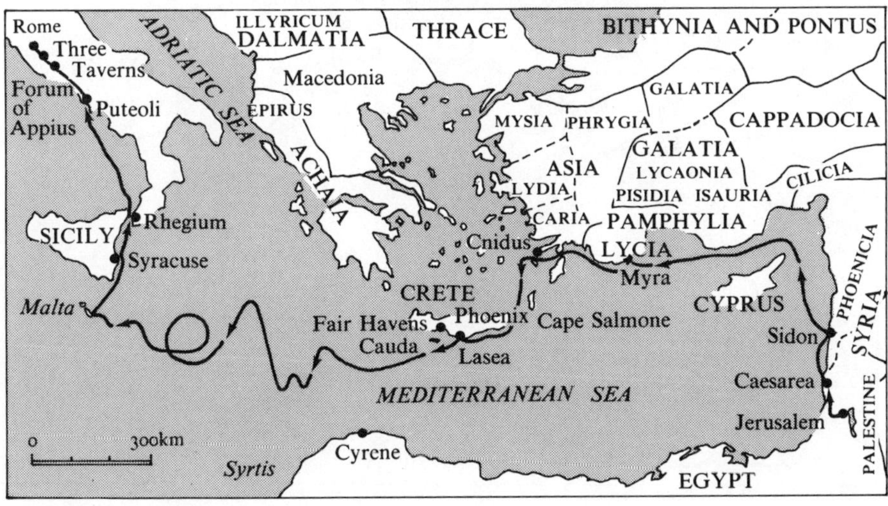

PALESTINE IN NEW TESTAMENT TIMES

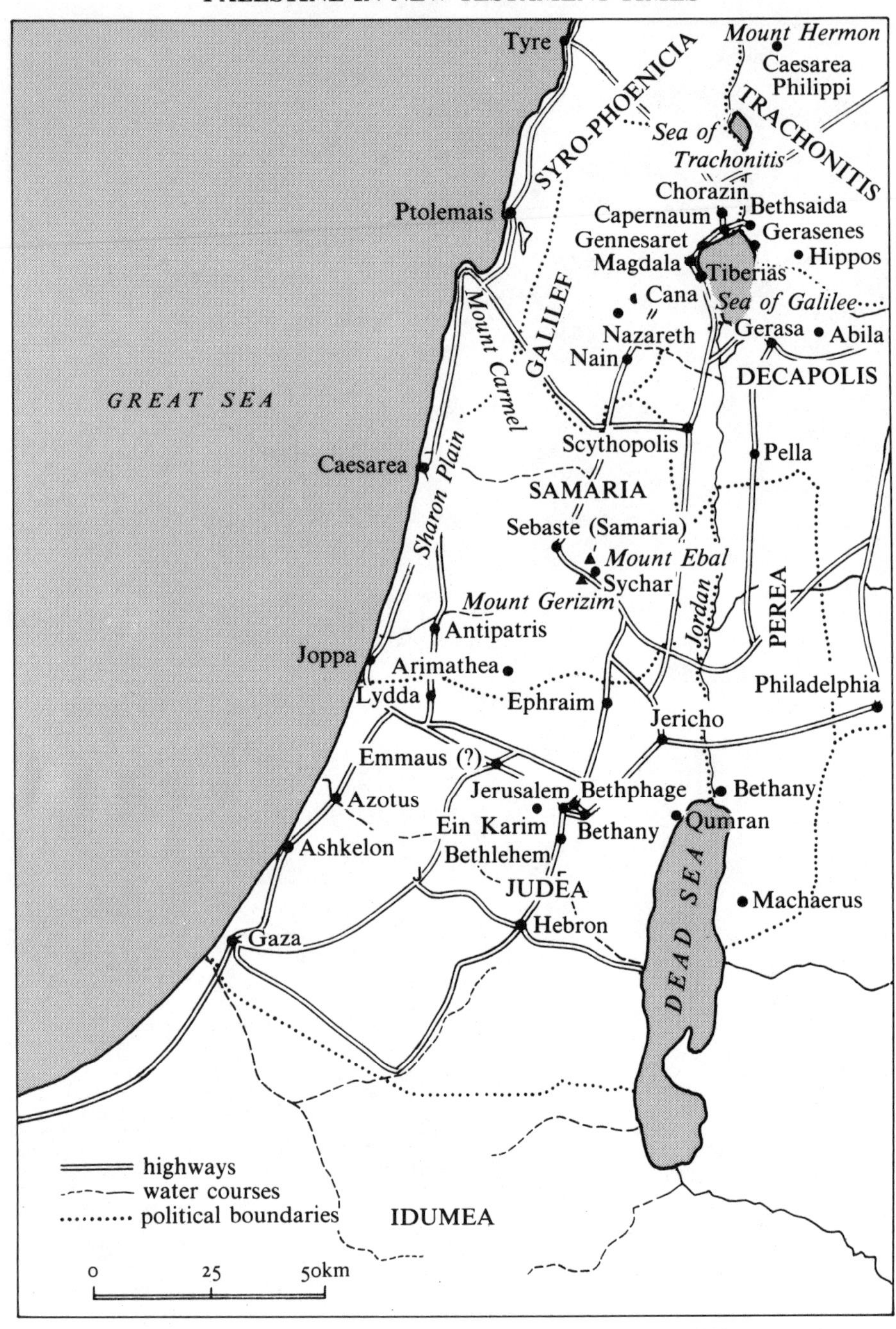

Tyre
Mount Hermon
Caesarea
Philippi
SYRO-PHOENICIA
TRACHONITIS
Sea of
Trachonitis
Chorazin
Bethsaida
Ptolemais
Capernaum
Gerasenes
Gennesaret
Magdala
Hippos
Tiberias
Cana
Sea of Galilee
GALILEE
Mount Carmel
Nazareth
Gerasa
Abila
Nain
DECAPOLIS
GREAT SEA
Scythopolis
Pella
Caesarea
Sharon Plain
SAMARIA
Sebaste (Samaria)
Mount Ebal
Sychar
Mount Gerizim
Jordan
PEREA
Antipatris
Joppa
Arimathea
Philadelphia
Lydda
Ephraim
Jericho
Emmaus (?)
Jerusalem
Bethphage
Bethany
Azotus
Qumran
Ein Karim
Bethany
Ashkelon
Bethlehem
JUDEA
DEAD SEA
Machaerus
Hebron
Gaza
highways
water courses
political boundaries
IDUMEA
0
25
50km

R
225.3
L57
c.1

60481

Lincoln Christian College